D1525438

America in the World

America in the World

SVEN BECKERT AND JEREMI SURI, *series editors*

Jeffrey A. Engel, Mark Atwood Lawrence, and Andrew Preston, editors, *America in the World: A History in Documents since 1898, Revised and Updated*

Mark Atwood Lawrence, *The End of Ambition: The United States and the Third World in the Vietnam Era*

Roberto Saba, *American Mirror: The United States and Brazil in the Age of Emancipation*

Dorothy Sue Cobble, *For the Many: American Feminists and the Global Fight for Democratic Equality*

Stefan J. Link, *Forging Global Fordism: Nazi Germany, Soviet Russia, and the Contest over the Industrial Order*

Katy Hull, *The Machine Has a Soul: American Sympathy with Italian Fascism*

Sara Lorenzini, *Global Development: A Cold War History*

Michael Cotey Morgan, *The Final Act: The Helsinki Accords and the Transformation of the Cold War*

A. G. Hopkins, *American Empire: A Global History*

Tore C. Olsson, *Agrarian Crossings: Reformers and the Remaking of the US and Mexican Countryside*

Kiran Klaus Patel, *The New Deal: A Global History*

Adam Ewing, *The Age of Garvey: How a Jamaican Activist Created a Mass Movement and Changed Global Black Politics*

Jürgen Osterhammel and Patrick Camiller, *The Transformation of the World: A Global History of the Nineteenth Century*

Donna R. Gabaccia, *Foreign Relations: American Immigration in Global Perspective*

Thomas Borstelmann, *The 1970s: A New Global History from Civil Rights to Economic Inequality*

Rachel St. John, *Line in the Sand: A History of the Western U.S.-Mexico Border*

Ian Tyrrell, *Reforming the World: The Creation of America's Moral Empire*

Andrew Zimmerman, *Alabama in Africa: Booker T. Washington, the German Empire, and the Globalization of the New South*

For a full list of titles in the series, go to: **https://press.princeton.edu/catalogs/series/title/america-in-the-world.html**

America in the World

A History in Documents since 1898, Revised and Updated

Edited by Jeffrey A. Engel,
Mark Atwood Lawrence, and Andrew Preston

Princeton University Press
Princeton and Oxford

Copyright © 2014, 2023 by Princeton University Press

Princeton University Press is committed to the protection of copyright and the intellectual property our authors entrust to us. Copyright promotes the progress and integrity of knowledge. Thank you for supporting free speech and the global exchange of ideas by purchasing an authorized edition of this book. If you wish to reproduce or distribute any part of it in any form, please obtain permission.

Requests for permission to reproduce material from this work should be sent to permissions@press.princeton.edu

Published by Princeton University Press
41 William Street, Princeton, New Jersey 08540
99 Banbury Road, Oxford OX2 6JX

press.princeton.edu

All Rights Reserved

ISBN 978-0-691-24744-1
ISBN (pbk.) 978-0-691-24873-8
ISBN (e-book) 978-0-691-24874-5

Library of Congress Control Number: 2023941302

British Library Cataloging-in-Publication Data is available

Editorial: Priya Nelson, Emma Wagh, and Morgan Spehar
Production Editorial: Karen Carter
Jacket/Cover Design: Chris Ferrante
Production: Lauren Reese
Copyeditor: Karen Verde

Jacket/cover images: (Left column, top to bottom) *New York Journal*, February 17, 1898. John Frost Newspapers / Alamy Stock Photo. Remarks by President Biden on America's Place in the World, February 4, 2021 / whitehouse.gov. "Columbia's Easter bonnet" from the cover of *Puck*, April 6, 1901 / Library of Congress. Global Trends 2040 website, March 2021 / Office of the Director of National Intelligence. Telegram from George Kennan Charge d'Affaires at United States Embassy in Moscow to the Secretary of State, February 22, 1946 / National Archives. Cover of The 9/11 Commission Report, July 22, 2004 / 9-11commission.gov. (Right column, top to bottom) The Platt Amendment, March 2, 1901 / National Archives. Sheet music for *I Didn't Raise My Boy to Be a Soldier*, 1915 / Library of Congress

This book has been composed in Sabon Next LT Pro and Helvetica Neue LT Std

10 9 8 7 6 5 4 3 2 1

Contents

Acknowledgments

One of the pleasures of international history is the limitless opportunity for collaboration. No single scholar can hope to know everything about a field as vast as the history of U.S. relations with the outside world. In fact, as we constantly rediscovered in the process of putting this book together and then in preparing the second edition in 2022, not even a three-member team of scholars who have focused on diverse aspects of American foreign policy can command anything close to the expertise necessary for a collection of this size and ambition. We therefore have inevitably relied on the knowledge, wisdom, and generosity of numerous colleagues. Our sincere thanks go to Frank Costigliola, Christopher Goscha, Madeleine Hsu, Christopher Lee, Erez Manela, Svetlana Savranskaya, Bartholomew Sparrow, and Matthew Tribbe. We are also grateful to Christian Ostermann and Laura Deal at the Cold War International History Project for their help in navigating CWIHP's unparalleled collections.

Jeffrey Engel would like to thank Ronna Spitz of SMU's Center for Presidential History, who organized and documented the seemingly endless quest for permissions, and Katherine Carte Engel, whose repeated feigning of interest during discussion of document foraging aided the project immeasurably. He also thanks the family of Edwin Marcus for their generosity in allowing republication of his work, as well as the library staffs of Princeton University, Southern Methodist University, Cambridge University, and the University of Edinburgh, where his contribution to this project was largely composed. Such peripatetic composition was only possible due to research support from Texas A&M University's Bush School of Government through funds donated by the family of Verlin and Howard Kruse, and the Office of the Provost of Southern Methodist University.

Mark Lawrence is grateful to Helen Pho for finding elusive documents, to Michelle Reeves for superb translation work on short notice, to David Willkie and Patrick Frank for their help in tracking down rights, and to the archival staffs at Indiana University, the University of Hawaii, and the University of Iowa for their invaluable assistance. He also thanks the Institute for Historical Studies at the University of Texas at Austin and the Stanley Kaplan Program in American Foreign Policy Williams College, both of which provided generous support while he was working on the first edition.

Andrew Preston would like to thank Satoshi Endo, Tim Harper, Barak Kushner, Lorenz Lüthi, Sarah Snyder, and Steven Ward for their advice on documents and their contexts, as well as the staffs at various libraries in

Cambridge, especially the University Library, the Seeley Historical Library, and the Forbes-Mellon Library at Clare College.

All of us are immensely grateful to the fantastic team at Princeton University Press. For the first edition, Brigitta Van Rheinberg consistently displayed the perfect blend of encouragement and patience as the project unfolded. We feel extremely fortunate to have worked with her and have no doubt that she shares an equal measure of credit for whatever merits this book possesses. We also thank Larissa Klein and her successor, Claudia Acevedo, who expertly guided the book through the final stages, not least by handling a torrent of emails with good cheer. Our thanks go too to several anonymous reviewers, whose advice had a major impact on the book. For the second edition, we are sincerely grateful to Priya Nelson, who suggested that we update and expand the book and then provided enthusiastic guidance at every step. Emma Wagh and Karen Carter helped us navigate all the complexities of a book with many moving parts, and Elizabeth Trammell expertly rounded up all the necessary permissions—no small undertaking. We also wish to thank Karen Verde for her superb copyediting of the second edition.

Introduction

THE LONG AMERICAN CENTURY

The questions have been there from the start. From the founding of the republic in the eighteenth century, Americans have debated their country's place in international affairs and the purpose of their foreign policy. Their rise to global prominence by the onset of the twentieth century only catalyzed competing arguments over if, and if so how, the United States should engage others—on their continent, within their own hemisphere, and, ultimately, globally.

The passage of time changed but never decided these debates. Indeed, the end of the Cold War—and the onrushing twenty-first century—only reinvigorated them. The Soviet Union's end, coupled with globalization and the apparent triumph of democracy, led many to wonder if the world still needed American power and influence spread across all the globe's time zones. Was such a global reach even in the country's own best interest? Former secretary of state Henry Kissinger, perhaps the world's most recognized living diplomat, worried that many of his fellow citizens thought their country too powerful and the world too peaceful to give much thought to what lay beyond their borders. "At the dawn of the new millennium, the United States is enjoying preeminence unrivaled by even the greatest empires of the past," he wrote in 2001 in a book with an intentionally provocative title: *Does America Need a Foreign Policy?*[1]

Perhaps it did, though not to confront the problems Kissinger expected. Only months after publication, the terrorist group al-Qaeda launched the devastating 9/11 attacks against targets in New York and Washington, D.C. Thousands died, and a new era began. But what kind of era would it be? Nothing could have shown Americans more clearly that they certainly needed a foreign policy following the Cold War, yet Kissinger (and, to be fair, most of the nation's national security establishment) had missed a great deal. His book made no mention of al-Qaeda or its leader, Osama bin Laden, and offered only a brief discussion of international terrorism. As Kissinger would be the first to admit, foreign policy priorities are apt to change, often suddenly and unpredictably.

[1] Henry Kissinger, *Does America Need a Foreign Policy? Toward a Diplomacy for the 21st Century* (New York: Simon & Schuster, 2001), 17.

When they do, as when World War II or the Cold War ended, after a shocking terrorist blow or a global pandemic, or as once-moribund great-power rivalries surged anew in the 2020s, Americans have found themselves locked in ferocious, albeit familiar, debates over how their country should act on the world stage. Such debates invariably hinge upon history. American successes and mistakes in past years helped latter-day strategists and politicians craft, justify, and legitimate plans for the present and future. Making claims about the past is common practice. Yet misperceptions about the history of American foreign relations are just as common; public debate, almost by its very nature, often lacks knowledge, context, or specificity.

Distortions, half-truths, and catechisms of national faith made without regard to evidence, offered by all parts of the political spectrum, typically prevail during highly politicized debates about America's "proper" role in the world. Three decades removed from their seemingly triumphant Cold War victory, and two decades after 9/11 shook the country and in turn the world, Republican and Democratic presidential candidates routinely submitted divergent foreign policy prescriptions for treating their ongoing international problems, offering different visions of America's place in the world, and of its past. Determined to "make America great again," which is inherently a claim about the past, Donald Trump additionally claimed during his final days in office that he had "restored American sovereignty at home and American leadership abroad" by making "America first" the hallmark of his diplomacy.[2] His successor disagreed, both with Trump's conclusion and his underlying approach. "I want the world to hear today: America is back," President Joe Biden declared soon after taking office, which meant back, as before, to the assumption it was the world's indispensable nation, responsible for safeguarding much more than its own interests. "The United States is determined to reengage," he told America's allies, "to consult with you, to earn back our position of trusted leadership."[3]

That Trump and Biden disagreed shocks no one who lived through the contentious 2020 election. Yet of far greater importance to historians, and to those who seek to understand America's past, is the simple truth that their words could easily have been uttered by political opponents in any decade since the Spanish-American War in 1898.

By bringing together important and revealing original documents from every era of that long American engagement with the world since the late nineteenth century, we hope that this second and updated edition, *America*

[2] "Foreign Policy," https://trumpwhitehouse.archives.gov/issues/foreign-policy/#:~:text=President%20Trump%20restored%20American%20sovereignty,security%2C%20prosperity%2C%20and%20peace.

[3] "Remarks by President Biden at the 2021 Virtual Munich Security Conference," February 19, 2021. https://www.whitehouse.gov/briefing-room/speeches-remarks/2021/02/19/remarks-by-president-biden-at-the-2021-virtual-munich-security-conference/

in the World: A History in Documents Since 1898, will contribute to a deeper understanding of America's role in the world by promoting the study of the past on its own terms and for its own sake and by informing present and future debates. Above all, we hope that readers, both students and the broader public, will come to appreciate through the following pages the sheer complexity of America's historical encounters with the outside world and the myriad factors—economic, political, cultural, ideological—that have driven U.S. behavior since the late nineteenth century.

Dating the rise of American international power is no easy task. When the Time-Life publishing baron Henry R. Luce proclaimed the advent of "the American century" in early 1941, he intended to suggest that the United States had suddenly arrived as a great power and was likely to dominate global affairs in the future.[4] By dating the emergence of the United States to the World War II era, however, Luce underestimated the historical spread of U.S. power and influence. In fact, the American century's origins lie farther back, in the late nineteenth century, when the nation's unprecedented industrial growth enabled its leaders to play an increasingly prominent world role. World War II may have marked a new highpoint of America's rise as a global superpower, but the process began much earlier.

Our book charts this process through an examination of the documentary record. Surveying what might be called the "long" American century from the 1890s to the third decade of the twenty-first century, we offer snapshots of the thoughts and perspectives of a wide variety of Americans who grappled with the complexities of their evolving global role. Americans, in the past as now, rarely agreed on how to use their power. The best way to appreciate these arguments is by listening to the voices that originally made them. It is instructive as well to heed foreign voices, which commented with increasing urgency and insight on the place of the United States in international affairs.

For ease of use—and because the first step for any student of history is to develop a timeline of events—documents are presented in chronological order within each chapter. But close reading reveals not a single line of narrative so much as the recurrence and intermingling of several themes that have cut across the history of U.S. relations with the outside world.

One central theme is the expanding definition of "national security," from a narrow concept of continental self-defense to an expansive, even limitless, global vision. Even outer space and the moon became battlegrounds for playing out American policies and influence during the Cold War. Another key

[4] Luce's phrase originally appeared in "The American Century," *Life*, February 17, 1941. In 1999, the journal *Diplomatic History* reprinted Luce's essay along with sixteen essays of commentary on the notion of an "American century." See "The American Century: A Roundtable (Part I)," *Diplomatic History* 23 (Spring 1999), 157–370; and "The American Century: A Roundtable (Part II)," *Diplomatic History* 23 (Summer 1999), 391–537.

theme is the concern Americans have often had for the influence of private capital and industry—what President Dwight D. Eisenhower famously called a "military-industrial complex"—on their nation's foreign policy. Equally, we are interested in exposing the ideological currents that have driven American engagement in the world or, conversely, given Americans pause about ever-expanding international ambitions. We also examine the waging of wars and opposition to them, the importance of human rights and democracy in the exercise of U.S. power, American efforts to respond to unforeseen challenges driven by technological change, and the intersections between race, religion, empire, and revolution in Americans' views of the world.

In choosing these themes, we have been guided partly by interest in a much-debated question that has preoccupied generations of historians: In making policy toward the outside world, have U.S. leaders been guided principally by ideology, material ambitions, or geostrategic calculation? Evidence exists for each possibility. Many of the documents provide windows into the ways in which these three types of motives weighed, and intermingled, in the minds of American decision makers. But we have also been guided by two newer concerns that have decisively reshaped the writing of U.S. foreign-relations history in the last few decades.

First, in keeping with a trend away from exclusive focus on decision-making elites, we include documents that reflect how Americans outside the rarified world of Washington thought about international affairs. We highlight the voices of academics, activists, clergy, novelists, poets, and songwriters in addition to presidents, cabinet secretaries, and military officers. To be sure, the book contains plenty of "classics," indisputably important landmark documents often written by easily recognizable figures familiar to any student of American foreign relations. By emphasizing the perspectives of Americans who never served in government alongside those of policy makers, however, we hope to capture a fuller, richer, and more nuanced interpretation of U.S. diplomatic history than is sometimes conveyed in textbooks or documentary collections surveying the history of American diplomacy.

Second, consistent with efforts by scholars to view the United States as just one participant within a complex web of international relationships, we include numerous non-American sources. The book in particular highlights materials from the Soviet bloc that became available following the end of the Cold War, and which in turn transformed historians' ability to write about the East-West conflict that dominated international affairs for half a century. But the book, especially in this updated version, also contains non-American documents from earlier and later periods. Our hope is that such documents from once-closed archives and new arenas—comprising approximately one quarter of the entire collection—will generate discussion of U.S. behavior by revealing what foreign observers, as well as Americans, thought about it.

This material reminds us that U.S. foreign policy generated a tremendous amount of comment abroad during the American century. As Canadian prime minister Pierre Trudeau once explained in a speech in Washington, D.C., "Living next to you is in some ways like sleeping with an elephant; no matter how friendly and even-tempered is the beast, one is affected by every twitch and grunt."[5] Like many clichés, this one bears more than a ring of truth. Americans make up roughly 4.5 percent of the world's population yet a far greater share of wealth, power, and influence. As one British commentator noted in 2004 during a presidential election that many believed would shape the fate of the entire world, non-Americans felt "increasingly helpless" at not having a say over the outcome. "[U]nless you happen to be a voter in a handful of swing states, there's little you can do about the final result. If you're not American, the situation is more acute" because "the actions of the US impact on our lives in overwhelming ways."[6]

We hope that the inclusion of non-American documents, from adversaries as well as allies, captures a sense of international sentiment and illustrates just how deep and profound America's effect on the rest of the world can be. However, we hasten to add that while our book examines foreign perceptions of U.S. behavior, it does not analyze policy decisions by other countries. Such analysis lies beyond this book's scope and size.

One of the most difficult challenges in compiling this book was to select a relatively small sample of documents from a monumentally vast pool of material. To address this problem, we have organized each chapter around one or two broad interpretive questions and selected material that in some way relates to that central agenda. Such questions are spelled out in the introduction to each chapter and, we hope, lend coherence to a project that clearly could spill in an infinite number of directions. If we have been successful, each chapter will read not as a loose collection of material organized around historical topics but as sustained considerations of major interpretive questions that have preoccupied historians of American foreign relations.

We hope, of course, that this approach proves useful to teachers and provokes classroom discussion. We also hope that our consideration of the role played by economic, ideological, and cultural factors in driving U.S. behavior abroad will dovetail with the flourishing debate within and beyond academic circles about which of these impulses has been most important in explaining American decision making. Finally, we hope that our juxtaposition of documents reflecting geostrategic calculation with other materials illuminating the political and cultural landscape of the United States will

[5] Pierre Trudeau, quoted in John Herd Thompson and Stephen J. Randall, *Canada and the United States: Ambivalent Allies*, 2nd ed. (Athens: University of Georgia Press, 1997), 250.

[6] Oliver Burkeman, "My Fellow Non-Americans . . . ," *Guardian*, October 13, 2004, 2.

promote consideration of the extent to which foreign policy grows from—and is restrained by—the nation's internal character. Put simply, domestic politics matter when considering foreign policy, and accordingly they play their part in our story as well.

Even as we have been heavily influenced by the long-standing preoccupations of diplomatic historians with questions of power, politics, and ideological perspective, we have also been guided by a sense of which questions about the past might resonate in future debates over American foreign relations. For this reason, we have included many documents that reflect on the questions of how deeply the United States should be involved in international affairs, how the nation should balance self-interest and principle, and how closely Americans' self-perceptions correspond to the opinions held by foreigners of the role the United States plays on the global stage. We readily acknowledge the futility of any effort to predict issues that will stand out in the future. After all, many of our selections provide abundant evidence that prognosticators about the global order have a decidedly mixed track record.

Future generations will undoubtedly pose questions about the past we cannot yet anticipate. Yet one point from this book is likely to stand the test of time: The American century has given rise to an extraordinary array of commentary that defies generalization. The documents that follow reflect a spectrum of opinion from ecstatic faith in the United States as global leader to certainty of American malfeasance. Who was right is perhaps a less interesting question than how various authors made their arguments, why they wrote as they did, and what kinds of responses they generated. Reckoning seriously with these matters will, we hope, enable new generations to deal meaningfully with problems inherited from the past. History is an imperfect guide, to be sure. But it remains the best we have and resides at the heart of any attempt to chart the future.

1

Motives of Expansion

The United States was never the passive, isolationist nation that the mythology of American history has often suggested. As early as 1776, American diplomats were busily attempting to woo European governments to support U.S. objectives. Over the following decades, moreover, the survival of the young republic depended on managing complex economic and military threats from abroad. Growing confidence encouraged increasingly ambitious uses of power. By the outbreak of the Civil War in 1861, U.S. presidents had sent forces into action in territories stretching from Cuba and Peru to the Marquesas Islands, Tripoli, and China.

Still, a decisive breaking point in the history of American interaction with the rest of the world occurred in the last few decades of the nineteenth century. A nation largely focused on economic relations with the outside world embraced an increasingly prominent role in international diplomacy, gradually joining the ranks of the European powers that had long vied for global influence. In addition, American leaders decided to equip the nation with naval forces suited not just to fighting small skirmishes but also to demonstrating America's arrival as a great power. Most impressively of all, the United States broke with its anticolonial traditions by acquiring Alaska, the Midway Atoll, and Hawaii. All of these transformations culminated in 1898, when the United States fought a major war against Spain and took control over vast new overseas territories.

What accounts for this transformation in the global role of the United States between the end of the Civil War in 1865 and the outbreak of the Spanish-American War in 1898? There is no single answer. Rather, U.S. activism sprang from various causes. One of them was America's rapidly expanding industrial economy, which seemed to many business moguls to require that the United States secure new markets overseas. Indeed, many powerful Americans believed that the United States could sustain its economic dynamism and avoid massive labor unrest only by acquiring new consumers for the nation's industrial output.

Powerful ideological currents in the late nineteenth century also encouraged international activism. In an era of pervasive social Darwinism, many Americans believed that their nation would inevitably weaken and die if it failed to compete vigorously with the other world powers, which were eagerly expanding their colonial possessions. The mark of a robust, energetic society seemed increasingly to be bold activism beyond its borders. American ambitions also flowed from more altruistic sources. As the nation's self-confidence grew and new technologies expanded opportunities for overseas travel, Americans increasingly concerned themselves with the moral condition of ostensibly "primitive" or "backward" foreign societies.

Yet another ideological source of overseas ambitions was a mounting anxiety about the "closing of the frontier." For centuries, in this view, the defining characteristic of American life had been the availability of unclaimed land, which gave all individuals the opportunity to succeed through hard work and thereby sustained the American creed of individualism. Once the entire continent was settled, as seemed to be the case in the 1890s, Americans increasingly viewed foreign territories as the next "frontier" that might absorb Americans' prodigious energies and preserve the nation's basic character.

Some combination of economic and ideological rationales convinced many Americans that their nation's future lay in global activism and even territorial expansion. Yet not everyone joined the chorus. Mounting determination to expand the nation's reach generated potent resistance rooted in fears that a quest for global power would betray the nation's ideals of self-determination and limited government. Hostility came as well from abroad, where critics viewed the United States as an arrogant upstart and peoples subjected to U.S. power often resented American heavy-handedness. In these tensions lay the seeds of disagreements that would swirl around the conduct of American foreign policy for many decades to come.

Document 1.1

AN APPEAL TO ANNEX THE DOMINICAN REPUBLIC

After 1865, some Americans continued to eye the Caribbean covetously, though for reasons different from the ones that had driven advocates of expanded slavery before the Civil War. In 1870, American expansionists focused their attention on the Dominican Republic, known at the time as Santo Domingo. Although Congress rejected the idea, President Ulysses S. Grant spoke enthusiastically about annexation in his State of the Union address on December 5, 1870.

During the last session of Congress a treaty for the annexation of the Republic of San Domingo to the United States failed to receive the requisite two-thirds vote of the Senate. I was thoroughly convinced then that the best interests of this country, commercially and materially, demanded its ratification. Time has only confirmed me in this view. . . . The Government of San Domingo has voluntarily sought this annexation. It is a weak power, numbering probably less than 120,000 souls, and yet possessing one of the richest territories under the sun, capable of supporting a population of 10,000,000 people in luxury. The people of San Domingo are not capable of maintaining themselves in their present condition, and must look for outside support. They yearn for the protection of our free institutions and laws, our progress and civilization. Shall we refuse them?

The acquisition of San Domingo is desirable because of its geographical position. It commands the entrance to the Caribbean Sea and the Isthmus transit of commerce. It possesses the richest soil, best and most capacious harbors, most salubrious climate, and the most valuable products of the forests, mine, and soil of any of the West India Islands.... It will give to us those articles which we consume so largely and do not produce, thus equalizing our exports and imports. In case of foreign war it will give us command of all the islands referred to, and thus prevent an enemy from ever again possessing himself of rendezvous upon our very coast....

San Domingo, with a stable government, under which her immense resources can be developed, will give remunerative wages to tens of thousands of laborers not now upon the island. This labor will take advantage of every available means of transportation to abandon the adjacent islands and seek the blessings of freedom and its sequence—each inhabitant receiving the reward of his own labor. Porto Rico and Cuba will have to abolish slavery, as a measure of self-preservation, to retain their laborers.

San Domingo will become a large consumer of the products of Northern farms and manufactories. The cheap rate at which her citizens can be furnished with food, tools, and machinery will make it necessary that contiguous islands should have the same advantages in order to compete in the production of sugar, coffee, tobacco, tropical fruits, etc. This will open to us a still wider market for our products. The production of our own supply of these articles will cut off more than one hundred millions of our annual imports, besides largely increasing our exports. With such a picture it is easy to see how our large debt abroad is ultimately to be extinguished. With a balance of trade against us ... equal to the entire yield of the precious metals in this country, it is not so easy to see how this result is to be otherwise accomplished.

The acquisition of San Domingo is an adherence to the "Monroe doctrine"; it is a measure of national protection; it is asserting our just claim to a controlling influence over the great commercial traffic soon to flow from west to east by way of the Isthmus of Darien; it is to build up our merchant marine; it is to furnish new markets for the products of our farms, shops, and manufactories; it is to make slavery insupportable in Cuba and Porto Rico at once, and ultimately so in Brazil; it is to settle the unhappy condition of Cuba and end an exterminating conflict; it is to provide honest means of paying our honest debts without overtaxing the people; it is to furnish our citizens with the necessaries of everyday life at cheaper rates than ever before; and it is, in fine, a rapid stride toward that greatness which the intelligence, industry, and enterprise of the citizens of the United States entitle this country to assume among nations.

Document 1.2

THE HIERARCHY OF RACES

Growing European and American interest in Asia, Africa, and other distant parts of the globe in the late nineteenth century spawned growing fascination with the peoples encountered in those areas. How were whites of European origin related to Africans, Asians, and others? What physical, intellectual, and cultural differences separated the purportedly "advanced" parts of the globe from the others? Among the authors to take up these questions was the Swiss-born Arnold Henry Guyot, who settled in the United States in the late 1840s and became a leading natural scientist at Princeton University. In the following excerpt from his 1873 book Physical Geography, *Guyot expounds on the relationships among the world's major racial groups.*

Under the influence of ever-varying external conditions, the human family,—while preserving in all climes, and under all circumstances, certain common features of body and mind, which mark them as one,—display an almost unlimited diversity of physical and mental qualities, and of social conditions.

The form and features show every gradation, from the symmetry, grace, and dignity of the ideal man, portrayed by the sculptors of ancient Greece, to the ugliness and deformity of the Hottentot and the Fuegian. The color of the skin varies from white tinted with rose, through brownish or yellowish hues, to an almost jet black.

The temperament is here ardent and impulsive, the emotions responding with the vivacity of childhood to every impression, whether joyous or sad; there it is cold, passive, as in old age, almost insensible alike to pain or pleasure.

The social condition varies from the refinement and culture of the European nations, to the degradation of the savage who roams the tropical forests, or burrows in the earth in the Arctic islands. . . .

The White race are distinguished by their tall stature, graceful proportions, and light, elastic step; their oval head and face, high broad forehead, symmetrical features, and ruddy cheeks; their abundant beard, and waving or slightly curling hair. . . .

The typical man . . . is distinguished by perfect regularity of features, and harmony in all the proportions of the figure, securing agility and strength in the highest degree, with the utmost beauty and grace. . . .

The law of perfection of type, in man, . . . forms an exception to that observed in the lower orders of creation. . . . The human family appears in its highest physical perfection, not within the Tropics, but in the Temperate Zone, in western Asia, the geographical center of the Old World.

The type degenerates gradually, with increasing distance, in all directions from this geographical centre; until, in the remotest regions of the globe, are found the ugliest, and the most deformed specimens of the human family. . . .

The Mongolic Race is more numerous than any other, and, including the various Mongoloid types, more widely dispersed than all others together. This race very anciently attained a comparatively high degree of civilization, and founded a powerful monarchy in China. They have, however, contributed little to the progress of mankind in general, owing to their isolation, their jealousy of foreign nations, and the policy of non-intercourse so rigidly observed by them even to the present time. . . .

The Negro Race have, by themselves, made only the first steps in civilization, and the great mass are still in the savage state. Where they have been brought under the influence of cultured nations, however, they have shown themselves capable of a high degree of progress. . . .

The Secondary Races have contributed nothing to the present condition of mankind; and none of the existing branches have taken more than the first steps in civilization, except under the influence of the White or Mongolic races.

Document 1.3

A Vision of Anglo-Saxon Triumph

Growing awareness of conditions in faraway parts of the world and the increasing feasibility of long-distance travel spurred the growth of a powerful American missionary movement in the late nineteenth century. Meanwhile, surging social Darwinism led many Americans to view their nation—or often the English-speaking "Anglo-Saxon" nations of the world—as waging a struggle for survival with other peoples. The Congregationalist clergyman Josiah Strong, who helped found the Social Gospel movement dedicated to applying Christian teachings to contemporary social problems, knit these two trends together in his 1885 book Our Country: Its Possible Future and Its Present Crisis. *The book urged Americans to undertake missionary work among benighted populations at home and abroad.*

It is not necessary to argue to those for whom I write that the two great needs of mankind, that all men may be lifted up into the light of the highest Christian civilization, are, first, a pure, spiritual Christianity, and, second, civil liberty. Without controversy, these are the forces which, in the past, have contributed most to the elevation of the human race, and they must continue to be, in the future, the most efficient ministers to its progress. It follows, then, that the Anglo-Saxon, as the great representative of these two ideas, the depository of these two great blessings, sustains peculiar relations to the world's future, is divinely commissioned to be, in a peculiar sense, his brother's keeper. . . .

[A] marked characteristic of the Anglo-Saxon is what may be called an instinct or genius for colonizing. His unequaled energy, his indomitable perseverance, and his personal independence, made him a pioneer. He excels all others in pushing his way into new countries. It was those in whom this tendency was strongest that came to America, and this inherited tendency has been further developed by the westward sweep of successive generations across the continent. . . .

Again, nothing more manifestly distinguishes the Anglo-Saxon than his intense and persistent energy; and he is developing in the United States an energy which, in eager activity and effectiveness, is peculiarly American. This is due partly to the fact that Americans are much better fed than Europeans, and partly to the undeveloped resources of a new country, but more largely to our climate, which acts as a constant stimulus. . . . Moreover, our social institutions are stimulating. In Europe the various ranks of society are, like the strata of the earth, fixed and fossilized. There can be no great change without a terrible upheaval, a social earthquake. Here society is like the waters of the sea, mobile. . . . Every one is free to become whatever he can make of himself; free to transform himself from a rail-splitter or a tanner or a canal-boy, into the nation's President. Our aristocracy, unlike that of Europe, is open to all comers. Wealth, position, influence, are prizes offered for energy; and every farmer's boy, every apprentice and clerk, every friendless and penniless immigrant, is free to enter the lists. Thus many causes co-operate to produce here the most forceful and tremendous energy in the world.

What is the significance of such facts? These tendencies infold the future; they are the mighty alphabet with which God writes his prophecies. May we not, by careful laying together of the letters, spell out something of his meaning? It seems to me that God, with infinite wisdom and skill, is training the Anglo-Saxon race for an hour sure to come in the world's future. . . . If I read not amiss, this powerful race will move down upon Mexico, down upon Central and South America, out upon the islands of the sea, over upon Africa and beyond. And can any one doubt that the result of this competition of races will be the "survival of the fittest"? . . . To this result no war of extermination is needful; the contest is not one of arms, but of vitality and civilization.

DOCUMENT 1.4

A CUBAN VIEW

Enthusiasts for the extension of U.S. power frequently focused their attention on Cuba, the Spanish-controlled island that some Americans had coveted for decades. U.S. ambitions were hardly lost on Cuban observers, many of whom feared that the end of Spanish rule might bring subjugation by a new foreign power. One sharp critic of U.S. imperial desires was José Martí, the Cuban journalist and poet who helped spark rebellion against Spain in the 1890s. Martí found much to admire in the United States, including a commitment to human freedom that he associated with Abraham Lincoln. But Martí resented U.S. dominance in Latin America, which he associated with Francis Cutting, leader of the Ameri- can Annexationist League. In the following letter, published in the New York Evening Post *on March 25, 1889, Martí juxtaposes these two aspects of the United States and criticizes the country for failing to help Cubans break free of Spain. He also denounces harsh attitudes among Americans about Cubans (especially Cubans living in the United States), focusing his criticism on an article that had been recently published by a Philadelphia newspaper called the* Manufacturer.

This is not the occasion to discuss the question of the annexation of Cuba. It is probable that no self-respecting Cuban would like to see his country annexed to a nation where the leaders of opinion share towards him the prejudices excusable only to vulgar jingoism or rampant ignorance. No honest Cuban will stoop to be received as a moral pest for the sake of the usefulness of his land in a community where his ability is denied, his morality insulted, and his character despised. There are some Cubans who, from honorable motives, from an ardent admiration for progress and liberty, from a prescience of their own powers under better political conditions, from an unhappy ignorance of the history and tendency of annexation, would like to see the island annexed to the United States. But those who have fought in war and learned in exile, who have built, by the work of hands and mind, a virtuous home in the heart of an unfriendly community; who by their successful efforts as scientists and merchants, as railroad builders and engineers, as teachers, artists, lawyers, journalists, orators, and poets, as men of alert intelligence and uncommon activity, are honored wherever their powers have been called into action and the people are just enough to understand them; ... those, more numerous than the others, do not desire the annexation of Cuba to the United States. They do not need it. They admire this nation, the greatest ever built by liberty, but they dislike the evil conditions that, like worms in the heart, have begun in this mighty republic their work of destruction. They have made of the heroes of this country their own heroes, and look to the success of the American commonwealth as the crowning glory of mankind; but they cannot honestly believe that excessive individualism, reverence for wealth, and the protracted exultation of a terrible victory are preparing the United States to be the typical nation of liberty, where no opinion is to be based in greed, and no triumph or acquisition reached against charity and justice. We love the country of Lincoln as much as we fear the country of Cutting.

We are not the people of destitute vagrants or immoral pigmies that the *Manufacturer* is pleased to picture; nor the country of petty talkers, incapable of action, hostile to hard work, that, in a mass with the other countries of Spanish America, we are by arrogant travelers and writers represented to be. We have suffered impatiently under tyranny; we have fought like men, sometimes like giants, to be freemen; we are passing that period of stormy repose, full of germs of revolt, that naturally follows a period of excessive and unsuccessful action . . . we deserve in our misfortune the respect of those who did not help us in our need.

Document 1.5

A CALL FOR NAVAL POWER

Dramatically expanding overseas trade and the apparent danger of failing to keep up with the military prowess of the other great powers convinced some Americans of the need to build a big navy. Unquestionably, the most influential and eloquent advocate of expanding America's seagoing power was Captain Alfred Thayer Mahan, a prolific historian, president of the U.S. Naval War College from 1886 to 1889 and 1892 to 1893, and friend of Theodore Roosevelt and other lead- ing politicians. Mahan's writings on the necessity of sea power remain classics a century after his death in 1914. In 1890, Mahan laid out some of his key ideas in an essay for the Atlantic Monthly *entitled "The United States Looking Outward."*

Indications are not wanting of an approaching change in the thoughts and policy of Americans as to their relations with the world outside their own borders. For the past quarter of a century, the predominant idea, which has asserted itself successfully at the polls and shaped the course of the government, has been to preserve the home market for the home industries. The employer and the workman alike have been taught to look at the various economical measures proposed from this point of view, to regard with hostility any step favoring the intrusion of the foreign producer upon their own domain, and rather to demand increasingly rigorous measures of exclusion than to acquiesce in any loosening of the chain that binds the consumer to them. The inevitable consequence has followed, as in all cases when the mind or the eye is exclusively fixed in one direction, that the danger of loss or the prospect of advantage in another quarter has been overlooked; and although the abounding resources of the country have maintained the exports at a high figure, this flattering result has been due more to the superabundant bounty of Nature than to the demand of other nations for our protected manufactures.

For nearly the lifetime of a generation, therefore, American industries have been thus protected, until the practice has assumed the force of a tradition, and is clothed in the mail of conservatism. In their mutual relations, these industries resemble the activities of a modern ironclad that has heavy armor, but inferior engines and guns; mighty for defence, weak for offence. Within, the home market is secured; but outside, beyond the broad seas, there are the markets of the world, that can be entered and controlled only by a vigorous contest, to which the habit of trusting to protection by statute does not conduce.

At bottom, however, the temperament of the American people is essentially alien to such a sluggish attitude.... The interesting and significant feature of this changing attitude is the turning of the eyes outward, instead of inward only, to seek the welfare of the country. To affirm the importance of distant markets, and the relation to them of our own immense powers of production, implies logically the recognition of the link that joins the products and the markets,—that is, the carrying trade; the three together constituting that chain of maritime power to which Great Britain owes her wealth and greatness. Further, is it too much to say that, as two of these links, the shipping and the markets, are exterior to our own borders, the acknowledgment of them carries with it a view of the relations of the United States to the world radically distinct from the simple idea of self-sufficingness? We shall not follow far this line of thought before there will dawn the realization of America's unique position, facing the older worlds of the East and West, her shores washed by the oceans which touch the one or the other, but which are common to her alone.

Coincident with these signs of change in our own policy there is a restlessness in the world at large which is deeply significant, if not ominous. It is beside our purpose to dwell upon the internal state of Europe, whence, if disturbances arise, the effect upon us may be but partial and indirect. But the great seaboard powers there do not stand on guard against their continental rivals only; they cherish also aspirations for commercial extension, for colonies, and for influence in distant regions, which may bring, and, even under our present contracted policy, already have brought them into collision with ourselves. . . .

There is no sound reason for believing that the world has passed into a period of assured peace outside the limits of Europe. Unsettled political conditions, such as exist in Haiti, Central America, and many of the Pacific islands, especially the Hawaiian group, when combined with great military or commercial importance as is the case with most of these positions, involve, now as always, dangerous germs of quarrel, against which it is prudent at least to be prepared. Undoubtedly, the general temper of nations is more averse from war than it was of old. If no less selfish and grasping than our predecessors, we feel more dislike to the discomforts and sufferings attendant upon a breach of peace; but to retain that highly valued repose and the undisturbed enjoyment of the returns of commerce, it is necessary to argue upon somewhat equal terms of strength with an adversary. It is the preparedness of the enemy, and not acquiescence in the existing state of things, that now holds back the armies of Europe. . . .

Despite a certain great original superiority conferred by our geographical nearness and immense resources,—due, in other words, to our natural advantages, and not to our intelligent preparations,—the United States is woefully unready, not only in fact but in purpose, to assert in the Caribbean and Central America a weight of influence proportioned to the extent of her interests. We have not the navy, and, what is worse, we are not willing to have the navy, that will weigh seriously in any disputes with those nations whose interests will conflict there with our own. We have not, and we are not anxious to provide, the defence of the seaboard which will leave the navy free for its work at sea. We have not, but many other powers have, positions, either within or on the borders of the Caribbean, which not only possess great natural advantages for the control of that sea, but have received and are receiving that artificial strength of fortification and armament which will make them practically inexpugnable. On the contrary, we have not on the Gulf of Mexico even the beginning of a navy yard which could serve as the base of our operations. . . .

It is perfectly reasonable and legitimate, in estimating our needs of military preparation, to take into account the remoteness of the chief naval and military nations from our shores, and the consequent difficulty of maintaining operations at such a distance. It is equally proper, in framing our policy, to consider the jealousies of the European family of states, and their consequent unwillingness to incur the enmity of a people so strong as ourselves; their dread of our revenge in the future, as well as their inability to detach more than a certain part of their forces to our shores without losing much of their own weight in the councils of Europe. . . . [But] it is folly to look upon [these considerations] as sufficient alone for our security. . . .

Though distant, our shores can be reached; being defenceless, they can detain but a short time a force sent against them. . . .

Yet, were our sea frontier as strong as it now is weak, passive self-defence, whether in trade or war, would be but a poor policy, so long as this world continues to be one of struggle and vicissitude. All around us now is strife; "the struggle of life," "the race of life," are phrases so familiar that we do not feel their significance till we stop to think about them. Everywhere nation is arrayed against nation; our own no less than others. . . . Are our people . . . so unaggressive that they are likely not to want their own way in matters where their interests turn on points of disputed right, or so little sensitive as to submit quietly to encroachment by others, in quarters where they long have considered their own influence should prevail?

Document 1.6

THE CLOSING OF THE AMERICAN FRONTIER

In 1890, the U.S. Census Bureau declared that the settlement of the trans-Mississippi West had put an end to the Western frontier. Frederick Jackson Turner, an eminent historian at the University of Wisconsin, picked up on the theme in a paper entitled "The Significance of the Frontier in American History," which he delivered as a speech at the 1893 meeting of the American Historical Association in Chicago and then published as an essay that has been reprinted innumerable times ever since. Turner worried that the "closing of the frontier" would destroy the ethic of individualism that was the nation's defining characteristic. It was a small step for many of Turner's contemporaries to argue that the nation must find new frontiers on which to concentrate its energies.

In a recent bulletin of the Superintendent of the Census for 1890 appear these significant words: "Up to and including 1880 the country had a frontier of settlement, but at present the unsettled area has been so broken into by isolated bodies of settlement that there can hardly be said to be a frontier line. In the discussion of its extent, its westward movement, etc., it can not, therefore, any longer have a place in the census reports." This brief official statement marks the closing of a great historic movement. Up to our own day American history has been in a large degree the history of the colonization of the Great West. The existence of an area of free land, its continuous recession, and the advance of American settlement westward, explain American development.

Behind institutions, behind constitutional forms and modifications, lie the vital forces that call these organs into life and shape them to meet changing conditions. The peculiarity of American institutions is the fact that they have been compelled to adapt themselves to the changes of an expanding people—to the changes involved in crossing a continent, in winning a wilderness, and in developing at each area of this progress out of the primitive economic and political conditions of the frontier into the complexity of city life....

So long as free land exists, the opportunity for a competency exists, and economic power secures political power. But the democracy born of free land, strong in selfishness and individualism, intolerant of administrative experience and education, and pressing individual liberty beyond its proper bounds, has its dangers as well as its benefits. Individualism in America has allowed a laxity in regard to governmental affairs which has rendered possible the spoils system and all the manifest evils that follow from the lack of a highly developed civic spirit....

From the conditions of frontier life came intellectual traits of profound importance. The works of travelers along each frontier from colonial days onward describe certain common traits, and these traits have, while softening down, still persisted as survivals in the place of their origin, even when a higher social organization succeeded. The result is that, to the frontier, the American intellect owes its striking characteristics. That coarseness and strength combined with acuteness and inquisitiveness, that practical, inventive turn of mind, quick to find expedients, that masterful grasp of material things, lacking in the artistic but powerful to effect great ends, that restless, nervous energy, that dominant individualism, working for good and for evil, and withal that buoyancy and exuberance which comes with freedom—these are traits of the frontier, or traits called out elsewhere because of the existence of the frontier.

Since the days when the fleet of Columbus sailed into the waters of the New World, America has been another name for opportunity, and the people of the United States have taken their tone from the incessant expansion which has not only been open but has even been forced upon them. He would be a rash prophet who should assert that the expansive character of American life has now entirely ceased. Movement has been its dominant fact, and, unless this training has no effect upon a people, the American energy will continually demand a wider field for its exercise. But never again will such gifts of free land offer themselves....

What the Mediterranean Sea was to the Greeks, breaking the bond of custom, offering new experiences, calling out new institutions and activities, that, and more, the ever retreating frontier has been to the United States directly, and to the nations of Europe more remotely. And now, four centuries from the discovery of America, at the end of a hundred years of life under the Constitution, the frontier has gone, and with its going has closed the first period of American history.

Document 1.7

OPPOSITION TO FOREIGN ADVENTURES

The failure to acquire Santo Domingo or Cuba in the 1860s and 1870s did not end speculation about adding new territories to the United States. Indeed, growing commercial and military power made the prospect appear more feasible than ever before. Some Americans viewed that possibility with great enthusiasm. Others worried that expanding the nation would carry numerous problems and could even eat away at core American ideals. One such skeptic was Carl Schurz, a German-born politician and essayist whose career included a term in the U.S. Senate, an ambassadorship to Spain, and a stint as editorial writer for Harper's. *In the following essay published in* Harper's *in October 1893, Schurz spelled out various reasons for anxiety about American ambitions in the Western Hemisphere.*

The patriotic ardor of those who would urge this Republic into the course of indiscriminate territorial aggrandizement to make it the greatest of the great Powers of the world deserves more serious consideration. To see his country powerful and respected among the nations of the earth, and to secure to it all those advantages to which its character and position entitle it, is the natural desire of every American. In this sentiment we are all agreed. There may, however, be grave differences of opinion as to how this end can be most surely, most completely and most worthily attained....

Let us admit, for argument's sake, that there is something dazzling in the conception of a great republic embracing the whole continent and the adjacent islands, and that the tropical part of it would open many tempting fields for American enterprise; let us suppose—a violent supposition, to be sure—that we could get all these countries without any trouble or cost. But will it not be well to look beyond? If we receive those countries as States of this Union, as we eventually shall have to do in case we annex them, we shall also have to admit the people inhabiting them as our fellow-citizens on a footing of equality. As our fellow-citizens they will not only govern themselves in their own States as best they can—the United States undertaking to guarantee them a republican form of government, and to protect them against invasion and domestic violence—but they will, through their Senators and Representatives in Congress, and through their votes in Presidential elections, and through their influence upon our political parties, help in governing the whole Republic, in governing us. And what kind of people are those we take in as equal members of our National household, our family circle?

It is a matter of universal experience that democratic institutions have never on a large scale prospered in tropical latitudes. The so-called republics existing under the tropical sun constantly vibrate between anarchy and despotism. When we observe there a protracted period of order and quiet, we find almost always something like martial law at the bottom of it. . . . It cannot be said that the people of the American tropics have lacked opportunity for the progressive development of democratic institutions. Ever since they threw off the Spanish yoke they have been their own masters. They have long been as free and unhampered as the people of the United States to rule their home affairs and to shape their own destinies. Why have they not succeeded, as we have, in developing the rich resources of their own countries and in building up stable democratic governments? The cause is obvious to every unprejudiced observer. . . .

I do not say that in the tropics there are not some persons who perform comparatively hard and steady work. But it is a well-known fact that the great mass of the people in those regions, in a state of freedom, labor just enough to satisfy their immediate wants; and these are very limited in a climate of perpetual summer, where most of the time food is easily obtainable, and where extremely little is needed in point of clothing and shelter. As in addition to this the high temperature discourages every strenuous and steady exertion, it is but natural that wherever in such climate labor is left to itself it should run into shiftlessness, and that efforts to stimulate or organize labor for production on a large scale should have a tendency to develop into some sort of coercion.

Neither do I say that in tropical countries there are not persons who understand the true theory of democratic government, or who are in favor of it. But democratic government cannot long be sustained by mere sentiment or political philosophy. It must live in the ways of thinking and the habits of the people who have to carry it on. And experience shows that the tropics will indeed breed individual men who know how to govern others, but not great masses of men who know how to govern themselves. . . .

In our present condition we have over all the great nations of the world one advantage of incalculable value. We are the only one that is not in any of its parts threatened by powerful neighbors; the only one not under any necessity of keeping up a large armament either on land or water for the security of its possessions; the only one that can turn all the energies of its population to productive employment; the only one that has an entirely free hand. This is a blessing for which the American people can never be too thankful. It should not be lightly jeoparded. . . .

Seeing the impossibility, under existing conditions, of striking against us a quick blow that would have any decisive consequences, and seeing also that a war carried on upon our own ground would, owing to our unlimited staying power, be practically a war without end, and present chances of combinations most dangerous to them—recognizing these obvious facts, all those powers will be naturally disposed to go to the extreme of honorable concession in order to avoid hostilities with the United States. In fact, we can hardly get into a war unless it be of our own seeking....

This advantage will be very essentially impaired if we present to a possible enemy a vulnerable point of attack which we have to defend, but cannot defend without going out of our impregnable stronghold, away from the seat of our power, to fight on ground on which the enemy may appear in superior strength, and have the conditions in his favor.... Attempts of the enemy to gain an important advantage by a sudden stroke, which would be entirely harmless if made on our continental stronghold, might have an excellent chance of success if made on our distant insular possession, and then the whole war could be made to turn upon that point, where the enemy might concentrate his forces as easily as we, or even more easily, and be our superior on the decisive field of operations. It is evident that thus the immense advantage we now enjoy of a substantially unassailable defensive position would be lost. We would no longer possess the inestimable privilege of being stronger and more secure than any other nation without a large and costly armament. Hawaii, or whatever other outlying domain, would be our Achilles' heel....

It is said that we need a large navy in any case for the protection of our commerce, and that if we have it for this purpose it may at the same time serve for the protection of outlying National domains without much extra expense.... Our commerce is not threatened by anybody or anything, unless it be the competition of other nations and the errors of our own commercial policy; and against these influences warships avail nothing. Nor do we need any warships to obtain favorable commercial arrangements with other nations. Our position of power under existing circumstances is such that no foreign nation will, at the risk of a quarrel with us, deny our commerce any accommodation we can reasonably lay claim to....

Document 1.8

A VIEW FROM GERMANY

Growing confidence among Americans about their nation's place in the international order was obvious to rival nations. Yet it was also clear that growing U.S. power was accompanied by social turbulence. Labor unrest, urban squalor, and massive disparities of wealth resulted from the nation's rapid industrialization over the course of the nineteenth century. But the problems were greatly exacerbated by a major economic depression beginning in 1893. The following cartoon, which appeared in the Berlin satirical weekly Kladderadatch *on July 15, 1894, contrasted apparent American prosperity with other realities that did not easily mesh with self-congratulatory expressions of U.S. nationalism. The caption reads, "Uncle Sam dreaming and awake."*

Onkel Sams Träumen und Erwachen.

Document 1.9

U.S. DOMINANCE IN THE WESTERN HEMISPHERE

In 1895, a diplomatic confrontation erupted between Venezuela and Great Britain over the boundary between Venezuela and its British-controlled eastern neighbor, British Guiana. U.S. leaders regarded British assertiveness as an affront to U.S. preponderance in the Western Hemisphere. Eager to exert U.S. authority but also to settle the matter peacefully, Secretary of State Richard Olney sent the following note to the U.S. ambassador in London on July 20, 1895, instructing the ambassador to inform the British government of the U.S. position. Later dubbed the "Olney Corollary" to the 1823 Monroe Doctrine, the note went far beyond the earlier proclamation barring European colonization in the Western Hemisphere by insisting that the United States had the right to mediate territorial disputes. Britain ultimately accepted the American position and submitted to arbitration.

That America is in no part open to colonization, though the proposition was not universally admitted at the time of its first enunciation, has long been universally conceded. We are now concerned, therefore, only with that other practical application of the Monroe doctrine the disregard of which by an European power is to be deemed an act of unfriendliness towards the United States.... The rule in question has but a single purpose and object. It is that no European power or combination of European powers shall forcibly deprive an American state of the right and power of self-government and of shaping for itself its own political fortunes and destinies....

The states of America, South as well as North, by geographical proximity, by natural sympathy, by similarity of governmental constitutions, are friends and allies, commercially and politically, of the United States. To allow the subjugation of any of them by an European power is, of course, to completely reverse that situation and signifies the loss of all the advantages incident to their natural relations to us. But that is not all. The people of the United States have a vital interest in the cause of popular self-government. They have secured the right for themselves and their posterity at the cost of infinite blood and treasure. They have realized and exemplified its beneficent operation by a career unexampled in point of national greatness or individual felicity. They believe it to be for the healing of all nations, and that civilization must either advance or retrograde accordingly as its supremacy is extended or curtailed....

The greater its enlightenment, the more surely every state perceived that its permanent interests require it to be governed by the immutable principles of right and justice. Each, nevertheless, is only too liable to succumb to the temptations offered by seeming special opportunities for its own aggrandizement, and each would rashly imperil its own safety were it not to remember that for the regard and respect of other states it must be largely dependent upon its own strength and power. To-day the United States is practically sovereign on this continent, and its fiat is law upon the subjects to which it confines its interposition. Why? It is not because of the pure friendship or good will felt for it. It is not simply by reason of its high character as a civilized state, nor because of wisdom and justice and equity are the invariable characteristics of the dealings of the United States. It is because, in addition to all other grounds, its infinite resources combined with its isolated position render it master of the situation and practically invulnerable as against any or all other powers.

All of the advantages of this superiority are at once imperiled if the principle be admitted that European powers may convert American states into colonies or provinces of their own. The principle would be eagerly availed of, and every power doing so would immediately acquire a base of military operations against us. What one power was permitted to do could not be denied to another, and it is not inconceivable that the struggle now going on for the acquisition of Africa might be transferred to South America. If it were, the weaker countries would unquestionably be soon absorbed, while the ultimate result might be the partition of all South America between the various European powers. The disastrous consequences to the United States of such a condition of things are obvious. The loss of prestige, of authority, and of weight in the councils of the family of nations, would be among the least of them. Our only real rivals in peace as well as enemies in war would be found located at our very doors. Thus far in our history we have been spared the burdens and evils of immense standing armies and all the other accessories of huge warlike establishments, and the exemption has largely contributed to our national greatness and wealth as well as to the happiness of every citizen. But, with the powers of Europe permanently encamped on American soil, the ideal conditions we have thus far enjoyed can not be expected to continue. We too must be armed to the teeth, we too must convert the flower or our male population into soldiers and sailors, and by withdrawing them from the various pursuits of peaceful industry we too must practically annihilate a large share of the productive energy of the nation.

Document 1.10

THE NECESSITY OF OVERSEAS MARKETS

The debilitating depression that began in 1893 led many Americans to ask what underlying problems in the American economy had caused such a calamity. Many businessmen and politicians pointed to the same culprit: overproduction. So mighty had American industry grown, they reasoned, that production had out- stripped the ability of the nation's consumers to purchase it. The result was periodic busts that shuttered factories, caused massive unemployment, and stirred labor unrest. One solution was to distribute wealth more evenly among the American population. But the favored solution among most industrialists was to capture new markets abroad for American goods. Charles R. Flint, president of the American Clipper Ship Line, laid out this reasoning in the following essay. The piece appeared in The Forum, *a New York–based magazine specializing in commentary about politics and economics, in May 1897, as the country suffered the fourth year of economic crisis.*

American commerce was first colonial, is now national, and must become international. In the earlier period of our industrial life, it was natural that the energies of our people should be applied mainly to the discovery and development of our vast and varied resources, to the construction of post-roads, canals, and great systems of railways, to the establishment and extension of inland navigation, to the building of towns and cities, and to the founding of manufacturing industries. One development stimulated another, and thus produced finally an era of unexampled prosperity. A period of depression followed, owing largely to the fact that "we were our own best customers"; our power of production and our output of manufactures far exceeded the demand for home consumption; and one-half of our industrial energy had to lie unemployed. Such is our situation today. The present, therefore, seems a most fitting time to discuss the influence of our export trade upon our national prosperity.

In this latest period of contraction, particularly during the past year, the importance of our exports has been brought home to our people.... During the past four years, if it had not been for the sustaining power of foreign orders, many factories would have been forced to close; thus breaking up organizations which it had required years to perfect, and throwing laborers out of work at a time when they would have been unable to obtain other employment.... Hitherto our trade in manufactured goods has been almost exclusively among ourselves; but during the recent years of depression the feeling has grown that the only way out of our straits is through commerce with all the world. Thus will be brought about an industrial revival that will end the present popular discontent....

We cannot remain wholly dependent for our active industrial life upon the home demand; and the markets of the world are open to us, ready to absorb the surplus products of our utmost manufacturing capacity. Economists recognize that the industrial greatness of a nation depends on the possession of the main sources of mechanical energy—coal and water power—and of abundant deposits of iron ore. That nation which has the cheaper fuel and cheaper iron has a steady advantage in the contest for supremacy in the world's trade....

Every dollar's worth of merchandise exported represents just so much wealth given by the foreigner in exchange for our own people's industry. It is, therefore, natural that we should supplement our great interstate commerce—the greatest commercial intercourse in the world conducted under the conditions of absolute free trade—by securing markets abroad. A comparatively small additional demand often turns bad times into good times. The total wealth of the United States is about $80,000,000,000; the total amount of money is about $2,300,000,000; yet at times, if the bank reserves of New York decline ten millions, anxiety is created in financial circles, and money required for legitimate wants of trade is unobtainable. But if the reserves advance ten millions, money becomes a drug in the market. So it is with our industries. A moderate increase in the sale of our products abroad would give an impulse to some of our industries, which would stimulate others and thus bring about a wholesome industrial activity.

In widening our field of distribution, there are several reasons why it is most important to create markets for our *manufactured* goods, including flour, canned foods, and other manufactures of farm products, as distinguished from "raw materials."

(1) The percentage of profit on manufactured goods is much larger than on raw materials. The French best appreciate this. Importing the crude products of other countries, they add to them features that please the eye and gratify the taste, and thus make a vastly greater profit than the producers of raw materials.

(2) There is a greater necessity to widen our market for manufactured goods. Raw materials are readily marketed; and though it requires much time and expense to build up a trade in manufactured goods, yet, when once developed, it is not only more profitable than that in raw materials, but is less vulnerable to competition. . . .

(3) The United States is becoming yearly more of a manufacturing nation. The value of our exports of manufactured products in 1870 was $68,279,764; in 1890, $151,102,376; and in 1896, $228,489,893. While these figures show a large increase, the largest shipment of manufactured goods in any one year ($228,489,893) is small as compared with our capacity and opportunities, and with the exports of manufactures by our competitors of Western Europe. The latter reach an annual value of $3,500,000,000. Our export trade is less than one-fifteenth this.

The vital question arises, How can this export trade be developed? The answer is: (1) By the establishment of international banking facilities based upon a currency of undoubted stability; (2) by controlling means of transportation; (3) by manufacturing what is most suitable for the needs of foreign markets; (4) by proper legislation, commercial treaties, and intelligent representation abroad; and (5) by manufacturing products of good quality at low cost. . . .

Document 1.11

A PROTEST AGAINST ANNEXATION OF HAWAII

Enthusiasts of U.S. expansion increasingly focused their attention on the Hawaiian (Sandwich) Islands in the 1880s and 1890s. The islands, also coveted by Britain and Japan, offered an ideal port and coaling station halfway across the Pacific Ocean and possessed lucrative sugar and fruit industries dominated by American planters. The American takeover began in 1887, when U.S. businessmen, backed by the threat of violence, coerced the Hawaiian king to sign what became known as the "bayonet constitution," stripping natives of most of their rights. Six years later, the new monarch, Queen Liliuokalani, was overthrown in a coup organized by white planters, who established a republic dominated by U.S.-born elites. A treaty annexing the islands to the United States was signed in 1897 and took effect the next year. On June 17, 1897, Liliuokalani sent President William McKinley the following note to protest U.S. behavior.

I, Liliuokalani of Hawaii, by the will of God named heir apparent on the tenth day of April, A. D. 1877, and by the grace of God Queen of the Hawaiian Islands on the seventeenth day of January, A. D. 1893, do hereby protest against the ratification of a certain treaty, which, so I am informed, has been signed at Washington by Messrs. Hatch, Thurston, and Kinney, purporting to cede those Islands to the territory and dominion of the United States. I declare such a treaty to be an act of wrong toward the native and part-native people of Hawaii, an invasion of the rights of the ruling chiefs, in violation of international rights both toward my people and toward friendly nations with whom they have made treaties, the perpetuation of the fraud whereby the constitutional government was overthrown and, finally, an act of gross injustice to me.

Because the official protests made by me on the seventeenth day of January, 1893, to the so-called Provisional Government was signed by me, and received by said government with the assurance that the case was referred to the United States of America for arbitration.

Because that protest and my communications to the United States Government immediately thereafter expressly declare that I yielded my authority to the forces of the United States in order to avoid bloodshed, and because I recognized the futility of a conflict with so formidable a power.

Because the President of the United States, the Secretary of State, and an envoy commissioned by them reported in official documents that my government was unlawfully coerced by the forces, diplomatic and naval, of the United States; that I was at the date of their investigations the constitutional ruler of my people. . . .

Because neither the above-named commission nor the government which sends it has ever received any such authority from the registered voters of Hawaii, but derives its assumed powers from the so-called committee of public safety, organized on or about the seventeenth day of January, 1893, said committee being composed largely of persons claiming American citizenship, and not one single Hawaiian was a member thereof, or in any way participated in the demonstration leading to its existence.

Because my people, about forty thousand in number, have in no way been consulted by those, three thousand in number, who claim the right to destroy the independence of Hawaii. My people constitute four-fifths of the legally qualified voters of Hawaii, and excluding those imported for the demands of labor, about the same proportion of the inhabitants.

Because said treaty ignores, not only the civic rights of my people, but, further, the hereditary property of their chiefs. Of the 4,000,000 acres composing the territory said treaty offers to annex, 1,000,000 or 915,000 acres has in no way been heretofore recognized as other than the private property of the constitutional monarch, subject to a control in no way differing from other items of a private estate.

Because it is proposed by said treaty to confiscate said property, technically called the crown lands, those legally entitled thereto, either now or in succession, receiving no consideration whatever for estates, their title to which has been always undisputed, and which is legitimately in my name at this date.

Because said treaty ignores, not only all professions of perpetual amity and good faith made by the United States in former treaties with the sovereigns representing the Hawaiian people, but all treaties made by those sovereigns with other and friendly powers, and it is thereby in violation of international law.

Because, by treating with the parties claiming at this time the right to cede said territory of Hawaii, the Government of the United States receives such territory from the hands of those whom its own magistrates (legally elected by the people of the United States, and in office in 1893) pronounced fraudulently in power and unconstitutionally ruling Hawaii.

Therefore I, Liliuokalani of Hawaii, do hereby call upon the President of that nation, to whom alone I yielded my property and my authority, to withdraw said treaty (ceding said Islands) from further consideration. I ask the honorable Senate of the United States to decline to ratify said treaty, and I implore the people of this great and good nation, from whom my ancestors learned the Christian religion, to sustain their representatives in such acts of justice and equity as may be in accord with the principles of their fathers, and to the Almighty Ruler of the universe, to him who judgeth righteously, I commit my cause.

Document 1.12

CRITICISM OF U.S. METHODS IN HAWAII

Hawaiians were not the only ones to criticize U.S. behavior in Hawaii. The New York–based humor magazine Puck *published the following cartoon on December 1, 1897, to underscore that fact that many Americans were skeptical about the acquisition. The presiding clergyman, labeled "McKinley," reads from a book entitled* Annexation Policy, *while Alabama senator John Tyler Morgan, a major proponent of acquiring Hawaii, holds a shotgun emblazoned with "bluster." The cartoon, drawn by C. J. Taylor, features the caption "Another Shotgun Wedding with Neither Party Willing."*

Document 1.13

THE DANGERS OF OVERCIVILIZATION

The dwindling of the Western frontier, rapid urbanization, and the transformation of the American economy led some Americans to fear that the nation was becoming too disconnected from its rugged past—in a word, too soft. A growing number of politicians and publicists called for a return to martial, manly values and urged that the United States welcome conflict and even war as cleansing experiences. One author who feared excessive civilization was the essayist and biographer Henry Childs Merwin. In June 1897, Merwin published the following article, entitled "On Being Civilized Too Much," in the Atlantic Monthly.

There are in all of us certain natural impulses, or instincts, which furnish in large measure the springs of human conduct; and these impulses, or instincts, as they may be called with some exaggeration, are apt to be dulled and weakened by civilization. While they are still strong in a man, he may be said to be close to nature, in the essential meaning of that expression. He has a certain spontaneous promptitude of action and of feeling, akin to that which is displayed by all dumb animals. Man is a compound of feeling and intellect. In the savage, feeling predominates, and the intellect plays a very subordinate part. But now take your savage in hand, cut his hair, put trousers on his legs, give him a common school education, an air-tight stove, and a daily newspaper, and presently his intellect will develop, and will exercise more and more control over his feelings. Pursue this process a little further, and soon you will have a creature who is what we call over-sophisticated and effete,—a being in whom the springs of action are, in greater or less degree, paralyzed or perverted by the undue predominance of the intellect. In every age and in every country, in the most civilized nations, and also, I suppose, in the most savage tribes, men will be found who illustrate all stages of this process. In fact, the difference is one between individuals more than between ages or races. Still, every age as well as every nation has a type of its own, which may be close to nature or far from nature. Man is at his best, does the greatest deeds and produces the greatest literature, when there is in him a perfect balance between the feelings and the intellect; when he is neither an emotional nor an intellectual being, but a happy compound of both....

To be close to nature is ... to preserve certain primeval impulses, or instincts.... Nature herself has decided against the man who has lost these primeval impulses. He does not survive, he does not conquer and overspread the earth: and this appears most plainly when the instinct of pugnacity is considered. This instinct we share with the beasts of the field. If a dog has a bone, and a strange dog comes up and tries to take it from him, the result is a fight, which ends in the killing or disabling, or perhaps simply in the intimidation of one animal, so that the other is left to enjoy the bone in contention. In that humble contest we find the principle of most great wars. When the instinct is weakened, when people get too far from nature, they hire others to fight for them, as the Romans did in their decadence; and when that stage is reached the end is not far off. Nature will not tolerate the suppression of the instinct of pugnacity.

But this instinct is far more beautifully shown in questions of honor than it is in questions of mere property; and here too we find ourselves at one with the inferior animals. Dogs can insult one another as well as men can; and they have the same instinct to resent an insult. You will sometimes see two dogs walking around each other on their toes and growling, until presently one flies at the other's throat, and they fight it out. The bravest man who ever died on the field of honor was actuated by the same impulse; and though dueling may be a bad and foolish manifestation or exercise of the instinct, still the instinct itself is a good one, and upon its existence depend, in the last analysis, the prosperity and permanence of nations. Before the time of the Civil War in this country, and even after the war had begun, the South thought that they would have an easy victory over the North, because, as the South supposed, the North had lost the instinct to pugnacity. They thought that we were so given over to trading and dickering, to buying and selling, that we could not fight. They thought that we were too far from nature to fight. The event proved that they were greatly in error. But nations have lost the instinct of pugnacity, they have become incapable of fighting; and when they have reached that stage, they have perished.

2

Imperial America

WAR WITH SPAIN AND THE PHILIPPINES

U.S. power had expanded enormously by the time the United States went to war with Spain, but it was not yet clear what role the rising nation would play on the international stage. Policy makers and pundits charged Spain with mercilessly misruling Cuba—a country many American policy makers desired for their own sphere of influence—as Spanish leaders countered independence-minded rebels with force by the late 1890s. Unrest brought even more brutal tactics, while instability contributed to economic woes for the island, whose lucrative trade with the United States suffered. The death of a hard-line nationalist prime minister in Madrid in 1897 cleared the way for the promise of Cuban independence by the start of 1898. Peace would not come easily, however. Ongoing instability on the island prompted further Spanish crackdowns, drawing even greater concern from the United States. In February 1898, President William McKinley announced that American naval vessels would sail to Havana, ostensibly to ensure the safety of American citizens, though clearly also as a reminder to Spanish officials that their actions would not go unnoticed. As the documentary record now makes clear, McKinley also longed to ensure that any Cuban state, devoid of Spanish rule, would remain under American influence if not direct American control.

Leading the American flotilla was the battleship USS Maine, *which moved to Cuba at the same time American strategists positioned additional naval forces near other Spanish outposts in Europe, Asia, and throughout the Pacific. Cuba was the spark, but planners were ready for a far wider conflagration. The first unexpected explosion sunk the* Maine, *which caught fire during the night of February 15 in the middle of Havana's harbor. American politicians and a wild-eyed press corps demanded revenge, even if little evidence existed at the time that Cuban or Spanish forces were at fault. Tensions erupted between Madrid and Washington, leading to mutual declarations of war by late April.*

Conflict erupted far beyond the Caribbean as American and Spanish forces fought at several key points throughout Spain's aging empire. The Philippines in particular proved a vital hotspot, with American forces routing the Spanish. American policy makers had long coveted the strategically placed archipelago of the Philippines and coaling stations at Guam and other Pacific atolls, considering them crucial refueling points on the long commercial route from the United States to mainland Asia. The teeming and seemingly untapped markets of China were the real goals of American merchants and empire builders. In time both Cuba and the Philippines came under American control, as well as a series of island possessions, building a virtual chain (for coaling and resupply) across the vast Pacific Ocean.

Within ten short weeks—what Secretary of State John Hay famously termed a "splendid little war"—Americans gained something new in their nation's history: an overseas empire. Prior expansion had almost invariably occurred within lands contiguous with the United States, or at the least (as in the case of California or Alaska) via as-yet-unincorporated areas. Such new territories were largely expected one day to join the Union. This was different. War and conquest brought new territories across the globe, and they were connected only by water. It brought as well new peoples whom few U.S. leaders expected would become full-bore Americans.

Control did not come as easily as conquest. In the Philippines, especially, local leaders initially embraced Americans as liberators but then balked when those liberators imposed their own rule. A bloody counterinsurgency campaign ensued. Both sides—those who supported American colonial rule and those who opposed it—battled for the hearts and minds of the Filipino people. Both committed atrocities. Accounts of massacres, tortured prisoners, and burned-out villages filled the pages of American newspapers, further fueling the intensity of the anti-imperialists. For a nation born of anticolonialism, the transition to empire was fraught with controversy. What to do with these possessions in the long term and, of equal importance, how to justify their acquisition and utilization among an American populace long opposed to overseas empires, would prove difficult questions for successive presidential administrations. One thing was certain: whether the United States was formally an empire or not, Washington controlled peoples, territory, trade, and politics far from American shores.

Document 2.1

HALTING A HUMANITARIAN CRISIS

While historians debate to this day the varied causes of the Spanish-American War—some arguing it was an American search for markets, others suggesting Cubans played the larger role in provoking U.S. intervention—widespread American concern over Spanish misrule of Cuba clearly helped drive popular sentiment within the United States. Such humanitarian concerns touched the American conscience and also usefully sold newspapers for publishers eager to relate increasingly horrific and lurid accounts of Spanish barbarity. American politicians and journalists swarmed the island, documenting their case for intervention. Tensions between the two nations finally broke in April 1898, when Spain and the United States declared war. The speech below, offered by Senator and former Secretary of War Redfield Proctor on March 17, 1898, exemplifies the humanitarian concerns that publicly drove the crisis beyond its tipping point, casting the Spanish military commander charged with pacifying the island, General Valeriano Weyler, as the principal villain.

Everything seems to go on much as usual in Havana. Quiet prevails and except for the frequent squads of soldiers marching to guard and police duty and their abounding presence in all public places, one sees little signs of war. Outside Havana all is changed. It is not peace, nor is it war. It is desolation and distress, misery and starvation. Every town and village is surrounded by a trocha, a sort of rifle pit, but constructed on a plan new to me, the dirt being thrown up on the inside and a barbed wire fence on the outer side of the trench.

These trochas have at every corner, and at frequent intervals along the sides, what are there called forts, but which are really small block-houses, many of them more like a large sentry box, loop-holed for musketry, and with a guard of from two to ten soldiers in each. The purpose of these trochas is to keep reconcentrados in as well as to keep the insurgents out.

From all the surrounding country the people have been driven into these fortified towns and held there to subsist as they can. They are virtually prison yards and not unlike one in general appearance, except that the walls are not so high and strong, but they suffice, where every point is in range of a soldier's rifle, to keep in the poor reconcentrado women and children.

Every railroad station is within one of these trochas and has an armed guard. Every train has an armored freight car, loop-holed for musketry, and filled with soldiers and with, as I observed usually, and was informed is always the case, a pilot engine a mile or so in advance. There are frequent block-houses enclosed by a trocha and with a guard along the railroad track. With this exception there is no human life or habitation between these fortified towns and villages throughout the whole of the four western provinces, except to a very limited extent among the hills, where the Spaniards have not been able to go and drive the people to the towns and burn their dwellings.

I saw no house or hut in the 400 miles of railroad rides from Pinar del Rio Province in the west across the full width of Havana and Matanzas Provinces, and to Sagua La Grando on the north shore and to Cienfuegos on the south shore of Santa Clara, except within the Spanish trochas. There are no domestic animals or crops on the rich fields and pastures except such as are under guard in the immediate vicinity of the towns.

In other words, the Spaniards hold in these four western provinces just what their army sits on. Every man, woman and child and every domestic animal, wherever their columns have reached, is under guard and within their so-called fortifications. To describe one place is to describe all. To repeat, it is neither peace nor war.

It is concentration and desolation. This is the "pacified" condition of the four western provinces. . . .

With large families or with more than one in this little space, the commonest sanitary provisions are impossible. Conditions are unmentionable in this respect. Torn from their homes, with foul earth, foul air, foul water and foul food, or none, what wonder that one-half have died and that one-quarter of the living are so diseased that they cannot be saved. A form of dropsy is a common disorder resulting from these conditions. Little children are still walking about with arms and chests terribly emaciated, eyes swollen and abdomen bloated to three times the natural size. The physicians say these cases are hopeless.

Deaths in the streets have not been uncommon. I was told by one of our consuls that people have been found dead about the markets in the morning where they had crawled hoping to get some stray bits of food from the early hucksters, and that there had been cases where they had dropped dead inside the market, surrounded by food.

These people were independent and self-supporting before Weyler's order. They are not beggars even now. There are plenty of professional beggars in every town among the regular residents, but these country people, the reconcentrados, have not learned the art. Rarely is a hand held out to you for alms when going among their huts, but the sight of them makes an appeal stronger than words. The hospitals—of these I need not speak; others have described their condition far better than I can.

It is not within the narrow limits of my vocabulary to portray it. I went to Cuba with a strong conviction that the picture had been overdrawn; that a few cases of starvation and suffering had inspired and stimulated the press correspondents, and that they had given free play to a strong, natural and highly cultivated imagination.

I could not believe that out of a population of one million six hundred thousand, 200,000 had died within these Spanish forts, practically prison walls, within a few months past, from actual starvation and disease caused by insufficient and improper food.

My inquiries were entirely outside of sensational sources. They were made of our medical officers, of our consuls, of city alcaldes (mayors), of relief commitees, of leading merchants and bankers, physicians and lawyers. Several of my informants were Spanish born, but every time came the answer that the case had not been overstated.

What I saw I cannot tell so that others can see it. It must be seen with one's own eyes to be realized.

Document 2.2

YELLOW JOURNALISM AND THE *MAINE*

The Spanish-American War represented a breaking point in the history of modern media. Pressed to sell papers, journalists and publishers scrambled not only to report news but also to capture—through sensationalized writing and images—eager readers throughout the nation's exploding metropolises. This style of writing and coverage, driven by sales rather than concern for the facts, became known as "yellow journalism." Writers sent to Cuba by media moguls William Randolph Hearst and Joseph Pulitzer competed to compose the most dramatic tales of suffering and woe, frequently featuring images of starving women and children, arbitrary executions, and scantily clad damsels suffering under the Spanish heel. Yellow journalism's most dramatic moment came following the loss of the USS Maine, *on February 15, 1898, when an explosion ripped through its forward gunpowder magazine. More than three quarters of the crew of 354 officers and sailors were lost. Newspaper headlines announcing the* Maine's *destruction, such as this front page from the* New York Journal, *demonstrate that the press and many Americans—including ranking officials such as Assistant Secretary of the Navy Theodore Roosevelt—leaped to the conclusion that foul play and murder were at hand.*

$50,000 REWARD.—WHO DESTROYED THE MAINE?—$50,000 REWARD.

EDITION FOR GREATER NEW YORK

NEW YORK JOURNAL

AND ADVERTISER.

DESTRUCTION OF THE WAR SHIP MAINE WAS THE WORK OF AN ENEMY.

$50,000!

$50,000 REWARD!
For the Detection of the Perpetrator of the Maine Outrage!

Assistant Secretary Roosevelt Convinced the Explosion of the War Ship Was Not an Accident.

The Journal Offers $50,000 Reward for the Conviction of the Criminals Who Sent 258 American Sailors to Their Death. Naval Officers Unanimous That the Ship Was Destroyed on Purpose.

$50,000!

$50,000 REWARD!
For the Detection of the Perpetrator of the Maine Outrage!

NAVAL OFFICERS THINK THE MAINE WAS DESTROYED BY A SPANISH MINE.

Hidden Mine or a Sunken Torpedo Believed to Have Been the Weapon Used Against the American Man-of-War—Officers and Men Tell Thrilling Stories of Being Blown Into the Air Amid a Mass of Shattered Steel and Exploding Shells—Survivors Brought to Key West Scout the Idea of Accident—Spanish Officials Protest Too Much—Our Cabinet Orders a Searching Inquiry—Journal Sends Divers to Havana to Report Upon the Condition of the Wreck.

Document 2.3

ROOSEVELT JUMPS THE GUN

The war began in the spring of 1898, but American policy makers—especially those who endorsed what Massachusetts Senator Henry Cabot Lodge termed a "Large Policy" designed to increase American global power—had clearly prepared for the conflict far earlier. In late February 1898, for example, Assistant Secretary of the Navy Theodore Roosevelt took the opportunity of his superior's absence from the office to ramp up the navy's readiness for war. Navy Secretary John Long, more hopeful for peace than Roosevelt, rescinded many of his underling's orders upon his return, though several, including the one below authorizing hostilities against Spanish holdings in the Pacific if war erupted, remained as general policy. Roosevelt sent this cable to Admiral George Dewey, commander of U.S. naval forces in Asia, on February 25, 1898, well before most public calls to war. In short, human suffering in Cuba grabbed the headlines, but behind the scenes American strategists viewed the brewing crisis as a welcome opportunity.

Dewey, Hong Kong

Secret and confidential. Order the squadron, except *Monacacy*, to Hong Kong. Keep full of coal. In event of declaration of war with Spain your duty will be to see that Spanish squadron does not leave Asiatic coast, and then offensive operations in Philippine Islands. Keep *Olympia* until further orders. Roosevelt.

Document 2.4

WHO WOULD RULE CUBA?

American policy makers had long opposed any transfer of colonial sovereignty over territories in the Western Hemisphere from one European state to another. Spain's faltering grasp on its own colonial holdings made strategists in Washington particularly fearful that another power might swoop in to control what Madrid could not; but, more fundamentally, on a broad strategic level they resisted true Cuban independence for the same reason: sovereignty without American control did not guarantee American security or potential economic gain. Thus, when negotiations commenced in Madrid between Spanish officials and Cuban independence parties, some within McKinley's administration urged the president to intervene in the bloody war before it was too late—to intervene, in other words, before Washington lost the opportunity to truly control the island. The following telegram from the American minister in Spain, Stewart Woodford, to President McKinley, composed March 17, 1897, states the case for American intervention—to suit American goals—in explicit terms.

The establishment of any form of protectorate still seems to me fraught with great and permanent danger. There is no general popular education in Cuba. The blacks and whites are quite even in numbers. The native Cubans and the Spanish residents are divided into hostile factions. Corruption in official rule has been for centuries the curse of Cuba. I do not believe that the population is to-day fit for self-government, and acceptance of a practical protectorate over Cuba seems to be very like the assumption of the responsible care of a madhouse. There are possibly conditions under which a practical protectorate may be a reasonable and desirable result. But time and reflection have strengthened my first impression into deliberate judgment, and I pray that no conditions may arise under which we shall be responsible for the practical peace and good government of the island unless we have full power of ownership which shall enable us to compel good government.

Peace is still a necessity. Peace can hardly be assured by the insurgents through and under an independent government. Autonomy has not yet secured peace. I have at last come to believe that the only certainty of peace is under our flag and that with courage and faith we can minimize the dangers of American occupation and assure the blessings of American constitutional liberty.

I am thus, reluctantly, slowly, but entirely a convert to the American ownership and occupation of the island. If we recognize independence, we may turn the island over to a part of its inhabitants against the judgment of many of its most educated and wealthy residents. If we advise the insurgents to accept autonomy we may do injustice to men who have fought hard and well for liberty, and they may not get justice from the insular government should it once obtain control of the island. We may in either event only foster conditions that will lead to continuous disorder. If we have war we must finally occupy and ultimately own the island. If today we could purchase at reasonable price we should avoid the horrors and the expense of war, and you, as a soldier, know what war is, even when waged for the holiest cause.

Documents 2.5, 2.6, and 2.7

IMAGES OF RACE AND EMPIRE

The war went well for American forces, who captured Cuba, Puerto Rico, and the Philippines within months. But what should be done with the spoils of war? This question proved a far more time-consuming issue than the war itself, since few pol-

icy makers expected that the new territories would become full parts of the union. These political cartoons, drawn by Charles Lewis Bartholomew before, during, and immediately after the war, offer a glimpse into public perception of Washington's official rationale for fighting and its new role as colonial power. At the same time, they starkly reveal general perceptions of race and Americans' sense of bringing civilization to less-developed peoples.

Document 2.8

MOUNTING FEARS OF EMPIRE

Shortly after news of Dewey's victory over the Spanish fleet at Manila reached American shores, famed journalist Walter Hines Page, editor of the Atlantic Monthly, *predicted problems the United States would face as an imperial power. His remarks, published in the June 1898 edition of the well-read magazine, not only proved prescient but also demonstrate that problems to come were hardly unknown within American decision-making circles.*

The problems that seem likely to follow the war are graver than those that have led up to it; and if it be too late to ask whether we entered into it without sufficient deliberation, it is not too soon to make sure of every step that we now take. The inspiring unanimity of the people in following their leaders proves to be as earnest and strong as it ever was under any form of government; and this popular acquiescence in war puts a new responsibility on those leaders, and may put our institutions and our people themselves to a new test. A change in our national policy may change our very character; and we are now playing with the great forces that may shape the future of the world—almost before we know it.

Yesterday we were going about the prosaic tasks of peace, content with our own problems of administration and finance, a nation to ourselves,—"commercials," as our enemies call us in derision. Today we are face to face with the sort of problems that have grown up in the management of world empires, and the policies of other nations are of intimate concern to us. Shall we still be content with peaceful industry, or does there yet lurk in us the adventurous spirit of our Anglo-Saxon forefathers? And have we come to a time when, no more great enterprises awaiting us at home, we shall be tempted to seek them abroad?

The race from which we are sprung is a race that for a thousand years has done the adventurous and outdoor tasks of the world. The English have been explorers, colonizers, conquerors of continents, founders of states. We ourselves, every generation since we came to America, have had great practical enterprises to engage us,—the fighting with Indians, the clearing of forests, the war for independence, the construction of a government, the extension of our territory, the pushing backward of the frontier, the development of an El Dorado (which the Spaniards owned, but never found), the long internal conflict about slavery, a great civil war, the building of railroads, and the compact unification of a continental domain. These have been as great enterprises and as exciting, coming in rapid succession, as any race of men has ever had to engage in,—as great enterprises for the play of the love of adventure in the blood as our kinsmen over the sea have had in the extension and the management of their world empire. The old outdoor spirit of the Anglo-Saxon has till lately found wider scope in our own history than we are apt to remember.

But now a generation has come to manhood that has had no part in any great adventure. In politics we have had difficult and important tasks, indeed, but they have not been exciting,—the reform of the civil service and of the system of currency, and the improvement of municipal government. These are chiefly administrative. In a sense they are not new nor positive tasks, but the correction of past errors. . . .

Within a week such a question, which we had hitherto hardly thought seriously to ask during our whole national existence, has been put before us by the first foreign war that we have had since we became firmly established as a nation. Before we knew the meaning of foreign possessions in a world ever growing more jealous, we have found ourselves the captors of islands in both great oceans; and from our home-staying policy of yesterday we are brought face to face with world-wide forces in Asia as well as in Europe, which seem to be working, by the opening of the Orient, for one of the greatest changes in human history. Until a little while ago our latest war dispatches came from Appomattox. Now our latest dispatches (when this is written) come from Manila. The news from Appomattox concerned us only. The news from Manila sets every statesman and soldier in the world to thinking new thoughts about us, and to asking new questions. And to nobody has the change come more unexpectedly than to ourselves. Has it come without our knowing the meaning of it? The very swiftness of these events and the ease with which they have come to pass are matters for more serious thought than the unjust rule of Spain in Cuba, or than any tasks that have engaged us since we rose to commanding physical power.

Document 2.9

"SHALL CUBA BE TAKEN FOR CHRIST?"

Occupation of foreign lands and control over their peoples generated a sense of opportunity as well as controversy. Commercial and strategic advantages of empire have been noted above. But many Americans considered conquest a chance to raise up foreign peoples to American standards—religious ones in particular. This published resolution from the September 1898 edition of the American Missionary *exemplifies the opportunity many such groups saw within America's newfound empire.*

The Alumni Association of Oberlin Theological Seminary recently passed the following vote:

"Voted: that the Alumni of Oberlin Theological Seminary suggest to the American Missionary Association the importance of organizing at once for an extension of its educational and evangelizing work into Cuba as soon as the deliverance of that island from the dominion of Spain will permit."

At the recent Triennial National Council of Congregational Churches held in Portland, Oregon, reference to the pressing of Christian educational work into Cuba was greeted with enthusiastic applause.

And now there come letters from those who desire to volunteer for service under the American Missionary Association to enter upon this work in Cuba and Porto Rico[*sic*]. This Association has not the power to issue bonds for the expense of such missionary campaigns, nor to levy taxes. The significance, however, of these new fields of work and the especial fitness of the American Missionary Association to enter them must be apparent to all our constituents. The inhabitants of both these islands are largely of a mixed race. The splendid band of young colored people in the South have been trained during the years in the American Missionary Association schools and are excellently qualified for carrying this Christian work among the peoples of these island regions.

They are acclimated, born and reared in the Southern climate. Some even are immune. Is it not a special providence that this band of young people have been trained for just such work as this opening to our Congregational Fellowship in Cuba and Porto Rico?

The volunteers for work in these islands, however, are not confined to any one race. The Oberlin Alumni suggest an "Oberlin Band" to be organized and sent into the field. From the far West and from the far East we receive letters from well-trained, earnest and godly teachers and preachers anxious to volunteer for this service.

The sinews of war for this magnificent Christian campaign are wanting. The responsibility of promptly entering these fields that God is opening to Christian conquest and an intelligent and free gospel rests upon those who can furnish these great sinews of war. Shall Cuba and Porto Rico be taken for Christ and an intelligent gospel?

Document 2.10

MCKINLEY EXPLAINS U.S. OCCUPATION OF THE PHILIPPINES

President William McKinley never enthusiastically sought war with Spain or possession of the colonial empire he ultimately controlled. His postconflict explanation, given at the end of a meeting with missionary leaders on November 21, 1899, reveals the history he wanted told: that he came to empire wholly unexpectedly and took up the burden unenthusiastically. As other documents show, others within his party and his nation embraced empire willingly. But McKinley's explanation demonstrates the complexity of the issue for Americans and their leaders at the time. Echoing the Progressive Era's language of improvement and uplift—paradoxically, the same language used to justify Jim Crow—McKinley's words also demonstrate that Americans believed they were spreading the blessings of liberty, Christianity, and civilization to an impoverished, benighted land. One idea comes through boldly in his statement: he would not relinquish the lands upon which the American flag had flown.

Hold a moment longer! Not quite yet, gentlemen! Before you go I would like to say just a word about the Philippine business. I have been criticized a good deal about the Philippines, but don't deserve it. The truth is I didn't want the Philippines, and when they came to us, as a gift from the gods, I did not know what to do with them. When the Spanish War broke out Dewey was at Hong Kong, and I ordered him to go to Manila and to capture or destroy the Spanish fleet, and he had to; because, if defeated, he had no place to refit on that side of the globe, and if the Dons were victorious they would likely cross the Pacific and ravage our Oregon and California coasts. And so he had to destroy the Spanish fleet, and did it! But that was as far as I thought then.

When I next realized that the Philippines had dropped into our laps I confess I did not know what to do with them. I sought counsel from all sides—Democrats as well as Republicans—but got little help. I thought first we would take only Manila; then Luzon; then other islands perhaps also. I walked the floor of the White House night after night until midnight; and I am not ashamed to tell you, gentlemen, that I went down on my knees and prayed Almighty God for light and guidance more than one night. And one night late it came to me this way—I don't know how it was, but it came: (1) That we could not give them back to Spain—that would be cowardly and dishonorable; (2) that we could not turn them over to France and Germany—our commercial rivals in the Orient—that would be bad business and discreditable; (3) that we could not leave them to themselves—they were unfit for self-government—and they would soon have anarchy and misrule over there worse than Spain's was; and (4) that there was nothing left for us to do but to take them all, and to educate the Filipinos, and uplift and civilize and Christianize them, and by God's grace do the very best we could by them, as our fellow-men for whom Christ also died. And then I went to bed, and went to sleep, and slept soundly, and the next morning I sent for the chief engineer of the War Department (our map-maker), and I told him to put the Philippines on the map of the United States (pointing to a large map on the wall of his office), and there they are, and there they will stay while I am President!

Document 2.11

A CRITIQUE FROM THE HEARTLAND

Opponents of Washington's new colonial empire quickly charged that the entire notion of Americans holding colonial possessions was anathema to the national character and the nation's own revolutionary past. Among the most prominent of such critics was William Jennings Bryan, Democratic nominee for president in 1896 and 1900 and ultimately Woodrow Wilson's first secretary of state after Democrats recaptured the White House in 1912. Bryan made anti-imperialism among his signature campaign issues in 1900, a race he lost to McKinley. He endorsed war to save Cuba and even volunteered to fight in what he considered a humanitarian mission. He deeply opposed seizure of the Philippines, however, believing that such an act was little more than naked imperialism. This article, published in the New York Journal *on Christmas 1898 but later reprinted throughout the country, demonstrates the way anti-imperialists, much like supporters of the "Large Policy," employed history and their interpretation of America's legacy as signposts for the future.*

The advocates of imperialism have sought to support their position by appealing to the authority of Jefferson. Of all the statesmen who have ever lived, Jefferson was the one most hostile to the doctrines embodied in the demand for a European colonial policy.

Imperialism as it now presents itself embraces four distinct propositions:

1. That the acquisition of territory by conquest is right.

2. That the acquisition of remote territory is desirable.

3. That the doctrine that governments derive their just powers from the consent of the governed is unsound.

4. That people can be wisely governed by aliens.

To all these propositions Jefferson was emphatically opposed. In a letter to William Short, written in 1791, he said:

"If there be one principle more deeply written than any other in the mind of every American, it is that we should have nothing to do with conquest."

Could he be more explicit? Here we have a clear and strong denunciation of the doctrine that territory should be acquired by force. . . .

But this is a time of great and rapid changes, and some may even look upon Blaine's official acts as ancient history. If so, let it be remembered that President McKinley only a year ago (December 6, 1897), in a message to Congress discussing the Cuban situation, said:

"I speak not of forcible annexation, for that is not to be thought of. That, by our code of morality, would be criminal aggression."

And yet some are now thinking of that which was then "not to be thought of." Policy may change, but does a "code of morality" change? In his recent speech at Savannah, Secretary Gage, in defending the new policy of the administration, suggested that "philanthropy and five percent" may go hand in hand. Surely we know not what a day may bring forth, if in so short a time "criminal aggression" can be transformed into "philanthropy and five percent." What beauty, what riches, the isles of the Pacific must possess if they can tempt our people to abandon not only the traditions of a century, but our standard of national morality! What visions of national greatness the Philippines must arouse if the very sight of them can lead our country to vie with the monarchies of the old world in the extension of sovereignty by force.

Jefferson has been called an expansionist, but our opponents will search in vain for a single instance where he advocated the acquisition of remote territory. On the contrary, he expressly disclaimed any desire for land outside of the North American continent.

Modest Jefferson! He had been Governor, Ambassador to France, Vice-President and President; he was ripe in experience and crowned with honors; but this modern law-giver, this immortal genius, hesitated to suggest laws for a people with whose habits, customs and methods of thought he was unfamiliar. And yet the imperialists of today, intoxicated by a taste of blood, are rash enough to enter upon the government of the Filipinos, confident of the nation's ability to compel obedience, even if it cannot earn gratitude or win affection. Plutarch said that men entertained three sentiments concerning the ancient gods: They feared them for their strength, admired them for their wisdom and loved them for their justice. Jefferson taught the doctrine that governments should win the love of men. What shall be the ambition of our nation—to be loved because it is just or to be feared because it is strong?

Document 2.12

THE "WHITE MAN'S BURDEN"

Americans pondered growing U.S. power as the nineteenth century came to a close, and so did others. Many European leaders in particular feared rising American power on the world stage, but some hoped that American power might be deployed for imperial goals similar to their own. One such imperial proponent was Rudyard Kipling, a famed poet of the British Empire. His "The White Man's Burden" pleaded with American officials to ponder their future role in the Philippines.

Kipling, who had lived in the United States from 1892 to 1896, believed Americans had a duty to control, develop, and ultimately civilize those they conquered. But a close reading of his text, first published in 1899, reveals that he did not believe the task easy or without pain.

Take up the White Man's burden—
Send forth the best ye breed
Go bind your sons to exile
To serve your captives' need;
To wait in heavy harness,
On fluttered folk and wild—
Your new-caught, sullen peoples,
Half-devil and half-child.

Take up the White Man's burden—
In patience to abide,
To veil the threat of terror
And check the show of pride;
By open speech and simple,
An hundred times made plain
To seek another's profit,
And work another's gain.

Take up the White Man's burden—
The savage wars of peace—
Fill full the mouth of Famine
And bid the sickness cease;
And when your goal is nearest
The end for others sought,
Watch sloth and heathen Folly
Bring all your hopes to nought.

Take up the White Man's burden—
No tawdry rule of kings,
But toil of serf and sweeper—
The tale of common things.
The ports ye shall not enter,
The roads ye shall not tread,
Go make them with your living,
And mark them with your dead.

Take up the White Man's burden—
And reap his old reward:
The blame of those ye better,
The hate of those ye guard—

The cry of hosts ye humour
(Ah, slowly!) toward the light:—
"Why brought he us from bondage,
Our loved Egyptian night?

Take up the White Man's burden—
Ye dare not stoop to less—
Nor call too loud on Freedom
To cloke your weariness;
By all ye cry or whisper,
By all ye leave or do,
The silent, sullen peoples
Shall weigh your gods and you.

Take up the White Man's burden—
Have done with childish days—
The lightly proferred laurel,
The easy, ungrudged praise.
Comes now, to search your manhood
Through all the thankless years
Cold, edged with dear-bought wisdom,
The judgment of your peers!

Document 2.13

PROTESTING THE TRANSFER OF SOVEREIGNTY

American forces took control of the Philippines from Spain in 1898. What seemed to some an opportunity to project American power into the Pacific, and to others an opportunity to missionize, appeared to many Filipinos merely the exchange of one colonial power for another. Felipe Agoncillo, for example, a lawyer who served as the Filipino representative to the Treaty of Paris negotiations that ended the Spanish-American War, repeatedly objected to any direct transfer of sovereignty of his homeland from Madrid to Washington. His pleas fell on deaf ears, including this official statement of protest issued in December of 1898.

If the Spaniards have not been able to transfer to the Americans the rights which they did not possess; if the latter have not militarily conquered positions in the Philippines; if the occupation of Manila was a resultant fact, prepared by the Filipinos; if the international officials and representatives of the Republic of the United States of America offered to recognize the independence and sovereignty of the Philippines, solicited and accepted their alliance, how they can now constitute themselves as arbiters of the control, administration, and future government of the Philippine islands?

If in the Treaty of Paris there had simply been declared the withdrawal and abandonment by the Spaniards of their domination—if they had such—over Filipino territory, if America, on accepting peace, had signed the treaty, without prejudice to the rights of the Philippines, and with a view to coming to a subsequent settlement with the existing Filipino National Government, no protest against their action would have been made. But in view of the terms of the Article III of the Protocol, the attitude of the American Commissioners, and the imperative necessity of safeguarding the national rights of my country, I take this protest, for the before-mentioned reasons but with the proper legal reservations, against the action taken and the resolutions passed by the Peace Commissioners at Paris and in the Treaty signed by them.

Document 2.14

AGUINALDO'S PROCLAMATION TO THE PHILIPPINE PEOPLE

American forces found controlling and governing the Philippines far harder than its acquisition. On January 1, 1899, a constitutional convention proclaimed an independent Philippine republic with Emilio Aguinaldo as president. Aguinaldo had been an American ally during the period of Spanish rule, but his refusal to accept American control made him an adversary and target of American military repression. After Washington refused to accept Filipino independence, he and his assembly declared war on the United States on February 4, 1899. He was eventually captured on March 23, 1901, following American use of many of the same brutal tactics of suppression condemned when used by the Spanish only years before. As his independence proclamation to the Philippine people, published on February 5, 1899, shows, Aguinaldo ultimately considered American rule little improvement over Spanish.

By my proclamation of yesterday I have published the outbreak of hostilities between the Philippine forces and the American forces of occupation in Manila, unjustly and unexpectedly provoked by the latter.

In my manifest of January 8 last I published the grievances suffered by the Philippine forces at the hands of the army of occupation. The constant outrages and taunts, which have caused the misery of the people of Manila, and finally the useless conferences and the contempt shown the Philippine government prove the premeditated transgression of justice and liberty.

I know that war has always produced great losses; I know that the Philippine people have not yet recovered from past losses and are not in the condition to endure others. But I also know by experience how bitter is slavery, and by experience I know that we should sacrifice all on the altar of our honor and of the national integrity so unjustly attacked.

I have tried to avoid, as far as it has been possible for me to do so, armed conflict, in my endeavors to assure our independence by pacific means and to avoid more costly sacrifices. But all my efforts have been useless against the measureless pride of the American government and of its representatives in these islands, who have treated me as a rebel because I defend the sacred interests of my country and do not make myself an instrument of their dastardly intentions.

Past campaigns will have convinced you that the people are strong when they wish to be so. Without arms we have driven from our beloved country our ancient masters, and without arms we can repulse the foreign invasion as long as we may wish to do so. Providence always has means in reserve and prompt help for the weak in order that they may not be annihilated by the strong; that justice may be done and humanity progress.

Document 2.15

"THE WHITE MAN'S BURDEN AS PROPHECY"

Senator Benjamin Tillman of South Carolina, known as "Pitchfork Ben" due to his fiery rhetoric, was a virulent proponent of segregation and white rule. Like Bryan and Kipling, he saw difficulties ahead following the McKinley administration's decision to control former Spanish colonies, though he added his own peculiar—though hardly unique—interpretation. The following speech, offered at nearly the same time as Aguinaldo's appeal for independence, not only demonstrates the tenor of racial politics at the time but also reinforces the point that domestic and foreign affairs are never wholly distinct. As this Senate speech from February 7, 1899, reveals, Tillman feared the racial consequences of integrating nonwhite Filipinos into American society, though he clearly also feared agricultural competition from colonies producing inside an American tariff wall.

As though coming at the most opportune time possible, you might say just before the treaty reached the Senate, or about the time it was sent to us, there appeared in one of our magazines a poem by Rudyard Kipling, the greatest poet of England at this time. This poem, unique, and in some places too deep for me, is a prophecy. I do not imagine that in the history of human events any poet has ever felt inspired so clearly to portray our danger and our duty. It is called "The White Man's Burden." With the permission of Senators I will read a stanza, and I beg Senators to listen to it, for it is well worth their attention. This man has lived in the Indies. In fact, he is a citizen of the world, and has been all over it, and knows whereof he speaks.

"Take up the White Man's burden—Send forth the best ye breed—Go, bind your sons to exile, To serve your captive's need; To wait, in heavy harness, On fluttered folk and wild—Your new-caught sullen peoples, Half devil and half child."

I will pause here. I intend to read more, but I wish to call attention to a fact which may have escaped the attention of Senators thus far, that with five exceptions every man in this chamber who has had to do with the colored race in this country voted against the ratification of the treaty [the Treaty of Paris, which was ratified February 6, 1899, and ended the Spanish-American War]. It was not because we are Democrats, but because we understand and realize what it is to have two races side by side that can not mix or mingle without deterioration and injury to both and the ultimate destruction of the civilization of the higher. We of the South have borne this white man's burden of a colored race in our midst since their emancipation and before.

It was a burden upon our manhood and our ideas of liberty before they were emancipated. It is still a burden, although they have been granted the franchise. It clings to us like the shirt of Nessus, and we are not responsible, because we inherited it, and your fathers as well as ours are responsible for the presence amongst us of that people. Why do we as a people want to incorporate into our citizenship ten millions more of different or of differing races, three or four of them?

But we have not incorporated them yet, and let us see what this English poet has to say about it, and what he thinks.

"Take up the White Man's burden—No iron rule of kings, But toil of serf and sweeper—The tale of common things. The ports ye shall not enter, The roads ye shall not tread, Go, make them with your living And mark them with your dead."

Ah, if we have no other consideration, if no feeling of humanity, no love of our fellows, no regard for others' rights, if nothing but our self-interest shall actuate us in this crisis, let me say to you that if we go madly on in the direction of crushing these people into subjection and submission we will do so at the cost of many, many thousands of the flower of American youth. There are 10,000,000 of these people, some of them fairly well civilized, and running to the extreme of naked savages, who are reported in our press dispatches as having stood out in the open and fired their bows and arrows, not flinching from the storm of shot and shell thrown into their midst by the American soldiers there.

The report of the battle claims that we lost only seventy-five killed and a hundred and odd wounded; but the first skirmish has carried with it what anguish, what desolation, to homes in a dozen states! How many more victims are we to offer up on this altar of Mammon or national greed? When those regiments march back, if they return with decimated ranks, as they are bound to come, if we have to send thousands and tens of thousands of re-enforcements there to press onward until we have subdued those ten millions, at whose door will lie these lives—their blood shed for what? An idea. If a man fires upon the American flag, shoot the last man and kill him, no matter how many Americans have to be shot to do it.

The city of Manila is surrounded by swamps and marshes, I am told. A few miles back lie the woods and jungles and mountains. These people are used to the climate. They know how to get about, and if they mean to have their liberties, as they appear to do, at what sacrifice will the American domination be placed over them? There is another verse of Kipling. I have fallen in love with this man. He tells us what we will reap:

"Take up the White Man's burden, And reap his old reward—The blame of those ye better, The hate of those ye guard—The cry of those ye humor (Ah, slowly!) toward the light:—'Why brought he us from bondage, Our loved Egyptian night?'"

Those peoples are not suited to our institutions. They are not ready for liberty as we understand it. They do not want it. Why are we bent on forcing upon them a civilization not suited to them and which only means in their view degradation and a loss of self-respect, which is worse than the loss of life itself?

I am nearly done. Nobody answers and nobody can. The commercial instinct which seeks to furnish a market and places for the growth of commerce or the investment of capital for the money making of the few is pressing this country madly to the final and ultimate annexation of these people regardless of their own wishes.

Document 2.16

A VIEW FROM THE JUNGLE

Kipling was right: the wars of peace proved savage indeed. By the latter half of 1899, much of the archipelago had erupted in open revolt against American control. The ensuing struggle was bloody, messy, and difficult to assess. It became in fact a "classic" example of a counterinsurgency, wherein local loyalties were frequently purchased during the day yet forgotten once night fell. American commanders responded by promising material improvements for the Filipino people, authorizing widespread sanitation work and educational opportunities, for example. When these failed to materialize or secure local support, further bribes and violence ensued. Villages deemed friendly to the American cause were protected. Areas deemed "hostile" to American plans were frequently burned to the ground. According to this New York Times *account of the Battle of Tirad Pass, published June 4, 1900, the war was bloody, confusing, and hardly as "splendid" as John Hay had called the war with Spain.*

Vigan, Luzon, June 2—Major March with his detachment of the Thirty-Third Regiment, overtook what is believed to have been Aguinaldo's party on May 19 at Lagat, about 100 miles Northeast of Vigan. The Americans killed or wounded an officer, supposed to be Aguinaldo, whose body was removed by his followers.

The rebels had one hundred men, Major March one hundred and twenty-five. The American commander reached Lagoagan, where Aguinaldo had made his headquarters since March 6, on May 7. Aguinaldo had fled seven hours before, leaving all the beaten trails, and traveling through the forests along the beds of streams. Towards evening, May 19, Major March struck Aguinaldo's outpost about a mile outside of Lagat, killing four Filipinos and capturing two. From the latter he learned that Aguinaldo had camped there for the night.

Although exhausted and half starved, Major March's men entered Lagat on the run. They saw the insurgents scattering into the bushes or over the plateau. A thousand yards beyond the town, on the mountain side, the figures of twenty-five Filipinos, dressed in white, with their leader on a gray horse were silhouetted against the sunset. The Americans fired a volley and saw the officer drop from his horse. His followers fled, carrying the body.

The Americans, on reaching the spot, caught the horse, which was richly saddled. Blood from a badly wounded man was on the animal and on the ground. The saddle bags contained Aguinaldo's diary and some private papers, including proclamations. One of these was addressed: "To the civilized nations." It protested against the American occupation of the Philippines. There were also found copies of Senator Beveridge's speech, translated into Spanish, and entitled: "The Death Knell of the Filipino People."

Major March, believing that the Filipinos had taken to a river which is a tributary to the Chico, followed it for two days, reaching Tiago, where he learned that a party of Filipinos had descended the river May 20, on a raft with the body of a dead or wounded man upon a litter, covered with palm leaves.

There Major March reviewed his command, shoeless and exhausted, and picked out twenty-four of the freshest men, with whom he beat the surrounding country for six days longer, but without finding any trace of the insurgents. The Americans pushed on and arrived at Aparri May 29.

The officer shot was either Aguinaldo or his Adjutant; as the horse was richly caparisoned, it is a fair assumption that it was Aguinaldo.

The soldiers of Gen. Young, Military Governor of Northwestern Luzon, captured early last month an insurgent officer with papers revealing Aguinaldo's whereabouts. Gen. Young immediately organized for pursuit, giving Major March a chance to finish the work begun in November. Major March left Candon May 10, hurrying North toward Laboagan, while Col. Hare, with a battalion divided into two parts, started from Rangued, Province of Abra, covering the trails westward. The garrisons in the Cagayan Valley were disposed in such a way as to guard the avenues of escape eastward.

Spies heralded the approach of Major March with signal fires. On reaching Laboagan, he apprehended a letter in Aguinaldo's handwriting, the ink of which was hardly dry, addressed to an officer of guerrillas of the Filipino army, and saying:

"There having arrived this morning at Laboagan a hostile column from Bokoc, I have set out with all my force. My road has no fixed destination."

This was signed "Colonel David," a soubriquet. Aguinaldo called at the Presidencia, from which he issued decrees and where his followers celebrated Easter with a banquet at a triangular table, when speeches were made eulogizing Gregorio del Pilar.

That night Major March's men slept in the bamboo, resuming the advance in the morning, and reaching Lagat, forty miles distant, in two days, although it was raining hard in the mountains all the time.

Aguinaldo's papers are very important. They show that he took refuge in Isabela Province, where he remained until he established himself at Laboagan, Province of Abra, where he proposed to direct the rainy season operations. Until recently he was ignorant of outside events, making no pretense of directing the insurrection, happy if, indeed, he might be able to keep alive among the hostile Igorrotes, who killed several of his followers.

Document 2.17

AGUINALDO'S SURRENDER

The youthful Filipino general was neither dead nor wounded. But in time he succumbed to American force, following his capture on March 23, 1901. Nearly a month later he took an oath of allegiance to the United States, ending his war and dealing a crucial blow to the anti-American cause. The war lasted for more than a year, but in this, his formal proclamation of surrender, the end of the Filipino independence movement appeared in sight.

To the Filipino People:

I believe that I am not in error in presuming that the unhappy fate to which my adverse fortune has led me is not a surprise to those who have been familiar day to day with the progress of the war. The lessons thus taught, the full meaning of which has recently come to my knowledge, suggested to me with irresistible force that the complete termination of hostilities and a lasting peace are not only desirable but absolutely essential to the welfare of the Philippines.

The Filipinos have never been dismayed by their weakness, nor have they faltered in following the path pointed out by their fortitude and courage. The time has come, however, in which they find their advance along the path impeded by an irresistible force—a force which, while it restrains them, yet enlightens the mind and opens another course by presenting to them the cause of peace. This cause has been joyfully embraced around the glorious and sovereign banner of the United States. In this manner they repose their trust in the belief that under its protection our people will attain all the promised liberties which they are even now beginning to enjoy.

The country has declared unmistakably in favor of peace; so be it. Enough of blood; enough of tears and desolation. This wish cannot be ignored by the men still in arms if they are animated by no other desire than to serve this noble people which has clearly manifested its will.

So also do I respect this will now that it is known to me, and after mature deliberation resolutely proclaim to the world that I cannot refuse to heed the voice of a people longing for peace, nor the lamentations of thousands of families yearning to see their dear ones in the enjoyment of the liberty promised by the generosity of the great American nation.

By acknowledging and accepting the sovereignty of the United States throughout the entire Archipelago, as I now do without any reservations whatsoever, I believe that I am serving thee, my beloved country. May happiness be thine!

Documents 2.18 and 2.19

TWAIN'S PARODIES

Americans were not blind to the irony that U.S. forces, compelled to battle in 1898 on behalf of revolutionaries seeking safety from brutal oppression, turned into oppressors in search of control over far-off lands and alien peoples. Mark Twain, perhaps the most famous American writer of the period, published this short letter in the New York Herald *at the close of 1900, and a year later published a scathing parody of the famous antislavery and pro-Union Civil War marching ballad, the "Battle Hymn of the Republic."*

I bring you the stately matron named Christendom, returning bedraggled, besmirched and dishonored from pirate raids in Kiao-Chow, Manchuria, South Africa and the Philippines, with her soul full of meanness, her pocket full of boodle and her mouth full of pious hypocrisies. Give her soap and a towel, but hide the looking-glass.

. . . . . .

Mine Eyes have seen the orgy
Of the launching of the sword;
He is searching out the hoardings

Where the stranger's wealth is stored;
He has loosed his fateful lightnings
And with woe and death has scored;
His lust is marching on.

I have seen him in the watchfires
Of a hundred circling camps;
They have builded him an altar in
The Eastern dews and damps;
I have read his doomful mission
By the dim and flaring lamps—
His night is marching on.

I have read his bandit gospel
Writ in burnished rows of steel;
"As ye deal with my pretentions,
So with you my wrath shall deal;
Let the faithless son of Freedom
Crush the patriot with his heel;
Lo, Greed is marching on!"

We have legalized the strumpet
And are guarding her retreat;
Greed is seeking out commercial
Souls before his judgment seat;
O, be swift, ye clods, to answer
Him! Be jubilant my feet!
Our god is marching on!

In a sordid slime harmonious
Greed was born in yonder ditch,
With a longing in his bosom—and
For others' goods an itch.
As Christ died to make men holy
Let men die to make us rich—
Our god is marching on.

3

Varieties of Empire

The Spanish-American War and the peace treaty that concluded it made clear that the United States had entered a new era. With its smashing victory over Spain, once the mightiest of the European nations, the United States arrived as a formidable power willing to send force beyond its shores to challenge a well-armed rival from across the ocean. With its decision to annex the Philippines, moreover, Washington set aside its anticolonial traditions and joined the ranks of imperial powers such as Britain, France, and Japan.

American belligerency and imperialism raised as many questions as it answered, however, about the nation's future direction. Would it seek additional colonial possessions in a bid to create a world-spanning empire? Would it fold newly acquired lands into the American constitutional order as it had done with territories on the North American mainland in the eighteenth and nineteenth centuries? Or would overseas territories and their indigenous populations have a different status? How would the United States reconcile its growing international ambitions with its long-standing principles of self-determination and detachment from great-power conflict?

Two answers gradually became clear in the first years of the new century. First, the United States did not pursue additional colonial conquests. Popular discontent with the bloody war in the Philippines diminished American enthusiasm for colonialism, and the territories added between 1865 and 1898—Alaska, Hawaii, the Philippines, Puerto Rico, Guam, and American Samoa—proved to be the last major U.S. acquisitions. Second, the Supreme Court made clear in a series of rulings that those new territories would not automatically, or even in time, become full-fledged parts of the United States. Rather, the American empire became a patchwork of administrative arrangements that set different territories on paths toward statehood (Alaska and Hawaii), independence (the Philippines), and loose association (Puerto Rico, Guam, and American Samoa).

Declining enthusiasm for formal conquest did not, of course, mean that Americans lost any of their determination to assert power globally. On the contrary, Americans only grew more ambitious as U.S. economic, diplomatic, naval, and cultural power grew in the years after 1898. How, then, did Americans pursue their global ambitions while stopping short of formal colonialism? The answers that Americans improvised between 1900 and the First World War enabled the United

States to expand its economic and political power around the globe without the material burdens or ideological controversies generated by conquest.

Close to U.S. shores, where American military and economic power was greatest, Washington devised various methods to control many Caribbean and Latin American nations. U.S. leaders sent American troops to occupy Cuba, Haiti, the Dominican Republic, and other ostensibly independent territories for extended periods, while in Panama just the suggestion of American military power set the stage for construction of the U.S.-dominated Panama Canal. At other times, the United States made subtler use of its enormous economic and diplomatic power to shape political destinies, a type of informal colonial control often described as "dollar diplomacy."

A different pattern emerged in the Far East, where, despite acquisition of the Philippines, the United States remained weak compared to its rivals, Britain, France, Germany, Russia, and Japan. Anxious that the United States would be shut out if the other powers carved up China into colonial holdings, Secretary of State John Hay proposed that all interested nations allow freedom of economic activity throughout China and respect China's territorial integrity. In this way, the United States—whose industrial power outclassed its military might—aimed to enjoy unfettered economic access to China without risking direct clashes with the other powers or the burdens of formal empire.

All of these methods stirred controversy and opposition to one degree or another, both within the United States and in countries subjected to growing U.S. power. Critics complained that the United States was no less an imperial power merely because its methods were informal and indirect. But the array of approaches followed by U.S. leaders set patterns of thought and behavior that would persist for many decades to come.

Document 3.1

SUMNER DECRIES AMERICAN IMPERIALISM

Debate over the annexation of the Philippines reverberated through the United States in 1899, giving rise to powerful oratory on all sides. One of the most eloquent antiannexation voices was that of William Graham Sumner, an eminent sociologist at Yale University and prolific author on a wide range of topics. In the following speech, delivered at Yale on January 16, 1899, Sumner takes a characteristically unsentimental approach to the Philippine question and considers what might become of the United States if it continued down the imperial path.

Spain was the first, for a long time the greatest, of the modern imperialistic states. The United States, by its historical origin, its traditions, and its principles, is the chief representative of the revolt and reaction against that kind of a state. I intend to show that, by the line of action now proposed to us, which we call expansion and imperialism, we are throwing away some of the most important elements of the American symbol and are adopting some of the most important elements of the Spanish symbol. We have beaten Spain in a military conflict, but we are submitting to be conquered by her on the field of ideas and policies.

Expansionism and imperialism are nothing but the old philosophies of national prosperity which have brought Spain to where she now is. Those philosophies appeal to national vanity and national cupidity. They are seductive, especially upon the first view and the most superficial judgment, and therefore it cannot be denied that they are very strong for popular effect. They are delusions, and they will lead us to ruin unless we are hardheaded enough to resist them. . . .

A statesman could not be expected to know in advance that we should come out of the war [of 1898] with the Philippines on our hands, but it belongs to his education to warn him that a policy of adventure and of gratuitous enterprise would be sure to entail embarrassments of some kind. What comes to us in the evolution of our own life and interests, that we must meet; what we go to seek which lies beyond that domain is a waste of our energy and a compromise of our liberty and welfare. . . .

There is another observation, however, about the war which is of far greater importance: that is, that it was a gross violation of self-government. We boast that we are a self-governing people, and in this respect, particularly, we compare ourselves with pride with older nations. What is the difference after all? The Russians, whom we always think of as standing at the opposite pole of political institutions, have self-government, if you mean by it acquiescence in what a little group of people at the head of the government agree to do. The war with Spain was precipitated upon us headlong, without reflection or deliberation, and without any due formulation of public opinion. Whenever a voice was raised in behalf of deliberation and the recognized maxims of statesmanship, it was howled down in a storm of vituperation and cant. Everything was done to make us throw away sobriety of thought and calmness of judgment and to inflate all expressions with sensational epithets and turgid phrases. It cannot be denied that everything in regard to the war has been treated in an exalted strain of sentiment and rhetoric very unfavorable to the truth. At present the whole periodical press of the country seems to be occupied in tickling the national vanity to the utmost by representations about the war which are extravagant and fantastic. . . . Patriotism is being prostituted into a nervous intoxication which is fatal to an apprehension of truth. It builds around us a fool's paradise, and it will lead us into errors about our position and relations just like those which we have been ridiculing in the case of Spain. . . .

There is not a civilized nation which does not talk about its civilizing mission just as grandly as we do. . . . We assume that what we like and practice, and what we think better, must come as a welcome blessing to Spanish-Americans and Filipinos. This is grossly and obviously untrue. They hate our ways. They are hostile to our ideas. Our religion, language, institutions, and manners offend them. They like their own ways, and if we appear amongst them as rulers, there will be social discord in all the great departments of social interest. The most important thing which we shall inherit from the Spaniards will be the task of suppressing rebellions. . . . If we believe in liberty, as an American principle, why do we not stand by it? Why are we going to throw it away to enter upon a Spanish policy of dominion and regulation? . . .

Document 3.2

THE UNITED STATES DEMANDS AN "OPEN DOOR" IN CHINA

Many Americans hoped that the acquisition of the Philippines in 1898 would enable the United States to expand its commercial activity in China. Conditions in China threatened American ambitions. Exploiting Chinese weakness, the major imperial powers had already established "spheres of interest" and seemed poised to carve up China as they had partitioned virtually all of Africa in the previous decades. Anxious that American commerce might be excluded under such a scenario, U.S. Secretary of State John Hay sent a diplomatic note on September 6, 1899, to each of the powers embroiled in China—Britain, France, Germany, Japan, Italy, and Russia. These demarches, later dubbed the Open Door Notes, requested that the powers respect the principle of equal opportunity for trade and commerce throughout China. The following is the note sent to U.S. ambassador in London to guide his appeal to the British government.

The Government of Her Britannic Majesty has declared that its policy and its very traditions precluded it from using any privileges which might be granted it in China as a weapon for excluding commercial rivals, and that freedom of trade for Great Britain in that Empire meant freedom of trade for all the world alike. While conceding by formal agreements, first with Germany and then with Russia, the possession of "spheres of influence or interest" in China in which they are to enjoy special rights and privileges, more especially in respect of railroads and mining enterprises, Her Britannic Majesty's Government has therefore sought to maintain at the same time what is called the "open-door" policy, to insure to the commerce of the world in China equality of treatment within said "spheres" for commerce and navigation. This latter policy is alike urgently demanded by the British mercantile communities and by those of the United States, as it is justly held by them to be the only one which will improve existing conditions, enable them to maintain their positions in the markets of China, and extend their operations in the future. While the Government of the United States will in no way commit itself to a recognition of exclusive rights of any power within or control over any portion of the Chinese Empire under such agreements as have within the last year been made, it can not conceal its apprehension that under existing conditions there is a possibility, even a probability, of complications arising between the treaty powers which may imperil the rights insured to the United states under our treaties with China.

This Government is animated by a sincere desire that the interests of our citizens may not be prejudiced through exclusive treatment by any of the controlling powers within their so-called "spheres of interest" in China, and hopes also to retain there an open market for the commerce of the world, remove dangerous sources of international irritation, and hasten thereby united or concerted action of the powers at Peking in favor of the administrative reforms so urgently needed for strengthening the Imperial Government and maintaining the integrity of China in which the whole western world is alike concerned. It believes that such a result may be greatly assisted by a declaration by the various powers claiming "spheres of interest" in China of their intentions as regards treatment of foreign trade therein. The present moment seems a particularly opportune one for informing Her Britannic Majesty's Government of the desire of the United States to see it make a formal declaration and to lend its support in obtaining similar declarations from the various powers claiming "spheres of influence" in China, to the effect that each in its respective spheres of interest or influence—

First. Will in no way interfere with any treaty port or any vested interest within any so-called "sphere of interest" or leased territory it may have in China.

Second. That the Chinese treaty tariff of the time being shall apply to all merchandise landed or shipped to all such ports as are within said "sphere of interest" (unless they be "free ports"), no matter to what nationality it may belong, and that duties so leviable shall be collected by the Chinese Government.

Third. That it will levy no higher harbor dues on vessels of another nationality frequenting any port in such "sphere" than shall be levied on vessels of its own nationality, and no higher railroad charges over lines built, controlled, or operated within its "sphere" on merchandise belonging to citizens or subjects of other nationalities transported through such "sphere" than shall be levied on similar merchandise belonging to its own nationals transported over equal distances.

Document 3.3

AN APPEAL FOR IMPERIAL EXPANSION

Among the most eloquent and original advocates of further American expansion was Brooks Adams, an eminent historian and descendent of two presidents. In the following excerpt from his book America's Economic Supremacy, *published in 1900, Adams lays out a gloomy vision of the nation's future if it failed to pursue a boldly expansionist policy and embrace its destiny as the new center of the world economy.*

Whether we like it or not, we are forced to compete for the seat of international exchanges, or, in other words, for the seat of empire. The prize is the most dazzling for which any people can contend, but it has usually been won only by the destruction of the chief competitor of the victor. Rome rose on the ruins of Carthage, and England on the collapse of Spain and France.

For upward of a thousand years the tendency of the economic center of the world has been to move westward, and the Spanish War has only been the shock caused by its passing the Atlantic. Probably, within two generations, the United States will have faced about, and its great interests will cover the Pacific, which it will hold like an inland sea. The natural focus of such a Pacific system would be Manila. Lying where all the paths of trade converge, from north and south, east and west, it is the military and commercial key to eastern Asia. Entrenched there, and backing on Europe, with force enough to prevent our competitors from closing the Chinese mainland against us by discrimination, there is no reason why the United States should not become a greater seat of wealth and power than ever was England, Rome, or Constantinople.

But to maintain such an empire presupposes an organization perfect in proportion to the weight it must support and the friction it must endure; and it is the perfecting of this organization, both military and civil, which must be the task of the next fifty years. For there is no possibility of self-deception. Our adversary is deadly and determined. Such are his jealousy of our power and his fear of our expansion, that to cripple us he would have gladly joined with Spain. But for the victory of Manila and the attitude of England, his fleets would last spring have been off our coasts. If we yield before him, he will stifle us.

If the coalition of France, Germany, and Russia succeeds in occupying and organizing the interior of China, if this coalition can control its trade and discriminate against our exports, it will have good prospects of throwing back a considerable surplus on our hands, for us to digest as best we can. In that event, America's possible destiny might be to approach the semi-stationary period of France, meanwhile entering into a competition with our rivals in regard to the cost of domestic life, of industrial production, and of public administration. In such a competition, success can only be won by surpassing the enemy in his own method, or in that concentration which reduces waste to a minimum. Such a concentration might, conceivably, be effected by the growth and amalgamation of great trusts until they absorbed the government, or it might be brought about by the central corporation, called the government, absorbing the trusts. In either event, the result would be approximately the same. The Eastern and Western continents would be competing for the most perfect system of state socialism.

Document 3.4

THE SECOND OPEN DOOR NOTE

The first round of Open Door Notes in 1899 was a modest success. Although competition for China's resources remained intense, none of the great powers rejected the U.S. proposal, and no partition of China occurred. The problem for U.S. policy makers was accelerating political unrest in China, most notably the antiforeign uprising known as the Boxer Rebellion. With rebels and foreign soldiers battling over large areas in 1900, American leaders feared that the great powers would be tempted to tighten their control over swaths of China, unraveling the loosely accepted open door principle. To discourage any such outcome, Secretary of State Hay issued a second round of notes on July 3, 1900, this time insisting especially that all of the powers respect the territorial integrity of China.

In this critical posture of affairs in China it is deemed appropriate to define the attitude of the United States as far as present circumstances permit this to be done. We adhere to the policy initiated by us in 1857, of peace with the Chinese nation, of furtherance of lawful commerce, and of promotion of lives and property of our citizens by all means guaranteed under extraterritorial treaty rights and by the law of nations. If wrong be done to our citizens we propose to hold the responsible authors to the uttermost accountability. We regard the condition at Peking as one of virtual anarchy, whereby power and responsibility are practically devolved upon the local provincial authorities. So long as they are not in overt collusion with rebellion and use their power to protect foreign life and property we regard them as representing the Chinese people, with whom we seek to remain in peace and friendship. The purpose of the President is, as it has been heretofore, to act concurrently with the other powers, first in opening up communica- tion with Pekin and rescuing the American officials, missionaries, and other Americans who are in danger; secondly, in affording all possible protection everywhere in China to American life and property; thirdly, in guarding and protecting all legitimate American interests; and fourthly, in aiding to prevent a spread of the disorders to the other provinces of the Empire and a recurrence of such disasters. It is, of course, too early to forecast the means of attaining this last result; but the policy of the Government of the United States is to seek a solution which may bring about permanent safety and peace to China, preserve Chinese territorial and administrative entity, protect all rights guaranteed to friendly powers by treaty and international law, and safeguard for the world the principle of equal and impartial trade with all parts of the Chinese Empire.

Document 3.5

THE FACE OF AMERICAN POWER

The brutal war in the Philippines caused some Americans to see their nation's recent rise to power in a new light, while questions about how to incorporate new territories into the American political system stirred controversy. But many Americans were confident of their nation's new global role. The following cartoon, published in the humor magazine Puck *in 1901, captures this view of American power.*

Document 3.6

BRUTALITY IN THE PHILIPPINES

By 1902, the war in the Philippines had become a grueling guerrilla conflict marked by shocking brutality on both sides. In the United States, pressure mounted for formal investigation of the tactics used by American troops. The U.S. Senate Committee on the Philippines, set up in 1899 to oversee U.S. administration of the colony, responded in 1902 with investigations into the behavior of American forces. Although closed to the public, newspaper reporters were permitted to cover the hearings, which featured sensational testimony about torture. Reports focused especially on the "water cure," an interrogation method that caused the sensation of drowning. The following story appeared in the New York Times *on May 4, 1902, under the headline "Discharged Soldier Tells Senate Committee How and Why the Torture Was Inflicted."*

WASHINGTON, May 3—L. E. Hallock of Boston, Mass., formerly a Sergeant and later a private in Company I, Twenty-sixth Volunteer Infantry, testified to-day before the Senate Committee on the Philippines concerning the practice of the water cure in the Philippine archipelago. He told of the infliction of the cure upon a dozen natives at the town of Leon, Province of Panay. He said they were captured and tortured in order to secure information of the murder of Private O'Herne of Company I, who had been not only killed, but roasted and otherwise tortured before death ensued. Capt. Glenn, in charge of a scouting party, had first secured a confession of participation in this crime by one native who had implicated twelve others. These were, the witness said, taken to Leon, where his company, under command of Capt. Gregg, was stationed, and there on the 21st and again on the 23d of August, 1900, the cure was administered by members of Company I under the orders of First Sergeant Januarius Manning.

Hallock added that he had witnessed the torture . . . and while it was in progress Capt. Gregg was at company headquarters, less than 100 yards distant.

"Did Capt. Gregg known [*sic*] of the torture?" Senator Rawlins asked.

"All the command knew it, and I don't see how he could have helped knowing it."

"What was the effect of the punishment?"

"The stomach would swell up, and in some cases I witnessed blood come from the mouth."

Asked what became of the Philippine prisoners to whom the cure was administered, he replied that they were placed in a guardhouse 20 by 25 feet in size, in which there was one window, and in which there were at times eighteen men confined. The twelve prisoners were kept for four or five months, and then they tried to escape. That effort had been successful on the part of some of them, but five or six fleeing prisoners were shot and killed. One of them had been killed while trying to get away when the squad was taken to the river for a bath, and the others when out at work, in a general rush for liberty.

"Were all the prisoners who did not escape killed?"

"I think so, with one exception; I think one was given his freedom."

Senator Lodge brought out the details of the murder of Private O'Herne. The witness said that in June, 1900, O'Herne, with two other members of the company, had been sent to Iloilo for mail, and that on their return on June 30 they were ambushed by 100 natives, and O'Herne's companions captured. O'Herne had made a dash to get away, and after escaping from the attacking party, had fallen in with other natives supposed to be friendly, but that instead of proving to be so they had devoted the entire next day to his torture and death, beginning at daylight by cutting him with bolos and then roasting him all day by a slow fire, not finishing up until night. All these details had, the witness said, been gathered from the confessions of the men to whom they had given the cure.

Replying to other questions, he said he had not known any one to die under the water cure. The prisoners were generally fed on rice and coffee, with an occasional meal of hard tack. He said they were all "fat." He also said he understood the orders to be to treat the natives well.

In reply to a question from Senator Burrows, Mr. Hallock said he had seen the bodies of four of the native prisoners who had been shot by the soldiers while trying to make their escape, but that he had not seen the actual shooting.

Document 3.7

The Platt Amendment

In 1898, Congress passed the Teller Amendment, which stipulated that the United States could not annex Cuba following the war with Spain. But the precise nature of the relationship between the United States and an independent Cuba remained an open question. Only in 1901, as a condition for the withdrawal of U.S. occupation troops from the island, were long-term arrangements clarified through the Platt Amendment, named for Connecticut Senator Orville Platt. Added to a joint congressional resolution, the amendment limited Cuban sovereignty and accorded the United States various privileges on the island. Though enormously controversial in Cuba, the amendment was ultimately incorporated into the Cuban constitution of 1902 and a U.S.-Cuban treaty signed on May 22, 1903.

[I]n fulfillment of the declaration contained in the joint resolution approved April twentieth, eighteen hundred and ninety-eight, . . . the President is hereby authorized to "leave the government and control of the island of Cuba to its people" so soon as a government shall have been established in said island under a constitution which, either as a part thereof or in an ordinance appended thereto, shall define the future relations of the United States with Cuba, substantially as follows:

I. That the government of Cuba shall never enter into any treaty or other compact with any foreign power or powers which will impair or tend to impair the independence of Cuba, nor in any manner authorize or permit any foreign power or powers to obtain by colonization or for military or naval purposes or otherwise, lodgement in or control over any portion of said island.

II. That said government shall not assume or contract any public debt, to pay the interest upon which, and to make reasonable sinking fund provision for the ultimate discharge of which, the ordinary revenues of the island, after defraying the current expenses of government shall be inadequate.

III. That the government of Cuba consents that the United States may exercise the right to intervene for the preservation of Cuban independence, the maintenance of a government adequate for the protection of life, property, and individual liberty, and for discharging the obligations with respect to Cuba imposed by the treaty of Paris on the United States, now to be assumed and undertaken by the government of Cuba.

IV. That all Acts of the United States in Cuba during its military occupancy thereof are ratified and validated, and all lawful rights acquired thereunder shall be maintained and protected.

V. That the government of Cuba will execute, and as far as necessary extend, the plans already devised or other plans to be mutually agreed upon, for the sanitation of the cities of the island, to the end that a recurrence of epidemic and infectious diseases may be prevented, thereby assuring protection to the people and commerce of Cuba, as well as to the commerce of the southern ports of the United States and the people residing therein.

VI. That the Isle of Pines shall be omitted from the proposed constitutional boundaries of Cuba, the title thereto being left to future adjustment by treaty.

VII. That to enable the United States to maintain the independence of Cuba, and to protect the people thereof, as well as for its own defense, the government of Cuba will sell or lease to the United States lands necessary for coaling or naval stations at certain specified points to be agreed upon with the President of the United States.

VIII. That by way of further assurance the government of Cuba will embody the foregoing provisions in a permanent treaty with the United States.

Document 3.8

A GERMAN VIEW OF AMERICAN POWER

The rise of American power inevitably drew the attention of European statesmen and intellectuals. European appraisals often expressed a complex mixture of awe, fear, and disdain for the new world power. So it was with German novelist and social critic Wilhelm von Polenz, whose 1903 book Das Land der Zukunft (The Land of the Future) *compared the historical trajectories of the United States and Germany.*

We cannot be surprised if this people is led by its unheard-of success to a ridiculous megalomania. With the exception of the War of Independence and the Civil War, when the existence of the States was at stake, American history is a long chain of good-fortune; but certainly such good fortune can only befall an alert, robust, and self-conscious nation. This nation, with happy instinct, very early understood its mission: to Americanize the continent on which it had grown up. The childhood of the growing nation had been the happiest possible, in spite of poverty. It had not been disturbed by hostile attacks . . . and injuries from foreign neighbours as those to which crowded Europe had been exposed throughout the Middle Ages. The first Indian wars, though bloody, at least steeled the strength of the young colonies and did not permit men to forget the use of weapons, or women that of prayer. The youth of America was free from any crusade-fanaticism such as caused our ancestors to neglect many other far more important tasks of civilization. Fortunately the young colonials were bound to the soil by the quantity of the work they found. No emperor led them across the Alps, no priest tempted them to the East. And they escaped the misfortune which befell the German people of being passed by foreign races which placed themselves before them like an iron bolt. . . . The modern American was born in the belief that not only America, but the whole of the western Hemisphere ought to belong to him. He is strengthened in this idea by the inferiority of the Central and South American races and nations. Two things have made the nation great and masterful: the climate and nature of his native country, and the happy instinct of the Anglo-Saxon to keep his race pure from non-Arian mixture. Bred in a temperate zone of the best blood of the civilized world this northern race must inevitably gain ascendancy over the mongrels of Central and South America and of the West Indian islands.

It is quite natural that the foreign policy of North America should show deep traces of the self-esteem encouraged by association with inferior races. There has never been a "red-tape" diplomatic school in North America, and so that "shirt-sleeve" policy has grown up which fills old-fashioned diplomatists with horror. What France was formerly, the United States seems becoming now: the *enfant terrible* among the Great Powers.

Document 3.9

QUESTIONING U.S. AIMS IN EAST ASIA

The Open Door Notes promised that the United States would pursue an even-handed, nonaggressive policy in China, but American behavior elsewhere suggested something different. Among Chinese critics of U.S. foreign policy was Liang Qichao, the eminent Chinese reformer and journalist who did as much as any intellectual to interpret the Western world for readers in his homeland during the late nineteenth and early twentieth centuries. Liang published the following commentary on American diplomacy following a seven-month tour of North America in 1903. Liang traversed the United States and Canada and visited with President Theodore Roosevelt on May 17. Although Roosevelt did not articulate his "corollary" to the Monroe Doctrine until the following year, Liang feared that growing American ambitions could lead to clashes reminiscent of battles provoked by earlier imperial forays into East Asia.

In personality Roosevelt is like Kaiser Wilhelm II of Germany. Of the heads of the various countries of the world, only these two men have great ambition and talent and the aura of one who would create a new epoch.... Since McKinley, the Republican Party has leaned toward an imperialistic policy; Roosevelt, in particular, assumes an extremely aggressive posture and is full of ambition. There is a chapter in his book called "The Life of Struggle." All his speeches take war as the means for building up a nation; from this his character can be seen....

As everyone knows, America has for several decades considered the Monroe Doctrine an inalienable diplomatic principle. During McKinley's and

Roosevelt's terms in office, however, the nature of the Monroe Doctrine underwent a considerable change, and this must be looked into if we want to understand world trends....

The original meaning of the Monroe Doctrine was "the Americas belong to the people of the Americas," but this has become transformed into "the Americas belong to the peoples of the United States." And who knows if this will not continue to change, day after day from now on, into "the world belongs to the United States"? ...

Hawaii and the Philippines have been annexed; how can they be taken away without overthrowing the hegemon? I fear that there will soon be a successor to our Opium War with England, battle of Tonkin Gulf with France, and battle of Kiaochaow Bay with Germany.

Document 3.10

CONDEMNATION OF U.S. METHODS IN PANAMA

U.S. interest in constructing a canal across the Isthmus of Panama, then a province of Colombia, mounted steadily in the late nineteenth century. American hopes appeared to be realized in early 1903, when the U.S. and Colombian governments reached an agreement authorizing construction of a waterway and giving the United States control for one hundred years. When the Colombian legislature rejected the deal, the Roosevelt administration sought a different path to its goal. U.S. leaders threw their support behind a small group of Panamanian conspirators who, backed by U.S. gunboats off shore, carried out a secessionist rebellion against the Colombian government. Washington quickly recognized the new state of Panama. While these events paved the way for the opening of the Panama Canal in 1914, liberals such as prominent Boston lawyer Moorfield Storey saw them as a shameful display of naked power. In 1904, Storey, a well-known anti-imperialist, published a stinging critique of American behavior in a pamphlet entitled "The Recognition of Panama."

The machinery of revolution was on board our gunboats. It was our forces that accomplished the independence of Panama....

What is this government now called "the new republic"? A self-con- stituted junta of three men.... They have no courts, no constitution, no frame of government, no legislature, no evidence of popular assent....

On the 5th [of November 1903] the United States received from Panama a formal announcement, signed by the three persons calling themselves a junta, that the Republic of Panama was established.

On the 6th the new government of Panama is recognized. Thus reads the dispatch of that date to our minister at Bogata:—

"The people of Panama, having by an apparently unanimous movement dissolved their political connection with the Republic of Colombia and resumed their independence, and having adopted a government of their own, republican in form."

Since when was a self-elected junta of three, supported by foreign bayonets against their lawful rulers, not elected by the people, and with absolute power unfettered by constitutional restraint, a government "republican in form"? What did our government know as to the sentiments of the people of Panama in less than two days after this junta had seized the power?

On the 17th of November the commissioners from the junta sent to negotiate a new treaty reached this country. The treaty was ready for them when they reached Washington; and it was negotiated, signed, and sealed between lunch and dinner. Its first article is as follows:—

"The United States guarantees and agrees to maintain the independence of the Republic of Panama."

Its second article cedes to the United States a strip of land across the isthmus. . . .

It is not necessary to point out that the revolution was hatched in New York. . . . We know that the plan was known to our authorities in advance, that they prepared to aid the revolutionists by force, that they did so, and that to their interposition the success of the revolution is due. . . .

International law has no meaning, if it does not bind the strong nation in its dealings with the weak,—if it is obeyed only when it is dangerous to disobey it. That great system of jurisprudence built up by the labors of enlightened statesmen and jurists during centuries rests upon principles of eternal justice; and, if its rules can be set aside from motives of interest or ambition whenever a great people or its rulers for the moment desire, there is no international law save "the highwayman's plea that 'might makes right.'" It should be the highest ambition of our great republic to be a leader among the peoples in scrupulous regard for the rights of the weak rather than in the reckless exercise of overwhelming power at their expense.

But we want the canal. That is true, but not at any cost. We want many good things in this world. We should like to see property more equally divided. We should like to see land held by men who would use it best for the interests of all rather than by the shiftless and inefficient. We should like to see criminals promptly punished. We should like to see men who have plundered their neighbors compelled to disgorge their ill-gotten gains. We should like to see corrupt politicians driven from public life. But we do not believe in securing these good things by lawless violence. We wish ours to be "a government of laws, and not of men." We believe in courts, not in irresponsible despotism; and we refuse to let the most honest reformer redistribute our property or punish our criminals as he thinks best. The crying evil of the time is the tendency of men to make their desires the standard for other men's duties, and to consider their wills backed by their hands a substitute for law. It is not safe to let a strong man decide what is just to the weak. Such a doctrine means anarchy. Justice is the same for individuals and nations, and a great power has no more right to rob a weak one than the prize-fighter has to plunder the minister.

The course of the administration is wrong legally and morally.

Document 3.11

THEODORE ROOSEVELT'S "COROLLARY" TO THE MONROE DOCTRINE

American fears of European meddling in the Western Hemisphere ran back to the early nineteenth century, when much of the Spanish Empire in the New World crumbled. In 1823, President James Monroe warned Europeans to keep their hands off the young and weak nations of Latin America—a policy known as the Monroe Doctrine. Eighty years later, the Roosevelt administration feared a new round of European intrusions due the inability of impoverished Latin American nations to repay loans from Britain, Germany, and other countries. In his State of the Union address on December 6, 1904, President Theodore Roosevelt restated American insistence that Europeans must not intervene in the hemisphere but made clear that the United States reserved the right to do so in order to promote order.

It is not true that the United States feels any land hunger or entertains any projects as regards the other nations of the Western Hemisphere save such as are for their welfare. All that this country desires is to see the neighboring countries stable, orderly, and prosperous. Any country whose people conduct themselves well can count upon our hearty friendship. If a nation shows that it knows how to act with reasonable efficiency and decency in social and political matters, if it keeps order and pays its obligations, it need fear no interference from the United States. Chronic wrongdoing, or an impotence which results in a general loosening of the ties of civilized society, may in America, as elsewhere, ultimately require intervention by some civilized nation, and in the Western Hemisphere the adherence of the United States to the Monroe Doctrine may force the United States, however reluctantly, in flagrant cases of such wrongdoing or impotence, to the exercise of an international police power. If every country washed by the Caribbean Sea would show the progress in stable and just civilization which with the aid of the Platt amendment Cuba has shown since our troops left the island, and which so many of the republics in both Americas are constantly and brilliantly showing, all question of interference by this Nation with their affairs would be at an end. Our interests and those of our southern neighbors are in reality identical. They have great natural riches, and if within their borders the reign of law and justice obtains, prosperity is sure to come to them. While they thus obey the primary laws of civilized society they may rest assured that they will be treated by us in a spirit of cordial and helpful sympathy. We would interfere with them only in the last resort, and then only if it became evident that their inability or unwillingness to do justice at home and abroad had violated the rights of the United States or had invited foreign aggression to the detriment of the entire body of American nations. It is a mere truism to say that every nation, whether in America or anywhere else, which desires to maintain its freedom, its independence, must ultimately realize that the right of such independence can not be separated from the responsibility of making good use of it.

In asserting the Monroe Doctrine, in taking such steps as we have taken in regard to Cuba, Venezuela, and Panama, and in endeavoring to circumscribe the theater of war in the Far East, and to secure the open door in China, we have acted in our own interest as well as in the interest of humanity at large. There are, however, cases in which, while our own interests are not greatly involved, strong appeal is made to our sympathies. Ordinarily it is very much wiser and more useful for us to concern ourselves with striving for our own moral and material betterment here at home than to concern ourselves with trying to better the condition of things in other nations. We have plenty of sins of our own to war against, and under ordinary circumstances we can do more for the general uplifting of humanity by striving with heart and soul to put a stop to civic corruption, to brutal lawlessness and violent race prejudices here at home than by passing resolutions and wrongdoing elsewhere. Nevertheless there are occasional crimes committed on so vast a scale and of such peculiar horror as to make us doubt whether it is not our manifest duty to endeavor at least to show our disapproval of the deed and our sympathy with those who have suffered by it. The cases must be extreme in which such a course is justifiable. There must be no effort made to remove the mote from our brother's eye if we refuse to remove the beam from our own. But in extreme cases action may be justifiable and proper. What form the action shall take must depend upon the circumstances of the case; that is, upon the degree of the atrocity and upon our power to remedy it.

Documents 3.12 and 3.13

LATIN AMERICAN PERCEPTIONS OF U.S. POLICY

President Roosevelt and other U.S. leaders invariably professed altruistic intentions in the hemisphere. But many Latin Americans saw other motives at work in U.S. policy decisions. The following cartoons, both of which were published in the aftermath of Roosevelt's 1904 declaration of his "corollary" to the Monroe Doctrine, suggest that U.S. intentions were anything but selfless. The lefthand cartoon comes from Sucesos, *a magazine published in Valparaiso, Chile. The cartoon on the right comes from* Caras y Caretas, *a magazine published in Buenos Aires, Argentina.*

Document 3.14

A CRITIQUE OF AMERICA'S CIVILIZING MISSION

The horrific war in the Philippines encouraged some Americans to seek gentler ways to exert American influence abroad. Progressive reformers called on the nation to abandon not just military methods but also its harsh judgments about other societies. One eloquent voice was that of Jane Addams, an ambitious reformer best known for establishing social programs for women and poor people in Chicago. Addams was also an influential participant in the peace movement that gathered force in the years before the First World War. The following selection comes from a speech delivered at a meeting of the Universal Peace Congress in Boston on October 5, 1904.

It is easy to kill a man. It is not easy to bring him forward in the paths of civilization. It is easy to have one broad road such as the British have laid out, and to say, "Some people are at this milestone, other people are at that milestone." But we know that civilization is no such thing; that it has no metes and bounds, but that it advances along devious paths. A man has not begun to read history aright, he does not know the very first rudiments of human life, if he imagines that we are all going to march down one narrow road. If we could only convert our men and women, and make them see that war is destructive, that peace is creative, that if a man commit himself to warfare he is committing himself to the played-out thing, and not to the new, vigorous and fine thing along the lines of the highest human development, we should have accomplished very much.

There is one moral pit into which we continually fall, a sort of hidden pit which the devil digs for the feet of the righteous. It is that we keep on in one way because we have begun that way and do not have the presence of mind enough to change when that path is no longer the right one. The traditional way, the historic way, is the way the Romans used when they went forward into Europe and levied taxes and then brought back to Rome all their treasure and all their finest blood. That is the easiest way.

But if we have the spirit of moral adventure, if we believe, as we pretend to believe in America, in democracy, then we shall be ready to take another course, even if it be much more difficult. I do not believe people can say that we no longer believe in democracy in America, but they can say that we no longer trust democracy. Almost every state in Europe has established forts in Africa or Asia or some other place. It seems to me that here in America is the place for experiment. Let us say, "We will trust the people although they are of a different color, although they are of a different tradition from ours." Perhaps we shall be able, through our very confidence, to nourish them into another type of government, not Anglo-Saxon even. Perhaps we shall be able to prove that some things that are not Anglo-Saxon are of great value, of great beauty. Let us not be like the men in commercial life, who say it is easy enough to go into a place after it has been swept clear by warships. You can force anything on natives when they have been once intimidated. But we must proceed in a different way. We must do our work on the highest plane. We have a higher ideal than the old one which has been incorporated in the rule of first gaining government control by force and making things safe. I can imagine that most young men would say that they will not go into these new regions until a warship has gone first. The man with courage would be the man who would prefer to go without the warships, just as a brave young man walks the streets of Chicago without arms, while the coward carries brass knuckles and a revolver in his hip pocket.

Document 3.15

DOLLAR DIPLOMACY

U.S. leaders frequently used military force to protect American interests abroad during the early twentieth century, but some preferred to rely on American economic power. Above all, the administration of President William H. Taft (1909–13) practiced what became known as "dollar diplomacy," especially in Latin America. Under this approach, U.S. leaders sought agreements by which American firms provided economic expertise and loans while Latin American governments encouraged American investment and placed customs collection, the main source of revenue for most nations, in the hands of U.S. officials. In the following mes- sage to the Senate on January 26, 1911, President Taft asks for approval of a treaty extending a loan to Honduras in return for Honduran acceptance of substantial American control over the country's economy.

I transmit herewith for the consideration of the Senate, with a view to eliciting its advice in regard thereto and obtaining its consent to the ratification thereof, a convention between the United States and the Republic of Honduras concerning a loan which the Republic contemplates making with citizens of the United States, to provide for the refundment of its debt and the placing of its finances on a sound and stable basis.

The weighty considerations of national and international policy which counsel the consummation of such an arrangement are so rational and just as not only to commend themselves to earnest attention, but to call for such elaboration and support as it is my duty to give in fulfillment of my constitutional obligation to consult the coordinate treaty-making power on a matter so intimately concerning the policies of this country in its relations with the neighboring nations of the Caribbean region.

From a very early period of our history it has been alike the policy and moral obligation of the United States to lend, when required, appropriate countenance and counsel to the Commonwealths of the West in all that tends to increase their stability, to promote their welfare, and to maintain and fortify their relations with one another.... It has been but natural that this community of sympathy and purpose should find expression, at any time of exceptional need, in trustful recourse to the impartial counsels of the United States, and that the successive administrations of this country, obeying the sentiments of the American people, should feel it appropriate in the spirit of reciprocal good will to befriend those States upon fitting occasion, within the necessary limitations of our own sound national policy....

Now that the linking of the oceans by the Isthmian Canal is nearing assured realization the conservation of stable conditions in the adjacent countries becomes a still more pressing need, and all that the United States has hitherto done in that direction is amply justified, if there were no other consideration, by the one fact that this country has acquired such vast interest in that quarter as to demand every effort on its part to make solid and durable the tranquillity [*sic*] of the neighboring countries. . . .

The financial embarrassment of Honduras has long been noteworthy. Insufficient revenue has induced repeated foreign loans, incurred without adequate provision for meeting the high interest exacted thereon, resulting in default of payment and in the incurment of still more onerous debts through still more burdensome loans placed on European markets at a large discount. As a consequence, Honduras is to-day a hopeless debtor to foreign countries, tottering under a heavy obligation which is not within its power to satisfy. That Honduras is absolutely incapable of acquitting anything like the face value of its indebtedness is fortunately evident to its creditors. They have long been disposed to acquiesce in a compromise for the adjustment of their claims, upon terms which obviously would be the more favorable as the security for the refunded obligations should become more substantial through the acquirement of some tangible assurance that the normal revenues of the State, pledged for the payment of the debt, would be integrally devoted to the assigned purpose without danger of impairment by internal turbulence or external pressure. . . .

That the domestic welfare of Honduras will be assured by a sound reorganization of its fiscal system is a self-evident proposition. Wastefulness and inefficiency in the collection of revenues can not fail to decrease the income of the State in even greater ratio than economy and efficiency operate to increase it. The good results of effective and safe fiscal reform are shown in the Dominican arrangement under which the augmented revenue not only adequately provides for the governmental needs but now yields a positive surplus actually greater in amount than the total revenue of the State prior to the initiation of the present system of collection. Moreover, the removal of the collecting function from local control takes away one of the main incentives to revolutionary disturbance, when the cupidity of turbulent malcontents is often excited by the material profit to be gained by an even brief control of the customhouses. In its political aspects, too, the Republic is freed from apprehensions of intervention on the part of creditor nations. Such intervention is an inherent right of sovereignty and, if unattended by territorial acquisition of American soil by a foreign power, this Government would not necessarily oppose it, especially if our own offers of help had been put aside. It is no part of the broad national policy of the United States to champion repudiation by its neighbors or to encourage them with the prospect of immunity for the irresponsible contraction of debts which they are not in a condition to discharge; but sound policy counsels our aiding them to get out of debt and keep out of debt. It can in no wise better our good repute to turn a deaf ear to their appeals for a helping hand to lift them from the slough of default into which misfortune may have plunged them; nor could it improve the good will in which we wish to live with our American congeners were we to leave them to make probably harsh terms with their alien creditors, with the alternative of remaining responsible to such international right of redress as the injured parties might invoke.

Besides the considerations of propriety, expediency, and interest which make the present arrangement with Honduras alike desirable and mutually advantageous, its wisdom as an evolution in the direction of far-sighted international policy is to be borne in mind. Honduras is not alone in financial embarrassment. The continual disturbances of other Central American States put them, also, although to a less degree, in the category of prospective borrowers. Within a year past, Guatemala has sought the friendly counsel of the United States regarding the terms of a projected foreign loan, and it is announced, as part of the program of national recuperation put forth by the newly installed constitutional Government of Nicaragua, that the aid of the United States will be asked in effecting a readjustment of the debts of that Republic. It needs no profuse argument to show that the financial rehabilitation of the greater part of Central America will work potential good for the stability and peace of all, and lead to that development of internal resources and expansion of foreign commerce of which they are all capable, and of which they all stand in need.

Document 3.16

MANAGING PUBLIC ATTITUDES

The outbreak of the Mexican Revolution in 1910 alarmed U.S. officials, who feared that turbulence across the border imperiled American investments and lives. After taking office in 1913, President Woodrow Wilson ordered military incursions to tilt the balance of political power in Mexico. In 1914, U.S. troops occupied the port of Veracruz. Two years later, American soldiers attacked across the Rio Grande after Mexican guerrillas raided Columbus, New Mexico. As the latter campaign progressed, Secretary of State Robert Lansing sent the following letter to Wilson on June 10, 1916, warning that the United States faced a growing public-relations problem in Latin America by engaging in acts that were widely condemned as imperialistic "interventions." Lansing worried especially that U.S. behavior violated the Democratic Party platform, which asserted that "intervention" was "revolting to the people of the United States."

As there appears to be an increasing probability that the Mexican situation may develop into a state of war I desire to make a suggestion for your consideration. It seems to me that we should avoid the use of the word "Intervention" and deny that any invasion of Mexico is for the sake of intervention.

There are several reasons why this appears to me expedient:

First. We have all along denied any purpose to interfere in the internal affairs of Mexico and the St. Louis platform declares against it. Intervention conveys the idea of such interference.

Second. Intervention would be humiliating to many Mexicans whose pride and sense of national honor would not resent severe terms of peace in case of being defeated in a war.

Third. American intervention in Mexico is extremely distasteful to all Latin America and might have a very bad effect upon our Pan-American program.

Fourth. Intervention, which suggests a definite purpose to "clean up" the country, would bind us to certain accomplishments which circumstances might make extremely difficult or inadvisable, and, on the other hand, it would impose conditions which might be found to be serious restraints upon us as the situation develops.

Fifth. Intervention also implies that the war would be made primarily in the interest of the Mexican people, while the fact is it would be a war forced on us by the Mexican Government, and, if we term it intervention, we will have considerable difficulty in explaining why we had not intervened before but waited until attacked.

It seems to me that the real attitude is that the *de facto* Government having attacked our forces engaged in a rightful enterprise or invaded our borders (as the case may be) we had no recourse but to defend ourselves and to do so it has become necessary to prevent future attacks by forcing the Mexican Government to perform its obligations. That is, it is simply a state of international war without purpose on our part other than to end the conditions which menace our national peace and the safety of our citizens, and that it is *not* intervention with all that that word implies.

I offer the foregoing suggestion, because I feel that we should have constantly in view the attitude we intend to take if worse comes to worse, so that we may regulate our present policy and future correspondence with Mexico and other American Republics with that attitude.

In case this suggestion meets with your approval I further suggest that we send to each diplomatic representative of a Latin American Republic in Washington a communication stating briefly our attitude and denying any intention to intervene. I enclose a draft of such a note. If this is to be done at all, it seems to me that it should be done at once, otherwise we will lose the chief benefit, namely, a right understanding by Latin America at the very outset.

4

The Rise and Fall of Wilsonianism

Woodrow Wilson arguably influenced U.S. foreign policy more than any other twentieth-century figure. His ideas shaped the country's vision of itself within the international system, stirred international and domestic opinion alike, and offered the language and values that would permeate foreign policy debates for generations to come. Yet Wilson largely failed to put his ideas into practice during his lifetime. This chapter explores this paradox, first by demonstrating some of the major ideas that comprise Wilsonianism and then by showing how those ideas became controversial during and after the peace conference that ended the First World War.

Wilson's ideals—and the stubbornness with which he advocated them—stemmed partly from his religious convictions. The son of a Presbyterian minister, Wilson believed he was God's instrument to bring peace and harmony to the world. But Wilson honed his ideas through a lifetime of academic study and writing. An accomplished political scientist and historian, Wilson came to national prominence as president of Princeton University before turning to politics. He was elected governor of New Jersey in 1910 and then to the presidency of the United States in 1912.

Wilson's moral fervor and dedication to rational problem solving converged first in the domestic policy initiatives that commanded his attention early in his presidency. Under the "New Freedom" banner, Wilson championed an agenda of progressive reform. Before long, however, menacing events beyond America's border led Wilson to turn his reformist energies from the domestic to the international arena. First, political turmoil in Mexico in 1913–14 seemed to demand action from Washington. Then, in July 1914, war broke out among the great powers of Europe. In Mexico, Wilson took action, dispatching troops to occupy the port of Veracruz and to pursue Mexican forces south of the U.S. border. In Europe, Wilson chose studious neutrality. But a common theme ran through both episodes. Wilson insisted that his nation was standing up for morality, decency, justice, and human progress.

As the First World War dragged on, Wilson grew increasingly bold in his contention that the United States had a uniquely benevolent role to play in leading the world toward a new, more peaceful world order. For a time, he argued that the United States could best play that role by staying removed from the fighting. But by early 1917, he had calculated that America should join the war—not simply to vanquish Germany but also to assure a key role at the peace conference where a new international order would be established. By the end of the fighting in November 1918, Wilson had articulated a remarkable vision of a reformed global order rooted in the principles of self-determination, free trade, disarmament, and collective security.

Those principles inspired considerable enthusiasm among European and American public opinion, as well as among nationalist leaders in colonized territories. But they encountered strong opposition where it counted most: among the governments of the other great powers and within Washington, D.C. Britain and France balked at many of Wilson's ideas about self-determination, free trade, and disarmament. The U.S. Senate balked, in turn, at Wilson's preferred mechanism for establishing international cooperation and collective responses to aggression—the League of Nations. Wary of surrendering America's freedom of action, the Senate rejected participation in the league after Wilson refused to compromise over the terms on which the United States would take part. Thus did Wilsonianism completely collapse in early 1920.

Many commentators praised Wilson as a man of profound vision whose ideals—though they may have seemed hopelessly utopian when first articulated—could provide a sound basis for a harmonious and progressive world order. Others sharply criticized him for promoting ideas with the potential to lead the United States into costly international commitments. These critiques, originating in the debates of 1918–20, have reverberated ever since.

Document 4.1

WILSON'S VISION OF AMERICA'S GLOBAL ROLE

On the Fourth of July 1914, a month before the outbreak of the First World War in Europe, Woodrow Wilson articulated his vision of the United States playing a uniquely progressive and moral role in world affairs. The speech, delivered to thousands of admirers at Philadelphia's Independence Hall, was inspired by an unfolding crisis in U.S.-Mexican relations, but it contained many ideas that would underpin Wilson's thinking in later years about the role the United States might play in a reconstructed world order.

It is one thing to be independent, and it is another thing to know what to do with your independence. It is one thing to come to your majority and another to know what you are going to do with your life and your energies. And one of the most serious questions for sober-minded men to address themselves to in the United States is this: what are we going to do with the influence and power of this great nation? Are we going to play by the old rule of using that power for our own aggrandizement and material benefit only? You know what that may mean. It may upon occasion mean that we shall use it to make the peoples of other nations suffer in the way in which we said it was intolerable to suffer when we uttered our Declaration of Independence. . . .

If American enterprise in foreign countries, particularly in those foreign countries which are not strong enough to resist us, takes the shape of imposing upon and exploiting the mass of the people of that country, it ought to be checked and not encouraged. I am willing to get anything for an American that money and enterprise can obtain, except the suppression of the rights of other men. . . .

My dream is that, as the years go on and the world knows more and more of America, it will also drink at these fountains of youth and renewal; that it will also turn to America for those moral inspirations which lie at the basis of all freedom; that the world will never fear America unless it feels that it is engaged in some enterprise which is inconsistent with the rights of humanity; and that America will come into the full light of the day when all shall know that she puts human rights above all other rights, and that her flag is the flag, not only of America, but of humanity.

Document 4.2

WILSON FORESEES A PEACEMAKING ROLE FOR THE UNITED STATES

Ten months into the war, millions lay dead on Europe's battlefields, and German submarines had sent numerous allied ships to the ocean floor. No end to the conflict seemed in sight. Across the Atlantic, Wilson defended his neutrality policy, attacked those who would use the war to divide Americans, and developed his vision of America as a peaceful example—and potential peacemaker—for the world. He laid out his evolving views in a speech in New York City on April 20, 1915.

Do you realize that, roughly speaking, we are the only great nation at present disengaged? . . . Therefore is it not likely that the nations of the world will some day turn to us for the cooler assessments of the elements engaged? I am not now thinking so preposterous a thought as that we should sit in judgment upon them—no nation is fit to sit in judgment upon any other nation—but that we shall some day have to assist in reconstructing the process of peace. Our resources are untouched; we are more and more becoming, by the force of circumstances, the mediating nation of the world in respect to finance. We must make up our minds what are the best things to do and what are the best ways to do them. We must put our money, our energy, our enthusiasm, our sympathy into these things, and we must have our judgments prepared and our spirits chastened against the coming of that day.

So that I am not speaking in a selfish spirit when I say that our whole duty, for the present, at any rate, must be summed up in this motto: "America first." Let us think of America before we think of Europe, in order that America may be fit to be Europe's friend when the day of tested friendship comes. The test of friendship is not now sympathy with the one side or the other, but getting ready to help both sides when the struggle is over. The basis of neutrality, gentlemen, is not indifference; it is not self-interest. The basis of neutrality is sympathy for mankind. It is fairness, it is good will at bottom. It is impartiality of spirit and of judgment. I wish that all of our fellow citizens could realize that. There is in some quarters a disposition to create distempers in this body politic. Men are even uttering slanders against the United States as if to excite her. Men are saying that if we should go to war upon either side, there would be a divided America—an abominable libel of ignorance! America is not all of it vocal just now. It is vocal in spots, but I, for one, have a complete and abiding faith in that great silent body of Americans who are not standing up and shouting and expressing their opinions just now, but are waiting to find out and support the duty of America. . . .

Document 4.3

ANTI-INTERVENTIONIST SENTIMENT

Americans found many reasons to avoid rushing headlong into the war. For some the key motive was disagreement with European policies; for others, it was opposition to war itself. One of the most popular songs of 1915, "I Didn't Raise My Boy to be a Soldier," embodied a strain of antimilitarism prevalent in American thinking since the country's founding, coupled with reference to the growing movement favoring international arbitration that swelled in influence in the years before the war. Former president William Taft was one such prominent proponent of arbitration, for example, and President Theodore Roosevelt had used the mechanism numerous times during his own White House tenure to resolve international disputes. Neither man had faced a crisis such as confronted Wilson in 1915, however, and, as the song demonstrates, Americans were far from unified on the war.

I Didn't Raise My Boy to be a Soldier

Ten million soldiers to the war have gone
Who may never return again.
Ten million mothers' hearts must break,
For the ones who died in vain.
Head bowed down in sorrow in her lonely years,
I heard a mother murmur thro' her tears:

Chorus:
I didn't raise my boy to be a soldier,
I brought him up to be my pride and joy,
Who dares to put a musket on his shoulder,
To shoot some other mother's darling boy?

Let nations arbitrate their future troubles,
It's time to lay the sword and gun away,
There'd be no war today,
If mothers all would say,
I didn't raise my boy to be a soldier.
(Chorus)

What victory can cheer a mother's heart,
When she looks at her blighted home?
What victory can bring her back,
All she cared to call her own?
Let each mother answer in the year to be,
Remember that my boy belongs to me!
(Chorus)

Document 4.4

WILSON CALLS FOR "PEACE WITHOUT VICTORY"

With reelection under his belt, Wilson turned his full attention to foreign policy in 1917. As the war dragged on, the United States supplied growing amounts of credit and war materiel to the Western powers. German leaders believed an unbridled submarine campaign might strangle France and force Britain from the war. Berlin would announce such a policy only eight days after Wilson gave this speech to the Senate on January 22, 1917. The address, one of Wilson's most famous and oft-quoted, elaborated his ideas about the central role to be played by the United States in constructing a durable peace.

It is inconceivable that the people of the United States should play no part in that great enterprise [establishing a new peaceful order among nations]. To take part in such a service will be the opportunity for which they have sought to prepare themselves by the very principles and purposes of their polity and the approved practices of their Government ever since the days when they set up a new nation in the high and honourable hope that it might in all that it was and did show mankind the way to liberty. They can not in honour withhold the service to which they are now about to be challenged. They do not wish to withhold it. But they owe it to themselves and the other nations of the world to state the conditions under which they will feel free to render it. . . .

The present war must first be ended; but we owe it to candour and to a just regard for the opinion of mankind to say that, so far as our participation in guarantees of future peace is concerned, it makes a great deal of difference in what way and upon what terms it is ended. The treaties and agreements which bring it to an end must embody terms which will create a peace that is worth guaranteeing and preserving, a peace that will win the approval of mankind, not merely a peace that will serve the several interests and immediate aims of the nations engaged. We shall have no voice in determining what those terms shall be, but we shall, I feel sure, have a voice in determining whether they shall be made lasting or not by the guarantees of a universal covenant; and our judgment upon what is fundamental and essential as a condition precedent to permanency should be spoken now, not afterwards when it may be too late. . . .

I do not mean to say that any American government would throw any obstacle in the way of any terms of peace the governments now at war might agree upon, or seek to upset them when made, whatever they might be. I only take it for granted that mere terms of peace between the belligerents will not satisfy even the belligerents themselves. Mere agreements may not make peace secure. It will be absolutely necessary that a force be created as a guarantor of the permanency of the settlement so much greater than the force of any nation now engaged or any alliance hitherto formed or projected that no nation, no probable combination of nations, could face or withstand it. If the peace presently to be made is to endure, it must be a peace made secure by the organized major force of mankind. . . .

[I]t must be a peace without victory. It is not pleasant to say this. I beg that I may be permitted to put my own interpretation upon it and that it may be understood that no other interpretation was in my thought. I am seeking only to face realities and to face them without soft concealments. Victory would mean peace forced upon the loser, a victor's terms imposed upon the vanquished. It would be accepted in humiliation, under duress, at an intolerable sacrifice, and would leave a sting, a resentment, a bitter memory upon which terms of peace would rest, not permanently, but only as upon quicksand. Only a peace between equals can last, only a peace the very principle of which is equality and a common participation in a common benefit. The right state of mind, the right feeling between nations, is as necessary for a lasting peace as is the just settlement of vexed questions of territory or of racial and national allegiance.

The equality of nations upon which peace must be founded if it is to last must be an equality of rights; the guarantees exchanged must neither recognize nor imply a difference between big nations and small, between those that are powerful and those that are weak. Right must be based upon the common strength, not upon the individual strength, of the nations upon whose concert peace will depend. Equality of territory or of resources there of course cannot be; nor any other sort of equality not gained in the ordinary peaceful and legitimate development of the peoples themselves. But no one asks or expects anything more than an equality of rights. Mankind is looking now for freedom of life, not for equipoises of power. . . .

I am proposing, as it were, that the nations should with one accord adopt the doctrine of President Monroe as the doctrine of the world: that no nation should seek to extend its polity over any other nation or people, but that every people should be left free to determine its own polity, its own way of development, unhindered, unthreatened, unafraid, the little along with the great and powerful.

I am proposing that all nations henceforth avoid entangling alliances which would draw them into competitions of power, catch them in a net of intrigue and selfish rivalry, and disturb their own affairs with influences intruded from without. There is no entangling alliance in a concert of power. When all unite to act in the same sense and with the same purpose, all act in the common interest and are free to live their own lives under a common protection.

I am proposing government by the consent of the governed; that freedom of the seas which in international conference after conference representatives of the United States have urged with the eloquence of those who are the convinced disciples of liberty; and that moderation of armaments which makes of armies and navies a power for order merely, not an instrument of aggression or selfish violence.

These are American principles, American policies. We could stand for no others. And they are also the principles and policies of forward-looking men and women everywhere, of every modern nation, of every enlightened community. They are the principles of mankind and must prevail.

Document 4.5

WILSON'S REQUEST FOR A DECLARATION OF WAR

With U.S. ships under threat from German submarines, Wilson took the podium in Congress to ask for war on April 2, 1917. Most of the packed crowd cheered and clapped; critics such as Senator Robert La Follette angrily chewed his gum with arms folded in opposition. The final votes were 82–6 in the Senate, 373–50 in the House. America was going to war not against the German people, Wilson declared, but against German leaders and on behalf of the interests of humankind.

The present German submarine warfare against commerce is a warfare against mankind.

It is a war against all nations. American ships have been sunk, American lives taken, in ways which it has stirred us very deeply to learn of, but the ships and people of other neutral and friendly nations have been sunk and overwhelmed in the waters in the same way. There has been no discrimination.

The challenge is to all mankind. Each nation must decide for itself how it will meet it. The choice we make for ourselves must be made with a moderation of counsel and a temperateness of judgement befitting our character and our motives as a nation. We must put excited feeling away. Our motive will not be revenge or the victorious assertion of the physical might of the nation, but only the vindication of right, of human right, of which we are only a single champion. . . .

There is one choice we cannot make, we are incapable of making: we will not choose the path of submission and suffer the most sacred rights of our Nation and our people to be ignored or violated. The wrongs against which we now array ourselves are no common wrongs; they cut to the very roots of human life.

With a profound sense of the solemn and even tragical character of the step I am talking and of the grave responsibilities which it involves, but in unhesitating obedience to what I deem my constitutional duty, I advise that the Congress declare the recent course of the Imperial German Government to be in fact nothing less than war against the government and people of the United States; that it formally accept the status of belligerent which has thus been thrust upon it; and that it take immediate steps not only to put the country in a more thorough state of defence but also to exert all its power and employ all its resources to bring the Government of the German Empire to terms and end the war. . . .

Our object . . . is to vindicate the principles of peace and justice in the life of the world as against selfish and autocratic power and to set up amongst the really free and self-governed peoples of the world such a concert of purpose and of action as will henceforth insure the observance of those principles. . . .

We have no quarrel with the German people. We have no feeling towards them but one of sympathy and friendship. It was not upon their impulse that their government acted in entering this war. It was not with their previous knowledge or approval.

It was a war determined upon as wars used to be determined upon in the old, unhappy days when peoples were nowhere consulted by their rulers and wars were provoked and waged in the interest of dynasties or of little groups of ambitious men who were accustomed to use their fellow men as pawns and tools. . . .

The world must be made safe for democracy. Its peace must be planted upon the tested foundations of political liberty. We have no selfish ends to serve. We desire no conquest, no dominion. We seek no indemnities for ourselves, no material compensation for the sacrifices we shall freely make. We are but one of the champions of the rights of mankind. We shall be satisfied when those rights have been made as secure as the faith and the freedom of nations can make them.

Document 4.6

THE "FOURTEEN POINTS"

By the time American soldiers began arriving in Europe with the hope of breaking the bloody stalemate on the western front, Wilson faced a new problem. In November 1917, a radical movement led by Vladimir Lenin had seized power in Russia. The Bolsheviks threatened to pull their country out of the war against Germany—a move that would deal a crushing blow to the Western military effort. But the president also worried that the Bolsheviks' bold calls for worldwide communist revolution threatened to undermine his simultaneous calls for a new global order based on liberal conceptions of self-determination and free trade. Feeling pressure from his new competitor, Wilson delivered his "Fourteen Points" speech to Congress on January 8, 1918. After a preamble that echoed much of his earlier idealist rhetoric, Wilson laid out an unprecedentedly specific plan for the postwar international order.

I. Open covenants of peace, openly arrived at, after which there shall be no private international understandings of any kind but diplomacy shall proceed always frankly and in the public view.

II. Absolute freedom of navigation upon the seas, outside territorial waters, alike in peace and in war, except as the seas may be closed in whole or in part by international action for the enforcement of international covenants.

III. The removal, so far as possible, of all economic barriers and the establishment of an equality of trade conditions among all the nations consenting to the peace and associating themselves for its maintenance.

IV. Adequate guarantees given and taken that national armaments will be reduced to the lowest point consistent with domestic safety.

V. A free, open-minded, and absolutely impartial adjustment of all colonial claims, based upon a strict observance of the principle that in determining all such questions of sovereignty the interests of the populations concerned must have equal weight with the equitable claims of the government whose title is to be determined.

VI. The evacuation of all Russian territory and such a settlement of all questions affecting Russia as will secure the best and freest cooperation of the other nations of the world in obtaining for her an unhampered and unembarrassed opportunity for the independent determination of her own political development and national policy and assure her of a sincere welcome into the society of free nations under institutions of her own choosing; and, more than a welcome, assistance also of every kind that she may need and may herself desire. The treatment accorded Russia by her sister nations in the months to come will be the acid test of their good will, of their comprehension of her needs as distinguished from their own interests, and of their intelligent and unselfish sympathy.

VII. Belgium, the whole world will agree, must be evacuated and restored, without any attempt to limit the sovereignty which she enjoys in common with all other free nations. No other single act will serve as this will serve to restore confidence among the nations in the laws which they have themselves set and determined for the government of their relations with one another. Without this healing act the whole structure and validity of international law is forever impaired.

VIII. All French territory should be freed and the invaded portions restored, and the wrong done to France by Prussia in 1871 in the matter of Alsace-Lorraine, which has unsettled the peace of the world for nearly fifty years, should be righted, in order that peace may once more be made secure in the interest of all.

IX. A readjustment of the frontiers of Italy should be effected along clearly recognizable lines of nationality.

X. The peoples of Austria-Hungary, whose place among the nations we wish to see safeguarded and assured, should be accorded the freest opportunity to autonomous development.

XI. Rumania, Serbia, and Montenegro should be evacuated; occupied territories restored; Serbia accorded free and secure access to the sea; and the relations of the several Balkan states to one another determined by friendly counsel along historically established lines of allegiance and nationality; and international guarantees of the political and economic independence and territorial integrity of the several Balkan states should be entered into.

XII. The Turkish portion of the present Ottoman Empire should be assured a secure sovereignty, but the other nationalities which are now under Turkish rule should be assured an undoubted security of life and an absolutely unmolested opportunity of autonomous development, and the Dardanelles should be permanently opened as a free passage to the ships and commerce of all nations under international guarantees.

XIII. An independent Polish state should be erected which should include the territories inhabited by indisputably Polish populations, which should be assured a free and secure access to the sea, and whose political and economic independence and territorial integrity should be guaranteed by international covenant.

XIV. A general association of nations must be formed under specific covenants for the purpose of affording mutual guarantees of political independence and territorial integrity to great and small states alike.

Document 4.7

A French Tribute to Wilson

When he arrived in Paris in December 1918, millions of Europeans threw flowers in the path of the man whom they expected to lead them into a new era of peace. For much of the European public, Wilson was no less than a savior—a man of great vision who promised to reform international affairs and usher in a new era of peace and prosperity. Even on the left, many Europeans expressed great admiration for the American president. The French novelist Anatole France, a socialist, extolled Wilson's ideas in the pages of L'Humanité, *a leading leftist newspaper, on December 14, 1918, a little more than a month after the end of the fighting.*

With respect and sympathy, we salute President Wilson, who entered the war in order to end it on terms beneficial to the people rather than to the industrial and financial elite who in every country reaped monstrous profits, and to build a peaceful and prosperous Europe on the ruins of imperialistic and militaristic Europe.

We salute the head of state who, even amid the heat of war, kept his vision fixed on justice and brought to the troubled world the sort of wisdom that alone can guarantee real progress and riches.

Everyone is familiar with the fourteen points that he believes necessary to establish a peace that is durable and, therefore, just; this is so because only a peace founded on justice can endure. The first of these articles is so crucial that all citizens, at this solemn moment, should meditate upon it. It calls for openness of diplomatic agreements. The seeds of war have always been sown amid the secrecy of the ministries. . . .

How great is our satisfaction to hear President Wilson protest such bloody deceptions and to pose a new principle: "Open covenants of peace, openly arrived at, after which there shall be no private international understandings of any kind but diplomacy shall proceed always frankly and in the public view."

A beneficent declaration for the salvation of millions and millions of human lives!

We also endorse with all our heart and spirit President Wilson's proposal that all nations should be allowed to determine for themselves the form of government under which they wish to live. May we never again see, in violation of this principle, soldiers of a sovereign nation extinguish freedom beyond their borders!

Finally, as for President Wilson's call for a League of Nations, we add our voice for such a union of peoples, whose first fragile bonds have been established through the worldwide efforts of Socialism and the Workers' International.

We salute, in Woodrow Wilson, the president of a great republic and a Citizen of the world!

Document 4.8

THE BOLSHEVIK PROBLEM

Although Russia was excluded from the Versailles Conference, the Bolshevik government cast a long shadow over the negotiations. Above all, events in Russia created serious problems for Wilson as he sought to apply his principles of self-determination and disarmament in Europe. With danger seeming to lurk in the East, the major European leaders—Prime Minister David Lloyd George of Britain, Italian Foreign Minister Giorgio Sonnino, and Premier Georges Clemenceau of France (joined in the cartoon below by Marshal Ferdinand Foch, a top French military commander)—were in no mood to follow Wilson's more pacific proposals. Wilson himself grew discouraged and joined with the European powers in redrawing the map of eastern Europe with foremost attention not to ethnic boundaries but to the military and economic viability of the new nations as bulwarks against Bolshevism. The following cartoon appeared in the American periodical Literary Digest *on January 11, 1919.*

Copyrighted by George Matthew Adams.

DISTURBING THE GLEE CLUB.

—Morris for the George Matthew Adams Service.

Document 4.9

THE FRENCH PRESIDENT'S VISION OF PEACE

The Versailles Conference opened on January 18, 1919, amid great fanfare and high hopes. Yet differences of opinion among the key powers quickly emerged. Most important, the French government made clear that it would demand a peace treaty that punished Germany and made Germans pay for damage inflicted on France over four years of war. In France alone, a million soldiers had died, and four thousand towns had been destroyed. In his speech welcoming delegates to Versailles on January 18, 1919, French President Raymond Poincaré echoed Wilson's calls for justice, but Poincaré laid out a vision of justice that differed significantly from

Wilson's. Treatment of Germany emerged as a major point of disagreement among the "Big Three"—France, the United States, and Britain—that dominated the negotiations.

It is not only governments, but free peoples, who are represented here. Through the test of danger they have learned to know and help one another. They want their intimacy of yesterday to assure the peace of tomorrow. Vainly would our enemies seek to divide us. If they have not yet renounced their customary manoeuvres, they will soon find that they are meeting today, as during the hostilities, a homogeneous block which nothing will be able to disintegrate.

Even before the armistice you placed that necessary unity under the standard of the lofty moral and political truths of which President Wilson has nobly made himself the interpreter.

And in the light of those truths you intend to accomplish your mission. You will, therefore, seek nothing but justice, "justice that has no favourites," justice in territorial problems, justice in financial problems, justice in economic problems.

But justice is not inert, it does not submit to injustice. What it demands first, when it has been violated, are restitution and reparation for the peoples and individuals who have been despoiled or maltreated. In formulating this lawful claim, it obeys neither hatred nor an instinctive or thoughtless desire for reprisals. It pursues a twofold object—to render to each his due, and not to encourage crime through leaving it unpunished.

What justice also demands, inspired by the same feeling, is the punishment of the guilty and effective guaranties against an active return of the spirit by which they were tempted; and it is logical to demand that these guaranties should be given, above all, to the nations that have been, and might again be most exposed to aggressions or threats, to those who have many times stood in danger of being submerged by the periodic tide of the same invasions.

What justice banishes is the dream of conquest and imperialism, contempt for national will, the arbitrary exchange of provinces between states as though peoples were but articles of furniture or pawns in a game....

An immortal glory will attach to the names of the nations and the men who have desired to co-operate in this grand work in faith and brotherhood, and who have taken pains to eliminate from the future peace causes of disturbance and instability.

This very day forty-eight years ago, on January 18, 1871, the German Empire was proclaimed by an army of invasion in the Chateau at Versailles. It was consecrated by the theft of two French provinces; it was thus vitiated from its origin and by the fault of the founders; born in injustice, it has ended in opprobrium.

Document 4.10

HO CHI MINH'S APPEAL FOR SELF-DETERMINATION

While Wilson's ideas encountered resistance at home and in Europe, they inspired enthusiasm among nationalist movements struggling against European colonialism. For them, Wilson's Fourteen Points seemed to promise a new era of national self-determination. Anxious to encourage the great powers to live up to this goal, expatriate nationalists living in Europe requested audiences with the statesmen gathered at Versailles and, when those appeals failed, publicized declarations of their demands. The most famous nationalist leader to do so was Nguyen Ai Quoc (Nguyen "the Patriot"), who later embraced another pseudonym, Ho Chi Minh. On June 18, 1919, he sent the following declaration, entitled "Demands of the Annamite [Vietnamese] People," to Robert Lansing, the U.S. secretary of state. Wilson's senior adviser wrote a brief reply acknowledging receipt of the material and a second note promising to share it with Wilson. But the correspondence went no further.

Since the Allies' victory, all subject peoples are trembling with hope before the prospect of an era of law and justice that ought to open for them by virtue of the formal and solemn commitments undertaken before the whole world by the various Entente powers during the fight of Civilization against Barbarism.

While waiting for the principle of national self-determination to pass from ideal to reality through effective recognition of the sacred right of all people to determine their own destiny, the people of the one-time Empire of Annam, today French Indochina, present to the Noble Governments of the Entente in general and to the honorable French Government in particular the following humble demands:

1. A general amnesty for all indigenous political prisoners.
2. Reform of Indochinese justice by extending to the native population the same legal guarantees enjoyed by Europeans, and the total suppression of the special courts which are instruments of terrorization and repression of the most responsible part of the Annamite population.
3. Freedom of the press and speech.
4. Freedom of association and assembly.
5. Freedom to emigrate and to travel abroad.
6. Freedom of education and the creation in every province of technical and professional schools for the native population.

7. Replacement of rule by decree with rule of law.

8. Creation of permanent positions for elected members of the native population to serve in the French parliament to keep it informed of indigenous demands.

Document 4.11

OPPOSITION FROM HENRY CABOT LODGE

After compromising on other key elements of his original peace plan, Wilson increasingly focused on winning approval for the League of Nations, which he considered the centerpiece of his vision. On this matter, he found opposition not in the capitals of Europe but within his own country. Most important, members of the U.S. Senate—where a two-thirds vote was required for approval of any treaty—voiced opposition to the league, especially after the president formally presented the treaty on July 10. A group of about twelve "irreconcilables" declared that they would oppose U.S. membership in an international organization of any sort. Another group—the "reservationists," led by Henry Cabot Lodge, the Republican chair of the Senate Foreign Relations Committee—also sharply criticized Wilson's proposal but allowed that he might revise it before the Senate had to vote. Lodge delivered the following speech to the Senate on August 12, 1919.

The independence of the United States is not only more precious to ourselves but to the world than any single possession. Look at the United States today. We have made mistakes in the past. We have had shortcomings. We shall make mistakes in the future and fall short of our own best hopes. But none the less is there any country today on the face of the earth which can compare with this in ordered liberty, in peace, and in the largest freedom?

Contrast the United States with any country on the face of the earth today and ask yourself whether the situation of the United States is not the best to be found. I will go as far as anyone in world service, but the first step to world service is the maintenance of the United States.

I have always loved one flag and I cannot share that devotion [with] a mongrel banner created for a League. . . .

I have never had but one allegiance—I cannot divide it now. I have loved but one flag and I cannot share that devotion and give affection to the mongrel banner invented for a league. Internationalism, illustrated by the Bolshevik and by the men to whom all countries are alike provided they can make money out of them, is to me repulsive.

National I must remain, and in that way I like all other Americans can render the amplest service to the world. The United States is the world's best hope, but if you fetter her in the interests and quarrels of other nations, if you tangle her in the intrigues of Europe, you will destroy her power for good and endanger her very existence. Leave her to march freely through the centuries to come as in the years that have gone.

Strong, generous, and confident, she has nobly served mankind. Beware how you trifle with your marvelous inheritance, this great land of ordered liberty, for if we stumble and fall freedom and civilization everywhere will go down in ruin. . . .

We hear much of visions and I trust we shall continue to have visions and dream dreams of a fairer future for the race. But visions are one thing and visionaries are another, and the mechanical appliances of the rhetorician designed to give a picture of a present which does not exist and of a future which no man can predict are as unreal and short-lived as the steam or canvas clouds, the angels suspended on wires and the artificial lights of the stage.

They pass with the moment of effect and are shabby and tawdry in the daylight. Let us at least be real. Washington's entire honesty of mind and his fearless look into the face of all facts are qualities which can never go out of fashion and which we should all do well to imitate. . . .

Our first ideal is our country, and we see her in the future, as in the past, giving service to all her people and to the world. Our ideal of the future is that she should continue to render that service of her own free will. She has great problems of her own to solve, very grim and perilous problems, and a right solution, if we can attain to it, would largely benefit mankind.

We would have our country strong to resist a peril from the West, as she has flung back the German menace from the East. We would not have our politics distracted and embittered by the dissensions of other lands. We would not have our country's vigour exhausted or her moral force abated, by everlasting meddling and muddling in every quarrel, great and small, which afflicts the world.

Our ideal is to make her ever stronger and better and finer, because in that way alone, as we believe, can she be of the greatest service to the world's peace and to the welfare of mankind.

Document 4.12

A British View of Wilson's Problems

European governments forced Wilson to compromise on much of his initial plan for the peace, but they went along with his ideas about the League of Nations. Indeed, the league was fully enshrined in the Treaty of Versailles, which was signed on June 28, 1919, and ratified by Britain, France, Italy, Japan, Germany, and other nations between July and October. Whether the U.S. Senate would ratify the plan and permit U.S. participation in the organization remained an open question, however. As suggested by the following cartoon, Wilson—whom many Europeans had regarded as a knight in shining armor—seemed to face a difficult challenge from his unruly and unpredictable foes at home. The cartoon appeared in the British journal Punch *on September 3, 1919.*

Document 4.13

WILSON'S DEFENSE OF THE LEAGUE

Unwilling to compromise with Lodge, Wilson, an accomplished orator, decided to take his case directly to the American people. On September 4, 1919, he set off on a grueling cross-country speaking tour to defend his vision of the League of Nations. More than anything, he defended the controversial Article 10 of the league's covenant—the provision that required signatory countries to assist other member nations if they were attacked from abroad. Lodge and other critics contended that this provision would lead the United States into unwanted conflicts. Wilson believed it was the cornerstone of a new global order and refused to alter it. With his accustomed tone of righteousness, the president delivered thirty-six speeches in just twenty-three days. His final event came in Pueblo, Colorado, where, after deliver-

ing his address on September 25, 1919, he collapsed. A week later he suffered a stroke that would greatly diminish his political effectiveness over the remainder of his life.

There is an organized propaganda against the League of Nations and against the treaty proceeding from exactly the same sources that the organized propaganda proceeded from which threatened this country here and there with disloyalty, and I want to say—I cannot say too often—any man who carries a hyphen about with him carries a dagger that he is ready to plunge into the vitals of this Republic whenever he gets ready. . . .

Do not think of this treaty of peace as merely a settlement with Germany. It is that. It is a very severe settlement with Germany, but there is not anything in it that she did not earn. Indeed, she earned more than she can ever be able to pay for, and the punishment exacted of her is not a punishment greater than she can bear, and it is absolutely necessary in order that no other nation may ever plot such a thing against humanity and civilization.

But the treaty is so much more than that. It is not merely a settlement with Germany; it is a readjustment of those great injustices which underlie the whole structure of European and Asiatic society. This is only the first of several treaties. They are all constructed upon the same plan. The Austrian treaty follows the same lines. The treaty with Hungary follows the same lines. . . .

What are those lines? They are based upon the purpose to see that every government dealt with in this great settlement is put in the hands of the people and taken out of the hands of coteries and of sovereigns who had no right to rule over the people.

It is a people's treaty, that accomplishes by a great sweep of practical justice the liberation of men who never could have liberated themselves, and the power of the most powerful nations has been devoted not to their aggrandizement but to the liberation of people whom they could have put under their control if they had chosen to do so. . . .

And what do they unite for? They enter into a solemn promise to one an- other that they will never use their power against one another for aggression; that they never will impair the territorial integrity of a neighbour; that they never will interfere with the political independence of a neighbour; that they will abide by the principle that great populations are entitled to determine their own destiny and that they will not interfere with that destiny; and that no matter what differences arise amongst them they will never resort to war without first having done one or other of two things—either submitted the matter of controversy to arbitration, in which case they agree to abide by the result without question, or submitted it to the consideration of the council of the League of Nations, laying before that council all the documents, all the facts, agreeing that the council can publish the documents and the facts to the whole world, agreeing that there shall be six months allowed for the mature consideration of those facts by the council, and agreeing that at the expiration of the six months, even if they are not then ready to accept the advice of the council with regard to the settlement of the dispute, they will still not go to war for another three months.

In other words, they consent, no matter what happens, to submit every matter of difference between them to the judgment of mankind, and just so certainly as they do that, my fellow citizens, war will be in the far background, war will be pushed out of that foreground of terror in which it has kept the world for generation after generation, and men will know that there will be a calm time of deliberate counsel. . . .

But, you say, "We have heard that we might be at a disadvantage in the League of Nations." Well, whoever told you that either was deliberately falsifying or he had not read the Covenant of the League of Nations. I leave him the choice. I want to give you a very simple account of the organization of the League of Nations and let you judge for yourselves.

It is a very simple organization. The power of the League, or rather the activities of the league, lie in two bodies. There is the council, which consists of one representative from each of the principal allied and associated powers—that is to say, the United States, Great Britain, France, Italy, and Japan, along with four other representatives of smaller powers chosen out of the general body of the membership of the League.

The council is the source of every active policy of the League, and no active policy of the League can be adopted without a unanimous vote of the council. That is explicitly stated in the Covenant itself. Does it not evidently follow that the League of Nations can adopt no policy whatever without the consent of the United States? . . .

Article ten is the heart of the whole matter. What is article ten? I never am certain that I can from memory give a literal repetition of its language, but I am sure that I can give an exact interpretation of its meaning. Article ten provides that every member of the league covenants to respect and preserve the territorial integrity and existing political independence of every other member of the league as against external aggression.

Not against internal disturbance. There was not a man at that table who did not admit the sacredness of the right of self determination, the sacredness of the right of any body of people to say that they would not continue to live under the Government they were then living under, and under article eleven of the Covenant they are given a place to say whether they will live under it or not. . . .

Whether you believe it or not, I know the relative size of my own ideas; I know how they stand related in bulk and proportion to the moral judgments of my fellow countrymen, and I proposed nothing whatever at the peace table at Paris that I had not sufficiently certain knowledge embodied the moral judgment of the citizens of the United States.

I had gone over there with, so to say, explicit instructions. Don't you remember that we laid down fourteen points which should contain the principles of the settlement? They were not my points. In every one of them I was conscientiously trying to read the thought of the people of the United States, and after I uttered those points I had every assurance given me that could be given me that they did speak the moral judgment of the United States and not my single judgment. . . .

What of our pledges to the men that lie dead in France? We said that they went over there not to prove the prowess of America or her readiness for another war but to see to it that there never was such a war again. It always seems to make it difficult for me to say anything, my fellow citizens, when I think of my clients in this case.

My clients are the children; my clients are the next generation. They do not know what promises and bonds I undertook when I ordered the armies of the United States to the soil of France, but I know, and I intend to redeem my pledges to the children; they shall not be sent upon a similar errand. . . .

Document 4.14

LODGE'S RESERVATIONS

As a Senate vote on the treaty drew near in November 1919, Senator Lodge codified the ideas of the "reservationists" in a formal fourteen-point statement to be voted upon by the Senate alongside the treaty. Issued on November 6, 1919, the reservations, excerpted below, addressed several of the critics' anxieties about the League of Nations but especially sought to blunt American responsibilities under the despised Article 10. True to form, Wilson rejected the proposals and urged Democrats to vote against the amended treaty. Together, Democrats and the "irreconcilables" defeated the treaty by a vote of 55–39.

1. [I]n case of notice of withdrawal from the League of Nations, . . . the United States shall be the sole judge as to whether all its international obligations and all its obligations under the said Covenant have been fulfilled, and notice of withdrawal by the United States may be given by a concurrent resolution of the Congress of the United States.

2. The United States assumes no obligation to preserve the territorial integrity or political independence of any other country or to interfere in controversies between nations—whether members of the League or not—under the provisions of Article 10, or to employ the military or naval forces of the United States under any article of the treaty for any purpose, unless in any particular case the Congress, which, under the Constitution, has the sole power to declare war or authorize the employment of the military or naval forces of the United States, shall . . . so provide. . . .

4. The United States reserves to itself exclusively the right to decide what questions are within its domestic jurisdiction and declares that all domestic and political questions relating wholly or in part to its internal affairs, including immigration, labor, coast traffic, the tariff, commerce, the suppression of traffic in women and children, and in opium and other dangerous drugs, and all other domestic questions, are solely within the jurisdiction of the United States and are not under this treaty to be submitted in any way either to arbitration or to the consideration of the Council or of the Assembly of the League of Nations, or any agency thereof, or to the decision or recommendation of any other power.

5. The United States will not submit to arbitration or to inquiry by the Assembly or by the Council of the League of Nations . . . any questions which in the judgment of the United States depend upon or relate to its long-established policy, commonly known as the Monroe Doctrine; said doctrine is to be interpreted by the United States alone and is hereby declared to be wholly outside the jurisdiction of [the] League of Nations. . . .

7. The Congress of the United States will provide by law for the appointment of the representatives of the United States in the Assembly and the Council of the League of Nations. . . .

9. The United States shall not be obligated to contribute to any expenses of the League of Nations . . . unless and until an appropriation of funds . . . shall have been made by the Congress of the United States.

10. If the United States shall at any time adopt any plan for the limitation of armaments proposed by the Council of the League of Nations . . . it reserves the right to increase such armaments without the consent of the Council whenever the United States is threatened with invasion or engaged in war. . . .

Document 4.15

A Poetic Tribute to the League of Nations

The defeat of the treaty on November 19, 1919, crushed the hopes of the League of Nations' supporters, who may have constituted a majority in the United States throughout the period. Wilson's backers accused senators of manipulating the league for partisan advantage in the 1920 elections. In a bit of doggerel entitled "Panatela" (a kind of cigar; the poem loosely takes a cigar's shape), Clark McAdams, a satirist for the St. Louis Post-Dispatch, *lauded the president on November 19, 1919, for standing up for principle. The poem criticizes not only Republicans but also Democrats—the "opposition" in the first stanza—for doing too little to back Wilson's plan.*

Panatela

—by Clark McAdams

Yes, Luella,
Mr. Wilson
Cheers us all
By showing fight;
After all,
The opposition isn't doing
As it might.
While the plot
Within the Senate
Moves as smoothly
As a rhyme,
Just imagine
What the people
Think about it
All the time!

In the average
Opinion
War is nothing
Much at all
But a want
Of understanding
As to matters
That befall.
Any nation
Could adjust them,
Were they under
Its control,
But we lack
Co-operation
On the planet as a whole.

That is all,
My little girlie;
Anybody with a head

Feels exactly that about it,
Notwithstanding
What is said.
Something like
The league of nations,
Same as sheriffs
Or police,
And despite
The politicians
Is the patent
Way to peace.

So we have it,
Sweet Luella:
While the
Presidential race
Rages early
In the Senate,
War has yet
To win its case.
Now the President
Has answered
And has called
Their little bluff,
Maybe all of us
Together
Will arise and cry,
"Enough!"

Anyway,
The 1920
Drive is falling
Pretty flat;
Most of us,
We hope,
Are looking
Rather further
On than that.
While we all
Belong to parties
And at best
Are pretty blind,
What we want
To do is something

For the good
Of humankind.

Document 4.16

A CRITIQUE OF WILSON'S LEADERSHIP

While some praised Wilson for remaining true to his ideals, others attacked him for his stubborn refusal to accept compromise. A cartoonist for the Chicago Tribune *took this view on November 20, 1919, pointing out that the president had abandoned several of his Fourteen Points during negotiations at Versailles. Why, then, wouldn't he compromise on the League of Nations? Many Americans asked similar questions and successfully demanded during the winter of 1919–20 that the*

Senate reconsider Lodge's compromise solution. Once again, however, Wilson refused to accept Lodge's proposal, and the Senate rejected the league, this time by a vote of 49–35—too small a majority to pass the measure.

Documents 4.17 and 4.18

WILSON'S INTERNATIONAL LEGACY

Wilson and the League of Nations became political sensations at home, but around the world the American president's pleas for revision of the international system and self-determination helped inspire a generation of nationalists and activists. His words circulated the globe, and in doing so helped foster a positive image of the United States throughout the colonized world. This image would in many ways come back to haunt American policy makers during the Cold War, when their defense of colonial regimes and the status quo seemed to many determined nationalists not only wrong but hypocritical. As these two documents show, Wilson's influence ranged far and wide. The first is a 1919 advertisement for a collection of Wilson's writings available in India, praising the American leader as a "modern apostle for freedom." The second is a letter of praise and obituary, published following Wilson's death in 1924 by Muhammad Husayn Haykal, an influential Egyptian journalist and nationalist.

President Wilson:

The Modern Apostle of Freedom

Dr. Woodrow Wilson is the most striking personality in the world at present time. He has been described as the "Man of the Hour," or the "Man of Destiny" by the admiring world which he has aroused with a remarkable message of peace and freedom. President Wilson's speeches are surely one of the finest and sweetest fruits of the deadly war, and it is universally hoped that his ideals will be realised as far as practicable at the Peace Conference. The speeches which Dr. Wilson delivered since American entry into the war have been collected and published in a single volume by the enterprising publishers, Messrs. Ganesh & Co., Madras, who have thereby done a service to civilisation. These speeches bring solace to a war weary world and hope to small and weak nationalities. They bring out indeed a new spiritual vision of human progress, and are not of an ephemeral or territorial interest. The book is therefore a welcome addition to the world's classics. It includes a spirited foreword by Dr. S. Subramania Iyer and an excellent character sketch of the President by Mr. K. Vyasa Rao. The get up of this book is splendid. Price Rs. 1. Ganesh & Co., Madras.—W. C. Reformer.

India for Indians

(Second Edition revised and enlarged.)

This is a collection of the speeches delivered by Mr. C. R. Das on Home Rule for India wherein he has also tellingly exposed the fallacy of Anglo-Indian Agitation against Indian aspirations. The book opens with an introduction by Babu Motilal Ghose, Editor, Amrita Bazar Patrika. Price As. 12

India's Claim for Home Rule

New India writes:—The growth of political literature in India is, in recent times, becoming very rapid and remarkable, and with the great National awakening in this land also has arisen a keen and fervent desire to spread it by means of cheap and useful books. Messrs. Ganesh & Co., the enterprising publishers of Madras, stimulated by this desire, have brought out many popular books on Indian problems and their recent venture is India's Claim for Home Rule. This book contains a comprehensive collection of speeches and writings of eminent Indians and veteran English publicists, with an attractive appendix and an exhaustive index. Price Rs. 2

The Soul of India

A vision of the past and future, by Mrs. Sarojini Naidu. Price As. 4

The Indian Nation Builders

This is the only Publication which gives the biographies and speeches of thirty six eminent Indians, with their portraits in three comprehensive volumes at such a cheap cost of Rs. 4-8, (Volume I, Rs. 1-8, Volume II, Rs. 1-8; Volume III, Rs. 1-8). Each Volume contains the biographies and select speeches of 12 eminent Indians with their portraits and is bound in cloth. Revised and enlarged edition.

Heroes of the Hour

This is a collection of exhaustive biographical studies of Mahatma Gandhi, Tilak Maharaj and Dr. S. Subramanya Aiyar wherein is given a [illegible] account of the [illegible] activities of these three heroes in building up the Indian Nation. Price Re. 1-8

GANESH & Co., Publishers

MADRAS

Thomas Woodrow Wilson passed away two days ago, bidding farewell to this tumultuous world where he fought to be a guiding light, leading men from the shadow of war toward peace. Yet humanity, like before the war, still yearns to see spilt blood, and still delights in righteous words as their actions take the path of iniquity.

Dr. Wilson, the former President of the United States, has died. Who does not know Dr. Wilson! Who did not have Dr. Wilson's name on their lips! Moreover, who did not see the great light spread by the spirit of that great man, and who did not stare at that light dumbfounded, its miraculous effects making them forget the treacherous nature of man, his attachment to his own trivial interests, his subjugation to his own lowest passions, and imagine that they could embrace the principles of this new Messiah and rise above daily life, transcending this foolish world in which they live into a new world of love, purity, and peace.

We all know Dr. Wilson. We all remember the time when we gazed at the Fourteen Points in awe. We all remember the great hopes built upon those principles, hopes which still grip the world. The violent conflict between East and West, between imperialism and self-determination, between slavery and freedom, between darkness and light; this violent conflict, which began on the day that the Great War ended and will continue until light triumphs and right prevails—is it not the consequence of these great principles, that some today see as illusions? They are not illusions. They are a force which has built up over the ages, created by general suffering and hopes, by individual dreams and yearnings, by the ideas of philosophers and the words of poets, by all the power, feeling, and desire of the human soul. And then, fate chose President Wilson to be their translator and spokesman.

Wilson's principles were not illusions. People believed in them as soon as they were uttered, because they answered the yearnings, thoughts, and hopes in their hearts. People believed in them; then, they failed to carry them out; then, they condemned them; then, they said they were mere illusions. This is the fate of every new idea. First, people notice it. Then they condemn it and stand in its way. Then they begin to support it. Finally, they appreciate its true value and organize their lives in accordance with it.

Wilson has died, but his thought remains, and it will no doubt triumph. Its triumph shall be a great victory to justice, good, and happiness. . . .

After the armistice, Dr. Wilson traveled to Europe in order to serve as his nation's spokesman at the peace conference. But unfortunately, he could not implement his principles, and was too weak to leave Europe to its misfortunes because America held debts from all the Allies and had an interest in retaining the alliance. When he returned to America he failed to have the Senate to ratify the Versailles Treaty. Thus collapsed one of his greatest hopes, perhaps the greatest among them. His call to the people failed, and in the end he suffered a stroke. But Wilson's failure to bring his country to accept the treaty does not at all diminish his stature. He will remain in history as one among the great guides of humanity. His name will live on in history forever.

• • • • • •

5

Isolation and Intervention

The Wilsonian moment was fleeting. After the Senate rejected the Treaty of Versailles, and with it American membership in the League of Nations, the U.S. government played a fitful role in international relations in the 1920s. There were important international issues to settle, yet among Americans there was little appetite for deeper, more meaningful involvement in world affairs, particularly in Europe. For example, in response to the chronic instability of the reparations system established at Versailles, by which Germany pledged to pay a continuing indemnity to Britain and France, Washington attempted to broker solutions in the 1924 Dawes Plan and the 1929 Young Plan. But these efforts did nothing to tackle the root causes of the crisis or establish a more permanent American role in European security.

Most problematic was the Great War, which continued to cast a long and ominous shadow. When Americans did become involved in international affairs, they did so with a determination never again to intervene in a distant war. During the heady 1920s, many believed it was possible that war could be ended, everywhere and for all time. In addition to disarmament, the interwar era was the heyday of other anti-interventionist doctrines, such as socialism, Christian pacifism, and the movement to outlaw war. In 1921–22, President Warren Harding hosted the Washington Naval Conference, which limited arms and warships in the Pacific. In 1928, Secretary of State Frank Kellogg successfully promoted a broadly multilateral treaty by which countries agreed to renounce war as an instrument of foreign policy. Yet these treaties had only limited impact.

The reluctance to become fully entwined in world politics, known as isolationism, deepened with the coming of the Great Depression in 1929, even though the Depression also fatally undermined the whole post–World War I system of international security and thus destabilized world order. The political and social turmoil of the early 1930s led to the emergence of radical alternatives to liberal democratic capitalism, such as fascism, in Europe and Japan. While many Americans remained committed to nonintervention, an increasing number called for the United States to respond. With the Japanese invasion of China in 1937, President Franklin D. Roosevelt joined those who believed the United States should oppose the dictators in some way, even if he did not yet want to commit the nation to war. Still, the isolationists and anti-interventionists formed a majority of public opinion.

With the "revisionist" powers of Germany, Italy, and Japan (so called because they wanted to revise, and even end, the Versailles and Washington treaties) taking the offensive, Americans in the 1930s were faced with a difficult choice between isolation and intervention. Much of the difficulty stemmed from the simple fact that while Americans had an interest in world affairs and expressed revulsion for Nazi Germany and imperial Japan, the United States itself was never at risk of attack or invasion. Thus, even as late as 1941, the year the United States entered World War II, it was unclear who would win the emotional, often acrimonious debate between isolationists and interventionists. One thing, however, was clear to all: whoever won the debate over isolationism or interventionism would determine the basis of U.S. foreign policy for the foreseeable future.

Document 5.1

RACE AND EMPIRE

After World War I, the United States supposedly went into a period of isolationism. But there was no isolationism in the Western Hemisphere. Instead, building on previous interventions, Presidents Harding, Coolidge, and Hoover deepened U.S. involvement in the region, particularly the Caribbean. Until Franklin D. Roosevelt announced the Good Neighbor Policy of nonintervention in Latin America, between 1906 and 1934 U.S. troops directly occupied and ruled Cuba (for eight years), the Dominican Republic (eight years), Nicaragua (fourteen years), and Haiti (nineteen years). Defenders of hemispheric intervention argued that the United States was simply upholding law and order in the region and that U.S. occupation was for those countries' own good. This was, they said, part of America's duty to spread civilization, much as the European empires claimed to be doing in Asia and Africa. Opponents simply called it racist imperialism, imposed not for the benefit of other people but at the behest of banks and corporate interests. Though less widespread than the debates over the Philippines a few decades earlier, these arguments revealed a great deal about the nation's attitudes toward foreign affairs in the interwar period. In this 1921 speech in Philadelphia, Marcus Garvey, a fierce critic of U.S. foreign policy in the Caribbean (especially Haiti) and leader of the Universal Negro Improvement Association, a major civil rights organization, lumps the United States in with the European empires in criticizing white rule around the world. Garvey's was an early voice of the national liberation movements that would transform the world in the decades following World War II. His speech concerns the Washington Conference on reducing naval armaments in the Pacific—and, Garvey and other critics charged, containing nonwhite Japan in the name of white, Western imperialism.

Now, what is about to take place? The bigger powers, the bigger nations, the more progressive races, after having satisfied themselves at the expense of the weaker ones, are about to get together and form themselves into a great combination, a great coterie. They are endeavoring to settle some plan by which they will not continue to rule by brute force, by armaments, through which they destroy themselves, but by some other method. But whom are they going to rule? They are going to rule the same people that they ruled when they had armaments, but only under different methods....

The world cannot disarm so long as one section of humanity oppresses the other section, because the oppressed section of humanity will always rebel and will use any power at its command for the freeing of itself. We want a conference of the Bigger Brotherhood of humanity. How can you disarm when you have robbed others, when you have plundered the lands and properties of others, and still hold them? So long as human nature remains as it is, the world cannot disarm. So long as the one man will inflict injustice upon the other, the world cannot disarm. When we practice justice, equity and mercy and love and charity, then the entire universe can disarm. I am in favor of disarmament. I do not want to see any guns and pistols and swords around. I am for such a conference, but I think at this time it is inopportune. There should have been another conference before this one.

The conference, where Europe would have met Asia, where Asia, Europe and Africa would be at the table of human justice, and where Europe would say to Asia, "Brother, take what is yours"; where Asia and Europe would say to Africa, "Brother, take what is yours." Until they do that, talking about disarmament is only a farce....

But if they expect Japan is going to disarm when Europe has its eye on Asia, they make a big mistake. Again, they have a second thought coming. Japan is not going to disarm until Asia controls Asia. What right have you in the other man's home? ...

I am advising the statesmen of the world—we are just fifty years out of slavery, and you may ignore me because I am a Negro—but I may tell you wise statesmen of the world that you had better discard your old-time tricks. Take my advice and call a conference of the larger humanity and start this world over anew. Start it out fair. Call the white man from Europe, the yellow and brown from Asia, call the black man from Africa and let us all sit together, and let Europe say, "Well, Africa, we have robbed you long enough." And because the African is so charitable, because he is so merciful, because he is so religious, because he is so human, he will say, "All right, I know you have robbed me; we are quits; we will start afresh." The African is large-hearted enough to do that, and he is waiting on them to suggest it. But you know every man has a limit to his patience. There is a limit to even God's patience; God Almighty put up with Lucifer until He could not do so any more; then He drew his sword. There is armament in heaven. There is armament among the angels. . . .

It is a very delicate proposition they are now discussing in Washington. We will support humanity, we will support the nations of the world when they deal out to us justice, true liberty, true democracy. If they fail to give us that we are going our way.

Document 5.2

THE WORLD RENOUNCES WAR

Though the United States was not isolationist in the decade following World War I, its involvement in world affairs was nonetheless limited in certain respects. American officials were willing to put themselves at the center of world politics, but they rejected initiatives that would have led to their management of the world system. Instead of a Wilsonian plan in which the United States would help guarantee international order, the interwar Republican presidents and their secretaries of state devised a system in which the United States would help create international norms without guaranteeing their enforcement. The Washington Conference treaties of 1921–22, the Dawes Plan of 1924, and the Young Plan of 1929 all tried to establish stability in Asia and Europe without committing Washington to its maintenance. None was as ambitious as the Kellogg-Briand Pact, which was signed in August 1928 and ratified by the Senate the following January. The pact may have failed to disprove Carl von Clausewitz's maxim that war was a continuation of politics by other means, but it still stands as the epitome of interwar idealism.

Deeply sensible of their solemn duty to promote the welfare of mankind;

Persuaded that the time has come when a frank renunciation of war as an instrument of national policy should be made to the end that the peaceful and friendly relations now existing between their peoples may be perpetuated;

Convinced that all changes in their relations with one another should be sought only by pacific means and be the result of a peaceful and orderly process, and that any signatory Power which shall hereafter seek to promote its national interests by resort to war a should be denied the benefits furnished by this Treaty;

Hopeful that, encouraged by their example, all the other nations of the world will join in this humane endeavor and by adhering to the present Treaty as soon as it comes into force bring their peoples within the scope of its beneficent provisions, thus uniting the civilized nations of the world in a common renunciation of war as an instrument of their national policy. . . .

ARTICLE I

The High Contracting Parties solemnly declare in the names of their respective peoples that they condemn recourse to war for the solution of international controversies, and renounce it, as an instrument of national policy in their relations with one another.

ARTICLE II

The High Contracting Parties agree that the settlement or solution of all disputes or conflicts of whatever nature or of whatever origin they may be, which may arise among them, shall never be sought except by pacific means.

ARTICLE III

The present Treaty shall be ratified by the High Contracting Parties named in the Preamble in accordance with their respective constitutional requirements, and shall take effect as between them as soon as all their several instruments of ratification shall have been deposited at Washington.

Document 5.3

GOOD NEIGHBORS

The onset of the Great Depression meant that Americans had little appetite for involvement in foreign affairs. Thus Franklin D. Roosevelt, who became president at the height of the economic crisis in 1933, had to balance growing isolationism with his own strongly internationalist instincts. Roosevelt believed that the United States had a responsibility to promote international stability, and he still needed to protect U.S. interests abroad, but he had to be careful not to get too far ahead of isolationist public opinion. One solution was the Good Neighbor Policy toward Latin America, which Roosevelt outlined in this speech from April 1933.

Common ideals and a community of interest, together with a spirit of cooperation, have led to the realization that the well-being of one Nation depends in large measure upon the well-being of its neighbors. It is upon these foundations that Pan Americanism has been built.

This celebration commemorates a movement based upon the policy of fraternal cooperation. In my Inaugural Address I stated that I would "dedicate this Nation to the policy of the good neighbor—the neighbor who resolutely respects himself and, because he does so, respects the rights of others—the neighbor who respects his obligations and respects the sanctity of his agreements in and with a world of neighbors." Never before has the significance of the words "good neighbor" been so manifest in international relations. Never have the need and benefit of neighborly cooperation in every form of human activity been so evident as they are today.

Friendship among Nations, as among individuals, calls for constructive efforts to muster the forces of humanity in order that an atmosphere of close understanding and cooperation may be cultivated. It involves mutual obligations and responsibilities, for it is only by sympathetic respect for the rights of others and a scrupulous fulfillment of the corresponding obligations by each member of the community that a true fraternity can be maintained.

The essential qualities of a true Pan Americanism must be the same as those which constitute a good neighbor, namely, mutual understanding, and, through such understanding, a sympathetic appreciation of the other's point of view. It is only in this manner that we can hope to build up a system of which confidence, friendship and good-will are the cornerstones.

Document 5.4

PEACE THROUGH TRADE

Free trade, another solution that tried to balance isolationism and internationalism, was the passion of Secretary of State Cordell Hull. Like most liberal internationalists of the time, Hull believed that the spread of free trade around the world would foster peace because it would spread prosperity, weaken economic competition, make natural resources available for all countries, and intertwine national economies to such an extent that war would become unthinkable. Free trade would also stimulate global commerce, Hull and Roosevelt predicted, and therefore help the United States overcome the Depression. In this 1934 speech, Hull explains the promise of free trade. But in the midst of the Depression, economic diplomacy proved to be too complicated to have much use, and often Washington passed measures that undercut free trade. In 1931, for example, Congress had raised protectionist trade barriers to record levels, and in 1933 Roosevelt pulled the United States off the gold standard and withdrew the U.S. delegation from the London Economic Conference, which aimed to stabilize world currencies.

At this moment, while on this side of the ocean there is a relatively peaceful condition, and neighborly and friendly ties among the nations are stronger and more genuine than ever before, we are obliged to feel deep concern that across the water, notwithstanding the terrible havoc and wreckage wrought by the war that began 20 years ago, and notwithstanding that the inventions of science will make future wars more terrible, there is so much reason for the gravest apprehension. Regardless of the fact that preparation for war but too often makes war inevitable, and the fact that preparation places a grievous burden on the people, armaments are being momentarily increased, and in practice the theory seems to be abandoned that nations, like individuals, should live not as potential enemies but as neighbors and friends. . . .

I wish to refer briefly to another problem belonging to the class I have just indicated, having both foreign and domestic aspects. In recent years a dangerous conception has become too prevalent, a strange economic conception that a nation can live to itself and virtually dispense with customary international relations. It is significant that none of the statesmen who made history in the period before and during the Revolution, and during a long later period were connected with the Federal Government, had any thought that this country could or should lead a self-contained existence. All of the evidence is directly to the contrary. They were devoted to their own land, but even though communication was slow with other lands, they completely realized that it was not possible for this country to develop without commercial, social, and cultural relations with Europe. They of course barred the possibility of political relationship. It is for the purpose of returning to the older conception which they held that it has just been decided by Congress that the Executive shall have authority to negotiate trade agreements with other nations, it being expected that by this method there can be effected a substantial expansion of international commercial dealings, and markets opened that in recent years have been to a large extent fenced about by insurmountable barriers.

Document 5.5

THE MERCHANTS OF DEATH

Despite Roosevelt and Hull's hopes, the Depression transformed the limited internationalism and search for peace of the 1920s, which the Roosevelt administration continued through the Good Neighbor Policy and promotion of free trade, into something close to full-fledged isolationism. The economic crisis also led many Americans to doubt the ethical behavior of private corporations. During World War I, which most Americans now believed had been a tragic and avoidable mistake, American banks and businesses profited enormously from supplying Britain and France with loans, supplies, resources, and food, but they did comparatively little business with Germany. Based on this line of thinking, a new theory emerged: America's entry into World War I had been a crusade not to make the world safe for democracy but to protect corporate profits. It also built on another theory, common in the more idealistic 1920s, that the international arms trade was a leading cause of war. These ideas had much in common with Garvey's critique of American imperialism in the Caribbean. They also fed powerful currents of isolationism, reflected in books such as H. C. Engelbracht and F. C. Hanighen's bestselling Merchants of Death: A Study of the International Armament Industry. *Vowing never again to be duped into supporting a foreign war, Senator Gerald Nye of North Dakota, a staunch isolationist, launched an official investigation into the causes of World War I. The findings of his report, released in February 1936, were explosive.*

THE SALES METHODS OF THE MUNITIONS COMPANIES

The Committee finds, under the head of sales methods of the munitions companies, that almost without exception, the American munitions companies investigated have at times resorted to such unusual approaches, questionable favors and commissions, and methods of "doing the needful" as to constitute, in effect, a form of bribery of foreign governmental officials or of their close friends in order to secure business....

The committee accepts the evidence that the same practices are resorted to by European munitions companies, and that the whole process of selling arms abroad thus, in the words of a Colt agent, has "brought into play the most despicable side of human nature; lies, deceit, hypocrisy, greed, and graft occupying a most prominent part in the transactions."

The committee finds such practices on the part of any munitions company, domestic or foreign, to be highly unethical, a discredit to American business, and an unavoidable reflection upon those American governmental agencies which have unwittingly aided in the transactions so contaminated.

The committee finds, further, that not only are such transactions highly unethical, but that they carry within themselves the seeds of disturbance to the peace and stability of those nations in which they take place....

The committee finds, further, that the intense competition among European and American munitions companies with the attendant bribery of governmental officials tends to create a corrupt officialdom, and thereby weaken the remaining democracies of the world at their head.

The committee finds, further, that the constant availability of munitions companies with competitive bribes ready in outstretched hands does not create a situation where the officials involved can, in the nature of things, be as much interested in peace and measures to secure peace as they are in increased armaments....

THEIR ACTIVITIES CONCERNING PEACE EFFORTS

The committee finds, under this head, that there is no record of any munitions company aiding any proposals for limitation of armaments, but that, on the contrary, there is a record of their active opposition by some to almost all such proposals, of resentment toward them, of contempt for those responsible for them, and of violation of such controls whenever established, and of rich profiting whenever such proposals failed. . . .

THE EFFECT OF ARMAMENTS ON PEACE

The committee finds, under the head of the effect of armament, on peace, that some of the munitions companies have occasionally had opportunities to intensify the fears of people for their neighbors and have used them to their own profit.

The committee finds, further, that the very quality which in civilian life tends to lead toward progressive civilization, namely the improvements of machinery, has been used by the munitions makers to scare nations into a continued frantic expenditure for the latest improvements in devices of warfare. The constant message of the traveling salesman of the munitions companies to the rest of the world has been that they now had available for sale something new, more dangerous and more deadly than ever before and that the potential enemy was or would be buying it.

While the evidence before this committee does not show that wars have been started solely because of the activities of munitions makers and their agents, it is also true that wars rarely have one single cause, and the committee finds it to be against the peace of the world for selfishly interested organizations to be left free to goad and frighten nations into military activity.

Document 5.6

THE LIMITS OF COLLECTIVE SECURITY

While the world crisis revived fears of repeating the horrors of the Great War and the merchants of death, it also slowly began to rehabilitate the reputation of those, like Woodrow Wilson, who in 1917 had believed they were fighting a war to end all wars and to make the world safe for democracy. Perhaps, some Americans began to think in the late 1930s, Wilsonian internationalism was not such a bad idea after all. Had the United States ratified the Treaty of Versailles and joined the League of Nations, they mused, perhaps the problems of the 1930s would not be happening at all. The rehabilitation of Wilson's reputation was complete by the end of the World War II. But the League of Nations, and the principle of collective security, first had to undergo a time of testing; when it failed that test, and that failure led to another world war, Roosevelt could argue for American leadership of a new international organization, the United Nations. The league's biggest challenge, which it failed to meet, came with the Italian invasion of Ethiopia in 1935. Though Italy was widely condemned, the members of the League of

Nations did nothing to stop it. Here, in May 1936, in an emotional appeal upon fleeing before the Italian invaders, Ethiopia's leader, Emperor Haile Selassie, puts a persistent dilemma facing the West in the sharpest possible terms. Selassie's message was transmitted to Washington by the ranking U.S. diplomat in Ethiopia, who betrays a few prejudices of his own.

In order to complete the records of the Department in this connection I am also quoting below what is probably the last public utterance of the Emperor before he went into exile. It was made to the Press on April 30th, the day he received me:

"Do not the peoples of the world yet realize that by fighting on until the bitter end I have not only been performing my sacred duty towards my own people, but have been standing guard in the last citadel of collective security? Are they so blind that they cannot see I have been facing my responsibilities to the whole of humanity?

"I wanted with all my heart to hold on until my tardy allies appeared. But if they never come then I say to you prophetically and without a trace of bitterness 'the West is doomed.'"

A truly great ruler and a polished Oriental gentleman has passed from the scene of world politics, and it will be extremely difficult to find his equal among the backward peoples who are striving toward progress and enlightenment.

Document 5.7

QUARANTINING THE AGGRESSOR

With national resources stretched, the interventionism of the Wilson years discredited, and the mood of the people isolationist, American liberal internationalism was waning. Beginning in 1935, with the causes of World War I uppermost in its mind, Congress passed the Neutrality Acts, which outlawed financial or material aid to countries at war. However, alarmed by the turn of world events and prompted by the Japanese invasion of China, in 1937 Roosevelt began a campaign to warn the American people about the dangers from abroad, primarily from Germany and Japan. With America itself immune to attack, Roosevelt had to frame the threat in terms other than the self-defense of the continental United States. Here, in a major speech in Chicago, he vowed to "quarantine" aggressive nations—even though he did not yet know how.

The political situation in the world, which of late has been growing progressively worse, is such as to cause grave concern and anxiety to all the peoples and nations who wish to live in peace and amity with their neighbors.

Some fifteen years ago the hopes of mankind for a continuing era of international peace were raised to great heights when more than sixty nations solemnly pledged themselves not to resort to arms in furtherance of their national aims and policies. The high aspirations expressed in the Briand-Kellogg Peace Pact and the hopes for peace thus raised have of late given way to a haunting fear of calamity. The present reign of terror and international lawlessness began a few years ago.

It began through unjustified interference in the internal affairs of other nations or the invasion of alien territory in violation of treaties; and has now reached a stage where the very foundations of civilization are seriously threatened. The landmarks and traditions which have marked the progress of civilization toward a condition of law, order and justice are being wiped away. . . .

If those things come to pass in other parts of the world, let no one imagine that America will escape, that America may expect mercy, that this Western Hemisphere will not be attacked and that it will continue tranquilly and peacefully to carry on the ethics and the arts of civilization. . . .

If those days are not to come to pass—if we are to have a world in which we can breathe freely and live in amity without fear—the peace-loving nations must make a concerted effort to uphold laws and principles on which alone peace can rest secure.

The peace-loving nations must make a concerted effort in opposition to those violations of treaties and those ignorings of humane instincts which today are creating a state of international anarchy and instability from which there is no escape through mere isolation or neutrality.

Those who cherish their freedom and recognize and respect the equal right of their neighbors to be free and live in peace, must work together for the triumph of law and moral principles in order that peace, justice and confidence may prevail in the world. There must be a return to a belief in the pledged word, in the value of a signed treaty. There must be recognition of the fact that national morality is as vital as private morality. . . .

There is a solidarity and interdependence about the modern world, both technically and morally, which makes it impossible for any nation completely to isolate itself from economic and political upheavals in the rest of the world, especially when such upheavals appear to be spreading and not declining. There can be no stability or peace either within nations or between nations except under laws and moral standards adhered to by all. International anarchy destroys every foundation for peace. It jeopardizes either the immediate or the future security of every nation, large or small. It is, therefore, a matter of vital interest and concern to the people of the United States that the sanctity of international treaties and the maintenance of international morality be restored. . . .

The situation is definitely of universal concern. The questions involved relate not merely to violations of specific provisions of particular treaties;

they are questions of war and of peace, of international law and especially of principles of humanity. It is true that they involve definite violations of agreements, and especially of the Covenant of the League of Nations, the Briand-Kellogg Pact and the Nine Power Treaty. But they also involve problems of world economy, world security and world humanity.

It is true that the moral consciousness of the world must recognize the importance of removing injustices and well-founded grievances; but at the same time it must be aroused to the cardinal necessity of honoring sanctity of treaties, of respecting the rights and liberties of others and of putting an end to acts of international aggression.

It seems to be unfortunately true that the epidemic of world lawlessness is spreading.

When an epidemic of physical disease starts to spread, the community approves and joins in a quarantine of the patients in order to protect the health of the community against the spread of the disease.

It is my determination to pursue a policy of peace. It is my determination to adopt every practicable measure to avoid involvement in war. It ought to be inconceivable that in this modern era, and in the face of experience, any nation could be so foolish and ruthless as to run the risk of plunging the whole world into war by invading and violating, in contravention of solemn treaties, the territory of other nations that have done them no real harm and are too weak to protect themselves adequately. Yet the peace of the world and the welfare and security of every nation, including our own, is today being threatened by that very thing. . . .

War is a contagion, whether it be declared or undeclared. It can engulf states and peoples remote from the original scene of hostilities. We are determined to keep out of war, yet we cannot insure ourselves against the disastrous effects of war and the dangers of involvement. We are adopting such measures as will minimize our risk of involvement, but we cannot have complete protection in a world of disorder in which confidence and security have broken down.

Document 5.8

A DISTANT MIRROR

To Roosevelt, it was clear who the aggressors were: Nazi Germany and imperial Japan. Along with Italy, Germany and Japan were known as the revisionist powers because they wanted to revise the terms of the post–World War I settlement. The Germans wanted to overcome the restraints of the Treaty of Versailles, the Italians wanted to claim what they believed was wrongly denied them after the war, and the Japanese wanted to nullify the terms of both the Versailles system and the Washington Conference. To Japan it seemed hypocritical for the Western powers, led by the United States, to deny it an empire in neighboring East Asia when Britain, France, and America had all carved their own empires there already. In this July 1938 speech by the Japanese prime minister, Prince Fumimaro Konoye, delivered on the first anniversary of Japan's invasion of China, it is the United States that is portrayed as the unjust aggressor. Note how Konoye's rhetoric is a kind of mirror image of Roosevelt's rhetoric, including the themes of humanitarianism and self-defense.

Thanks to the skillful strategic operations of the Imperial forces and the efforts of all the men, Japan has won continued victories. At present the fall of Hankow is imminent. As the nation is aware, the Chiang [Kai-shek] regime is the Government which has dared to destroy the Yellow river embankments and does not care about sacrificing thereby in the muddy flood the lives of hundreds of thousands of innocent fellow-nationals. Such an outrageous and cruel act will never be permitted by man or Heaven. There is no reason why such a Government should last. Under ordinary circumstance, the Chiang regime would have collapsed long ago. But the fact that the regime still exists is due to the aid of foreign Powers, upon which it depends, and which use every available means to perpetuate its existence at the cost of the welfare of the entire Chinese nation.

Of the foreign Powers, there are such friendly nations as Germany and Italy which approve the Empire's national policy and collaborate with us in joint defense against Communism. But there are still other nations which do not yet understand our true intention and are engrossed in the acquisition of new rights and interests in China as well as in the protection of already-acquired rights and interests in that country. Who knows but that those nations, knowing the feeble power of the Chiang regime, by giving further help to the regime in an attempt to prolong the hostilities and weaken the national power of Japan, will not try thus to threaten Japan's national safety?

Faced by this serious fact of national emergency, the nation cannot rest contented with the number of victories gained, inflated over the success. The current Incident is known as the China Incident, but the other party is not necessarily the Chiang regime only. Behind the Chiang regime there exists extremely complex and manifold international relations involving international interests. . . .

Document 5.9

THE ILLOGIC OF AMERICAN INTERVENTION

It was not only the Japanese who remained unconvinced. Roosevelt's Chicago speech did not change many minds at home, either, and despite the alarming events overseas most Americans continued to oppose intervention in Europe and Asia.

However, there was more than one kind of isolationism, some of which could scarcely be called "isolationist" at all. Some "isolationists," such as former President Herbert Hoover, agreed that the world was becoming more interconnected and that the United States could not remain isolated, but did not agree that the United States would be affected by Nazi Germany, much less invaded, as a result. Conservative internationalists like Hoover also feared Roosevelt's concentration of power, in both the New Deal and in foreign policy, within the White House at the expense of Congress. These fears would reverberate strongly with the rise of the "imperial presidency" during the Cold War. Hoover explained his position in this 1939 address to the Council on Foreign Relations in Chicago.

I wish to talk on peace. We are deluged with talk of war. Our minds are being prepared to accept war as inevitable. We need to keep our heads. . . .

I have no need to cite the malevolent forces rampant in the world. In twenty nations desperate peoples have surrendered personal liberty for some form of authoritarian government. They are placing their trust in dictatorship clothed in new ideologies of Utopia. Some of them are making war or are aggressively threatening other nations. The world is taut with fear. Five times more men are under arms than before the great war.

We in America are indignant at the brutalities of these systems and their cruel wrongs to minorities. We are fearful of the penetration of their ideologies. We are alarmed at their military preparations and their aggressiveness. . . .

We have need to strip emotion from these questions as much as we can. They are questions of life or death not only to men but also to nations.

We have need to appraise coolly these dangers. We have need of sober, analytical debate upon the policies of government toward them. We must do so without partisanship.

Amid these agitations, President Roosevelt has now announced a new departure in foreign policies. . . .

Let me say at once that if our defense requires it every American will willingly bear that burden though it contributes to lower the standard of living of every American and though it plunges us further into debt.

But the proper degree of our military preparedness depends first upon what our foreign policies are to be, and second, upon where and from what our dangers come. When these are determined then the size of our armament is for our army and navy experts to say. Without these determinations they can give no competent advice.

Our foreign policies in these major dimensions must be determined by the American people and the Congress, not by the President alone. The citizens can also in some degree appraise our dangers. After all, it is the people who are made poor and who sacrifice their lives and the lives of their sons. . . .

But to determine the issue, let me propose some questions that the American people deserve to have answered.

1. Shall we reverse our traditional policies at this time?

2. Shall we set ourselves up to determine who the aggressor is in the world?

3. Shall we engage in embargoes, boycotts, economic sanctions against aggressor nations?

4. Shall we do this where the Western Hemisphere is not attacked?

5. Shall we provide an armament greater than that necessary to protect the Western Hemisphere from military invasion?

6. Shall we take collective action with other nations to make these more-than-words-and-short-of-war policies effective?

7. Are we to be the policemen of the world? . . .

Before we answer these questions and before we venture into these paths of force and conflict, even short of war, we should realistically examine how serious the so-called imminent dangers are from aggressive nations.

Our dangers are obviously in two forms—the penetration of their ideologies, which would destroy democracies, and their military aggressiveness.

And their military aggressiveness has to be appraised in two aspects. First, the direct dangers to the Western Hemisphere, and, second, our further concern in the dangers to our sister democracies in Europe and Asia.

The first segment of this danger is the ideologies. The penetration of these ideologies, whether it be the communism of Russia, the national socialism of Germany or the fascism of Italy, is an internal problem for each country where they penetrate. Ideas cannot be cured with battleships or airplanes. I say this, as I do not assume that we intend to attack dictators or extirpate ideologies in their home sources. That would lead the world to worse destruction than the religious wars of the Middle Ages.

Our job of defense against these un-American ideologies is to eliminate Communist, Socialist and Fascist ideas and persons from our own institutions. It is to maintain the ideals of free men, which make this unprofitable soil for such alien seed.

I am confident that if the lamp of liberty can be kept alight these ideologies will yet die of their own falsity. They spring not from moral and spiritual inspirations but from the cupidity of men. In any event no additional appropriations for arms will settle those problems.

The second segment of danger is that of military attack of the dictatorships upon the democracies.

And we may first explore the imminent dangers of military attack upon the Western democracies. And again we should consider it in the light of realism rather than the irritating words that emanate from world capitals. . . .

Do not think I believe the situation is not dangerous in Europe. Far from it. But it is not so imminent as the speeches abroad might make it appear. And what is not imminent is often preventable.

Obviously, our dangers are much less than those of the overseas democracies. The Western Hemisphere is still protected by a moat of 3,000 miles of ocean on the east and 6,000 miles on the west. No airplane has yet been built that can come one-third the way across the Atlantic and one-fifth of the way across the Pacific with destructive bombs and fly home again. In any event, these dictatorships have nothing to gain by coming 3,000 miles or 6,000 miles to attack the Western Hemisphere. So long as our defenses are maintained they have everything to lose.

Document 5.10

THE CHURCHES AGAINST WAR

A majority of Americans refused to support intervention even after war broke out in Europe in September 1939, but many within that majority were liberal internationalists who believed the United States must remain actively involved in world politics. They resolutely opposed the use of conflict or coercion—such as the resort to war or the use of economic sanctions—but neither did they call for pure isolation from world affairs. Many of these anti-interventionists were Christian pacifists and peace activists who had been horrified by the pointless carnage of World War I. Their views, which included a strong belief in world government, were aptly expressed by the Federal Council of Churches, an organization that represented approximately one-third of all American Protestants, in a letter to Roosevelt shortly after the outbreak of war in Europe.

Dear Mr. President,

By authorization of the Executive Committee of the Federal Council of the Churches of Christ in America we assure you that we welcome your statement on the occasion of the outbreak of hostilities in Europe to the effect that you hope the United States will keep out of this war and believe that it will do so. We are grateful for your assurance that every effort of our government will be directed toward that end.

We support you in your purpose that our government shall not join in this war. Our desire to prevent the involvement of the United States in military conflict does not mean that we seek physical safety for ourselves at a time when millions of people in other lands are being subjected to the privations and perils of war; nor does it mean that we condone the exploitation of the needs of other nations for private gain. We seek to keep the United States at peace in the hope that our nation may thereby render a greater service to mankind.

We are urging our churches to support your appeal that citizens of our country refrain from exploiting the present crisis for their own financial profit. We believe that appropriate measures designed to prevent such exploitation should be adopted. For the sake of peace, for the sake of our national honor, for the sake of a sound domestic economy, we believe it is imperative that wars elsewhere be not made the occasion for our profiteering.

We also support you in your purpose, expressed in your radio broadcast of September 3, that "the influence of America should be consistent in seeking for humanity a final peace which will eliminate, as far as it is possible to do so, the continued use of force between nations." Our churches support the policy of international cooperation implied in this declaration. We therefore urge our government to indicate, at the earliest opportunity, the terms upon which it is prepared to cooperate with other nations in the establishment of peace in Europe and in the Far East and in the development of some form of political world order in which certain aspects of the sovereignty of the individual state would be limited in the interests of world community.

We assure you, Mr. President, of our prayers that you and our other leaders responsible for the determination of national governmental policy may be guided by the Spirit of God to choose such measures as will enable the United States to serve most effectively the ends of justice, liberty and goodwill for all peoples.

Document 5.11

AMERICA FIRST

There were also large numbers of people, such as Father Charles Coughlin, the popular "Radio Priest," who could genuinely claim to be isolationists because they did not want the United States to become actively engaged in world affairs at all. But increasingly involved it was: first in 1939 through the "cash-and-carry" policy; then in 1940 with the destroyers-for-bases agreement with Britain, a major re- armament program in the United States, and the first peacetime draft in American history; and finally in 1941 with the extension of lend-lease aid to Britain and the Soviet Union. Alarmed by Roosevelt's erosion of the Neutrality Acts and gradual escalation of U.S. involvement in the war, many of these hardcore isolationists joined the group America First and followed the speeches of the celebrated aviator Charles Lindbergh. Though not all such isolationists were racists, powerful currents of xenophobia and anti-Semitism could be found in much isolationist rhetoric. On September 11, 1941, in a widely reported speech sponsored by the America First Committee in Des Moines, Iowa, Lindbergh accused Jews, the British, and Roosevelt himself of manipulating the United States into entering an unnecessary war.

It is now two years since this latest European war began. From that day in September, 1939, until the present moment, there has been an ever-increasing effort to force the United States into the conflict. That effort has been carried on by foreign interests and by a small minority of our own people, but it has been so successful that, today, our country stands on the verge of war.

At this time, as the war is about to enter its third winter, it seems appropriate to review the circumstances that have led us to our present position. Why are we on the verge of war? Was it necessary for us to become so deeply involved? Who is responsible for changing our national policy from one of neutrality and independence to one of entanglement in European affairs?

Personally, I believe there is no better argument against our intervention than a study of the causes and developments of the present war. I have often said that if the true facts and issues were placed before the American people, there would be no danger of our involvement. . . .

When this war started in Europe, it was clear that the American people were solidly opposed to entering it. Why shouldn't we be? We had the best defensive position in the world; we had a tradition of independence from Europe; and the one time we did take part in a European war left European problems unsolved, and debts to America unpaid. . . .

But there were various groups of people here and abroad whose interests and beliefs necessitated the involvement of the United States in the war. I shall point out some of these groups tonight, and outline their methods of procedure. In doing this, I must speak with utmost frankness, for in order to counteract their efforts, we must know exactly who they are.

The three most important groups who have been pressing this country toward war are the British, the Jewish and the Roosevelt administration. Behind these groups, but of lesser importance, are a number of capitalists, Anglophiles, and intellectuals who believe that their future and the future of mankind depends upon the domination of the British empire. . . .

Let us consider these groups, one at a time. First, the British: It is obvious and perfectly understandable that Great Britain wants the United States in the war on her side. England is now in a desperate position. Her population is not large enough, and her armies are not strong enough to invade the continent of Europe and win the war she declared against Germany. Her geographical position is such that she cannot win the war by the use of aviation alone, regardless of how many planes we send her. Even if America entered the war, it is improbable that the Allied armies could invade Europe and overcome the Axis powers.

But one thing is certain. If England can draw this country into the war she can shift to our shoulders a large portion of the responsibility for waging it, and for paying its cost. As you all know, we were left with the debts of the last European war and unless we are more cautious in the future than we have been in the past we will be left with the debts of the present one....

The second major group I mentioned is the Jewish. It is not difficult to understand why Jewish people desire the overthrow of Nazi Germany. The persecution they suffered in Germany would be sufficient to make bitter enemies of any race. No person with a sense of the dignity of mankind can condone the persecution of the Jewish race in Germany. But no person of honesty and vision can look on their pro-war policy here today without seeing the dangers involved in such a policy, both for us and for them.

Instead of agitating for war, the Jewish groups in this country should be opposing it in every possible way, for they will be among the first to feel its consequences. Tolerance is a virtue that depends upon peace and strength. History shows that it cannot survive war and devastation. A few farsighted Jewish people realize this and stand opposed to intervention. But the majority still do not. Their greatest danger to this country lies in their large ownership and influence in our motion pictures, our press, our radio, and our government....

The Roosevelt administration is the third powerful group which has been carrying this country toward war. Its members have used the war emergency to obtain a third presidential term for the first time in American history. They have used the war to add unlimited billions to a debt which was already the highest we had ever known. And they have used the war to justify the restrictions of congressional power, and the assumption of dictatorial procedures on the part of the President and his appointees.

The power of the Roosevelt administration depends upon the maintenance of a wartime emergency. The prestige of the Roosevelt administration depends upon the success of Great Britain to whom the President attached his political future at a time when most people thought that England and France would easily win the war. The danger of the Roosevelt administration lies in its subterfuge. While its members have promised us peace they have led us to war heedless of the platform upon which they were elected....

Men and women of Iowa: Only one thing holds this country from war today. That is the rising opposition of the American people. Our system of democracy and representative government is on test today as it has never been before. We are on the verge of a war in which the only victor would be chaos and prostration. We are on the verge of a war for which we are still unprepared, and for which no one has offered a feasible plan for victory—a war which cannot be won without sending our soldiers across the ocean to force a landing on a hostile coast against armies stronger than our own.

Document 5.12

A SINGLE WORLD CONFLICT

Despite the strength of the anti-interventionist opinion, Roosevelt backed the Allies, and the United States increasingly found itself drawn into the war. Perhaps the most significant idea to develop from this process was a truly global conception of American security. As we have seen, American policy makers began to form a global mindset in the 1890s. But until 1940–41, Americans' global engagement was episodic. It was Roosevelt who fit all the pieces together to formulate a doctrine of national security that had no geographical limits. Roosevelt also enhanced Wilson's ideological views by arguing that in an interconnected and interdependent world—in other words, a globalized world—the defense of American territory and the defense of American values were inseparable and equally important. Thanks to the Japanese, Roosevelt was able to turn theory into practice. Here, in this January 1941 letter to U.S. Ambassador Joseph C. Grew in Tokyo, Roosevelt lays out his view that American national security now had no geographical limits.

Dear Joe . . .

I believe that the fundamental proposition is that we must recognize that the hostilities in Europe, in Africa, and in Asia are all parts of single world conflict. We must, consequently, recognize that our interests are menaced both in Europe and in the Far East. We are engaged in the task of defending our way of life and our vital national interests wherever they are seriously endangered. Our strategy of self-defense must be a global strategy which takes account of every front and takes advantage of every opportunity to contribute to our total security.

You [ask] the question whether our getting into war with Japan would so handicap our help to Britain in Europe as to make the difference to Britain between victory and defeat. In this connection it seems to me that we must consider whether, if Japan should gain possession of the region of the Netherlands East Indies and the Malay Peninsula, the chances of England's winning in her struggle with Germany would not be decreased thereby. . . .

The British need assistance along the lines of our generally established policies at many points, assistance which in the case of the Far East is certainly well within the realm of "possibility" so far as the capacity of the United States is concerned. Their defense strategy must in the nature of things be global. Our strategy of giving them assistance toward ensuring our own security must envisage both sending of supplies to England and helping to prevent a closing of channels of communication to and from various parts of the world, so that other important sources of supply will not be denied to the British and be added to the assets of the other side. . . .

As I have indicated above, the conflict is world-wide, not merely a European war. . . . I am giving you my thoughts at this length because the problems which we face are so vast and so interrelated that any attempt even to state them compels one to think in terms of five continents and seven seas.

Document 5.13

THE ATLANTIC CHARTER

Before Pearl Harbor, Roosevelt envisioned the United States acting as the "arsenal of democracy": it would not send troops overseas but provide Germany's enemies with enough money and materiel to win. By this time, isolationist support was starting to crack. 1941 was the crucial year in which the United States finally joined the war. In his State of the Union address in January, Roosevelt announced the "Four Freedoms"—freedom of speech, freedom of religion, freedom from fear, and freedom from want—that Americans would defend against tyranny all around the world. In June, Germany invaded the Soviet Union, bringing the Soviets into an alliance with Britain. And in August, on a warship off the coast of Newfoundland, Roosevelt held a conference with British Prime Minister Winston Churchill. There, they drafted the Atlantic Charter, a manifesto of ideals and values that constituted the Allies' war aims—even though the United States was not yet officially at war.

The President and the Prime Minister have had several conferences. They have considered the dangers to world civilization arising from the policies of military domination by conquest upon which the Hitlerite government of Germany and other governments associated therewith have embarked, and have made clear the stress which their countries are respectively taking for their safety in the face of these dangers.

They have agreed upon the following joint declaration:

Joint declaration of the President of the United States of America and the Prime Minister, Mr. Churchill, representing His Majesty's Government in the United Kingdom, being met together, deem it right to make known certain common principles in the national policies of their respective countries on which they base their hopes for a better future for the world.

First, their countries seek no aggrandizement, territorial or other;

Second, they desire to see no territorial changes that do not accord with the freely expressed wishes of the peoples concerned;

Third, they respect the right of all peoples to choose the form of government under which they will live; and they wish to see sovereign rights and self government restored to those who have been forcibly deprived of them;

Fourth, they will endeavor, with due respect for their existing obligations, to further the enjoyment by all States, great or small, victor or vanquished, of access, on equal terms, to the trade and to the raw materials of the world which are needed for their economic prosperity;

Fifth, they desire to bring about the fullest collaboration between all nations in the economic field with the object of securing, for all, improved labor standards, economic advancement and social security;

Sixth, after the final destruction of the Nazi tyranny, they hope to see established a peace which will afford to all nations the means of dwelling in safety within their own boundaries, and which will afford assurance that all the men in all lands may live out their lives in freedom from fear and want;

Seventh, such a peace should enable all men to traverse the high seas and oceans without hindrance;

Eighth, they believe that all of the nations of the world, for realistic as well as spiritual reasons must come to the abandonment of the use of force. Since no future peace can be maintained if land, sea or air armaments continue to be employed by nations which threaten, or may threaten, aggression outside of their frontiers, they believe, pending the establishment of a wider and permanent system of general security, that the disarmament of such nations is essential. They will likewise aid and encourage all other practicable measures which will lighten for peace-loving peoples the crushing burden of armaments.

Franklin D. Roosevelt

Winston S. Churchill

Document 5.14

"HITLERISM CAN BE STOPPED"

In October 1941, Roosevelt gave perhaps his most openly interventionist speech before the attack on Pearl Harbor. With Hoover, Lindbergh, and the isolationists in mind (take note of the thinly veiled reference to Lindbergh and his popularity in Germany), Roosevelt took pains to argue that America's physical safety was under threat from the Nazis. But by this point, his conflation of ideological and territorial security was complete: both America's values, especially its traditions of religious tolerance and pluralism, and its physical safety were at risk from the same threat.

Five months ago tonight I proclaimed to the American people the existence of a state of unlimited national emergency.

Since then much has happened. Our Army and Navy are temporarily in Iceland in the defense of the Western Hemisphere.

Hitler has attacked shipping in areas close to the Americas in the North and South Atlantic.

Many American-owned merchant ships have been sunk on the high seas. One American destroyer was attacked on September fourth. Another destroyer was attacked and hit on October seventeenth. Eleven brave and loyal men of our Navy were killed by the Nazis.

We have wished to avoid shooting. But the shooting has started. And history has recorded who fired the first shot. In the long run, however, all that will matter is who fired the last shot. . . .

If our national policy were to be dominated by the fear of shooting, then all of our ships and those of our sister Republics would have to be tied up in home harbors. Our Navy would have to remain respectfully—abjectly—behind any line which Hitler might decree on any ocean as his own dictated version of his own war zone.

Naturally we reject that absurd and insulting suggestion. We reject it because of our own self-interest, because of our own self-respect, and because, most of all, of our own good faith. Freedom of the seas is now, as it has always been, a fundamental policy of your Government and mine.

Hitler has often protested that his plans for conquest do not extend across the Atlantic Ocean. His submarines and raiders prove otherwise. So does the entire design of his new world order.

For example, I have in my possession a secret map made in Germany by Hitler's Government—by the planners of the new world order. It is a map of South America and a part of Central America, as Hitler proposes to reorganize it. Today in this area there are fourteen separate countries. But the geographical experts of Berlin have ruthlessly obliterated all existing boundary lines; they have divided South America into five vassal states, bringing the whole continent under their domination. And they have also so arranged it that the territory of one of these new puppet states includes the Republic of Panama and our great life line—the Panama Canal.

That is his plan. It will never go into effect.

This map, my friends, makes clear the Nazi design not only against South America but against the United States as well.

Your Government has in its possession another document, made in Germany by Hitler's Government. It is a detailed plan, which, for obvious reasons, the Nazis did not wish and do not wish to publicize just yet, but which they are ready to impose, a little later, on a dominated world—if Hitler wins. It is a plan to abolish all existing religions—Catholic, Protestant, Mohammedan, Hindu, Buddhist, and Jewish alike. The property of all churches will be seized by the Reich and its puppets. The cross and all other symbols of religion are to be forbidden. The clergy are to be forever liquidated, silenced under penalty of the concentration camps, where even now so many fearless men are being tortured because they have placed God above Hitler.

In the place of the churches of our civilization, there is to be set up an International Nazi Church—a church which will be served by orators sent out by the Nazi Government. And in the place of the Bible, the words of *Mein Kampf* will be imposed and enforced as Holy Writ. And in the place of the cross of Christ will be put two symbols—the swastika and the naked sword.

The god of Blood and Iron will take the place of the God of Love and Mercy. Let us well ponder that statement which I have made tonight.

These grim truths which I have told you of the present and future plans of Hitlerism will of course be hotly denied tonight and tomorrow in the controlled press and radio of the Axis powers. And some Americans—not many—will continue to insist that Hitler's plans need not worry us—that we should not concern ourselves with anything that goes on beyond rifle shot of our own shores.

The protestations of these few American citizens will, as usual, be paraded with applause through the Axis press and radio during the next few days, in an effort to convince the world that the majority of Americans are opposed to their duly chosen Government, and in reality are only waiting to jump on Hitler's band wagon when it comes this way.

The motive of such Americans is not the point at issue. The fact is that Nazi propaganda continues in desperation to seize upon such isolated statements as proof of American disunity.

The Nazis have made up their own list of modern American heroes. It is, fortunately, a short list. I am glad that it does not contain my name.

All of us Americans, of all opinions, in the last analysis are faced with the choice between the kind of world we want to live in and the kind of world which Hitler and his hordes would impose upon us.

None of us wants to burrow under the ground and live in total darkness like a comfortable mole.

The forward march of Hitler and of Hitlerism can be stopped—and it will be stopped.

Very simply and very bluntly—we are pledged to pull our own oar in the destruction of Hitlerism.

And when we have helped to end the curse of Hitlerism we shall help to establish a new peace which will give to decent people everywhere a better chance to live and prosper in security and in freedom and in faith.

6

World War II

Before 1941 ended, Germany controlled Europe, having done in weeks what a previous generation of German militarists had failed to accomplish in years: the conquest of rival France and the near capture of Moscow. Among the continent's great powers, only Great Britain remained beyond Adolf Hitler's control. Conflict raged in Asia too. Japanese forces had invaded China in 1937. Weak international reaction effectively killed off the dwindling influence of the League of Nations and opened the door to further Japanese aggression. As the global situation grew darker, American policy makers faced monumental questions of war and peace: how to keep out of war; then how to win the war; and finally how to ensure war would not erupt yet again.

President Franklin D. Roosevelt strongly believed it was only a matter of time before America entered the conflict, though, as noted in chapter 5, he never seriously feared a direct German (or later Japanese) invasion of the United States. What truly frightened Roosevelt, more than the specter of bombing or direct enemy invasion, was what a full Axis victory in Europe and Asia might mean for American society. To survive in such a world, Roosevelt reasoned, the United States would require authoritarian rule of its own sufficient to create a garrison state capable of withstanding further Axis incursions. To remain free, in other words, would require sacrificing the very way of life Americans valued most. He sided with Britain and its allies not only out of sympathy for their cause but also out of a genuine fear for what their defeat might mean for the United States. Similar fears of totalitarian rule abroad diminishing American freedoms at home would in time drive early Cold War policy makers, many trained under Roosevelt's tutelage.

Foremost in Roosevelt's mind once the war began—of equal priority with victory itself—was securing a stable postwar environment so that the mistakes of the past peace would not once more return to haunt another generation. This goal meant not only eliminating immediate security threats but also establishing an equitable economic order. Roosevelt believed it also meant eliminating colonialism, which he considered a root cause of international strife. On this point in particular, Roosevelt found little common ground with several of his key wartime allies, thus sowing the seeds of postwar controversy. Indeed, as the documents below show, his primary allies, including Britain's Winston Churchill and the Soviet Union's Joseph Stalin, proved quite comfortable discussing and even negotiating for national interests, spheres of influence, and outright colonial rule, but only when the Americans were not around.

One of the war's many tragedies was that acts capable of stirring controversy at the onset of the conflict raised few qualms by its end. Attacks against civilians proved one such example. Roosevelt's first public statement on the outbreak of war in September of 1939 termed aerial bombing of cities nothing less than "inhuman barbarism." Yet by war's end American air fleets joined those from other nations in making the barbaric routine. Cities throughout Europe and Asia were decimated. By 1945, hundreds of thousands of Japanese civilians had lost their lives in nightly American raids purposefully designed to instigate deadly firestorms. Then in August appeared the ultimate weapon, the atomic bomb, capable of leveling an entire city at a single blast. International relations, and life itself, would never be the same again following eruption of the atomic mushroom cloud. When added to the indelible image of concentration camp survivors and the mass graves of those less fortunate, the mushroom cloud and the half-starved prisoner symbolized the war's true cost and the almost unfathomable implications of future conflict.

Document 6.1

JAPANESE DISCUSSION OF THE TRIPARTITE PACT

World War II arguably began in Asia, with Japan's invasion of China in 1937. In late September 1940, Tokyo struck again, seizing French Indochina. Washington responded with sharp sanctions, cutting off exports of scrap iron and steel to Japan. The Roosevelt administration held off on embargoing oil, upon which the Japanese economy relied, believing that move likely to prompt further Japanese aggression. By the close of September 1940, Tokyo formally sided with Berlin and Rome, publicizing their Tripartite Pact, informally termed the Axis Pact under the notion that the world would soon revolve around the new axis of power formed by the three. Records of the Imperial Conference, the Japanese government's highest decision-making body, demonstrate Tokyo's recognition that its decision put the nation on a direct collision course with the United States. The following discussion took place on September 19, 1940.

Prime Minister Konoye: We can anticipate that trade relations with Britain and the United States will deteriorate even more. If worst comes to worst, it may become impossible to obtain any imported goods. At the present time our country depends to a large extent on Britain and the United States for her principal war materials. Accordingly, we cannot help but experience considerable difficulties. We have been aware of this problem, and we have increased our domestic production and added to our stockpiles. Hence, if we tighten controls over consumption by the military, the Government, and the people, and if we limit consumption to the most critical areas, we should be able to meet military needs for an extended period; and in the event of a war with the United States, we should be able to supply the military and thus withstand a rather prolonged war.

Director of the Planning Board Hoshino: Since scrap iron is the principal raw material for steel, our steel production will suffer if the United States bans the export of scrap iron. But as the Prime Minister has explained, we should be able to produce a considerable amount of steel because we have expanded our steel-producing capacity, and because we can use production methods that do not call for scrap iron. Our planning estimates for this year call for a steel production of 5.4 million tons. However, if the United States bans the export of scrap iron, production will drop to 4 million tons for the first year of the plan; and because of the decrease in our stockpiles it will remain at that figure for the second year, even though our production capacity is expanded. If we resort to emergency measures, we should be able to maintain current levels. . . .

Since the domestic production of petroleum is low, oil presents even more difficulties than steel and nonferrous metals. . . . The oil situation is as I have already explained. If there should be a fairly prolonged war, it will be necessary to get oil from northern Sakhalin and the Netherlands East Indies. . . . In short, it will be essential to acquire a large amount of oil any way we can. The Netherlands East Indies and Northern Sakhalin are the places one thinks of first; once we have made up our minds, we will have to get oil from these places.

President of the Privy Council Hara: Although what I was going to ask has been covered in the questions put by the Navy Chief of Staff, I should like to add that this Pact is a treaty of alliance with the United States as its target. Germany and Italy hope to prevent American entry into the war by making this Pact public. Recently the United States has been acting as a watchdog in Eastern Asia in place of Great Britain. She has applied pressure to Japan, but she has probably been restraining herself in order to prevent Japan from joining Germany and Italy. But when Japan's position becomes clear with the announcement of this Pact, she will greatly increase her pressure on us, she will greatly step up her aid to Chiang, and she will obstruct Japan's war effort. I presume the United States, which has not declared war on Germany and Italy, will put economic pressure on Japan without declaring war on us. She will probably ban the export of oil and iron, and will refuse to purchase goods from us. She will attempt to weaken us so over the long term so that we will not be able to endure war. The Director of the Planning Board has said that all available steps will be taken to obtain iron and steel, but the results are uncertain. Also, the Foreign Minister's statement shows that we cannot obtain iron and oil right away, and that in any case the amount will be restricted. The capital in Netherlands East Indies oil is British and American, and the Dutch Government has fled to England; so I think it will be impossible to obtain oil from the Netherlands East Indies by peaceful means.

Document 6.2

SUMNER WELLES DECRIES GERMANY'S INVASION OF THE SOVIET UNION

Everything about World War II changed in late June 1941, when Germany invaded the Soviet Union, with which Hitler had signed a nonaggression pact in 1939. The Wehrmacht quickly drove toward Moscow, beginning the policy of ethnic cleansing that culminated in the killing of millions and would later be dubbed the Holocaust. In the following speech by U.S. Undersecretary of State Sumner Welles on June 23, 1941, the West's ambivalence about Moscow's communist regime clearly shines through, though so too does the more pressing danger posed by the tripartite powers.

If any further proof could conceivably be required of the real purposes and projects of the present leaders of Germany for world domination, it is now furnished by Hitler's treacherous attack upon Soviet Russia.

We see once more, beyond peradventure of doubt, with what intent the present Government of Germany negotiates "non-aggression pacts." To the leaders of the German Reich sworn engagements to refrain from hostile acts against other countries—engagements regarded in a happier and in a civilized world as contracts to the faithful observance of which the honor of nations themselves was pledged—are but a symbol of deceit and constitute a dire warning on the part of Germany of hostile and murderous intent. To the present German Government the very meaning of the word "honor" is unknown.

This Government has often stated, and in many of his public statements the President has declared, that the United States maintains that freedom to worship God as their consciences dictate is the great and fundamental right of all peoples. This right has been denied to their peoples by both the Nazi and the Soviet Governments. To the people of the United States this and other principles and doctrines of communistic dictatorship are as intolerable and as alien to their own beliefs as are the principles and doctrines of Nazi dictatorship. Neither kind of imposed overlordship can have or will have any support or any sway in the mode of life or in the system of government of the American people.

But the immediate issue that presents itself to the people of the United States is whether the plan for universal conquest, for the cruel and brutal enslavement of all peoples, and for the ultimate destruction of the remaining free democracies, which Hitler is now desperately trying to carry out, is to be successfully halted and defeated.

That is the present issue which faces a realistic America. It is the issue at this moment which most directly involves our own national defense and the security of the New World in which we live.

In the opinion of this Government, consequently, any defense against Hitlerism, any rallying of the forces opposing Hitlerism, from whatever source these forces may spring, will hasten the eventual downfall of the present German leaders, and will therefore redound to the benefit of our own defense and security. Hitler's armies are today the chief dangers of the Americas.

Document 6.3

AMERICAN STRATEGISTS WARN AGAINST PRESSURING JAPAN

On July 19, 1941, the Navy Department's War Plans Division advised Roosevelt against including oil in any economic sanctions, believing this a red-line issue from which neither side could subsequently retreat. Perceiving the need to further "quarantine" despotic regimes, as he had proposed (without detail) years before, Roosevelt endorsed the embargo nonetheless, cutting all oil exports to Japan by September of 1941.

EFFECT OF FURTHER RESTRICTIONS ON EXPORTS

(a) The most important fields for exercising further restrictions on exports are petroleum products and raw cotton, which accounted for 74% and 13%, respectively, of the trade in May, 1941.

(b) It is generally believed that shutting off the American supply of petroleum will lead promptly to an invasion of the Netherlands East Indies. While probable, this is not necessarily a sure immediate result. Japan doubtless knows that wells and machinery probably would be destroyed. If then engaged in war in Siberia, the necessary force for southward adventures might not be immediately available. Furthermore, Japan has oil stocks for about eighteen months' war operations. Export restrictions of oil by the United States should be accompanied by similar restrictions by the British and Dutch.

(c) Restrictions on the export of raw cotton would probably be serious for Japan only if India, Peru, and Brazil should apply the same restrictions. Cotton stocks in Japan are believed to be rather low at present.

(d) It will, of course, be recognized that an embargo on exports will automatically stop imports from Japan.

(e) An embargo on exports will have an immediate severe psychological reaction in Japan against the United States. It is almost certain to intensify the determination of those now in power to continue their present course. Furthermore, it seems certain that, if Japan should then take military measures against the British and Dutch, she would also include military action against the Philippines, which would immediately involve us in a Pacific war. Whether or not such action will be taken immediately will doubtless depend on Japan's situation at that time with respect to Siberia.

(f) Additional export restrictions would hamper Japan's war effort, but not to a very large extent since present restrictions are accomplishing the same result, except with regard to oil, raw cotton and wood pulp. Thus, the economic weapon against Japan has largely been lost, and the effect of complete embargo would be not very great from a practical standpoint.

CONCLUSIONS

(a) Present export restrictions, plus reductions of available ship tonnage for use in Japanese trade have greatly curtailed both exports and imports.

(b) The effect of an embargo would hamper future Japanese war effort, though not immediately, and not decisively.

(c) An embargo would probably result in a fairly early attack by Japan on Malaya and the Netherlands East Indies, and possibly would involve the United States in early war in the Pacific.

If war in the Pacific is to be accepted by the United States, actions leading up to it should, if practicable, be postponed until Japan is engaged in war in Siberia. It may well be that Japan has decided against an early attack on the British and Dutch, but has decided to occupy Indo-China and to strengthen her position there, and also to attack the Russians in Siberia. Should this prove to be the case, it seems probable that the United States could engage in war in the Atlantic, and that Japan would not intervene for the time being, even against the British.

RECOMMENDATION

That trade with Japan not be embargoed at this time.

Document 6.4

NOT YET A BELLIGERENT BUT PLANNING FOR THE POSTWAR WORLD

American planners considered the potential post–World War II world long before joining the fight. In August 1941, Roosevelt and British Prime Minister Winston Churchill met off the coast of Newfoundland. The resulting document, and the struggle in the United States between isolation and engagement, is discussed in chapter 5. As the following document—notes by Undersecretary of State Sumner Welles on a conversation with the president on August 11, 1941—reveals, American policy makers signed the charter in order to counter the immediate Axis threat, but it also suggests that a broader vision for a stable international system was never far from mind.

I subsequently went to see the President. . . . I said I felt it necessary for me to ask him whether he did not believe that a very considerable opposition on the part of extreme isolationists in the United States would result from that portion of point seven which declares in the judgment of the United States that it is essential that aggressor nations be disarmed. I said that if a great power like the United States publicly declares that something is essential, the inference is that that power is going to do something itself about it. I said it appeared to me more than likely that the isolationists will insist that this public statement by the President meant that the United States would go to war in order to disarm not only Germany but even possibly Japan and theoretically, at least, even the Soviet Union if that country should later once more embark upon aggression on its neighbors. The President replied that the whole intent of point seven, as he saw it, was to make clear what the objective would be if the war was won and that he believed people in the United States would take that point of view. He further said he felt the realism inherent in article seven was one which would be apparent to the enormous majority of the American people and that they would enthusiastically support the need for the disarmament of aggressor nations.

I said I also had been surprised and somewhat discouraged by a remark that the President had casually made in our morning's conference—if I had understood him correctly—which was that nothing could be more futile than the reconstitution of a body such as the Assembly of the League of Nations. I said to the President that it seemed to me that if he conceived of the need for a transition period upon the termination of the war during which period Great Britain and the United States would undertake the policing of the world, it seemed to me that it would be enormously desirable for the smaller Powers to have available to them an Assembly in which they would all be represented and in which they could make their complaints known and join in recommendations as to the policy to be pursued by the major Powers who were doing the police work. I said it seemed to me that an organization of that kind would be the most effective safety valve that could be devised.

The President said that he agreed fully with what I said and that all that he had intended by the remark he made this morning was to make clear his belief that a transition period was necessary and that during that transition period no organizations such as the Council or the Assembly of the League could undertake the powers and prerogatives with which they had been entrusted during the existence of the League of Nations.

Document 6.5

THE UNITED NATIONS DECLARATION

The Japanese attack on Hawaii on December 7, 1941, thrust the United States into the war. Having set the ideological parameters of their war effort, Anglo-American policy makers began formally securing allies and allied pledges to their shared vision of a postwar world. Proclaiming themselves the United Nations, these countries—their number increasing over time—vowed to fight against fascism, but along the lines outlined by the Atlantic Charter. Formally, at least, the war effort against the Axis powers would be fought for ideals proclaimed by Roosevelt and Churchill. The United Nations issued the following declaration on January 1, 1942.

The Governments signatory hereto,

Having subscribed to a common program of purposes and principles embodied in the Joint Declaration of the President of United States of America and the Prime Minister of the United Kingdom of Great Britain and Northern Ireland dated August 14, 1941, known as the Atlantic Charter.

Being convinced that complete victory over their enemies is essential to defend life, liberty, independence and religious freedom, and to preserve human rights and justice in their own lands as well as in other lands, and that they are now engaged in a common struggle against savage and brutal forces seeking to subjugate the world,

DECLARE:

(1) Each Government pledges itself to employ its full resources, military or economic, against those members of the Tripartite Pact and its adherents with which such government is at war.

(2) Each Government pledges itself to cooperate with the Governments signatory hereto and not to make a separate armistice or peace with the enemies.

The foregoing declaration may be adhered to by other nations which are, or which may be, rendering material assistance and contributions in the struggle for victory over Hitlerism.

DONE at Washington, January First, 1942

Document 6.6

WARTIME LONGING AND LOSS

The war meant strategy and planning to top-level policy makers, but it meant change, separation, and the possibility of death for millions of American servicemen and servicewomen and the families and loved ones they left at home. Among the most popular songs of the era proved to be "Don't Sit Under the Apple Tree (with Anyone Else but Me)," released to wide acclaim by Glenn Miller's band in 1942 and later popularized by the Andrews Sisters. The song's lyrics date to 1939, but in December 1941, after the Pearl Harbor attack, the line "Till I come marchin' home" was added. The song's popularity soared. In 1943 a parody, "They Just Chopped Down the Old Apple Tree," comically told the story of a young girl writing her soldier overseas that he need not worry about her staying true, as the tree they pledged to marry under no longer stood anyway. World War II has come to be known as the Good War, a clear conflict of good against evil and the culminating act of what later pundits termed the "greatest generation." As this song shows, however, longing, sexual tension, and even betrayal underlay much of the personal anxiety experienced by everyday men and women in the midst of what many considered a moral crusade. More than 400,000 American servicemen and servicewomen never returned home from World War II.

Don't Sit Under the Apple Tree

{male vocals}
Don't sit under the apple tree
with anyone else but me
Anyone else but me,
anyone else but me
No! No! No!
Don't sit under the apple tree
with anyone else but me
Till I come marchin' home

Don't go walkin' down Lover's Lane
with anyone else but me
Anyone else but me,
anyone else but me
No! No! No!
Don't go walkin' down Lover's Lane
with anyone else but me
Till I come marchin' home

I just got word from a guy who heard
from the guy next door to me
The girl he met just loves to pet
and it fits you to-a-tee
So, don't sit under the apple tree
with anyone else but me
Till I come marchin' home

{female vocals}
Don't give out with those lips of yours
to anyone else but me
Anyone else but me,
anyone else but me
No! No! No!
Watch the girls on the foreign shores,
you'll have to report to me
When you come marchin' home

Don't hold anyone on your knee,
you better be true to me
You better be true to me,
you better be true to me
Don't hold anyone on your knee,
you're gettin' the third degree
When you come marchin' home

You're on your own where there is no phone
and I can't keep tab on you
Be fair to me, I'll guarantee
this is one thing that I'll do
I won't sit under the apple tree
with anyone else but you
Till you come marchin' home

{all}
Don't sit under the apple tree

with anyone else but me
I know the apple tree
is reserved for you and me
And I'll be true
till you come marchin' home

Documents 6.7 and 6.8

CORRESPONDENCE BETWEEN ROOSEVELT AND GANDHI

Many within the colonized world perceived World War II to be an opportunity. For example, Mohandas K. Gandhi, leader of the most powerful independence movement in India, hoped to find an ally in the American president after reading the Atlantic Charter, the United Nations Declaration, and Roosevelt's rhetoric decrying imperialism. While sympathetic, Roosevelt well knew that Churchill valued Britain's empire, and India in particular, to the hilt. Even as the Allies pondered the postwar world, they and those they sided with against the Axis powers did not always envision identical futures. Gandhi and Roosevelt carried on the following exchange in the second half of 1942.

Mohandas K. Gandhi to Franklin D. Roosevelt, July 1, 1942

Dear Friend,

I twice missed coming to your great country. I have the privilege of having numerous friends there both known and unknown to me. Many of my countrymen have received and are still receiving higher education in America. I know too that several have taken shelter there. I have profited greatly by the writings of Thoreau and Emerson. I say this to tell you how much I am connected with your country. Of Great Britain I need say nothing beyond mentioning that in spite of my intense dislike of British rule, I have numerous personal friends in England whom I love as dearly as my own people. I had my legal education there. I have therefore nothing but good wishes for your country and Great Britain. You will therefore accept my word that my present proposal, that the British should unreservedly and without reference to the wishes of the people of India withdraw their rule, is prompted by the friendliest intention. I would like to turn into good will the ill will which, whatever may be said to the contrary, exists in India towards Great Britain and thus enable the millions of India to play their part in the present war.

My personal position is clear. I hate all war. If, therefore, I could persuade my countrymen, they would make a most effective and decisive contribution in favour of an honourable peace. But I know that all of us have not a living faith in non-violence. Under foreign rule however we can make no effective contribution of any kind in this war, except as helots.

The policy of the Indian National Congress, largely guided by me, has been one of non-embarrassment to Britain, consistently with the honourable working of the Congress, admittedly the largest political organization, of the longest standing in India. The British policy as exposed by the Cripps mission and rejected by almost all parties has opened our eyes and has driven me to the proposal I have made. I hold that the full acceptance of my proposal and that alone can put the Allied cause on an unassailable basis. I venture to think that the Allied declaration that the allies are fighting to make the world safe for freedom of the individual and for democracy sounds hollow, so long as India and, for that matter, Africa are exploited by Great Britain, and America has the Negro problems in their own home. But in order to avoid all complications, in my proposal I have confined myself only to India. If India becomes free, the rest must follow, if it does not happen simultaneously.

In order to make my proposal fool-proof I have suggested that, if the Allies think it necessary, they may keep their troops, at their own expense, in India, not for internal order but for preventing Japanese aggression and defending China. So far as India is concerned, she must become free even as America and Great Britain are. The Allied troops will remain in India during the war under treaty with the free Indian Government that may be formed by the people of India without any outside interference, direct or indirect.

It is on behalf of this proposal that I write this to enlist your active sympathy.

. . . . . .

Franklin D. Roosevelt to Mohandas K. Gandhi, August 1, 1942

My Dear M. Gandhi:

I have received your letter of July 1, 1942, which you have thoughtfully sent me in order that I may better understand your plans, which I well know may have far-reaching effect upon developments important to your country and to mine.

I am sure that you will agree that the United States has consistently striven for and supported policies of fair dealing, of fair play, and of all related principles looking towards the creation of harmonious relations between nations. Nevertheless, now that war has come as a result of Axis dreams of world conquest, we, together with many other nations, are making a supreme effort to defeat those who would deny forever all hope of freedom throughout the world. I am enclosing a copy of an address of July 23 by the Secretary of State, made with my complete approval, which illustrates the attitude of this Government.

I shall hope that our common interest in democracy and righteousness will enable your countrymen and mine to make common cause against a common enemy.

Document 6.9

AIRWAYS TO PEACE

American policy makers perceived a newfound responsibility to reshape the world in large part because the world seemed physically closer than ever before. In 1943, New York City's Museum of Modern Art offered a landmark exhibit, entitled Airways to Peace, *which described in detail the changing map and vocabulary of the new world. This sense of global intimacy, intertwined with American perceptions of insecurity, only increased as the twentieth century wore on and as opportunities for global travel advanced in stride with the growing fear of a world filled with nuclear weapons and intercontinental missiles. As the June 1943 press release for the museum's airways exhibit shows, the war shrank the world for Americans, though opportunity always ran hand in hand with vulnerability.*

AIRWAYS TO PEACE EXHIBITION WITH TEXT BY WENDELL L. WILLKIE OPENS AT MUSEUM OF MODERN ART

Today's great panorama of the world of the air, from its beginning in ancient myths of bird-men to its present struggle for air supremacy and its future possibilities for world peace, will be spread before the visitor in *Airways to Peace: An Exhibition of Geography for the Future*, opening today (Friday, July 2) at the Museum of Modern Art, 11 West 53 Street.

Wendell L. Willkie has written the text, which will be mounted on the walls as a running commentary on the various sections of the exhibition. The opening and closing paragraphs of Mr. Willkie's text are as follows:

> "We have always known two kinds of geography. Nature drew the oceans, continents, mountains, rivers and plains. Men etched in cities and national boundaries. For our well-being, we have tried to harmonize natural and man-made geography.
>
> "But the modern airplane creates a new geographical dimension. A navigable ocean of air blankets the whole surface of the globe. There are no distant places any longer: the world is small and the world is one. The American people must grasp these new realities if they are to play their essential part in winning the war and building a world of peace and freedom. This exhibition tells the story of airways to peace. . . .
>
> "Peace must be planned on a world basis. Continents and oceans are plainly only parts of a whole seen from the air. And it is inescapable that

there can be no peace for any part of the world unless the foundations of peace are made secure throughout all parts of the world. Our thinking in the future must be world-wide."

An automatic question-and-answer device will enable visitors to test the knowledge they have derived from the exhibition. Some of the questions concern the relative distance from the North Pole of Vladivostok and Venice; the relative distance from New York of Dakar and Berlin; and the percentage of the world's land area occupied by Europe.

The exhibition is divided into five sections, a prologue and a conclusion:

Prologue, which introduces the purpose of the exhibition, i.e., to explain to the layman in graphic form the basic factors of air-age geography, an understanding of which is essential to winning the war and making a successful peace.

I. *How Man Has Drawn His World:* Maps and globes from the *Ga-Sur Clay Tablet* of 2500 B.C. to the latest air maps of the world. The distortions of flat maps are explained and the importance of the globe to an understanding of global geography is emphasized. A 15-foot globe into which the visitor can walk shows the nations of the world and air routes which link them.

II. *The Development of Flight:* From the prehistoric pterodactyl and Icarus, the flying man of Greek mythology, to the giant air transport of tomorrow. From December 17, 1903, when the Wright brothers flew the first heavier-than-air machine, the progress of American aviation has been spectacular. United States airplane production this year is seven times greater than our automobile production before the war. By our fortunate geographic location no less than by national temperament, America's destiny seems to be the air world.

III. *Theatres of War:* Background terrain and natives in a score of countries all over the earth where American men are now fighting.

IV. *Global Strategy:* Germany's geo-political theories and the repudiation of them by the resources and strategy of the United Nations.

V. *The Nature of the Air:* A series of colored panels showing the earth as a ball of atmosphere with a solid center, and the clouds and air currents which aviators must understand.

Conclusion: Photo-mural and text which indicate that in a world internationalized by the airplane peace can only be built on dynamic idealism.

Document 6.10

ROOSEVELT'S VISION OF A POSTWAR UNITED NATIONS

The British were first of the wartime Big Three to fight the Nazis, but their power was eclipsed by the United States and the Soviet Union. In late 1943, Stalin and Roosevelt met for the first time. Stalin pleaded for an immediate American-led invasion of western Europe, designed to force Germany into a two-front land war in Europe. Roosevelt hoped to keep Soviet forces in the war absent such an immediate invasion (it finally occurred in June of 1944), while keeping the Soviets engaged as well in the international system long after the fighting eventually ended. Both leaders—this record of their conversation from November 29, 1943, reveals—thought as much about potential future conflicts as the one their nations were currently fighting.

The President . . . said the question of a post-war organization to preserve peace had not been fully explained and dealt with and he would like to discuss with the Marshal the prospect of some organization based on the United Nations.

The President then outlined the following general plan:

There would be a large organization composed of some 35 members of the United Nations which would meet periodically at different places, discuss and make recommendations to a smaller body.

Marshal Stalin inquired whether this organization was to be world-wide or European, to which the President replied, world-wide.

The President continued that there would be set up an executive committee composed of the Soviet Union, the United States, United Kingdom, and China, together with two additional European states, one South American, one Near East, one Far Eastern country, and one British Dominion. He mentioned that Mr. Churchill did not like this proposal for the reason that the British Empire only had two votes. This Executive Committee would deal with all non-military questions such as agriculture, food, health, and economic questions, as well as the setting up of an International Committee. This Committee would likewise meet in various places.

Marshall Stalin inquired whether this body would have the right to make decisions binding on the nations of the world.

The President replied, yes and no. It could make recommendations for settling disputes with the hope that the nations concerned would be guided thereby, but that, for example, he did not believe [the] Congress of the United States would accept as binding a decision of such a body. The President then turned to the third organization which he termed "The Four Policemen," namely the Soviet Union, the United States, Great Britain, and China. This organization would have the power to deal immediately with any threat to the peace and any sudden emergency which requires this action. He went on to say that in 1935, when Italy attacked Ethiopia, the only machine in existence was the League of Nations. He personally had begged France to close the Suez Canal, but they instead referred it to [the] League which disputed the question and in the end did nothing. The result was that the Italian Armies went through the Suez Canal and destroyed Ethiopia. The President pointed out that had the machinery of the Four Policemen, which he had in mind, been in existence, it would have been possible to close the Suez Canal. The President then summarized briefly the idea that he had in mind.

Marshall Stalin said that he did not think that the small nations of Europe would like the organization composed of the Four Policemen. He said, for example, that a European state would probably resent China having the right to apply certain machinery to it. And in any event, he did not think China would be very powerful at the end of the war. He suggested as a possible alternative, the creation of European or a Far Eastern Committee and a European or a Worldwide organization. He said that in the European Commission there would be the United States, Great Britain, the Soviet Union and possibly one other European state.

The President said that the idea just expressed by Marshal Stalin was somewhat similar to Mr. Churchill's idea of a Regional Committee, one for Europe, one for the Far East, and one for the Americas. Mr. Churchill had also suggested that the United States be a member of the European Commission, but he doubted if the United States Congress would agree to the United States' participation in an exclusively European Committee which might be able to force the dispatch of American troops to Europe.

The President added that it would take a terrible crisis such as the present before Congress would ever agree to that step.

Marshall Stalin pointed out that the world organization suggested by the President, and in particular the Four Policemen, might also require the sending of American troops to Europe.

The President pointed out that he had only envisaged the sending of American planes and ships to Europe, and that England and the Soviet Union would have to handle the land armies in the event of any future threat to peace. He went on to say that if the Japanese had not attacked the United States, he doubted very much if it would have been possible to send any American forces to Europe. The President added that he saw two methods of dealing with possible threats to the peace. In one case if the threat arose from a revolution or developments in a small country, it might be possible to apply the quarantine method, closing the frontiers of the countries in question and imposing embargoes. In the second case, if the threat was more serious, the four powers, acting as policemen, would send an ultimatum to the nation in question and if refused, [it] would result in the immediate bombardment and invasion of that country.

Marshall Stalin said that yesterday he had discussed the question of safeguarding against Germany with Mr. Churchill and found him optimistic on the subject in that Mr. Churchill believed that Germany would not rise again. He, Stalin, personally thought that unless prevented, Germany would completely [recover] within 15 to 20 years, and that therefore we must have something more serious than the type of organization proposed by the President. He pointed out that the first German aggression had occurred in 1870 and then 42 [*sic*] years later in the 1st World War, whereas only 21 years had elapsed between the end of the last war and the beginning of the present. He added that he did not believe the period between the revival of German strength would be any longer in the future and therefore he did not consider the organizations outlined by the President were enough.

He went on to say that what was needed was the control of certain strong physical points either within Germany or along German borders, or even farther away, to insure that Germany would not embark on another course of aggression. He mentioned specifically Dakar as one of those points. He added that the same method should be applied in the case of Japan and that the islands in the vicinity of Japan should remain under strong control to prevent Japan's embarking on a course of aggression.

He stated that any commission or body which was set up to preserve peace should have the right to not only make decisions but to occupy such strong points against Germany and Japan.

The President said he agreed 100% with Marshall Stalin.

Documents 6.11 and 6.12

ROOSEVELT CONFRONTS EMPIRE HEAD-ON

American policy makers were not so naive as to believe that generations of colonialism could be eliminated overnight. In the following two documents, the first from January 1944 and the second from a year later, Roosevelt reveals his concerns about the future of empire and Washington's imperial allies. Indochina, and in particular Vietnam, would dominate the attention of successive American presidents to come. The first document is a memorandum that Roosevelt sent to Secretary of State Cordell Hull on January 24, 1944. The second is an excerpt from a press conference that Roosevelt gave on February 23, 1945.

I saw Halifax [Lord Halifax, British Ambassador to the United States] last week and told him quite frankly that it was perfectly true that I had, for over a year, expressed the opinion that Indo-China should not go back to France but that it should be administered by an international trusteeship. France has had the country—thirty million inhabitants—for nearly one hundred years, and the people are worse off than they were at the beginning.

As a matter of interest, I am wholeheartedly supported in this view by Generalissimo Chiang Kai-shek and by Marshal Stalin. I see no reason to play in with the British Foreign Office in this matter. The only reason they seem to oppose it is that they fear the effect it would have on their own possessions and those of the Dutch. They have never liked the idea of trusteeship because it is, in some instances, aimed at future independence. This is true in the case of Indo-China.

Each case must, of course, stand on its own feet, but the case of Indo-China is perfectly clear. France has milked it for one hundred years. The people of Indo-China are entitled to something better than that.

. . . . . .

Roosevelt: With the Indo-Chinese, there is a feeling they ought to be independent but are not ready for it. I suggested at the time [1943], to Chiang, that Indo-China be set up under a trusteeship—have a Frenchman, one or two Indo-Chinese, and a Chinese and a Russian because they are on the coast, and maybe a Filipino and an American—to educate them for self-government. It took fifty years for us to do it in the Philippines.

Stalin liked the idea. China liked the idea. The British don't like it. It might bust up their empire, because if the Indo-Chinese were to work together and eventually get their independence, the Burmese might do the same thing to England. The French have talked about how they expect to recapture Indo-China, but they haven't got any shipping to do it with. It would only get the British mad. Chiang would go along. Stalin would go along. As for the British, it would only make the British mad. Better to keep quiet just now.

Documents 6.13 and 6.14

CONFRONTING THE HOLOCAUST

World War II fostered unspeakable horrors, as modernity and violence coupled to wreak unprecedented death and destruction. Tens of millions of civilians died, perhaps as many from starvation and other wartime deprivations as from combat. Many were purposefully murdered, including more than twelve million victims of the German ethnic cleansing known as the Holocaust. Jews above all, but also communists, Gypsies, homosexuals, religious and political dissidents, and the physically and mentally infirm, were targeted for destruction, among others. The British and American governments certainly knew of the deliberate extermination of whole European populations by 1943. As the following documents from August of 1944 demonstrate, Jewish advocacy groups in particular pleaded with the Roosevelt administration for direct air attacks on German concentration camps and their connected transit networks, hoping that disruption of the extermina- tion would help save lives. Specifically, below are two letters: one from the World Jewish Congress on August 9, 1944, to Assistant Secretary of War John McCloy, and McCloy's reply a week later. Administration officials largely refused such requests, reasoning that most lives would ultimately be saved by a speedy end to the war. The government, which wrestled with these moral issues, meanwhile forged ahead with its own plans to develop the atomic bomb.

From The World Jewish Congress to the Honorable John J. McCloy

I beg to submit to your consideration the following excerpt from a message which we received under date of July 29 from Mr. Ernest Frischer of the Czechoslovak State Council through the War Refugee Board:

"I believe that destruction of gas chambers and crematoria in Oswiecim by bombing would have a certain effect now. Germans are exhuming and burning corpses in an effort to conceal their crimes. This could be prevented by destruction of crematoria and then Germans might possibly stop further mass extermination especially since so little time is left to them. Bombing of railway communications in this same area would also be of importance and of military interest."

Sincerely yours,

A. Leon Kubowitski

Head, Rescue Department

• • • • • •

August 14, 1944

Dear Mr. Kubowitski

I refer to your letter of August 9 in which you request consideration of a proposal made by Mr. Ernest Frischer that certain installations and railroad centers be bombed.

The War Department had been approached by the War Refugee Board, which raised the question of the practicability of this suggestion. After a study it became apparent that such an operation could be executed only by the diversion of considerable air support essential to the success of our forces now engaged in decisive operations elsewhere and would in any case be of such doubtful efficacy that it would not warrant the use of our resources. There has been considerable opinion to the effect that such an effort, even if practicable, might provoke even more vindictive action by the Germans.

The War Department fully appreciates the humanitarian motives which promoted the suggested operation, but for the reasons stated above it has not been felt that it can or should be undertaken, at least at this time.

Sincerely,

John J. McCloy

Document 6.15

CHURCHILL, STALIN, AND DIVVYING UP EUROPE

Both Churchill and Stalin could speak in ways capable of motivating their populaces, but they reasoned more often in terms of hard power. Their meeting in October 1944 in Moscow provided opportunity to discuss, without an American present, their visions of how to divvy up the spoils of war. They agreed on the fol-

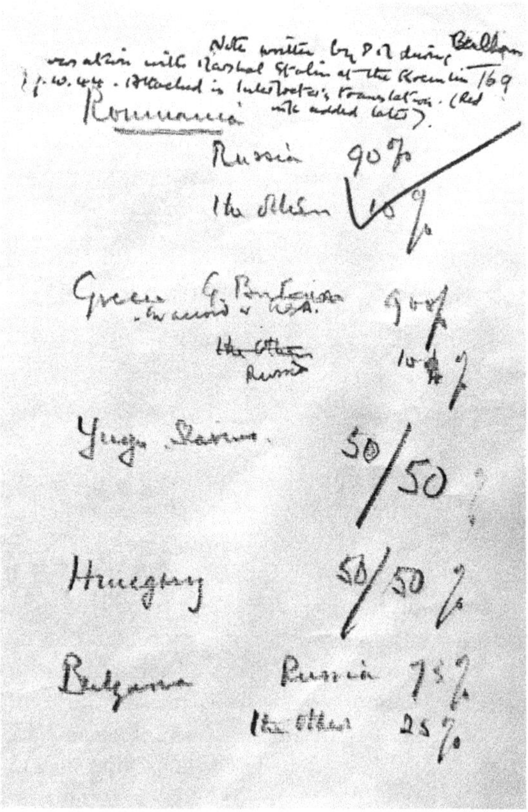

lowing percentages for their respective control of eastern and southern Europe, in a document composed by Churchill, and according to his memoirs, endorsed by Stalin with tick marks after each number. The Soviets denied the agreement ever existed, and neither leader ever explained what a percentage of influence might mean in practice. The document, written on October 9, 1944, thus reveals more about how global leaders interacted outside the public view and how they thought about the structure of the postwar world.

Document 6.16

THE WORLD OF BRETTON WOODS

While top leaders discussed the dissolution of empire, many American strategists worked feverishly during the war to develop an economic system capable of sustaining a just, long-term peace. Many axiomatically believed World War II arose from the economic inequalities that flowed from the settlement that had ended World War I. They also generally accepted, as influential State Department policy maker Will Clayton put it, "The international economic policies of nations have more to do with creating conditions which lead to war than any other single factor." In summer 1944, therefore, Americans led an international conference at Bretton Woods, New Hampshire, designed to forge a blueprint for postwar economic stability, which—as these closing remarks by Treasury Secretary Henry Morgenthau from July 22 demonstrate—was as much about peace as prosperity.

I am gratified to announce that the Conference at Bretton Woods has completed successfully the task before it.

It was, as we knew when we began, a difficult task, involving complicated technical problems. We came to work out methods which would do away with the economic evils—the competitive currency devaluation and destructive impediments to trade—which preceded the present war. We have succeeded in that effort.

The actual details of a financial and monetary agreement may seem mysterious to the general public. Yet at the heart of it lie the most elementary bread and butter realities of daily life. What we have done here in Bretton Woods is to devise machinery by which men and women everywhere can exchange freely, on a fair and stable basis, the goods which they produce through fair labor. And we have taken the initial step through which the nations of the world will be able to help one another in economic development to their mutual advantage and for the enrichment of all. . . .

Yet none of us has found any incompatibility between devotion to our own country and joint action. Indeed, we have found on the contrary that the only genuine safeguard for our national interests lies in international cooperation. We have to recognize that the wisest and most effective way to protect our national interests is through international cooperation—that is to say, through united effort for the attainment of common goals. This has been the great lesson taught by the war, and is, I think, the great lesson of contemporary life—that the people of the earth are inseparably linked to one another by a deep, underlying community of purpose. This community of purpose is no less real and vital in peace than in war, and cooperation is no less essential to its fulfillment.

To seek the achievement of our aims separately through the planless, senseless rivalry that divided us in the past, or through the outright economic aggression which turned neighbors into enemies would be to invite ruin again upon us all. Worse, it would be once more to start our steps irretraceably down the steep, disastrous road to war. That sort of extreme nationalism belongs to an era that is dead....

I take it as an axiom that this war is ended; no people—therefore no government of the people—will again tolerate prolonged or wide-spread unemployment. A revival of international trade is indispensable if full employment is to be achieved in a peaceful world and with standards of living which will permit the realization of man's reasonable hopes.

What are the fundamental conditions under which the commerce among nations can once more flourish?

First, there must be a reasonable stable standard of international exchange to which all countries can adhere without sacrificing the freedom of action necessary to meet their internal economic problems.

This is the alternative to the desperate tactics of the past—competitive currency depreciation, excessive tariff barriers, uneconomic barter deals, multiple currency practices, and unnecessary exchange restrictions—by which governments vainly sought to maintain employment and uphold living standards. In the final analysis, these tactics only succeeded in contributing to world-wide depression and even war. The International Monetary Fund agreed upon at Bretton Woods will help remedy this situation.

Second, long-term financial aid must be made available at reasonable rates to those countries whose industry and agriculture have been destroyed by the ruthless torch of an invader or by the heroic scorched earth policy of their defenders.

Long-term funds must be made available also to promote sound industry and increase industrial and agricultural production in nations whose economic potentialities have not yet been developed. It is essential to us all that these nations play their full part in the exchange of goods throughout the world.

They must be enabled to produce and to sell if they are to be able to purchase and consume. The International Bank for Reconstruction and Development is designed to meet this need....

This monetary agreement is but one step, of course, in the broad program of international action necessary for the shaping of a free future. But it is an indispensable step in the vital test of our intentions. We are at a crossroad, and we must go one way or the other. The Conference at Bretton Woods has erected a signpost . . . pointing down a highway broad enough for all men to walk in step and side by side. If they will set out together, there is nothing on earth that need stop them.

Document 6.17

ECONOMIC INTERDEPENDENCE AND POLITICAL INDEPENDENCE

Dean Acheson proved to be one of the most influential American diplomats of the twentieth century, leading efforts on the part of the administration of President Harry S. Truman to establish the institutions that guided American diplomacy through the remainder of the century. During World War II, he worked as an assistant secretary of state in his area of expertise: international economics. In this dramatic congressional testimony from November 30, 1944, Acheson lectured one representative on the intertwined nature, in his mind, of economic power and traditional American freedoms.

Mr. Acheson: [I]t seems clear that we are in for a very bad time, so far as the economic and social position of the country is concerned. We cannot go through another ten years like the ten years at the end of the twenties and the beginning of the thirties, without having the most far-reaching consequences upon our economic and social system.

When we look at that problem we may say it is a problem of markets. You don't have a problem of production. The United States has unlimited creative energy. The important thing is markets. We have got to see that what the country produces is used and is sold under financial arrangements which make its production possible. . . . You must look to foreign markets. . . .

[W]e could argue for quite a while that under a different system in this country you could use the entire production of the country in the United States.

[Representative Francis] Worley: What do you mean by that?

Mr. Acheson: I take it the Soviet Union could use its entire production internally.

If you wish to control the entire trade and income of the United States, which means the life of the people, you could probably fix it so that everything produced here would be consumed here, but that would completely change our constitution, our relations to property, human liberty, our very conceptions of law.

And nobody contemplates that. Therefore, you find you must look to other markets and those markets are abroad.

It happens that these other markets are quite as anxious for our goods as we are to sell to them. They always have been to some extent, but now that is true as never before.

This war has created a colossal demand such as has never existed before. But it is only a wish and not an economic demand unless there is purchasing power behind it. . . .

But the first thing that I want to bring out is that we need these markets for the output of the United States. If I am wrong about that, then all the argument falls by the wayside, but my contention is that we cannot have full employment and prosperity in the United States without the foreign markets. That is point one, and if anyone wants to challenge me on that we will go over it again. . . .

Mr. Worley: You don't think there would be a peace agreement without collateral agreements of an economic nature?

Mr. Acheson: I don't see how it would work, Mr. Chairman. If we tried to do that it would really mean that we would be relying exclusively on the use of force. I don't believe that would work.

Document 6.18

THE ATOMIC BOMB

Roosevelt never lived to see the United Nations of his dreams formally established; he died on April 12, 1945, and Truman became president. Wholly by coincidence, at nearly the same moment as the UN Charter's acceptance, Secretary of War Henry Stimson wrote the new president seeking immediate opportunity to discuss the new and awesome power that would soon be at Washington's disposal: the atomic bomb. What follows is Stimson's initial memorandum to Truman, delivered on April 25, 1945, to facilitate that meeting.

Within four months we shall in all probability have completed the most terrible weapon ever known in human history, one bomb of which could destroy a whole city.

Although we have shared its development with the UK, physically the US is at present in the position of controlling the resources with which to construct and use it and no other nation could reach this position for some years.

Nevertheless it is practically certain that we could not remain in this position indefinitely.

a. Various segments of its discovery and production are widely known among many scientists in many countries, although few scientists are now acquainted with the whole process which we have deployed.

b. Although its construction under present methods requires great scientific and industrial effort and raw materials, which are temporarily within the possession and knowledge of the US and UK, it is extremely probable that much easier and cheaper methods of production will be discovered by scientists in the future, together with the use of materials of much wider distribution. As a result, it is extremely probable that the future will make it possible to be constructed by smaller nations or even groups, or at least by a large nation in a much shorter time.

As a result, it is indicated that the future may see a time when such a weapon may be constructed in secret and used suddenly and effectively with devastating power by a willful nation or group against an unsuspecting nation or group of much greater size and material power. With its aid even a very powerful unsuspecting nation might be conquered within a very few days by a very much smaller one, although probably the only nation which could enter into production within the next few years is Russia.

The world in its present state of moral advancement compared with its technical development would be eventually at the mercy of such a weapon. In other words, modern civilization might be completely destroyed.

To approach any world peace organization of any pattern now likely to be considered, without any appreciation by the leaders of our country of the power of this new weapon, would seem to be unrealistic. No system of control heretofore considered would be adequate to control this menace. Both inside any particular country and between the nations of the world, the control of this weapon will undoubtedly be a matter of the greatest difficulty and would involve such thorough-going rights of inspection and internal controls as we have never heretofore contemplated.

Furthermore, in the light of our present position with reference to this weapon, the question of sharing it with other nations and, if so shared, upon what terms, becomes a primary question of our foreign relations. Also our leadership in the war and in the development of this weapon has placed a certain moral responsibility upon us which we cannot shirk without very serious responsibility for any disaster to civilization which it would further.

On the other hand, if the problem of the proper use of this weapon can be solved, we would have the opportunity to bring the world into a pattern in which the peace of the world and our civilization can be saved.

Document 6.19

Visions of a Future Apocalypse

World War II left Americans triumphant yet afraid. As Acheson noted (in document 6.17, above), they feared a return to the depression of the 1930s. Yet they also feared the world might someday bring to them the kind of devastation they had largely avoided during the war. The atomic bomb brought these fears to the fore, auguring in any future war, should it escalate out of control, unprecedented destruction. It is impossible to appreciate the Cold War that soon followed, the manic fear of Soviet attack and of communism at home, without appreciating the new threat to home and security felt by many Americans even amid the victorious close of World War II. The widely read Life *magazine crystallized such fears in its November 19, 1945, issue. In an article entitled "The 36-Hour War," the magazine predicted a brief future war that would leave cities like New York (with the famous lions astride the entrance to the New York Public Library) little more than radioactive hellscapes.*

7

The Beginning of the Cold War

The Soviet-American alliance against Nazi Germany fractured within a few months after the end of the Second World War, and the two superpowers settled into a bitter rivalry that American newspaper columnist Walter Lippmann dubbed a "cold war." This deterioration resulted from numerous sources of disagreement, some of them rooted long before 1945. The two nations had regarded each other warily ever since the Bolshevik Revolution of 1917 had brought communists to power in Russia and established a national ideology opposed to the American creed of free enterprise and democracy. The outbreak of global war in 1941 thrust Washington and Moscow together as partners against fascism, yet old resentments festered.

The Cold War resulted not just from past disagreements, however, but also from conflicting visions of the future. U.S. and Soviet leaders advanced contrasting ideas about how to remake the world once the fighting came to an end. For Joseph Stalin, ensuring the physical security of the Soviet Union was paramount. He aimed to destroy German power, assert control over eastern Europe, and extend Soviet influence toward the Mediterranean, oil-rich Southwest Asia, and the Far East.

This desire for territorial domination, rooted in a profound sense of insecurity honed by repeated invasions of the Soviet Union, contrasted sharply with U.S. plans for the postwar order. Convinced that global catastrophe—first the Great Depression and then the Second World War—had resulted from nations pursuing narrow economic and territorial advantages, U.S. leaders hoped to establish an open world order based on free trade, self-determination, and international cooperation. Like Woodrow Wilson in an earlier day, U.S. officials believed that the universal application of such principles would serve the interests not only of the United States but also of the whole international community. Soviet leaders took a dim view of U.S. intentions, echoing earlier critics of U.S. foreign policy by charging that American preferences amounted to a new form of imperialism designed to open the world to capitalist penetration.

This chapter examines the evolution of American thinking as these competing visions of the future generated friction between 1944 and 1949. At first, American leaders believed it might be possible to find common ground with the Soviets. By 1947, however, U.S. officials largely gave up on the possibility of compromise and embraced the policy of containment. The Truman administration concluded that the Soviet Union was implacably determined to expand and that the best alternative for the West was to oppose the Soviets wherever they threatened to add new territory to the communist bloc. Over time, U.S. policy makers hoped, frustration of Soviet designs would cause Moscow to abandon its aggressive intentions.

By some measures, these efforts were a great success. Economic aid distributed through the Marshall Plan and the extension of American military power via the North Atlantic Treaty Organization (NATO) helped moor western Europe firmly in the U.S. geopolitical order, while Japan made a remarkable transition from mortal enemy to close ally of the United States within a few years. Yet many Americans felt less secure as time passed, convinced by 1950 that revelations of Soviet espionage in the United States, Soviet acquisition of the atomic bomb, and the communist triumph in the Chinese civil war indicated that Moscow, not Washington, had the upper hand. Americans increasingly abandoned hope of a peaceful new era in international relations, embraced fervent anticommunism, and prepared themselves to wage another long struggle against foreign enemies.

Document 7.1

A SYMPATHETIC VIEW OF THE SOVIET UNION

Many Americans expressed a favorable view of the Soviet Union during the Second World War, when the two nations made common cause against Germany. Popular American books, articles, and films depicted Russia as a land not of menacing communists but of honorable patriots much like Americans. Among prominent U.S. citizens to advance this view was Wendell L. Willkie, the Republican nominee for president in 1940. The following passage comes from One World, *Willkie's widely read 1943 book recounting his travels to the Soviet Union and other countries as an emissary of President Franklin D. Roosevelt.*

I had not sufficiently taken into account [before the trip], in appraising modern Russia, that it is ruled by and composed almost entirely of people whose parents had no property, no education, and only a folk heritage. That there is hardly a resident of Russia today whose lot is not as good or better than his parents' lot was prior to the revolution. The Russian individual, like all individuals, naturally finds some good in a system that has improved his own lot, and has a tendency to forget the ruthless means by which it has been brought about. This may be difficult for an American to believe or like. . . .

But I had not gone to Russia to remember the past. Besides my concrete assignment for the President, I had gone determined to find an answer for myself to the actual problems posed for our generation of Americans by the simple fact that the Soviet Union, whether we like it or not, exists.

Some of these answers I believe I found, at least to my own satisfaction. I can sum up the three most important in a few sentences.

First, Russia is an effective society. It works. It has survival value. The record of Soviet resistance to Hitler has been proof enough of this to most of us, but I must admit in all frankness that I was not prepared to believe before I went to Russia what I now know about its strengths as a going organization of men and women.

Second, Russia is our ally in this war. The Russians, more sorely tested by Hitler's might even than the British, have met the test magnificently. Their hatred of Fascism and the Nazi system is real and deep and bitter....

Third, we must work with Russia after the war. At least it seems to me that there can be no continued peace unless we learn to do so....

In Moscow I had two long talks with Joseph Stalin. Much of what was said I am not at liberty to report. But about the man himself there is no reason to be cautious. He is one of the significant men of his generation....

Among the other leaders I met and talked to at any great length were Viacheslav Molotov, the Foreign Minister, Andrei Vishinsky and Solomon Lozovsky, his assistants, Marshal Voroshilov, the former Commissar of Supply and head of the Soviet foreign-trade apparatus. Each of these is an educated man, interested in the foreign world, completely unlike in manner, appearance, and speech the uncouth, wild Bolshevik of our cartoons....

No, we do not need to fear Russia. We need to learn to work with her against our common enemy, Hitler. We need to learn to work with her in the world after the war. For Russia is a dynamic country, a vital new society, a force that cannot be bypassed in any future world.

Document 7.2

TOWARD A HARDER LINE

As the Allies advanced on Germany in 1944 and early 1945, U.S.-Soviet disagreements mounted over plans for the postwar settlement, especially the political status of eastern Europe. At first, many U.S. policy makers believed that the solution was to drive a harder bargain with the Soviets by insisting that continued cooperation depended on greater respect for American positions. The U.S. ambassador in Moscow, W. Averell Harriman, expressed this view in a dispatch to Harry L. Hopkins, one of President Roosevelt's closest advisers, on September 10, 1944.

Now that the end of the war is in sight our relations with the Soviets have taken a startling turn evident during the last 2 months. They have held up our requests with complete indifference to our interests and have shown an unwillingness even to discuss pressing problems.... I have been conscious since early in the year of a division among Stalin's advisers on the question of cooperation with us. It is now my feeling that those who oppose the kind of cooperation we expect have recently been getting their way and the policy appears to be crystallizing to force us and the British to accept all Soviet policies backed by the strength and prestige of the Red Army. . . .

I am convinced that we can divert this trend but only if we materially change our policy toward the Soviet Government. I have evidence that they have misinterpreted our generous attitude toward them as a sign of weakness, and acceptance of their policies.

Time has come when we must make clear what we expect of them as the price of our good will. Unless we take issue with the present policy there is every indication the Soviet Union will become a world bully wherever their interests are involved. This policy will reach into China and the Pacific as well when they can turn their attention in that direction. No written agreement[s] can be of any value unless they are carried out in a spirit of give and take and recognition of the interests of other people.

I am disappointed but not discouraged. The job of getting the Soviet Government to play a decent role in international affairs is however going to be more difficult than we had hoped. The favorable factors are still the same. Ninety percent of the Russian people want friendship with us and it is much to the interest of the Soviet Government to develop it. It is our problem to strengthen the hand of those around Stalin who want to play the game along our lines and to show Stalin that the advice of the counselors of a tough policy is leading him into difficulties. . . .

When it comes to the question of what we should do in dealing with the situation I am not going to propose any drastic action but a firm but friendly *quid pro quo* attitude. In some cases where it has been possible for us to show a firm hand we have been making definite progress.

Document 7.3

THE "LONG TELEGRAM"

In February 1946, officials in Washington asked the U.S. embassy in Moscow why the Soviet government was failing to cooperate with American plans for the postwar international order. On the receiving end was George Kennan, a career foreign service officer who had risen to be the second-ranking American official in Moscow. Kennan replied with an extraordinary 5,300-word cable later dubbed the "long telegram." Kennan drew on his long experience in the Soviet Union and eastern Europe to lay out a distinctive view of Russian history and culture, challenging Harriman's contention that the United States simply needed to bargain more aggressively with Moscow.

At bottom of Kremlin's neurotic view of world affairs is traditional and instinctive Russian sense of insecurity. Originally, this was insecurity of a peaceful agricultural people trying to live on vast exposed plain in neighborhood of fierce nomadic peoples. To this was added, as Russia came into contact with economically advanced West, fear of more competent, more powerful, more highly organized societies in that area. But this latter type of insecurity was one which afflicted rather Russian rulers than Russian people; for Russian rulers have invariably sensed that their rule was relatively archaic in form, fragile and artificial in its psychological foundation, unable to stand comparison or contact with political systems of Western countries. For this reason they have always feared foreign penetration, feared direct contact between Western world and their own, feared what would happen if Russians learned truth about world without or if foreigners learned truth about world within. And they have learned to seek security only in patient but deadly struggle for total destruction of rival power, never in compacts and compromises with it.

It was no coincidence that Marxism, which had smoldered ineffectively for half a century in Western Europe, caught hold and blazed for first time in Russia. Only in this land which had never known a friendly neighbor or indeed any tolerant equilibrium of separate powers, either internal or international, could a doctrine thrive which viewed economic conflicts of society as insoluble by peaceful means. After establishment of Bolshevist regime, Marxist dogma, rendered even more truculent and intolerant by Lenin's interpretation, became a perfect vehicle for sense of insecurity with which Bolsheviks, even more than previous Russian rulers, were afflicted. In this dogma, with its basic altruism of purpose, they found justification for their instinctive fear of outside world, for the dictatorship without which they did not know how to rule, for cruelties they did not dare not to inflict, for sacrifice they felt bound to demand. In the name of Marxism they sacrificed every single ethical value in their methods and tactics. Today they cannot dispense with it. It is fig leaf of their moral and intellectual respectability. . . .

In summary, we have here a political force committed fanatically to the belief that with US there can be no permanent *modus vivendi*, that it is desirable and necessary that the internal harmony of our society be disrupted, our traditional way of life be destroyed, the international authority of our state be broken, if Soviet power is to be secure. This political force has complete power of disposition over energies of one of world's greatest peoples and resources of world's richest national territory, and is borne along by deep and powerful currents of Russian nationalism. In addition, it has an elaborate and far flung apparatus for exertion of its influence in other countries, an apparatus of amazing flexibility and versatility, managed by people whose experience and skill in underground methods are presumably without parallel in history. Finally, it is seemingly inaccessible to considerations of reality in its basic reactions. For it, the vast fund of objective fact about human society is not, as with us, the measure against which outlook is constantly being tested and re-formed, but a grab bag from which individual items are selected arbitrarily and tendenciously to bolster an outlook already preconceived. This is admittedly not a pleasant picture. Problem of how to cope with this force [is] undoubtedly greatest task our diplomacy has ever faced and probably greatest it will ever have to face. . . . I cannot attempt to suggest all answers here. But I would like to record my conviction that problem is within our power to solve—and that without recourse to any general military conflict. And in support of this conviction there are certain observations of a more encouraging nature I should like to make:

(1) Soviet power, unlike that of Hitlerite Germany, is neither schematic nor adventurist. It does not work by fixed plans. It does not take unnecessary risks. Impervious to logic of reason, and it is highly sensitive to logic of force. For this reason it can easily withdraw—and usually does when strong resistance is encountered at any point. Thus, if the adversary has sufficient force and makes clear his readiness to use it, he rarely has to do so. If situations are properly handled there need be no prestige-engaging showdowns.

(2) Gauged against western world as a whole, Soviets are still by far the weaker force. Thus, their success will really depend on degree of cohesion, firmness and vigor which western world can muster. And this is factor which it is within our power to influence.

(3) Success of Soviet system, as form of internal power, is not yet finally proven. It has yet to be demonstrated that it can survive supreme test of successive transfer of power from one individual or group to another. . . . We here are convinced that never since termination of civil war have mass of Russian people been emotionally farther removed from doctrines of Communist Party than they are today. In Russia, party has now become a great and—for the moment—highly successful apparatus of dictatorial administration, but it has ceased to be a source of emotional inspiration. Thus, internal soundness and permanence of movement need not yet be regarded as assured.

(4) All Soviet propaganda beyond Soviet security sphere is basically negative and destructive. It should therefore be relatively easy to combat it by any intelligent and really constructive program.

Document 7.4

AN APPEAL FOR PEACE

The tough approaches advocated by Harriman and Kennan did not please all U.S. leaders. Perhaps the most prominent dissenter against the drift of U.S. policy was Henry Wallace, the former vice president who served as secretary of commerce after the Second World War. In a speech at Madison Square Garden in New York City on September 12, 1946, Wallace criticized the Truman administration's foreign policy—so much so that Truman promptly fired him. Wallace continued to champion friendly relations with Moscow during his campaign as the Progressive Party candidate for the presidency in 1948, but his views were increasingly out of sync with the popular mood. He captured only 2.4 percent of the popular vote.

To achieve lasting peace, we must study in detail just how the Russian character was formed—by invasions of Tartars, Mongols, Germans, Poles, Swedes, and French; by the czarist rule based on ignorance, fear and force; by the intervention of the British, French and Americans in Russian affairs from 1919 to 1921; by the geography of the huge Russian land mass situated strategically between Europe and Asia; and by the vitality derived from the rich Russian soil and the strenuous Russian climate. Add to all this the tremendous emotional power which Marxism and Leninism gives to the Russian leaders—and then we can realize that we are reckoning with a force which cannot be handled successfully by a "Get tough with Russia" policy. "Getting tough" never bought anything real and lasting—whether for schoolyard bullies or businessmen or world powers. The tougher we get, the tougher the Russians will get. . . .

The real peace treaty we now need is between the United States and Russia. On our part, we should recognize that we have no more business in the *political* affairs of Eastern Europe than Russia has in the *political* affairs of Latin America, Western Europe and the United States. We may not like what Russia does in Eastern Europe. Her type of land reform, industrial expropriation, and suppression of basic liberties offends the great majority of the people of the United States. But whether we like it or not the Russians will try to socialize their sphere of influence just as we try to democratize our sphere of influence. This applies also to Germany and Japan. We are striving to democratize Japan and our area of control in Germany, while Russia strives to socialize eastern Germany. . . .

Russian ideas of social-economic justice are going to govern nearly a third of the world. Our ideas of free enterprise democracy will govern much of the rest. The two ideas will endeavor to prove which can deliver the most satisfaction to the common man in their respective areas of political dominance. But by mutual agreement, this competition should be put on a friendly basis and the Russians should stop conniving against us in certain areas of the world just as we should stop scheming against them in other parts of the world. Let the results of the two systems speak for themselves. . . .

Under friendly peaceful competition the Russian world and the American world will gradually become more alike. The Russians will be forced to grant more and more of the personal freedoms; and we shall become more and more absorbed with the problems of social-economic justice.

Russia must be convinced that we are not planning for war against her and we must be certain that Russia is not carrying on territorial expansion or world domination through native communists faithfully following every twist and turn in the Moscow party line. But in this competition, we must insist on an open door for trade throughout the world. There will always be an ideological conflict—but that is no reason why diplomats cannot work out a basis for both systems to live safely in the world side by side.

Document 7.5

A SOVIET VIEW OF U.S. INTENTIONS

Among the first readers of Kennan's "Long Telegram" were Soviet leaders, who obtained the top-secret document through intelligence channels. On orders from Moscow, the Soviet ambassador in Washington, Nikolai Vasilovich Novikov, quickly set to work writing a comparable cable analyzing U.S. motives and behavior. It remains unclear whether the telegram, dispatched on September 27, 1946, reflects Novikov's sense of what his superiors wished to read or his true understanding of U.S. policy.

Reflecting the imperialistic tendency of American monopoly capital, U.S. foreign policy has been characterized in the postwar period by a desire for world domination. This is the real meaning of repeated statements by President Truman and other representatives of American ruling circles that the US has a right to world leadership. All the forces of American diplomacy, the Army, Navy, and Air Force, industry, and science have been placed at the service of this policy. With this objective in mind broad plans for expansion have been developed, to be realized both diplomatically and through the creation of a system of naval and air bases far from the US, an arms race, and the creation of newer and newer weapons. . . .

This situation does not completely match the expectations of those reactionary circles who hoped during the Second World War that they would be able to remain apart from the main battles in Europe and Asia for a long time. Their expectation was that the United States of America, if it was not able to completely avoid participation in the war, would enter it only at the last moment when it might be able to influence its outcome without great effort, completely securing its own interests. It was intended thereby that the main rivals of the US would be crushed in this war or weakened to a great degree and that due to this circumstance the US would be the most powerful factor in deciding the main issues of the postwar world. These expectations also were based on the assumption quite widespread in the US during the first period of the war that the Soviet Union, which had been attacked by German fascism in June 1941, would be weakened as a result of the war or even completely destroyed.

Reality has not borne out all the expectations of the American imperialists. . . .

Europe came out of the war with a thoroughly shattered economy, and the economic devastation which resulted during the war cannot soon be repaired. All the countries of Europe and Asia are feeling an enormous need for consumer goods, industrial and transportation equipment, etc. Such a situation opens up a vista for American monopoly capital of enormous deliveries of goods and the importation of capital to these countries, which would allow [American monopoly capital] to be introduced into their economies.

The realization of this opportunity would mean a serious strengthening of the economic position of the US throughout the entire world and would be one of the stages in the path toward establishing American world supremacy. . . .

On the other hand, the expectations of those American circles have not been justified which were based on the Soviet Union being destroyed during the war or coming out of it so weakened that it was forced to bow to the US for economic aid. In this event it could have dictated such conditions which would provide the US with an opportunity to carry out its expansion in Europe and Asia without hindrance from the USSR.

In reality, in spite of all the economic difficulties of the postwar period associated with the enormous damage caused by the war and the German fascist occupation the Soviet Union continues to remain economically independent from the outside world and is restoring its economy by its own means. . . .

The increase in peacetime military potential and the organization of a large number of naval and air bases both in the US and beyond its borders are clear indicators of the US desire to establish world domination.

For the first time in the country's history in the summer of 1946 Congress adopted a law to form a peacetime army not of volunteers but on the basis of universal military conscription. . . . The colossal growth of expenditures for the Army and Navy, comprising $13 billion in the 1946–1947 budget (about 40% of the entire budget of $36 billion) and is more than 10 times the corresponding expenditures in the 1938 budget, when it did not even reach $1 billion.

These enormous budget sums are being spent along with the maintenance of a large Army, Navy, and Air Force and also the creation of a vast system of naval and air bases in the Atlantic and Pacific Oceans. According to available official plans, in the coming years 228 bases, support bases, and radio stations are to be built in the Atlantic Ocean and 258 in the Pacific Ocean. The majority of these bases and support bases are located outside the United States. . . .

The current policy of the American government with respect to the USSR is also directed at limiting or displacing Soviet influence from neighboring countries. While implementing it the US is trying to take steps at various international conferences or directly in these very same countries which, on the one hand, manifest themselves in the support of reactionary forces in former enemy or allied countries bordering the USSR with the object of creating obstacles to the processes of democratizing these countries but, on the other, in providing positions for the penetration of American capital into their economies. . . .

The numerous statements by American government, political, and military leaders about the Soviet Union and its foreign policy in an exceptionally hostile spirit are quite typical of the current attitude of American ruling circles toward the USSR. . . . The primary goal of this anti-Soviet campaign of American "public opinion" consists of exerting political pressure on the Soviet Union and forcing it to make concessions. Another, no less important goal of the campaign is a desire to create an atmosphere of a fear of war among the broad masses who are tired of war, which would make it easier for the government to take steps to maintain the great military potential in the US.

Document 7.6

THE TRUMAN DOCTRINE

U.S. fears of Soviet expansionism escalated in early 1947, when the British government informed the Truman administration that it could no longer bear the costs of an active diplomatic, economic, and military role in southeastern Europe, a region of traditional British influence. The British announcement seemed to clear the way for the Soviet Union to gain control of the area. On March 12, 1947, Truman went before Congress to request $400 million to buoy the Turkish and Greek governments. In his speech, he not only laid out his concerns about southeastern Europe but also, using unprecedentedly bold rhetoric to describe the U.S.-Soviet conflict, insisted that the United States must support anticommunist forces elsewhere, a view that became known as the Truman Doctrine.

At the present moment in world history nearly every nation must choose between alternative ways of life. The choice is too often not a free one.

One way of life is based upon the will of the majority, and is distinguished by free institutions, representative government, free elections, guarantees of individual liberty, freedom of speech and religion, and freedom from political oppression.

The second way of life is based upon the will of a minority forcibly imposed upon the majority. It relies upon terror and oppression, a controlled press and radio; fixed elections, and the suppression of personal freedoms.

I believe that it must be the policy of the United States to support free peoples who are resisting attempted subjugation by armed minorities or by outside pressures.

I believe that we must assist free peoples to work out their own destinies in their own way.

I believe that our help should be primarily through economic and financial aid which is essential to economic stability and orderly political processes.

The world is not static, and the status quo is not sacred. But we cannot allow changes in the status quo in violation of the Charter of the United Nations by such methods as coercion, or by such subterfuges as political infiltration. In helping free and independent nations to maintain their freedom, the United States will be giving effect to the principles of the Charter of the United Nations.

It is necessary only to glance at a map to realize that the survival and integrity of the Greek nation are of grave importance in a much wider situation. If Greece should fall under the control of an armed minority, the effect upon its neighbor, Turkey, would be immediate and serious. Confusion and disorder might well spread throughout the entire Middle East.

Moreover, the disappearance of Greece as an independent state would have a profound effect upon those countries in Europe whose peoples are struggling against great difficulties to maintain their freedoms and their independence while they repair the damages of war.

It would be an unspeakable tragedy if these countries, which have struggled so long against overwhelming odds, should lose that victory for which they sacrificed so much. Collapse of free institutions and loss of independence would be disastrous not only for them but for the world. Discouragement and possibly failure would quickly be the lot of neighboring peoples striving to maintain their freedom and independence.

Should we fail to aid Greece and Turkey in this fateful hour, the effect will be far reaching to the West as well as to the East.

We must take immediate and resolute action.

I therefore ask the Congress to provide authority for assistance to Greece and Turkey in the amount of $400,000,000 for the period ending June 30, 1948. In requesting these funds, I have taken into consideration the maximum amount of relief assistance which would be furnished to Greece out of the $350,000,000 which I recently requested that the Congress authorize for the prevention of starvation and suffering in countries devastated by the war. . . .

This is a serious course upon which we embark.

I would not recommend it except that the alternative is much more serious. The United States contributed $341,000,000,000 toward winning World War II. This is an investment in world freedom and world peace.

The assistance that I am recommending for Greece and Turkey amounts to little more than 1 tenth of 1 per cent of this investment. It is only common sense that we should safeguard this investment and make sure that it was not in vain.

The seeds of totalitarian regimes are nurtured by misery and want. They spread and grow in the evil soil of poverty and strife. They reach their full growth when the hope of a people for a better life has died. We must keep that hope alive.

Document 7.7

A DOWNWARD SPIRAL

By 1947, U.S.-Soviet relations were deteriorating at an alarming rate. Most Americans placed the responsibility for this pattern on the Soviets, blaming Moscow for a series of provocative acts that had destroyed prospects for a new era of peace and security. This cartoon, drawn by New Zealander David Low and published in

INSEPARABLES

London's Evening Standard *on April 25, 1947, offers a variation on this theme, suggesting that Western hostility did much to generate Soviet antagonism. The figure at the center of the cartoon is Soviet Foreign Minister Vyacheslav Molotov.*

Document 7.8

THE MARSHALL PLAN

The Second World War devastated the economies of Europe, and reconstruction proved agonizingly slow in the first two postwar years. The unusually harsh winter of 1946–47 raised the specter of total collapse and social unrest. Washington worried that such developments would invite communist takeovers and cripple the U.S. economy by closing down crucial markets for American exports. To boost recovery, the Truman administration conceived the European Recovery Program, better known as the Marshall Plan. Under the scheme, the United States distributed approximately $13 billion, most of which was used to purchase American goods, to seventeen countries over four years. In the following speech delivered at Harvard University on June 5, 1947, U.S. Secretary of State George C. Marshall spelled out the problems confronting Europe and the rationale for the U.S. program, which sought not only to boost economic recovery but also to encourage political cooperation among participating nations.

The town and city industries are not producing adequate goods to exchange with the food producing farmer. Raw materials and fuel are in short supply. Machinery is lacking or worn out. The farmer or the peasant cannot find the goods for sale which he desires to purchase. So the sale of his farm produce for money which he cannot use seems to him an unprofitable transaction. He, therefore, has withdrawn many fields from crop cultivation and is using them for grazing. . . . Meanwhile people in the cities are short of food and fuel. So the governments are forced to use their foreign money and credits to procure these necessities abroad. This process exhausts funds which are urgently needed for reconstruction. Thus a very serious situation is rapidly developing which bodes no good for the world. The modern system of the division of labor upon which the exchange of products is based is in danger of breaking down.

The truth of the matter is that Europe's requirements for the next three or four years of foreign food and other essential products—principally from America—are so much greater than her present ability to pay that she must have substantial additional help or face economic, social, and political deterioration of a very grave character.

The remedy lies in breaking the vicious circle and restoring the confidence of the European people in the economic future of their own countries and of Europe as a whole. The manufacturer and the farmer throughout wide areas must be able and willing to exchange their products for currencies the continuing value of which is not open to question.

Aside from the demoralizing effect on the world at large and the possibilities of disturbances arising as a result of the desperation of the people concerned, the consequences to the economy of the United States should be apparent to all. It is logical that the United States should do whatever it is able to do to assist in the return of normal economic health in the world, without which there can be no political stability and no assured peace. Our policy is directed not against any country or doctrine but against hunger, poverty, desperation and chaos. Its purpose should be the revival of a working economy in the world so as to permit the emergence of political and social conditions in which free institutions can exist. Such assistance, I am convinced, must not be on a piecemeal basis as various crises develop. Any assistance that this Government may render in the future should provide a cure rather than a mere palliative. Any government that is willing to assist in the task of recovery will find full co-operation, I am sure, on the part of the United States Government. Any government which maneuvers to block the recovery of other countries cannot expect help from us. Furthermore, governments, political parties, or groups which seek to perpetuate human misery in order to profit therefrom politically or otherwise will encounter the opposition of the United States.

It is already evident that, before the United States Government can proceed much further in its efforts to alleviate the situation and help start the European world on its way to recovery, there must be some agreement among the countries of Europe as to the requirements of the situation and the part those countries themselves will take in order to give proper effect to whatever action might be undertaken by this Government. It would be neither fitting nor efficacious for this Government to undertake to draw up unilaterally a program designed to place Europe on its feet economically. This is the business of the Europeans. The initiative, I think, must come from Europe. The role of this country should consist of friendly aid in the drafting of a European program and of later support of such a program so far as it may be practical for us to do so. The program should be a joint one, agreed to by a number, if not all European nations.

Document 7.9

"THE SOURCES OF SOVIET CONDUCT"

George Kennan's "Long Telegram" impressed many U.S. policy makers in Washington, including Navy Secretary James Forrestal, who urged Kennan to elaborate on his ideas in a longer report. Kennan obtained permission from Forrestal to publish the resulting essay in the journal Foreign Affairs *in July 1947. Although the essay appeared under the pseudonym "X," since it did not necessarily reflect official government views, it quickly became clear that Kennan was the author and that his opinions enjoyed a good deal of support within the Truman administration. In the essay, Kennan repeated some of the themes covered in the earlier telegram but devoted much more attention to the question of how the United States should respond to the Soviet danger.*

Soviet diplomacy [is] at once easier and more difficult to deal with than the diplomacy of individual aggressive leaders like Napoleon and Hitler. On the one hand it is more sensitive to contrary force, more ready to yield on individual sectors of the diplomatic front when that force is felt to be too strong, and thus more rational in the logic and rhetoric of power. On the other hand it cannot be easily defeated or discouraged by a single victory on the part of its opponents. And the patient persistence by which it is animated means that it can be effectively countered not by sporadic acts which represent the momentary whims of democratic opinion but only by intelligent long-range policies on the part of Russia's adversaries—policies no less steady in their purpose, and no less variegated and resourceful in their application, than those of the Soviet Union itself.

In these circumstances it is clear that the main element of any United States policy toward the Soviet Union must be that of long-term, patient but firm and vigilant containment of Russian expansive tendencies. It is important to note, however, that such a policy has nothing to do with outward histrionics: with threats or blustering or superfluous gestures of outward "toughness." While the Kremlin is basically flexible in its reaction to political realities, it is by no means unamenable to considerations of prestige. Like almost any other government, it can be placed by tactless and threatening gestures in a position where it cannot afford to yield even though this might be dictated by its sense of realism. The Russian leaders are keen judges of human psychology, and as such they are highly conscious that loss of temper and of self-control is never a source of strength in political affairs. They are quick to exploit such evidences of weakness. For these reasons it is a *sine qua non* of successful dealing with Russia that the foreign government in question should remain at all times cool and collected and that its demands on Russian policy should be put forward in such a manner as to leave the way open for a compliance not too detrimental to Russian prestige....

In the light of the above, it will be clearly seen that the Soviet pressure against the free institutions of the western world is something that can be contained by the adroit and vigilant application of counter-force at a series of constantly shifting geographical and political points, corresponding to the shifts and maneuvers of Soviet policy, but which cannot be charmed or talked out of existence. The Russians look forward to a duel of infinite duration, and they see that already they have scored great successes. It must be borne in mind that there was a time when the Communist Party represented far more of a minority in the sphere of Russian national life than Soviet power today represents in the world community. . . .

It would be an exaggeration to say that American behavior unassisted and alone could exercise a power of life and death over the Communist movement and bring about the early fall of Soviet power in Russia. But the United States has it in its power to increase enormously the strains under which Soviet policy must operate, to force upon the Kremlin a far greater degree of moderation and circumspection than it has had to observe in recent years, and in this way to promote tendencies which must eventually find their outlet in either the breakup or the gradual mellowing of Soviet power. For no mystical, Messianic movement—and particularly not that of the Kremlin—can face frustration indefinitely without eventually adjusting itself in one way or another to the logic of that state of affairs.

Thus the decision will really fall in large measure in this country itself. The issue of Soviet-American relations is in essence a test of the overall worth of the United States as a nation among nations. To avoid destruction the United States need only measure up to its own best traditions and prove itself worthy of preservation as a great nation.

Document 7.10

SPY SCARES AT HOME

After initial ambivalence, Americans warmed quickly to the anticommunist cause. Crucial to this changing public mood was a sense that the United States was under dire threat from communists operating secretly within American society. Such fears stemmed partly from mounting evidence that Americans, including high-ranking government officials, had spied for the Soviets in the 1930s and early 1940s. Spectacular revelations came out especially in public hearings conducted by the Committee on Un-American Activities in the House of Representatives. In the following transcript of a hearing conducted on July 31, 1948, Elizabeth Bentley, an American who was drawn to antifascist causes in the 1930s, discussed her activities as a spy for Moscow between 1938 and 1945. Her questioners are Robert E. Stripling, the chief investigator for the committee, and Representative John E. Rankin, a Democrat from Mississippi.

Mr. Stripling: Miss Bentley, were you ever a member of the Communist Party of the United States?

Miss Bentley: Yes; I was.

Mr. Stripling: When did you join?

Miss Bentley: March, 1935. . . .

Mr. Stripling: Would you tell the committee the circumstances under which you were recruited into the party?

Miss Bentley: Yes. I had come back from a year in Italy quite upset about Fascist conditions there. On my return I met a number of Communists . . . and they got me into the American League Against War and Fascism, which was interested in my impressions of Italy. After that they gradually got me into the Communist Party. . . .

Mr. Stripling: Miss Bentley, are you acquainted with an individual or were you acquainted with an individual named Jacob Golos?

Miss Bentley: Yes; I was.

Mr. Stripling: When did you first meet Jacob Golos?

Miss Bentley: In October 1938.

Mr. Stripling: Would you give us the circumstances under which you met him, please?

Miss Bentley: Yes. I think about 3 or 4 months before I met him I had, through Columbia University, obtained a position with the Italian Library of Information, which I had discovered to be a part of the Italian Government Propaganda Ministry. I had discovered they were circulating Fascist propaganda, and I had gone to Communist Party headquarters and requested someone who could use this information to be distributed to anti-Fascist organizations for their use. I was then introduced to Mr. Jacob Golos. . . .

Mr. Stripling: Did Mr. Golos ever ask you to perform any special duties for him in connection with any work that he was doing for the Communist Party in behalf of the Soviet Union?

Miss Bentley: Later on; yes. . . .

Mr. Stripling: When was that?

Miss Bentley: At about the start of the Russian-German war which would be around June or July of 1941.

Mr. Stripling: What did he ask you to do?

Miss Bentley: He asked me to take charge of individuals and groups. This was a gradual process, not all at once. It was to take charge of individuals and groups who were employed in the United States Government and in positions to furnish information.

Mr. Stripling: What kind of information?

Miss Bentley: All sorts of information—political, military, whatever they could lay their hands on. . . .

Mr. Stripling: Would you tell the committee how this espionage organization operated and your participation in it?

Miss Bentley: It started with actual Government employees in about July 1941, when he told me that he had received from [U.S. Communist Party leader] Earl Browder the name of a man working for the United States Government, who was interested in helping in getting information to Russia and who could organize a group of other Government employees to help in this work.

Mr. Rankin: What kind of employees?

Miss Bentley: Government employees. . . .

Mr. Stripling: Who was the individual?

Miss Bentley: N. Gregory Silvermaster. . . .

Mr. Stripling: In what agency of the Government was Mr. Silvermaster employed at that time?

Miss Bentley: He was with the Farm Security Administration in the Agriculture Department, and then in 1943, briefly, perhaps 6 months or so, he was in the [Bureau of Economic Warfare]. . . .

Mr. Rankin: I want to know where he is now. . . . Is he on the Federal pay roll now? . . .

Mr. Stripling: Mr. Rankin, he resigned last year when his salary was cut from $10,000 to $8,000. . . . At the time he resigned he was in [the War Assets Administration].

Mr. Rankin: You mean he was a member of the Communist Party at that time?

Miss Bentley: Yes.

Mr. Rankin: An agent of the Communist International? . . .

Miss Bentley: Probably an agent of the NKVD would be more correct.

Mr. Rankin: That is the Russian Communist secret police?

Miss Bentley: That is correct.

Mr. Rankin: Communists are dedicated to the overthrow of this Government; is that right?

Miss Bentley: That is right.

Mr. Stripling: Now, Miss Bentley, will you continue with your testimony? ... You were a courier?

Miss Bentley: I was the person who made trips to Washington and picked up the material and brought it back to Mr. Golos.

Mr. Stripling: How often did you come to Washington?

Miss Bentley: About every 2 weeks.

Mr. Stripling: Can you name any other individuals that you know of your own knowledge were members of this group, this espionage group?

Miss Bentley: Yes....

Mr. Stripling: Were there any ... individuals in the Treasury Department who were working with your group?

Miss Bentley: Yes; Harry Dexter White.

Mr. Stripling: What was Mr. White's position?

Miss Bentley: I believe he was Assistant Secretary of the Treasury.

Document 7.11

AMERICAN DESPAIR OVER CHINA

China's long-running civil war culminated on October 1, 1949, when Mao Zedong's communist armies completed their conquest of the mainland and proclaimed the formation of the People's Republic of China. Coming on top of the successful Soviet test of an atomic bomb in August 1949, developments in China seemed to many Americans to indicate that the tide of the Cold War was suddenly running strongly against the West. Yet the communist victory in China was neither as abrupt nor surprising as many Americans believed. Policy makers had foreseen that outcome for many months. In the following report issued on February 28, 1949, the National Security Council acknowledged the inevitability of Mao's triumph and considered how Washington should respond.

As anticipated, the Communists have shattered, although they have not yet completely destroyed, the power of the National Government. They now look southward across the Yangtze and westward across the mountains watching the fragmentation of non-communist China and pondering by what means and at what tempo they should proceed to bring the rest of

China under their sway. These are tactical questions, the answers to which turn on a variety of complex and fluid factors. . . . It is sufficient here to recognize that (a) preponderant power has now clearly passed to the Communists, (b) although a remnant of the National Government may survive in South China or Formosa for months or years to come, it will at best be a local regime with its claims to international recognition based on insubstantial legalisms and (c) eventually most or all of China will come under Communist rule.

The fruits of victory in a revolution are responsibility. Now for the Communists comes the pay-off. Manchuria and North China are already theirs. They have moved from caves to chancelleries and for the first time are confronted with urban and national problems. For a long time to come these problems are going to grow rather than diminish. . . . The disciplined administration of their sprawling domain, possessing no tradition of strong, centralized government but rather beset by stubborn regional tendencies, is likely to constitute a formidable task for Mao Tse-tung. The Chinese Communists are not taking over an existing centralized state apparatus as the Communists in Czechoslovakia did but are having to build from the ground up. . . .

The natural points of conflict between the Chinese Communists and the USSR have not yet developed. The vestiges of American "intervention" still serve the Chinese communists as a rationalization for equating their interests with those of the USSR. This is so notwithstanding obvious Kremlin cupidity in northern Manchuria, its extra-territorial activities in Sinkiang and the dispatch of the Soviet Ambassador with the National Foreign Office to Canton. The full force of nationalism remains to be released in Communist China. . . .

Our present position is not a happy one. The new China emerging in the north is deeply suspicious of and hostile to us—and is likely to continue to be so for a long time to come. As for our policy of aid to the Nationalists, it is now beyond question of doubt that any further military program for the Chinese mainland will in the foreseeable future (a) be ineffectual, (b) eventually contribute to the military strength of the Communists and (c) perhaps most important of all, solidify the Chinese people in support of the Communists and perpetuate the delusion that China's interests lie with the USSR.

It is even questionable whether we have anything to gain from political support of any of the remaining anti-communist public figures in China. . . . The only vital political resistance to the Chinese Communists is something that is not yet evident. That force will take time to appear and develop; but inevitably it will, simply because a China under the Communists will breed it just as surely as Chiang's Kuomintang was the forcing ground of the Communists. It will and must necessarily be a grass-roots movement finding its expression in native Chinese forms.

We shall therefore find ourselves before long entering upon a period when the Kremlin and we shall find ourselves in reversed roles. The Kremlin is going to try to influence, probably more than we, the course of events in China. And it will not be easy, as we can testify with feeling. We shall be seeking to discover, nourish and bring to power a new revolution, a revolution which may eventually have to come to a test of arms with the Chinese Communists, if it cannot in the meantime so modify the composition and character of the Chinese Communists that they become a truly independent government, existing in amicable relations with the world community.

This is obviously a long-term proposition. There is, however, no short-cut. Consequently we have no sound alternative but to accommodate our native impatience to this fact. The Kremlin waited twenty-five years for the fulfillment of its revolution in China. We may have to persevere as long or longer.

Document 7.12

PROTESTING THE NATO ALLIANCE

The Soviet blockade of West Berlin and other signs of mounting East-West tensions in Europe led the Truman administration to abandon America's long tradition of avoiding peacetime military alliances and to back U.S. membership in the North Atlantic Treaty, signed on April 4, 1949. That step unsurprisingly angered Soviet leaders. In the following letter to U.S. Secretary of State Dean Acheson four days before the signing, the Soviet ambassador in Washington, Alexander Paniushkin, spells out Soviet objections to the treaty.

Among the great powers only the Soviet Union is excluded from the number of the parties to this treaty, which may only be explained by the fact that this Treaty is directed against the Soviet Union. . . .

To justify the conclusion of the North Atlantic Treaty, reference is made to the fact that the Soviet Union has defensive treaties with the countries of people's democracy. However, these references are completely untenable.

All the treaties of the Soviet Union on friendship and mutual assistance with the countries of people's democracy have a bilateral character and are directed solely against the possibility of a repetition of German aggression, the danger of which no single peace-loving nation can forget. In this connection the possibility of interpreting them as treaties in any degree directed against the Allies of the USSR in the last war, against the United States or Great Britain or France, is entirely excluded. . . .

[T]he North Atlantic Treaty is not a bilateral but a multilateral treaty which creates a closed grouping of states and, what is particularly important, entirely ignores the possibility of a repetition of German aggression, not having consequently as its aim the prevention of a new German aggression. . . .

The carrying out under present peace-time conditions by the United States in cooperation with Great Britain and France of extensive military measures, including an increase in all types of armed forces, the drafting of a plan for the utilization of the atomic weapon, the stockpiling of atomic bombs, which are a purely offensive weapon, the construction of a network of military air and naval bases, and so forth—have by no means a defensive character. . . .

The North Atlantic Treaty is designed to frighten states which do not agree to submit to the dictates of the Anglo-American grouping of powers, which aspire to world domination, although the second World War, which ended with the defeat of fascist Germany, which also aspired to world domination, confirmed anew the untenability of such pretensions. . . .

At the same time one cannot but see the groundlessness of the anti-Soviet motives of the North Atlantic Treaty, since as everyone knows the Soviet Union does not intend to attack anyone and in no way threatens either the United States of America, Great Britain, France, or other parties to the Treaty.

Document 7.13

AN APPEAL FOR CALM

By 1949, anticommunist fervor was increasingly sweeping the United States, a process that would culminate in the McCarthyite heyday of the early 1950s. Those who dissented from the general drift of American politics did so at the risk of their reputations and sometimes their jobs. Nevertheless, a few individuals and publications spoke up about the increasingly intolerant mood in the United States. One such publication was the Hartford Courant, *which printed an editorial on June 19, 1949, entitled "Are We Afraid of Freedom?"*

Over all of us hangs the threat of communism. Though the cold war with Soviet Russia is not now being fought with arms, it is a deadly war. The overwhelming proportion of the American people have been convinced by three decades of Soviet history, and especially by Soviet actions in the four years since the war, that the masters of Russia plot our downfall. Whatever twisted ideals may lie behind communism, its aim is to conquer the world and make it a police state ruled from Moscow. Where opposing forces are weak, the Communist threat takes the shape of military might. But most dangerous is the insidious penetration of ideas.

How are we to defend ourselves against this double attack? If we stop to think, we know it is silly to fear Russian arms. Despite Russia's vast resources, it is inconceivable that there is a present danger that the Russian Army, Navy, and Air Force—even with the atomic bomb—can conquer us. The real danger is not the armed strength of the Russian national state but the subtle, intangible penetration of ideas.

It is when it comes to defending ourselves against this attack on the mind that Americans differ among themselves. Many among us rush to em- brace the seemingly natural way of seeking to stamp out Communist ideas. Hence the current wave of loyalty purges, censorship, suppression, snooping, and intimidation. Yet these are the very stuff of which the police state is made. If we resort to them, we shall fasten upon ourselves the very chains we want to keep off.

The only way to fight dangerous ideas is with ideas that are more magnetic. And we have them, if we will but trust them. They run through our history from the beginning. . . . Yet now many would, in the name of freedom, turn their backs on freedom. The House Committee on Un-American Activities would examine textbooks in schools and colleges. We laughed at, and scorned, Hitler's book burnings. But in what essential is this different? And so it is in all the other places, whether in the Atomic Energy Commission, elsewhere in government, in labor, and wherever Americans look with distrust upon their neighbors. . . .

Why should we fear communism? It is neither so new nor so fearsome as it seems. All that is new is the technique of fifth-column infiltration. And even that is only a new twist in the old game of conquest. The basic threat of ideas we have met before in our history. It is no defense to persecute individuals for what they think or for their motives, still less because some self-appointed patriot points an accusing finger at them. . . .

Acts of spying or of sedition are punishable now as they always have been. Through it all we shall be strongest if we prosecute individuals, not for what they say or think, but only for what they do. When acts of subversion are proved in court, let punishment be swift, sure, and relentless. . . .

In this land of freedom the danger from communism is not nearly so great as the danger from suppression. To fear communism is to ascribe to it a strength it does not have. It is fantastic to suppose that Americans can be tricked into trading freedom, the hope of mankind that they hold in trust, for communism. Students in our schools and colleges, our people in government or out of it, are not such fools and weaklings as to fall for the dark, conspiratorial philosophy of communism—unless by prohibition we indicate to them that it has a fascination we dare not face. If communism were really as strong as that, nothing we could do, no wall of defense we built, no suppression by methods as ruthless as those of Russia's own secret police, could keep it out.

Document 7.14

MCCARTHY'S ACCUSATIONS

McCarthyism involved countless individuals and organizations and was supported by innumerable ordinary Americans. Yet Joseph McCarthy, the junior senator from Wisconsin, was indisputably the most celebrated and visible anticommunist activist of the Red Scare era of the late 1940s and early 1950s. McCarthy seized the spotlight especially after delivering the following speech in Wheeling, West Virginia, on February 9, 1950. Although some details of the speech are still disputed (including the number of communists whom he claimed to have identified in the State Department), there is no question that he delivered a stinging attack on the Truman administration's handling of U.S. foreign policy, reaping immediate short-term political benefits.

Five years after a world war has been won, men's hearts should anticipate a long peace—and men's minds should be free from the heavy weight that comes with war. But this is not such a period—for this is not a period of peace. This is a time of "the cold war." This is a time when all the world is split into two vast, increasingly hostile armed camps—a time of a great armament race.

Today we can almost physically hear the mutterings and rumblings of an invigorated god of war. You can see it, feel it, and hear it all the way from the Indochina hills, from the shores of Formosa, right over into the very heart of Europe itself.

The one encouraging thing is that the "mad moment" has not yet arrived for the firing of the gun or the exploding of the bomb which will set civilization about the final task of destroying itself. . . .

The great difference between our western Christian world and the atheistic Communist world is not political, gentlemen, it is moral. For instance, the Marxian idea of confiscating the land and factories and running the entire economy as a single enterprise is momentous. Likewise, Lenin's invention of the one-party police state as a way to make Marx's idea work is hardly less momentous. . . .

The real, basic difference, however, lies in the religion of immoralism . . . invented by Marx, preached feverishly by Lenin, and carried to unimaginable extremes by Stalin. This religion of immoralism, if the Red half of the world triumphs—and well it may, gentlemen—this religion of immoralism will more deeply wound and damage mankind than any conceivable economic or political system....

Today we are engaged in a final, all-out battle between communistic atheism and Christianity. The modern champions of communism have selected this as the time, and ladies and gentlemen, the chips are down—they are truly down....

Six years ago ... there was within the Soviet orbit, 180,000,000 people. Lined up on the antitotalitarian side there were in the world at that time, roughly 1,625,000,000 people. Today, only six years later, there are 800,000,000 people under the absolute domination of Soviet Russia—an increase of over 400 percent. On our side, the figure has shrunk to around 500,000,000. In other words, in less than six years, the odds have changed from 9 to 1 in our favor to 8 to 5 against us. This indicates the swiftness of the tempo of Communist victories and American defeats in the cold war....

The reason why we find ourselves in a position of impotency is not because our only powerful potential enemy has sent men to invade our shores ... but rather because of the traitorous actions of those who have been treated so well by this Nation. It has not been the less fortunate, or members of minority groups who have been traitorous to this Nation, but rather those who have had all the benefits that the wealthiest Nation on earth has had to offer ... the finest homes, the finest college education and the finest jobs in government we can give.

This is glaringly true in the State Department. There the bright young men who are born with silver spoons in their mouths are the ones who have been most traitorous....

I have here in my hand a list of 205 ... a list of names that were made known to the Secretary of State as being members of the Communist Party and who nevertheless are still working and shaping policy in the State Department.

8

The Korean War and the Cold War of the 1950s

The Cold War took an ominous turn in 1950. Open hostilities erupted on the Korean Peninsula, which had been split at the thirty-eighth parallel at the end of World War II. Troops and tanks from the communist north poured into the pro-Western south. What many historians interpret today as a civil war between Koreans immediately appeared to policy makers around the world, and in Washington in particular, as part of a global communist assault orchestrated by Beijing and Moscow. American policy makers responded with force, vowing to defend the southern regime, while plotting as well a long-term evolution of American society and military planning capable of defeating the global communist threat over time.

They soon split over exactly how much force they might best employ in Korea and beyond. President Harry S. Truman in particular wanted South Korea liberated, but not at the cost of a broader war in Asia against Chinese and Soviet troops. Others, most notably the American commander in the region, General Douglas MacArthur, believed there should be no limits on the American war effort against global communism. This clash between Truman and MacArthur became one of the signature moments in the struggle between civilian and military control of American war making in the nation's history. The struggle also encapsulated the broad questions of the 1950s for American policy makers: how much was enough to secure American interests and Washington's allies, and how much—in defense spending, domestic surveillance of communist threats, or the size of government itself—would undermine the very freedom they hoped to defend. At the moment MacArthur lost his job for too often and too vocally endorsing a wholesale assault on communism, including perhaps even the use of atomic weapons, Truman's White House embraced the National Security Council's NSC-68, a global blueprint for vastly expanding the national security state. Such debates continued within Washington's highest policy-making circles even after Republicans regained control of the White House under Dwight D. Eisenhower.

Eisenhower in fact presided over the very massive expansion of federal power he personally loathed. He had long preached against the dangers of a "garrison state," yet he proved largely powerless in the end to constrain the Cold War state's reach into most facets of American life. By the close of his presidency, federal power was pervasive as never before in arenas as diverse as transportation policy, higher education, science funding, and industrial planning. He entered office on a wave of optimism, catalyzed later in 1953 when Joseph Stalin's death seemed to create an opening for reduced East-West tensions and a toned-down Cold War. Soviet and American leaders even met in Switzerland for face-to-face talks, but though the "spirit of Geneva" offered promise of improved relations, little of substance resulted. Both countries wielded increasingly powerful militaries as the decade wore on, each increasingly wary of the other.

More government power did not equal greater security. To many Americans and many neutral observers throughout the world, communism held the upper hand in the global struggle. It was the Soviet Union that launched the world's first outer-space satellite. So too did communists control China and other populous regions of Asia. They seemed on the march throughout the continent, ejecting French colonials from Indochina and threatening to expand throughout Southeast Asia. Eastern Europe and the Soviet Union itself enjoyed unprecedented rates of growth, spurred by the reconstruction of their war-torn region. Victory seemed hardly assured in the global Cold War struggle pitting capitalism against communism, but thoughtful observers placing bets at the close of the 1950s might have received good odds by betting on Moscow and Beijing.

Document 8.1

TRUMAN RESPONDS TO FIGHTING IN KOREA

Pyongyang's assault took American policy makers by surprise. They immediately interpreted the attack as part of a global communist effort to undermine Washington and its allies throughout the world. In his first official statement following the attack, President Truman described the immediate actions his government and military took to defend Seoul's government, but of equal import, he also described the global nature of the conflict and the worldwide response as an effort to save the still teething United Nations. In a speech on June 27, 1950, that used language similar to his 1947 Truman Doctrine, the president described the communist assault as proof of his earlier warnings.

In Korea the Government forces, which were armed to prevent border raids and to preserve internal security, were attacked by invading forces from North Korea. The Security Council of the United Nations called upon the invading troops to cease hostilities and to withdraw to the 38th parallel. This they have not done, but on the contrary have pressed the attack. The Security Council called upon all members of the United Nations to render every assistance to the United Nations in the execution of this resolution. In these circumstances I have ordered United States air and sea forces to give the Korean Government troops cover and support.

The attack upon Korea makes it plain beyond all doubt that communism has passed beyond the use of subversion to conquer independent nations and will now use armed invasion and war. It has defied the orders of the Security Council of the United Nations issued to preserve international peace and security. In these circumstances the occupation of Formosa by Communist forces would be a direct threat to the security of the Pacific area and to United States forces performing their lawful and necessary functions in that area.

Accordingly I have ordered the 7th Fleet to prevent any attack on Formosa. As a corollary of this action I am calling upon the Chinese Government on Formosa to cease all air and sea operations against the mainland. The 7th Fleet will see that this is done. The determination of the future status of Formosa must await the restoration of security in the Pacific, a peace settlement with Japan, or consideration by the United Nations.

I have also directed that United States Forces in the Philippines be strengthened and that military assistance to the Philippine Government be accelerated.

I have similarly directed acceleration in the furnishing of military assistance to the forces of France and the Associated States in Indochina and the dispatch of a military mission to provide close working relations with those forces.

I know that all members of the United Nations will consider carefully the consequences of this latest aggression in Korea in defiance of the Charter of the United Nations. A return to the rule of force in international affairs would have far-reaching effects. The United States will continue to uphold the rule of law.

Document 8.2

WASHINGTON'S ORDERS FOR MACARTHUR

Truman saw Beijing's and Moscow's fingerprints all over Pyongyang's invasion, but this did not mean he desired a global war against communism. On the contrary, American forces were woefully ill-prepared to fight in Korea, and to some eyes equally unprepared to counter potential communist assaults elsewhere in the world, including Europe. The overall American theater commander, General MacArthur, was thus instructed to find some means of liberating South Korea without enlarging the war. Rollback of communism might have been on MacArthur's agenda even as he struggled to maintain a foothold on the peninsula, but it clearly caused great consternation among American strategists back in Washington. MacArthur was one of the most storied—and self-confident—military commanders in American history. An avowed anticommunist, he considered his knowledge of Asia superior to that of anyone in Washington and believed his strategic decision making superior even to the president's. Truman had to treat his wildly popular commander carefully, and thus with communist troops retreating north following the successful Inchon invasion, the two met face-to-face in October 1950 at Wake Island to ensure concurrence on American policy on ending the war without encouraging Chinese or Soviet participation. This summary of their discussion reflects not only MacArthur's general optimism but also the respectful yet tense tone both the commander in chief and the theater commander employed with each other.

The President asked General MacArthur to state the rehabilitation situation with reference to Korea.

General MacArthur: It cannot occur until the military operations have ended. I believe that formal resistance will end throughout North and South Korea by Thanksgiving. There is little resistance left in South Korea—only about 15,000 men—and those we do not destroy, the winter will. We now have about 60,000 prisoners in compounds.

In North Korea, unfortunately, they are pursuing a forlorn hope. They have about 100,000 men who were trained as replacements. They are poorly trained, led and equipped, but they are obstinate and it goes against my grain to have to destroy them. They are only fighting to save face. Orientals prefer to die than to lose face....

It is my hope to be able to withdraw the Eighth Army to Japan by Christmas. That will leave the X Corps, which will be reconstituted, composed of the Second and Third divisions and UN detachments. I hope the United Nations will hold elections by the first of the year. Nothing is gained by military occupation. All occupations are failures. (The President nodded agreement)....

[Army] Secretary [Frank] Pace: When the Army's responsibility ends, could the Army provide aid in psychological rehabilitation? Should KMAG [Korean Military Advisory Group] continue?

General MacArthur: The KMAG group has been wonderful. As far as the military mission is concerned, I think it should be continued indefinitely. I want to pay high tribute to that group. I believe that 500 officers and men should be continued indefinitely. At the start of rehabilitation the Army will have to continue until the civil rehabilitation is organized. It should be organized as rapidly as possible. The United Nations should take it over. You will have a hard job getting good men to serve in Korea. It is not a nice place....

The President: What are the chances for Chinese or Soviet interference?

General MacArthur: Very little. Had they interfered in the first or second months it would have been decisive. We are no longer fearful of their intervention. We no longer stand hat in hand. The Chinese have 300,000 men in Manchuria. Of these probably not more than 100/125,000 are distributed along the Yalu River. Only 50/60,000 could be gotten across the Yalu River. They have no Air Force. Now that we have bases for our Air Force in Korea, if the Chinese tried to get down to Pyongyang there would be the greatest slaughter.

With the Russians it is a little different. They have an Air Force in Siberia and a fairly good one, with excellent pilots equipped with some jets and B-25 and B-29 planes. They can put 1,000 planes in the air with some 2/300 more from the Fifth and Seventh Soviet Fleets. They are probably no match for our Air Force. The Russians have no ground troops available for North Korea. They would have difficulty putting troops into the field. It would take six weeks to get a division across and six weeks brings the winter. The only other combination would be Russian air support of Chinese ground troops. Russian air is deployed in a semicircle through Mukden and Harbin, but the coordination between the Russian air and the Chinese ground would be so flimsy that I believe Russian air would bomb the Chinese as often as they would bomb us. Ground support is a very difficult thing to do. Our Marines do it perfectly. They have been trained for it. Our own Air and Ground Forces are not as good as the Marines but they are effective. Between untrained Air and Ground Forces an air umbrella is impossible without a lot of joint training. I believe it just wouldn't work with Chinese Communist ground and Russian air. We are the best.

[Presidential Aide W. Averell] Harriman: What about war criminals?

General MacArthur: Don't touch the war criminals. It doesn't work. The Nurnberg trials and Tokyo trials were no deterrent. In my own right I can handle those who have committed atrocities and, if we catch them, I intend to try them immediately by military commission. . . .

The President: I would like to hear your views, General, on a possible Pacific pact, or some other arrangements similar to that in the Atlantic.

General MacArthur: A Pacific pact would be tremendous, but due to the lack of homogeneity of the Pacific nations, it would be very difficult to put into effect. If the President would make an announcement like the Truman Doctrine, which would be a warning to the predatory nations, it would have a great effect. It is not possible to get a pact, since they are so non-homogeneous. They have no military forces. Only the United States has the forces. All they want is the assurance of security from the United States. The President should follow up this conference with a ringing pronouncement. I believe that at this time, after the military successes and the President's trip, it would have more success than a Pacific pact....

MR. HARRIMAN: When you speak of the Truman Doctrine, do you mean direct external aggression or do you mean the type of thing that has been going on in Indo-China and has previously occurred in Greece to which the Truman Doctrine was directed?

GENERAL MACARTHUR: I am referring to direct aggression. The situation in Indo-China is puzzling. The French have 150,000 of their best troops there with an officer of the highest reputation in command. Their forces are twice what we had in the perimeter and they are opposed by half of what the North Koreans had. I cannot understand why they do not clean it up. They should be able to do so in four months yet we have recently seen a debacle. This brings up a question of far deeper concern. What is the capacity and caliber of the French Army? In the First World War they were excellent. In the Second World War they were poor. The present French soldier is doubtful. If the French won't fight we are up against it because the defense of Europe hinges upon them. They have the flower of the French Army in Indochina and they are not fighting. If this is so, no matter what supplies we pour in they may be of no use. The loss of territory in itself is nothing, but the French failure is broader than this. I cannot understand it.

THE PRESIDENT: I cannot understand it either.

ADMIRAL [ARTHUR] RADFORD: The French seem to have no popular backing from the local Indo-Chinese. The French must train native troops. The rest of Southeast Asia—Burma, Siam—is wide open if the Chinese Communists pursue a policy of aggression. We probably have more chance of assisting in Indo-China than anywhere else. We must stiffen the backbone of the French....

THE PRESIDENT: This is the most discouraging thing we face. [Presidential emissary Philip] Jessup and others have worked on the French tooth and nail to try and persuade them to do what the Dutch had done in Indonesia but the French have not been willing to listen. If the French Prime Minister comes to see me, he is going to hear some very plain talk. I am going to talk cold turkey to him. If you don't want him to hear that kind of talk, you had better keep him away from me.

Document 8.3

MACARTHUR'S WAR PLANS

Total victory seemed in sight in November 1950, and MacArthur informed Washington of his decision to drive to the Yalu River, the historic Chinese-Korean border. The White House did not disapprove of this decision, but what stands out is the language and rationale MacArthur used to justify his conquest of Korea. Dramatic rhetoric in this November 9, 1950, message to the Joint Chiefs of Staff reveals at once the magnitude of the global struggle many perceived underway as the Cold War grew in scope, the potential stakes of failure, and the potential political costs of opposing any effort to defeat communism by whatever means necessary. Fearful of an escalating global struggle, Truman relieved MacArthur of his command when the general once too often refused to follow his commander in chief's orders not to call for a broadening of the war beyond the Korean Peninsula.

In my opinion it would be fatal to weaken the fundamental and basic policy of the United Nations to destroy all resisting armed forces in Korea and bring that country into a united and free nation. I believe that with my air power, now unrestricted so far as Korea is concerned except as to hydroelectric installations, I can deny reinforcements coming across the Yalu in sufficient strength to prevent the destruction of those forces now arrayed against me in North Korea. I plan to launch my attack for this purpose on or about November 15 with the mission of driving to the border and securing all of North Korea. Any program short of this would completely destroy the morale of my forces and its psychological consequence would be inestimable. It would condemn us to an indefinite retention of our military forces along difficult defense lines in North Korea and would unquestionably arouse such resentment among the South Koreans that their forces would collapse or might even turn against us. It would therefore necessitate immediately a large increment of increase in foreign troops. That the Chinese Communists after having achieved the complete success of establishing themselves within North Korea would abide by any delimitations upon further expansion southward would represent wishful thinking at its very worst.

The widely reported British desire to appease the Chinese Communists by giving them a strip of Northern Korea finds its historical precedent in the action taken at Munich on 29 Sept 1938 by Great Britain, France and Italy where in the Sudeten Lands, the strategically important Bohemian mountain bastion, were ceded to Germany without the participation of Czechoslo- vakia and indeed against the protest of the [government]. Within 10 months following acquisition of that vital strategic bastion, Germany had seized the resulting impotent Czechoslovakia declaring it had ceased to exist as a sovereign state and that the Reich forces would thereafter preserve order. Of that settlement our own State Department had this to say in its public document "Postwar Foreign Policy Preparation [1939–1945]," page 14:

"The crisis occasioned by the German occupation of Austria in March 1938 was followed by the Munich crisis in Sept., when the weakness of peaceful efforts toward just settlements in the face of determined aggression was unmistakably demonstrated."

This observation of the State Department points unmistakably to the lessons of history. I am unaware of a single exception which would cast doubt upon the validity of this concept. In the case of the United Nations such action would carry within itself the germs of its own ultimate destruction, for which it would bare its own weakness requiring that it limit the imposition of its decisions and orders upon the weak, not the strong. It is tribute to aggression which encourages that very international lawlessness which it is the fundamental duty of the United Nations to curb.

To give up any portion of North Korea to the aggression of the Chinese Communists would be the greatest defeat of the free world in recent times. . . .

I recommend with all the earnestness that I possess that there be no weakening at this critical moment and that we press on to complete victory which I believe can be achieved if our determination and indomitable will do not desert us.

Document 8.4

A British Intervention in Washington

Unbeknownst to MacArthur's command, tens of thousands of Chinese troops had infiltrated North Korea without notice by November 1950. On November 1, more than a week before MacArthur boasted of victory and assailed his critics as "appeasers," American and Chinese troops directly fought for the first time. The latter did not follow up their initial successes, choosing instead to pull back despite the opportunity of routing some American troops. MacArthur pressed forward undaunted, announcing a "home by Christmas" campaign. On November 25 the Chinese attacked in force, sending the United Nations command reeling. The war quickly entered a more desperate and bloodier phase. Word of UN forces' retreat down the Korean Peninsula fueled rumor that MacArthur would stem the tide with atomic weapons. Fearful that the very expanded war no one desired was suddenly upon them, British Prime Minister Clement Attlee flew at once to Washington to confer with Truman. Minutes from their meeting reveal divisions between the two close allies not only over what to do with Korea but also over how to wage the Cold War more broadly. Truman appeared dovish to MacArthur; but in this December 4, 1950, meeting with Attlee, the president appeared practically as a warmonger, deploying a version of the domino theory popularized by the subsequent administration.

The Prime Minister said that he was very glad to be here and appreciated the President's willingness to see him. He, like the President, felt that they must take a broad view on a wide horizon. A first point was the maintenance of the prestige and authority of the United Nations. (The President expressed agreement.) The United States is the principal instrument for supporting the United Nations, and the United Kingdom is giving what help it can. This problem has now become very difficult with the Chinese Communists coming in. It is common to our thinking that we wish the Korean business to be limited to asserting the authority of the United Nations against aggression in Korea. We all realize that other forces might come in and might bring another world war. We are very eager to avoid the extension of the conflict. If our forces become engaged in China, it will weaken us elsewhere. (The President agreed.) As the President has said, the United Kingdom and France have other Asian interests, but it would help the Russians if we were fully engaged in Asia. (The President again agreed.). . . . We must not get so involved in the East as to lay ourselves open to attack in the West. The West is, after all, the vital part in our line against communism. . . .

Secretary Acheson, at the request of the President, commented on the points which had been made by the Prime Minister. In the first place, we had to bear in mind that the central enemy is not the Chinese but the Soviet Union. All the inspiration for the present action comes from there. There has no doubt been some arrangement between the Chinese and the Russians to make the Chinese think they have strong Russian support. While their counterattack goes well, there is little limit to what they will try to do; if they can drive us out, they will do so. No one knows how much further they might be inclined to go. The situation is already serious. Regarding the question of all-out war against China, if this meant land, sea, and air action, there were not many of the President's advisers who would urge him to follow that course. . . .

He wished to return again to the attitude of the Chinese Communists. He agreed that they do not think of this as being the United Nations against them. He referred to the editorial which appeared in *Pravda* yesterday, and the theme that the matter should be treated as an issue of military power between the Soviet Union, the Chinese Communists, and the United States. The Chinese Communists were not looking at the matter as Chinese but as communists who are subservient to Moscow. All they do is based on the Moscow pattern, and they are better pupils even than the Eastern European satellites. The Russians are no doubt pleased with the idea that we might be fully engaged in war with the Chinese Communists who are acting as their satellites. The questions raised by the Prime Minister were very grave. He referred to the reports of the talks between Sir B. N. Rau and General Wu of the Chinese Communist delegation in New York. The means we should utilize should be considered in the broadest terms in relation to the whole Far East. If Formosa were turned over as a result of aggression, this fact would be exploited in a most devastating way. It is hard to believe that this is merely a burst of Chinese military fervor; and if we give them Formosa and make other concessions, they would then become calm and peaceful. On the contrary, if we give concessions, they will become increasingly aggressive. We may not be able to do anything about this on the mainland, but we can on the islands.

If we yield to the Chinese communists, he questioned whether we would be able to keep the Japanese and the Filipinos in hand. . . .

The Prime Minister inquired what the reaction of people would be if we continued to hold the beachhead with continuing losses. Wouldn't there be a demand for all-out war against China?

The President said that such demands are now being made. We need a united effort at home. Huge appropriations are being made. He hoped that the line could be held in Korea until the situation was better for negotiation. All of his military advisers tell him that there is no chance to do this, but he still wanted to try. . . .

Attlee: opinions differ on the extent to which Chinese Communists are satellites. He inquired when is it that you scratch a communist and find a nationalist.

The President believes they are satellites of Russia and will be satellites so long as the present Peiping regime is in power. He thought they were complete satellites. The only way to meeting communism is to eliminate it. After Korea, it would be Indochina, then Hong Kong, then Malaya.

Document 8.5

FAULKNER'S FEARS

The American writer William Faulkner received the Nobel Prize for Literature at the close of 1950. He used the occasion to suggest the atomic age had brought something profoundly different to the human experience: "There is only one question: When will I be blown up?" Faulkner's words, delivered on December 10, 1950, epitomized the way nuclear-tinged superpower tensions pervaded American life during the 1950s and beyond.

I feel that this award was not made to me as a man, but to my work—a life's work in the agony and sweat of the human spirit, not for glory and least of all for profit, but to create out of the materials of the human spirit something which did not exist before. So this award is only mine in trust. It will not be difficult to find a dedication for the money part of it commensurate with the purpose and significance of its origin. But I would like to do the same with the acclaim too, by using this moment as a pinnacle from which I might be listened to by the young men and women already dedicated to the same anguish and travail, among whom is already that one who will someday stand here where I am standing.

Our tragedy today is a general and universal physical fear so long sustained by now that we can even bear it. There are no longer problems of the spirit. There is only the question: When will I be blown up? Because of this, the young man or woman writing today has forgotten the problems of the human heart in conflict with itself which alone can make good writing because only that is worth writing about, worth the agony and the sweat.

He must learn them again. He must teach himself that the basest of all things is to be afraid; and, teaching himself that, forget it forever, leaving no room in his workshop for anything but the old verities and truths of the heart, the old universal truths lacking which any story is ephemeral and doomed—love and honor and pity and pride and compassion and sacrifice. Until he does so, he labors under a curse. He writes not of love but of lust, of defeats in which nobody loses anything of value, of victories without hope and, worst of all, without pity or compassion. His griefs grieve on no universal bones, leaving no scars. He writes not of the heart but of the glands.

Until he relearns these things, he will write as though he stood among and watched the end of man. I decline to accept the end of man. It is easy enough to say that man is immortal simply because he will endure: that when the last dingdong of doom has clanged and faded from the last worthless rock hanging tideless in the last red and dying evening, that even then there will still be one more sound: that of his puny inexhaustible voice, still talking.

I refuse to accept this. I believe that man will not merely endure: he will prevail. He is immortal, not because he alone among creatures has an inexhaustible voice, but because he has a soul, a spirit capable of compassion and sacrifice and endurance.

Document 8.6

NSC-68

Even before the Korean War broke out, U.S. officials were rethinking their entire Cold War strategy. But the fighting in Korea gave new urgency to the exercise and led to the adoption of a policy statement formally known as National Security

Council Document 68. This document, far too lengthy to reprint here, cast the Soviet threat as existential for the United States and called for unprecedented levels of military spending to counter communism in the 1950s and beyond. The urgency felt by many U.S. policy makers is captured in the following letter by Stuart Symington, chairman of the National Security Resources Board (and later a senator from Missouri). Symington's letter, dated September 5, 1950, accompanied a draft of NSC-68 that was sent to top officials in the Truman administration.

For many years a group of determined men have been pushing with practical realism the religion of communism.

Over 30 years ago some of this group obtained control of one of the world's great nations—Russia.

Since then the most outstanding characteristics of their actions have been:

The extermination of anything which stood in their way toward their often declared objective—a world communist state.

The rapid advancement they have made toward their ultimate goal, as characterized by such developments as:

- In the past 10 years, the communist or communist controlled peoples of the world have increased some 188 million people to over 800 million people.
- In nearly every country of importance in the world the communists now have a well organized, well trained, and militant minority which takes maximum advantage of the tolerance of democratic governments; this is to the extent that the United States and other countries might be sabotaged at the start of a general war to the point where successful continuance of the conflict would be impossible.
- Through clever, consistent, and determined propaganda, more people in the world may now well believe that communism is a better form of government for them than is democracy.

The Soviets have, outside their own country, millions of well trained men organized to fight the battle of communism. As a result, they can continue to bleed the democracies without committing their own troops.

The Soviets are steadily increasing the power of their own army, navy and air force, as well as their stock of atomic bombs and the equipment to deliver the latter. With relatively minor exceptions, everything would now seem to be going according to their schedule for world conquest. Attainment of an adequate stock of atomic bombs appears the only remaining requirement in their plan for world conquest.

To those who have followed these developments over recent years, the grave danger of the current world situation is all too apparent.

If Korea taught us anything, it is that the peace loving democracies cannot afford to wait for additional Soviet aggression before mobilizing to meet that aggression. We must build, now, a defense sufficient not only to cope with other Koreas, but also one which can form the basis for an ultimatum to the Soviets that we will hold them responsible for, and subject to retaliation in case of additional aggression.

An analysis of the scope and character of the current United States military build-up, however, indicates a contemplated build-up that is not adequate to meet the present world situation, particularly when the United States, supposedly the strongest nation, is now with difficulty maintaining its position against Russia's weakest satellite. . . .

The Resources Board believes this current planning will result in a defensive program that is inadequate to meet the current menace to the nation's security.

We believe that the current communist aggression in Korea, plus possible aggression against such other localities as Formosa, Indochina, Japan, Iran, Turkey, Greece, Yugoslavia, Germany, and the United States itself, adds up to a danger that is not being recognized by such piecemeal plans for preparedness.

Document 8.7

IKE WOULD GO TO KOREA

The war dragged on, resembling at times the bloody trench warfare of the First World War. Peace talks appeared stalled, and in late October 1952, the Republican nominee for president, former General Dwight D. Eisenhower, verily secured electoral vic- tory by pledging to personally deliver peace in Korea. In this address of October 25, Eisenhower also signaled to the American electorate and to the watching world that his administration was prepared to wage a renewed Cold War struggle against global communism even if he succeeded in ending the conflict in Korea.

World War II should have taught us all one lesson. The lesson is this: To vacillate, to hesitate—to appease even by merely betraying unsteady purpose—is to feed a dictator's appetite for conquest and to invite war itself. That lesson—which should have firmly guided every great decision of our leadership through these later years—was ignored in the development of the Administration's policies for Asia since the end of World War II. Because it was ignored, the record of these policies is a record of appalling failure. . . .

When the enemy struck, on that June day of 1950, what did America do? It did what it always has done in all its times of peril. It appealed to the heroism of its youth. This appeal was utterly right and utterly inescapable. It was inescapable not only because this was the only way to defend the idea of collective freedom against savage aggression. That appeal was inescapable because there was now in the plight into which we had stumbled no other way to save honor and self-respect.

The answer to that appeal has been what any American knew it would be. It has been sheer valor—valor on all the Korean mountainsides that, each day, bear fresh scars of new graves. Now—in this anxious autumn—from these heroic men there comes back an answering appeal. It is no whine, no whimpering plea. It is a question that addresses itself to simple reason. It asks: Where do we go from here? When comes the end? Is there an end?

My answer—candid and complete—is this: The first task of a new Administration will be to review and re-examine every course of action open to us with one goal in view: To bring the Korean war to an early and honorable end. This is my pledge to the American people. For this task a wholly new Administration is necessary. The reason for this is simple. The old Administration cannot be expected to repair what it failed to prevent. Where will a new Administration begin? It will begin with its President taking a simple, firm resolution. The resolution will be: To forego the diversions of politics and to concentrate on the job of ending the Korean war—until that job is honorably done. That job requires a personal trip to Korea.

I shall make that trip. Only in that way could I learn how best to serve the American people in the cause of peace. I shall go to Korea.... As the next Administration goes to work for peace, we must be guided at every instant by that lesson I spoke of earlier. The vital lesson is this: To vacillate, to appease, to placate is only to invite war—vaster war—bloodier war. In the words of the late Senator [Arthur H.] Vandenberg, appeasement is not the road to peace; it is only surrender on the installment plan. I will always reject appeasement....

In rendering their verdict, the people must judge with courage and with wisdom. For—at this date—any faltering in America's leadership is a capital offense against freedom. In this trial, my testimony, of a personal kind, is quite simple. A soldier all my life, I have enlisted in the greatest cause of my life—the cause of peace. I do not believe it a presumption for me to call the effort of all who have enlisted with me—a crusade.

I use that word only to signify two facts. First: We are united and devoted to a just cause of the purest meaning to all humankind. Second: We know that—for all the might of our effort—victory can come only with the gift of God's help. In this spirit—humble servants of a proud ideal—we do soberly say: This is a crusade.

Document 8.8

EISENHOWER'S CHANCE FOR PEACE

Having promised a global crusade against communism—indeed, Eisenhower would use similar language in private correspondence with British Prime Minister Winston Churchill—the president took office speaking of peace and of a new opportunity for resolution of the Cold War. Soviet leader Joseph Stalin died in March, and his passing spawned optimism throughout Western capitals that perhaps the Cold War would die with him. Eisenhower's speech of April 1953 offers arguably his fullest articulation of his belief that militarism and freedom were at odds. As a career soldier he had seen his share of war and destruction; he knew war's cost. That he oversaw one of the nation's largest military expansions, in particular of nuclear weaponry, underlay the tension he felt throughout his presidency between securing American liberty and protecting American security.

This has been the way of life forged by 8 years of fear and force.

What can the world, or any nation in it, hope for if no turning is found on this dread road?

The worst to be feared and the best to be expected can be simply stated.

The worst is atomic war.

The best would be this: a life of perpetual fear and tension; a burden of arms draining the wealth and the labor of all peoples; a wasting of strength that defies the American system or the Soviet system or any system to achieve true abundance and happiness for the peoples of this earth.

Every gun that is made, every warship launched, every rocket fired signifies, in the final sense, a theft from those who hunger and are not fed, those who are cold and are not clothed.

This world in arms is not spending money alone.

It is spending the sweat of its laborers, the genius of its scientists, the hopes of its children.

The cost of one modern heavy bomber is this: a modern brick school in more than 30 cities.

It is two electric power plants, each serving a town of 60,000 population.

It is two fine, fully equipped hospitals.

It is some fifty miles of concrete pavement.

We pay for a single fighter plane with a half million bushels of wheat.

We pay for a single destroyer with new homes that could have housed more than 8,000 people.

This is, I repeat, the best way of life to be found on the road the world has been taking.

This is not a way of life at all, in any true sense. Under the cloud of threatening war, it is humanity hanging from a cross of iron. These plain and cruel truths define the peril and point the hope that come with this spring of 1953.

This is one of those times in the affairs of nations when the gravest choices must be made, if there is to be a turning toward a just and lasting peace.

It is a moment that calls upon the governments of the world to speak their intentions with simplicity and with honesty.

It calls upon them to answer the question that stirs the hearts of all sane men: is there no other way the world may live?

Document 8.9

DIEN BIEN PHU

Korea was not the Cold War's only hotspot. The war in Northeast Asia ended in a tense armistice in 1953, but global attention and superpower tensions soon moved south. French efforts to reclaim their empire in Indochina, lost to the Japanese in 1941 and then challenged by local nationalists thereafter, came to a conclusion in 1954. Impending defeat at the military outpost of Dien Bien Phu left French leaders in Paris and Saigon reeling, though not before pleading with American officials for direct military intervention. Having largely sponsored and paid for the French effort to date, Washington declined, ironically setting the stage for a direct American takeover of the anticommunist effort in the years to come. As the following April 26, 1954, diary entry from White House Press Secretary James Hagerty makes clear, American policy makers wanted victory in Vietnam, but just as in Korea they proved unable to pay the costs necessary and unsure if victory could even be purchased at any price.

The President said that the French "are weary as hell." He said that it didn't look as though Dienbienphu could hold out for more than a week and would fall possibly sooner. Reported that the British thought that the French were not putting out as much as they could, but that he did not necessarily agree with their viewpoint. "The French go up and down every day—they are very volatile. They think they are a great power one day and they feel sorry for themselves the next day." The President said that if we were to put one combat soldier into Indochina, then our entire prestige would be at stake, not only in that area but throughout the world. . . . The President said the situation looked very grim this morning, but that he and Dulles were doing everything they could to get the free countries to act in concert. In addition, he said "there are plenty of people in Asia, and we can train them to fight well. I don't see any reason for American ground troops to be committed in Indochina, don't think we need it, but we can train their forces and it may be necessary for us eventually to use some of our planes or aircraft carriers off the coast and some of our fighting craft we have in that area for support."

Document 8.10

EUROPE CAUGHT BETWEEN THE SUPERPOWERS

While Washington and Moscow sparred over Asia, many Europeans perceived themselves caught between ever expanding atomic arsenals. In 1955 the French writer and intellectual Raymond Aron fully articulated his view that many Europeans considered the Cold War a fight over who might someday control their graves.

The memories which the peoples have stored up from preceding conflicts and the presentiments which they now harbor as regards a future conflict account for the profound difference between the American and the European consciousness.

For the United States, the two wars of the twentieth century were colonial wars. They were waged—especially the second one—according to the unwritten law of the American economy, namely, the reduction of human costs by the increase of expenditure on machines. A type of combat that does not count the costs of materiel in order to save the lives of soldiers will certainly not be squeamish about the destruction of enemy lives and property in theaters of operation. Such a war of materiel whenever it is being waged upon foreign soil will be waged efficiently, without scruples and without hesitation. It poses some pressing questions for these peoples whose countries serve as battlefields. . . .

The Americans are probably right when they remind us that there is, in the atomic age, one alternative which is worse than war, namely defeat. But Europeans are not wrong when they hold that, in this age, avoidance of war is better than victory. Nor are they wrong when they question the worth of a strategy which places greatest emphasis upon the preparation of that kind of war which would be so horrible that no one will dare start it—except as a last gesture of desperation. . . .

Since two atomic bombs were dropped upon cities the world awaits, perhaps wrongly, the repetition, in the case of total war, of these horrible massacres. It is difficult to imagine an atomic world war without envisaging the destruction of the civilization which we know. . . .

It is possible to compress our findings into the following general statements: Strategies aimed at whole populations, and not merely at armies, have increased tremendously the terrors of war. Secondly, war threatens the very life of civilizations when it is conducted with means of destruction that are vastly superior to available means of construction, and when it effaces the traditions and withers the feeling of security underlying the existence of the human community. We cannot rid ourselves of the dismal feeling that we have entered this danger zone. Are Europeans more deeply convinced that history has reached a crisis than are the American people? Perhaps. The nearness of danger often distorts judgment; it also sharpens awareness of the essential.

Document 8.11

SPUTNIK

Communism appeared on the march in the mid-1950s, nowhere more so than in the embryonic space race. On October 4, 1957, Soviet scientists launched Sputnik, the world's first man-made satellite capable of achieving low Earth orbit. The machine itself, visible with binoculars from the ground, did little more than periodically beep as it circled the globe. But as this cartoon published in the New York

Times *during the second week of October 1957 suggests, if Soviet officials could launch satellites into space aboard high-powered rockets, missiles might be next, and perhaps the day of American vulnerability had finally arrived.*

Documents 8.12

UNREST BEHIND THE IRON CURTAIN

Though chastened by their experience in Korea, many American policy makers, including Secretary of State John Foster Dulles, actively discussed "rolling back" communism from areas considered conquered by Moscow after World War II. American policy makers enthusiastically encouraged the kind of independence and separatism that arose behind the Iron Curtain during the mid-1950, in places such as Poland and Hungary. Buoyed by the prospect of American support, Hungarian nationalists declared independence from the Soviet bloc in late 1956. They were subsequently dispersed and massacred by Soviet troops, leaving little more than the dramatic words of their leader, Imre Nagy, who broadcast this message on November 4, 1959, only hours before his capture by Soviet forces.

This fight is the fight for freedom by the Hungarian people against the Russian intervention, and it is possible that I shall only be able to stay at my post for one or two hours. The whole world will see how the Russian armed forces, contrary to all treaties and conventions, are crushing the resistance of the Hungarian people. They will also see how they are kidnapping the Prime Minister of a country which is a Member of the United Nations, taking him from the capital, and therefore it cannot be doubted at all that this is the most brutal form of intervention. I should like in these last moments to ask the leaders of the revolution, if they can, to leave the country. I ask that all that I have said in my broadcast, and what we have agreed on with the revolutionary leaders during meetings in Parliament, should be put in a memorandum, and the leaders should turn to all the peoples of the world for help and explain that today it is Hungary and tomorrow, or the day after tomorrow, it will be the turn of other countries because the imperialism of Moscow does not know borders, and is only trying to play for time.

Document 8.13

WASHINGTON DEBATES, LAMENTS, AND DEBATES FURTHER

Eisenhower's White House monitored events in Eastern Europe closely, and as the following record of discussion within the National Security Council reveals, rollback was not merely a theoretical matter for those trapped behind the Iron Cur-

tain. But like Korea and Dien Bien Phu, neither did it appear to American policy makers worthy of risking nuclear war over. A recent review of Voice of America and Radio Free Europe broadcasts from 1956 reveals no instance where American material support was promised to Hungary's revolutionaries; at the same time, nearly 40 percent of Hungarian refugees queried after their failed revolt believed the Americans had made just such a promise. In this November 8, 1956, discussion, American leaders recognized their moral complicity in the failed Hungarian uprising but also their limited practical options.

Mr. Dulles went on to describe briefly the European reaction to what the Soviets had done in Hungary, concluding that these Soviet actions had reduced Soviet prestige in Western Europe to its lowest point in years. He ended with the prediction that the rebellion in Hungary would be extinguished in a matter of days, if not in hours. Nevertheless, the Soviets would be faced with a problem in Hungary for many, many years to come. In turn, the situation presents the United States with the problem of what more we can do. . . .

The President said that this was indeed a bitter pill for us to swallow. We say we are at the end of our patience, but what can we do that is really constructive? Should we break off diplomatic relations with the USSR? What would be gained by this action? The Soviets don't care. The whole business was shocking to the point of being unbelievable. And yet many people seemed unconvinced. For example, said the President, he had just had a message from [Indian Prime Minister Jawaharlal] Nehru—or was it a point he made in a recent speech? Wherever it came from, Nehru said that what was really happening in Hungary was obscure. Could anything be blinder? The President also cited [Soviet] Premier [Nikolai] Bulganin's message to him received this morning, in which Bulganin stated in effect that what was going on in Hungary was none of the business of the United States.

Document 8.14

A COLD STABILITY AND ITS CRITICS

By the close of the 1950s, crises like those of Hungary and Sputnik wore on the American people who, like their president, largely understood that the Cold War would be a long and perhaps enduring struggle. Both Moscow and Washington directed empires and militaries too robust for the other to conquer, surely not at an acceptable price, because as President Eisenhower warned, the risk of any crisis spinning out of control far outweighed most potential gains. Out of power for eight years, Democratic challengers for the White House saw things differently. John F. Kennedy ultimately gained his party's nomination, and charged his opponent, Vice President Richard Nixon, with representing an administration unwilling to act—

in Southeast Asia, in Latin America (and Cuba in particular), and in the nuclear arms race itself—in defense of American vital interests. Kennedy accused the White House of allowing a "missile gap," with Soviet strategic forces outpacing American, tipping, he argued, the Cold War's delicate balance too far to Moscow's advantage. Eisenhower and Nixon knew no such missile gap existed yet could not refute Kennedy's charge without simultaneously revealing how they knew: through espionage and the intense clandestine scrutiny of Soviet forces from above. On the campaign trail, therefore, Kennedy frequently held the upper hand in debates, charging Republicans with doing too little to actively win the Cold War and promising a more vigorous foreign policy should he win. This moment in their second presidential debate, October 7, 1960, reveals the way each sought to recast the Cold War struggle in his own terms. Two years and one week later, Kennedy would tell the world that Soviet missile sites were being developed in Cuba, bringing the world closer to the nuclear brink than ever before or since.

Mr. Nixon: No matter how well we're doing in the cold war, we're not doing as well as we should. And that will always be the case as long as the Communists are on the international scene, in the aggressive tac—uh—tendencies that they presently are following. Now as far as the present situation is concerned, I think it's time that we nail a few of these distortions about the United States that have been put out. First of all, we hear that our prestige is at an all-time low. Senator Kennedy has been hitting that point over and over again. I would suggest that after Premier Kush—Khrushchev's uh—performance in the United Nations, compared with President Eisenhower's eloquent speech, that at the present time Communist prestige in the world is at an all-time low and American prestige is at an all-time high. Now that, of course, is just one factor, but it's a significant one. When we look, for example, at the vote on the Congo. We were on one side; they were on the other side. What happened? There were seventy votes for our position and none for theirs. Look at the votes in the United Nations over the past seven and a half years. That's a test of prestige. Every time the United States has been on one side and they've been on the other side, our position has been sustained. Now looking to what we ought to do in the future. In this cold war we have to recognize where it is being fought and then we have to develop programs to deal with it. It's being fought primarily in Asia, in Africa, and in Latin America. What do we need? What tools do we need to fight . . . ? Well we need, for example, economic assistance; we need technical assistance; we need exchange; we need programs of diplomatic and other character which will be effective in that area. Now Senator Kennedy a moment ago referred to the fact that there was not an adequate Voice of America program for Latin America. I'd like to point out that in the last six years, the Democratic Congresses, of which he'd been a member, have cut twenty million dollars off of the Voice of America programs. They also have cut four billion dollars off of mutual security in these last six years. They also have cut two billion dollars off of defense. Now when they talk about our record here, it is well that they recognize that they have to stand up for their record as well. So let me summarize by saying this: I'm not satisfied with what we're doing in the cold war because I believe we have to step up our activities and launch an offensive for the minds and hearts and souls of men. It must be economic; it must be technological; above all it must be ideological. But we've got to get help from the Congress in order to do this.

Mr. Frank McGee, Debate Moderator: Senator Kennedy?

Mr. Kennedy: Of course Mr. Nixon is wholly inaccurate when he says that the Congress has not provided more funds in fact than the President recommended for national defense. Nineteen fifty-three we tried to put an appropriation of five billion dollars for our defenses. I was responsible for the amendment . . . in 1954 to strengthen our ground forces. The Congress of the United States appropriated six hundred and seventy-seven million dollars more than the President was willing to use up till a week ago. Secondly, on the question of our position in the United Nations. We all know about the vote held this week—of the five neutralists—and it was generally regarded as a defeat for the United States. Thirdly, in 1952, there were only seven votes in favor of the admission of Red China into the United Nations. Last year there were twenty-nine and tomorrow when the preliminary vote is held you will see a strengthening of that position or very closely to it. We have not maintained our position and our prestige. A Gallup Poll taken in February of this year asking the—in eight out of nine countries—they asked the people, who do they think would be ahead by 1970 militarily and scientifically, and a majority in eight of the nine countries said the Soviet Union would be by 1970. Governor Rockefeller has been far more critical in June of our position in the world than I have been. The Rockefeller Brothers report, General Ridgway, General Gavin, the Gaither Report, various reports of Congressional committees all indicate that the relative strength of the United States both militarily, politically, psychologically, and scientifically and industrially—the relative strength of the so—of United States compared to that of the Soviet Union and the Chinese Communists together—has deteriorated in the last eight years and we should know it, and the American people should be told the facts.

Document 8.15

PASSING THE TORCH

Eisenhower left office in early 1961, distraught that the Cold War appeared more dangerous than ever and dismayed in particular over the way the conflict was changing American society. He warned in his farewell address against the vast "military-industrial complex" for which profits and political stability accrued from ever-present Cold War tensions. But he also left office deeply worried about the encroaching power of communism, particularly in Southeast Asia. On January 19, 1961, just days before leaving office, Eisenhower met privately with incoming President John F. Kennedy. The following memorandum summarizes their encounter.

President Eisenhower opened the discussion on Laos by stating that the United States was determined to preserve the independence of Laos. It was his opinion that if Laos should fall to the Communists, then it would be just a question of time until South Vietnam, Cambodia, Thailand and Burma would collapse. He felt that the Communists had designs on all of Southeast Asia, and that it would be a tragedy to permit Laos to fall.

President Eisenhower gave a brief review of the various moves and coups that had taken place in Laos involving the Pathet Lao, Souvanna Phouma, Boun Oum, and Kong Le. He said that the evidence was clear that Communist China and North Vietnam were determined to destroy the independence of Laos. He also added that the Russians were sending in substantial supplies in support of the Pathet Lao in an effort to overturn the government.

President Eisenhower said it would be fatal for us to permit Communists to insert themselves in the Laotian government. He recalled that our experience had clearly demonstrated that under such circumstances the Communists always ended up in control. He cited China as an illustration. . . .

Secretary [of State Christian] Herter stated, with President Eisenhower's approval, that we should continue every effort to make a political settlement in Laos. He added, however, that if such efforts were fruitless, then the United States must intervene in concert with our allies. If we were unable to persuade our allies, then we must go it alone.

At this point, President Eisenhower said with considerable emotion that Laos was the key to the entire area of Southeast Asia. He said that if we permitted Laos to fall, then we would have to write off all the area. He stated that we must not permit a Communist take-over. He reiterated that we should make every effort to persuade member nations of SEATO or the ICC to accept the burden with us to defend the freedom of Laos.

As he concluded these remarks, President Eisenhower stated it was imperative that Laos be defended. He said that the United States should accept this task with our allies, if we could persuade them, and alone if we could not. He added that "our unilateral intervention would be our last desperate hope" in the event we were unable to prevail upon the other signatories to join us. . . .

This phase of the discussion was concluded by President Eisenhower in commenting philosophically upon the fact that the morale existing in the democratic forces in Laos appeared to be disappointing. He wondered aloud why, in interventions of this kind, we always seem to find that the morale of the Communist forces was better than that of the democratic forces. His explanation was that the Communist philosophy appeared to produce a sense of dedication on the part of its adherents, while there was not the same sense of dedication on the part of those supporting the free forces. He stated that the entire problem of morale was a serious one and would have to be taken into consideration as we became more deeply involved.

9

The Nationalist Challenge

The most intense years of the Cold War coincided with another momentous development: the powerful assertion of autonomy by Asian, African, and Latin American nations. Many such nations gained their independence from colonial rule from the 1940s to the 1970s. The remarkable pace at which new countries came into existence does not, however, fully capture the enormity of the transformation wrought by the emergence of an energized "Global South" or "Third World." Even nations that had secured their independence from imperial rule decades earlier demanded greater respect and a bigger international role.

This development created opportunities and challenges for Washington and Moscow, both of which hoped to harness the Third World to their purposes. The superpowers wanted access to economic resources and military bases. But they were at least as preoccupied by a less tangible desire to pull the countries of Latin America, Asia, and Africa into their geopolitical orbits as a way to demonstrate the universal validity of the economic and political systems that they espoused.

The challenges were especially acute for the United States, since many developing nations had reason to be hostile to the West. The Western alliance, after all, was comprised partly of the very powers from which many new countries had just gained their independence. By contrast, many identified with the Soviet revolutionary tradition and embraced economic policies closer to the Soviet than the American model.

This chapter explores how Americans responded to these challenges and how observers at home and abroad critiqued those responses. As in earlier periods, U.S. leaders were torn between conflicting impulses with regard to colonized and formerly colonized regions. On the one hand, they often sympathized with the desire of Third World nations to shatter the remaining vestiges of colonialism and praised them for following on a revolutionary path blazed by the United States in 1776. On the other hand, U.S. officials worried that impassioned nationalists were dangerously prone to extremism, which could, in turn, open the door to communist influence. Washington's solution was often to promote moderation by supporting the basic principle of independence but working constantly to blunt radical impulses and to reshape Third World nations in the Western mold.

Starting in the late 1950s, U.S. officials gradually developed a range of options that they drew upon, in different mixes at different times, as they struggled to guide Third World nations along this moderate course. One approach, prevalent in the 1960s, was to send vast economic aid to poor nations. U.S. leaders hoped such as-

sistance would win friends among recipient nations, help restructure their economies along Western lines, and damp down social unrest that seemed to feed radicalism. The United States also sent military aid to Third World nations in order to curry favor and help well-disposed governments combat radicalism among their own populations. In a few cases, Washington resorted to outright intervention—whether by small numbers of intelligence agents or large military forces—to manipulate local politics or suppress leftists.

All of these efforts generated fierce criticism. Soviet and Chinese leaders accused the United States of hypocritically frustrating the ambitions of young nations and declared their support for "wars of liberation" against Western domination. Third World leaders voiced similar complaints, though many espoused nonalignment rather than outright support for the communist bloc. Within the United States, meanwhile, some Americans echoed anti-imperial sentiments of an earlier day by charging that Washington, despite its liberal pretensions, often obstructed progress for poor nations. Other Americans complained that Washington cared far too much about the sensitivities of distant, inconsequential countries.

Document 9.1

THE CASE FOR AN "EVOLUTIONARY APPROACH"

By the early 1950s, U.S. officials could easily see that the era of Western colonialism was ending. Asian nations such as India, Burma, and Indonesia had already secured their independence in the first five years after the Second World War, and it required little imagination to see that a similar process would soon play out elsewhere. That prospect stirred a mix of enthusiasm and anxiety in Washington. In a speech delivered on October 30, 1953, Henry A. Byroade, the assistant secretary of state for Near Eastern, South Asian, and African Affairs in the Eisenhower administration, laid out a general U.S. policy aimed at balancing competing objectives.

When we Americans turn our thoughts to international relations, one problem stands out above all others. Our principal concern is the threat of Soviet aggression. . . . Americans are therefore sometimes surprised to learn that there are vast areas of the world where the Soviet threat is given secondary emphasis. Throughout parts of Africa, the Near East, South Asia and the Far East, human interests and emotions are focused primarily on such questions as "imperialism," "colonialism," and "nationalism." In many of these areas, the principal motivating force is the desire of dependent peoples to end foreign domination and achieve political and economic self-determination.

This movement toward self-determination is one of the most powerful forces in twentieth century affairs. When the history of our era is finally written, it may prove to have been the most significant of all.

There is a paradox in the fact that the upsurge for national self-determination among the dependent peoples comes at this stage of human history. We know that Western nations, which have long possessed sovereign independence, are coming to recognize that self-sufficiency is a myth. We are moving steadily toward increasing association and interdependence among ourselves. In fact, several of the older nations are now engaged in creating new forms of association in which portions of national sovereignty are voluntarily surrendered.

We must frankly recognize that the hands of the clock of history are set at different hours in different parts of the world. We ourselves believe that peace, prosperity, and human freedom can be assured only within a concert of free peoples which transcends national boundaries. However, we must accept the fact that many of our friends in Asia and Africa tend to view national independence as a magic solution to all their difficulties. The problem is to avoid serious conflict between these viewpoints. We hope that the peoples now seeking self-determination will achieve it and exercise it in such a way as to strengthen rather than weaken the bonds of international cooperation. . . .

The movement towards self-determination has recently encountered an even more strange and potentially more tragic paradox. At the same time that Western colonialism of the old type is disappearing, a new form of imperialism has begun to extend a clutching hand to every quarter of the globe. I am referring to the new Soviet colonialism. This new colonialism is more subtle and more poisonous than the old because it often masquerades under the guise of nationalism itself. . . .

Since old-style colonialism is on its way out, and nothing can restore it, the real choice today lies between continued progress toward self-determination, and surrender to the new Communist imperialism.

The policies of the United States Government toward colonial questions have not always been clearly understood. In part, this may be explained by the fact that each area of the world presents its own peculiar problems and circumstances. It is not possible to develop any general rule of thumb which will be applicable to all nations and areas. Our basic policy however is relatively simple. We believe in eventual self-determination for all peoples, and we believe that evolutionary development to this end should move forward with minimum delay. . . .

People here and abroad frequently ask: "Why *evolution*? Why not grant all dependent peoples immediate sovereignty? By what right does one nation continue to exercise jurisdiction over a foreign territory?"

This question cannot readily be answered on abstract ethical grounds. No government has a God-given right to rule peoples other than its own. The old concept of the "white man's burden" is obsolete, and provides no valid justification for colonialism. But if the question defies pure ethics, it may nevertheless be answered on practical and human grounds. It is a hard, inescapable fact that premature independence can be dangerous, retrogressive and destructive.

Unless we are willing to recognize that there is such a thing as premature independence, we cannot think intelligently or constructively about the status of dependent peoples. For example, there are areas in which there is no concept of community relationships beyond the family or the tribe. There are regions where human beings are unable to cope with disease, famine and other forces of nature. Premature independence for these peoples would not serve the interests of the United States nor the interests of the free world as a whole. Least of all would it serve the interests of the dependent peoples themselves. . . .

[W]hen dependent peoples attain self-determination, we want it to be *real*, and we want it to endure. If they choose independence, we want them to be able to maintain their independence against the new Soviet imperialism and any other form of tyranny. We do not want the vast labor and pain expended in the struggle for freedom to be wasted by the premature creation of a state which will collapse like a stack of cards at the first hint of difficulty. . . . If a few additional years of evolution can make the difference between a self-determination that endures and a reversion to dependency or chaos, the years will not be wasted. . . .

[L]et us be frank in recognizing our stake in the strength and stability of certain European nations which exercise influence in the dependent areas. These European nations are our allies. They share many common interests with us. They will probably represent, for many years to come, the major source of free world defensive power outside our own. We cannot blindly disregard their side of the colonial question without injury to our own security. In particular, we cannot ignore the legitimate economic interests which European nations possess in certain dependent territories. Nor can we forget the importance of these interests to the European economy which we have contributed so much to support.

Document 9.2

NEHRU'S DEFENSE OF NONALIGNMENT

Many Third World nations, especially in Asia and Africa, wanted to avoid alignment with either of the Cold War blocs. The push for geopolitical independence came to fruition in 1961, when twenty-five nations formally established the Non-Aligned Movement. But many of the basic ideas had been articulated six years earlier at the landmark meeting of African and Asian leaders held in Bandung, Indonesia. In a speech at Bandung on April 22, 1955, Indian leader Jawaharlal Nehru made an impassioned case against participation in the Cold War.

I belong to neither [Cold War bloc] and I propose to belong to neither whatever happens in the world. If we have to stand alone, we will stand by ourselves, whatever happens (and India has stood alone without any aid against a mighty Empire, the British Empire) and we propose to face all consequences. . . .

We do not agree with the communist teachings, we do not agree with the anti-communist teachings, because they are both based on wrong principles. . . . We will defend ourselves with whatever arms and strength we have, and if we have no arms we will defend ourselves without arms. . . .

My country has made mistakes. Every country makes mistakes. I have no doubt we will make mistakes; we will stumble and fall and get up. The mistakes of my country and perhaps the mistakes of other countries here do not make a difference; but the mistakes the Great Powers make do make a difference to the world and may well bring about a terrible catastrophe. I speak with the greatest respect [for] these Great Powers because they are not only great in military might but in development, in culture, in civilization. But I do submit that greatness sometimes brings quite false values, false standards. When they begin to think in terms of military strength—whether it be the United Kingdom, the Soviet Union or the U.S.A.—then they are going away from the right track and the result of that will be that the overwhelming might of one country will conquer the world. Thus far the world has succeeded in preventing that; I cannot speak for the future. . . .

So far as I am concerned, it does not matter what war takes place; we will not take part in it unless we have to defend ourselves. If I join any of these big groups I lose my identity; I have no identity left, I have no views left. . . . If all the world were to be divided up between these two big blocs what would be the result? The inevitable result would be war. Therefore every step that takes place in reducing that area in the world which may be called the *unaligned area* is a dangerous step and leads to war. It reduces that objective, that balance, that outlook which other countries without military might can perhaps exercise.

Honorable members laid great stress on moral force. It is with military force that we are dealing now, but I submit that moral force counts and the moral force of Asia and Africa must, in spite of the atomic and hydrogen bombs of Russia, the U.S.A. or another country, count!

Many members present here do not obviously accept the communist ideology, while some of them do. For my part I do not. I am a positive person, not an "anti" person. I want positive good for my country and the world. Therefore, are we, the countries of Asia and Africa, devoid of any positive position except being pro-communist or anti-communist? Has it come to this, that the leaders of thought who have given religions and all kinds of things to the world have to tag on to this kind of group or that and be hangers-on of this party or the other carrying out their wishes and occasionally giving an idea? It is most degrading and humiliating to any self-respecting people or nation. It is an intolerable thought to me that the great countries of Asia and Africa should come out of bondage into freedom only to degrade themselves or humiliate themselves in this way.

Document 9.3

A CRITIQUE OF U.S. DIPLOMACY IN THE THIRD WORLD

By the late 1950s, Americans watched anxiously as East-West tensions spilled into Asia, Africa, and Latin America. Washington had resisted Soviet expansionism in western Europe and the Far East, but Americans doubted that their country could achieve such good results in the developing world. Among other problems, U.S. officials seemed to have little knowledge about, or sensitivity to, the problems afflicting poor nations. Many commentators complained that Americans had grown too lazy, materialistic, and arrogant to act effectively in distant, alien parts of the world. The opening pages of the best-selling novel The Ugly American, *published in 1958, captured widespread worries that the United States was poorly prepared for the next stage of the Cold War. The passage relates the experiences of the U.S. ambassador to the fictional Southeast Asian nation of Sarkhan (capital at Haidho), whose pro-U.S. government was under threat from a communist insurgency.*

The Honorable Louis Sears, American Ambassador to Sarkhan, was angry. Even though the airconditioner [*sic*] kept his office cool, he felt hot and irritable. He smoothed out the editorial page of the *Sarkhan Eastern Star*, the most widely distributed paper in Haidho, and studied the cartoon carefully.

I don't give a damn what the Prime Minister and all those little advisers of his say, Ambassador Sears said to himself, that damned *Eastern Star* is a Red paper, and that cartoon looks too much like me to be an accident.

He jerked his head away from the paper, with a tic of anger, and turned toward the window. The lawn of the Embassy swept down to the main road of Haidho in a long, pure green carefully trimmed wave. On each side it broke into a froth of color . . . the red and purple of bougainvillea, the softer colors of hibiscus, the myriad orchids hanging in elegant parasitic grace from banyan trees, the crisp straight lines of bamboo trees. At the end of the lawn the pickets of a wrought-iron fence separated Embassy grounds from the confusion and noise of the road.

From the countryside an unbroken line of women were moving into Haidho, as they did every morning, carrying on their backs faggots of wood, or baskets of vegetables—radishes, spring onions, and beans laid out in simple perfection on moist leaves. Occasionally a woman went by with a basket of fish on her head, the tiny silvery bodies catching the early morning sun. Whenever a man passed he was on a bicycle, making his way along the chattering lines of women.

Strange little monkeys, Ambassador Sears thought, forgetting for a moment his pique at the cartoon. Women do all the work, men have all the fun.

The only motorized vehicles he could see were trucks which had been given to the Sarkhanese government by the American military advisory group. They went down the road at a fast clip, their horns blaring steadily as if they had been turned on when the engine was started. They carried military supplies toward the north; neat boxes of hand grenades, bundles of barbed wire, barrels of gasoline and oil, big rectangular boxes which contained disassembled 50-caliber machine guns.

And all of it made in America, Ambassador Sears thought. At once his anger returned and he looked down again at the *Eastern Star*. The cartoon was obvious. Although he could not read Sarkhanese beyond a few words forced upon him by constant repetition, the point was clear. The cartoon showed a short, fat American, his face perspiring, and his mouth open like a braying mule's, leading a thin, gracefully-built Sarkhanese man by the tether around his neck toward a sign bearing two of the few Sarkhanese words the ambassador could recognize—"Coca Cola." Underneath the short fat man was a single English word: "Lucky."

Lucky, Lucky Louis had been Ambassador Sears' nickname when he was in politics in the United States. For eighteen years he had been a popular and successful senator; but it was said about him that he always won his elections by a lucky fluke. When Sears, a Democrat, first won, Drew Pearson had said that he had been elected because he was lucky enough to be a Democrat in a Democratic year. In his second race his Republican opponent had dropped dead ten days before the election, which even Sears has recognized as luck. His opponent's wife had got involved in a scandal during his third campaign. But, as Sears had noticed wryly, no one had thought it was bad luck when he lost the fourth time up.

Actually Sears had not been too much worried when he lost this last election. He had been in politics long enough to know that the party owed him something. Two days after the election, with his voting record under his arm, he called on the National Committee.

The political strategists were ready for him.

"What kind of a job would you like, Lucky?" they asked.

"A Federal judgeship with a nice long tenure," he answered promptly.

"Okay, but there won't be an opening for two years. In the meantime, Lucky, how would you like to be an ambassador?"

"Me, an ambassador?" said Sears, immediately picturing himself appearing in a morning coat and striped trousers before the court of St. James, or running the big handsome embassy building in Paris. Sears was a shrewd enough politician to keep any look of expectation from crossing his face. "Now look, boys, an ambassador has to spend a lot more than he makes. That's all right, if you've got a philanthropist who might stand the gaff for me; but you know my personal situation. After eighteen years, everything I've gotten has gone into the party."

The strategists nodded without comment. It was a remark they heard often, but it never failed to touch them.

"There's an ambassadorship open in Sarkhan," the strategists said. "It pays $17,500 and you ought to be able to save money on that. There's an entertainment allowance of $15,000, and you can buy liquor tax free. There's also an ambassador's mansion which you get rent free."

"Where the hell is Sarkhan?"

"It's a small country out toward Burma and Thailand."

"Now, you know I'm not prejudiced, but I just don't work well with blacks."

"They're not black, they're brown. Well, if you don't want it, we can fix you up as a legal assistant to . . ."

"I'll take it."

Document 9.4

THE CHANGING BALANCE OF WORLD POWER

Among the reasons for U.S. anxiety about the rise of the Third World was a sense that the balance of power would shift drastically within the United Nations, where the United States and its allies had enjoyed a sizeable majority since the

organization's founding at the end of the Second World War. This cartoon, drawn by British cartoonist Michael Cummings and published in the London Daily Express *on August 10, 1958, shows British Prime Minister Harold Macmillan and U.S. President Dwight D. Eisenhower precariously holding their position against a large mix of Third World and communist leaders. A blindfolded U.N. Secretary General Dag Hammarskjold holds the scales of global justice.*

Document 9.5

SOVIET SUPPORT FOR "NATIONAL LIBERATION WARS"

Joseph Stalin had little enthusiasm for expanding communist influence in the poor, mostly agricultural nations of Asia, Africa, and Latin America. That attitude changed drastically in the late 1950s, when a new Soviet leader, Nikita Khrushchev, sought to throw Soviet support behind radical movements in the Third World and build enduring partnerships. In a speech on January 6, 1961, Khrushchev predicted the ultimate victory of revolutionary forces over Western reaction. Although the speech may have been intended mainly to impress Chinese leaders with Soviet revolutionary ardor, U.S. officials took careful note of the speech, which seemed to affirm growing Soviet ambitions in the Third World.

Now a word about national liberation wars. The armed struggle by the Vietnamese people or the war of the Algerian people, which is already in its seventh year, serve as the latest examples of such wars. These wars began as an uprising by the colonial peoples against their oppressors and changed into guerrilla warfare. Liberation wars will continue to exist as long as imperialism exists, as long as colonialism exists. These are revolutionary wars. Such wars are not only admissible but inevitable, since the colonialists do not grant independence voluntarily. Therefore, the peoples can attain their freedom and independence only by struggle, including armed struggle. . . .

These are uprisings against rotten reactionary regimes, against the colonizers. The Communists fully support such just wars and march in the front rank with the peoples waging liberation struggles. . . .

Comrades, the peoples which achieved national independence have become a new and powerful force in the struggle for peace and social progress. The national liberation movement deals more and more blows against imperialism, helps consolidation of peace, contributes to speeding mankind's development along the path of social progress. Asia, Africa, and Latin America are now the most important centers of revolutionary struggle against imperialism. In the postwar period about 40 countries won national independence. Almost 1.5 billion people have wrenched themselves out of colonial slavery. . . .

New remarkable pages are opening in the history of mankind. It is easy to imagine what majestic deeds these peoples will perform after they completely evict the imperialists from their countries, when they feel that they are masters of their own fate.

This vastly multiplies the progressive forces of mankind. For example, take Asia. This ancient cradle of civilization. What inexhaustible strength lies hidden in the peoples of this continent! And will the Arab people with their heroic traditions, and all the peoples of the Middle East, which have already freed or are freeing themselves from political and economic dependence on imperialism, play any lesser role in the solution of tasks now facing mankind?

A remarkable phenomenon of our time is the awakening of the peoples of Africa. Dozens of states in north and central Africa have already achieved independence. The south of Africa is seething and there is no doubt that the fascist prisons in the Union of South Africa will collapse, that Rhodesia, Uganda, and other parts of Africa will become free.

The forces of the national liberation movement are greatly increasing owing to the fact that one more front of active struggle against American imperialism has been formed in recent years. Latin America has become this front. Until recently that vast continent was identified by one concept: America. This concept greatly expressed its substance: Latin America was bound hand and foot by Yankee imperialism. By their struggle, the Latin American peoples are showing that the American continent is not an appendage of the United States. Latin America is reminiscent of an active volcano: the lava of the liberation struggle has swept away dictatorial regimes in a number of Latin American countries.

Document 9.6

KENNEDY'S CALL TO ACTION

The sense of crisis in the Third World and the apparent need for dynamic leaders to cope with this and other unfamiliar global problems helped propel John F. Kennedy to the White House in 1960. The president did not disappoint those who expected a new tone of vigor and ingenuity. In his famous inauguration speech on January 20, 1961, Kennedy promised to devote almost limitless attention and resources to promote progress in Asia, Africa, and Latin America. Indeed, the speech amounted to a liberal manifesto of sorts, reverberating with confidence about America's capacity to master even the weightiest international challenges.

Let the word go forth from this time and place, to friend and foe alike, that the torch has been passed to a new generation of Americans—born in this century, tempered by war, disciplined by a hard and bitter peace, proud of our ancient heritage—and unwilling to witness or permit the slow undoing of those human rights to which this nation has always been committed, and to which we are committed today at home and around the world.

Let every nation know, whether it wishes us well or ill, that we shall pay any price, bear any burden, meet any hardship, support any friend, oppose any foe to assure the survival and the success of liberty.

This much we pledge—and more.

To those old allies whose cultural and spiritual origins we share, we pledge the loyalty of faithful friends. United there is little we cannot do in a host of cooperative ventures. Divided there is little we can do—for we dare not meet a powerful challenge at odds and split asunder.

To those new states whom we welcome to the ranks of the free, we pledge our word that one form of colonial control shall not have passed away merely to be replaced by a far more iron tyranny. We shall not always expect to find them supporting our view. But we shall always hope to find them strongly supporting their own freedom—and to remember that, in the past, those who foolishly sought power by riding the back of the tiger ended up inside.

To those people in the huts and villages of half the globe struggling to break the bonds of mass misery, we pledge our best efforts to help them help themselves, for whatever period is required—not because the communists may be doing it, not because we seek their votes, but because it is right. If a free society cannot help the many who are poor, it cannot save the few who are rich.

To our sister republics south of our border, we offer a special pledge—to convert our good words into good deeds—in a new alliance for progress—to assist free men and free governments in casting off the chains of poverty. But this peaceful revolution of hope cannot become the prey of hostile powers. Let all our neighbors know that we shall join with them to oppose aggression or subversion anywhere in the Americas. And let every other power know that this Hemisphere intends to remain the master of its own house.

To that world assembly of sovereign states, the United Nations, our last best hope in an age where the instruments of war have far outpaced the instruments of peace, we renew our pledge of support—to prevent it from becoming merely a forum for invective—to strengthen its shield of the new and the weak—and to enlarge the area in which its writ may run. . . .

In your hands, my fellow citizens, more than mine, will rest the final success or failure of our course. Since this country was founded, each generation of Americans has been summoned to give testimony to its national loyalty. The graves of young Americans who answered the call to service surround the globe.

Now the trumpet summons us again—not as a call to bear arms, though arms we need—not as a call to battle, though embattled we are—but a call to bear the burden of a long twilight struggle, year in and year out, "rejoicing in hope, patient in tribulation"—a struggle against the common enemies of man: tyranny, poverty, disease and war itself.

Can we forge against these enemies a grand and global alliance, North and South, East and West, that can assure a more fruitful life for all mankind? Will you join in that historic effort?

Document 9.7

THE CHALLENGE OF MODERNIZATION

If Kennedy's inaugural speech furnished the call to action, other officials provided specific ideas about how the United States should go about promoting development in the Third World. Kennedy's deputy national security adviser, Walt W. Rostow, was ideally suited to this task. As an eminent economist at the Massachusetts Institute of Technology during the 1950s, Rostow had played a key role in developing "modernization theory," which held that all nations were traveling the same road from economic backwardness to industrial capitalism. In a speech to the graduating class at the U.S. Army Special Warfare School on June 28, 1961, Rostow laid out some of his key ideas about the problems afflicting Third World nations and the steps the United States must take to push them along the path to Western-style modernity.

What is happening throughout Latin America, Africa, the Middle East, and Asia is this: Old societies are changing their ways in order to create and maintain a national personality on the world scene and to bring to their peoples the benefits modern technology can offer. This process is truly revolutionary. It touches every aspect of the traditional life—economic, social, and political. The introduction of modern technology brings about not merely new methods of production but a new style of family life, new links between the villages and the cities, the beginnings of national politics, and a new relationship to the world outside.

Like all revolutions, the revolution of modernization is disturbing. Individual men are torn between the commitment to the old familiar way of life and the attractions of a modern way of life. The power of old social groups—notably the landlord, who usually dominates the traditional society—is reduced. Power moves toward those who can command the tools of modern technology, including modern weapons. Men and women in the villages and the cities, feeling that the old ways of life are shaken and that new possibilities are open to them, express old resentments and new hopes.

This is the grand arena of revolutionary change which the Communists are exploiting with great energy. They believe that their techniques of organization—based on small disciplined cadres of conspirators—are ideally suited to grasp and to hold power in these turbulent settings. They believe that the weak transitional governments that one is likely to find during this modernization process are highly vulnerable to subversion and to guerrilla warfare. And whatever Communist doctrines of historical inevitability may be, Communists know that their time to seize power in the underdeveloped areas is limited. They know that, as momentum takes hold in an underdeveloped area—and the fundamental social problems inherited from the traditional society are solved—their chances to seize power decline.

It is on the weakest nations, facing their most difficult transitional moments, that the Communists concentrate their attention. They are the scavengers of the modernization process. They believe that the techniques of political centralization under dictatorial control—and the projected image of Soviet and Chinese Communist economic progress—will persuade hesitant men, faced by great transitional problems, that the Communist model should be adopted for modernization, even at the cost of surrendering human liberty. They believe that they can exploit effectively the resentments built up in many of these areas against colonial rule and that they can associate themselves effectively with the desire of the emerging nations for independence, for status on the world scene, and for material progress.

This is a formidable program; for the history of this century teaches us that communism is not the long-run wave of the future toward which societies are naturally drawn. But it is one particular form of modern society to which a nation may fall prey during the transitional process. Communism is best understood as a disease of the transition to modernization.

What is our reply to this historical conception and strategy? What is the American purpose and the American strategy? We, too, recognize that a revolutionary process is under way. We are dedicated to the proposition that this revolutionary process of modernization shall be permitted to go forward in independence, with increasing degrees of human freedom. We seek two results: first, that truly independent nations shall emerge on the world scene; and, second, that each nation will be permitted to fashion, out of its own culture and its own ambitions, the kind of modern society it wants. The same religious and philosophical beliefs which decree that we respect the uniqueness of each individual make it natural that we respect the uniqueness of each national society. Moreover, we Americans are confident that, if the independence of this process can be maintained over the coming years and decades, these societies will choose their own version of what we would recognize as a democratic, open society. . . .

The United States has the primary responsibility for assisting the economies of those hard-pressed states on the periphery of the Communist bloc, which are under acute military or quasi-military pressure which they cannot bear from their own resources; for example, South Korea, Viet-Nam, Taiwan, Pakistan, Iran. The United States has a special responsibility of leadership in bringing not merely its own resources but the resources of all the free world to bear in aiding the long-run development of those nations which are serious about modernizing their economy and their social life. . . .

Finally, the United States has a role to play—symbolized by your presence here and by mine—in learning to deter guerrilla warfare, if possible, and to deal with it, if necessary.

I do not need to tell you that the primary responsibility for dealing with guerrilla warfare in the underdeveloped areas cannot be American. There are many ways in which we can help—and we are searching our minds and our imaginations to learn better how to help; but a guerrilla war must be fought primarily by those on the spot. This is so for a quite particular reason. A guerrilla war is an intimate affair, fought not merely with weapons but fought in the minds of the men who live in the villages and in the hills, fought by the spirit and policy of those who run the local government. An outsider cannot, by himself, win a guerrilla war. He can help create conditions in which it can be won, and he can directly assist those prepared to fight for their independence. We are determined to help destroy this international disease.

Document 9.8

THE NEW LEFT CRITIQUE

The Kennedy administration's efforts to craft a more energetic U.S. policy in the Third World drew criticism from left and right. On the left, detractors sometimes welcomed the administration's progressive rhetoric but often condemned actions that seemed to differ little from the heavy-handed methods of the early 1950s. Criticism of U.S. policy making gained strength in the 1960s as American students and intellectuals, comprising a "New Left" in American politics, focused on the injustices of life in the United States and called for profound changes in American behavior at home and abroad. One of the most eloquent expressions of this rising spirit of dissent was the 1962 "Port Huron Statement," a lengthy manifesto issued by Students for a Democratic Society and written mostly by activist Tom Hayden.

While weapons have accelerated man's opportunity for self-destruction, the counter-impulse to life and creation are superbly manifest in the revolutionary feelings of many Asian, African and Latin American peoples. Against the individual initiative and aspiration, and social sense of organicism characteristic of these upsurges, the American apathy and stalemate stand in embarrassing contrast. . . .

With rare variation, American foreign policy in the Fifties was guided by a concern for foreign investment and a negative anti-communist political stance linked to a series of military alliances, both undergirded by military threat. We participated unilaterally—usually through the Central Intelligence Agency—in revolutions against governments in Laos, Guatemala, Cuba, Egypt, Iran. We permitted economic investment to decisively affect our foreign policy: fruit in Cuba, oil in the Middle East, diamonds and gold in South Africa (with whom we trade more than with any African nation). . . .

Since the Kennedy administration began, the American government seems to have initiated policy changes in the colonial and underdeveloped areas. It accepted "neutralism" as a tolerable principle; it sided more than once with the Angolans in the United Nations; it invited Souvanna Phouma to return to Laos after having overthrown his neutralist government there; it implemented the Alliance for Progress that President Eisenhower proposed when Latin America appeared on the verge of socialist revolutions; it made derogatory statements about the Trujillos; it cautiously suggested that a democratic socialist government in British Guiana might be necessary to support; in inaugural oratory, it suggested that a moral imperative was involved in sharing the world's resources with those who have been previously dominated. These were hardly sufficient to heal the scars of past activity and present associations, but nevertheless they were motions away from the Fifties. But quite unexpectedly, the President ordered the Cuban invasion, and while the American press railed about how we had been "shamed" and defied by that "monster Castro," the colonial peoples of the world wondered whether our foreign policy had really changed from its old imperialist ways. . . .

Ever since the colonial revolution began, American policy makers have reacted to new problems with old "gunboat" remedies, often thinly disguised. The feeble but desirable efforts of the Kennedy administration to be more flexible are coming perhaps too late, and are of too little significance to really change the historical thrust of our policies. The hunger problem is increasing rapidly mostly as a result of the worldwide population explosion that cancels out the meager triumphs gained so far over starvation. . . .

The world is in transformation. But America is not. It can race to industrialize the world, tolerating occasional authoritarianisms, socialisms, neutralisms along the way—or it can slow the pace of the inevitable and default to the eager and self-interested Soviets and, much more importantly, to mankind itself. Only mystics would guess we have opted thoroughly for the first. Consider what our people think of this, the most urgent issue on the human agenda. Fed by a bellicose press, manipulated by economic and political opponents of change, drifting in their own history, they grumble about "the foreign aid waste," or about "that beatnik down in Cuba," or how "things will get us by" . . . thinking confidently, albeit in the usual bewilderment, that Americans can go right on like always, five percent of mankind producing forty percent of its goods.

Document 9.9

LINKS TO THE CIVIL RIGHTS MOVEMENT

Rapid decolonization during the 1960s coincided with the rise of the movement for African American civil rights in the United States. Although the two trends sprang from separate causes, they became intertwined in the minds of many activists and political leaders within the United States and abroad. Nationalists in Asia, Africa, and Latin America voiced strong support for African American demands, which mirrored their own insistence on greater respect and autonomy. Meanwhile, U.S. leaders backed civil rights reforms partly because of their desire to blunt communist criticism of segregation in the United States and to curry favor with nonwhite nationalists throughout the Third World. U.S. Secretary of State Dean Rusk made this logic clear on July 10, 1963, when he testified before a Senate committee in favor of a civil rights bill pending in Congress.

As matters stand . . . racial discrimination here at home has important effects on our foreign relations. This is not because such discrimination is unique to the United States. Discrimination on account of race, color, religion, national or tribal origin may be found in other countries. But the United States is widely regarded as the home of democracy and the leader of the struggle for freedom, for human rights, for human dignity. We are expected to be the model—no higher compliment could be paid to us. So our failure to live up to our proclaimed ideals are noted—and magnified and distorted.

One of the epochal developments of our time has been the conversion of the old colonial empires into a host of new independent nations—some 50 since the Second World War. The vast majority of these newly independent peoples are nonwhite, and they are determined to eradicate every vestige of the notion that the white race is superior or entitled to special privileges because of race. Were we as a nation "in their shoes," we would do the same.

This tremendous transformation in the world has come about under the impulse of the fundamental beliefs set forth in the second and third sentences of our Declaration of Independence. These universal ideas which we have done so much to nurture have spread over the earth. The spiritual sons of the American Revolution are of every race. For let us remind ourselves that the great declaration said "all men are created equal and are endowed by their Creator with certain unalienable rights"; it did not say, "all men except those who are not white."

Freedom, in the broadest and truest sense, is the central issue in the world struggle in which we are engaged. We stand for government by the consent of the governed, for government by law, for equal opportunity, for the rights and worth of the individual human being. These are aspirations shared, I believe, by the great majority of mankind. . . .

I believe that the forces of freedom are making progress. I am confident that if we [persevere] in the efforts we are now making, we shall eventually achieve the sort of world we seek—a world in which all men will be safe in freedom and peace.

But in waging this world struggle we are seriously handicapped by racial or religious discrimination in the United States. Our failure to live up to the pledges of our Declaration of Independence and our Constitution embarrasses our friends and heartens our enemies.

In their efforts to enhance their influence among the nonwhite peoples and to alienate them from us, the Communists clearly regard racial discrimination in the United States as one of their most valuable assets. . . .

If progress should stop, if Congress should not approve legislation designed to remove remaining discriminatory practices, questions would inevitably arise in many parts of the world as to the real convictions of the American people. In that event, hostile propaganda might be expected to hurt us more than it has hurt us until now.

Document 9.10

A BELLWETHER NATION

On March 6, 1957, Kwame Nkrumah, the prime minister of Ghana, declared his country's independence from Britain, making the nation the first in sub-Saharan Africa to break free of European rule. U.S. leaders worked hard to cultivate Nkrumah's cooperation, viewing Ghana as a bellwether among the new nations of the developing world in its attitude toward the East-West rivalry. Within a few years, however, goodwill gave way to tension as Nkrumah tightened his grip on power and Washington grew less tolerant of Ghana's nonalignment and socialist economic policies. In the following letter to President Lyndon Johnson on February 26, 1964, Nkrumah complained about American methods in his country, a precursor of Nkrumah's later accusations that the Central Intelligence Agency conspired with his political opponents to organize the coup that overthrew him in 1966.

In my first meeting with President Kennedy, I explained how dangerous it is for the emerging States of Africa to take sides in the diplomatic manoeuvres and political disputes among the Great Powers. One of our principal aims has been to protect ourselves from the dangers of involvement in these manoeuvres and disputes. It follows from this that Ghana must establish good relations with all countries of the world, irrespective of the political systems of their governments.

You will appreciate, Mr. President, that the success of this policy depends on the extent of mutual respect which can be shown in the relationships that subsist between ourselves and the Governments which wish to maintain links with us.

It is on this issue that I must express some concern about that which has come to notice within recent times as a result of the activities of certain United States citizens in Ghana. There appears to be two conflicting establishments representing the United States in our part of the world. There is the United States Embassy as a diplomatic institution doing foreign diplomatic business with us; there is also the C.I.A. organisation which functions presumably within or outside this recognised body. This latter organisation, that is, the C.I.A., seems to devote all its attention to fomenting ill-will, misunderstanding and even clandestine and subversive activities among our people to the impairment of the good relations which exist between our two Governments.

If my analysis of this situation is correct, and all the indications are that it is, then I could not, Mr. President, view this without some alarm. Neither will any other Government in a developing State, however weak its economic position, accept this situation without demur. We of the independent African States wish to be left alone to pursue policies and courses which we know to be in the best interests of our people, and at the same time conducive to the maintenance of good relations with other governments of the world. . . .

It should be obvious to any one who has followed the history of Africa's development with impartiality that a planned economy and rapid industrial and agricultural development can be best achieved through a socialist course.

Mr. President, the ravages of colonialism and its effect on the territories now emerging from colonialism make it difficult and almost impossible for us in Africa to follow the traditional path of capitalist development. We must therefore ensure that the public sector of the productive economy expands at the maximum possible rate, especially in the strategic areas of production upon which our economy essentially depends. It is my primary ambition, therefore, to secure and maintain the economic independence of Ghana in such a manner as to forestall the danger of the growth of those social antagonisms which can result from the unequal distribution of economic power among our people.

Within the framework of this position there is an open door for foreign investment in Ghana. . . . Ghana welcomes foreign investors in a spirit of partnership; they can earn their profits here, provided they leave us an agreed portion for promoting the welfare and happiness of the majority of our people, as against the greedy ambitions of the few.

Document 9.11

SKEPTICISM ABOUT U.S. FOREIGN AID

On the right, critics of U.S. policy toward the Third World often excoriated the Kennedy and Johnson administrations for working too hard to gain the favor of antagonistic and ungrateful leftists such as Egypt's Gamal Abdel Nasser and Indonesia's Sukarno. Some Third World leaders, said the detractors, were only too happy to accept American aid but usually offered nothing in return except verbal attacks on the United States. "Dixiecrat" Senator Herman Talmadge of Georgia voiced such an opinion in a speech to fellow senators on January 8, 1965, during deliberations over legislation dealing with U.S. foreign assistance programs.

It is inconceivable to think that such bad days have fallen upon the foreign relations of the United States that we would have to endure the threats, insults, and curses of dictators.

It is more shocking that we would even consider the continuance of our foreign aid programs in nations that not only do not profess to be our friends, but which by word and deed make no secret about being our enemies.

Regardless of how eloquently anyone may attempt to justify it, I cannot swallow the idea of sending American dollars and American food into dictatorships which take our assistance with one hand and slap us with the other. It sticks in my throat.

I submit . . . that it is a shame and a disgrace to the American people. This is the strongest, the most free, the richest, the greatest nation on the face of the earth. The United States has never assumed the role of a lackey, and it ill befits our position of world leadership to go hat in hand to anyone.

The recent outrages perpetrated against the United States and our friends and allies by Nasser's Egypt demand the immediate end to our aid program in that country.

Nasser ever increases his alignment with the Soviet Union and Red China, and repeatedly acts against the best interests of the free world. He boasted of joining the Chinese Communists in sending arms to support the bloody and bestial war against the legally constituted government in the Congo. He has taken our aid and turned it into Russian arms to further Egyptian aggression against Yemen and Israel. He stood by while the John F. Kennedy Library was burned and destroyed in Cairo last November. His air force in December shot down without provocation a private plane owned by a Texas oil company. And then, to add insult to injury, Nasser told the United States to take our aid and go drink from the sea, or in effect, to go jump in the lake.

In the past 12 years, Nasser's Egypt has received approximately one billion dollars in aid from the United States, and food is still being shipped to Nasser at the rate of about $150 million a year....

Earlier this year, Sukarno of Indonesia told the United States to take our foreign aid and go to Hell. Despite this insult, despite Sukarno's continued aggression against our ally Malaysia, and notwithstanding his support of the warmongering policies of Red China in Asia, Indonesia and its left-wing government is being aided and abetted by U.S. dollars. Nearly $900 million has been pumped into Indonesia, and according to the Agency for International Development, we spent more than $10 million upon Sukarno in fiscal year 1964, and scheduled the same amount for fiscal 1965....

Document 9.12

THE TEMPTATION OF AUTHORITARIAN REGIMES

John F. Kennedy promised that the United States would try to bolster democracy throughout the Third World. In practice, however, Washington found it difficult to accomplish this goal. One reason was the weakness of democratic institutions and traditions in many Third World nations. Another reason was the temptation to support or install right-wing authoritarian governments that would loyally serve U.S. interests around the world. As the United States bogged down in Vietnam, reliable governments in other regions gained even more allure than previously. This cartoon, drawn by Herbert Block ("Herblock") for the Washington Post, *captures a logic that led the Kennedy, Johnson, and Nixon administrations to tolerate, or even form close partnerships with, a growing number of antidemocratic leaders throughout Asia, Africa, and Latin America.*

When I'm in charge, there's absolutely no danger of democratic government being subverted.

Document 9.13

BLACK NATIONALISM AND THE THIRD WORLD

Controversies over U.S. policy in the Third World intensified in the same years that saw civil rights activism sweep across the United States. The precise connection between the two phenomena inspired a great deal of commentary. White liberals argued that Cold War pressures, especially the need to win friends among the dozens of newly emerging nonwhite nations, made it more important than ever to support racial reform at home. African American moderates, anxious to preserve their partnership with the liberal establishment, tended to downplay any connection between their cause and decolonization struggles overseas. By contrast, black radicals insisted that their fight for dignity and opportunity was part of the larger global fight against oppression. In the following 1968 interview, conducted at a time of intense social conflict in the United States, the Black Panther leader Huey Newton expounds on this link. Shortly after the interview, Newton was convicted of killing a policeman in Oakland, California.

There are two kinds of nationalism, revolutionary nationalism and reactionary nationalism. Revolutionary nationalism is first dependent upon a people's revolution with the end goal being the people in power. Therefore to be a revolutionary nationalist you would by necessity have to be a socialist. If you are a reactionary nationalist you are not a socialist and your end goal is the oppression of the people....

A good example of revolutionary nationalism was the revolution in Algeria when Ben Bella took over. The French were kicked out but it was a people's revolution because the people ended up in power. The leaders that took over were not interested in the profit motive where they could exploit the people and keep them in a state of slavery. They nationalized the industry and plowed the would-be profits into the community. That's what socialism is all about in a nutshell. The people's representatives are in office strictly on the leave of the people. The wealth of the country is controlled by the people and they are considered whenever modifications in the industries are made....

Black people in America and colored people throughout the world suffer not only from exploitation, but they suffer from racism. Black people here in America, in the black colony, are oppressed because we're black and we're exploited. The whites [who sympathize with black activists] are rebels, many of them from the middle class and as far as any overt oppression this is not the case. So therefore I call their rejection of the system somewhat of an abstract thing. They're looking for new heroes. They're looking to wash away the hypocrisy that their fathers have presented to the world. In doing this they see the people who are really fighting for freedom. They see the people who are really standing for justice and equality and peace throughout the world. They are the people of Vietnam, the people of Africa, and the black people in the black colony here in America....

The imperialistic or capitalistic system occupies areas. It occupies Vietnam now. They occupy them by sending soldiers there, by sending policemen there. The policemen or soldiers are only a gun in the establishment's hand. They make the racist secure in his racism. The gun in the establishment's hand makes the establishment secure in its exploitation. The first problem it seems is to remove the gun from the establishment's hand. Until lately the white radical has seen no reason to come into conflict with the policemen in his own community. The reason I said until recently is because there is friction now in the mother country between the young white revolutionaries and the police. Because now the white revolutionaries are attempting to put some of their ideas into action, and there's the rub. We say that it should be a permanent thing....

Black power is really people's power. The Black Panther Program, Panther Power as we call it, will implement this people's power. We have respect for all of humanity and we realize that the people should rule and determine their destiny. Wipe out the controller. To have Black Power doesn't humble or subjugate anyone to slavery or oppression. Black Power is giving power to people who have not had power to determine their destiny. We advocate and we aid any people who are struggling to determine their destiny. This is regardless of color. The Vietnamese say Vietnam should be able to determine its own destiny. Power of the Vietnamese people. We also chant power of the Vietnamese people. The Latins are talking about Latin America for the Latin Americans. Cuba, Si and Yanqui, No. It's not that they don't want the Yankees to have any power[;] they just don't want them to have power over them. They can have power over themselves. We in the black colony of American want to be able to have power over our destiny and that's black power.

Document 9.14

AN INVESTIGATION OF U.S. METHODS

Critics of American policy in Asia, Africa, and Latin America frequently charged that Washington abused its power by orchestrating coups and attempting to kill revolutionary leaders. Such accusations were impossible to substantiate given the secrecy that surrounded U.S. intelligence operations. Only in the early 1970s did Congress investigate the executive branch's behavior earlier in the Cold War. The resulting reports documented numerous abuses in many Third World countries. One of the most striking studies examined attempts in the early 1960s to assassinate leaders in the Congo, Cuba, the Dominican Republic, and South Viet- nam. This report, prepared by a committee under the chairmanship of Democratic Senator Frank Church, was made public in November 1975.

United States strategy for conducting the Cold War called for the establishment of interlocking treaty arrangements and military bases throughout the world. Concern over the expansion of an aggressive Communist monolith led the United States to fight two major wars in Asia. In addition, it was considered necessary to wage a relentless cold war against Communist expansion wherever it appeared in the "back alleys of the world." This called for a full range of covert activities in response to the operations of Communist clandestine services.

[In the 1950s and 1960s], the United States felt impelled to respond to threats which were, or seemed to be, skirmishes in a global Cold War against Communism. Castro's Cuba raised the spectre of a Soviet outpost at America's doorstep. Events in the Dominican Republic appeared to offer an additional opportunity for the Russians and their allies. The Congo, freed from Belgian rule, occupied the strategic center of the African continent, and the prospect of Communist penetration there was viewed as a threat to American interests in emerging African nations. There was great concern that a Communist takeover in Indochina would have a "domino effect" throughout Asia. Even the election in 1970 of a Marxist president in Chile was seen by some as a threat similar to that of Castro's takeover in Cuba.

The Committee regards the unfortunate events dealt with in this Interim Report as an aberration, explainable at least in part, but not justified, by the pressures of the time. The Committee believes that it is still in the national interest of the United States to help nations achieve self-determination and resist Communist domination. However, it is clear that this interest cannot justify resorting to the kind of abuses covered in this report. Indeed, the Committee has resolved that steps must be taken to prevent those abuses from happening again....

The evidence establishes that the United States was implicated in several assassination plots. The Committee believes that, short of war, assassination is incompatible with American principles, international order, and morality. It should be rejected as a tool of foreign policy.

Our inquiry also reveals serious problems with respect to United States involvement in coups directed against foreign governments....

The Committee believes the truth about the assassination allegations should be told because democracy depends upon a well-informed electorate. We reject any contention that the facts disclosed in this report should be kept secret because they are embarrassing to the United States. Despite the temporary injury to our national reputation, the Committee believes that foreign peoples will, upon sober reflection, respect the United States more for keeping faith with its democratic ideal than they will condemn us for the misconduct revealed....

The evidence concerning each alleged assassination can be summarized as follows:

Patrice Lumumba (Congo/Zaire).—In the Fall of 1960, two CIA officials were asked by superiors to assassinate Lumumba. Poisons were sent to the Congo and some exploratory steps were taken toward gaining access to Lumumba. Subsequently, in early 1961, Lumumba was killed by Congolese rivals. It does not appear from the evidence that the United States was in any way involved in the killing.

Fidel Castro (Cuba).—United States Government personnel plotted to kill Castro from 1960 to 1965. American underworld figures and Cubans hostile to Castro were used in these plots, and were provided encouragement and material support by the United States.

Rafael Trujillo (Dominican Republic).—Trujillo was shot by Dominican dissidents on May 31, 1961. From early in 1960 and continuing to the time of the assassination, the United States Government generally supported these dissidents. Some Government personnel were aware that the dissidents intended to kill Trujillo. Three pistols and three carbines were furnished by American officials, although a request for machine guns was later refused. There is conflicting evidence concerning whether the weapons were knowingly supplied for use in the assassination and whether any of them were present at the scene.

Ngo Dinh Diem (South Vietnam).—Diem and his brother, Nhu, were killed on November 2, 1963, in the course of a South Vietnamese Generals' coup. Although the United States Government supported the coup, there is no evidence that American officials favored the assassination. Indeed, it appears that the assassination of Diem was not part of the Generals' pre-coup planning but was instead a spontaneous act which occurred during the coup and was carried out without United States involvement or support.

General Rene Schneider (Chile).—On October 25, 1970, General Schneider died of gunshot wounds inflicted three days earlier while resisting a kidnap attempt. Schneider, as Commander-in-Chief of the Army and a constitutionalist opposed to military coups, was considered an obstacle in efforts to prevent Salvador Allende from assuming the office of President of Chile. The United States Government supported, and sought to instigate a military coup to block Allende. U.S. officials supplied financial aid, machine guns and other equipment to various military figures who opposed Allende. Although the CIA continued to support coup plotters up to Schneider's shooting, the record indicates that the CIA had withdrawn active support of the group which carried out the actual kidnap attempt on October 22, which resulted in Schneider's death. Further, it does not appear that any of the equipment supplied by the CIA to coup plotters in Chile was used in the kidnapping. There is no evidence of a plan to kill Schneider or that United States officials specifically anticipated that Schneider would be shot during the abduction.

10

Years of Crisis

A slight relaxation of East-West tensions in the mid-1950s gave way to new confrontations that made the early 1960s the most dangerous years of the Cold War. Accelerating hostility resulted from the confluence of several developments. One was the rapid crumbling of European empires, a process that dissolved old sources of stability in large swaths of the world and opened new arenas for superpower competition. A second cause of mounting confrontation was discord between the Soviet Union and China as the two powers competed for leadership of the communist world. Each sought to legitimize its claim to supremacy by demonstrating superior revolutionary ardor and willingness to risk war by confronting the capitalist West. Yet another source of tension was the rapid development of new weapons technologies, which made both superpowers increasingly anxious about the overall balance of military power.

Perhaps most important of all, new conflicts resulted from changes in leadership on both sides. In the Soviet Union, the mercurial Nikita Khrushchev proved far more willing than his predecessors to provoke the West and run risks after he consolidated power in 1957. On the U.S. side, President John F. Kennedy, embodying a new spirit of liberal activism, expanded U.S. military capabilities, deepened American commitments throughout the developing world, and cultivated a reputation for muscular anticommunism.

Growing hawkishness in both Moscow and Washington fueled a series of crises from 1958 to 1962. This chapter explores U.S. decision making regarding the two most dangerous points of conflict, Berlin and Cuba. The documents shed light especially on two crucial questions: Why did American leaders believe that Soviet gains in either location would imperil U.S. security, and why did the crises come to peaceful conclusions despite serious dangers of war?

The period of near-constant crisis began when Khrushchev presented President Dwight D. Eisenhower with an ultimatum: if the Western powers did not agree to withdraw from West Berlin within six months, Moscow would turn the entire city over to the East German government, dissolving U.S., British, and French privileges dating from the end of the Second World War. The Western powers responded defiantly, insisting on their rights in West Berlin. Khrushchev backed away from his ultimatum a few months later but then renewed it in June 1961, when he confronted Kennedy at a summit meeting in Vienna. The ensuing confrontation ended only after construction of the Berlin Wall in August.

An even more serious crisis erupted in October 1962, when U.S. surveillance aircraft discovered that the Soviet Union was constructing missile bases in Cuba, just ninety miles from American shores. U.S. leaders, who had tried to overthrow the Castro regime by launching the Bay of Pigs invasion eighteen months earlier, concluded that the United States could not tolerate the missiles. The main question was how to get rid of them. Some policy makers favored a military strike against Cuba, despite the risk that an attack could lead to war with the Soviet Union. Others, including the president, insisted on trying for a peaceful resolution before resorting to military action. The latter group prevailed, and the crisis ended without fighting.

To their critics at home and abroad, U.S. leaders ran horrific risks over territories that held little tangible value to the United States or its allies. U.S. officials judged, however, that Berlin and Cuba were crucial to American interests in the broader struggle against communism. Whether or not they were correct, the twin crisis convinced leaders on both sides that the Cold War had become too dangerous and that steps must be taken to ease hostilities.

Document 10.1

A VISION OF NUCLEAR APOCALYPSE

The threat of nuclear combat increasingly seized the popular imagination during the 1950s and early 1960s as more information became available about the likely effects of such a war on everyday life. In a remarkable flurry of work, novelists and filmmakers depicted the outbreak and consequences of war. Films such as On the Beach *(1959) attracted large audiences, as did novels such as* Fail-Safe (1962). *The following selection comes from* Alas, Babylon, *Pat Frank's 1959 novel describing the effects of nuclear war on the fictional town of Fort Repose, Florida, on the Timucuan River. The scene, centering on the novel's protagonist, Randy, and his dog Graf, describes the first horrific moments of a war that would devastate the entire nation.*

At first Randy thought someone was shaking the couch. Graf, nestled under his arm, whined and slipped to the floor. Randy opened his eyes and elevated himself on his elbow. He felt stiff and grimy from sleeping in his clothes. Except for the dachshund, tail and ears at attention, the room was empty. Again the couch shook. The world outside still slept, but he discerned movement in the room. His fishing rods, hanging by their tips from a length of pegboard, inexplicably swayed in rhythm. He had heard such phenomena accompanied earthquakes, but there had never been an earthquake in Florida. Graf lifted his nose and howled.

Then the sound came, a long, deep, powerful rumble increasing in crescendo until the windows rattled, cups danced in their saucers, and the bar glasses rubbed rims and tinkled in terror. The sound slowly ebbed, then boomed to a fiercer climax, closer.

Randy found himself on his feet, throat dry, heart pounding. This was not the season for thunder, nor were storms forecast. Nor was this thunder. He stepped out onto the upstairs porch. To his left, in the east, an orange glow heralded the sun. In the south, across the Timucuan and beyond the horizon, a similar glow slowly faded. His sense refused to accept a sun rising and a sun setting. For perhaps a minute the spectacle numbed reaction.

What had jolted Randy from his sleep—he would not learn all the facts for a long, a very long time after—were two nuclear explosions, both in the megaton range, the warheads of missiles lobbed in by submarines. The first obliterated the SAC base at Homestead, and incidentally sank and returned to the sea a considerable area of Florida's tip. Ground Zero of the second missile was Miami's International Airport, not far from the heart of the city. Randy's couch had been shaken by shock waves transmitted through the earth, which travel faster than through the air, so he had been awake when the blast and sound arrived a little later. Gazing at the glow to the south, Randy was witnessing, from a distance of almost two hundred miles, the incineration of a million people.

Document 10.2

A U.S.-SOVIET RELATIONSHIP IN FLUX

The United States maintained a formidable lead over Moscow in both the quantity and quality of its nuclear weaponry, but that advantage seemed to be imperiled in the early 1960s as the Soviets expanded their arsenal. Just as worrying to American officials, new technologies such as intercontinental ballistic missiles (ICBMs), submarine-launched missiles, and defensive antimissile systems—all of which had either been recently developed or were imaginable within a few years—made the future unpredictable. In the following report, completed on January 17, 1961, the Central Intelligence Agency surveys the innumerable uncertainties confronting Washington.

Despite a widespread feeling that allout [*sic*] nuclear war is unlikely, the problem posed by the accumulation of offensive weapons of mass destruction by the great powers will remain the major problem of the 1960's. Although we have been unable to agree upon an estimate of the size of the Soviet ICBM program (estimates range from 200—or perhaps even less—to 700 on launcher for mid-1963), the Soviet capability even at the lowest estimated figure will pose a grave threat to the US. To illustrate, if one assumes the number on launcher to be 200 and applies reasonable rates of reliability to the missile, the USSR could detonate in the US in the target area some 1,000 to 1,250 megatons. The even greater delivery capability provided by shorter range missiles and nuclear weapons deliverable by aircraft or submarines and ships poses an additional threat to the US, to US bases overseas, to US allies, and indeed to most of the northern hemisphere.

So far as we can see now, if the USSR undertook to deliver such an attack, the US could do little to prevent enormous damage. A US preemptive attack—that is, an attack delivered when a Soviet attack was believed to be imminent—would not prevent such damage unless the various types of Soviet missile launchers had been precisely located, and there is doubt that a high proportion could be so located. Antiballistic missile systems of presently unproven effectiveness will probably be available about the middle of the decade, but such early systems almost certainly will not be sufficiently developed or widely-enough deployed to give assurances of destroying or neutralizing more than a small proportion of the missiles which the USSR will be capable of launching. . . .

There is much ignorance and uncertainty among military and civilian leaders throughout the world—in both Communist and non-Communist countries—about the present and future world military situation. This is due in part to security restrictions between governments and even within governments, in part to the complex technical and operational factors involved in modern military actions, and in part to the fact that the destructive potential of modern weapons is unprecedented in human history. Even among the politically and militarily sophisticated, there is considerable puzzlement and disagreement about the deterrent effect of present and future nuclear capabilities, about the proper behavior of states in critical situations, and about the most suitable and effective strategic doctrines and weapons systems to develop.

These problems must trouble the Soviet leaders as much as they trouble those of the West. We do not believe that the Soviet leaders conceive the ICBM to be the final answer to their military problems, and we doubt that they have formed definite ideas about their force structure ten years hence or about the precise role they will assign to military power in their campaign to establish world communism. They now see themselves as emerging from a period of strategic inferiority, and they surely consider it a prime objective not to let the US draw ahead once more. As long as the weapons race persists, they will not be content with a strategic equilibrium, or with the progress they have hitherto made in weapons development. Beyond that, they will continue to carry on scientific and weapons research and development programs with a high sense of urgency in order to find new weapons systems and defenses against existing ones. . . .

In the decade ahead some such weapons—for example, one providing defense against missiles—may achieve operational status and tend to upset the nuclear missile terror balance we have described. From what we know of Soviet ideas, however, we conclude that during the next five years—and perhaps longer—the Soviet leaders will conceive of their long-range striking capability in terms of deterrence and of employment in a heavy blow should they finally conclude that deterrence had failed, rather than in terms of the deliberate initiation of general war. In their view, a condition of mutual deterrence will provide an umbrella under which they can wage a vigorous campaign, using a wide variety of methods, throughout the non-Communist world.

In such circumstances the Soviet leaders will have substantial advantages. They can create crises and issue threats over comparatively minor matters with a reasonable degree of confidence that one or more of the Western powers will give way because of the risks of general war involved in resisting. In circumstances where they judge the risk is not too great they might engage in military action, possibly with Soviet forces but more probably with other bloc forces or with local revolutionary armed groups. In any case where it appears that the choice for resisters was one between massive nuclear destruction and compromise of principle (including surrender of territory), large numbers of people around the world would choose the latter.

It is now widely held that, in order to prevent such a paralyzing choice from being presented, it is necessary to have limited war capabilities, so that comparatively minor threats can be countered with appropriate means. But in recent years limited war capabilities in the West have been declining rather than rising. There has been a trend toward the reduction of budgetary allocations for the modernization and mobility of limited-war-capable forces. . . .

Even if substantial limited war forces should be available, many of the principles of their political and military use in a nuclear age remain to be developed and to be accepted. It is clear, for example, that only limited objectives can be won by limited means, and that pursuit of broad objectives or extension of the conflict beyond a well defined area of combat threatens expansion into a major war and poses for both sides the question of undertaking a large-scale pre-emptive attack on the enemy's homeland. . . .

A major problem during the next decade is also posed by the probability that additional nations will acquire a nuclear weapons capability. . . . Related to these problems of limited war and the spread of nuclear capabilities is the problem of preventing miscalculation which might precipitate general war unintentionally. . . . Another concern is that general war may come about by sheer accident. The worry here is that with an increasing number and variety of space capsules in orbit or being fired into orbit, with an increasing number of missiles nuclear-armed and on the ready, with strategic air forces airborne and armed with nuclear weapons, with a new and untested ballistic missile early warning system in operation, war could come about through communications failures or anomalies, irrational action by local crews or commanders, or errors in judgment, without either side wishing this to happen.

Document 10.3

THE VIENNA SUMMIT

Many observers hoped that meetings between Kennedy and Khrushchev in June 1961 would ease East-West tensions. They were badly disappointed. At the Vienna Summit, Khrushchev, apparently eager to intimidate the young American leader and to rub salt in American wounds from the failed Bay of Pigs invasion two months earlier, confronted Kennedy over numerous issues and brazenly threatened war. Tensions ran especially high over Berlin and Cuba. In the following excerpt from the minutes of a meeting on June 3, the two leaders discuss dangers that might arise from a shifting global situation—a condition that Khrushchev compared to other historic watersheds—and especially from revolutionary upheavals in the developing world.

[Kennedy] said it would be useful to discuss the problem underlying the [global] situation and consider the specifics perhaps later. . . . [S]uch specifics might include Germany and nuclear tests. The President then recalled Mr. Khrushchev's earlier reference to the death of feudalism. He said he understood this to mean that capitalism was to be succeeded by Communism. This was a disturbing situation because the French Revolution, as the Chairman well knew, had caused great disturbances and upheavals throughout Europe. Even earlier the struggle between Catholics and Protestants had caused the Hundred Year War. Thus it is obvious that when systems are in transition we should be careful, particularly today when modern weapons are at hand. Whatever the results of the present competition—and no one can be sure what it will be—both sides should act in such a way as to prevent them from coming into direct contact and thus prejudicing the establishment of lasting peace, which, the President said, was his ambition.

Mr. Khrushchev interjected that he fully understood this.

Even the Russian Revolution had produced convulsions, even intervention by other countries, the President continued. He then said that he wanted to explain what he meant by "miscalculation". In Washington, he has to attempt to make judgments of events, judgments which may be accurate or not; he made a misjudgment with regard to the Cuban situation. He has to attempt to make judgments as to what the USSR will do next, just as he is sure that Mr. Khrushchev has to make judgments as to the moves of the US. The President emphasized that the purpose of this meeting was to introduce greater precision in these judgments so that our two countries could survive this period of competition without endangering their national security.

Mr. Khrushchev responded by saying that this was a good idea and that this was what he called demonstration of patience and understanding. However, judging by some of the President's statements, the Soviet Union understood the situation differently. The US believes that when people want to improve their lot, this is a machination by others. Mr. Khrushchev said that he liked the President's statement in his message to Congress to the effect that it was difficult to defend ideas not supporting better standards of living. However, the President drew the wrong conclusion. He believes that when people rise against tyrants, that is a result of Moscow's activities. This is not so. Failure by the US to understand this generates danger. The USSR does not foment revolution but the United States always looks for outside forces whenever certain upheavals occur. . . .

[An] example of this situation is Cuba. A mere handful of people, headed by Fidel Castro, overthrew the Batista regime because of its oppressive nature. During Castro's fight against Batista, US capitalist circles, as they are called in the USSR, supported Batista and this is why the anger of the Cuban people turned against the United States. The President's decision to launch a landing in Cuba only strengthened the revolutionary forces and Castro's own position, because the people of Cuba were afraid that they would get another Batista and lose the achievements of the revolution. Castro is not a Communist but US policy can make him one. US policy is grist on the mill of Communists, because US actions prove that Communists are right. . . .

The President had said that the US had attacked Cuba because it was a threat to American security. Can six million people really be a threat to the mighty US? The United States has stated that it is free to act, but what about Turkey and Iran? These two countries are US followers, they march in its wake, and they have US bases and rockets. If the US believes that it is free to act, then what should the USSR do? The US has set a precedent for intervention in the internal affairs of other countries. . . .

The President reminded Mr. Khrushchev of the announced policy of the USSR that it would not tolerate governments hostile to it in areas which it regards as being of national interest to it. He inquired what the USSR's reaction would be if a government associated with the West were established in Poland. The United States stands for the right of free choice for all peoples and if Castro had acted in that spirit, he might have obtained endorsement. . . . The President concluded by saying that it was critical to have the changes occurring in the world and affecting the balance of power take place in a way that would not involve the prestige or the treaty commitments of our two countries. The changes should be peaceful. . . .

Document 10.4

RALLYING AMERICANS TO THE DEFENSE OF BERLIN

Khrushchev's renewed threat to turn all of Berlin over to East German authority produced intense alarm in Washington, where Kennedy and his advisers were determined to keep West Berlin in the Western camp despite its isolation inside the Soviet bloc. On July 25, 1961, Kennedy went before a nationwide television audience to state his willingness to negotiate with the USSR but also his refusal to back down in the face of Soviet threats. The president announced specific steps to bolster U.S. military forces, including a sharp rise in defense spending and expansion of each branch of the armed forces, but also laid out the general case for the American presence in Berlin.

We are [in Berlin] as a result of our victory over Nazi Germany—and our basic rights to be there, deriving from that victory, include both our presence in West Berlin and the enjoyment of access across East Germany. These rights have been repeatedly confirmed and recognized in special agreements with the Soviet Union. Berlin is not a part of East Germany, but a separate territory under the control of the allied powers. Thus our rights there are clear and deep-rooted. But in addition to those rights is our commitment to sustain—and defend, if need be—the opportunity for more than two million people to determine their own future and choose their own way of life.

Thus, our presence in West Berlin, and our access thereto, cannot be ended by any act of the Soviet government. The NATO shield was long ago extended to cover West Berlin—and we have given our word that an attack upon that city will be regarded as an attack upon us all.

For West Berlin, lying exposed 110 miles inside East Germany, surrounded by Soviet troops and close to Soviet supply lines, has many roles. It is more than a showcase of liberty, a symbol, an island of freedom in a Communist sea. It is even more than a link with the Free World, a beacon of hope behind the Iron Curtain, an escape hatch for refugees.

West Berlin is all of that. But above all it has now become—as never before—the great testing place of Western courage and will, a focal point where our solemn commitments stretching back over the years since 1945, and Soviet ambitions now meet in basic confrontation. . . .

So long as the Communists insist that they are preparing to end by themselves unilaterally our rights in West Berlin and our commitments to its people, we must be prepared to defend those rights and those commitments.

We will at all times be ready to talk, if talk will help. But we must also be ready to resist with force, if force is used upon us....

The new preparations that we shall make to defend the peace are part of the long-term build-up in our strength which has been underway since January. They are based on our needs to meet a world-wide threat, on a basis which stretches far beyond the present Berlin crisis. Our primary purpose is neither propaganda nor provocation—but preparation....

[I]n the days and months ahead, I shall not hesitate to ask the Congress for additional measures, or exercise any of the executive powers that I possess to meet this threat to peace. Everything essential to the security of freedom must be done; and if that should require more men, or more taxes, or more controls, or other new powers, I shall not hesitate to ask them. The measures proposed today will be constantly studied, and altered as necessary. But while we will not let panic shape our policy, neither will we permit timidity to direct our program....

We have another sober responsibility. To recognize the possibilities of nuclear war in the missile age, without our citizens knowing what they should do and where they should go if bombs begin to fall, would be a failure of responsibility. In May, I pledged a new start on Civil Defense. Last week, I assigned, on the recommendation of the Civil Defense Director, basic responsibility for this program to the Secretary of Defense, to make certain it is administered and coordinated with our continental defense efforts at the highest civilian level. Tomorrow, I am requesting of the Congress new funds for the following immediate objectives: to identify and mark space in existing structures—public and private—that could be used for fall-out shelters in case of attack; to stock those shelters with food, water, first-aid kits and other minimum essentials for survival; to increase their capacity; to improve our air-raid warning and fallout detection systems, including a new household warning system which is now under development; and to take other measures that will be effective at an early date to save millions of lives if needed.

Document 10.5

A SOVIET VIEW OF JOHN F. KENNEDY

By early August 1961, U.S.-Soviet tensions had reached new heights concerning Berlin. Privately, Khrushchev was probably convinced that his best move was to build a barrier between East and West Berlin since a wall would secure the stability of East Germany without directly antagonizing the West. Facing pressure from the East German and Chinese governments, however, he had to maintain a posture of hawkish defiance. In a speech to fellow communist leaders at an extraordinary meeting of the Warsaw Pact on August 4, Khrushchev laid out a complicated view of the United States and especially Kennedy. He reported especially on his recent conversations with U.S. envoy John J. McCloy and Italian Prime Minister Amintore Fanfani.

[It was always clear that the West] would intimidate us, call out all spirits against us to test our courage, our acumen and our will. . . . As for me and my colleagues in the state and party leadership, we think that the adversary proved to be less staunch than we had estimated. . . . We expected there would be more blustering and . . . so far the worst spurt of intimidation was in the Kennedy speech [on July 25, 1961]. . . . Kennedy spoke [to frighten] us and then got scared himself.

Immediately after Kennedy delivered his speech I spoke with McCloy. . . . "You want to frighten us," I [said to McCloy]. "You convinced yourself that Khrushchev will never go to war . . . so you scare us [expecting] us to retreat. True, we will not declare war, but we will not withdraw either, if you push it on us. We will respond to your war in kind.

I told him to let Kennedy know . . . that if he starts a war then he would probably become the last president of the United States of America. I know he reported it accurately. In America they are showing off vehemently, but yet people close to Kennedy are beginning to pour cold war like a fire-brigade.

[I told Fanfani that] Kennedy himself acknowledged that there is equality of forces, i.e. the Soviet Union has as many hydrogen and atomic weapons as they have. I agree with that, [although] we did not crunch numbers. [But, if one recognizes that equality] let us speak about equal opportunities. Instead [Western leaders] behave as if they were a father dealing with a toddler: if it doesn't come their way, they threaten to pull our ears. . . . We already passed that age, we wear long trousers, not short ones. . . .

[War is] hardly possible, because it would be a duel of ballistic missiles. We are strong on that. . . . America would be at a disadvantage to start a war with this weapon. . . . They know it and admit it. . . .

The outcome of modern war will be decided by atomic weapons. Does it make sense if there is one more division or less [in Germany]? If the entire French army cannot cope with Algerians, armed with knives, then how do they expect to scare us with a division. It is ludicrous, not frightening. . . .

I told Fanfani that [the United States] is a barely governed state. . . . Kennedy himself hardly influences the direction and development of policies in the American state. . . . [A]nything is possible in the United States. . . .

As for Kennedy, he is rather an unknown quantity in politics. So I feel empathy with him in his situation, because he is too much of a lightweight both for the Republicans as well as for the Democrats. And the state is too big, the state is powerful, and it poses certain dangers.

Document 10.6

THE U.S. RESPONSE TO THE BERLIN WALL

The erection of the Berlin Wall, starting on August 13, 1961, put the Kennedy administration in a difficult bind. On the one hand, U.S. officials were shocked by the brutal division of the city and felt pressure to take action in response. On the other hand, they recognized that the wall did not directly infringe Western rights in the city and understood that acceptance of the division might help end the crisis. The dilemma became especially acute on August 16, when West Berlin Mayor Willy Brandt criticized U.S. inaction in a letter to Kennedy. On August 18, Kennedy responded in a letter expressing a mix of determination and caution.

The measures taken by the Soviet Government and its puppets in East Berlin have caused revulsion here in America. This demonstration of what the Soviet Government means by freedom for a city, and peace for a people, proves the hollowness of Soviet pretensions; and Americans understand that this action necessarily constitutes a special blow to the people of West Berlin, connected as they remain in a myriad of ways to their fellow Berliners in the eastern sector. So I understand entirely the deep concerns and sense of trouble which prompted your letter.

Grave as the matter is, however, there are, as you say, no steps available to us which can force a significant material change in the present situation. Since it represents a resounding confession of failure and of political weakness, this brutal border closing evidently represents a basic Soviet decision which only war could reverse. Neither you nor we, nor any of our Allies, have ever supposed that we should go to war on this point.

Yet the Soviet action is too serious for inadequate responses. My own objection to most of the measures which have been proposed . . . is that they are mere trifles compared to what has been done. Some of them, moreover, seem unlikely to be fruitful even in their own terms. This is our present judgment, for example, on the question of an immediate appeal to the United Nations, although we shall continue to keep this possibility under lively review.

On careful consideration I myself have decided that the best immediate response is a significant reinforcement of the Western garrisons. The importance of this reinforcement is symbolic—but not symbolic only. We know that the Soviet Union continues to emphasize its demand for the removal of Allied protection from West Berlin. We believe that even a modest reinforcement will underline our rejection of this concept.

At the same time, and of even greater basic importance, we shall continue and accelerate the broad buildup of the military strength of the West upon which we are decided, and which we view as the necessary answer to the long-range Soviet threat to Berlin and to us all. . . .

More broadly, let me urge it upon you that we must not be shaken by Soviet actions which in themselves are a confession of weakness. West Berlin today is more important than ever, and its mission to stand for freedom has never been so important as now. The link of West Berlin to the Free World is not a matter of rhetoric. Important as the ties to the East have been, painful as is their violation, the life of the city, as I understand it, runs primarily to the West—its economic life, its moral basis, and its military security. You may wish to consider and to suggest concrete ways in which these ties might be expanded in a fashion that would make the citizens of West Berlin more actively conscious of their role, not merely as an outpost of freedom, but as a vital part of the Free World and all its enterprises.

Document 10.7

THINKING THE UNTHINKABLE

Fearful that the Berlin Wall would not end the crisis, U.S. officials continued to prepare intensively for the possibility of war with the Soviet Union. Some national security experts worried that the existing U.S. plan for waging nuclear war, the so-called Single Integrated Operational Plan (SIOP), was too rigid, giving the president no option other than a massive retaliatory blow in response to a Soviet nuclear attack. Under these circumstances, officials such as National Security Council aide Carl Kaysen began to explore the possibility that the United States might launch a limited first strike against the Soviet Union if tensions mounted uncontrollably. Kaysen sent the following memo to Kennedy's top military adviser, General Maxwell Taylor, on September 5, 1961.

The plan which now determines the use of our strategic striking power in the event of war is SIOP-62. This plan, prepared well before the present Berlin crisis, is built around two concepts that may well be inappropriate to the current situation. First, the plan is essentially a second-strike plan, which envisages a response to an attack on us, the size of which depends essentially on the amount of warning of enemy attack we receive. The minimum warning assumed is one hour: this suffices to generate the alert force of nearly 900 vehicles carrying almost 1500 weapons. In 28 hours the full force of some 2300 vehicles carrying about 3400 weapons can be launched. Second, the plan calls for strikes against a single set of targets, the "optimum mix" of Sino-Soviet air and missile bases, and cities, and the various force generation options determine how far down the list the targets are struck, and the degree of their coverage by more than one weapon to assure achievement of planned damage levels. The single target list embodies the notion of "massive retaliation," the threat of which is expected to deter attack. At least two sets of circumstances that seem likely to arise in the context of the struggle over Berlin suggest the need for supplementary and alternate plans. The first is the problem raised by a false alarm, whether arising from a deliberate feint or a misinterpretation of events, that results first in the launching of SAC and then a decision to recall it at the positive control line. The second is the broader question of whether we might wish to strike first, and thus how appropriate both the target list and the operational concept of the SIOP are in that case.

If the present state of tension over Berlin persists over a period of months, it is likely that, at some point, a Soviet action will appear to threaten an attack on the United States with sufficient likelihood and imminence to cause us to launch [Strategic Air Command], and initiate the SIOP. After some lapse of time, we may conclude that we had been wrong, and, under the positive control arrangements, recall the force. There is, roughly, a six-hour interval between bases and the positive control line for aircraft in the first wave. After recall and return to base, that part of the force which had been launched would require a stand-down of about eight hours before it was again ready for launch. Thus, there would be a significant degradation of our capability for a short period of time after such a false alarm. . . .

Further, in the nature of the SIOP, that part of the force which was still in reserve might not be ready to attack an appropriate set of targets, since their initially assigned targets would have been chosen under the assumption that the vehicles in question were part of the follow-on force, coming after the targets assigned to the first wave had already been attacked. These consequences of a false alarm suggest two dangers: First, the value to the Soviets of a feint; second, the danger that we will have a tendency to refuse to interpret any alarm as a false alarm, once the force has been launched, since the temporary degradation of our striking capacity consequent on a recall may be unacceptable in the situation which provoked the alarm.

The second and broader question is whether a second-strike plan of massive retaliation is appropriate to our current position. Our military contingency plans for Berlin call for a number of ground force actions of increasing scope and magnitude. Their basic aim is to force the Soviets to withdraw the impediments to our access to West Berlin which have called them forth. Implicitly, they rest on the expectation that the Soviets will not respond, at least to the earlier steps, by initiating general war. If each increase in the scale of our action is met by a corresponding and always dominating increase in the Soviet response, we will clearly be forced at some point to move from local to general action. Is the SIOP the appropriate form of this action? If the SIOP were executed as planned, the alert force would be expected (in the statistical sense) to kill 37% of the population of the Soviet Union (including 55% of the urban population) and the full force 54% (including 71% of the urban population), and the two forces, respectively, to destroy 75% and 82% of the buildings, as measured by floor space. (Further, there is reason to believe that these figures are underestimated; the casualties, for example, include only those of the first 72 hours). Is this really an appropriate next step after the repulse of a three-division attack across the zonal border between East and West Germany? Will the President be ready to take it? The force of these questions is underlined by the consideration that the scale and nature of the SIOP are such as inevitably to alert the Soviets to its initiation. . . . Thus Soviet retaliation is inevitable; and most probably, it will be directed against our cities and those of our European Allies. . . .

What is required in these circumstances is something quite different. We should be prepared to initiate general war by our own first strike, but one planned for this occasion, rather than planned to implement a strategy of massive retaliation. We should seek the smallest possible list of targets, focusing on the long-range striking capacity of the Soviets, and avoiding, as much as possible, casualties and damage in Soviet civil society. We should maintain in reserve a considerable fraction of our own strategic striking power; this will deter the Soviets from using their surviving forces against our cities; our efforts to minimize Soviet civilian damage will also make such abstention more attractive to them, as well as minimizing the force of the irrational urge for revenge. The SIOP now provides for no reserve forces, except insofar as aircraft return and can be recycled into operation.

Document 10.8

THE STAKES IN CUBA

On October 16, 1962, U.S. intelligence officials informed Kennedy that the Soviet Union was constructing missile bases in Cuba. Within hours, the president began meeting with top advisers to consider how to manage what all of them regarded as a major crisis in U.S.-Soviet relations. Those meetings, captured by a White House taping system, continued for the next thirteen days. In the following excerpts from October 16, Kennedy and his aides speculate on the significance of Soviet medium-range ballistic missiles (MRBMs) in Cuba and the reasons why the Soviets had taken such a provocative step. Besides the president, speakers include National Security Adviser McGeorge Bundy; Defense Secretary Robert S. McNamara; a military adviser, General Maxwell Taylor; and two influential undersecretaries of state, George Ball and U. Alexis Johnson.

BUNDY: What is the strategic impact on the position of the United States of MRBMs in Cuba? How gravely does this change the strategic balance?

MCNAMARA: Mac, I asked the chiefs that this afternoon, in effect. They said, "substantially." My own personal view is: not at all.

BUNDY: Not so much.

. . . .

TAYLOR: I think from a cold-blooded point of view, Mr. President, you're quite right in saying that these are just a few more missiles targeted on the United States. However, they can become a very, rather important, adjunct and reinforcement to the strike capability of the Soviet Union. We have no idea how far they will go. But more than that, these are, to our nation it means a great deal more, as we all are aware, if they have them in Cuba and not over in the Soviet Union.

BUNDY: Oh, I ask the question with an awareness of the political—[chuckles].

KENNEDY: Well, let's say—I understand, but let's just say that they get these in there. And then you can't—They get sufficient capacity, so we can't, with warheads. Then you don't want to knock them out because that's too much of a gamble. Then they just begin to build up those air bases there, and then put more and more. I suppose they really—Then they start getting ready to squeeze us in Berlin. Doesn't that—You may say it doesn't make any difference if you get blown up by an ICBM flying from the Soviet Union or one from 90 miles away. Geography doesn't mean that much—.

TAYLOR: We would have to target them with our missiles and have the same kind of pistol pointed at the head situation as they have in the Soviet Union at the present time.

BUNDY: No question. If this thing goes on, an attack on Cuba becomes general war. And that's really the question: whether—

KENNEDY: That's why it shows the Bay of Pigs was really right. If we had done it right. That was [a choice between] better and better, and worse and worse.

TAYLOR: I'm impressed with this, Mr. President. We have a war plan over there for you. [It] calls for a quarter of a million American soldiers, marines, and airmen to take an island we launched 1,800

Cubans against, a years and a half ago. We changed our evaluations about it.

. . . .

KENNEDY: Why does he put these in there, though? . . . It's just as if we suddenly began to put a major number of MRBMs in Turkey. Now that'd be goddamn dangerous, I would think.

BUNDY: Well, we did, Mr. President.

JOHNSON: We did it. We did it in England.

KENNEDY: Yeah, but that was five years ago.

U. A. JOHNSON: That's when we were short. We put them in England too when we were short of ICBMs.

KENNEDY: But that was during a different period then.

JOHNSON: But doesn't [Khrushchev] realize he has a deficiency of ICBMs vis-à-vis our capacity perhaps? In view of that he's got lots of MRBMs and this is a way to balance it out a bit.

BUNDY: I'm sure his generals have been telling him for a year and a half that he was missing a golden opportunity to add to his strategic capability.

BALL: Yes, I think you look at this possibility that this is an attempt to add to his strategic capabilities. A second consideration is that it is simply a trading ploy, that he wants this in so that he can—

JOHNSON: It's not inconsistent. If he can't trade then he's still got the other.

DOCUMENT 10.9

PLANNING FOR AN ATTACK ON CUBA

On October 22, the Kennedy administration deferred military options in favor of a blockade to isolate Cuba and block the arrival of additional missile equipment. But a U.S. attack remained a distinct possibility as the superpower standoff continued during the following days. Among those policy makers charged with studying military options was Treasury Secretary Douglas Dillon, whose team of experts produced a discussion paper entitled "Scenario for Airstrike against Offensive Missile Bases and Bombers in Cuba." Presented to the Executive Committee on October 25, the study weighed the pros and cons of an air attack.

ADVANTAGES

1. Carries out President's pledge to eliminate offensive threat to U.S. and Hemisphere from Cuba and avoids any erosion of U.S. momentum and position. The pledge carried out shows that U.S. has will to fight and to protect vital interests (of great importance vis-à-vis Berlin).

2. Since directed at offensive weapons, keeps issue focused on Soviet nuclear presence in Cuba in defiance of [Organization of American States] and majority of Security Council.

3. Sharp, possible one time action, may carry smaller risks of further escalation than a series of confrontations over a period of time. Soviet decision to risk major war unlikely to be decisively affected by this action in an area non-vital to the Soviets.

4. Prompt action will avoid danger of a growth of hands-off Cuba movement throughout Latin America which might make it increasingly difficult to strike at offensive weapons. Present willingness of Latin Americans to support strong action probably cannot be maintained indefinitely.

5. Signals clearly that U.S. not prepared to bargain bases in Cuba for positions in Berlin, NATO and elsewhere.

6. It could demonstrate to Cubans, Castro and others, the weakness of Soviet position in Cuba. In the absence of a strong Soviet reaction in defense of Cuba, we would start the process of disenchantment and disaffection requisite to undermining Castro and Cuban reliance on the Soviet Union. We would also weaken any tendencies to rely on Soviets elsewhere in the world.

7. Removes a military threat to U.S. from Cuban territory.

8. Denies Khrushchev a possible cheap victory through successful maintenance of offensive weapons in Cuba.

DISADVANTAGES

1. This action may force Khrushchev to react strongly and could result in some type of war. Khrushchev will not order launch of a missile from Cuba unless he is ready for war essentially on other grounds. There is greater likelihood of a riposte in kind. However, it is unlikely that the risks of major war are greater than through escalation of a blockade.

2. There is remote possibility that some local Soviet commander in Cuba may order firing of a missile.

3. Adverse effect on U.S. image of initiation of use of force against a small country. This can be minimized by making attack selective and focused on Soviet offensive weapons. At same time there would be positive increments to our image from demonstration of clear willingness to take on the Soviets in protection of our vital interests.

4. Unless carefully handled could damage long-range U.S.-Cuban relations.

5. May not totally eliminate offensive weapons thus calling for follow up attacks and/or invasion, unless full and unlimited international inspection is agreed to.

Document 10.10

THE CRUCIAL MEETING

A resolution to the Cuban crisis fell into place on October 27, the climactic day of the confrontation. President Kennedy agreed to promise not to invade Cuba and to pull U.S. nuclear missiles out of Turkey in return for a Soviet commitment to withdraw the missiles from Cuba. These terms were communicated to the Soviet government by the president's brother, Attorney General Robert F. Kennedy, during a late-night meeting with Soviet Ambassador Anatoly Dobrynin in Washington. Dobrynin's dispatch to Moscow describing the meeting makes clear the attorney general's insistence that the U.S. commitment to withdraw missiles from Turkey would have to remain secret. Khrushchev announced his acceptance of the formula the next morning and never revealed the missile swap.

Late this evening R. Kennedy invited me to come see him. The conversation occurred in private. . . .

"I want," R. Kennedy emphasized, "to set forth the current alarming situation as seen by the president, who wants N. S. Khrushchev to know about it. The situation now boils down to the following. . . ."

"The US government is committed to getting rid of those [missile] bases—even, as a last resort, to bombing them, since, I repeat, they pose a major threat to US national security. But to the bombing of these bases, during the course of which Soviet specialists might be harmed, the Soviet government will undoubtedly respond in kind, somewhere in Europe. A real war will begin, in which ultimately millions of Americans and Russians will be killed. We want to avoid that by all means necessary. I'm sure that the government of the USSR has the same desire. However, a delay in finding a solution is very risky (here R. Kennedy noted as if in passing that there are many irrational heads among the generals—and not even only among the generals—who are "spoiling for a fight"). The situation could get out of control, with irreparable repercussions."

"To that end," R. Kennedy said, "the president feels that an appropriate basis for the regulation of the whole Cuban conflict could be N. S. Khrushchev's letter from October 26 and the President's letter in reply, which was sent to N. S. Khrushchev today through the U.S. Embassy in Moscow. The main thing for us," R. Kennedy emphasized, "is to receive as soon as possible the Soviet government's agreement to terminate further work on the construction of the missile bases in Cuba and to take measures under international control that would make the use of such weapons impossible. In exchange, in addition to repealing all 'quarantine' measures, the US government is ready to give assurances that there will not be any kind of invasion of Cuba and that the other countries of the Western Hemisphere—and the US government is certain of this—are ready to give the same assurances."

"And how does this pertain to Turkey?" I asked R. Kennedy.

"If that is the only obstacle to achieving the aforementioned accommodation, then the president doesn't see any insurmountable difficulties in resolving the issue," R. Kennedy answered. "The main difficulty for the president is the public discussion of the Turkey question. The deployment of missile bases in Turkey was formally established by a special decision of the NATO Council. To now announce a unilateral decision by the president of the USA to withdraw missile bases from Turkey—this would strike a blow to the entire structure of NATO and to the US position as leader of NATO, in which, as the Soviet government undoubtedly knows well, much controversy exists. In short, the announcement of such a decision would seriously undermine NATO.

"However, President Kennedy is ready to reach an agreement on that issue with N. S. Khrushchev. I think that the withdrawal of these bases from Turkey," R. Kennedy said, "would require 4–5 months. This is the minimum amount of time necessary for the US government to do this, considering the procedures that exist within the framework of NATO. On the whole Turkey issue," added Kennedy, "if Premier N.S. Khrushchev agrees with everything that has been laid out, we can continue the exchange of opinions between him and the president, using him, R. Kennedy and the Soviet ambassador. However, the president can't say anything publicly about this Turkey plan," R. Kennedy repeated. R. Kennedy then warned that his message about

Turkey is highly confidential; aside from him and his brother, only 2 or 3 other people in Washington know about it.

"That's everything I was requested to pass on to N. S. Khrushchev," concluded Kennedy. "The president also requested that N. S. Khrushchev give him an answer (through the Soviet ambassador and R. Kennedy) if possible within the next day (Sunday) on these points, in order to have a businesslike and essentially clear answer and not to get dragged into a verbose discussion, which would only prolong the entire affair. Unfortunately, the current serious situation is such that there remains very little time to resolve the whole issue. Regretfully, events are developing too rapidly. The request for a reply tomorrow," R. Kennedy stressed, "is exactly that—a request, and not any sort of ultimatum or deadline. The president hopes that the head of the Soviet government will understand him correctly."

I noted that it goes without saying that the Soviet government would not accept any sort of ultimatum and that it was good that the American government realized that. I also reminded him of N. S. Khrushchev's appeal in his last letter to the president to exercise statecraft in resolving this issue. Then R. Kennedy was told that the president's thoughts would be made available to the head of the Soviet government. He was also told that when a reply is forthcoming, I will immediately contact him. To that end, R. Kennedy gave me the telephone number of a direct line to the White House. . . .

It should be said that during our meeting R. Kennedy was extremely agitated; at any rate, it was the first time I had seen him in such a state. It is true that about twice he tried to return to the subject of "deception" (that he talked about so persistently during our last meeting), but he did so cursorily and without hectoring. He didn't even try to argue about various issues, as he usually does, but persistently returned to one topic: time is short and we must not squander it.

Document 10.11

KHRUSHCHEV ASSESSES THE CUBAN CRISIS

Most of the world viewed the resolution of the Cuban Missile Crisis as a victory for the United States, an interpretation that left Khrushchev on the defensive when communist officials from throughout the Soviet bloc arrived in Moscow at the end of October to commemorate the 1917 Bolshevik Revolution. On October 30, 1962, Khrushchev tried to justify his conduct during a meeting with Czechoslovak communist leader Antonín Novotny. In the following excerpt from the minutes of that conversation, the Soviet leader reviews the crisis and states various reasons for his decision to withdraw the missiles.

Naturally we wanted the presence of our missiles with atomic warheads to remain secret. That is obviously impossible in Cuba. They were hardly the most powerful missiles, but the Americans calculated well when it came to their range—they could have reached Washington and New York.

We now know the subsequent course of events. We had to act very quickly. That is also why we even used radio to contact the president, because the other means might have been too slow. This time we really were on the verge of war.

We received a letter from [Fidel] Castro in which he told us that the USA would attack Cuba within twenty-four hours. That would mean nuclear war. We could not be certain that they would not do so. The presence of our missiles provoked them too much; the Americans thus sensed the winds of war from up close. It was necessary to act quickly. That is why we issued the statement [on October 28] that we would dismantle the missiles if the USA declared it swore not to attack Cuba. . . .

In the letter, Fidel Castro proposed that we ourselves should be the first to start an atomic war. Do you know what that would mean? That probably cannot even be expressed at all. We were completely aghast. Castro clearly has no idea about what thermonuclear war is. After all, if a war started, it would primarily be Cuba that would vanish from the face of the Earth. At the same time, it is clear that with a first strike one cannot today knock the opponent out of the fight. There can always be a counter-strike, which can be devastating. There are, after all, missiles in the earth, which intelligence does not know about; there are missiles on submarines, which cannot be knocked out of the fight right away, and so on. What would we gain if we ourselves started a war? After all, millions of people would die, in our country too. Can we even contemplate a thing like that? Could we allow ourselves to threaten the world of socialism which was hard won by the working class? Only a person who has no idea what nuclear war means, or who has been so blinded, for instance, like Castro, by revolutionary passion, can talk like that. . . .

How should one assess the result of these six days which shook the world? Who won? I am of the opinion that we won. One must start from the final aims we set ourselves. What aim did the Americans have? To attack Cuba and get rid of the Cuban Republic, to establish a reactionary regime in Cuba. Things did not work as they planned. Our main aim was to save Cuba, to save the Cuban revolution. That is why we sent missiles to Cuba. We achieved our objective—we wrenched the promise out of the Americans that they would not attack Cuba and that other countries on the American continent would also refrain from attacking Cuba. That would not have happened without our missiles in Cuba. The USA would have attacked Cuba. The proximity of our missiles made them understand, perhaps for the first time, that we have weapons that are at least as strong as theirs.

Document 10.12

PRESSURES FOR CONFRONTATION

The Cuban Missile Crisis, like the Berlin Crisis before it, was often depicted as a standoff between two larger-than-life men, Kennedy and Khrushchev. But much commentary suggested that the two leaders were mere puppets of powerful yet secretive forces operating behind the scenes, such as military chiefs, industrialists, media barons, and ideological extremists. Indeed, during the Cuban crisis both Kennedy and Khrushchev speculated that the other man could only go so far toward compromise due to fears of domestic critics. The eminent cartoonist David Low, who was born in New Zealand but achieved fame in Britain, captured this possibility in a cartoon published in the Guardian *on November 13, 1962.*

THE GUARDIAN ✫ ✫ Tuesday November 13 1962

ADVISERS AND CONSENTERS

Document 10.13

AN APPEAL FOR DÉTENTE

Following the Cuban Missile Crisis, both Kennedy and Khrushchev realized more clearly than ever the risks of war and sought to ease Cold War tensions. To some extent, both seem to have understood that the danger of nuclear war made it impossible for either side to challenge the other's core interests around the world. In June 1963, Washington and Moscow established a telephone hotline to assure that leaders could communicate directly during crises, and a few months later they signed a treaty limiting the testing of nuclear weapons. Kennedy made his new approach to the Cold War clear in one of his most famous speeches, delivered as a commencement address at American University in Washington, D.C., on June 10, 1963.

I have . . . chosen this time and this place to discuss a topic on which ignorance too often abounds and the truth is too rarely perceived—yet it is the most important topic on earth: world peace.

What kind of peace do I mean? What kind of peace do we seek? Not a Pax Americana enforced on the world by American weapons of war. Not the peace of the grave or the security of the slave. I am talking about genuine peace, the kind of peace that makes life on earth worth living, the kind that enables men and nations to grow and to hope and to build a better life for their children—not merely peace for Americans but peace for all men and women—not merely peace in our time but peace for all time.

I speak of peace because of the new face of war. Total war makes no sense in an age when great powers can maintain large and relatively invulnerable nuclear forces and refuse to surrender without resort to those forces. It makes no sense in an age when a single nuclear weapon contains almost ten times the explosive force delivered by all the allied air forces in the Second World War. It makes no sense in an age when the deadly poisons produced by a nuclear exchange would be carried by wind and water and soil and seed to the far corners of the globe and to generations yet unborn.

Today the expenditure of billions of dollars every year on weapons acquired for the purpose of making sure we never need to use them is essential to keeping the peace. But surely the acquisition of such idle stockpiles—which can only destroy and never create—is not the only, much less the most efficient, means of assuring peace.

I speak of peace, therefore, as the necessary rational end of rational men. I realize that the pursuit of peace is not as dramatic as the pursuit of war—and frequently the words of the pursuer fall on deaf ears. But we have no more urgent task.

Some say that it is useless to speak of world peace or world law or world disarmament—and that it will be useless until the leaders of the Soviet Union adopt a more enlightened attitude. I hope they do. I believe we can help them do it. But I also believe that we must reexamine our own attitude—as individuals and as a Nation—for our attitude is as essential as theirs. And every graduate of this school, every thoughtful citizen who despairs of war and wishes to bring peace, should begin by looking inward—by examining his own attitude toward the possibilities of peace, toward the Soviet Union, toward the course of the cold war and toward freedom and peace here at home.

First: Let us examine our attitude toward peace itself. Too many of us think it is impossible. Too many think it unreal. But that is a dangerous, defeatist belief. It leads to the conclusion that war is inevitable—that mankind is doomed—that we are gripped by forces we cannot control.

We need not accept that view. Our problems are manmade—therefore, they can be solved by man. And man can be as big as he wants. No problem of human destiny is beyond human beings. Man's reason and spirit have often solved the seemingly unsolvable—and we believe they can do it again.

I am not referring to the absolute, infinite concept of peace and good will of which some fantasies and fanatics dream. I do not deny the value of hopes and dreams but we merely invite discouragement and incredulity by making that our only and immediate goal.

Let us focus instead on a more practical, more attainable peace—based not on a sudden revolution in human nature but on a gradual evolution in human institutions—on a series of concrete actions and effective agreements which are in the interest of all concerned. There is no single, simple key to this peace—no grand or magic formula to be adopted by one or two powers. Genuine peace must be the product of many nations, the sum of many acts. It must be dynamic, not static, changing to meet the challenge of each new generation. For peace is a process—a way of solving problems. . . .

Second: Let us reexamine our attitude toward the Soviet Union. . . . No government or social system is so evil that its people must be considered as lacking in virtue. As Americans, we find communism profoundly repugnant as a negation of personal freedom and dignity. But we can still hail the Russian people for their many achievements—in science and space, in economic and industrial growth, in culture and in acts of courage. . . .

Third: Let us reexamine our attitude toward the cold war, remembering that we are not engaged in a debate, seeking to pile up debating points. We are not here distributing blame or pointing the finger of judgment. We must deal with the world as it is, and not as it might have been had the history of the last 18 years been different.

We must, therefore, persevere in the search for peace in the hope that constructive changes within the Communist bloc might bring within reach solutions which now seem beyond us. We must conduct our affairs in such a way that it becomes in the Communists' interest to agree on a genuine peace. Above all, while defending our own vital interests, nuclear powers must avert those confrontations which bring an adversary to a choice of either a humiliating retreat or a nuclear war. To adopt that kind of course in the nuclear age would be evidence only of the bankruptcy of our policy—or of a collective death-wish for the world.

11

The Vietnam War

America's long, painful involvement in Southeast Asia began in the late 1940s, when U.S. officials decided that, despite its small size and apparent insignificance, Vietnam represented a key battleground in the global crusade against communism. After World War II, U.S. officials had pressured France to relinquish control of its colonies in Indochina (Cambodia, Laos, and Vietnam). But when it seemed that the alternative to French colonialism was Soviet- and Chinese-sponsored communism under the leadership of Ho Chi Minh, the administration of President Harry S. Truman reluctantly backed France. However, in 1954, after a grisly eight-year war, France faced total defeat. The last straw was the fall of the French garrison at Dien Bien Phu, a frontier outpost surrounded by the remote jungle highlands of northern Vietnam, in May 1954.

Meeting shortly afterward in Geneva, the great powers agreed to settle the Franco-Vietnamese war by partitioning Vietnam into two zones at the seventeenth parallel; the terms of reunification would be decided by a national referendum two years later. The communist-led Viet Minh ruled North Vietnam, officially known as the Democratic Republic of Vietnam, while a noncommunist regime under the American-backed Ngo Dinh Diem governed South Vietnam. Fearing a communist victory and confident of his own authority by 1956, Diem cancelled the referendum and mounted a campaign to rid South Vietnam of communists. Just as the Cold War had divided Germany and Korea, by the end of the 1950s the two Vietnams appeared to be two separate countries without a common destiny. In response, North Vietnam, prompted by southern communist insurgents reel- ing from Diem's anticommunist campaign, decided to resume the drive to reunify all of Vietnam. In 1960, Vietnamese communists established the southern-based National Liberation Front—soon nicknamed the Vietcong—and in 1964 North Vietnam began sending troops and large amounts of supplies to fuel the insurgency in the south.

From the outside, it seemed that Washington was united in its decision to preserve a noncommunist South Vietnam at almost all costs. But internally, U.S. officials argued bitterly among themselves over what to do. Between 1954 and 1961, the administration of President Dwight D. Eisenhower embarked on a "nation-building" program to transform South Vietnam into a viable independent state. But Diem himself proved to be a major obstacle, especially given that he was an authoritarian Roman Catholic in a country that was 90 percent Buddhist.

Nonetheless, the Kennedy administration increased direct economic and military aid to Saigon and sent many more U.S. military advisers. Kennedy was not eager to escalate in Vietnam, but he felt he had little choice.

In November 1963, both Diem and Kennedy were assassinated. Chaos replaced Diem, and communist forces threatened to overrun South Vietnam. Lyndon Johnson replaced Kennedy, vowing not to be the first president to lose a war. But Johnson was just as wary of Vietnam as Kennedy had been, and he tried to avoid a much deeper commitment for over a year. However, a series of events between February and July 1965 convinced him that South Vietnam would collapse without U.S. intervention, and by that time he was equally convinced that the consequences of South Vietnam's collapse would be disastrous for American credibility and prestige all over the world. Without anyone planning for it, Vietnam had become the most important brick in the whole foundation of U.S. national security. The American phase of the war ended only in 1973, when, following détente and the opening to China, the Cold War conditions that had made Vietnam important dissipated. North Vietnam conquered South Vietnam in April 1975, and Vietnam became one country again.

The war did more damage to U.S. foreign policy than any other in American history and deeply divided Americans at home, from each other as well as from a government they had once trusted. How did Vietnam, a small, impoverished, faraway country with no direct ties to the United States, assume such importance in the minds of American policy makers? Why did they persist with a commitment to holding the line against communism in Vietnam when they privately held such deep doubts about success? How did people outside Washington, both Americans and others around the world, perceive the Vietnam War? How did it affect their views of the United States and the Cold War?

Document 11.1

THE DOMINO THEORY

In April 1954, as the battle of Dien Bien Phu raged in a remote corner of North Vietnam near the border with Laos, the eight-year war between France and the Democratic Republic of Vietnam was nearing its end. President Eisenhower now found himself at a crossroads. Should the United States allow the communist-led Viet Minh to govern all of Vietnam? Or should America step in, pick up where the French left off, and prevent a communist takeover? Allowing the Viet Minh to win would be a major blow to containment, less than five years after Mao Zedong's Communist Party had taken power in China. Yet the strategic relevance of Vietnam was not self-evident. With all this in mind, Eisenhower decided on a compromise, drawing the line against communist expansion in Vietnam but without committing U.S. military power to accomplish that goal. In a news conference on April 7, 1954, he explained why, laying out a logic that would form the basis of U.S. strategic thinking for the next twenty years.

Q. Robert Richards, Copley Press: Mr. President, would you mind commenting on the strategic importance of Indochina to the free world? I think there has been, across the country, some lack of understanding on just what it means to us.

The President: You have, of course, both the specific and the general when you talk about such things.

First of all, you have the specific value of a locality in its production of materials that the world needs.

Then you have the possibility that many human beings pass under a dictatorship that is inimical to the free world.

Finally, you have broader considerations that might follow what you would call the "falling domino" principle. You have a row of dominoes set up, you knock over the first one, and what will happen to the last one is the certainty that it will go over very quickly. So you could have a beginning of a disintegration that would have the most profound influences.

Now, with respect to the first one, two of the items from this particular area that the world uses are tin and tungsten. They are very important. There are others, of course, the rubber plantations and so on.

Then with respect to more people passing under this domination, Asia, after all, has already lost some 450 million of its peoples to the Communist dictatorship, and we simply can't afford greater losses.

But when we come to the possible sequence of events, the loss of Indochina, of Burma, of Thailand, of the Peninsula, and Indonesia following, now you begin to talk about areas that not only multiply the disadvantages that you would suffer through loss of materials, sources of materials, but now you are talking really about millions and millions and millions of people.

Finally, the geographical position achieved thereby does many things. It turns the so-called island defensive chain of Japan, Formosa, of the Philippines and to the southward; it moves in to threaten Australia and New Zealand.

It takes away, in its economic aspects, that region that Japan must have as a trading area or Japan, in turn, will have only one place in the world to go—that is, toward the Communist areas in order to live.

So, the possible consequences of the loss are just incalculable to the free world.

Document 11.2

THE KENNEDY COMMITMENT

By 1961, the communist-nationalist insurgency in South Vietnam was in full swing, which meant that seven years after Eisenhower outlined the domino theory, the United States found itself at yet another crossroads: Should it commit more to the defense of South Vietnam, perhaps even by sending U.S. ground troops to join the fighting? Should it pressure the authoritarian Diem to change his ways? American policy making was further complicated by the fact that in 1961 a new president, John F. Kennedy, was in the White House. To get a better picture of what was going on in South Vietnam, in the fall of 1961 Kennedy sent two of his closest foreign policy advisers, former Army General Maxwell D. Taylor and Deputy National Security Adviser Walt W. Rostow, to take a closer look. Taylor's recommendations, outlined in this letter to Kennedy, included measures that would significantly deepen the American commitment in Vietnam.

My Dear Mr. President:

I am submitting herewith the report of the mission which visited South Vietnam, Thailand, and Hong Kong in the period 15 October to 3 November 1961....

My recommendations, already laid before you by cable, represent the emergency program which we feel our Government should implement without delay. After you have reached a decision on this program, it will be a major challenge to our governmental machinery in Washington to see that the many segments of the program which involve many departments and agencies are executed with maximum energy and proper timing....

While we feel that the program recommended represents those measures which should be taken in our present knowledge of the situation in Southeast Asia, I would not suggest that it is the final word. Future needs beyond this program will depend upon the kind of settlement we obtain in Laos and the manner in which Hanoi decides to adjust its conduct to that settlement. If the Hanoi decision is to continue the irregular war declared on South Viet-Nam in 1959 with continued infiltration and covert support of guerrilla bands in the territory of our ally, we will then have to decide whether to accept as legitimate the continued guidance, training, and support of a guerrilla war across an international boundary, while the attacked react only inside their borders. Can we admit the establishment of the common law that the party attacked and his friends are denied the right to strike the source of aggression, after the fact of external aggression is clearly established? It is our view that our government should undertake with the Vietnamese the measures outlined herein, but should then consider and face the broader question beyond.

We cannot refrain from expressing, having seen the situation on the ground, our common sense of outrage at the burden which this kind of aggression imposes on a new country, only seven years old, with a difficult historical heritage to overcome, confronting the inevitable problems of political, social, and economic transition to modernization. It is easy and cheap to destroy such a country whereas it is difficult undisturbed to build a nation coming out of a complex past without carrying the burden of a guerrilla war. . . .

It is my judgment and that of my colleagues that the United States must decide how it will cope with Khrushchev's "wars of liberation" which are really para-wars of guerrilla aggression. This is a new and dangerous Communist technique which bypasses our traditional political and military responses. While the final answer lies beyond the scope of this report, it is clear to me that the time may come in our relations to Southeast Asia when we must declare our intention to attack the source of guerrilla aggression in North Viet-Nam and impose on the Hanoi Government a price for participating in the current war which is commensurate with the damage being inflicted on its neighbors to the south.

In closing, let me add that our party left Southeast Asia with the sense of having viewed a serious problem but one which is by no means hopeless. We have many assets in this part of the world which, if properly combined and appropriately supported, offer high odds for ultimate success.

Basically the forces at work in Vietnam, Thailand, and Hong Kong are extremely positive in character. Everywhere there is new activity and momentum. In the long run there is no reason to believe that the rate of growth and the degree of modernization in non-Communist Asia as a whole will be outpaced by developments in Communist Asia. There is no need for fatalism that, somehow, Southeast Asia will inevitably fall into Communist hands. We have the means to make it otherwise.

Document 11.3

WHOSE WAR IS IT?

Kennedy did not agree to send troops, but he approved almost all the other recommendations of the Taylor-Rostow report. Yet the vast increase in American involvement did nothing to improve the situation in South Vietnam. In May 1963, a clash between government security forces and Buddhist monks in the city of Hue triggered a widespread revolt. Diem's crackdown only aggravated tensions and led several Buddhist monks to burn themselves to death in protest. Kennedy now found himself the patron of a deeply unpopular ruler, and the United States came under increasing domestic and international pressure to withdraw its support for Diem.

None of Washington's policies had worked, and once again the president was faced with a difficult dilemma: further U.S. intervention would be costly, difficult, and controversial, but withdrawal would almost certainly mean the fall of South Vietnam to communism. Kennedy had significantly increased the U.S. commitment to Vietnam, but he was unsure about authorizing yet another increase. In a September 1963 interview with Walter Cronkite of CBS Television News, Kennedy expressed his ambivalence.

MR. CRONKITE: Mr. President, the only hot war we've got running at the moment is of course the one in Viet-Nam, and we have our difficulties there, quite obviously.

THE PRESIDENT: I don't think that unless a greater effort is made by the Government [of South Vietnam] to win popular support that the war can be won out there. In the final analysis, it is their war. They are the ones who have to win it or lose it. We can help them, we can give them equipment, we can send our men out there as advisers, but they have to win it, the people of Viet-Nam, against the Communists.

We are prepared to continue to assist them, but I don't think that the war can be won unless the people support the effort and, in my opinion, in the last 2 months, the government has gotten out of touch with the people.

The repressions against the Buddhists, we felt, were very unwise. Now all we can do is to make it very clear that we don't think this is the way to win. It is my hope that this will become increasingly obvious to the government, that they will take steps to try to bring back popular support for this very essential struggle.

MR. CRONKITE: Do you think this government still has time to regain the support of the people?

THE PRESIDENT: I do. With changes in policy and perhaps with personnel I think it can. If it doesn't make those changes, I would think that the chances of winning it would not be very good.

MR. CRONKITE: Hasn't every indication from Saigon been that President Diem has no intention of changing his pattern?

THE PRESIDENT: If he does not change it, of course, that is his decision. He has been there 10 years and, as I say, he has carried this burden when he has been counted out on a number of occasions.

Our best judgment is that he can't be successful on this basis. We hope that he comes to see that, but in the final analysis it is the people and the government itself who have to win or lose this struggle. All we can do is help, and we are making it very clear, but I don't agree with those who say we should withdraw. That would be a great mistake. I know people don't like Americans to be engaged in this kind of an effort. Forty-seven Americans have been killed in combat with the enemy, but this is a very important struggle even though it is far away.

We took all this—made this effort to defend Europe. Now Europe is quite secure. We also have to participate—we may not like it—in the defense of Asia.

Mr. Cronkite: Mr. President, have you made an assessment as to what President de Gaulle was up to in his statement on Viet-Nam last week?

The President: No. I guess it was an expression of his general view, but he doesn't have any forces there or any program of economic assistance, so that while these expressions are welcome, the burden is carried, as it usually is, by the United States and the people there. But I think anything General de Gaulle says should be listened to, and we listened.

What, of course, makes Americans somewhat impatient is that after carrying this load for 18 years, we are glad to get counsel, but we would like a little more assistance, real assistance. But we are going to meet our responsibility anyway.

It doesn't do us any good to say, "Well, why don't we all just go home and leave the world to those who are our enemies."

Document 11.4

DOUBTS

It may have been "their war," but the South Vietnamese could do little to stem the communist insurgency on their own. In response, Kennedy reluctantly authorized a coup, and on November 1, 1963, Diem was overthrown and murdered. Three weeks later, Kennedy himself was assassinated. Unexpectedly thrust into power, Lyndon Johnson vowed to maintain the U.S. commitment, but he had no clear idea how to make the existing policy work. He was not confident or optimistic, but instead wary of entering a difficult conflict he feared America might not win. Here, in a May 1964 telephone conversation, he expresses some of his doubts to National Security Adviser McGeorge Bundy.

LBJ: I'll tell you the more that I stayed awake last night thinking of this thing, the more I think of it, I don't know what in the hell—it looks to me like we're getting into another Korea. It just worries the hell out of me. I don't see what we can ever hope to get out of there with, once we're committed. I believe that the Chinese Communists are coming into it. I don't think we can fight them ten thousand miles away from home . . . I don't think it's worth fighting for and I don't think that we can get out. It's just the biggest damned mess that I ever saw.

BUNDY: It is. It's an awful mess.

LBJ: And we just got to think about—I was looking at this sergeant of mine this morning. Got six little old kids over there and he's getting out my things and bringing me in my night reading . . . and I just thought about ordering his kids in there and what in the hell am I ordering him out there for? What the hell is Vietnam worth to me? What is Laos worth to me? What is it worth to this country? No, we've got a treaty but, hell, everybody else's got a treaty out there and they're not doing anything about it. Of course if you start running from the Communists, they may just chase you right into your own kitchen.

BUNDY: Yeah, that's the trouble. And that is what the rest of that half of the world is going to think if this thing comes apart on us. That's the dilemma.

Document 11.5

"SUSTAINED REPRISAL"

In the winter of 1965, after a year of uncertainty and postponing major decisions, and with the situation in South Vietnam deteriorating rapidly, Johnson found himself at precisely the same crossroads that had once faced Eisenhower and Kennedy. And like his predecessors, he ultimately decided he could not abandon South Vietnam. In February 1965, Johnson sent Bundy to South Vietnam to take another look. While he was there, the Vietcong attacked a U.S. air base at Pleiku, killing eight Americans and wounding many more. After the attack, Bundy's recommendation outlined the policy that would lead to the United States taking control of the war from South Vietnam.

En route from Saigon to Washington . . .

The situation in Vietnam is deteriorating, and without new U.S. action defeat appears inevitable—probably not in a matter of weeks or perhaps even months, but within the next year or so. There is still time to turn it around, but not much.

The stakes in Vietnam are extremely high. The American investment is very large, and American responsibility is a fact of life which is palpable in the atmosphere of Asia, and even elsewhere. The international prestige of the United States, and a substantial part of our influence, are directly at risk in Vietnam. There is no way of unloading the burden on the Vietnamese themselves, and there is no way of negotiating ourselves out of Vietnam which offers any serious promise at present. It is possible that at some future time a neutral non-Communist force may emerge, perhaps under Buddhist leadership, but no such force currently exists, and any negotiated U.S. withdrawal today would mean surrender on the installment plan.

The policy of graduated and continuing reprisal outlined in Annex A is the most promising course available, in my judgment. That judgment is shared by all who accompanied me from Washington, and I think by all members of the country team.

The events of the last twenty-four hours have produced a practicable point of departure for this policy of reprisal, and for the removal of U.S. dependents. They may also have catalyzed the formation of a new Vietnamese government. If so, the situation may be at a turning point. . . .

For the last year—and perhaps for longer—the overall situation in Vietnam has been deteriorating. The Communists have been gaining and the anti-Communist forces have been losing. As a result there is now great uncertainty among Vietnamese as well as Americans as to whether Communist victory can be prevented. There is nervousness about the determination of the U.S. Government. There is recrimination and fear among Vietnamese political leaders. There is an appearance of wariness among some military leaders. There is a worrisome lassitude among the Vietnamese generally. There is a distressing absence of positive commitment to any serious social or political purpose. Outside observers are ready to write the patient off. All of this tends to bring latent anti-Americanism dangerously near to the surface.

To be an American in Saigon today is to have a gnawing feeling that time is against us. Junior officers in all services are able, zealous and effective within the limits of their means. Their morale is sustained by the fact that they know that they are doing their jobs well and that they will not have to accept the responsibility for defeat. But near the top, where responsibility is heavy and accountability real, one can sense the inner doubts of men whose outward behavior remains determined. . . .

The prospect in Vietnam is grim. The energy and persistence of the Viet Cong are astonishing. They can appear anywhere—and at almost any time. They have accepted extraordinary losses and they come back for more. They show skill in their sneak attacks and ferocity when cornered. Yet the weary country does not want them to win.

There are a host of things the Vietnamese need to do better and areas in which we need to help them. The place where we can help most is in the clarity and firmness of our own commitment to what is in fact as well as in rhetoric a common cause. There is one grave weakness in our posture in Vietnam which is within our own power to fix—and that is a widespread belief that we do not have the will and force and patience and determination to take the necessary action and stay the course.

This is the overriding reason for our present recommendation of a policy of sustained reprisal. Once such a policy is put in force, we shall be able to speak in Vietnam on many topics and in many ways, with growing force and effectiveness.

One final word. At its very best the struggle in Vietnam will be long. It seems to us important that this fundamental fact be made clear and our understanding of it be made clear to our own people and to the people of Vietnam. Too often in the past we have conveyed the impression that we expect an early solution when those who live with this war know that no early solution is possible. It is our own belief that the people of the United States have the necessary will to accept and to execute a policy that rests upon the reality that there is no short cut to success in South Vietnam.

Document 11.6

THE CASE FOR WITHDRAWAL

Johnson agreed with Bundy's recommendation to launch an air war of "sustained reprisal," and Operation Rolling Thunder, a massive bombing campaign against North Vietnam that would continue for the next three years, began on March 2, 1965. A week later, on March 8, 1965, the first U.S. ground troops waded ashore at Danang, beginning the Americanization of the Vietnam War. Bundy had recommended military escalation because he saw Vietnam as both an important battleground in the Cold War and a test of American credibility, and Johnson, despite his profound doubts, agreed. But not everyone did, even at the very highest levels of the Johnson administration. It is a myth that, beyond the radical antiwar fringe, there was a consensus for war before 1965 and that it collapsed in 1968 because of high U.S. casualties. Here, in a February 1965 memo to the president, Vice President Hubert Humphrey outlines a way out for Johnson.

A. DOMESTIC POLITICAL CONSEQUENCES . . .

I would like to share with you my views on the political consequences of certain courses of action that have been proposed in regard to U.S. policy in Southeast Asia. I refer both to the domestic political consequences here in the United States and to the international political consequences. . . .

The Johnson Administration is associated both at home and abroad with a policy of progress toward detente with the Soviet bloc, a policy of limited arms control, and a policy of new initiatives for peace. A full-scale military at- tack on North Vietnam—with the attendant risk of an open military clash with Communist China—would risk gravely undermining other U.S. policies. It would eliminate for the time being any possible exchange between the President and Soviet leaders; it would postpone any progress on arms control; it would encourage the Soviet Union and China to end their rift; it would seriously hamper our efforts to strengthen relations with our European allies; it would weaken our position in the United Nations; it might require a call-up of reservists if we were to get involved in a large-scale land war—and a consequent increase in defense expenditures; it would tend to shift the Administration's emphasis from its Great Society oriented programs to further military outlays; finally and most important it would damage the image of the President of the United States—and that of the United States itself....

American wars have to be politically understandable by the American public. There has to be a cogent, convincing case if we are to have sustained public support. In World Wars I and II we had this. In Korea we were moving under UN auspices to defend South Korea against dramatic, across-the-border conventional aggression. Yet even with those advantages, we could not sustain American political support for fighting the Chinese in Korea in 1952.

Today in Vietnam we lack the very advantages we had in Korea. The public is worried and confused. Our rationale for action has shifted away now even from the notion that we are there as advisers on request of a free government—to the simple argument of our "national interest." We have not succeeded in making this "national interest" interesting enough at home or abroad to generate support....

Politically, people can't understand why we would run grave risks to support a country which is totally unable to put its own house in order. The chronic instability in Saigon directly undermines American political support for our policy....

Politically, it is always hard to cut losses. But the Johnson Administration is in a stronger position to do so than any Administration in this century. 1965 is the year of minimum political risk for the Johnson Administration. Indeed it is the first year when we can face the Vietnam problem without being preoccupied with the political repercussions from the Republican right. As indicated earlier, the political problems are likely to come from new and different sources if we pursue an enlarged military policy very long (Democratic liberals, Independents, Labor, Church groups)....

The best possible outcome a year from now would be a Vietnam settlement which turns out to be better than was in the cards because the President's political talents for the first time came to grips with a fateful world crisis and so successfully. It goes without saying that the subsequent domestic political benefits of such an outcome, and such a new dimension for the President, would be enormous.

If on the other hand, we find ourselves leading from frustration to escalation, and end up short of a war with China but embroiled deeper in fighting with Vietnam over the next few months, political opposition will steadily mount. It will underwrite all the negativism and disillusionment which we already have about foreign involvement generally—with direct spillover effects politically for all the Democratic internationalist programs to which we are committed—AID, UN, disarmament, and activist world policies generally.

B. INTERNATIONAL POLITICAL IMPLICATIONS OF VIETNAM

What is our goal, our ultimate objective in Vietnam? Is our goal to restore a military balance between North and South Vietnam so as to go to the conference table later to negotiate a settlement? I believe it is the latter. If so, what is the optimum time for achieving the most favorable combination of factors to achieve this goal?

If ultimately a negotiated settlement is our aim, when do we start developing a political track, in addition to the military one, that might lead us to the conference table? I believe we should develop the political track earlier rather than later. We should take the initiative on the political side and not end up being dragged to a conference as an unwilling participant. This does not mean we should cease all programs of military pressure. But we should distinguish carefully between those military actions necessary to reach our political goal of a negotiated settlement, and those likely to provoke open Chinese military intervention.

Document 11.7

UNSOLICITED NEIGHBORLY ADVICE

Canadian Prime Minister Lester B. Pearson, a North Atlantic Treaty Organization member and the leader of America's closest ally, shared Humphrey's concerns. Here, in an April 1965 speech accepting a peace award from Temple University, Pearson criticized North Vietnamese aggression but called for the United States to halt Operation Rolling Thunder. This was an important turning point, for if unassuming and normally loyal Canada was turning against the war, it did not bode well for the United States.

There are many factors which I am not in a position to weigh. But there does appear to be at least a possibility that a suspension of such air strikes against North Vietnam, at the right time, might provide the Hanoi authorities with an opportunity, if they wish to take it, to inject some flexibility into their policy without appearing to do so as the direct result of military pressure.

If such a suspension took place for a limited time, then the rate of incidents in South Vietnam would provide a fairly accurate way of measuring its usefulness and the desirability of continuing it. I am not, of course, proposing any compromise on points of principle, nor any weakening of resistance to aggression in South Vietnam, indeed, resistance may require increased military strength to be used against the armed and attacking Communists. I merely suggest that a measured and announced pause in one field of military action at the right time might facilitate the development of diplomatic resources which cannot easily be applied to the problem under the existing circumstances. . . .

With a cease-fire followed by political negotiations, with the countries in the area given an international guarantee of neutrality and assurance of aid for peaceful development, then the danger, destruction and distress of the present hour might be replaced by peace, hope and progress.

Document 11.8

WHY AMERICA FIGHTS

Within a month, it was clear that Operation Rolling Thunder would not be able to stop the insurgency, force Hanoi to the negotiating table, or shore up morale and political stability in Saigon. Yet Johnson was now too deeply committed to withdraw. Instead, he and his advisers began quietly searching for ways to conduct the war more effectively, including the deployment of large numbers of U.S. ground troops. With unease growing at home, and with political elites and foreign allies becoming critical both in public and in private, Johnson used a major speech at Johns Hopkins University in April 1965 to explain and justify U.S. policy in more idealistic terms that could also offer Hanoi a face-saving way to avert a full-scale war.

Tonight Americans and Asians are dying for a world where each people may choose its own path to change.

This is the principle for which our ancestors fought in the valleys of Pennsylvania. It is the principle for which our sons fight tonight in the jungles of Viet-Nam.

Viet-Nam is far away from this quiet campus. We have no territory there, nor do we seek any. The war is dirty and brutal and difficult. And some 400 young men, born into an America that is bursting with opportunity and promise, have ended their lives on Viet-Nam's steaming soil.

Why must we take this painful road?

Why must this Nation hazard its ease, and its interest, and its power for the sake of a people so far away?

We fight because we must fight if we are to live in a world where every country can shape its own destiny. And only in such a world will our own freedom be finally secure.

This kind of world will never be built by bombs or bullets. Yet the infirmities of man are such that force must often precede reason, and the waste of war, the works of peace.

We wish that this were not so. But we must deal with the world as it is, if it is ever to be as we wish. . . .

Why are these realities our concern? Why are we in South Viet-Nam?

We are there because we have a promise to keep. Since 1954 every American President has offered support to the people of South Viet-Nam. We have helped to build, and we have helped to defend. Thus, over many years, we have made a national pledge to help South Viet-Nam defend its independence.

And I intend to keep that promise.

To dishonor that pledge, to abandon this small and brave nation to its enemies, and to the terror that must follow, would be an unforgivable wrong.

We are also there to strengthen world order. Around the globe, from Berlin to Thailand, are people whose well-being rests, in part, on the belief that they can count on us if they are attacked. To leave Viet-Nam to its fate would shake the confidence of all these people in the value of an American commitment and in the value of America's word. The result would be increased unrest and instability, and even wider war.

We are also there because there are great stakes in the balance. Let no one think for a moment that retreat from Viet-Nam would bring an end to conflict. The battle would be renewed in one country and then another. The central lesson of our time is that the appetite of aggression is never satisfied. To withdraw from one battlefield means only to prepare for the next. We must say in southeast Asia—as we did in Europe—in the words of the Bible: "Hitherto shalt thou come, but no further."

There are those who say that all our effort there will be futile—that China's power is such that it is bound to dominate all southeast Asia. But there is no end to that argument until all of the nations of Asia are swallowed up.

There are those who wonder why we have a responsibility there. Well, we have it there for the same reason that we have a responsibility for the defense of Europe. World War II was fought in both Europe and Asia, and when it ended we found ourselves with continued responsibility for the defense of freedom. . . .

Our objective is the independence of South Viet-Nam, and its freedom from attack. We want nothing for ourselves—only that the people of South Viet-Nam be allowed to guide their own country in their own way.

We will do everything necessary to reach that objective. And we will do only what is absolutely necessary. . . .

This war, like most wars, is filled with terrible irony. For what do the people of North Viet-Nam want? They want what their neighbors also desire: food for their hunger; health for their bodies; a chance to learn; progress for their country; and an end to the bondage of material misery. And they would find all these things far more readily in peaceful association with others than in the endless course of battle. . . .

These countries of southeast Asia are homes for millions of impoverished people. Each day these people rise at dawn and struggle through until the night to wrestle existence from the soil. They are often wracked by disease, plagued by hunger, and death comes at the early age of 40.

Stability and peace do not come easily in such a land. Neither independence nor human dignity will ever be won, though, by arms alone. It also requires the work of peace. The American people have helped generously in times past in these works. Now there must be a much more massive effort to improve the life of man in that conflict-torn corner of our world. . . .

For our part I will ask the Congress to join in a billion dollar American investment in this effort as soon as it is underway.

And I would hope that all other industrialized countries, including the Soviet Union, will join in this effort to replace despair with hope, and terror with progress.

The task is nothing less than to enrich the hopes and the existence of more than a hundred million people. And there is much to be done.

The vast Mekong River can provide food and water and power on a scale to dwarf even our own TVA [Tennessee Valley Authority].

The wonders of modern medicine can be spread through villages where thousands die every year from lack of care.

Schools can be established to train people in the skills that are needed to manage the process of development.

And these objectives, and more, are within the reach of a cooperative and determined effort.

Document 11.9

WHY NORTH VIETNAM FIGHTS

In essence, Johnson had offered to bring the New Deal and the Great Society to Southeast Asia. For a seasoned American politician such as Johnson, this made perfect sense: North Vietnam would trade war and devastation for peace, modernization, and prosperity. But for the North Vietnamese, Johnson's offer amounted to little more than a bribe. They pursued two inseparable goals, national reunification under communist rule, and neither would be achieved by accepting Johnson's peace offering. Their swift response to Johnson's Johns Hopkins speech, outlined as North Vietnamese Prime Minister Pham Van Dong's "Four Points," left little room for compromise.

1. Recognition of the basic national rights of the Vietnamese people: peace, independence, sovereignty, unity and territorial integrity. According to the [1954] Geneva Agreements, the U.S. Government must withdraw from South Vietnam all U.S. troops, military personnel and weapons of all kinds, dismantle all U.S. military bases there, cancel its "military alliance" with South Vietnam. It must end its policy of intervention and aggression in South Vietnam. According to the Geneva Agreements, the U.S. Government must stop its acts of war against North Vietnam, completely cease all encroachments on the territory and sovereignty of the Democratic Republic of Vietnam.
2. Pending the peaceful reunification of Vietnam, while Vietnam is still temporarily divided into two zones the military provisions of the 1954 Geneva Agreements on Vietnam must be strictly respected; the two zones must refrain from joining any military alliance with foreign countries, and there must be no foreign military bases, troops and military personnel in their respective territory.
3. The internal affairs of South Vietnam must be settled by the South Vietnamese people themselves, in accordance with the programme of the South Vietnam National Front for Liberation [the Vietcong], without any foreign interference.
4. The peaceful reunification of Vietnam is to be settled by the Vietnamese people in both zones, without any foreign interference.

Document 11.10

AGAINST WAR

By this time, opposition to the war in Vietnam, and to containment and the military-industrial complex more generally, had begun to form. Peace activists and students had already been protesting against segregation and nuclear weapons for several years, and in the mid-1960s they broadened their movement considerably to mount massive opposition to the war. The movement's values and rhetoric echoed the anticorporate and antiwar radicalism of the 1930s and anticipated the anti-globalization protests of the 1990s. Antiwar songs flourished in the 1960s and 1970s, among them "Draft Morning" by the Byrds, "Kill for Peace" by the Fugs, "I-Feel-Like-I'm-Fixin'-to-Die Rag" by Country Joe and the Fish, "Waist Deep in the Big Muddy" by Pete Seeger, "Give Peace a Chance" by John Lennon, "Where Are You Now, My Son?" by Joan Baez, and "Ohio" by Crosby, Stills, Nash, and Young. The folk singer Phil Ochs recorded several major antiwar songs, including "Cops of the World," "Draft Dodger Rag," "I Ain't Marching Anymore," "Talkin' Vietnam," and "White Boots Marching in a Yellow Land." Even country singer Loretta Lynn, by no means a radical or even antiwar, had a hit with "Dear Uncle Sam," a mournful story about the high costs of the war sung from the perspective of a wife whose husband has been killed in Vietnam. To Bob Dylan, the problems with U.S. foreign policy in places like Southeast Asia were part of a much larger system, as seen in his 1963 song "Masters of War."

Come you masters of war
You that build all the guns
You that build the death planes
You that build the big bombs
You that hide behind walls
You that hide behind desks
I just want you to know
I can see through your masks

You that never done nothin'
But build to destroy
You play with my world
Like it's your little toy
You put a gun in my hand
And you hide from my eyes
And you turn and run farther
When the fast bullets fly

Like Judas of old
You lie and deceive
A world war can be won
You want me to believe
But I see through your eyes
And I see through your brain
Like I see through the water
That runs down my drain

You fasten the triggers
For the others to fire
Then you set back and watch
When the death count gets higher
You hide in your mansion

As young people's blood
Flows out of their bodies
And is buried in the mud

Document 11.11

THE WAR AND THE DAMAGE DONE

Antiwar protest continued to build throughout the decade. In an April 1967 speech to an organization of antiwar clergy, the civil rights leader Martin Luther King Jr. delivered one of the most eloquent and powerful critiques of the war. Giving this speech was a painful moment for King, for it meant breaking with Johnson, who had done more for African Americans than any president since Abraham Lincoln. But by this time, King felt that the war had nearly destroyed all of the promise and potential of the civil rights movement and the Great Society.

I come to this magnificent house of worship tonight because my conscience leaves me no other choice. I join you in this meeting because I am in deepest agreement with the aims and work of the organization which has brought us together: Clergy and Laymen Concerned about Vietnam. The recent statements of your executive committee are the sentiments of my own heart, and I found myself in full accord when I read its opening lines: "A time comes when silence is betrayal." And that time has come for us in relation to Vietnam.

The truth of these words is beyond doubt, but the mission to which they call us is a most difficult one. Even when pressed by the demands of inner truth, men do not easily assume the task of opposing their government's policy, especially in time of war. Nor does the human spirit move without great difficulty against all the apathy of conformist thought within one's own bosom and in the surrounding world. Moreover, when the issues at hand seem as perplexed as they often do in the case of this dreadful conflict, we are always on the verge of being mesmerized by uncertainty; but we must move on. . . .

There is at the outset a very obvious and almost facile connection between the war in Vietnam and the struggle I, and others, have been waging in America. A few years ago there was a shining moment in that struggle. It seemed as if there was a real promise of hope for the poor—both black and white—through the poverty program. There were experiments, hopes, new beginnings. Then came the buildup in Vietnam, and I watched this program broken and eviscerated, as if it were some idle political plaything of a society gone mad on war, and I knew that America would never invest the necessary funds or energies in rehabilitation of its poor so long as adventures like Vietnam continued to draw men and skills and money like some demonic destructive suction tube. So, I was increasingly compelled to see the war as an enemy of the poor and to attack it as such.

Perhaps the more tragic recognition of reality took place when it became clear to me that the war was doing far more than devastating the hopes of the poor at home. It was sending their sons and their brothers and their husbands to fight and to die in extraordinarily high proportions relative to the rest of the population. We were taking the black young men who had been crippled by our society and sending them eight thousand miles away to guarantee liberties in Southeast Asia which they had not found in southwest Georgia and East Harlem. And so we have been repeatedly faced with the cruel irony of watching Negro and white boys on TV screens as they kill and die together for a nation that has been unable to seat them together in the same schools. And so we watch them in brutal solidarity burning the huts of a poor village, but we realize that they would hardly live on the same block in Chicago. I could not be silent in the face of such cruel manipulation of the poor. . . .

I am convinced that if we are to get on the right side of the world revolution, we as a nation must undergo a radical revolution of values. We must rapidly begin the shift from a thing-oriented society to a person-oriented society. When machines and computers, profit motives and property rights, are considered more important than people, the giant triplets of racism, extreme materialism, and militarism are incapable of being conquered. . . .

A true revolution of values will soon look uneasily on the glaring contrast of poverty and wealth. With righteous indignation, it will look across the seas and see individual capitalists of the West investing huge sums of money in Asia, Africa, and South America, only to take the profits out with no concern for the social betterment of the countries, and say, "This is not just." It will look at our alliance with the landed gentry of South America and say, "This is not just." The Western arrogance of feeling that it has everything to teach others and nothing to learn from them is not just.

A true revolution of values will lay hands on the world order and say of war, "This way of settling differences is not just." This business of burning human beings with napalm, of filling our nation's homes with orphans and widows, of injecting poisonous drugs of hate into the veins of peoples normally humane, of sending men home from dark and bloody battlefields physically handicapped and psychologically deranged, cannot be reconciled with wisdom, justice, and love. A nation that continues year after year to spend more money on military defense than on programs of social uplift is approaching spiritual death.

America, the richest and most powerful nation in the world, can well lead the way in this revolution of values. There is nothing except a tragic death wish to prevent us from reordering our priorities so that the pursuit of peace will take precedence over the pursuit of war. There is nothing to keep us from molding a recalcitrant status quo with bruised hands until we have fashioned it into a brotherhood.

This kind of positive revolution of values is our best defense against communism. War is not the answer. Communism will never be defeated by the use of atomic bombs or nuclear weapons. Let us not join those who shout war and, through their misguided passions, urge the United States to relinquish its participation in the United Nations. These are days which demand wise restraint and calm reasonableness. We must not engage in a negative anticommunism, but rather in a positive thrust for democracy, realizing that our greatest defense against communism is to take offensive action in behalf of justice. We must with positive action seek to remove those conditions of poverty, insecurity, and injustice, which are the fertile soil in which the seed of communism grows and develops.

These are revolutionary times. All over the globe men are revolting against old systems of exploitation and oppression, and out of the wounds of a frail world, new systems of justice and equality are being born. The shirtless and barefoot people of the land are rising up as never before. The people who sat in darkness have seen a great light. We in the West must support these revolutions.

It is a sad fact that because of comfort, complacency, a morbid fear of communism, and our proneness to adjust to injustice, the Western nations that initiated so much of the revolutionary spirit of the modern world have now become the arch antirevolutionaries. This has driven many to feel that only Marxism has a revolutionary spirit. Therefore, communism is a judgment against our failure to make democracy real and follow through on the revolutions that we initiated. Our only hope today lies in our ability to recapture the revolutionary spirit and go out into a sometimes hostile world declaring eternal hostility to poverty, racism, and militarism. With this powerful commitment we shall boldly challenge the status quo and unjust mores, and thereby speed the day when "every valley shall be exalted, and every mountain and hill shall be made low, and the crooked shall be made straight, and the rough places plain."

Document 11.12

VIETNAM AND WORLD REVOLUTION

Just as serious was protest from the non-Western world. Ernesto "Che" Guevara was a Marxist revolutionary who had helped lead the Cuban Revolution and now sought to export communist-nationalist revolution throughout the Global South.

In this 1967 speech, he positioned the United States at the center of international injustice, advocated violence in resistance to what he saw as American imperialism, and looked to Vietnamese defiance for inspiration.

Almost two years ago the U.S. started bombing systematically the Democratic Republic of Vietnam, in yet another attempt to overcome the resistance of the South and impose, from a position of strength, a meeting at the conference table. At first, the bombardments were more or less isolated occurrences and were represented as reprisals for alleged provocations from the North. Later on, as they increased in intensity and regularity, they became one gigantic attack carried out by the air force of the United States day after day for the purpose of destroying all vestiges of civilization in the northern zone of the country. This is an episode of the infamously notorious "escalation."

The material aspirations of the Yankee world have been fulfilled to a great extent despite the unflinching defense of the Vietnamese. . . .

There is a sad reality: Vietnam—a nation representing the aspirations, the hopes of a whole world of forgotten peoples—is tragically alone. This nation must endure the furious attacks of U.S. technology with practically no possibility of reprisals in the South and only some of defense in the North—but always alone.

The solidarity of all progressive forces of the world with the people of Vietnam is today similar to the bitter irony of the plebeians urging on the gladiators in the Roman arena. It is not a matter of wishing success to the victim of aggression, but of sharing his fate; one must accompany him to his death or to victory.

When we analyze the lonely situation of the Vietnamese people, we are overcome by anguish at this illogical fix in which humanity finds itself.

U.S. imperialism is guilty of aggression—its crimes are enormous and cover the whole world. We already know all that, gentlemen! But this guilt also applies to those who, when the time came for a definition, hesitated to make Vietnam an inviolable part of the socialist camp, running, of course, the risks of war on a global scale—but also forcing a decision on imperialism. . . .

And what great people these are! What stoicism and courage! And what a lesson for the world is contained in this struggle! Not for a long time shall we be able to know if President Johnson ever seriously thought of bringing about some of the reforms needed by his people—to iron out the barbed class contradictions that grow each day with explosive power. The truth is that the improvements announced under the pompous title of the "Great Society" have been poured down the drain of Vietnam.

The largest of all imperialist powers feels in its own guts the bleeding inflicted by a poor and underdeveloped country; its fabulous economy feels the strain of the war effort. Murder is ceasing to be the most convenient business for its monopolies. Defensive weapons, and never in adequate numbers, are all these extraordinary Vietnamese soldiers have—besides love for their homeland, their society, and unsurpassed courage. But imperialism is bogging down in Vietnam, is unable to find a way out, and desperately seeks one that will overcome with dignity this dangerous situation in which it now finds itself. . . .

Everything indicates that peace, this unstable peace which bears that name for the sole reason that no worldwide conflagration has taken place, is again in danger of being destroyed by some irrevocable and unacceptable step taken by the United States.

What role shall we, the exploited people of the world, play? The peoples of the three continents focus their attention on Vietnam and learn their lesson. Because imperialists blackmail humanity by threatening it with war, the wise reaction is not to fear war. The general tactics of the people should be to launch a constant and firm attack on all fronts where the confrontation is taking place.

In those places where this meager peace we have has been violated, what is our duty? To liberate ourselves at any price. . . .

This means a long war. And, we repeat once more, a cruel war. Let no one fool himself at the outset and let no one hesitate to begin in fear of the consequences it may bring to his people. It is almost our sole hope for victory. We cannot elude the call of this hour. Vietnam is pointing it out with its endless lesson of heroism, its tragic and everyday lesson of struggle and death for the attainment of final victory. . . .

What a luminous, near future would be visible to us if two, three, or many Vietnams appeared throughout the world with their share of death and immense tragedies, their everyday heroism and repeated blows against imperialism, obliging it to disperse its forces under the attack and the increasing hatred of all peoples of the earth!

Document 11.13

THE PRO-WAR MOVEMENT

The war met with vehement criticism at home and abroad, but not everyone opposed it. U.S. allies in Asia—such as Australia, New Zealand, the Philip- pines, South Korea, and Thailand—sent troops to fight with the U.S. military in South Vietnam, while Singapore offered rhetorical and diplomatic support. Just as important were the war's supporters in the United States. Among them was Reverend Harold Ockenga, a founder of the National Association of Evangelicals and a leading voice of what would become known as the Religious Right. To conservatives like Ockenga, the war was just and necessary, and Johnson's only fault was in waging it in a deliberately limited fashion. Ockenga visited South Vietnam in March 1968, shortly after the Tet Offensive, and filed this report. Note the references to prominent liberals and Democrats—such as John Kenneth Galbraith, an economist at Harvard University who had been John F. Kennedy's ambassador to India, and senators Robert and Edward Kennedy—who called for a U.S. withdrawal to end the war.

The great concern expressed here is that the U.S. government will work out a compromise with the VC, bringing them into a coalition government. Then everything for which this people has fought and suffered will be lost. The more our press and our leaders at home talk of negotiation, the weaker the Vietnamese people's desire to resist will become. Men like John K. Galbraith who prophesy the collapse of the government and the defeat of the American military do a great disservice to a heroic people and a great cause. The Kennedy brothers weaken our cause by their calls for negotiation.

What is the solution to the vexing problem? Three alternatives seem to offer themselves. First, withdraw. Take the defeat. Swallow our pride. Admit we made a mistake. This would be tragic for Viet Nam and for all Southeast Asia. Communism would take over. Even now the Communists are holding large areas of Laos and are infiltrating Thailand.

Second, negotiate. That is, bring the VC into the government of South Viet Nam. As in China, so here this would ultimately mean a Communist takeover.

Third, go for victory. If we have any right to be here at all, we should fight to win, not merely to hold an area. I am convinced that the present strategy will never win this war. The heart of resistance must be struck, not the periphery. This means blockading Haiphong harbor, from where the war supplies come. It means crossing the DMZ. It means destroying the enemy strongholds in Laos and Cambodia. And it means chancing a bigger war and an encounter with Russia and China. With the facts fully before the great powers, there would be a possibility of negotiation and neutralization.

Why should 200,000,000 Americans continue to live as usual while 15,000 Americans die and 100,000 are wounded in Viet Nam? These men have as much right to live as you and I. If we must hazard their lives, we must hazard our security, too.

Let us ask the ultimate questions and give courageous answers. Then let us act upon our conclusions. The carnage can be stopped only by victory or by withdrawal.

Document 11.14

"WE WILL NOT BE HUMILIATED"

By the spring of 1968, after the Tet Offensive showed that the Vietcong and North Vietnam were not on the verge of defeat, a majority of Americans simply wanted the United States to withdraw from Vietnam. Richard Nixon was elected presi- dent that November in part because people trusted him to do so. In partnership with his national security adviser, Henry Kissinger, Nixon vowed to bring "peace with honor" to Vietnam by removing U.S. forces without triggering a collapse of South Vietnam—in other words, they wanted to achieve the same goal that Eisenhower, Kennedy, and Johnson had sought before them. Nixon and Kissinger feared that a quick American withdrawal would damage American credibility around the world. Their solution, called "Vietnamization," aimed to increase funding to Saigon and turn over fighting to the South Vietnamese army as U.S. troops departed; that way, the United States could end an unpopular and expensive war without inflicting damage to its international reputation. To provide South Vietnam with cover and give Vietnamization a chance to work, Nixon authorized a significant escalation of the war in other ways, many of which Johnson had explicitly ruled out (but supporters like Ockenga had urged). The two most important were a vast increase in the military campaign against North Vietnam (through increased aerial bombing and the mining of Haiphong) and the extension of the war into neighboring Cambodia and Laos. Here, in an April 1970 address to the nation, Nixon explains his decision to send U.S. troops into Cambodia.

A majority of the American people, a majority of you listening to me, are for the withdrawal of our forces from Vietnam. The action I have taken tonight is indispensable for the continuing success of that withdrawal program.

A majority of the American people want to end this war rather than to have it drag on interminably. The action I have taken tonight will serve that purpose.

A majority of the American people want to keep the casualties of our brave men in Vietnam at an absolute minimum. The action I take tonight is essential if we are to accomplish that goal.

We take this action not for the purpose of expanding the war into Cambodia but for the purpose of ending the war in Vietnam and winning the just peace we all desire. We have made—we will continue to make every possible effort to end this war through negotiation at the conference table rather than through more fighting on the battlefield. . . .

The answer of the enemy has been intransigence at the conference table, belligerence in Hanoi, massive military aggression in Laos and Cambodia, and stepped-up attacks in South Vietnam, designed to increase American casualties.

This attitude has become intolerable. We will not react to this threat to American lives merely by plaintive diplomatic protests. If we did, the credibility of the United States would be destroyed in every area of the world where only the power of the United States deters aggression. . . .

The action that I have announced tonight puts the leaders of North Vietnam on notice that we will be patient in working for peace; we will be conciliatory at the conference table, but we will not be humiliated. We will not be defeated. We will not allow American men by the thousands to be killed by an enemy from privileged sanctuaries.

The time came long ago to end this war through peaceful negotiations. We stand ready for those negotiations. We have made major efforts, many of which must remain secret. I say tonight: All the offers and approaches made previously remain on the conference table whenever Hanoi is ready to negotiate seriously.

But if the enemy response to our most conciliatory offers for peaceful negotiation continues to be to increase its attacks and humiliate and defeat us, we shall react accordingly.

My fellow Americans, we live in an age of anarchy, both abroad and at home. We see mindless attacks on all the great institutions which have been created by free civilizations in the last 500 years. Even here in the United States, great universities are being systematically destroyed. Small nations all over the world find themselves under attack from within and from without.

If, when the chips are down, the world's most powerful nation, the United States of America, acts like a pitiful, helpless giant, the forces of totalitarianism and anarchy will threaten free nations and free institutions throughout the world.

It is not our power but our will and character that is being tested tonight. The question all Americans must ask and answer tonight is this: Does the richest and strongest nation in the history of the world have the character to meet a direct challenge by a group which rejects every effort to win a just peace, ignores our warning, tramples on solemn agreements, violates the neutrality of an unarmed people, and uses our prisoners as hostages?

If we fail to meet this challenge, all other nations will be on notice that despite its overwhelming power the United States, when a real crisis comes, will be found wanting.

During my campaign for the Presidency, I pledged to bring Americans home from Vietnam. They are coming home.

I promised to end this war. I shall keep that promise.

I promised to win a just peace. I shall keep that promise.

We shall avoid a wider war. But we are also determined to put an end to this war.

Document 11.15

THE WAR'S ENDING

By 1973, Kissinger had negotiated an end to the war, and the last American troops were gone by the spring. However, Vietnamization did not work, and in April 1975 North Vietnam captured Saigon and unofficially reunified the country. As Gerald Ford announced to a euphoric audience at Tulane University in April 1975, America's longest war—at that point—was finally over.

Today, America can regain the sense of pride that existed before Vietnam. But it cannot be achieved by refighting a war that is finished as far as America is concerned. As I see it, the time has come to look forward to an agenda for the future, to unify, to bind up the Nation's wounds, and to restore its health and its optimistic self-confidence.

In New Orleans, a great battle was fought after a war was over. In New Orleans tonight, we can begin a great national reconciliation. The first engagement must be with the problems of today, but just as importantly, the problems of the future. That is why I think it is so appropriate that I find myself tonight at a university which addresses itself to preparing young people for the challenge of tomorrow.

I ask that we stop refighting the battles and the recriminations of the past. I ask that we look now at what is right with America, at our possibilities and our potentialities for change and growth and achievement and sharing. I ask that we accept the responsibilities of leadership as a good neighbor to all peoples and the enemy of none. I ask that we strive to become, in the finest American tradition, something more tomorrow than we are today.

Instead of my addressing the image of America, I prefer to consider the reality of America. It is true that we have launched our Bicentennial celebration without having achieved human perfection, but we have attained a very remarkable self-governed society that possesses the flexibility and the dynamism to grow and undertake an entirely new agenda, an agenda for America's third century.

So, I ask you to join me in helping to write that agenda. I am as determined as a President can be to seek national rediscovery of the belief in ourselves that characterized the most creative periods in our Nation's history. The greatest challenge of creativity, as I see it, lies ahead.

We, of course, are saddened indeed by the events in Indochina. But these events, tragic as they are, portend neither the end of the world nor of America's leadership in the world.

12

The Era of Détente

By 1969, U.S. foreign policy was facing its most serious set of challenges since World War II. The most obvious problem was Vietnam. The stalemated war was a drag on the economy as well as damaging to America's international credibility and domestic tranquility. But other problems beset America. Spurred by its humiliation in the Cuban Missile Crisis, the Soviet Union achieved nuclear parity with the United States; no longer could American policy makers assume their strategic superiority. Europe (led by West Germany) and Japan were prospering at the expense of an increasingly lethargic American economy. European allies, moreover, were moving away from the protective U.S. nuclear umbrella and directly challenging Washington's leading role in the Atlantic alliance: France had recently pulled out of the North Atlantic Treaty Organization's military command, and West Germany was about to embark upon Ostpolitik, *a policy of carving out better relations with the communist world free of Washington's restraints. At home, meanwhile, young people were in open revolt and many of America's cities were gripped by racial strife and armed insurrection. All around the world, it seemed that American interests—military, political, and economic—were under fire, sometimes even in full retreat.*

Perhaps most important, the process we now refer to as globalization was just beginning to be felt. Thanks to breakneck advances in technology, particularly in the fields of computers, communications, and transportation, the world seemed to be getting smaller. Related was the process of deindustrialization, in which the American economy underwent an often painful transition from heavy industry and manufacturing to technology, finance, and services.

This was the situation President Richard Nixon inherited upon taking office in January 1969. In response, he and his chief foreign policy adviser, Henry Kissinger, devised a new grand strategy, based on a doctrine of realism, that would continue to pursue U.S. interests and security while also recognizing the limits of U.S. resources. The best way for America to regain the initiative, Nixon and Kissinger reasoned, would be to change the rules of the game. With this in mind, they set out to improve relations with both the Soviets and Chinese—a tactic known as triangulation—who for different reasons now feared each other more than they feared the United States. The overall policy, generally known as détente, intended to regain geopolitical leverage for the United States by putting it back at the very heart of international relations. Yet détente also had deeper roots that were grounded in widespread fears of nuclear war that heightened with the Missile Crisis and China's first successful test of a nuclear weapon in 1964.

For a time, Nixon and Kissinger's new approach seemed to succeed brilliantly. But it was not without its critics, at home or abroad. Many Americans, conservatives and liberals alike, felt that an amoral, realist U.S. foreign policy that did not emphasize values and ideals in its pursuit of interests was a mistake. In particular, conservatives loathed dealing with communist regimes and sacrificing traditional anticommunist allies such as Taiwan. Liberals protested against Nixon and Kissinger's support of right-wing dictators and neglect of human rights, especially in Latin America, in the name of international stability.

Whatever the merits of these arguments, it was increasingly clear that America's role in the world—indeed, the world system itself—had changed fundamentally in the 1970s. A new synthesis for U.S. foreign policy took shape by the end of the decade that blended the era's two great preoccupations: Nixon and Kissinger's pursuit of nuclear arms control and peaceful superpower relations, and their opponents' desire to spread human rights.

Document 12.1

TRANSCENDING DIFFERENCES

As we saw in chapter 10, John F. Kennedy sought a new relationship with the Soviet Union. The Missile Crisis had brought the superpowers closer to nuclear war than at any other point in the Cold War, and he was determined that it would not happen again. Lyndon Johnson shared Kennedy's concerns about nuclear war. By virtue of his personal temperament and political liberalism, Johnson was an optimist, and he saw no reason why the United States and the Soviet Union could not settle their differences rationally and peacefully. Just as the Great Society would bring a new era of peace and justice to the United States, so too would Johnson ease America's tensions with the Soviets. He continued Kennedy's message that Americans and Soviets shared many aspirations and did not want war. Johnson outlined his view of détente in a 1966 interview with the magazine America Illustrated *that was intended for distribution in the Soviet Union. But however sincere Johnson was about détente, he could not pursue it successfully as long as he was waging war in Vietnam. The irony was that a war in Southeast Asia, fought in the name of preventing the spread of communism, ultimately prevented full détente with the Soviet Union.*

Q. Mr. President, 10 years have elapsed since the United States and the Soviet Union began to exchange "America" magazine and "Soviet Life" in an effort to achieve better understanding between our countries.

I wonder, sir, if you would comment on the state of relations between the two countries over the past decade?

A. That's a question frequently asked, and one which is always difficult to answer. It is easy to be a hopeful optimist—and just as easy to be a fearful pessimist. What is important in these complicated times is to be a realist. Time and again, in many parts of the world, we and the Soviet Union find ourselves on the opposite sides of a question. But, over the years, we've gained a lot of experience in working out many of our differences. And we've taken a few very important constructive steps together. . . .

Q. What do you consider to be some of the future possibilities for additional constructive steps?

A. I think we must work toward progress in the field of disarmament and in greater cooperative efforts between our two countries in space exploration, medical research, and communications. This administration strongly supports these efforts. And then, too, there are what you might call the basics.

You know, in Texas, when we go to buy a farm, we don't put too much importance on the manmade disappointments—like a rundown barn or a badly fenced pasture. A good farmer goes out to the fields and sees what's growing. He stoops down and tastes a little bit of the soil. He looks at the stock and the streams and the spring. If these are ample or can be made so by the sweat of his brow, the farmer knows the place holds a future. I grew up on that land. Some of it was mighty poor and rocky—but some of it was good. I learned not to be afraid of disappointments—of the weeds and rocks—but to value the good soil and the hard, constructive work.

I think there's considerable good soil for U.S.-Soviet relations to grow and prosper with the right cultivation and care. We have more in common than we sometimes realize. I have considerable faith in the people of the Soviet Union. We are both large countries. We both possess an incredible variety of natural resources. Our people are energetic, generous, and talented. We Americans really came to know and to admire the Russian people in World War II. And, I hope, they share some of the same feeling for us. So, I would say that our people are more naturally friends than enemies. I would like to see us exchange goods and ideas and technology—all of the means to achieving common progress and prosperity. . . .

Q. Do you think then, sir, that we have reached a point in our relations with the Soviets where both sides accept the proposition that nuclear war is impossible?

A. There is no question but that the American people and the Russian people are absolutely opposed to war. I wish I could say that nuclear war is impossible. The United States, as I said before, will never start any war, nuclear or otherwise. But this world of ours is filled with dangers. We can never know what may suddenly erupt to bring new tensions and threats to the peace. . . .

Q. What about the ideological barriers, Mr. President? Do you think we can really find social and political accord with the Soviet Union as long as we are in such diverse ideological camps?

A. I think both sides must realize that neither is going to convert the other. The United States has no interest in remaking the Soviet Union in our image. And I don't see any evidence that America will go Communist. I think that the real interests of nations transcend the ideological differences. For instance, some of the nations with which we work closely have moved toward planned economies. But this makes no difference to us—or to them. We work together out of mutual trust and respect and because we share many of the same ideals and aspirations.

We Americans believe that our democracy and our system of a mixed economy with a wide scope for free enterprise works best for us. But we support and respect the rights of all peoples freely to choose their own system. We oppose the practice of imposing one's system on others. If everyone would abide by the principle of self-determination and reject aggression and subversion, the world would be a happier place.

Document 12.2

China and "Containment without Isolation"

Even before he became president in 1969, Richard Nixon looked toward a new future for U.S. foreign policy. Recognizing that America's domestic, international, and economic liabilities would make it impossible to continue pursuing containment in an unlimited fashion, Nixon began preparing the ground for an American diplomatic revolution with a series of speeches and articles in the 1960s. As he argued in a 1967 article in Foreign Affairs, *the centerpiece would be a new relationship with communist China, with which the United States did not even have diplomatic relations.*

Any American policy toward Asia must come urgently to grips with the reality of China. This does not mean, as many would simplistically have it, rushing to grant recognition to Peking, to admit it to the United Nations and to ply it with offers of trade, all of which would serve to confirm its rulers in their present course. It does mean recognizing the present and potential danger from Communist China, and taking measures designed to meet that danger. It also means distinguishing carefully between long-range and short-range policies, and fashioning short-range programs so as to advance our long-range goals.

Taking the long view, we simply cannot afford to leave China forever outside the family of nations, there to nurture its fantasies, cherish its hates and threaten its neighbors. There is no place on this small planet for a billion of its potentially most able people to live in angry isolation. But we could go disastrously wrong if, in pursuing this long-range goal, we failed in the short range to read the lessons of history.

The world cannot be safe until China changes. Thus our aim, to the extent that we can influence events, should be to induce change. The way to do this is to persuade China that it must change: that it cannot satisfy its imperial ambitions, and that its own national interest requires a turning away from foreign adventuring and a turning inward toward the solution of its own domestic problems.

If the challenge posed by the Soviet Union after World War II was not precisely similar, it was sufficiently so to offer a valid precedent and a valuable lesson. Moscow finally changed when it, too, found that change was necessary. This was essentially a change of the head, not of the heart. Internal evolution played a role, to be sure, but the key factor was that the West was able to create conditions, notably in the shoring up of European defenses, the rapid restoration of European economies and the cementing of the Atlantic Alliance, that forced Moscow to look to the wisdom of reaching some measure of accommodation with the West. We are still far from reaching a full détente, but at least substantial progress has been made. . . .

Some counsel conceding to China a "sphere of influence" embracing much of the Asian mainland and extending even to the island nations beyond; others urge that we eliminate the threat by preemptive war. Clearly, neither of these courses would be acceptable to the United States or to its Asian allies. Others argue that we should seek an anti-Chinese alliance with European powers, even including the Soviet Union. Quite apart from the obvious problems involved in Soviet participation, such a course would inevitably carry connotations of Europe vs. Asia, white vs. non-white, which could have catastrophic repercussions throughout the rest of the non-white world in general and Asia in particular. If our long-range aim is to pull China back into the family of nations, we must avoid the impression that the great powers or the European powers are "ganging up;" the response should clearly be one of active defense rather than potential offense, and must be untainted with any suspicion of racism.

For the United States to go it alone in containing China would not only place an unconscionable burden on our own country, but also would heighten the chances of nuclear war while undercutting the independent development of the nations of Asia. The primary restraint on China's Asian ambitions should be exercised by the Asian nations in the path of those ambitions, backed by the ultimate power of the United States. This is sound strategically, sound psychologically and sound in terms of the dynamics of Asian development. Only as the nations of non-communist Asia become so strong, economically, politically and militarily, that they no longer furnish tempting targets for Chinese aggression, will the leaders in Peking be persuaded to turn their energies inward rather than outward. And that will be the time when the dialogue with mainland China can begin.

For the short run, then, this means a policy of firm restraint, of no reward, of a creative counterpressure designed to persuade Peking that its interests can be served only by accepting the basic rules of international civility. For the long run, it means pulling China back into the world community, but as a great and progressing nation, not as the epicenter of world revolution.

"Containment without isolation" is a good phrase and a sound concept, as far as it goes. But it covers only half the problem. Along with it, we need a positive policy of pressure and persuasion, of dynamic detoxification, a marshaling of Asian forces both to keep the peace and to help draw off the poison from the Thoughts of Mao.

Dealing with Red China is something like trying to cope with the more explosive ghetto elements in our own country. In each case a potentially destructive force has to be curbed; in each case an outlaw element has to be brought within the law; in each case dialogues have to be opened; in each case aggression has to be restrained while education proceeds; and, not least, in neither case can we afford to let those now self-exiled from society stay exiled forever. We have to proceed with both an urgency born of necessity and a patience born of realism, moving step by calculated step toward the final goal.

Document 12.3

THE NIXON DOCTRINE

If Nixon was going to reformulate U.S. foreign policy for an era of limits and multipolarity, he was first going to have to withdraw the United States from Vietnam. The war was not only a source of unrest at home, but also an irritant with Moscow and Beijing. But as we saw in chapter 11, Nixon did not want to withdraw from Vietnam suddenly or quickly. Instead, he felt he needed to do so in a way that upheld American power in the Pacific, and by extension the rest of the world. In the summer of

1969, he embarked on a tour of Asia. During a stopover on the Pacific island of Guam, he revealed the basis of his new strategy—"Vietnamization," which meant that the United States would support its allies but not send U.S. troops to do their fighting—that would, he hoped, allow détente to proceed on a sound footing. The Nixon Doctrine, as this plan became known, applied to all U.S. allies in Asia.

The United States is going to be facing, we hope before too long—no one can say how long, but before too long—a major decision: What will be its role in Asia and in the Pacific after the end of the war in Vietnam? We will be facing that decision, but also the Asian nations will be wondering about what that decision is.

When I talked to Prime Minister [John] Gorton [of Australia], for example, he indicated, in the conversations he had had with a number of Asian leaders, they all wondered whether the United States, because of its frustration over the war in Vietnam, because of its earlier frustration over the war in Korea—whether the United States would continue to play a significant role in Asia, or whether the United States, like the French before, and then the British, and, of course, the Dutch—whether we would withdraw from the Pacific and play a minor role.

This is a decision that will have to be made, of course, as the war comes to an end. But the time to develop the thinking which will go into that decision is now. I think that one of the weaknesses in American foreign policy is that too often we react rather precipitately to events as they occur. We fail to have the perspective and the long-range view which is essential for a policy that will be viable.

As I see it, even though the war in Vietnam has been, as we all know, a terribly frustrating one, and, as a result of that frustration, even though there would be a tendency for many Americans to say, "After we are through with that, let's not become involved in Asia," I am convinced that the way to avoid becoming involved in another war in Asia is for the United States to continue to play a significant role.

I think the way that we could become involved would be to attempt withdrawal, because, whether we like it or not, geography makes us a Pacific power. . . .

So, what I am trying to suggest is this: As we look at Asia, it poses, in my view, over the long haul, looking down to the end of the century, the greatest threat to the peace of the world, and, for that reason the United States should continue to play a significant role. It also poses, it seems to me, the greatest hope for progress in the world—progress in the world because of the ability, the resources, the ability of the people, the resources physically that are available in this part of the world. And for these reasons, I think we need policies that will see that we play a part and a part that is appropriate to the conditions that we will find. . . .

The second factor is one that is going to, I believe, have a major impact on the future of Asia, and it is something that we must take into account. Asians will say in every country that we visit that they do not want to be dictated to from the outside, Asia for the Asians. And that is what we want, and that is the role we should play. We should assist, but we should not dictate....

But as far as our role is concerned, we must avoid that kind of policy that will make countries in Asia so dependent upon us that we are dragged into conflicts such as the one that we have in Vietnam.

Document 12.4

A NEW ERA

With the assistance of National Security Adviser (and later Secretary of State) Henry Kissinger, and building upon Kennedy and Johnson's new approach to the Cold War, Nixon declared that America needed a foreign policy that combined strength with openness and resolve with dialogue. He unveiled this new approach in his first annual foreign policy report to Congress in February 1970.

When I took office, the most immediate problem facing our nation was the war in Vietnam. No question has more occupied our thoughts and energies during this past year.

Yet the fundamental task confronting us was more profound. We could see that the whole pattern of international politics was changing. Our challenge was to understand that change, to define America's goals for the next period, and to set in motion policies to achieve them. For all Americans must understand that because of its strength, its history and its concern for human dignity, this nation occupies a special place in the world. Peace and progress are impossible without a major American role.

This first annual report on U.S. foreign policy is more than a record of one year. It is this Administration's statement of a new approach to foreign policy to match a new era of international relations.

A NEW ERA

The postwar period in international relations has ended.

Then, we were the only great power whose society and economy had escaped World War II's massive destruction. Today, the ravages of that war have been overcome. Western Europe and Japan have recovered their economic strength, their political vitality, and their national self-confidence. Once the recipients of American aid, they have now begun to share their growing resources with the developing world. Once almost totally dependent on American military power, our European allies now play a greater role in our common policies, commensurate with their growing strength.

Then, new nations were being born, often in turmoil and uncertainty. Today, these nations have a new spirit and a growing strength of independence. Once, many feared that they would become simply a battleground of cold-war rivalry and fertile ground for Communist penetration. But this fear misjudged their pride in their national identities and their determination to preserve their newly won sovereignty.

Then, we were confronted by a monolithic Communist world. Today, the nature of that world has changed—the power of individual Communist nations has grown, but international Communist unity has been shattered. Once a unified bloc, its solidarity has been broken by the powerful forces of nationalism. The Soviet Union and Communist China, once bound by an alliance of friendship, had become bitter adversaries by the mid-1960's. The only times the Soviet Union has used the Red Army since World War II have been against its own allies—in East Germany in 1953, in Hungary in 1956, and in Czechoslovakia in 1968. The Marxist dream of international Communist unity has disintegrated.

Then, the United States had a monopoly or overwhelming superiority of nuclear weapons. Today, a revolution in the technology of war has altered the nature of the military balance of power. New types of weapons present new dangers. Communist China has acquired thermonuclear weapons. Both the Soviet Union and the United States have acquired the ability to inflict unacceptable damage on the other, no matter which strikes first. There can be no gain and certainly no victory for the power that provokes a thermonuclear exchange. Thus, both sides have recognized a vital mutual interest in halting the dangerous momentum of the nuclear arms race.

Then, the slogans formed in the past century were the ideological accessories of the intellectual debate. Today the "isms" have lost their vitality—indeed the restlessness of youth on both sides of the dividing line testifies to the need for a new idealism and deeper purposes.

This is the challenge and the opportunity before America as it enters the 1970's.

Document 12.5

DÉTENTE WITH THE SOVIET UNION

One of Nixon and Kissinger's priorities was to construct a new relationship with the Soviet Union. In large part, their desire to do so was rooted in the same concerns about nuclear warfare that had spurred Kennedy and Johnson's attempts to build détente. Nixon and Kissinger also wanted to use détente to leverage a settlement in Vietnam. But they had another motivation, American vulnerability, that had been caused partly by the Kennedy and Johnson administrations (the Vietnam War) and partly by the new international system in which the United States was not as dominant militarily and economically. Nixon and Kissinger felt that Americans had to be more realistic about their position in the world. No longer could they shoulder the burden of containment alone; no longer could they demonize their communist adversaries and refuse to engage them in dialogue. Here, in a letter to Secretary of Defense Melvin Laird, Nixon explains his approach.

I believe that the tone of our public and private discourse about and with the Soviet Union should be calm, courteous and non-polemical. This will not prevent us from stating our views clearly and, if need be, firmly; nor will it preclude us from candidly affirming our attitude—negatively if warranted—toward the policies and actions of the Soviet Union. But what I said in my Inaugural address concerning the tone and character of our domestic debates should also govern the tone and character of our statements in the international arena, most especially in respect of the Soviet Union.

I believe that the basis for a viable settlement is a mutual recognition of our vital interests. We must recognize that the Soviet Union has interests; in the present circumstances we cannot but take account of them in defining our own. We should leave the Soviet leadership in no doubt that we expect them to adopt a similar approach toward us. This applies also to the concerns and interests of our allies and indeed of all nations. They, too, are entitled to the safeguarding of their legitimate interests. In the past we have often attempted to settle things in a fit of enthusiasm, relying on personal diplomacy. But the "spirit" that permeated various meetings lacked a solid basis of mutual interest and, therefore, every summit meeting was followed by a crisis in less than a year.

I am convinced that the great issues are fundamentally interrelated. I do not mean by this to establish artificial linkages between specific elements of one or another issue or between tactical steps that we may elect to take. But I do believe that crisis or confrontation in one place and real cooperation in another cannot long be sustained simultaneously. I recognize that the previous Administration took the view that when we perceive a mutual interest on an issue with the USSR, we should pursue agreement and attempt to insulate it as much as possible from the ups and downs of conflicts elsewhere. This may well be sound on numerous bilateral and practical matters such as cultural or scientific exchanges. But, on the crucial issues of our day, I believe we must seek to advance on a front at least broad enough to make clear that we see some relationship between political and military issues. I believe that the Soviet leaders should be brought to understand that they cannot expect to reap the benefits of cooperation in one area while seeking to take advantage of tension or confrontation elsewhere. Such a course involves the danger that the Soviets will use talks on arms as a safety valve on intransigence elsewhere. I note, for example, that the invasion of Hungary was followed by abortive disarmament talks within nine months. The invasion of Czechoslovakia was preceded by the explorations of a summit conference (in fact, when Ambassador [Anatoly] Dobrynin [of the Soviet Union] informed President Johnson of the invasion of Czechoslovakia, he received the appointment so quickly because the President thought his purpose was to fix the date of a summit meeting). Negotiation and the search for agreement carry their own burdens; the Soviets—no less than we—must be ready to bear them.

I recognize the problem of giving practical substance to the propositions set forth in the previous paragraph. Without attempting to lay down inflexible prescriptions about how various matters at issue between ourselves and the USSR should be connected, I would like to illustrate what I have in mind in one case of immediate and widespread interest—the proposed talks on strategic weapons. I believe our decision on when and how to proceed does not depend exclusively on our review of the purely military and technical issues, although these are of key importance. This decision should also be taken in the light of the prevailing political context and, in particular, in light of progress toward stabilizing the explosive Middle East situation, and in light of the Paris talks [on Vietnam]. I believe I should retain the freedom to ensure, to the extent that we have control over it, that the timing of talks with the Soviet Union on strategic weapons is optimal. This may, in fact, mean delay beyond that required for our review of the technical issues. Indeed, it means that we should—at least in our public position—keep open the option that there may be no talks at all.

Document 12.6

A NEW ECONOMY

The pressures of globalization required a new approach to the economy as well. Economic growth continued through the 1960s, but two pressures had begun to take their toll by the beginning of Nixon's presidency. First, the Vietnam War had created large imbalances in the economy, mostly because government spending rose dramatically but Johnson did not raise taxes, thereby creating deficits and stimulating inflation. Second, international banks and other countries, even allies like France, had put tremendous pressure on America's currency by converting their dollar reserves into gold, payable by the U.S. Treasury. A third problem, deindustrialization, was also emerging into view. With manufacturing costs far cheaper in the developing world, American companies began to build their products overseas; at the same time, foreign companies were now producing products, such as electronic equipment or automobiles, of equal or even superior quality to their American competitors. Deindustrialization resulted in the closing of hundreds of U.S. factories and the loss of thousands of jobs. As a result of these three problems, the American economy entered its most difficult crisis since the Great Depression. Nixon's response included a radical measure that emulated one of Franklin D. Roosevelt's: taking the United States off the gold standard. With it, Nixon ended one of the pillars of the post–World War II international order, the Bretton Woods system. Here, in this 1971 speech that shocked nearly everyone, Nixon explains his decision.

America today has the best opportunity in this century to achieve two of its greatest ideals: to bring about a full generation of peace, and to create a new prosperity without war.

This not only requires bold leadership ready to take bold action—it calls forth the greatness in a great people.

Prosperity without war requires action on three fronts: We must create more and better jobs; we must stop the rise in the cost of living; we must protect the dollar from the attacks of international money speculators.

We are going to take that action—not timidly, not half-heartedly, and not in piecemeal fashion. We are going to move forward to the new prosperity without war as befits a great people—all together, and along a broad front.

The time has come for a new economic policy for the United States. Its targets are unemployment, inflation, and international speculation. And this is how we are going to attack those targets. . . .

The third indispensable element in building the new prosperity is closely related to creating new jobs and halting inflation. We must protect the position of the American dollar as a pillar of monetary stability around the world.

In the past 7 years, there has been an average of one international monetary crisis every year. Now who gains from these crises? Not the workingman; not the investor; not the real producers of wealth. The gainers are the international money speculators. Because they thrive on crises, they help to create them.

In recent weeks, the speculators have been waging an all-out war on the American dollar. The strength of a nation's currency is based on the strength of that nation's economy—and the American economy is by far the strongest in the world. Accordingly, I have directed the Secretary of the Treasury to take the action necessary to defend the dollar against the speculators.

I have directed Secretary Connally to suspend temporarily the convertibility of the dollar into gold or other reserve assets, except in amounts and conditions determined to be in the interest of monetary stability and in the best interests of the United States.

Now, what is this action—which is very technical—what does it mean for you?

Let me lay to rest the bugaboo of what is called devaluation.

If you want to buy a foreign car or take a trip abroad, market conditions may cause your dollar to buy slightly less. But if you are among the overwhelming majority of Americans who buy American-made products in America, your dollar will be worth just as much tomorrow as it is today.

The effect of this action, in other words, will be to stabilize the dollar.

Now, this action will not win us any friends among the international money traders. But our primary concern is with the American workers, and with fair competition around the world.

To our friends abroad, including the many responsible members of the international banking community who are dedicated to stability and the flow of trade, I give this assurance: The United States has always been, and will continue to be, a forward-looking and trustworthy trading part- ner. In full cooperation with the International Monetary Fund and those who trade with us, we will press for the necessary reforms to set up an urgently needed new international monetary system. Stability and equal treatment is in everybody's best interest. I am determined that the American dollar must never again be a hostage in the hands of international spec- ulators.

I am taking one further step to protect the dollar, to improve our balance of payments, and to increase jobs for Americans. As a temporary measure, I am today imposing an additional tax of 10 percent on goods imported into the United States. This is a better solution for international trade than direct controls on the amount of imports.

This import tax is a temporary action. It isn't directed against any other country. It is an action to make certain that American products will not be at a disadvantage because of unfair exchange rates. When the unfair treatment is ended, the import tax will end as well.

As a result of these actions, the product of American labor will be more competitive, and the unfair edge that some of our foreign competition has will be removed. This is a major reason why our trade balance has eroded over the past 15 years.

At the end of World War II the economies of the major industrial nations of Europe and Asia were shattered. To help them get on their feet and to protect their freedom, the United States has provided over the past 25 years $143 billion in foreign aid. That was the right thing for us to do.

Today, largely with our help, they have regained their vitality. They have become our strong competitors, and we welcome their success. But now that other nations are economically strong, the time has come for them to bear their fair share of the burden of defending freedom around the world. The time has come for exchange rates to be set straight and for the major nations to compete as equals. There is no longer any need for the United States to compete with one hand tied behind her back.

Document 12.7

THE VIEW FROM MOSCOW

Nixon and Kissinger did not operate in a vacuum, of course. Détente could only work if the Soviets were also willing to negotiate the terms for a new, more peaceful, and more stable relationship. Here, in this excerpt from his memoirs, Anatoly Dobrynin, the Kremlin's ambassador to every U.S. president from John F. Kennedy to Ronald Reagan and a key architect of détente, expresses some of the Soviet Union's hopes, fears, and frustrations.

[Soviet Premier Leonid] Brezhnev was not much of a theorist, but he had lived through a devastating war and knew beyond doubt that our people put peace before all other things. Having assumed his position [in 1964], he spent a couple of years gingerly examining the intricate workings of international life. But even by the middle of Johnson's term and surely by the beginning of Nixon's presidency he had come to a rather strong conviction about the need to improve relations with the West and especially the United States, although he rendered appropriate homage to what then were considered ideologically sound Marxist-Leninist positions.

Several factors made Brezhnev and the highest officials of the party and state adjust their approach to foreign policy.

First, a nuclear war was utterly unacceptable, as the Cuban crisis had clearly demonstrated. Second, there was the enormous burden of military expenditures, which both sides unsuccessfully tried to reduce at the start of Johnson's presidency. Third, the process of improving relations between the Soviet Union and Western Europe, especially with the Federal Republic of [West] Germany through the so-called Berlin Agreements, would become extremely complicated if the United States were to try to impede it, and the American position was largely determined by the prospects for strategic arms limitation talks. Fourth, there was a sharp aggravation in Soviet-Chinese relations in the late 1960s and early 1970s, and it was essential to avert or neutralize any collusion between Washington and Beijing. Fifth, the improvement of relations with the United States would undoubtedly consolidate the prestige of Brezhnev's leadership within the Soviet Union. . . .

Soviet-American relations reached a level of amity in 1973 never before achieved in the postwar era. Events demonstrated the viability of the policy of détente, although there were some relapses, mainly on the American side. Indeed, the very idea of détente in terms of its practical implementation came to Americans out of the blue and caught many completely unaware.... [B]y far the most remarkable influence on the developments in the United States was made by Watergate, which provoked a crisis of American constitutional democracy. At first the break-in on May 28, 1972, at the Democratic Party's headquarters in Washington's Watergate apartment building, had seemed only a minor event. The burglars were later discovered to have been acting on behalf of Nixon's inner circle of political operatives, but even then I did not pay much attention to the first reports of the trail leading toward the White House. I thought it inconceivable that Nixon, a man of great political experience, would permit his office to become involved in such a petty venture.

The Soviet Union and its government had great difficulty understanding how public opinion in the United States could have gotten rid of President Nixon, surely one of the most able leaders of his time in foreign affairs even if he was also one of the most reckless in his climb to the top. Here was the president, elected for the second term by a significant majority, threatened by impeachment for what was seen as a minor affair. His use of the CIA, the FBI, and the considerable powers of his own office to remain in the White House was considered in the Soviet Union at that time a fairly natural thing for the chief of state to do. Who cared if there was a breach of the Constitution? So our inclination was to think that Watergate was some kind of intrigue organized by his political enemies to overthrow him. And in Moscow, most of those enemies were considered anyway to be the opponents of better relations with the Soviet Union. Although in the short run all this had no serious effect on the process of détente, it was eventually recognized as capable of exploding the process at any time. It was of course the time bomb that finally destroyed the presidency of the man who in our minds was the principal force in the United States behind the policy of détente.

Document 12.8

The Opening to China

With the Sino-Soviet split, Nixon and Kissinger sensed an opportunity: they would relax relations with both Moscow and Beijing with the intention of making each compete for American affections against the other. This strategy of triangulation aimed to give the United States leverage over both the Soviets and the Chinese. Nixon and Kissinger hoped that warmer relations with the communist great powers would also apply pressure on Hanoi to negotiate an end to the Vietnam War. In June 1971, Nixon and Kissinger received word through the Pakistani government that China was indeed interested in opening a new dialogue. To prepare for a summit between Nixon and China's leader, Mao Zedong, Kissinger secretly traveled to China in July 1971 for historic talks with Chinese Premier Zhou Enlai.

My Talks with Chou En-lai . . .

I am frank to say that this visit was a very moving experience. The historic aspects of the occasion; the warmth and dignity of the Chinese; the splendor of the Forbidden City, Chinese history and culture; the heroic stature of Chou En-lai; and the intensity and sweep of our talks combined to make an indelible impression on me and my colleagues.

These forty-eight hours, and my extensive discussions with Chou in particular, had all the flavor, texture, variety and delicacy of a Chinese banquet. Prepared from the long sweep of tradition and culture, meticulously cooked by hands of experience, and served in splendidly simple surroundings, our feast consisted of many courses, some sweet and some sour, all interrelated and forming a coherent whole. It was a total experience, and one went away, as after all good Chinese meals, very satisfied but not at all satiated.

We have laid the groundwork for you and Mao to turn a page in history. But we should have no illusions about the future. Profound differences and years of isolation yawn between us and the Chinese. They will be tough before and during the summit on the question of Taiwan and other major issues. And they will prove implacable foes if our relations turn sour. My assessment of these people is that they are deeply ideological, close to fanatic in the intensity of their beliefs. At the same time they display an inward security that allows them, within the framework of their principles, to be meticulous and reliable in dealing with others.

Furthermore, the process we have now started will send enormous shock waves around the world. It may panic the Soviet Union into sharp hostility. It could shake Japan loose from its heavily American moorings. It will cause a violent upheaval in Taiwan. It will have major impact on our other Asian allies, such as Korea and Thailand. It will increase the already substantial hostility in India. Some quarters may seek to sabotage the summit over the coming months.

However, we were well aware of these risks when we embarked on this course. We were aware too that the alternative was unacceptable—continued isolation from one-quarter of the world's most talented people and a country rich in past achievements and future potential.

And even the risks can be managed and turned to our advantage if we maintain steady nerves and pursue our policies responsibly. With the Soviet Union we will have to make clear the continued priorities we attach to our concrete negotiations with them. Just as we will not collude with them against China, so we have no intention of colluding with China against them. If carefully managed, our new China policy could have a longer term beneficial impact on Moscow. . . .

For Asia and for the world we need to demonstrate that we are enlarging the scope of our diplomacy in a way that, far from harming the interests of other countries, should instead prove helpful to them.

Our dealings, both with the Chinese and others, will require reliability, precision, finesse. If we can master this process, we will have made a revolution.

Document 12.9

National Insecurity

As Dobrynin had recognized, détente and the opening to China were not popular with all Americans. Many did not like relinquishing American strategic superiority through nuclear arms control; with the Soviet Union boasting far greater conventional forces in Europe, critics of détente feared that relinquishing U.S. nuclear superiority would lead to communist aggression and American insecurity. One of the most prominent critics was Senator Henry M. Jackson, a Democrat from Washington state. As this 1972 debate on the Senate floor shows, Jackson was especially concerned with the negotiations over nuclear arms control that lay at the heart of détente. He wanted to safeguard the U.S. advantage in multiple independently targetable reentry vehicles, or MIRVs, that could launch several nuclear warheads from a single missile; doing so also meant protecting America's superiority in advanced weapons technology. Underlying Jackson's opposition to détente was a profound distrust of the Soviet Union, and of communism more generally, that had more in common with the rhetoric of the early Cold War than the era of détente. The focus of this debate was Jackson's proposed amendment to an arms control treaty with the Soviets that Kissinger had negotiated; Jackson was effectively trying to nullify the compromises Kissinger made in the pursuit of stability. But not all of Jackson's colleagues agreed. In this extraordinary passage from the debate, Senator Alan Cranston, a fellow Democrat from California, criticizes Jackson's proposed amendment as a threat to peace and praises the Soviet Union—though whether raising the protein content of a citizen's diet could offset the suppression of basic human rights such as freedoms of speech and religion was left unsettled.

The assistant clerk read as follows:

"At the end of S.J. Res. 241 insert a new section as follows:

"The Government and the people of the United States ardently desire a stable international strategic balance that maintains peace and deters aggression. The Congress supports the stated policy of the United States that, were a more complete strategic offensive arms agreement not achieved within the five years of the interim agreement, and were the survivability of the strategic deterrent forces of the United States to be threatened as a result of such failure, this could jeopardize the supreme national interests of the United States; the Congress recognizes the difficulty of maintaining a stable strategic balance in a period of rapidly developing technology; the Congress recognizes the principle of United States–Soviet Union equality reflected in the antiballistic missile treaty, and urges and requests the President to seek a future treaty that, inter alia, would not limit the United States to levels of intercontinental strategic forces inferior to the limits provided for the Soviet Union; and the Congress considers that the success of these agreements and the attainment of more permanent and comprehensive agreements are dependent upon the maintenance of a vigorous research and development and modernization program leading to a prudent strategic posture." . . .

Mr. Jackson: [O]ur amendment, sponsored by 44 Senators, has as its central provision a request to the President to seek a future SALT treaty that would involve equal limits on the intercontinental strategic forces of the United States and the Soviet Union. . . .

The amendment rejects the notion that we should accept numerical inferiority in a long-term treaty because we now, before the follow-on negotiations have even begun, have technological superiority. The amendment rejects the shortsighted notion that our temporary advantage in numbers of MIRV warheads can compensate in a SALT II treaty for permanent Soviet superiority in numbers and throw weight. We must not base our security on an ephemeral advantage, while the Soviets base theirs on permanent ones. . . .

Mr. Cranston: I was in the Soviet Union last week and I should like to express some thoughts concerning my soundings and findings there. . . . The people I met there were talking about the very issues we are discussing on the Senate floor.

I came back from the Soviet Union with my own convictions reinforced that . . . it would be harmful to our future scaling down of the arms race to adopt the Jackson amendment. . . .

Plainly, the Soviet Union and the United States have entered a period of testing—testing each other's good faith, testing each other's promises, testing the possibilities for a world without overkill, even testing the possibilities for a world without any arms at all.

This testing period is very delicate. Everyone I talked to in Russia who was informed on the subject stressed that one serious incident could set back progress for 10 years. Something comparable to the U-2 incident or the Czech invasion could crush our new hopes for peace. . . .

And we should ratify the interim agreement without the Jackson amendment. The amendment, I am convinced, threatens the current effort to reduce tensions between our two powerful nations. . . .

The Soviet Union is still a repressive dictatorship.

The treatment meted out to gifted men like Alexander Solzhenitsyn and the Medvedev brothers is deplorable.

Talented, dissident intellectuals who have not captured Western attention fare much worse.

And the treatment of Soviet Jews and other minority groups is shocking.

But there seems little doubt that, in terms of economics, life for the ordinary person inside the U.S.S.R. is better than it was either under the czars or under Stalin.

The repression of free speech is repugnant to me, and to all of us.

But Soviet leaders are, at any rate, groping toward a better life for the Russian consumer.

For example, the Soviet Government has pledged to increase the protein content of the Soviet diet by 25 percent within 5 years.

I saw many new housing developments.

And I was told that many frank and vigorous debates are permitted on ways of unsnarling local administration and overcoming the petty bureaucracy that stifles Soviet life.

So it appears that the Soviet Government is slowly moving toward a better life for its people at home and a more peaceful atmosphere abroad.

This is a critical time.

Document 12.10

DÉTENTE, OR HUMAN RIGHTS?

The debate between Senators Jackson and Cranston hit upon the central dilemma of the diplomacy Nixon and Kissinger had crafted in a new age of American vulnerability. Détente with the Soviets required a healthy working relationship. In turn, this meant that the U.S. government had to refrain from openly criticizing communist ideology and practices, which entailed significant and widespread abuses of basic human rights. But American opponents of détente were deeply uncomfortable with the moral compromises that came with turning a blind eye to Moscow's appalling human rights record. Human rights activists were also troubled that the United States had refrained from criticizing its allies, many of whom were reliably anticommunist but brutally authoritarian regimes. Instead of Nixon and Kissinger's search for peace through stability, they called on Washington to promote peace through justice. The passages below, from a 1974 bipartisan congressional report, are an example of the new crusade for human rights. Note especially the new and quite radical notion that respect for national sovereignty should not take priority over respect for individual dignity—a notion that would come to define many of the wars once the Cold War ended fifteen years later.

Gross violations of human rights persist in every corner of the globe. Although an essential aim of any government should be to guarantee the free exercise of basic rights, governments frequently deny those rights to their own people. Government oppression is not limited to any particular ideological persuasion. Governments of the right, center, and left have been responsible for violating the fundamental rights of men and women....

The most abhorrent violations which exist today are: Racial discrimination, apartheid, and denial of self-determination; massacre of racial, religious, and ethnic groups; summary executions, torture, and denial of due process against political dissidents; and excessively harmful weaponry and methods of warfare against both civilians and combatants.

Protection of human rights is essentially the responsibility of each government with respect to its own citizens; however, when a government is itself the perpetrator of the violations, the victim has no recourse but to seek redress from outside his national boundaries. Men and women of decency find common cause in coming to the aid of the oppressed despite national differences. Through their own governments and international organizations, they have both the opportunity and responsibility to help defend human rights throughout the world....

The human rights factor is not accorded the high priority it deserves in our country's foreign policy. Too often it becomes invisible on the vast foreign policy horizon of political, economic, and military affairs. Proponents of pure power politics too often dismiss it as a factor in diplomacy. Unfortunately, the prevailing attitude has led the United States into embracing governments which practice torture and unabashedly violate almost every human rights guarantee pronounced by the world community. Through foreign aid and occasional intervention—both covert and overt—the United States supports those governments. Our relations with the present Governments of South Vietnam, Spain, Portugal, the Soviet Union, Brazil, Indonesia, Greece, the Philippines, and Chile exemplify how we have disregarded human rights for the sake of other assumed interests....

Respect for human rights is fundamental to our own national tradition. It is expressed unequivocally in our Constitution. Respect for human rights in other countries is a rightful concern of Americans not because of any assumed mission on our part to impose our own standards on others; rather, it is that not only have many other countries used our Bill of Rights as a model for their constitutions, but international standards have been established by the U.N. Charter and other treaties which obligate governments to uphold most of the same rights which are basic in our own system.

Furthermore, an increasingly interdependent world means that disregard for human rights in one country can have repercussions in others. The horrible atrocities of Nazi Germany and the tragic massacre in Bangladesh are examples of how gross violations of human rights precipitated bloody wars. The situations in southern Africa of racism and colonialism have the potential for international conflagration. Thus, consideration for human rights in foreign policy is both morally imperative and practically necessary.

Document 12.11

TROUBLE IN THE HEARTLAND

Kissinger soon found himself defending détente against its increasingly vocal domestic critics, mostly within his own Republican Party. In 1975, he embarked on a "heartland tour" of Midwestern states, where skepticism of détente ran high, to explain his foreign policy. The greatest human right, Kissinger argued in a speech to the Upper Midwest Council in Minneapolis, was the freedom from nuclear terror.

The incredible destructiveness of modern weapons has transformed international politics. We must maintain our military strength. But we have an obligation, in our own interest as well as the world's, to work with other nations to control both the growth and the spread of nuclear weapons.

In our relations with the Communist powers we must never lose sight of the fact that in the thermonuclear age general war would be disastrous to mankind. We have an obligation to seek a more productive and stable relationship despite the basic antagonism of our values.

Thirty years of economic and political evolution have brought about a new diffusion of power and initiative. At the same time, interdependence imposes upon all nations the reality that they must prosper together or suffer together. The destinies of the world's nations have become inevitably intertwined. Thus, the capacity of any one nation to shape events is more limited, and consequently our own choices are more difficult and complex.

To deal with this agenda we require strength of purpose and conviction. A nation unsure of its values cannot shape its future. A people confused about its direction will miss the opportunity to build a better and more peaceful world. This is why perhaps our deepest challenge is our willingness to face the increasing ambiguity of the problem of ends and means. . . .

We no longer live in so simple a world. We remain the strongest nation and the largest single factor in international affairs. Our leadership is perhaps even more essential than before. But our strategic superiority has given way to nuclear balance. Our political and economic predominance has diminished as others have grown in strength, and our dependence on the world economy has increased. Our margin of safety has shrunk.

Document 12.12

DÉTENTE AND HUMAN RIGHTS

Kissinger's speeches did little to reassure Americans who doubted the morality of his foreign policies. They continued to do so even after President Gerald Ford signed the 1975 Helsinki Accords, in which the United States recognized the legitimacy of Soviet rule and communist borders in Europe in exchange for a Soviet promise to respect human rights within the borders of the USSR and its European satellites. However, neither Ford nor Kissinger was especially committed to Helsinki's human rights provisions, as evidenced by their acquiescence in communist human rights violations and their support for right-wing dictators in the Third World. But Ford lost the 1976 election to Jimmy Carter, which created a window of opportunity for a new direction in U.S. foreign policy. As seen in this May 1977 speech at Notre Dame University, Carter made a much more robust commitment to the promotion and protection of human rights, and comprehensively linked it to the continuation of détente and nuclear arms control, peace in the Middle East, official recognition of communist China, and globalization itself.

I want to speak to you today about the strands that connect our actions overseas with our essential character as a nation. I believe we can have a foreign policy that is democratic, that is based on fundamental values, and that uses power and influence, which we have, for humane purposes. We can also have a foreign policy that the American people both support and, for a change, know about and understand.

I have a quiet confidence in our own political system. Because we know that democracy works, we can reject the arguments of those rulers who deny human rights to their people.

We are confident that democracy's example will be compelling, and so we seek to bring that example closer to those from whom in the past few years we have been separated and who are not yet convinced about the advantages of our kind of life.

We are confident that the democratic methods are the most effective, and so we are not tempted to employ improper tactics here at home or abroad.

We are confident of our own strength, so we can seek substantial mutual reductions in the nuclear arms race. . . .

Being confident of our own future, we are now free of that inordinate fear of communism which once led us to embrace any dictator who joined us in that fear. I'm glad that that's being changed.

For too many years, we've been willing to adopt the flawed and erroneous principles and tactics of our adversaries, sometimes abandoning our own values for theirs. We've fought fire with fire, never thinking that fire is better quenched with water. This approach failed, with Vietnam the best example of its intellectual and moral poverty. But through failure we have now found our way back to our own principles and values, and we have regained our lost confidence. . . .

We can no longer separate the traditional issues of war and peace from the new global questions of justice, equity, and human rights.

It is a new world, but America should not fear it. It is a new world, and we should help to shape it. It is a new world that calls for a new American foreign policy—a policy based on constant decency in its values and on optimism in our historical vision.

We can no longer have a policy solely for the industrial nations as the foundation of global stability, but we must respond to the new reality of a politically awakening world.

We can no longer expect that the other 150 nations will follow the dictates of the powerful, but we must continue—confidently—our efforts to inspire, to persuade, and to lead.

Our policy must reflect our belief that the world can hope for more than simple survival and our belief that dignity and freedom are fundamental spiritual requirements. Our policy must shape an international system that will last longer than secret deals.

We cannot make this kind of policy by manipulation. Our policy must be open; it must be candid; it must be one of constructive global involvement, resting on five cardinal principles.

I've tried to make these premises clear to the American people since last January. Let me review what we have been doing and discuss what we intend to do.

First, we have reaffirmed America's commitment to human rights as a fundamental tenet of our foreign policy. In ancestry, religion, color, place of origin, and cultural background, we Americans are as diverse a nation as the world has even seen. No common mystique of blood or soil unites us. What draws us together, perhaps more than anything else, is a belief in human freedom. We want the world to know that our Nation stands for more than financial prosperity. . . .

Second, we've moved deliberately to reinforce the bonds among our democracies. In our recent meetings in London [the multilateral International

Economic Summit Meeting], we agreed to widen our economic cooperation, to promote free trade, to strengthen the world's monetary system, to seek ways of avoiding nuclear proliferation. We prepared constructive proposals for the forthcoming meetings on North-South problems of poverty, development, and global well-being. And we agreed on joint efforts to reinforce and to modernize our common defense. . . .

Third, we've moved to engage the Soviet Union in a joint effort to halt the strategic arms race. This race is not only dangerous, it's morally deplorable. We must put an end to it. . . .

Fourth, we are taking deliberate steps to improve the chances of lasting peace in the Middle East. Through wide-ranging consultation with leaders of the countries involved—Israel, Syria, Jordan, and Egypt—we have found some areas of agreement and some movement toward consensus. The negotiations must continue.

Through my own public comments, I've also tried to suggest a more flexible framework for the discussion of the three key issues which have so far been so intractable: the nature of a comprehensive peace—what is peace; what does it mean to the Israelis; what does it mean to their Arab neighbors; secondly, the relationship between security and borders—how can the dispute over border delineations be established and settled with a feeling of security on both sides; and the issue of the Palestinian homeland. . . .

And fifth, we are attempting, even at the risk of some friction with our friends, to reduce the danger of nuclear proliferation and the worldwide spread of conventional weapons. . . .

It's important that we make progress toward normalizing relations with the People's Republic of China. We see the American and Chinese relationship as a central element of our global policy and China as a key force for global peace. We wish to cooperate closely with the creative Chinese people on the problems that confront all mankind. And we hope to find a formula which can bridge some of the difficulties that still separate us.

13

Escalating and Ending the Cold War

Détente had crumbled by 1979. Soviet forces invaded Afghanistan that year, and President Jimmy Carter responded with renewed American military spending. He declared a "doctrine" of his own, pledging American military intervention—potentially including a direct nuclear response—against any nation threatening the security of the oil-rich Persian Gulf. The warning was a shot across Moscow's bow, though more trying to the Kremlin was Washington's ensuing aid to anti-Soviet mujahideen *fighting the Soviets in Afghanistan. Islamic enthusiasts in particular rallied to fight the atheistic invaders, and American officials were only too happy to arm and supply anyone willing to fight Soviet forces.*

Marred by malaise and his inability to secure the release of American hostages held in Iran, Carter lost the White House to Ronald Reagan in 1980. Reagan, who had nearly bested Ford for his party's 1976 nomination, promised conservative renewal and pledged no tolerance for communism in any form. "So far détente's been a one-way street that the Soviet Union has used to pursue its own aims," Reagan declared at his first White House press conference. "I know of no Soviet leader since the revolution, and including the present leadership, that has not more than once repeated in the various Communist congresses they hold their determination that their goal must be the promotion of world revolution and a one-world Socialist or Communist state."

Reagan was determined to stop communism in its tracks. He escalated American military spending and put détente firmly on the back burner. Whether his actions contributed to the Soviet Union's eventual downfall remains in dispute, but one thing is clear: by the end of his term Soviet-American relations stood on a new footing of conciliation and stability, the Cold War appeared closer to its end than ever before, and as even Reagan admitted, the notion that the Soviets represented "evil" in the world, as he had stated in 1983, was a statement from "another time."

Changes behind the Iron Curtain itself undoubtedly did more to speed communism's collapse than anything Washington undertook. The Soviet economy staggered through the 1980s, accelerating calls for reform throughout Moscow's empire. Following a series of aged and infirm leaders in the Kremlin, Soviet officials elevated Mikhail Gorbachev to their leadership position in 1985. Gorbachev promised change, but no one—perhaps not even Gorbachev himself—precisely knew how far he would push, and perhaps of equal importance, how far conservative forces within his country would allow him to alter the very basis of their socialist state. Gorbachev forever walked a tightrope between assuring Western policy makers of his sincerity and safeguarding his own political standing at home.

In Eastern Europe, such calls for dramatic reform led to the downfall of communism. In China, on the other hand, similar pleas led only to a violent crackdown, though in the end a more market-based economy largely devoid of liberal freedoms emerged in place of orthodox communism. By 1991 the Cold War itself came to an end—though no one of significance in Western policy-making circles predicted such a rapid demise—when the Soviet Union ceased to exist, replaced by a loose confederation of former Soviet states with Russia as the dominant regional power. A new world emerged, with American power undisputed, China growing but isolated, Europe united and devoid of the Soviet threat for the first time in generations, and the Soviet Union itself gone but with tens of thousands of Soviet-era nuclear weapons still in place. The new post–Cold War world that emerged, therefore, held promise, but uncertainty as well.

Document 13.1

CZECHOSLOVAKIA'S CHARTER 77

Socialism was an uneven fit for much of Eastern Europe. East Germany, to paint with a broad brush, became a model totalitarian state, more ideologically doctrinaire than its Soviet master. Romania and Albania became over time authoritarian regimes socialist in name only, dedicated primarily to the glorification and survival of the ruling regimes. Hungary, Poland, and Czechoslovakia, meanwhile, frequently struggled to toe Moscow's line, evidenced by Soviet military interventions into each. Much indigenous hostility grew simply from rejection of Soviet rule, but many behind the Iron Curtain despised socialism's restraints. Among the most dramatic of these rejections was that of Czechoslovakia's Charter 77, founded by leading Czech intellectuals including future president Vaclav Havel in January 1977. The group's founding manifesto, excerpted here, was smuggled out of the country and published in Western newspapers. Havel and his collaborators demanded that their government adhere to the Helsinki Accords, a hallmark of détente. They were soon jailed in response, though their protest gave weight to Western supporters, including Reagan himself, who argued for vigorous opposition to Soviet rule.

On 13.10.1976, there were published in the Codex of Laws of the CSSR no. 120, an "International Pact on Civil and Political Rights" and an "International Pact on Economic, Social, and Cultural Rights," which had been signed on behalf of Czechoslovakia in 1968, confirmed at Helsinki in 1975 and which came into force in our country on 23.3.1976. Since that time our citizens have had the right and our state the duty to be guided by them.

The freedoms and rights of the peoples guaranteed by these pacts are important factors of civilization for which, throughout history, many progressive forces have been striving and their enactment can be of great assistance to the humanistic development of our society. We therefore welcome the fact that the Czechoslovak Socialist Republic has expressed adherence to these pacts.

But their publication reminds us with new urgency how many fundamental civil rights for the time being are—unhappily—valid in our country only on paper. Completely illusory, for example, is the right to freedom of expression, guaranteed by article 19 of the first pact.

Tens of thousands of citizens are not allowed to work in their own branches simply because they hold opinions which differ from official opinions. At the same time they are frequently the object of the most varied forms of discrimination and persecution on the part of the authorities and social organizations; they are deprived of any possibility of defending themselves and are virtually becoming the victims of apartheid.

Hundreds of thousands of other citizens are denied the right to "freedom from fear" [the preamble of the first pact], because they are forced to live in constant danger that if they express their opinions they will lose their possibility to work and other possibilities.

In contradiction to article 13 of the second pact, guaranteeing to all the right to education, there are countless young people who are prevented from studying because of their opinions or even those of their parents. There are citizens without number who must live in the fear that if they express themselves according to their convictions, they themselves or their children would be deprived of the right to education.

The implementation of the right "to seek, receive and spread information and ideas of all kinds, regardless of frontiers, either orally, in writing or in print, or by means of art" [part 2, article 13 of the first pact] is subject to persecution, not only outside the courts but judicially too, often under the guise of criminal charges (as is borne out, among others, by the trials of young musicians now going on). . . .

Some citizens—either privately, at their places of work or publicly—this letter being virtually possible only in foreign information media—call attention to the systematic violation of human rights and democratic freedoms and, in concrete cases, demand rectification. But in the majority of cases there is no response to their appeals or they themselves are subjected to investigation.

Responsibility for the observance of civil rights in a country naturally falls, in the first place, on the political and state power. But not on it alone. Each and every one of us has a share of responsibility for the general situation and thus, too, for the observance of the pacts which have been enacted and are binding not only on for the government but for all citizens.

The feeling of co-responsibility, faith in the idea of civic involvement and the will to exercise it and the common need to seek new and more effective means for it [*sic*] expression led us to the idea of setting up Charter 77, the origin of which we are announcing today.

Charter 77 is a free, informal and open association of people of different convictions, different faiths and different professions, who are linked by the desire, individually or jointly, to insist on the respecting of civil and human rights in our country and throughout the world, rights recognised for man both by the enacted international pacts, the Final Act of the Helsinki Conference and many other international documents against wars, violence, and social and spiritual oppression and which are expressed as a whole in the United Nations Declaration of Human Rights. . . .

Document 13.2

AN AMERICAN IN IRAN

Even as dissidents in Eastern Europe increasingly chafed under Soviet domination, once stable sections of the American sphere of influence also struggled for autonomy and change as the 1970s came to a close. Nowhere did this struggle play out more dramatically than in Iran in 1979. Long a key American ally in the volatile Middle East, Mohammad Reza Pahlavi, the Shah of Iran, was ousted by Islamic fundamentalists in February of 1979. Spurred by Ayatollah Khomeini's increasingly biting criticism of the United States for sheltering the shah, students and protestors stormed the American embassy in Tehran in November, ultimately taking fifty-two American citizens hostage; 444 days later, the hostages were released, though not before President Jimmy Carter's reputation crumbled, with Iranian-American relations yet to recover. What follows is a diary entry of one hostage, Robert C. Ode, noting his first experiences in captivity.

November 4, 1979: When we were about 1 ½ blocks from the Consular Section we were surrounded by a group of the students, who were armed, and told to return to the Compound. When we protested a shot was fired into the air above our heads.

It was raining moderately at the time. We were taken back to the Compound, being pushed and hurried along the way and forced to put our hands above our heads and then marched to the Embassy residence. After arriving at the residence I had my hands tied behind my back so tightly with a nylon cord that circulation was cut off. I was taken upstairs and put alone in a rear bedroom and after a short time was blindfolded. After protesting strongly that the cord was too tight, the cord was removed and the blindfold taken off when they tried to feed me some dates and I refused to eat anything I couldn't see. I strongly protested the violation of my diplomatic immunity, but these protests were ignored. I was then required to sit in a chair facing the bedroom wall. Then another older student came in and when I again protested the violation of my diplomatic immunity he confiscated my U.S. Mission Tehran ID card. My hands were again tied and I was taken to the Embassy living room on the ground floor where a number of other hostages were gathered. Some students attempted to talk with us, stating how they didn't hate Americans—only our government, President Carter, etc. We were given sandwiches and that night I slept on the living room floor. We were not permitted to talk to our fellow hostages and from then on our hands were tied day and night and only removed while we were eating or had to go to the bathroom.

November 13, 1979: We also received a visit from the Pope's representative—a fat dumpy little Italian who saw me reading a book, tapped me on the arm and clucked "molto buono" and "pazienza." We had three representatives from diplomatic missions in Tehran. Was told one was Belgian, another Syrian, and the third one I don't recall. They just walked through—had no conversation with us, and just looked at us as though we were animals in a zoo! On or about November 14, I was taken downstairs and asked to sign a statement requesting our Government to return the Shah so that we could be freed. I told my captors that it was useless since I knew that our Government not do so, but that I was willing to sign the petition just because I knew that it was a useless gesture. I noted that my name was #36 on the list of signers. At another time I had to complete a mimeographed form giving personal data such as my name, birth date, position in the Embassy and my duties. I again protested the violation of my diplomatic immunity in writing on this form.

Document 13.3

SOVIET TROUBLES AND FEARS

Soviet officials faced a quandary as the 1980s began. Many acknowledged, privately at least, the immense burdens Cold War military spending placed upon their struggling economy. At the same time, however, ranking Soviet officials also took Reagan at his word. They feared the militarization of the Cold War that he promised would either lead to great financial hardships should Moscow keep pace, or worse yet that Reagan might very well be inclined to start the war against communism his harsh rhetoric seemed to promise. Some historians, politicians, and pundits credit Reagan with winning the Cold War by his willingness to spend the Soviets into oblivion through expensive programs such as his Strategic Defense Initiative ("Star Wars"), announced in 1983 as a means of shielding the United States and its allies from nuclear attack. As the following excerpt from a July 1981 conversation between KGB Chairman Yuri Andropov (who would soon take the reins of power within the Kremlin) and his East German counterpart Erich Mielke demonstrates, however, Soviet officials already recognized the cost of Cold War parity and the perils of falling behind.

Yuri Andropov: The most complex program is that we cannot avoid the strains of military expenditures for us and the other socialist countries. Reagan has confirmed that he will spend 220 billion dollars for the military. Thus, we must do it all as well and provide our defense industry with corresponding means. We must not fall behind.

The balance of forces is currently as follows:

Aircraft = slight advantage for the US

Tanks/submarines = parity

Missiles = parity

The Americans know that parity exists. We cannot allow us to be overtaken. If we did not have to make these expenditures, we could solve all the other problems in 2 or 3 years.

On top of that, there is the assistance for Vietnam, Laos, Kampuchea, Angola, Cuba, Afghanistan, Ethiopia, and others. Poland recently received 4 billion dollars so that it could remain creditworthy. . . .

The struggle will be long and arduous.

We are prepared for this.

We have to explain to the peoples [of the world] why the imperialists were initially in favor of détente and are now coming out against it. This has nothing to do with the different US Presidents, of course. It is related to objective processes developing in the world. The correlation of forces is changing, and the imperialists realize this. When the US agreed to the policy of détente, it had to realize that socialism's strengths are real. Then there was the American defeat in Vietnam. They thought they could achieve their objectives through a policy of détente. They sought many freedoms for their diplomats analogous to those conceded to journalists. None of this was conceded to them.

Reagan's vulgar speeches show the true face of the military-industrial complex. They have long sought such a figure. Now, they have finally found it in the form of Reagan.

Document 13.4

RESPONSE TO THE CRACKDOWN IN POLAND

Much like presidents before him, Ronald Reagan struggled to find some practical means of influencing events behind the Iron Curtain without drastically escalating tensions with the Soviets. Reagan and his aides also feared escalating tensions with their European allies, many of whom—fearful of nearby Soviet tanks and troops and eager to preserve economic ties with Moscow, including a nearly constructed gas pipeline flowing from east to west—proved hesitant to anger Moscow too greatly by siding too strongly with reformers in Eastern Europe. In late December of 1981 such tensions came to a head when Poland's government imposed martial law as a response to the growing protests of the Solidarity labor movement, led by future Polish President Lech Wałęsa. Officials in Warsaw acted, they claimed at the time, in order to avert an even more violent Soviet intervention. American officials, as seen in this National Security Council discussion from December 22, 1981, perceived the Kremlin as wholly responsible for everything that occurred within its empire.

The President: It seems to me on this we make up our minds on what is right to do. We say to the Soviets tomorrow, right, we will proceed with actions, without spelling them out—actions that will isolate them politically and economically. We reduce political contact; we do all we can to persuade our Allies to come along, unless and until martial law is ended in Poland and they return to an antebellum state. We have to deal with our own labor movement. They are shutting off shipments to Poland, though church shipments are still going through.

[Secretary of State Alexander] Haig: Yes they are still going. Last shipment was one week ago.

The President: I don't know whether Red Cross aid is going or not.

The Vice President [George H. W. Bush]: Cardinal Krol mentioned they were getting receipts for the food deliveries.

The President: For that handled via their own distribution?

Haig: Another thing I would like to call to your attention, Mr. President. It is vitally important that whatever we do, we do officially to Brezhnev and Jaruzelksi so that they are on notice. They should be offered an alternative. We should include a deadline by which we expect a response. Now, if we want to get out a list of actions we are taking tomorrow night before we have a response to our threats, we risk losing the Europeans before we even get started.

You can lay out the human rights considerations tomorrow night. That keeps us flexible. Keeps our options open with no public threats.

You can highlight that you hold the Soviets responsible, but it is too soon for threats unless you want to break with our Allies.

THE PRESIDENT: The thing that bothers me—the constant question is—that we continue to deplore, but isn't there anything we can do in practice? Those "chicken littles" in Europe, will they still be "chicken littles" if we lead and ask them to follow our lead?

HAIG: The answer, Mr. President, is "yes and no." They are not the most courageous people (European leaders), but they have more at stake than we do. They are closer to Poland than we are.

THE PRESIDENT: I know.

HAIG: We ought to be careful (with our demands) until we decide we want a break with them over this matter (if that is what it comes to).

THE PRESIDENT: If they (the Polish government) don't cancel martial law, can we yet do these things?

HAIG: We will be in for a long, tortuous period with the continuation of martial law and negotiations (between Solidarity and the Polish Government) going on. It is difficult for us to kick over the traces now—to go all out—and then be accused of triggering what will probably happen anyway (a Soviet intervention into Poland).

[SECRETARY OF DEFENSE CASPAR] WEINBERGER: Concerning our Allies and the stakes we have in this matter, we have over half a million people in Europe. It is comfortable for the Europeans to do nothing. If you take the lead and give a strong speech, they will be in an uncomfortable (moral) position and they may be dragged along with our actions.

We should be taking stronger action than just wringing our hands. That (wringing our hands) is what the Soviets want. They (the Polish government) can begin meaningless negotiations with Solidarity that will please Europe. We should have a list of nine things we can do. Each is, in itself, a pin prick, but they cause anguish and pain. They evidence our seriousness. They influence public and industrial labor movements. It is morally right to take a stand—a position of leadership.

It is easy to delay, to do nothing. If we delay, we will allow them to crush the movement in Poland. We won't push them (the Soviets) into intervening in Poland. (They will do it if it suits their needs). As Ambassador Spasowski has said, they will march in for their own reasons, not because of what we do....

THE PRESIDENT: If we really believe this is the last chance of a lifetime, that this is a revolution started against this "damned force," we should let our allies know they, too, will pay a price if they don't go along; that we have long memories.

DOCUMENT 13.5

REAGAN AT WESTMINSTER

Washington imposed economic sanctions on Poland and the Soviet Union following the imposition of martial law in 1981, but few European states followed suit. Reagan believed the time had come for more vigorous opposition to communism. Taking his case for an anticommunist crusade to Europe, he offered one of the most rhetorically dramatic speeches from a man well trained to deliver a lasting message. The speech, delivered in London on June 8, 1982, endured as one of the clearest articulations of Reagan's core anticommunism.

We're approaching the end of a bloody century plagued by a terrible political invention—totalitarianism. Optimism comes less easily today, not because democracy is less vigorous, but because democracy's enemies have refined their instruments of repression. Yet optimism is in order, because day by day democracy is proving itself to be a not-at-all-fragile flower. From Stettin on the Baltic to Varna on the Black Sea, the regimes planted by totalitarianism have had more than 30 years to establish their legitimacy. But none—not one regime—has yet been able to risk free elections. Regimes planted by bayonets do not take root....

We have not inherited an easy world. If developments like the Industrial Revolution, which began here in England, and the gifts of science and technology have made life much easier for us, they have also made it more dangerous. There are threats now to our freedom, indeed to our very existence, that other generations could never even have imagined....

It may not be easy to see; but I believe we live now at a turning point.

In an ironic sense Karl Marx was right. We are witnessing today a great revolutionary crisis, a crisis where the demands of the economic order are conflicting directly with those of the political order. But the crisis is happening not in the free, non-Marxist West, but in the home of Marxist-Leninism, the Soviet Union. It is the Soviet Union that runs against the tide of history by denying human freedom and human dignity to its citizens. It also is in deep economic difficulty. The rate of growth in the national product has been steadily declining since the Fifties and is less than half of what it was then. . . .

Now, I don't wish to sound overly optimistic, yet the Soviet Union is not immune from the reality of what is going on in the world. It has happened in the past—a small ruling elite either mistakenly attempts to ease domestic unrest through greater repression and foreign adventure, or it chooses a wiser course. It begins to allow its people a voice in their own destiny. Even if this latter process is not realized soon, I believe the renewed strength of the democratic movement, complemented by a global campaign for freedom, will strengthen the prospects for arms control and a world at peace.

I have discussed on other occasions, including my address on May 9th, the elements of Western policies toward the Soviet Union to safeguard our interests and protect the peace. What I am describing now is a plan and a hope for the long term—the march of freedom and democracy which will leave Marxism-Leninism on the ash heap of history as it has left other tyrannies which stifle the freedom and muzzle the self-expression of the people. . . .

Document 13.6

A PATH FROM CONFRONTATION

Reagan thought of the Cold War as a crusade of good against evil. Others of his age feared the danger of confrontation more than the promise of a successful crusade. Antinuclear activists rallied during Reagan's first term, around the world but in western Europe and the United States especially, arguing that the risks of nuclear-armed struggle far outweighed any potential gains. An old saw of the Cold War was "better dead than red." Many influential voices disagreed. A case in point is the document below, a widely publicized and controversial open letter published by the National Conference of Catholic Bishops of the United States in May 1983. Totaling more than 44,000 words, "The Challenge of Peace: God's Promise and Our 'Response'" explored the nature of faith, war, and struggles of peace and nonviolence, but its overriding message, presented here in its first and final sections, was clear: nuclear Armageddon felt too close at hand for comfort, or for fiery rhetoric.

As Catholic bishops we write this letter as an exercise of our teaching ministry. The Catholic tradition on war and peace is a long and complex one; it stretches from the Sermon on the Mount to the statements of Pope John Paul II. We wish to explore and explain the resources of the moral-religious teaching and to apply it to specific questions of our day. In doing this we realize, and we want readers of this letter to recognize, that not all statements in this letter have the same moral authority. At times we state universally binding moral principles found in the teachings of the Church; at other times the pastoral letter makes specific applications, observations and recommendations which allow for diversity of opinion on the part of those who assess the factual data of situations differently. However, we expect Catholics to give our moral judgments serious consideration when they are forming their own views on specific problems. . . .

The nuclear age is an era of moral as well as physical danger. We are the first generation since Genesis with the power to virtually destroy God's creation. We cannot remain silent in the face of such danger. Why do we address these issues? We are simply trying to live up to the call of Jesus to be peacemakers in our own time and situation.

What are we saying? Fundamentally, we are saying that the decisions about nuclear weapons are among the most pressing moral questions of our age. While these decisions have obvious military and political aspects, they involve fundamental moral choices. In simple terms, we are saying that good ends (defending one's country, protecting freedom, etc.) cannot justify immoral means (the use of weapons which kill indiscriminately and threaten whole societies). We fear that our world and nation are headed in the wrong direction. More weapons with greater destructive potential are produced every day. More and more nations are seeking to become nuclear powers. In our quest for more and more security, we fear we are actually becoming less and less secure.

In the words of our Holy Father, we need a "moral about face." The whole world must summon the moral courage and technical means to say "no" to nuclear conflict; "no" to weapons of mass destruction; "no" to an arms race which robs the poor and the vulnerable; and "no" to the moral danger of a nuclear age which places before humankind indefensible choices of constant terror or surrender. Peacemaking is not an optional commitment. It is a requirement of our faith. . . .

As we come to the end of our pastoral letter we boldly propose the beginning of this work. The evil of the proliferation of nuclear arms becomes more evident every day to all people. No one is exempt from their danger. If ridding the world of the weapons of war could be done easily, the whole human race would do it gladly tomorrow. Shall we shrink from the task because it is hard?

Document 13.7

REAGAN AND THATCHER

Change appeared at hand behind the Iron Curtain in the mid-1980s, never more dramatically than in the elevation of Soviet leader Mikhail Gorbachev in 1985. Even before becoming general secretary in Moscow, Gorbachev enjoyed a powerful reputation as a reformer and leader for the future. He journeyed to London in 1984, enjoying wide-ranging discussions with Britain's prime minister, Margaret Thatcher. Thatcher and Reagan enjoyed a special bond: both were deeply conservative; both were deeply enthralled by market solutions and opposition to communist rule (though critics often accused them of deploying authoritarian methods of their own). Thatcher lobbied Reagan to give Gorbachev a fair hearing, suggesting he was cut from a different cloth than the communist leaders who came before. Though clearly skeptical, Reagan in time took Thatcher's advice. As this December 22, 1984, record of their conversation reveals, Thatcher was also wary of Reagan's recently announced Strategic Defense Initiative, publicly termed "Star Wars," a prospective defensive shield against nuclear attack that would help bring the Soviets to the nuclear bargaining table, only to drive the two sides apart.

Turning to Gorbachev's visit to the UK, Mrs. Thatcher said he was an unusual Russian in that he was much less constrained, more charming, open to discussion and debate, and did not stick to prepared notes. His wife was equally charming. The Prime Minister noted that she often says to herself the more charming the adversary, the more dangerous. Over the private lunch at Chequers, she had raised a number of pointed questions. She asked Gorbachev why the Soviet Union denies its people the right to emigrate. She had underlined that the West simply cannot understand or accept the Soviet policy of refusing people the right to leave. She contrasted the Soviet policy with the situation in the West, where many countries have had to stop people from coming in. Gorbachev replied that 89 percent of those who applied for permits to leave received them. Noting that she had no way to cross-check Gorbachev's statistics, she told the President that Gorbachev's claim clearly conflicted with information she receives from British Jewish groups. She commented that she had further suggested that it was a sign of weakness to feel the need to keep one's people in.

Mrs. Thatcher contrasted Gorbachev with Gromyko, whom she observed would have sharply replied that emigration was an internal matter and not open for discussion. Gorbachev was not willing to debate the point, but he did allow her to discuss it without cutting her off. He also avoided the usual Soviet reaction of citing lengthy position of principle. . . .

Turning to the Geneva talks, the President said since the Soviets had fared so poorly in recent months in the propaganda battles associated with disarmament talks, he feared that they were looking at Geneva as mainly a propaganda forum. This is one of the reasons they launched such an attack against what has become commonly known as "Star Wars." He emphasized that Star Wars was not his term and was clearly not what he had in mind. He continued that there has never been a weapon for which another weapon against it had not been developed. Therefore, in view of all the advances in technology, he asked for a study of new defensive systems. Its aim would strictly be to strengthen deterrence. So far, initial research has been promising and, as he had stated many times, if it proves successful he would be willing to put this new technology into international hands. The President said we are not violating the ABM treaty and have no intention of doing so. The new Strategic Defense Initiative also has a moral context. We must search for ways to build a more stable peace. Our goal is to reduce, and eventually eliminate nuclear weapons. Chernenko now claims that this is also a Soviet goal. We have told them if they are really serious about reductions, we are ready. Gromyko had told him, said the President, that we cannot continue to sit on two mountains of weapons. The President said he replied, "let us then begin to lower and eventually eliminate these mountains." . . .

Mrs. Thatcher noted that she had a special interest in learning more details about the U.S. SDI program. Gorbachev had told her "tell your friend President Reagan not to go ahead with space weapons." He suggested if you develop SDI the Russians would either develop their own, or more probably, develop new offensive systems superior to SDI. General Keegan (former head of USAF Intelligence), whom she had seen several times, had informed her about Soviet advances and she was interested in learning more about SDI.

Document 13.8

EARLY CIA ASSESSMENT OF GORBACHEV'S ECONOMIC AGENDA

Gorbachev posed a fundamental quandary for American officials. He promised reform and ultimately promised improved East-West relations. Yet if successful as a reformer, many hawks within Reagan's administration argued, he would develop a far more powerful Soviet state capable of sustaining the Cold War through the twenty-first century. As the following assessment composed by the Central Intelligence Agency asserted in September 1985, no one in the West (or in the world, for that matter) could answer the first fundamental question about Gorbachev's reforms: would they work?

Since coming to power, Mikhail Gorbachev has set in motion the most aggressive economic agenda since the Khrushchev era. The key elements are:

- A reallocation of investment resources aimed at accelerating S&T [science and technology] and modernizing the country's stock of plant and equipment.

- A revitalization of management and planning to rid the Soviet bureaucracy of incompetence and petty tutelage and put more operational control of enterprise in the hands of managers on the scene.
- A renewal of Andropov's anticorruption and discipline campaigns, coupled with a new temperance campaign, to increase and perhaps improve worker effort. . . .

Soviet officialdom probably was caught off guard by Gorbachev's sweeping condemnation of past economic policies, particularly considering the recent economic rebound, and was surprised that he apparently was ready to take action so early in his tenure. Despite the urgency of his rhetoric, he seems aware that implementing his programs too rapidly carries substantial economic and political risks:

- He has prepared the party and bureaucracy for substantial change by bluntly laying out the need for management reorganization and renewal, but has yet to provide specific details on controversial issues that would provide a basis for organized resistance.
- He has moved aggressively to replace old-line economic managers but has yet to replace Council of Ministers Chairman Tikhonov, regarded by most Soviets as a major political obstacle to economic change.
- He has talked about the potential need for "profound" changes in the area of economic reform, while strongly supporting the need to maintain central control. . . .

Gorbachev could employ various options to address these issues, but all contain serious pitfalls. East European countries could be ordered to shoulder a larger part of the economic burden, including increased exports of equipment to the USSR, but their own deep economic problems increase the likelihood of confrontation between Moscow and its allies. A drive to increase imports of Western technology would come at a time when the prospects for expanding hard currency exports, particularly oil, look dim. A shift of resources from defense to civilian uses could have considerable positive impact over the long run, but even the suggestion of such a shift might damage Gorbachev's relations with the military and risk deep divisions within the Politburo. Finally, major economic reforms to promote managerial effectiveness would encounter strong resistance on political and ideological grounds, particularly since they threaten the institutional prerogatives and thus the privileged position of the Soviet elite.

Indications that Gorbachev has decided on and gained consensus for more radical changes could include:

- New, dramatic initiatives to reach an accord at Geneva and concrete proposals for reduced tensions at the November meetings between the US President and the General Secretary, which might signal a willingness and desire to reduce the Soviet resource commitment to defense and create an atmosphere for expanded commerce with the West.

- Select legalization of private-sector activity, particularly in regard to consumer services, which would indicate a willingness to confront past economic orthodoxy in order to improve consumer welfare and thereby economic performance.
- Breaking the monopoly of the foreign trade apparatus, which would signal an increased reliance on managerial independence at some cost to centralized control.

Continued reliance on marginal tinkering despite clear indications that the plan for economic revitalization is faltering would indicate that Gorbachev, like Brezhnev before him, has succumbed to a politically expedient but economically ineffective approach.

Documents 13.9 and 13.10

GORBACHEV BEHIND CLOSED DOORS

Gorbachev was sincere about reform, demanding both perestroika, *a restructuring of Soviet political and economic life, and* glasnost, *a new openness throughout Soviet society. For him international and domestic affairs were forever intrinsically linked. He believed it was necessary to improve East-West relations in order to cut military spending and to divert resources into the faltering civilian economy. Moreover, he believed that the Soviet Union could no longer afford, either economically or politically, to maintain its domination of Eastern Europe, and he envisioned fundamental alteration of Moscow's relationship with the region. What he proposed was little more than heresy to many old-line communists and Soviet strategists. The following two documents should be considered together. They are a memorandum Gorbachev wrote to the Communist Party's central committee on June 26, 1986, outlining his vision of reformed relations with Eastern Europe's socialist states, and notes taken at the ensuing debate among Soviet leaders on July 3, 1986, which demonstrates Gorbachev's ideals and his passion for change.*

Over the past four decades, world socialism has turned into a powerful international formation. There are solid foundations for the new system in the majority of socialist countries, the leading role of the party has been consolidated, and maturity and national self-awareness have grown. The socialist countries have withstood serious internal and external trials and not one of them has returned to the old order. Bilateral and multilateral communications among socialist states have developed broadly, and countries have formed international organizations—the Warsaw Treaty and the Council for Mutual Economic Assistance.

All of these are our strengths. But we cannot deny the fact that in recent years, as the scientific-technological revolution has opened new vistas for developing the socialist system, that developing has instead slowed down. Regrettably, it must be said that to a certain degree centrifugal forces have become evident within the framework of world socialism. There is a real danger of a weakening of its influence on the overall trend of international affairs.

What is the cause of this? This is not a simple question; it cannot be disposed of with a one-word answer. However, undoubtedly one of the main causes is that the nature of relations established during the period of world socialist formation is coming into conflict with the necessities of life.

In the beginning, the Soviet Union, the largest and most experienced socialist state, led the fraternal countries by the hand, as it were. And they thought it necessary to follow our example, recommendations, and advice in everything. Economic relations developed with an accent on the USSR providing resource support through raw materials and fuel, and developing primary industries.

Such a system of political and economic cooperation was reasonable for the beginning stages of the formation of the world socialist system. But it became less and less justified as the fraternal countries gained power, as their economic strength and political stability increased and their international authority grew.

All of the Politburo members have a good deal of experience in communicating with the leadership of the fraternal parties and know well that over time there was less sincerity, frankness, and trust in our relations.

The regularity of contacts with fraternal party leaders was disrupted, and the meetings that took place often bore the stamp of showiness and formalities. The necessity of such contacts is especially urgent under present circumstances, when for objective reasons a period of change in leadership is taking place in the majority of countries.

We should admit honestly that Moscow has been viewed as a kind of conservative power that hindered reforms that were ripe for implementation. Some of our allies, afraid of a domineering approach, cautiously introduced certain correctives into the practice of building socialism. Instead of jointly discussing topical issues of socialist development we often assumed the function of sole custodian of Marxist-Leninist teachings; at the same time we judged everything from our own standpoint, inadequately considering the novelty of the issues and the specific character of the fraternal countries. We did not very seriously and respectfully take into consideration their own searches [for solutions].

All of these shortcomings have built up over the years and have done real damage. Take this fact, for example: it has been 15 years since we agreed to embark on the path of socialist economic integration, but this process is sharply behind the integration process of Western Europe. In essence in many aspects we continue to be at the commodity exchange stage. At the same time, since the CMEA countries were not able to make a collective technological leap forward and the Soviet side was not able to meet our friends' demands for up-to-date technology and equipment, those countries developed a tendency to resolve pressing social-economic problems by switching to the track of intensive management through credits from the West. It is well known what difficult consequences this has had for Poland, and to some extent other countries of the community. . . .

The solution suggests itself: a genuine turning point in the entire system of collaboration with our allies is needed.

. . . .

GORBACHEV: We all became aware that we had entered a new stage with the socialist countries. What went on before could not continue. The methods that were used in Czechoslovakia and Hungary now are no good; they will not work!

[SOVIET AMBASSADOR TO THE UNITED STATES ANATOLY] DOBRYNIN: We need to act like NATO: constant, daily integration of foreign policy work through different mechanisms, discussion of all international events and actions.

GORBACHEV: A new society is forming, which will develop on its own foundation . . . the mechanisms of bilateral relations are becoming more complex. . . . What was in the past is now causing discontent, encouraging centrifugal forces. . . . Nothing will work out if we work within the old framework. We cannot use the remnants of the Comintern . . . "administrative methods of leadership" with our friends. Fidel was right: the CPSU's influence can only be ideological, only through example! Everything else is an illusion. And we don't need it, this kind of "leadership." It would mean carrying them on our back.

The economy is the most important [factor]. Here there is a major lag in coordination and integration. And this hinders, and will continue to hinder, all other aspects of relations. From the conception of *perestroika* to its realization is still a long way. We are behind. The central question is—what are the main issues? Exactly so. The country is abuzz, it is waiting. This is serious, intense work. It is here that the weak links are making themselves felt.

Document 13.11

REYKJAVIK

Reagan and Gorbachev both considered themselves transformative figures, and each desired radical change of the international system. Gorbachev's goal was salvation of socialism through reform. Reagan wanted communism's eradication, but increasingly over the course of his presidency came to fear an even greater threat: global nuclear war. The harsh rhetoric and military escalations of his first term spawned a new intensity to the Cold War that very nearly led to inadvertent strikes—particularly in 1983, when, after Reagan termed the Kremlin an "evil empire," North Atlantic Treaty Organization (NATO) military exercises nearly prompted a Soviet nuclear response from officials in Moscow who were all too ready to believe Reagan's crusading rhetoric. In time the two leaders met for arms talks, and realizing their mutual desire for dramatic change, nearly agreed in Reykjavik, Iceland, in October 1986 to eliminate all strategic nuclear weapons by 2000. As the following U.S. record of their October 12 negotiation makes plain, they nearly pulled off an unprecedented accord, faltering at the last moment over "Star Wars."

The President said that he thought the two sides were very close to an agreement.

Gorbachev noted that an addition should be made to the text which the Soviet side had just translated to the effect that during the next few years after the ten-year period the two sides should negotiate a mutually acceptable solution concerning their future course of action. The US side feels that this should be SDI. The Soviet side might want something else. But the Soviet formula would permit finding a mutually acceptable solution for future activity after the ten-year period. Why would this not be satisfactory to the US?

The President replied that if both sides had completely eliminated nuclear weapons and there was no longer any threat, why would there be any concern if one side built a safeguard, a defensive system against non-existent weapons, in case there might be a need for it in the future? The President had a different picture: perhaps after the ten-year period the Soviet side would want to build new missiles, and would not want the US to have defenses against them. But he preferred to see a different formula. Ten years from now he would be a very old man. He and Gorbachev would come to Iceland and each of them would bring the last nuclear missile from each country with them. Then they would give a tremendous party for the whole world.

Gorbachev interjected that he thought the two sides were close to reaching a common formula. He did not think the US should suspect the Soviet Union of having evil designs. If it had such designs, it would not have gone so far in proposing reductions of strategic and medium-range missiles.

The president continued to describe his vision of their meeting in Iceland ten years from now. He would be very old by then and Gorbachev would not recognize him. The President would say, "Hello, Mikhail." And Gorbachev would say, "Ron, is it you?" And then they would destroy the last missiles.

Gorbachev replied that he did not know if we would live another ten years.

The President said he was counting on living that long. . . .

[Soviet Foreign Minister Eduard] Shevardnadze said he wanted to say just one thing. The two sides were so close to accomplishing an historic task, to decisions of such historic significance, that if future generations read the minutes of these meetings, and saw how close we had come but how we did not use these opportunities, they would never forgive us. . . .

The President said he had believed, and had said so in Geneva, that he and Gorbachev had the possibility of getting along as no two American and Soviet leaders ever had before. He had asked Gorbachev for a favor, which was important to him and to what he could do with Gorbachev in the future. Gorbachev had refused him that favor.

Gorbachev replied that if the President had come to him and said things are hard for American farmers, and asked him to buy some American grain, he would have understood. But what the President was asking him to agree to on behalf of the USSR was to allow the US, at a time when they were proceeding to deep reductions and elimination of nuclear weapons—to conduct full-scale research and development, including development of a space-based ABM system, which would permit the US to destroy the Soviet Union's offensive nuclear potential. The President would not like it if Gorbachev had asked that of him. It would cause nervousness and suspicion. It was not an acceptable request. It could not be met. The President was not asking for a favor, but for giving up on a point of principle. . . .

The President said he was asking Gorbachev to change his mind as a favor to him, so that hopefully they could go on and bring peace to the world.

Gorbachev said he could not do it. If they could agree to ban research in space, he would sign in two minutes. They should add to the text, "the testing in space of all space components of missile defense is prohibited, except research and testing conducted in laboratories," as in the draft. The point was not one of words, but of principle.

Document 13.12

GORBACHEV AT THE UNITED NATIONS

Perestroika *and* glasnost *stumbled at home. The Soviet standard of living, never high by Western standards, dropped during Gorbachev's tenure, the price to his mind of dramatic though necessary economic reforms. Naturally his popularity at home plummeted as well, forcing the Soviet leader to look abroad for foreign policy successes large enough to sustain his legitimacy within his own country. In time he called for a complete overhaul of modern international relations, delivering what the* New York Times *termed "surrender" in the broad Cold War struggle. By offering sweeping visions such as the speech below, delivered to the United Nations General Assembly on December 7, 1988, Gorbachev became among the most popular leaders in the world, at least outside his own borders.*

The history of the past centuries and millennia has been a history of almost ubiquitous wars, and sometimes desperate battles, leading to mutual destruction. They occurred in the clash of social and political interests and national hostility, be it from ideological or religious incompatibility. All that was the case, and even now many still claim that this past—which has not been overcome—is an immutable pattern. However, parallel with the process of wars, hostility, and alienation of peoples and countries another process, just as objectively conditioned, was in motion and gaining force: the process of the emergence of a mutually connected and integral world.

Further world progress is now possible only through the search for a consensus of all mankind, in movement toward a new world order. We have arrived at a frontier at which controlled spontaneity leads to a dead end. The world community must learn to shape and direct the process in such a way as to preserve civilization, to make it safe for all and more pleasant for normal life. It is a question of cooperation that could be more accurately called "co-creation" and "co-development." The formula of development "at another's expense" is becoming outdated. In light of present realities, genuine progress by infringing upon the rights and liberties of man and peoples, or at the expense of nature, is impossible. . . .

The compelling necessity of the principle of freedom of choice is also clear to us. The failure to recognize this, to recognize it, is fraught with very dire consequences, consequences for world peace. Denying that right to the peoples, no matter what the pretext, no matter what the words are used to conceal it, means infringing upon even the unstable balance that is, has been possible to achieve.

Freedom of choice is a universal principle to which there should be no exceptions. We have not come to the conclusion of the immutability of this principle simply through good motives. We have been led to it through impartial analysis of the objective processes of our time. The increasing varieties of social development in different countries are becoming an ever more perceptible feature of these processes. This relates to both the capitalist and socialist systems. The variety of sociopolitical structures which has grown over the last decades from national liberation movements also demonstrates this. This objective fact presupposes respect for other people's views and stands, tolerance, a preparedness to see phenomena that are different as not necessarily bad or hostile, and an ability to learn to live side by side while remaining different and not agreeing with one another on every issue.

The de-ideologization of interstate relations has become a demand of the new stage. We are not giving up our convictions, philosophy, or traditions. Neither are we calling on anyone else to give up theirs. Yet we are not going to shut ourselves up within the range of our values. That would lead to spiritual impoverishment, for it would mean renouncing so powerful a source of development as sharing all the original things created independently by each nation. In the course of such sharing, each should prove the advantages of his own system, his own way of life and values, but not through words or propaganda alone, but through real deeds as well. That is, indeed, an honest struggle of ideology, but it must not be carried over into mutual relations between states. Otherwise we simply will not be able to solve a single world problem; arrange broad, mutually advantageous and equitable cooperation between peoples; manage rationally the achievements of the scientific and technical revolution; transform world economic relations; protect the environment; overcome underdevelopment; or put an end to hunger, disease, illiteracy, and other mass ills. Finally, in that case, we will not manage to eliminate the nuclear threat and militarism. . . .

Our country is undergoing a truly revolutionary upsurge. The process of restructuring is gaining pace. We started by elaborating the theoretical concepts of restructuring; we had to assess the nature and scope of the problems, to interpret the lessons of the past, and to express this in the form of political conclusions and programs. This was done. The theoretical work, the re-interpretation of what had happened, the final elaboration, enrichment, and correction of political stances have not ended. They continue. However, it was fundamentally important to start from an overall concept, which is already now being confirmed by the experience of past years, which has turned out to be generally correct and to which there is no alternative.

In order to involve society in implementing the plans for restructuring it had to be made more truly democratic. Under the badge of democratization, restructuring has now encompassed politics, the economy, spiritual life, and ideology. We have unfolded a radical economic reform, we have accumulated experience, and from the new year we are transferring the entire national economy to new forms and work methods. Moreover, this means a profound reorganization of production relations and the realization of the immense potential of socialist property. . . .

Esteemed Mr. Chairman, esteemed delegates: I finish my first speech at the United Nations with the same feeling with which I began it: a feeling of responsibility to my own people and to the world community. We have met at the end of a year that has been so significant for the United Nations, and on the threshold of a year from which all of us expect so much. One would like to believe that our joint efforts to put an end to the era of wars, confrontation and regional conflicts, aggression against nature, the terror of hunger and poverty, as well as political terrorism, will be comparable with our hopes. This is our common goal, and it is only by acting together that we may attain it. Thank you.

Document 13.13

SKEPTICISM AND OPPORTUNITY WITHIN GEORGE H. W. BUSH'S WHITE HOUSE

People throughout the world took Gorbachev at his word, making 1989 among the most revolutionary and dramatic in modern history. Crowds of protestors took to the streets in Eastern Europe and in time in China as well, each demanding reform. Within Washington's highest policy-making circles, however, skepticism initially held sway. Many of George H. W. Bush's appointees, and the president himself, believed Reagan had gone too far; that he'd been too trusting of Gorbachev; and that the Soviet leader was unlikely to succeed in any event. They urged Bush to rethink Reagan's warm embrace of glasnost *and* perestroika, *retaining Washington's upper hand both militarily and economically. The time to let up on an opponent, the most hawkish among them argued, was not when it was near to admitting defeat. At the same time, the president himself, led in part by National Security Adviser Brent Scowcroft, increasingly appreciated the historic opportunity 1989 offered. As this memorandum from Scowcroft's staff to Bush on March 20, 1989 makes plain, Gorbachev's reforms offered dangers, to be sure—not least the threat of widespread international instability and fear that Gorbachev's "common European home" might exclude American influence—but it also offered opportunities to remake the international system not seen since 1945.*

Europe and the United States (and Canada) are joined inseparably by history, culture, demography, values, and security needs. The basic lesson of two world wars was that American power is essential to any stable equilibrium on the continent. The postwar era's success is founded on recognition of this fact. In years to come, only we can balance the inherent strength of what is still, and likely will remain, the dominant military power on the Eurasian landmass—the Soviet Union. Geopolitical realities will endure. Of course, Gorbachev is less threatening than his predecessors. So, in its day, was the Weimar Republic. . . .

The NATO Summit and your public speaking opportunities before and after it can articulate our view of how Europe should evolve over the next decade. Here are some ideas about possible elements we think might appear in a Summit declaration.

1. A POLITICAL GOAL FOR THE YEAR 2000

The weakness in Gorbachev's notion of a "common European home" is that its occupancy is defined by geography; also, if the East Europeans could, they would evict the Soviets from their part of the home. The Americans, on the other hand, can only be guests in a home so defined. The real glue that binds the Atlantic Alliance is commonality of values, not geography. This premise suggests that we advocate the existence of a "Commonwealth of Free Nations"; The Atlantic Alliance forms the core of this group, but it embraces any country that truly shares our values. Within Europe, the CSCE process offers guideposts for Eastern movement toward a true sense of shared ideals. We hope that all the countries of Eastern Europe will be part of this commonwealth as they, one by one, rejoin the Western cultural and political tradition that is part of their heritage.

2. THE DIVISION OF GERMANY

Even if we make strides in overcoming the division of Europe through greater openness and pluralism, we cannot have a vision for Europe's future that does not include an approach to the "German question." Here we cannot promise immediate political reunification, but we should offer some promise of change, of movement. As Giovanni Agnelli said here in early February, although virtually no West German expects German reunification to happen in this century, there is no German of any age who does not dream of it in his soul. The formal Allied position has long been that we want the German people to regain their unity through self-determination. I think we can, working with Bonn, improve on this formula, make it more pointed, and send a clear signal to the Germans that we are ready to do more if the political climate allows it. We can, for example, pledge our support for the *right* of the German people to self-determination and encourage Germans to take concrete *steps* to express that right. We can stress, at the same time, that the problem is not just one of borders. It is a problem of a nation divided by barriers that range from land mines to currency restrictions. Amidst all the enthusiasm about "glasnost," it is sobering to remember that, in February 1989, East German border guards again shot down and killed a youth for trying to cross the Wall.

3. DEALING WITH GORBACHEV

Some still ask whether we want Soviet reforms to succeed. We should give a clear answer: Yes, we welcome perestroika to the degree that it humanizes the USSR at home and demilitarizes the USSR abroad. This does not translate into subsidies for Gorbachev's efforts. It means that we hope someday to be able to deal with the Soviet Union on the same normal and equal terms that we use for relations with other states. . . .

In his memoirs, *Present at the Creation*, Dean Acheson remarked that, in 1945, their task "began to appear as just a bit less formidable than that described in the first chapter of Genesis. That was to create a world out of chaos; ours, to create half a world, a free half, out of the same material without blowing the whole to pieces in the process." When those creators of the 1940s and 1950s rested, they had done much. We now have unprecedented opportunities to do more, to pick up the task where they left off, while doing what must be done to protect a handsome inheritance.

Document 13.14

TIANANMEN SQUARE

Polish voters elected a democratic government on June 4, 1989. That same night, in Beijing, tanks and troops violently crushed an indigenous protest movement. Hundreds perished; thousands more were imprisoned or eventually exiled. Chinese students, followed in time by workers and educators, took to the streets in the spring of 1989 demanding reform. Though they wisely displayed placards (in English) linking their movement to the protestors of Eastern Europe and beyond, hoping to gain international legitimacy in the process, in truth the Chinese reformers were by and large domestically focused, hoping to eliminate some of the excesses of Deng Xiaoping's recent moves toward market reforms. Whereas communists in Eastern Europe largely relinquished power, albeit reluctantly, in 1989, culminating most dramatically with the peaceful fall of the Berlin Wall in November, hard-liners in Beijing retained power through force. They proved at once their own resilience, but also—for American policy makers in particular—the potential pitfalls of too rapid a push for reform of communist states. As this telegram from the American embassy in Beijing on June 4, 1989, demonstrates, the consequences for the protesters throughout China were dire, though not wholly unexpected.

As of about 0330 hours local troops were in control of Tiananmen Square, but people remained in the surrounding streets. Sporadic gunfire continued to be heard throughout the city. By 0430 troops had taken up position across Changan Boulevard facing east with a line of APCs behind them. Students in turn lined up facing West towards the troops. Meanwhile, a large convoy of troops began entering Tiananmen Square from the West. Some 10,000 troops in the square formed concentric rings, one facing inward towards some 3,000 remaining demonstrators, and the other facing outward. At 0530 a column of about 50 APCs, tanks, and trucks entered Tiananmen from the East. Demonstrators shouted angrily at the convoy and PLA troops in Tiananmen opened a barrage of rifle and machine gun fire. When this gunfire ended at 0545, a number of casualties remained lying on the ground. At 0620, a second column of about 40 APCs, tanks, and trucks entered Tiananmen by the same route and the students again moved into the road. PLA troops in Tiananmen opened fire with rifles and machine guns, once more causing a large number of casualties.

A similar stand-off continued throughout the morning and afternoon of June 4. POLOFF [political officer] reported from the Beijing Hotel that at 1300 and again at 1500 demonstrators approached troops in Tiananmen Square. The demonstrators shouted in defiance at the troops who, in each instance, eventually opened fire on the crowds. This pattern appears to have persisted since earlier in the day according to other diplomatic reports. As the crowds on Changan East of Tiananmen would approach the troops, the troops would move forward, often opening fire, and the crowds would retreat hurriedly. At 1030 massive machine-gun fire was reported. Troops then advanced in formation. The crowds fled in panic and soon the whole of Changan Boulevard was temporarily clear.

Document 13.15

THE DREAM OF A DEMOCRATIC REVOLUTION

The events in Tiananmen Square demonstrated the nightmare of protest and change run headlong into totalitarian rule. Throughout Eastern Europe, conversely, dreams of reform far exceeded expectation. In Poland, Hungary, East Germany, Czechoslovakia, and then ultimately throughout the entire Soviet bloc, demonstrators inspired by Gorbachev and desirous of a new democratic future took to the streets demanding change. They largely got what they hoped for, with democracies taking root where communist regimes once held sway. The world indeed appeared to be waking up to a new future or, as the British rock band Jesus Jones sang in 1991, "waking up from history."

Right Here, Right Now

A woman on the radio talks about revolution
When it's already passed her by

Bob Dylan didn't have this to sing about
You know it feels good to be alive

I was alive and I waited, waited
I was alive and I waited for this
Right here, right now
There is no other place I want to be
Right here, right now
Watching the world wake up from history

I saw the decade in, when it seemed the world could change
At the blink of an eye
And if anything
Then there's your sign of the times

I was alive and I waited, waited
I was alive and I waited for this
Right here, right now
There is no other place I want to be
Right here, right now
Watching the world wake up from history

14

Globalization after the Cold War

For four decades, the global conflict with the Soviet Union gave definition and purpose to U.S. foreign policy. But the fall of the Berlin Wall in 1989, and with it communist rule throughout Eastern Europe, as well as the collapse of the Soviet Union two years later, freed American officials from their Cold War moorings. Quite naturally, the demise of communism produced euphoria among many Americans, who thought they had arrived at what political scientist Francis Fukuyama called "the end of history." But it also created confusion and uncertainty. With no obvious adversary in sight, the question facing the nation was how to remake American foreign policy for a new era.

To some, the answer was obvious: retrenchment. A loose, ill-fitting alliance of conservative Republicans and liberal Democrats, mostly perched at the ideological extremes of their respective parties, pushed for America's withdrawal from the world. Liberals hoped for a "peace dividend" that would fund ambitious domestic reforms. Many conservatives, on the other hand, were disturbed by the growth of the state as a result of World War II and the Cold War and sought to curb the scope of the federal government now that those world crises had finally passed. Though their ultimate reasons differed, some Americans hoped that the end of the Cold War would initiate something of a retreat from world affairs. For the first time in fifty years, "isolationism" wielded significant authority in debates over U.S. foreign relations.

Retrenchment, however, was never seriously considered by presidents George H. W. Bush and Bill Clinton. Indeed, rarely did the United States intervene as often and as widely as it did in the decade following the end of the Cold War. Beginning with the invasion of Panama in 1989, the U.S. military intervened in Somalia and Haiti, attacked Afghanistan and Sudan, and fought three major wars—one in the Middle East and two in the Balkans.

Both Bush and Clinton were internationalists who wanted to use American power to steer the direction of world politics. However, there were some key differences between them. Like Nixon and Kissinger before him, Bush was a realist who believed that international relations were driven by nation-states pursuing power and security. He believed in American ideals but did not assume they should guide U.S. foreign policy. Though Bush sounded idealistic in calling for the establishment of a "new world order," he did little to make that happen.

Clinton also believed in pursuing the national interest, but he defined the concept more broadly to cover the expansion of liberal democracy, international trade, and deregulated free markets. Whether Americans liked it or not, globalization was linking everyone and everything into a single world community. Clinton and his advisers embraced globalization. As a system that both built upon and expanded openness, they assumed that globalization would inevitably lead to the spread of American values such as democracy and capitalism. In turn, the spread of such values—and the acceptance of democracy and free markets in places such as Latin America, Africa, Russia, and East Asia—would enhance American prosperity and national security because it would ensure the prosperity and security of friendly nations. The logic of the Washington Consensus (deregulation and free trade) and "democratic peace theory" was simple: The more friendly nations there were, the less America had to worry about them. In place of containment, then, Clinton devised a new American grand strategy by promoting globalization.

Two things, however, were immediately clear. First, Clinton's objectives of engagement and enlargement, including the expansion of NATO, were not popular with everyone. Resistance to both the Washington Consensus and the democratic peace meant, paradoxically, that the attempt to spread these ideas for peace often occurred through the use of force. At the same time, other global problems—such as the persistence of genocide, the rise of ethno-racial tension, and the emergence of new challenges linked to the environment, in particular a phenomenon that would soon be called "global warming"—posed serious obstacles to American hopes for globalization.

Second, while Europe and East Asia had dominated U.S. officials' strategic vision for the previous five decades, the Middle East was quickly becoming the region most vital to American security. Bush and Clinton faced a series of challenges in the Middle East, including the ongoing conflict between Israelis and Palestinians, the challenge from Iraq, and transnational fundamentalist Islamic terrorism. None of these problems were new, but they all escalated in the years following the end of the Cold War, presenting the United States with a new set of complex challenges.

Document 14.1

A NEW GLOBAL ERA

Even before the Berlin Wall collapsed in the fall of 1989, numerous intellectuals were speculating about the new international agenda that would replace the Cold War. Some anticipated a new era of international competition as long-suppressed resentments and rivalries came to the surface. Others worried about an array of global problems—environmental degradation, population growth, migration, and disease—that had received little attention during decades when politics and resources had been focused on the East-West conflict. One such commentator was the biologist Jessica Tuchman Mathews, who had served as director of the National Security Council's Office of Global Issues in the Carter administration. In an essay entitled "Redefining Security," published in Foreign Affairs *in the spring of 1989, Mathews urged that the United States and nations around the world acknowledge the urgency of such challenges and embrace a new era of multilateralism to address them.*

The 1990s will demand a redefinition of what constitutes national security. In the 1970s the concept was expanded to include international economics as it became clear that the U.S. economy was no longer the independent force it had once been, but was powerfully affected by economic policies in dozens of other countries. Global developments now suggest the need for another analogous, broadening definition of national security to include resource, environmental and demographic issues.

The assumptions and institutions that have governed international relations in the postwar era are a poor fit with these new realities. Environmental strains that transcend national borders are already beginning to break down the sacred boundaries of national sovereignty, previously rendered porous by the information and communication revolutions and the instantaneous global movement of financial capital. The once sharp dividing line between foreign and domestic policy is blurred, forcing governments to grapple in international forums with issues that were contentious enough in the domestic arena. . . .

Despite the headlines of 1988—the polluted coastlines, the climatic extremes, the accelerating deforestation and flooding that plagued the planet—human society has not arrived at the brink of some absolute limit to its growth. The planet may ultimately be able to accommodate the additional five or six billion people projected to be living here by the year 2100. But it seems unlikely that the world will be able to do so unless the means of production change dramatically. Global economic output has quadrupled since 1950 and it must continue to grow rapidly simply to meet basic human needs, to say nothing of the challenge of lifting billions from poverty. But economic growth as we currently know it requires more energy use, more emissions and wastes, more land converted from its natural state, and more need for the products of natural systems. Whether the planet can accommodate all of these demands remains an open question.

Individuals and governments alike are beginning to feel the cost of substituting for (or doing without) the goods and services once freely provided by healthy ecosystems. Nature's bill is presented in many different forms: the cost of commercial fertilizer needed to replenish once naturally fertile soils; the expense of dredging rivers that flood their banks because of soil erosion hundreds of miles upstream; the loss in crop failures due to the indiscriminate use of pesticides that inadvertently kill insect pollinators; or the price of worsening pollution, once filtered from the air by vegetation. Whatever the immediate cause for concern, the value and absolute necessity for human life of functioning ecosystems is finally becoming apparent.

Moreover, for the first time in its history, mankind is rapidly—if inadvertently—altering the basic physiology of the planet. Global changes currently taking place in the chemical composition of the atmosphere, in the genetic diversity of species inhabiting the planet, and in the cycling of vital chemicals through the oceans, atmosphere, biosphere and geosphere, are unprecedented in both their pace and scale. If left unchecked, the consequences will be profound and, unlike familiar types of local damage, irreversible. . . .

If such resource and population trends are not addressed, as they are not in so much of the world today, the resulting economic decline leads to frustration, resentment, domestic unrest or even civil war. Human suffering and turmoil make countries ripe for authoritarian government or external subversion. Environmental refugees spread the disruption across national borders. Haiti, a classic example, was once so forested and fertile that it was known as the "Pearl of the Antilles." Now deforested, soil erosion in Haiti is so rapid that some farmers believe stones grow in their fields, while bulldozers are needed to clear the streets of Port-au-Prince of topsoil that flows down from the mountains in the rainy season. While many of the boat people who fled to the United States left because of the brutality of the Duvalier regimes, there is no question that—and this is not widely recognized—many Haitians were forced into boats by the impossible task of farming bare rock. Until Haiti is reforested, it will never be politically stable.

Haitians are by no means the world's only environmental refugees. In Indonesia, Central America and sub-Saharan Africa, millions have been forced to leave their homes in part because the loss of tree cover, the disappearance of soil, and other environmental ills have made it impossible to grow food. Sudan, despite its civil war, has taken in more than a million refugees from Ethiopia, Uganda and Chad. Immigrants from the spreading Sahel make up one-fifth of the total population in the Ivory Coast. Wherever refugees settle, they flood the labor market, add to the local demand for food and put new burdens on the land, thus spreading the environmental stress that originally forced them from their homes. Resource mismanagement is not the only cause of these mass movements, of course. Religion and ethnic conflicts, political repression and other forces are at work. But the environmental causes are an essential factor. . . .

The planet is not destined to a slow and painful decline into environmental chaos. There are technical, scientific and economical solutions that are feasible to many current trends, and enough is known about promising new approaches to be confident that the right kinds of research will produce huge payoffs. . . .

But if the technological opportunities are boundless, the social, political and institutional barriers are huge. Subsidies, pricing policies and economic discount rates encourage resource depletion in the name of economic growth, while delivering only the illusion of sustainable growth. Population control remains a controversial subject in much of the world. The traditional prerogatives of nation states are poorly matched with the needs for regional cooperation and global decision-making. And ignorance of the biological underpinning of human society blocks a clear view of where the long-term threats to global security lie.

Overcoming these economic and political barriers will require social and institutional inventions comparable in scale and vision to the new arrangements conceived in the decade following World War II. Without the sharp political turning point of a major war, and with threats that are diffuse and long term, the task will be more difficult. But if we are to avoid irreversible damage to the planet and a heavy toll in human suffering, nothing less is likely to suffice. . . .

On the political front, the need for a new diplomacy and for new institutions and regulatory regimes to cope with the world's growing environmental interdependence is even more compelling. Put bluntly, our accepted definition of the limits of national sovereignty as coinciding with national borders is obsolete. . . . The majority of environmental problems demand regional solutions which encroach upon what we now think of as the prerogatives of national governments. This is because the phenomena themselves are defined by the limits of watershed, ecosystem, or atmospheric transport, not by national borders. Indeed, the costs and benefits of alternative policies cannot often be accurately judged without considering the region rather than the nation. . . .

The United States, in particular, will have to assign a far greater prominence than it has heretofore to the practice of multilateral diplomacy. This would mean changes that range from the organization of the State Department and the language proficiency of the Foreign Service, to the definition of an international role that allows leadership without primacy, both in the slogging work of negotiation and in adherence to final outcomes. Above all, ways must soon be found to step around the deeply entrenched North-South cleavage and to replace it with a planetary sense of shared destiny. Perhaps the successes of the U.N. specialized agencies can be built upon for this purpose. But certainly the task of forging a global energy policy in order to control the greenhouse effect, for example, is a very long way from eradicating smallpox or sharing weather information.

Document 14.2

A NEW WORLD ORDER?

Iraq invaded Kuwait at the beginning of August 1990. This aggression presented the first test of the post–Cold War international order and, as such, offered the United States its first chance to reshape the international system to suit new realities. President Bush spent the ensuing months building a significant military force in the Persian Gulf and assembling a coalition of allies, a process known as Operation Desert Shield. After a United Nations resolution backed the use of force, war broke out on January 17, 1991. Code-named Operation Desert Storm, the U.S. assault lasted five weeks and ended with an overwhelming victory for Washington and its allies. These efforts occurred under the banner of Bush's vision for a "new world order," which blended ideals and interests, such as the security of Middle Eastern oil supplies. In a landmark speech before a joint session of Congress on September 11, 1990, Bush set the tone for Washington's management of the international system for the rest of the decade and beyond, despite his realist principles.

Our objectives in the Persian Gulf are clear, our goals defined and familiar: Iraq must withdraw from Kuwait completely, immediately, and without condition. Kuwait's legitimate government must be restored. The security and stability of the Persian Gulf must be assured. And American citizens abroad must be protected. These goals are not ours alone. They've been endorsed by the United Nations Security Council five times in as many weeks. Most countries share our concern for principle. And many have a stake in the stability of the Persian Gulf. This is not, as Saddam Hussein would have it, the United States against Iraq. It is Iraq against the world. . . .

We stand today at a unique and extraordinary moment. The crisis in the Persian Gulf, as grave as it is, also offers a rare opportunity to move toward an historic period of cooperation. Out of these troubled times, our fifth objective—a new world order—can emerge: a new era—freer from the threat of terror, stronger in the pursuit of justice, and more secure in the quest for peace. An era in which the nations of the world, East and West, North and South, can prosper and live in harmony. A hundred generations have searched for this elusive path to peace, while a thousand wars raged across the span of human endeavor. Today that new world is struggling to be born, a world quite different from the one we've known. A world where the rule of law supplants the rule of the jungle. A world in which nations recognize the shared responsibility for freedom and justice. A world where the strong respect the rights of the weak. This is the vision that I shared with President Gorbachev in Helsinki. He and other leaders from Europe, the Gulf, and around the world understand that how we manage this crisis today could shape the future for generations to come.

The test we face is great, and so are the stakes. This is the first assault on the new world that we seek, the first test of our mettle. Had we not responded to this first provocation with clarity of purpose, if we do not continue to demonstrate our determination, it would be a signal to actual and potential despots around the world. America and the world must defend common vital interests—and we will. America and the world must support the rule of law—and we will. America and the world must stand up to aggression—and we will. And one thing more: In the pursuit of these goals America will not be intimidated.

Vital issues of principle are at stake. Saddam Hussein is literally trying to wipe a country off the face of the Earth. We do not exaggerate. Nor do we exaggerate when we say Saddam Hussein will fail. Vital economic interests are at risk as well. Iraq itself controls some 10 percent of the world's proven oil reserves. Iraq plus Kuwait controls twice that. An Iraq permitted to swallow Kuwait would have the economic and military power, as well as the arrogance, to intimidate and coerce its neighbors—neighbors who control the lion's share of the world's remaining oil reserves. We cannot permit a resource so vital to be dominated by one so ruthless. And we won't.

Recent events have surely proven that there is no substitute for American leadership. In the face of tyranny, let no one doubt American credibility and reliability. Let no one doubt our staying power. We will stand by our friends. One way or another, the leader of Iraq must learn this fundamental truth. From the outset, acting hand in hand with others, we've sought to fashion the broadest possible international response to Iraq's aggression. The level of world cooperation and condemnation of Iraq is unprecedented. Armed forces from countries spanning four continents are there at the request of King Fahd of Saudi Arabia to deter and, if need be, to defend against attack. Moslems and non-Moslems, Arabs and non-Arabs, soldiers from many nations stand shoulder to shoulder, resolute against Saddam Hussein's ambitions. . . .

I cannot predict just how long it will take to convince Iraq to withdraw from Kuwait. Sanctions will take time to have their full intended effect. We will continue to review all options with our allies, but let it be clear: we will not let this aggression stand.

Our interest, our involvement in the Gulf is not transitory. It predated Saddam Hussein's aggression and will survive it. Long after all our troops come home—and we all hope it's soon, very soon—there will be a lasting role for the United States in assisting the nations of the Persian Gulf. Our role then: to deter future aggression. Our role is to help our friends in their own self-defense. And something else: to curb the proliferation of chemical, biological, ballistic missile and, above all, nuclear technologies.

Let me also make clear that the United States has no quarrel with the Iraqi people. Our quarrel is with Iraq's dictator and with his aggression. Iraq will not be permitted to annex Kuwait. That's not a threat, that's not a boast, that's just the way it's going to be.

Document 14.3

THE PITY OF WAR

Many expected the end of the Cold War to inaugurate an era of lasting peace, and victory in the Gulf War to exorcise the painful ghosts of defeat in Vietnam. Neither assumption proved to be accurate. From the invasion of Panama in December 1989 to the escalation of the war in Afghanistan in 2009, rarely a year passed in the post–Cold War era in which the United States was not at war. And though these many "small" wars were supposed to rely on technology instead of manpower, and were therefore supposed to be "clean" and "surgical," with few U.S. casualties, they carried their own traumas and tragedies. In this excerpt from Jarhead, *his memoir of the Gulf War, former marine Anthony Swofford expressed the deep ambivalence felt by those charged with waging even the most popular and successful of American wars.*

The man fires a rifle for many years, and he goes to war, and afterward he turns the rifle in at the armory and he believes he's finished with the rifle. But no matter what else he might do with his hands—love a woman, build a house, change his son's diaper—his hands remember the rifle and the power the rifle proffered. The cold weight, the buttstock in the shoulder, the sexy slope and fall of the trigger guard. Where do rifles come from? the man's son asks. . . .

We fire and fire the AKs, a factory of firepower, the fierce scream of metal downrange and discharged cartridges and sand flying everywhere, now all of us shooting in the air, shooting straight up and dancing in circles, dancing on one foot, with the mad, desperate hope that the rounds will never descend, screaming, screaming at ourselves and each other and the dead Iraqis surrounding us, screaming at ourselves and the dead world surrounding us, screaming at ourselves, at the corpses surrounding us and the dead world.

I throw my rifle onto the discard pile and run toward the Humvee, and I dive under the vehicle as the fire line continues to send a wall of metal into the air, and I weep, and I hear my screaming friends, those men I love, and I know we'll soon carry that mad scream home with us, but that no one will listen because they'll want to hear the crowd-roar of victory. . . .

We arrived in California, and the bus trip from San Bernardino to Twentynine Palms took many hours because along the desert roads thousands of citizens had gathered to welcome home the heroes. I recalled pictures from World War II victory parades in New York City, and our twenty yellow buses rambling through the desert were a letdown in comparison.

People threw cases of cheap beer and bottles of cheap booze and plastic yellow ribbons and flags into the buses, and occasionally a marine lifted a willing woman into our bus. The woman would smile and congratulate us on our hero status. . . .

As we neared Twentynine Palms, Crocket pulled a Vietnam vet onto the bus, a hard Vietnam vet, a man obviously on and off the streets for many years, in and out of VA hospitals. The man had no shoes on his dirty feet and wore tattered jeans and a faded camouflage blouse of indeterminate origin. Tears fell from the man's eyes and rolled down his deeply wrinkled and hurt face, the surface of his face not unlike the topography of the Desert. The man was somewhat drunk, but obviously less drunk than he was used to being. He steadied himself by gripping Crocket's shoulder, and he opened his dry mouth but no words issued forth. The bus quieted. He closed his mouth and licked his cracked lips and yelled to the bus, "Thank you, thank you jarheads, for making them see we are not bad animals."

Crocket helped the man reenter the crowd. I hoped that even though the spectacle of the excited citizens was worth nothing to me, it might help the Vietnam vet heal his wounds.

Document 14.4

THE PALESTINIAN-ISRAELI PEACE PROCESS

In the late 1970s, Jimmy Carter recognized the growing importance of the Middle East to U.S. interests. By brokering the Camp David Peace Accords between Egypt and Israel, he positioned Washington as an intermediary between Israel and the Arabs. Yet Israel remained a staunch ally of the United States. From the Carter presidency onward, American presidents needed to balance their obligations to Israel with their commitment to finding a solution to the turmoil in the Middle East. Reagan made little progress, but Bush (with the Madrid peace conference in 1991) and Clinton pushed vigorously for a comprehensive settlement in the region. Alongside frequent wars and other military interventions, then, U.S. involvement in the Middle East would be marked by its sponsorship of an indefinite "peace process." Following lengthy and difficult secret negotiations in Oslo, the Israelis and Palestinians signed their first-ever bilateral agreement on August 20, 1993. Three weeks later, on September 13, Clinton hosted an official signing ceremony at the White House, where he delivered the following remarks.

Today the leadership of Israel and the Palestine Liberation Organization will sign a declaration of principles on interim Palestinian self-government. It charts a course toward reconciliation between two peoples who have both known the bitterness of exile. Now both pledge to put old sorrows and antagonisms behind them and to work for a shared future shaped by the values of the Torah, the Koran, and the Bible. . . .

We know a difficult road lies ahead. Every peace has its enemies, those who still prefer the easy habits of hatred to the hard labors of reconciliation. But Prime Minister Rabin has reminded us that you do not have to make peace with your friends. And the Koran teaches that if the enemy inclines toward peace, do thou also incline toward peace.

Therefore, let us resolve that this new mutual recognition will be a continuing process in which the parties transform the very way they see and understand each other. Let the skeptics of this peace recall what once existed among these people. There was a time when the traffic of ideas and commerce and pilgrims flowed uninterrupted among the cities of the Fertile Crescent. In Spain and the Middle East, Muslims and Jews once worked together to write brilliant chapters in the history of literature and science. All this can come to pass again.

Mr. Prime Minister, Mr. Chairman, I pledge the active support of the United States of America to the difficult work that lies ahead. The United States is committed to ensuring that the people who are affected by this agreement will be made more secure by it and to leading the world in marshaling the resources necessary to implement the difficult details that will make real the principles to which you commit yourselves today.

Together let us imagine what can be accomplished if all the energy and ability the Israelis and the Palestinians have invested into your struggle can now be channeled into cultivating the land and freshening the waters, into ending the boycotts and creating new industry, into building a land as bountiful and peaceful as it is holy. Above all, let us dedicate ourselves today to your region's next generation. In this entire assembly, no one is more important than the group of Israeli and Arab children who are seated here with us today.

Mr. Prime Minister, Mr. Chairman, this day belongs to you. And because of what you have done, tomorrow belongs to them. We must not leave them prey to the politics of extremism and despair, to those who would derail this process because they cannot overcome the fears and hatreds of the past. We must not betray their future. For too long, the young of the Middle East have been caught in a web of hatred not of their own making. For too long, they have been taught from the chronicles of war. Now we can give them the chance to know the season of peace. For them we must realize the prophecy of Isaiah that the cry of violence shall no more be heard in your land, nor wrack nor ruin within your borders. The children of Abraham, the descendants of Isaac and Ishmael, have embarked together on a bold journey. Together today, with all our hearts and all our souls, we bid them *shalom*, *salaam*, peace.

Document 14.5

FROM CONTAINMENT TO ENLARGEMENT

Though Bush's "new world order" failed to take root, its emphases on multilateralism, U.S. power, and the promotion of world stability through the pursuit of justice provided the ideological basis for post–Cold War U.S. foreign policy. Still, uncertainty continued to surround the world system in general and U.S. foreign policy in particular. Pessimists worried about the spread of chaos and strife now that the Cold War was no longer keeping religious, ethnic, and nationalist conflicts in check. Harvard University political scientist Samuel P. Huntington warned of a "clash of civilizations," while journalist Robert D. Kaplan predicted "the coming anarchy." But others were more optimistic. They included Francis Fukuyama, a neoconservative intellectual and former Bush administration official, who argued that the world was witnessing "the end of history," a period in which all of liberal democracy's challengers—fascism, communism, theocracy—had exhausted themselves. Building on foundations laid by Bush, the Clinton administration sought to chart a new course for the United States in the world, one that recognized Huntington and Kaplan's dangers but emphasized Fukuyama's possibilities. Its main visionary was National Security Adviser Tony Lake, who announced the strategy of enlargement in a September 1993 speech at Johns Hopkins University.

I have come to speak with you today because I believe our nation's policies toward the world stand at an historic crossroads. For half a century America's engagement in the world revolved around containment of a hostile Soviet Union. Our efforts helped block Soviet expansionism, topple Communist repression and secure a great victory for human freedom.

Clearly, the Soviet Union's collapse enhances our security. But it also requires us to think anew because the world is new.

In particular, with the end of the Cold War, there is no longer a consensus among the American people around why, and even whether our nation should remain actively engaged in the world. Geography and history always have made Americans wary of foreign entanglements. Now economic anxiety fans that wariness. Calls from the left and right to stay at home rather than engage abroad are re-enforced by the rhetoric of Neo-Know-Nothings.

Those of us who believe in the imperative of our international engagement must push back. For that reason, as President Clinton sought the presidency, he not only pledged a domestic renaissance, but also vowed to engage actively in the world in order to increase our prosperity, update our security arrangements and promote democracy abroad. . . .

Let us begin by taking stock of our new era. Four facts are salient. First, America's core concepts—democracy and market economics—are more broadly accepted than ever. Over the past ten years the number of democracies has nearly doubled. Since 1970, the number of significant command economies dropped from 10 to 3.

This victory of freedom is practical, not ideological: billions of people on every continent are simply concluding, based on decades of their own hard experience, that democracy and markets are the most productive and liberating ways to organize their lives.

Their conclusion resonates with America's core values. We see individuals as equally created with a God-given right to life, liberty and the pursuit of happiness. So we trust in the equal wisdom of free individuals to protect those rights: through democracy, as the process for best meeting shared needs in the face of competing desires; and through markets as the process for best meeting private needs in a way that expands opportunity.

Both processes strengthen each other: democracy alone can produce justice, but not the material goods necessary for individuals to thrive; markets alone can expand wealth, but not that sense of justice without which civilized societies perish.

Democracy and market economics are ascendant in this new era, but they are not everywhere triumphant. There remain vast areas in Asia, Africa, the Middle East and elsewhere where democracy and market economics are at best new arrivals—most likely unfamiliar, sometimes vilified, often fragile.

But it is wrong to assume these ideas will be embraced only by the West and rejected by the rest. Culture does shape politics and economics. But the idea of freedom has universal appeal. Thus, we have arrived at neither the end of history nor a clash of civilizations, but a moment of immense democratic and entrepreneurial opportunity. We must not waste it.

The second feature of this era is that we are its dominant power. Those who say otherwise sell America short. The fact is, we have the world's strongest military, its largest economy and its most dynamic, multiethnic society. We are setting a global example in our efforts to reinvent our democratic and market institutions. Our leadership is sought and respected in every corner of the world. . . .

The third notable aspect of this era is an explosion of ethnic conflicts. As Senator [Daniel Patrick] Moynihan and others have noted, the end of the Cold War and the collapse of various repressive regimes has removed the lid from numerous caldrons of ethnic, religious or factional hatreds. In many states of the former Soviet Union and elsewhere, there is a tension between the desire for ethnic separatism and the creation of liberal democracy, which alone can safely accommodate and even celebrate differences among citizens.

A major challenge to our thinking, our policies and our international institutions in this era is the fact that most conflicts are taking place within rather than among nations.

These conflicts are typically highly complex; at the same time, their brutality will tug at our consciences. We need a healthy wariness about our ability to shape solutions for such disputes, yet at times our interests or humanitarian concerns will impel our unilateral or multilateral engagement.

The fourth feature of this new era is that the pulse of the planet has accelerated dramatically and with it the pace of change in human events. Computers, faxes, fiber optic cables and satellites all speed the flow of information. The measurement of wealth, and increasingly wealth itself, consists in bytes of data that move at the speed of light.

The accelerated pace of events is neither bad nor good. Its sharp consequences can cut either way. It means both doctors and terrorists can more quickly share their technical secrets. Both prodemocracy activists and skinhead anarchists can more broadly spread their views. Ultimately, the world's acceleration creates new and diverse ways for us to exert our influence, if we choose to do so—but increases the likelihood that, if we do not, rapid events, instantly reported, may overwhelm us. As the President has suggested, we must decide whether to make change our ally or allow ourselves to become its victims. . . .

In such a world, our interests and ideals compel us not only to be engaged, but to lead. And in a real-time world of change and information, it is all the more important that our leadership be steadied around our central purpose.

That purpose can be found in the underlying rationale for our engagement throughout this century. As we fought aggressors and contained communism, our engagement abroad was animated both by calculations of power and by this belief: to the extent democracy and market economics hold sway in other nations, our own nation will be more secure, prosperous and influential, while the broader world will be more humane and peaceful.

The expansion of market-based economics abroad helps expand our exports and create American jobs, while it also improves living conditions and fuels demands for political liberalization abroad. The addition of new democracies makes us more secure because democracies tend not to wage war on each other or sponsor terrorism. They are more trustworthy in diplomacy and do a better job of respecting the human rights of their people. . . .

Throughout the Cold War, we contained a global threat to market democracies; now we should seek to enlarge their reach, particularly in places of special significance to us.

The successor to a doctrine of containment must be a strategy of enlargement—enlargement of the world's free community of market democracies. . . .

I see four components to a strategy of enlargement.

First, we should strengthen the community of major market democracies—including our own—which constitutes the core from which enlargement is proceeding.

Second, we should help foster and consolidate new democracies and market economies, where possible, especially in states of special significance and opportunity.

Third, we must counter the aggression—and support the liberalization—of states hostile to democracy and markets.

Fourth, we need to pursue our humanitarian agenda not only by providing aid, but also by working to help democracy and market economics take root in regions of greatest humanitarian concern....

In his farewell address in January, 1953, Harry Truman predicted the collapse of Communism. "I have a deep and abiding faith in the destiny of free men," he said. "With patience and courage, we shall some day move on into a new era."

Now that era is upon us. It is a moment of unparalleled opportunity. We have the blessing of living in the world's most powerful and respected nation at a time when the world is embracing our ideals as never before. We can let this moment slip away. Or we can mobilize our nation in order to enlarge democracy, enlarge markets, and enlarge our future. I am confident that we will choose the road best travelled.

Document 14.6

THE CLASH OF CIVILIZATIONS

Not everyone was cheered by the end of the Cold War. Some disagreed with Lake's belief that American engagement and the expansion of liberalism would create a better world. Instead of greater peace and prosperity, argued Harvard political scientist Samuel P. Huntington, the world would see a return of very old types of racial and ethnic conflict that the Cold War had long suppressed and that now had a chance to explode into the open once again.

World politics is entering a new phase, and intellectuals have not hesitated to proliferate visions of what it will be—the end of history, the return of traditional rivalries between nation states, and the decline of the nation state from the conflicting pulls of tribalism and globalism, among others. Each of these visions catches aspects of the emerging reality. Yet they all miss a crucial, indeed a central, aspect of what global politics is likely to be in the coming years.

It is my hypothesis that the fundamental source of conflict in this new world will not be primarily ideological or primarily economic. The great divisions among humankind and the dominating source of conflict will be cultural. Nation states will remain the most powerful actors in world affairs, but the principal conflicts of global politics will occur between nations and groups of different civilizations. The clash of civilizations will dominate global politics. The fault lines between civilizations will be the battle lines of the future. . . .

With the end of the Cold War, international politics moves out of its Western phase, and its centerpiece becomes the interaction between the West and non-Western civilizations and among non-Western civilizations. In the politics of civilizations, the peoples and governments of non-Western civilizations no longer remain the objects of history as targets of Western colonialism but join the West as movers and shapers of history. . . .

What do we mean when we talk of a civilization? A civilization is a cultural entity. Villages, regions, ethnic groups, nationalities, religious groups, all have distinct cultures at different levels of cultural heterogeneity. The culture of a village in southern Italy may be different from that of a village in northern Italy, but both will share in a common Italian culture that distinguishes them from German villages. European communities, in turn, will share cultural features that distinguish them from Arab or Chinese communities. Arabs, Chinese and Westerners, however, are not part of any broader cultural entity. They constitute civilizations. A civilization is thus the highest cultural grouping of people and the broadest level of cultural identity people have short of that which distinguishes humans from other species. It is defined both by common objective elements, such as language, history, religion, customs, institutions, and by the subjective self-identification of people. People have levels of identity: a resident of Rome may define himself with varying degrees of intensity as a Roman, an Italian, a Catholic, a Christian, a European, a Westerner. The civilization to which he belongs is the broadest level of identification with which he intensely identifies. People can and do redefine their identities and, as a result, the composition and boundaries of civilizations change. . . .

As people define their identity in ethnic and religious terms, they are likely to see an "us" versus "them" relation existing between themselves and people of different ethnicity or religion. The end of ideologically defined states in Eastern Europe and the former Soviet Union permits traditional ethnic identities and animosities to come to the fore. Differences in culture and religion create differences over policy issues, ranging from human rights to immigration to trade and commerce to the environment. Geographical propinquity gives rise to conflicting territorial claims from Bosnia to Mindanao. Most important, the efforts of the West to promote its values of democracy and liberalism as universal values, to maintain its military predominance and to advance its economic interests engender countering responses from other civilizations. Decreasingly able to mobilize support and form coalitions on the basis of ideology, governments and groups will increasingly attempt to mobilize support by appealing to common religion and civilization identity.

Document 14.7

THE "PROBLEM FROM HELL"

Nothing seemed to corroborate "the clash of civilizations" and "the coming anarchy" more than the bloodbath in the small central African nation of Rwanda. In the spring of 1994, a power struggle between the minority Tutsis, who had long dominated Rwandan politics, and the majority Hutus resulted in a massacre. Between April and July, Hutu militias slaughtered at least 500,000 Tutsis. This raised the specter of genocide and what the human rights scholar and activist Samantha Power—later President Barack Obama's ambassador to the United Nations—called "the problem from hell": events in Rwanda clearly represented a humanitarian disaster of the most serious kind, but what should other nations do about it? This was a particular quandary for the United States, which alone had the means possibly to stop the genocide but lacked any clear or compelling interest to do so, other than humanitarianism, while any intervention was sure to face violent resistance from the Hutus. Advocates of humanitarian intervention pressed vigorously for action, but that could only work if the world's most powerful nation and the leader of the West led the way. General Romeo Dallaire, the Canadian commander of the United Nations force, was particularly insistent in calling for direct intervention to stop the killings. But in the wake of the "Black Hawk down" debacle in Somalia, when eighteen U.S. troops lost their lives in a humanitarian mission only six months earlier, the Clinton administration remained reluctant and in the end decided not to intervene in Rwanda. In this record of a conversation between U.S. military officials and two UN officials—Assistant Secretary-General of Peacekeeping Operations Iqbal Riza and Military Adviser to the Secretary-General Maurice Baril—the difference of these views is clear.

After brief introductions the UN team stated that the UN would not withdraw from Rwanda. They did not support the proposed U.S. option of providing humanitarian assistance from outside the country (outside-in) and sought our approval for their option of humanitarian operations emanating from within the country out towards the border areas (inside-out). A/S Risa's [*sic*] rationale for the UN's option was that the UN had to get at the heart of the problem as soon as possible. He said the UN was morally obligated to stop the killing of civilians and alleviate the humanitarian crisis. Those problems are not as severe in the border areas that the U.S. had proposed in its option. Arguably, the UN option was riskier, commented General Baril but the circumstances required immediate action. The UN was working to achieve consent of both the RPF [Rwandan Patriotic Front] and the GOR [government of Rwanda] for the UN operation to be headquartered in Kigali along with 2–3 regional location bases. When pressed by the U.S. delegation for details on the concept of [the] operation General Baril commented that the proposed resolution's force of 5,500 was the number of troops the UN believed they could get from troop contributors, not necessarily what was needed to provide nation wide security and humanitarian assistance. He commented that troop availability (type and amount) and the resources they'd require (from transport to equipment and training) were the UN's major concerns.

Document 14.8

BOSNIA AND THE MORAL IMPERATIVE

Where and when should the United States use its military power? After Rwanda, this became the focus of debate for many in the West. Should it intervene only when American national interests or U.S. security were at risk? If so, genocide would

continue unimpeded. Or should it become involved in humanitarian and political crises in which it had no direct involvement? If so, it raised the possibility of becoming bogged down in bloody and difficult wars in which civilians would almost inevitably die and which the American public would be unlikely to support. The wars in the former country of Yugoslavia, which was breaking apart and creating horrific suffering in one of its provinces, Bosnia-Herzegovina, brought the issue to the forefront of American attention. Though people at the time did not always realize it, their debates over whether to intervene in humanitarian crises established one of the most enduring themes of U.S. foreign policy ever since. This 1993 editorial cartoon captures the complexity and moral anguish of debates that had no easy answers. In the end, the Clinton administration launched a military campaign in 1995 to end the war and the ethnic cleansing of Bosnian Muslims at the hands of Bosnian Serbs.

DOCUMENT 14.9

"THE ENVIRONMENT AS A HOSTILE POWER"

Analysts like Jessica Tuchman Mathews correctly observed that humanity was changing the world's environment and doing so at a faster rate than ever before; thanks to globalization, the process of environmental degradation was accelerating even more. Yet even after the Cold War, it was still unclear what effects the growing environmental crisis would have on international security. In a landmark 1994 article in The Atlantic Monthly, *journalist Robert Kaplan argued that the environment was threatening to create a new kind of geopolitics centered on environmental catastrophe.*

For a while the media will continue to ascribe riots and other violent upheavals abroad mainly to ethnic and religious conflict. But as these conflicts multiply, it will become apparent that something else is afoot, making more and more places like Nigeria, India, and Brazil ungovernable.

Mention "the environment" or "diminishing natural resources" in foreign-policy circles and you meet a brick wall of skepticism or boredom. To conservatives especially, the very terms seem flaky. Public-policy foundations have contributed to the lack of interest, by funding narrowly focused environmental studies replete with technical jargon which foreign-affairs experts just let pile up on their desks.

It is time to understand "the environment" for what it is: *the* national-security issue of the early twenty-first century. The political and strategic impact of surging populations, spreading disease, deforestation and soil erosion, water depletion, air pollution, and, possibly, rising sea levels in critical, overcrowded regions like the Nile Delta and Bangladesh—developments that will prompt mass migrations and, in turn, incite group conflicts—will be the core foreign-policy challenge from which most others will ultimately emanate, arousing the public and uniting assorted interests left over from the Cold War. In the twenty-first century water will be in dangerously short supply in such diverse locales as Saudi Arabia, Central Asia, and the southwestern United States. A war could erupt between Egypt and Ethiopia over Nile River water. Even in Europe tensions have arisen between Hungary and Slovakia over the damming of the Danube, a classic case of how environmental disputes fuse with ethnic and historical ones. The political scientist and erstwhile Clinton adviser Michael Mandelbaum has said, "We have a foreign policy today in the shape of a doughnut—lots of peripheral interests but nothing at the center." The environment, I will argue, is part of a terrifying array of problems that will define a new threat to our security, filling the hole in Mandelbaum's doughnut and allowing a post–Cold War foreign policy to emerge inexorably by need rather than by design.

Document 14.10

"ASIAN VALUES" VERSUS THE WASHINGTON CONSENSUS

As the war in Rwanda illustrated, there was nothing inevitable or smooth about the spread of American or Western values. China was busy establishing a system of authoritarian capitalism, which combined rigorous political control with dynamic economic growth. Yet perhaps the fiercest opponent of the U.S. worldview was Malaysian Prime Minister Mahathir bin Mohamad, who undermined Washington's claim to world leadership and defended "Asian values." In 1994, in a speech designed to be a direct challenge to Lake's strategy of enlargement, Mahathir doubted that what was good for Washington was also good for the world.

As the world has numerous communities and the state of their development differs widely, it is natural to expect that their concepts of human rights, of justice, and of obligation to the community to differ and differ widely. . . .

Developed countries can do with weak governments or no government. But developing countries cannot function without strong authority on the part of government. Unstable and weak governments will result in chaos, and chaos cannot contribute to the development and well-being of developing countries. Divisive politics will occupy the time and minds of everyone, as we can witness in many a developing country today.

The developing countries, by and large, want to practise democracy, but must they practise only the liberal forms prescribed by the West, forms which will retard their development and continued independence? But they are continuously being harassed through economic pressures including withdrawal of aid and loans, by carping criticisms and deliberate misinformation by the Western media and by campaigns on the part of Western NGOs, who sometimes finance pressure groups within the country to obstruct the government which they label as undemocratic. Even if the government is replaced, the new government would still be harassed. . . .

The record of the democratic governments of the West is not very inspiring. Unless their own interests are at stake, as in Kuwait, they would not risk anything in the cause of democracy. Is it any wonder that many countries are leery of the liberal system propounded by the Western democrats? . . .

After the collapse of the Soviet Union and the much vaunted victory over Iraq, the Western powers declared that the independence of nations notwithstanding, they have a right to interfere in the internal affairs of a country if there is evidence of human rights violation. This is very noble but the method is questionable. What qualifies the Western liberal democrats to become both judge and executor of the behaviour of nations and citizens of other countries? If there is to be interference in the internal affairs of nations, should not the U.N. be the right body to lay down the rules and to act? But the mild objections by insignificant nations were brushed aside. And so, among other things, people in distant lands who unknowingly breach the laws of powerful nations are tried in absentia and sentenced. The implication of this is frightening. When you can be tried under the laws of another country where you have no rights, you have lost your freedom and your independence. You have become colonised again. . . .

This then is the reality and irony of Western human rights. On the one hand other Governments are threatened because of some minor breach of human rights; on the other hand, when Western interest is not at stake they are prepared to allow the most brutal violation of human rights to take place before their very eyes.

It is rather difficult for us to agree and to accept these double standards. And this unwillingness to accede has brought on a tirade of accusations about Asian recalcitrance. It would seem that Asians have no right to define and practise their own sets of values about human rights. What, we are asked, are Asian values? The question is rhetorical because the implication is that Asians cannot possibly understand human rights, much less set up their own values. . . .

No one, no country, no people and no civilisation has a right to claim that it has a monopoly of wisdom as to what constitute human rights. Certainly from the records and the performance of the Western liberals, they are least capable of defining and preaching human rights. Indeed, at the moment they have no right at all to talk of human rights, much less judge others on this issue.

Document 14.11

OPPOSING ENLARGEMENT

The end of the Cold War raised questions about the future of the North Atlantic Treaty Organization, the alliance created in 1949 to tie the United States to the defense of Europe and to resist communist expansion. Some Americans celebrated NATO's successes and insisted that, far from being disbanded as an obsolete relic of a bygone era, it should be expanded to include nations that had once belonged to the Warsaw Pact. Others worried that the expansion of NATO would foster new tensions and divisions in Europe at just the moment when a new era of harmony appeared within reach. On June 26, 1997, fifty prominent politicians, policy makers, and scholars representing a wide array of political outlooks issued the following open letter urging President Clinton to suspend discussions to bring nations such as Poland and the Czech Republic into the alliance. Signatories included former secretary of defense Robert S. McNamara; senators Bill Bradley, Gary Hart, Mark Hatfield, and Sam Nunn; former CIA director Stansfield Turner; and former presidential advisers Paul H. Nitze and Paul Warnke.

Dear Mr. President,

We, the undersigned, believe that the current U.S. led effort to expand NATO, the focus of the recent Helsinki and Paris Summits, is a policy error of historic proportions. We believe that NATO expansion will decrease allied security and unsettle European stability for the following reasons:

In Russia, NATO expansion, which continues to be opposed across the entire political spectrum, will strengthen the nondemocratic opposition, undercut those who favor reform and cooperation with the West, bring the Russians to question the entire post–Cold War settlement, and galvanize resistance in the Duma to the START II and III treaties; In Europe, NATO expansion will draw a new line of division between the "ins" and the "outs," foster instability, and ultimately diminish the sense of security of those countries which are not included;

In NATO, expansion, which the Alliance has indicated is open-ended, will inevitably degrade NATO's ability to carry out its primary mission and will involve U.S. security guarantees to countries with serious border and national minority problems, and unevenly developed systems of democratic government;

In the U.S., NATO expansion will trigger an extended debate over its indeterminate, but certainly high, cost and will call into question the U.S. commitment to the Alliance, traditionally and rightly regarded as a centerpiece of U.S. foreign policy.

Because of these serious objections, and in the absence of any reason for rapid decision, we strongly urge that the NATO expansion process be suspended while alternative actions are pursued. These include:

- opening the economic and political doors of the European Union to Central and Eastern Europe;
- developing an enhanced Partnership for Peace program;
- supporting a cooperative NATO-Russian relationship; and
- continuing the arms reduction and transparency process, particularly with respect to nuclear weapons and materials, the major threat to U.S. security, and with respect to conventional military forces in Europe.

Russia does not now pose a threat to its western neighbors and the nations of Central and Eastern Europe are not in danger. For this reason, and the others cited above, we believe that NATO expansion is neither necessary nor desirable and that this ill-conceived policy can and should be put on hold.

Document 14.12

NO LOGO

Challenges to the Washington Consensus also came from within the West, including the United States. North Americans and Europeans vehemently attacked globalization, which they equated with Americanization, as a fundamentally unjust basis for international society. These critics embraced an alternative form of globalization that sought to spread democracy and human rights but not free markets, capitalism, or corporate power. In November 1999, at a special meeting of the World Trade Organization (WTO), the Western antiglobalization movement climaxed in the so-called Battle in Seattle, where peaceful demonstrations turned into violent riots. To promote their own vision of an anticorporate new world order, activists such as the Canadian journalist and filmmaker Naomi Klein, a frequent contributor to newspapers in the United States and Great Britain, formed transnational alliances that in many ways mirrored groups like the International Monetary Fund, the G-8, and the WTO. In this excerpt from her bestselling book No Logo, *she offers a searing critique of globalization as Americanization.*

Usually, reports about this global web of logos and products are couched in the euphoric marketing rhetoric of the global village, an incredible place where tribespeople in remotest rain forests tap away on laptop computers, Sicilian grandmothers conduct E-business, and "global teens" share, to borrow a phrase from a Levi's Web site, "a world-wide style culture." Everyone from Coke to McDonald's to Motorola has tailored their marketing strategy around this post-national vision, but it is IBM's long-running "Solutions for a Small Planet" campaign that most eloquently captures the equalizing promise of the logo-linked globe.

It hasn't taken long for the excitement inspired by these manic renditions of globalization to wear thin, revealing the cracks and fissures beneath its high-gloss façade. More and more over the past four years, we in the West have been catching glimpses of another kind of global village, where the economic divide is widening and cultural choices are narrowing.

This is a village where some multinationals, far from leveling the global playing field with jobs and technology for all, are in the process of mining the planet's poorest back country for unimaginable profits. . . .

I have become convinced that it is in these logo-forged global links that global citizens will eventually find sustainable solutions for this sold planet. . . . What conditions have set the stage for this backlash? Successful multinational corporations are increasingly finding themselves under attack, whether it's a cream pie in Bill Gates's face or the incessant parodying of the Nike swoosh—what are the forces pushing more and more people to become suspicious or even downright enraged at multinational corporations, the very engines of our global growth? Perhaps more pertinently, what is liberating so many people—particularly young people—to act on that rage and suspicion? . . .

It is a daunting task but it does have an upside. The claustrophobic sense of despair that has so often accompanied the colonization of public space and the loss of secure work begins to lift when one starts to think about the possibilities for a truly globally minded society, one that would include not just economics and capital, but global citizens, global rights and global responsibilities as well. It has taken many of us a while to find our footing in this new international arena, but thanks in large part to the crash course provided by the brands, we are closer than ever before.

Document 14.13

THE INDISPENSABLE NATION

Critics did little to blunt the Clinton administration's foreign policy. Instead, following the successful 1995 intervention in Bosnia, and Clinton's reelection in 1996, U.S. officials redoubled their efforts to create a world system based on the spread of liberal democracy, free trade, and deregulated open markets. Even the intractable, perennial problem of Iraq seemed little more than an obstacle. Though Saddam Hussein had remained in power since the 1991 Gulf War, he was reined in by UN sanctions and British and American warplanes. By 1998, after a series of confrontations with the United States, Iraq tried to break free from these constraints. In discussing a military solution to the Iraq problem with Matt Lauer of NBC's

Today Show, *Secretary of State Madeleine Albright used the term "indispensable nation" to describe America's mission in the world.*

MR. LAUER: On "Close Up" this morning—the showdown with Iraq. As UN Secretary-General Kofi Annan heads to Baghdad in a last-ditch diplomatic effort to end the standoff, Secretary of State Madeleine Albright is traveling around the United States making the administration's case for a possible strike against Saddam Hussein. Madame Secretary, good morning to you, good to see you.

SECRETARY ALBRIGHT: Good morning, Matt, nice to see you. . . .

Matt, we would like to solve this peacefully. But if we cannot, we will be using force; and the American people will be behind us, and I think that they understand that. . . .

[W]e had a half-a-million troops there in 1991. And the decision was that they could not take out Saddam Hussein. And I don't think, frankly, that if we got into it, that the American people would want us to send in huge numbers of forces. So we are doing what must be done.

First of all, we would like to have a diplomatic, peaceful solution and have him give unfettered access to these places, so that we could tell what is happening with his weapons of mass destruction. But otherwise, the purpose of a very substantial strike will be to substantially reduce his weapons of mass destruction threat and his threat to the neighbors. We think that is an appropriate goal, and our goal—and we've said this, Matt—may not seem really decisive; but what we're try- ing to do here is contain Saddam Hussein. We've managed to do that for seven years. This has been a successful policy. Whenever he puts his head up, we push him back. . . .

I think the problem with the idea is that we would have to end up being an occupying force. The Americans don't want to do that. I don't think the American people would want us to do that. But after the substantial strike, I think we have a much better chance of having the inspectors go back in or make sure that these weapons are not reconstituted by being willing to do another strike.

This is a very serious problem. None of us are saying that there are easy solutions to it, but we have to contain Saddam Hussein. And, as I've said many times, we are prepared to deal, ready to deal with a post-Saddam regime. . . .

MR. LAUER: Will you speak for me, Madame Secretary, to the parents of American men and women who may soon be asked to go into harm's way, and who get the feeling that many countries in the rest of the world are standing by silently while their children are once again being asked to clean up a mess for the rest of the world?

SECRETARY ALBRIGHT: Well, let me say that there are, a couple of dozen countries that are with us on this that are providing a variety of equipment, support and are willing to be with us. So there is a misunderstanding about saying that there is no coalition; there is. And the truth is that in the Gulf War, we did most of the work, too. There's no question that we, with the British and French, did a large proportion of the work.

Let me say that we are doing everything possible so that American men and women in uniform do not have to go out there again. It is the threat of the use of force and our line-up there that is going to put force behind the diplomacy. But if we have to use force, it is because we are America; we are the indispensable nation. We stand tall and we see further than other countries into the future, and we see the danger here to all of us. I know that the American men and women in uniform are always prepared to sacrifice for freedom, democracy and the American way of life.

DOCUMENT 14.14

LIBERAL INTERVENTIONISM

The apparent solution to the problem of "moral imperative gridlock," and perhaps the most important vision for U.S. foreign policy, was not devised by an American. In April 1999, the Economic Club of Chicago invited British Prime Minister Tony Blair to deliver a speech. By that time, the North Atlantic Treaty Organization (NATO) had been bombing Serbia for two months. The issue was Kosovo, a province of Serbia that was almost entirely ethnically Albanian and religiously Muslim and that had been advocating independence. In response, Serbia cracked down with a campaign of ethnic cleansing. The United States was officially in charge of the war, but its most ardent supporter was Blair. In fact, Blair felt that Clinton was not doing enough in the Balkans and that the United States was holding NATO back from a more aggressive campaign, including the use of ground troops. In his Chicago speech, Blair's marriage of power with principle laid out an ambitious plan for liberal interventionism—war for humanitarian reasons—in a globalized world. His vision of liberal interventionism essentially gave teeth to Lake's strategy of enlargement. Blair's speech also demonstrated that Americans were not the only ones who thought of the United States as the "indispensable nation."

While we meet here in Chicago this evening, unspeakable things are happening in Europe. Awful crimes that we never thought we would see again have reappeared—ethnic cleansing, systematic rape, mass murder.

I want to speak to you this evening about events in Kosovo. But I want to put these events in a wider context—economic, political and security—because I do not believe Kosovo can be seen in isolation.

No one in the West who has seen what is happening in Kosovo can doubt that NATO's military action is justified. Bismarck famously said the Balkans were not worth the bones of one Pomeranian Grenadier. Anyone who has seen the tear stained faces of the hundreds of thousands of refugees streaming across the border, heard their heartrending tales of cruelty or contemplated the unknown fates of those left behind, knows that Bismarck was wrong.

This is a just war, based not on any territorial ambitions but on values. We cannot let the evil of ethnic cleansing stand. We must not rest until it is reversed. We have learned twice before in this century that appeasement does not work. If we let an evil dictator range unchallenged, we will have to spill infinitely more blood and treasure to stop him later. . . .

Twenty years ago we would not have been fighting in Kosovo. We would have turned our backs on it. The fact that we are engaged is the result of a wide range of changes—the end of the Cold War; changing technology; the spread of democracy. But it is bigger than that.

I believe the world has changed in a more fundamental way. Globalisation has transformed our economies and our working practices. But globalisation is not just economic. It is also a political and security phenomenon.

We live in a world where isolationism has ceased to have a reason to exist. By necessity we have to co-operate with each other across nations.

Many of our domestic problems are caused on the other side of the world. Financial instability in Asia destroys jobs in Chicago and in my own constituency in County Durham. Poverty in the Caribbean means more drugs on the streets in Washington and London. Conflict in the Balkans causes more refugees in Germany and here in the US. These problems can only be addressed by international co-operation.

We are all internationalists now, whether we like it or not. We cannot refuse to participate in global markets if we want to prosper. We cannot ignore new political ideas in other counties if we want to innovate. We cannot turn our backs on conflicts and the violation of human rights within other countries if we want still to be secure. . . .

We are witnessing the beginnings of a new doctrine of international community. By this I mean the explicit recognition that today more than ever before we are mutually dependent, that national interest is to a significant extent governed by international collaboration and that we need a clear and coherent debate as to the direction this doctrine takes us in each field of international endeavour. Just as within domestic politics, the notion of community—the belief that partnership and co-operation are essential to advance self-interest—is coming into its own; so it needs to find its own international echo. Global financial markets, the global environment, global security and disarmament issues: none of these can he solved without intense international co-operation....

At the end of this century the US has emerged as by far the strongest state. It has no dreams of world conquest and is not seeking colonies. If anything Americans are too ready to see no need to get involved in affairs of the rest of the world. America's allies are always both relieved and gratified by its continuing readiness to shoulder burdens and responsibilities that come with its sole superpower status. We understand that this is something that we have no right to take for granted, and must match with our own efforts. That is the basis for the recent initiative I took with President Chirac of France to improve Europe's own defence capabilities.

As we address these problems at this weekend's NATO Summit we may be tempted to think back to the clarity and simplicity of the Cold War. But now we have to establish a new framework. No longer is our existence as states under threat. Now our actions are guided by a more subtle blend of mutual self interest and moral purpose in defending the values we cherish. In the end values and interests merge. If we can establish and spread the values of liberty, the rule of law, human rights and an open society then that is in our national interests too. The spread of our values makes us safer. As John Kennedy put it, "Freedom is indivisible and when one man is enslaved who is free?"

The most pressing foreign policy problem we face is to identify the circumstances in which we should get actively involved in other people's conflicts. Non-interference has long been considered an important principle of international order. And it is not one we would want to jettison too readily. One state should not feel it has the right to change the political system of another or foment subversion or seize pieces of territory to which it feels it should have some claim. But the principle of non-interference must be qualified in important respects. Acts of genocide can never be a purely internal matter. When oppression produces massive flows of refugees which unsettle neighbouring countries then they can properly be described as "threats to international peace and security." When regimes are based on minority rule they lose legitimacy—look at South Africa.

Looking around the world there are many regimes that are undemocratic and engaged in barbarous acts. If we wanted to right every wrong that we see in the modern world then we would do little else than intervene in the affairs of other countries. We would not be able to cope.

So how do we decide when and whether to intervene? I think we need to bear in mind five major considerations.

First, are we sure of our case? War is an imperfect instrument for righting humanitarian distress; but armed force is sometimes the only means of dealing with dictators. Second, have we exhausted all diplomatic options? We should always give peace every chance, as we have in the case of Kosovo. Third, on the basis of a practical assessment of the situation, are there military operations we can sensibly and prudently undertake? Fourth, are we prepared for the long term? In the past we talked too much of exit strategies. But having made a commitment we cannot simply walk away once the fight is over; better to stay with moderate numbers of troops than return for repeat performances with large numbers. And finally, do we have national interests involved? The mass expulsion of ethnic Albanians from Kosovo demanded the notice of the rest of the world. But it does make a difference that this is taking place in such a combustible part of Europe....

This has been a very broad-ranging speech, but maybe the time is right for that. One final word on the USA itself. You are the most powerful country in the world, and the richest. You are a great nation. You have so much to give and to teach the world; and I know you would say, in all modesty, a little to learn from it too. It must be difficult and occasionally irritating to find yourselves the recipient of every demand, to be called upon in every crisis, to be expected always and everywhere to do what needs to be done. The cry "What's it got to do with us" must be regularly heard on the lips of your people and be the staple of many a politician running for office.

Yet just as with the parable of the individuals and the talents, so those nations which have the power, have the responsibility. We need you engaged. We need the dialogue with you. Europe over time will become stronger and stronger; but its time is some way off.

I say to you: never fall again for the doctrine of isolationism. The world cannot afford it. Stay a country, outward-looking, with the vision and imagination that is in your nature. And realise that in Britain you have a friend and an ally that will stand with you, work with you, fashion with you the design of a future built on peace and prosperity for all, which is the only dream that makes humanity worth preserving.

Document 14.15

THE RISE OF AL-QAEDA

The Clinton administration and Tony Blair promoted one version of globalization, while Mahathir bin Mohamad, Naomi Klein, and others had offered their own alternatives. But the antithesis to enlargement, the democratic peace, the Washington Consensus, and the Middle East peace process came from a terrorist group called al-Qaeda ("The Base" in Arabic). Led by Osama bin Laden, a radi-

cal Islamic fundamentalist from Saudi Arabia who had fought the Soviets in Afghanistan in the 1980s, al-Qaeda used many of the same techniques as the Clinton administration—for example, global finance and communications networks—to challenge American hegemony in the Middle East. To bin Laden, Americans were heirs to the Christian Crusaders from Europe who had invaded Muslim lands a thousand years earlier. Even worse was America's close alliance with Israel, which bin Laden and his followers believed perpetuated economic and political injustice against Muslims everywhere. This document, "Jihad against Jews and Crusaders," was bin Laden's second fatwa, or religious ruling, against the United States; he delivered the first, a "Declaration of Jihad," in August 1996. Though he had helped fund the terrorist bombing of the World Trade Center in 1993, the first major al-Qaeda attack against U.S. targets came in August 1998, six months after issuing the "Jihad against Jews and Crusaders." In Arabic, jihad *simply means "struggle," but in this context bin Laden clearly meant for these fatwas to be declarations of war.*

Praise be to Allah, who revealed the Book, controls the clouds, defeats factionalism, and says in His Book: "But when the forbidden months are past, then fight and slay the pagans wherever ye find them, seize them, beleaguer them, and lie in wait for them in every stratagem (of war)"; and peace be upon our Prophet, Muhammad Bin-'Abdallah, who said: I have been sent with the sword between my hands to ensure that no one but Allah is worshipped, Allah who put my livelihood under the shadow of my spear and who inflicts humiliation and scorn on those who disobey my orders.

The Arabian Peninsula has never—since Allah made it flat, created its desert, and encircled it with seas—been stormed by any forces like the crusader armies spreading in it like locusts, eating its riches and wiping out its plantations. All this is happening at a time in which nations are attacking Muslims like people fighting over a plate of food. In the light of the grave situation and the lack of support, we and you are obliged to discuss current events, and we should all agree on how to settle the matter.

No one argues today about three facts that are known to everyone; we will list them, in order to remind everyone:

First, for over seven years the United States has been occupying the lands of Islam in the holiest of places, the Arabian Peninsula, plundering its riches, dictating to its rulers, humiliating its people, terrorizing its neighbors, and turning its bases in the Peninsula into a spearhead through which to fight the neighboring Muslim peoples.

If some people have in the past argued about the fact of the occupation, all the people of the Peninsula have now acknowledged it. The best proof of this is the Americans' continuing aggression against the Iraqi people using the Peninsula as a staging post, even though all its rulers are against their territories being used to that end, but they are helpless.

Second, despite the great devastation inflicted on the Iraqi people by the crusader-Zionist alliance, and despite the huge number of those killed, which has exceeded 1 million . . . despite all this, the Americans are once again trying to repeat the horrific massacres, as though they are not content with the protracted blockade imposed after the ferocious war or the fragmentation and devastation.

So here they come to annihilate what is left of this people and to humiliate their Muslim neighbors.

Third, if the Americans' aims behind these wars are religious and economic, the aim is also to serve the Jews' petty state and divert attention from its occupation of Jerusalem and murder of Muslims there. The best proof of this is their eagerness to destroy Iraq, the strongest neighboring Arab state, and their endeavor to fragment all the states of the region such as Iraq, Saudi Arabia, Egypt, and Sudan into paper statelets and through their disunion and weakness to guarantee Israel's survival and the continuation of the brutal crusade occupation of the Peninsula.

All these crimes and sins committed by the Americans are a clear declaration of war on Allah, His messenger, and Muslims. And ulema have throughout Islamic history unanimously agreed that the jihad is an individual duty if the enemy destroys the Muslim countries. This was revealed by Imam Bin-Qadamah in "Al-Mughni," Imam al-Kisa'i in "Al-Bada'i," al-Qurtubi in his interpretation, and the shaykh of al-Islam in his books, where he said: "As for the fighting to repulse [an enemy], it is aimed at defending sanctity and religion, and it is a duty as agreed [by the ulema]. Nothing is more sacred than belief except repulsing an enemy who is attacking religion and life."

On that basis, and in compliance with Allah's order, we issue the following fatwa to all Muslims:

The ruling to kill the Americans and their allies—civilians and military—is an individual duty for every Muslim who can do it in any country in which it is possible to do it, in order to liberate the al-Aqsa Mosque and the holy mosque [Mecca] from their grip, and in order for their armies to move out of all the lands of Islam, defeated and unable to threaten any Muslim. This is in accordance with the words of Almighty Allah, "and fight the pagans all together as they fight you all together," and "fight them until there is no more tumult or oppression, and there prevail justice and faith in Allah."

This is in addition to the words of Almighty Allah: "And why should ye not fight in the cause of Allah and of those who, being weak, are ill-treated (and oppressed)?—women and children, whose cry is: 'Our Lord, rescue us from this town, whose people are oppressors; and raise for us from thee one who will help!'"

We—with Allah's help—call on every Muslim who believes in Allah and wishes to be rewarded to comply with Allah's order to kill the Americans and plunder their money wherever and whenever they find it. We also call on Muslim ulema, leaders, youths, and soldiers to launch the raid on Satan's U.S. troops and the devil's supporters allying with them, and to displace those who are behind them so that they may learn a lesson.

Shaykh Usamah Bin-Muhammad Bin-Ladin

Ayman al-Zawahiri, amir of the Jihad Group in Egypt

Abu-Yasir Rifa'i Ahmad Taha, Egyptian Islamic Group

Shaykh Mir Hamzah, secretary of the Jamiat-ul-Ulema-e-Pakistan

Fazlur Rahman, amir of the Jihad Movement in Bangladesh

15

The Age of Terror

On September 11, 2001, the challenges of globalization culminated explosively. That day, nineteen al-Qaeda terrorists hijacked four civilian airliners in the United States. Using the planes as missiles on a suicide mission, with three of them they destroyed the Twin Towers of the World Trade Center in New York and a large section of the Pentagon just outside Washington, D.C.; after a struggle between passengers and terrorists, the fourth plane crashed in a field in rural Pennsylvania.

The American response was swift. In order to defeat terrorism and its state sponsors, President George W. Bush, who succeeded Bill Clinton after winning the 2000 election, authorized an invasion of Afghanistan, home to al-Qaeda's main base of operation. He also mounted a worldwide campaign, largely covert but conducted with the intelligence agencies of several other countries, to eradicate terrorist networks in North America, Europe, Africa, and Asia. At first, the so-called War on Terror and the war in Afghanistan enjoyed broad public support. But in 2002, as it became clear that the Bush administration was using 9/11 to justify an invasion of Iraq, which seemed to have no connection to al-Qaeda, the United States had to operate against fierce popular and political resistance around the world. Even several traditional U.S. allies publicly rebuked the Bush administration over Iraq and worked to prevent an invasion, while massive antiwar protests erupted across the United States and the world even before the U.S.-led invasion in March 2003.

Following a relatively straightforward invasion, Bush's difficulties grew after the United States occupied Iraq. U.S. troops and weapons inspectors could not locate any weapons of mass destruction (WMD), which had been the main justification for war. Widespread looting and lawlessness broke out in Baghdad after U.S. troops overthrew Saddam Hussein's government and police but did not step in to maintain order. Most troubling of all was the emergence of an intensely violent insurgency. The sheer diversity of the insurgency confounded occupation officials, and many Iraqis from very different sections of society opposed foreign rule: minority Sunnis who had been loyal to Saddam, majority Shiites who wanted to seize the reins of power after years of repression, and shifting coalitions of Islamic fundamentalists, al-Qaeda affiliates, and Ba'athist militants who all wanted to destroy the American-led occupation even if it meant destroying Iraq along with it. As the insurgency gained in strength and U.S. casualties grew, and with the rationale for war discredited when inspectors failed to locate any WMD stockpiles or uncover any direct evidence linking Saddam's government to the attacks of 9/11, Bush and his advisers increasingly turned to humanitarianism and democracy promotion to explain their decision to invade. A war that had initially been launched on grounds of national security had, thanks to its failings, now become an ideological crusade to remake Iraq, and in turn the Middle East.

Yet as radical as Bush's foreign policy seemed, the 9/11 attacks and wars in Afghanistan and Iraq did little to change the fundamental direction of U.S. foreign policy. Since 1989, Democrats and Republicans may have argued bitterly about how U.S. foreign policy should be implemented, but they mostly agreed on what its basic objectives should be: the spread of global free-market capitalism, free trade, and liberal democracy, all backed—and enforced, if necessary—by U.S. military power. Instead of blunting these overall objectives, the War on Terror seemed to offer the Bush administration an opportunity to pursue them with unprecedented vigor. The irony, however, was that in pursuing its goals so aggressively, the administration created profound hostility and resistance in other countries. As a result, in its search for security from terrorism and a world order more amenable to American interests and ideals, after 9/11 the United States found itself waging endless wars in the Middle East.

Document 15.1

THE NEOCONSERVATIVE MANIFESTO

Conservatives were deeply unhappy with President Bill Clinton's foreign policy. While some, such as libertarians and traditionalists, wanted retrenchment from world affairs in order to curtail the power of the federal government, others called for an even more assertive American role in the world. Neoconservatives, so called because they had once been liberals and Democrats but were now conservatives and Republicans, wedded traditional nationalism with liberal ideas about spreading justice, democracy, and liberty throughout the world. Their worldview was in many ways more similar to liberal interventionism than it was to more traditionalist conservatism. But the neoconservatives differed from liberals, too, in that they believed much more strongly in the uses of American military power, adhered unabashedly to American exceptionalism, distrusted multilateralism and international organizations such as the United Nations, and did not believe that globalization would lead humanity toward a better future. Two of the most prominent neoconservative voices were William Kristol and Robert Kagan, who published this neocon manifesto in 1996.

In a way, the current situation is reminiscent of the mid-1970s. But Ronald Reagan mounted a bold challenge to the tepid consensus of that era—a consensus that favored accommodation to and coexistence with the Soviet Union, accepted the inevitability of America's declining power, and considered any change in the status quo either too frightening or too expensive.

Proposing a controversial vision of ideological and strategic victory over the forces of international communism, Reagan called for an end to complacency in the face of the Soviet threat, large increases in defense spending, resistance to communist advances in the Third World, and greater moral clarity and purpose in U.S. foreign policy. He championed American exceptionalism when it was deeply unfashionable. Perhaps most significant, he refused to accept the limits on American power imposed by the domestic political realities that others assumed were fixed. . . .

Twenty years later, it is time once again to challenge an indifferent America and a confused American conservatism. . . . Conservatives will not be able to govern America over the long term if they fail to offer a more elevated vision of America's international role.

What should that role be? Benevolent global hegemony. Having defeated the "evil empire," the United States enjoys strategic and ideological predominance. The first objective of U.S. foreign policy should be to preserve and enhance that predominance by strengthening America's security, supporting its friends, advancing its interests, and standing up for its principles around the world. . . .

In a world in which peace and American security depend on American power and the will to use it, the main threat the United States faces now and in the future is its own weakness. American hegemony is the only reliable defense against a breakdown of peace and international order. The appropriate goal of American foreign policy, therefore, is to preserve that hegemony as far into the future as possible. To achieve this goal, the United States needs a neo-Reaganite foreign policy of military supremacy and moral confidence. . . .

American foreign policy should be informed with a clear moral purpose, based on the understanding that its moral goals and its fundamental national interests are almost always in harmony. The United States achieved its present position of strength not by practicing a foreign policy of live and let live, nor by passively waiting for threats to arise, but by actively promoting American principles of governance abroad—democracy, free markets, respect for liberty. . . . Support for American principles around the world can be sustained only by the continuing exertion of American influence.

Document 15.2

"WE WILL NOT FAIL"

Bush unveiled his response to 9/11 in a special address to a joint session of Congress on September 20. It was an unusually emotional speech that projected resolve in the face of tragedy, laid the ideological and strategic foundations for America's next three major wars—against terrorism, Afghanistan, and Iraq—and steeled Americans for a conflict of indefinite duration. More obliquely, Bush also hinted at the need to practice the dark arts of counterterrorism, tactics that would erupt in controversy a few years later.

Tonight we are a country awakened to danger and called to defend freedom. Our grief has turned to anger, and anger to resolution. Whether we bring our enemies to justice, or bring justice to our enemies, justice will be done. . . .

Americans have many questions tonight. Americans are asking: Who attacked our country? The evidence we have gathered all points to a collection of loosely affiliated terrorist organizations known as al Qaeda. They are the same murderers indicted for bombing American embassies in Tanzania and Kenya, and responsible for bombing the USS Cole.

Al Qaeda is to terror what the mafia is to crime. But its goal is not making money; its goal is remaking the world—and imposing its radical beliefs on people everywhere. . . .

The leadership of al Qaeda has great influence in Afghanistan and supports the Taliban regime in controlling most of that country. In Afghanistan, we see al Qaeda's vision for the world.

Afghanistan's people have been brutalized—many are starving and many have fled. Women are not allowed to attend school. You can be jailed for owning a television. Religion can be practiced only as their leaders dictate. A man can be jailed in Afghanistan if his beard is not long enough.

The United States respects the people of Afghanistan—after all, we are currently its largest source of humanitarian aid—but we condemn the Taliban regime. It is not only repressing its own people, it is threatening people everywhere by sponsoring and sheltering and supplying terrorists. By aiding and abetting murder, the Taliban regime is committing murder.

And tonight, the United States of America makes the following demands on the Taliban: Deliver to United States authorities all the leaders of al Qaeda who hide in your land. Release all foreign nationals, including American citizens, you have unjustly imprisoned. Protect foreign journalists, diplomats and aid workers in your country. Close immediately and permanently every terrorist training camp in Afghanistan, and hand over every terrorist, and every person in their support structure, to appropriate authorities. Give the United States full access to terrorist training camps, so we can make sure they are no longer operating.

These demands are not open to negotiation or discussion. The Taliban must act, and act immediately. They will hand over the terrorists, or they will share in their fate. . . .

Our war on terror begins with al Qaeda, but it does not end there. It will not end until every terrorist group of global reach has been found, stopped and defeated.

Americans are asking, why do they hate us? They hate what we see right here in this chamber—a democratically elected government. Their leaders are self-appointed. They hate our freedoms—our freedom of religion, our freedom of speech, our freedom to vote and assemble and disagree with each other. . . .

These terrorists kill not merely to end lives, but to disrupt and end a way of life. With every atrocity, they hope that America grows fearful, retreating from the world and forsaking our friends. They stand against us, because we stand in their way. . . .

Americans are asking: How will we fight and win this war? We will direct every resource at our command—every means of diplomacy, every tool of intelligence, every instrument of law enforcement, every financial influence, and every necessary weapon of war—to the disruption and to the defeat of the global terror network.

This war will not be like the war against Iraq a decade ago, with a decisive liberation of territory and a swift conclusion. It will not look like the air war above Kosovo two years ago, where no ground troops were used and not a single American was lost in combat.

Our response involves far more than instant retaliation and isolated strikes. Americans should not expect one battle, but a lengthy campaign, unlike any other we have ever seen. It may include dramatic strikes, visible on TV, and covert operations, secret even in success. We will starve terrorists of funding, turn them one against another, drive them from place to place, until there is no refuge or no rest. And we will pursue nations that provide aid or safe haven to terrorism. Every nation, in every region, now has a decision to make. Either you are with us, or you are with the terrorists. From this day forward, any nation that continues to harbor or support terrorism will be regarded by the United States as a hostile regime. . . .

This is not, however, just America's fight. And what is at stake is not just America's freedom. This is the world's fight. This is civilization's fight. This is the fight of all who believe in progress and pluralism, tolerance and freedom. . . .

After all that has just passed—all the lives taken, and all the possibilities and hopes that died with them—it is natural to wonder if America's future is one of fear. Some speak of an age of terror. I know there are struggles ahead, and dangers to face. But this country will define our times, not be defined by them. As long as the United States of America is determined and strong, this will not be an age of terror; this will be an age of liberty, here and across the world.

Great harm has been done to us. We have suffered great loss. And in our grief and anger we have found our mission and our moment. Freedom and fear are at war. The advance of human freedom—the great achievement of our time, and the great hope of every time—now depends on us. Our nation—this generation—will lift a dark threat of violence from our people and our future. We will rally the world to this cause by our efforts, by our courage. We will not tire, we will not falter, and we will not fail.

Document 15.3

THE WAR COUNCIL

U.S. foreign policy after 9/11 will always be linked with the Iraq War, but a push to oust Saddam Hussein was already an option during the Clinton presidency. The Clinton administration eventually attacked Iraq in December 1998, through four days of heavy bombing in an operation code-named Operation Desert Fox, but the Bush administration had more ambitious goals. Fearing further attacks, yet also seeing an opportunity to resolve a long-standing strategic issue, Bush officials quickly moved to link the 9/11 attacks to Iraq. The 9/11 Commission, a bipartisan investigative body created by Congress, published its findings in 2004. Its report included an analysis of the administration's thinking in the days and weeks following 9/11 and revealed the influential role played by the Deputy Secretary of Defense Paul Wolfowitz.

By late in the evening of September 11, the President had addressed the nation on the terrible events of the day. Vice President Cheney described the President's mood as somber. The long day was not yet over. When the larger meeting that included his domestic department heads broke up, President Bush chaired a smaller meeting of top advisers, a group he would later call his "war council." . . .

In this restricted National Security Council meeting, the President said it was a time for self-defense. The United States would punish not just the perpetrators of the attacks, but also those who harbored them. Secretary Powell said the United States had to make it clear to Pakistan, Afghanistan, and the Arab states that the time to act was now. He said we would need to build a coalition. The President noted that the attacks provided a great opportunity to engage Russia and China. Secretary Rumsfeld urged the President and the principals to think broadly about who might have harbored the attackers, including Iraq, Afghanistan, Libya, Sudan, and Iran. He wondered aloud how much evidence the United States would need in order to deal with these countries, pointing out that major strikes could take up to 60 days to assemble.

President Bush chaired two more meetings of the NSC on September 12. In the first meeting, he stressed that the United States was at war with a new and different kind of enemy. The President tasked principals to go beyond their pre-9/11 work and develop a strategy to eliminate terrorists and punish those who support them. As they worked on defining the goals and objectives of the upcoming campaign, they considered a paper that went beyond al Qaeda to propose the "elimination of terrorism as a threat to our way of life," an aim that would include pursuing other international terrorist organizations in the Middle East.

Rice chaired a Principals Committee meeting on September 13 in the Situation Room to refine how the fight against al Qaeda would be conducted. The principals agreed that the overall message should be that anyone supporting al Qaeda would risk harm. The United States would need to integrate diplomacy, financial measures, intelligence, and military actions into an overarching strategy. The principals also focused on Pakistan and what it could do to turn the Taliban against al Qaeda. They concluded that if Pakistan decided not to help the United States, it too would be at risk. . . .

President Bush had wondered immediately after the attack whether Saddam Hussein's regime might have had a hand in it. Iraq had been an enemy of the United States for 11 years, and was the only place in the world where the United States was engaged in ongoing combat operations. As a former pilot, the President was struck by the apparent sophistication of the operation and some of the piloting, especially [Hani] Hanjour's high-speed dive into the Pentagon. He told us [the 9/11 Commission] he recalled Iraqi support for Palestinian suicide terrorists as well. Speculating about other possible states that could be involved, the President told us he also thought about Iran. . . .

On the afternoon of 9/11, according to contemporaneous notes, Secretary Rumsfeld instructed General [Richard] Myers to obtain quickly as much information as possible. The notes also indicate that he told Myers that he was not simply interested in striking empty training sites. He thought the U.S. response should consider a wide range of options and possibilities. The secretary said his instinct was to hit Saddam Hussein at the same time—not only Bin Ladin. . . .

Secretary Powell recalled that Wolfowitz—not Rumsfeld—argued that Iraq was ultimately the source of the terrorist problem and should therefore be attacked. Powell said that Wolfowitz was not able to justify his belief that Iraq was behind 9/11. "Paul was always of the view that Iraq was a problem that had to be dealt with," Powell told us. "And he saw this as one way of using this event as a way to deal with the Iraq problem." Powell said that President Bush did not give Wolfowitz's argument "much weight." Though continuing to worry about Iraq in the following week, Powell said, President Bush saw Afghanistan as the priority.

Document 15.4

THE "AXIS OF EVIL"

Although some administration officials worked behind the scenes to broaden the war on terror to include Iraq within days of 9/11, Bush himself did not publicly do so until January 2002, when he identified Iran, Iraq, and North Korea as an "axis of evil."

Our nation will continue to be steadfast and patient and persistent in the pursuit of two great objectives. First, we will shut down terrorist camps, disrupt terrorist plans, and bring terrorists to justice. And, second, we must prevent the terrorists and regimes who seek chemical, biological or nuclear weapons from threatening the United States and the world. . . .

My hope is that all nations will heed our call, and eliminate the terrorist parasites who threaten their countries and our own. Many nations are acting forcefully. Pakistan is now cracking down on terror, and I admire the strong leadership of President [Pervez] Musharraf.

But some governments will be timid in the face of terror. And make no mistake about it: If they do not act, America will.

Our second goal is to prevent regimes that sponsor terror from threatening America or our friends and allies with weapons of mass destruction. Some of these regimes have been pretty quiet since September the 11th. But we know their true nature. North Korea is a regime arming with missiles and weapons of mass destruction, while starving its citizens.

Iran aggressively pursues these weapons and exports terror, while an unelected few repress the Iranian people's hope for freedom.

Iraq continues to flaunt its hostility toward America and to support terror. The Iraqi regime has plotted to develop anthrax, and nerve gas, and nuclear weapons for over a decade. This is a regime that has already used poison gas to murder thousands of its own citizens—leaving the bodies of mothers huddled over their dead children. This is a regime that agreed to international inspections—then kicked out the inspectors. This is a regime that has something to hide from the civilized world.

States like these, and their terrorist allies, constitute an axis of evil, arming to threaten the peace of the world. By seeking weapons of mass destruction, these regimes pose a grave and growing danger. They could provide these arms to terrorists, giving them the means to match their hatred. They could attack our allies or attempt to blackmail the United States. In any of these cases, the price of indifference would be catastrophic.

We will work closely with our coalition to deny terrorists and their state sponsors the materials, technology, and expertise to make and deliver weapons of mass destruction. We will develop and deploy effective missile defenses to protect America and our allies from sudden attack. And all nations should know: America will do what is necessary to ensure our nation's security. . . .

The last time I spoke here, I expressed the hope that life would return to normal. In some ways, it has. In others, it never will. Those of us who have lived through these challenging times have been changed by them. We've come to know truths that we will never question: evil is real, and it must be opposed. . . .

In a single instant, we realized that this will be a decisive decade in the history of liberty, that we've been called to a unique role in human events. Rarely has the world faced a choice more clear or consequential.

Document 15.5

A GRAND STRATEGY

Almost exactly a year after 9/11, in September 2002 the Bush administration released its National Security Strategy (NSS). Presidential administrations frequently offer such overarching statements—they are required by Congress to do so—but rarely has such a document been as revealing, or as politically important, as this one in 2002. As a "grand strategy" for the age of terror, it purported to map out a future for both America's role in the world and how the world system itself would function. Most important, the NSS outlined a radical new version of the strategy of "preemption," a controversial idea first articulated in 2002 by Bush in a speech at West Point in June and Vice President Dick Cheney in a speech before the Veterans of Foreign Wars in August of that year.

The United States possesses unprecedented—and unequaled—strength and influence in the world. Sustained by faith in the principles of liberty, and the value of a free society, this position comes with unparalleled responsibilities, obligations, and opportunity. The great strength of this nation must be used to promote a balance of power that favors freedom.

For most of the twentieth century, the world was divided by a great struggle over ideas: destructive totalitarian visions versus freedom and equality.

That great struggle is over. The militant visions of class, nation, and race which promised utopia and delivered misery have been defeated and discredited. America is now threatened less by conquering states than we are by failing ones. We are menaced less by fleets and armies than by catastrophic technologies in the hands of the embittered few. We must defeat these threats to our Nation, allies, and friends.

This is also a time of opportunity for America. We will work to translate this moment of influence into decades of peace, prosperity, and liberty. The U.S. national security strategy will be based on a distinctly American internationalism that reflects the union of our values and our national interests. The aim of this strategy is to help make the world not just safer but better. Our goals on the path to progress are clear: political and economic freedom, peaceful relations with other states, and respect for human dignity....

In the 1990s we witnessed the emergence of a small number of rogue states that, while different in important ways, share a number of attributes. These states:

- brutalize their own people and squander their national resources for the personal gain of the rulers;
- display no regard for international law, threaten their neighbors, and callously violate international treaties to which they are party;
- are determined to acquire weapons of mass destruction, along with other advanced military technology, to be used as threats or offensively to achieve the aggressive designs of these regimes;
- sponsor terrorism around the globe; and
- reject basic human values and hate the United States and everything for which it stands....

We must be prepared to stop rogue states and their terrorist clients before they are able to threaten or use weapons of mass destruction against the United States and our allies and friends. Our response must take full advantage of strengthened alliances, the establishment of new partnerships with former adversaries, innovation in the use of military forces, modern technologies, including the development of an effective missile defense system, and increased emphasis on intelligence collection and analysis....

Traditional concepts of deterrence will not work against a terrorist enemy whose avowed tactics are wanton destruction and the targeting of innocents; whose so-called soldiers seek martyrdom in death and whose most potent protection is statelessness. The overlap between states that sponsor terror and those that pursue WMD compels us to action.

For centuries, international law recognized that nations need not suffer an attack before they can lawfully take action to defend themselves against forces that present an imminent danger of attack. Legal scholars and international jurists often conditioned the legitimacy of preemption on the existence of an imminent threat—most often a visible mobilization of armies, navies, and air forces preparing to attack.

We must adapt the concept of imminent threat to the capabilities and objectives of today's adversaries. Rogue states and terrorists do not seek to attack us using conventional means. They know such attacks would fail. Instead, they rely on acts of terror and, potentially, the use of weapons of mass destruction—weapons that can be easily concealed, delivered covertly, and used without warning.

The targets of these attacks are our military forces and our civilian population, in direct violation of one of the principal norms of the law of warfare. As was demonstrated by the losses on September 11, 2001, mass civilian casualties is the specific objective of terrorists and these losses would be exponentially more severe if terrorists acquired and used weapons of mass destruction.

The United States has long maintained the option of preemptive actions to counter a sufficient threat to our national security. The greater the threat, the greater is the risk of inaction—and the more compelling the case for taking anticipatory action to defend ourselves, even if uncertainty remains as to the time and place of the enemy's attack. To forestall or prevent such hostile acts by our adversaries, the United States will, if necessary, act preemptively.

The United States will not use force in all cases to preempt emerging threats, nor should nations use preemption as a pretext for aggression. Yet in an age where the enemies of civilization openly and actively seek the world's most destructive technologies, the United States cannot remain idle while dangers gather.

Document 15.6

DEMOCRACY'S PROMISE

As pressure mounted for an invasion of Iraq, and as U.S. troops deployed to the Middle East, the Bush administration emphasized security: Saddam Hussein possessed weapons of mass destruction and intended to use them against the United States and its allies. But the administration also made another argument, albeit less frequently, based on promoting democracy in a region dominated by autocrats: if the United States could help establish a stable democracy in the heart of the Muslim Middle East, the thinking went, it would transform the entire region and initiate an era of peace. Here, in a speech shortly before the invasion, Bush outlined his vision for a new Iraq and a new Middle East.

The current Iraqi regime has shown the power of tyranny to spread discord and violence in the Middle East. A liberated Iraq can show the power of freedom to transform that vital region, by bringing hope and progress into the lives of millions. America's interests in security, and

America's belief in liberty, both lead in the same direction: to a free and peaceful Iraq.

The first to benefit from a free Iraq would be the Iraqi people, themselves. Today they live in scarcity and fear, under a dictator who has brought them nothing but war, and misery, and torture. Their lives and their freedom matter little to Saddam Hussein—but Iraqi lives and freedom matter greatly to us. . . .

Rebuilding Iraq will require a sustained commitment from many nations, including our own: we will remain in Iraq as long as necessary, and not a day more. America has made and kept this kind of commitment before—in the peace that followed a world war. After defeating enemies, we did not leave behind occupying armies, we left constitutions and parliaments. We established an atmosphere of safety, in which responsible, reform-minded local leaders could build lasting institutions of freedom. In societies that once bred fascism and militarism, liberty found a permanent home.

There was a time when many said that the cultures of Japan and Germany were incapable of sustaining democratic values. Well, they were wrong. Some say the same of Iraq today. They are mistaken. The nation of Iraq—with its proud heritage, abundant resources and skilled and educated people—is fully capable of moving toward democracy and living in freedom.

The world has a clear interest in the spread of democratic values, because stable and free nations do not breed the ideologies of murder. They encourage the peaceful pursuit of a better life. And there are hopeful signs of a desire for freedom in the Middle East. Arab intellectuals have called on Arab governments to address the "freedom gap" so their peoples can fully share in the progress of our times. Leaders in the region speak of a new Arab charter that champions internal reform, greater politics participation, economic openness, and free trade. And from Morocco to Bahrain and beyond, nations are taking genuine steps toward politics reform. A new regime in Iraq would serve as a dramatic and inspiring example of freedom for other nations in the region. . . .

Success in Iraq could also begin a new stage for Middle Eastern peace, and set in motion progress towards a truly democratic Palestinian state. The passing of Saddam Hussein's regime will deprive terrorist networks of a wealthy patron that pays for terrorist training, and offers rewards to families of suicide bombers. And other regimes will be given a clear warning that support for terror will not be tolerated. . . .

We go forward with confidence, because we trust in the power of human freedom to change lives and nations. By the resolve and purpose of America, and of our friends and allies, we will make this an age of progress and liberty. Free people will set the course of history, and free people will keep the peace of the world.

Document 15.7

DEMOCRACY'S PARADOX

The Bush administration was confident that the war would free the Iraqi people from the rule of a tyrant; on the eve of the invasion, for example, Vice President Cheney claimed that U.S. troops would be "greeted as liberators." It did not quite turn out that way, and even groups who had suffered terribly under Saddam Hussein's rule, such as the majority Shiites, resisted the American occupation of their country. In the cartoon below, Tom Toles, an editorial cartoonist at the Washington Post, *captured the painful irony of promoting democracy to a people who did not necessarily want it or appreciate the efforts of the Americans who promoted it.*

DOCUMENT 15.8

"DODGY DOSSIERS"

As we saw in chapter 14, America's strongest partner in the new world order was Great Britain—particularly its prime minister, Tony Blair. Blair was an early convert to the belief that only an invasion of Iraq could solve the region's problems and reduce international insecurity. However, since British public opinion remained skeptical about Blair's case for action against Iraq, in September 2002 and February 2003 the Labour Party government released official dossiers that highlighted the ways in which Iraq presented a clear and present danger. Supposedly based on high-grade secret intelligence, these dossiers claimed that Iraq had reconstituted its nuclear weapons program and could launch a surprise WMD attack with only a forty-five-minute advance warning time. It later turned out that these and several other high-profile claims by the Bush administration and Blair government (which often worked in tandem) were either gross exaggerations of credible intelligence or assertions based on discredited or unverifiable sources. In the end, none turned out to be true. In 2004, public and political pressure led to the creation of an official inquiry, headed by Lord Butler of Brockwell, to investigate what the British press dubbed the "dodgy dossiers." This excerpt from the Butler Inquiry's report, based largely on Blair's own testimony, explains why the British government went to such lengths to paint Saddam Hussein's Iraq as an imminent threat.

The Prime Minister told us that, even before the attacks of 11 September 2001, his concern in this area was increasingly causing him to examine more proactive policy options. He also described to us the way in which the events of 11 September 2001 led him to conclude that policy had to change. He and other witnesses told us of the impact on policy-making of the changed calculus of threat that emerged from those attacks—of the risk of unconventional weapons in due course becoming available to terrorists and extremists seeking to cause mass casualties unconstrained by the fear of alienating their supporters or the public, or by considerations of personal safety. The Prime Minister's view was that a stand had to be taken, and a more active policy put in place to prevent the continuing development and proliferation of nuclear, biological and chemical weapons and technology in breach of the will of the international community. . . .

The Government's conclusion in the spring of 2002 that stronger action (although not necessarily military action) needed to be taken to enforce Iraqi disarmament was not based on any new development in the current intelligence picture on Iraq. In his evidence to us, the Prime Minister endorsed the view expressed at the time that what had changed was not the pace of Iraq's prohibited weapons programmes, which had not been dramatically stepped up, but tolerance of them following the attacks of 11 September 2001. When the Government concluded that action going beyond the previous policy of containment needed to be taken, there were many grounds for concern arising from Iraq's past record and behaviour. There was a clear view that, to be successful, any new action to enforce Iraqi compliance with its disarmament obligations would need to be backed with the credible threat of force. But there was no recent intelligence that would itself have given rise to a conclusion that Iraq was of more immediate concern than the activities of some other countries.

Other factors clearly influenced the decision to focus on Iraq. The Prime Minister told us that, whilst on some perspectives the activities of other states might be seen as posing more direct challenges to British interests, the Government, as well as being influenced by the concerns of the US Government, saw a need for immediate action on Iraq because of the wider historical and international context, especially Iraq's perceived continuing challenge to the authority of the United Nations. The Government also saw in the United Nations and a decade of Security Council Resolutions a basis for action through the United Nations to enforce Iraqi compliance with its disarmament obligations.

The Government considered in March 2002 two options for achieving the goal of Iraqi disarmament—a toughening of the existing containment policy; and regime change by military means. Ministers were advised that, if regime change was the chosen policy, only the use of overriding force in a ground campaign would achieve the removal of Saddam Hussein and Iraq's re-integration with the international community. Officials noted that regime change of itself had no basis in international law; and that any offensive military action against Iraq could only be justified if Iraq were held to be in breach of its disarmament obligations under United Nations Security Council Resolution 687 or some new resolution. Officials also noted that for the five Permanent Members of the Security Council and the majority of the 15 members of the Council to take the view that Iraq was in breach of its obligations under Resolution 687, they would need to be convinced that Iraq was in breach of its obligations; that such proof would need to be incontrovertible and of large-scale activity; but that the intelligence then available was insufficiently robust to meet that criterion.

Document 15.9

THE MORAL MAZE

Further complications awaited the United States. The Bush administration claimed that the wars on terror and in Afghanistan and Iraq were fought in order to safeguard liberty as well as American security. But in doing so, the U.S. government began employing tactics that were widely considered either illegal or unethical. Terrorists broke the basic rules of warfare, argued the proponents of aggressive tactics such as torture and "extraordinary rendition"—seizing persons and secretly removing them from one country in order to move them to another, often for the purposes of "enhanced interrogation." In many cases, American officials relied on methods such as "waterboarding," which simulated the sensation of drowning. Such practices began coming to light in the spring of 2004, when U.S. military police at Abu Ghraib Prison outside Baghdad were discovered to be using torture to secure information from suspected al-Qaeda terrorists and Saddam loyalists. One of their techniques involved the wiring of a hooded prisoner; although the wires were not live, the prisoners thought they were and that they were about to be electrocuted. This editorial cartoon by Nick Anderson highlights how revelations of torture undermined America's claim to the protector of democracy and human rights.

Document 15.10

THE VIEW FROM BAGHDAD

With the U.S.-led Coalition Provisional Authority (CPA) now the governing authority in Baghdad, Iraqis contemplated life without Saddam Hussein for the first time in decades. Anthony Shadid, a Pulitzer Prize–winning reporter for the Washington Post, *was born in Oklahoma to Lebanese immigrants; as an English and Arabic speaker, he had a unique perspective on Iraqi life after the invasion. He lived in Baghdad in 2003 and 2004 and had easy access into the lives of ordinary Iraqis. In this excerpt from his book* Night Draws Near, *Shadid relates the story of Fuad and Suad Mohammed, a married couple who represented the divisions within Iraq about both Saddam Hussein and the United States.*

Fuad looked out the window, which like most glass in Baghdad was covered by tape. There was little respite from the war that day—neither in Mansur nor the rest of Baghdad. "All the time, boom, boom, boom," he said, in a tone of patient observation.

Unsolicited, his grievances poured out, as if the moment and the isolation had made bold talk more permissible. He despised the government, he said, and didn't understand why Saddam would not step down, "for the sake of his people and the sake of his country." A Shiite Muslim, Fuad listed the crimes of his government—exiling tens of thousands of his fellow Shiites to Iran, its brutal rule, eight years of war, and, of course, the invasion of Kuwait. Iraq's resources and wealth had been squandered, he said, and its people deprived, spiritually and materially. With a sense of nostalgia, he recalled what he made forty years ago as a doctor: eighty dinars a month, the equivalent of $350. Today, he told me, doctors' salaries were no more than a few dollars a month. His own pension, after a thirty-two year career, was about ten dollars every three months, and he was among the better off. And now, with a long life behind him, he had to brace for a battle over Baghdad that many, in private moments, believed was suicidal, orchestrated by Saddam's vanity.

"We hate this person," Fuad said matter-of-factly. "We want him off us. He's not only a dictator, but he's given nothing to the people." He stopped for a moment, glancing at the pictures of his children and his grandchildren lining the wall, then repeated himself and shook his head. "They hate him. Even the soldiers, they hate him. We've had enough. Really, we've had enough." . . .

Across town, Fuad . . . was reveling in what seemed to him a hopeful moment. His wife, Suad, had returned from Beirut, where she had spent the war with relatives. . . . This was my first time seeing Fuad since the government's collapse, and he was jubilant. "There's victory! There's victory!" he proclaimed. "All of us are reborn again." With familiar exuberance, his optimism untempered, he threw out his arms and raised them toward the ceiling, provoking the smiles of those around him. In the same breath, he dismissed the naysayers as inveterate pessimists, still stumbling before Saddam's shadow even with the dictator gone.

Lines for gas snaked along the streets, even in Fuad's wealthy neighborhood of Mansur, and his home was still cloaked in dark, as it had been during the bombing. But Fuad, far more avuncular than on our previous visit, seemed unscathed. He reclined on his sofa, never losing his smile. He was reassuring; at times, he even seemed giddy.

America? "I call it my government," Fuad boasted.

Bush? "From the bottom of my heart, I really respect, I adore this man, more than you," he declared. "I have a new birth certificate from the tenth of April."

"Don't talk to him," said his wife, Suad, shaking her head. "He's an American."

An effervescent woman with a sharp wit, Suad was as skeptical as Fuad was optimistic: they occupied the positions that shaped the two most familiar ends of the spectrum of opinion toward the aftermath. . . .

Leaning forward in her chair, she described her return to Baghdad after the war. She recalled the charred hulks of cars wrecked in the fighting, the scars of bombings, the wounds from looting, and a city left dark at night. Nobody was out after nine p.m. "It was horrible," she remembered. "I cried, I cried."

Fuad listened, then spoke again, seemingly at random.

"People think the Americans can do everything," he said.

"Not everything! Not everything!" Suad retorted, her frustration growing. "Just the electricity. Sick people, newborn babies. I'm not talking about myself. Telephones. We haven't got any telephones. We have to go outside. Bring mobiles. Why can't they bring mobiles?"

"People want everything at once," Fuad answered.

"This is just simple electricity," she said to him sharply. "We can't call our daughters. We have to cross the bridge to Jadriya to talk to them."

Fuad nodded. He would not be persuaded, even if he was still listening. . . . "As long as America is here, everything will be better, and the future will be brighter."

"Fuad, you say this, but the people don't," his wife said, shaking her head. "The people can't accept it. This is not me. This is the people."

"The people?" he countered. "What do the people want? They want to be happier. They want luxury. For thirty-five years, we didn't get any benefit. What did he do for Baghdad? He did nothing. Thirty-five years." He dragged out the last words, in a voice that suggested a lifetime lost.

Suad paused, looking down. "I don't like Saddam," she said. "But if Saddam were here, he would fix the telephones in two months. I don't say Saddam is good, but . . ." She left the sentence unfinished and shrugged her shoulders.

"They will bring new telephones in one month," Fuad said. "Of course, they will."

As the conversation ended, Suad laughed and looked at her husband, then turned to me. "Take him to America!" she said, flipping her hand dismissively.

Document 15.11

OCCUPATION AND ITS DISCONTENTS

Even the war's staunchest supporters conceded that the occupation of Iraq did not go according to plan. The Defense Department, particularly its Office of Special Plans, had predicted a smooth occupation in which Iraqis would cooperate with Americans in building a new Iraq. In 2002, Kenneth Adelman, an adviser to Secretary of Defense Donald Rumsfeld, had even predicted the invasion and occupation would be "a cakewalk." But others, such as the State Department's Future of Iraq Project and a major Council on Foreign Relations study, had more accurately foreseen the difficulties that quickly bedeviled American plans. In this excerpt from his account of his time working in Baghdad, Larry Diamond, a professor at Stanford University and a leading authority on global democracy, expressed his feelings on why the Bush administration's hopes for Iraq had failed.

We never listened carefully to the Iraqi people, or to the figures in the country that they respected. We never won their trust and confidence. We failed to move with the necessary dispatch to transfer power to an Iraqi interim government, chosen through an acceptable, consultative process that could have been mediated by the United Nations. We did not give the world body the kind of role that could have spared us from many mistakes, and from being perceived as an occupying power, until we ran into serious difficulty with our own plans—and by then it was too little, too late. Against the advice of most experts on Iraq and the region, we dissolved the Iraqi Army, purged from public life a broad swath of the existing elite, and indeed wound up alienating and marginalizing a whole section of the country—the best organized and best armed—until a series of readjustments that were, again, too little, too late. Against the advice of most people who knew Iraq well (including the politicians in exile with whom we had been working), and flying in the face of a proud and defiant national history that we barely studied, we established ourselves as an occupying power in every respect and so ensured that we would face a dedicated, violent resistance—without enough troops to cope.

As a result, an organized resistance emerged—as the UN mission had warned that it would—undermining postwar reconstruction at every turn. Electricity grids could not be revived, oil facilities could not be repaired, reconstruction jobs could not be commissioned, supplies could not be delivered, civil society could not organize, and a transition to democracy could not move forward because of the pervasive terrorist, criminal, and insurgent violence. America was simply overmatched in a postwar conflict for which it was grossly unprepared. . . .

The largely unilateral rush to war created predictable problems from the outset. But I now believe that the truly cardinal sin was going to war so unprepared for the postwar—despite all the detailed warnings to which the administration had access. . . .

Imagine that a person was about to go on a long car ride, took his car into a mechanic, and said, "Get me ready quickly for this long trip." Then the mechanic called back and said, "I am working on it, but your brake linings are gone—you really must have new brakes." And the driver said, "Forget it. There's no time and money for that. Just change the fluids and give me the car." Then imagine that the driver plowed through a crosswalk because he couldn't stop his car, and killed several children. His actions would be considered gross, criminal negligence, punishable under the law. . . . There are laws against individuals and corporations who take grossly negligent actions. There are no laws—and there probably cannot be—against negligence, however gross, on the part of government officials at the highest level. But in the broader calculus of moral responsibility, which is the greater offense?

Document 15.12

"AMERICA'S VITAL INTERESTS AND OUR DEEPEST BELIEFS ARE NOW ONE"

When U.S. forces did not find any WMDs in Iraq, this failure not only embarrassed the Bush administration but also removed its primary justification for war. As a result, security concerns faded from American rhetoric and were replaced by arguments about democracy promotion, as seen here in Bush's second Inaugural Address in 2005. Bush was tapping into an old concept in American foreign policy, one that had been first articulated by Woodrow Wilson and Franklin D. Roosevelt: that the protection of morality and interests were inseparable, and that the spread of American values was the best way to ensure U.S. security.

At this second gathering, our duties are defined not by the words I use, but by the history we have seen together. For a half century, America defended our own freedom by standing watch on distant borders. After the shipwreck of communism came years of relative quiet, years of repose, years of sabbatical—and then there came a day of fire.

We have seen our vulnerability—and we have seen its deepest source. For as long as whole regions of the world simmer in resentment and tyranny—prone to ideologies that feed hatred and excuse murder—violence will gather, and multiply in destructive power, and cross the most defended borders, and raise a mortal threat. There is only one force of history that can break the reign of hatred and resentment, and expose the pretensions of tyrants, and reward the hopes of the decent and tolerant, and that is the force of human freedom.

We are led, by events and common sense, to one conclusion: The survival of liberty in our land increasingly depends on the success of liberty in other lands. The best hope for peace in our world is the expansion of freedom in all the world.

America's vital interests and our deepest beliefs are now one. From the day of our Founding, we have proclaimed that every man and woman on this earth has rights, and dignity, and matchless value, because they bear the image of the Maker of Heaven and earth. Across the generations we have proclaimed the imperative of self-government, because no one is fit to be a master, and no one deserves to be a slave. Advancing these ideals is the mission that created our Nation. It is the honorable achievement of our fathers. Now it is the urgent requirement of our nation's security, and the calling of our time.

So it is the policy of the United States to seek and support the growth of democratic movements and institutions in every nation and culture, with the ultimate goal of ending tyranny in our world.

Document 15.13

NO BLOOD FOR OIL

Even before the invasion in 2003, the Bush administration encountered popular resistance in the United States and around the world. Antiwar protests were the largest since the Vietnam era. Critics pointed out that many administration officials had ties to large energy corporations and charged that Bush had invaded Iraq at their behest. This idea gave rise to the most common antiwar refrain, "No blood for oil." Undeterred, in his 2007 State of the Union address, Bush announced a "surge" of twenty thousand additional U.S. troops to Iraq in an effort to mount bigger counterinsurgency operations. Prompted by the death of his son, who had been serving in Iraq, Andrew J. Bacevich, a Vietnam veteran, professor of history and international relations at Boston University, and outspoken critic of Bush's foreign policy, touched on all these themes in this 2007 newspaper op-ed.

As a citizen, I have tried since Sept. 11, 2001, to promote a critical understanding of U.S. foreign policy. I know that even now, people of good will find much to admire in Bush's response to that awful day. They applaud his doctrine of preventive war. They endorse his crusade to spread democracy across the Muslim world and to eliminate tyranny from the face of the Earth. They insist not only that his decision to invade Iraq in 2003 was correct but that the war there can still be won. Some—the members of the "the-surge-is-already-working" school of thought—even profess to see victory just over the horizon.

I believe that such notions are dead wrong and doomed to fail. In books, articles and op-ed pieces, in talks to audiences large and small, I have said as much. "The long war is an unwinnable one," I wrote in this section of the *Washington Post* in August 2005. "The United States needs to liquidate its presence in Iraq, placing the onus on Iraqis to decide their fate and creating the space for other regional powers to assist in brokering a political settlement. We've done all that we can do."

Not for a second did I expect my own efforts to make a difference. But I did nurse the hope that my voice might combine with those of others—teachers, writers, activists and ordinary folks—to educate the public about the folly of the course on which the nation has embarked. I hoped that those efforts might produce a political climate conducive to change. I genuinely believed that if the people spoke, our leaders in Washington would listen and respond.

This, I can now see, was an illusion.

The people have spoken, and nothing of substance has changed. The November 2006 midterm elections signified an unambiguous repudiation of the policies that landed us in our present predicament. But half a year later, the war continues, with no end in sight. Indeed, by sending more troops to Iraq (and by extending the tours of those, like my son, who were already there), Bush has signaled his complete disregard for what was once quaintly referred to as "the will of the people."

To be fair, responsibility for the war's continuation now rests no less with the Democrats who control Congress than with the president and his party. After my son's death, my state's senators, Edward M. Kennedy and John F. Kerry, telephoned to express their condolences. Stephen F. Lynch, our congressman, attended my son's wake. Kerry was present for the funeral Mass. My family and I greatly appreciated such gestures. But when I suggested to each of them the necessity of ending the war, I got the brushoff. More accurately, after ever so briefly pretending to listen, each treated me to a convoluted explanation that said in essence: Don't blame me.

To whom do Kennedy, Kerry and Lynch listen? We know the answer: to the same people who have the ear of George W. Bush and Karl Rove—namely, wealthy individuals and institutions.

Money buys access and influence. Money greases the process that will yield us a new president in 2008. When it comes to Iraq, money ensures that the concerns of big business, big oil, bellicose evangelicals and Middle East allies gain a hearing. By comparison, the lives of U.S. soldiers figure as an afterthought.

Memorial Day orators will say that a G.I.'s life is priceless. Don't believe it. I know what value the U.S. government assigns to a soldier's life: I've been handed the check. It's roughly what the Yankees will pay Roger Clemens per inning once he starts pitching next month.

Money maintains the Republican/Democratic duopoly of trivialized politics. It confines the debate over U.S. policy to well-hewn channels. It preserves intact the clichés of 1933–45 about isolationism, appeasement and the nation's call to "global leadership." It inhibits any serious accounting of exactly how much our misadventure in Iraq is costing. It ignores completely the question of who actually pays. It negates democracy, rendering free speech little more than a means of recording dissent.

This is not some great conspiracy. It's the way our system works.

Document 15.14

THE LONG WAR CONTINUES

America's struggle in the Middle East became a series of wars without end that consumed U.S. resources with little prospect of victory. Bush left office in 2009 with the conflicts in Iraq and Afghanistan still raging and was succeeded by Barack Obama. Although he was a Democrat who had opposed the Iraq War, Obama continued, and even escalated, many of Bush's policies. Obama used unmanned aerial drone strikes against overseas terrorist targets with greater frequency and in 2009 announced a surge of thirty thousand additional troops to fight the war in Afghanistan. Obama's foreign policies disappointed many of those who had expected him to chart a new path away from the perceived excesses of the Bush era. The Nobel Institute in Oslo, which awards the annual Nobel Peace Prize, typified those hopes when it awarded Obama the prize for 2009. But in his acceptance speech, Obama carefully explained why he did not believe an era of perpetual peace was necessarily at hand.

[P]erhaps the most profound issue surrounding my receipt of this prize is the fact that I am the Commander-in-Chief of the military of a nation in the midst of two wars. One of these wars is winding down. The other is a conflict that America did not seek; one in which we are joined by 42 other countries—including Norway—in an effort to defend ourselves and all nations from further attacks.

Still, we are at war, and I'm responsible for the deployment of thousands of young Americans to battle in a distant land. Some will kill, and some will be killed. And so I come here with an acute sense of the costs of armed conflict—filled with difficult questions about the relationship between war and peace, and our effort to replace one with the other. . . .

I do not bring with me today a definitive solution to the problems of war. What I do know is that meeting these challenges will require the same vision, hard work, and persistence of those men and women who acted so boldly decades ago. And it will require us to think in new ways about the notions of just war and the imperatives of a just peace.

We must begin by acknowledging the hard truth: We will not eradicate violent conflict in our lifetimes. There will be times when nations—acting individually or in concert—will find the use of force not only necessary but morally justified.

I make this statement mindful of what Martin Luther King Jr. said in this same ceremony years ago: "Violence never brings permanent peace. It solves no social problem: it merely creates new and more complicated ones." As someone who stands here as a direct consequence of Dr. King's life work, I am living testimony to the moral force of non-violence. I know there's nothing weak—nothing passive—nothing naïve—in the creed and lives of Gandhi and King.

But as a head of state sworn to protect and defend my nation, I cannot be guided by their examples alone. I face the world as it is, and cannot stand idle in the face of threats to the American people. For make no mistake: Evil does exist in the world. A non-violent movement could not have halted Hitler's armies. Negotiations cannot convince al Qaeda's leaders to lay down their arms. To say that force may sometimes be necessary is not a call to cynicism—it is a recognition of history; the imperfections of man and the limits of reason.

16

The Liberal Order in Crisis

Barack Obama hoped to shift the regional focus of American foreign policy away from Europe and the Middle East and toward Asia instead, but his overall policy aims fit neatly with his post-1945 predecessors. Atop his list sat American leadership. The postwar international system of alliances and market integration, however damaged by the economic fallout of the Great Recession and Washington's troubled War on Terror, remained the best means of securing peace and stability. That system worked best, he believed, when the United States thoughtfully and judiciously deployed its power in line with, or at least not in opposition to, its allies. It failed when Americans didn't listen or acted rashly and unilaterally.

American foreign policy changed once Obama left office in 2017, in part due to ongoing changes within the international system, but more substantially when Donald J. Trump became the nation's forty-fifth president. Trump was unusual and planned to govern that way. A celebrity and businessman, before winning the White House in 2016 he had never won elected office, served in the military, or held any government post. This dearth of experience was part of his appeal. America was broken, he said, and needed new leadership. "It's time to shake the rust off America's foreign policy," he campaigned. "It's time to invite new voices and new visions into the fold."

Why? Because, Trump said, since the end of the Cold War American leaders had been "a complete and total disaster," in his words possessing "No vision. No purpose. No direction. No strategy." Past leaders had failed to control the southern border with Mexico, ballooned the national debt, and squandered American blood and treasure in pointless wars. They had also put a middle-class lifestyle out of reach for vast numbers of native-born Americans, especially those without higher education, who increasingly felt out of place—or out of privilege—in a country that was less white, statistically speaking, than at any time since the eighteenth century. Conservative religious groups and nationalists each found reason to back Trump, who argued that since the culture wars of the 1960s and the economic malaise of the 1970s, the nation had lost its way. It was time to "make America great again," he said.

"Great" was not in fact that promise's key word. It was, instead, "again." The United States of America had been better in the past, Trump argued, and under his leadership would reclaim the greatness that was every real American's birthright. Enthralled by globalism, corrupted by personal gain, incompetent, or perhaps

never too patriotic in the first place, Republicans and Democrats alike had forgotten the fundamental purpose of foreign policy, Trump said, which was to put "America first." The challenges he had inherited, he asserted, "really showed what previous mistakes were made over many years—and even decades—by other administrations." But "the one common thread behind all these problems was a failure to protect and promote the interests of the American people and American workers."

Trump governed for a single term. Twice impeached, he was the only president in more than a generation to lose his reelection bid, and the only one in the country's long history to refuse a peaceful handover of power to his successor. This relatively short tenure complicates any assessment of his short- and long-term impact on the broad trajectory of American foreign affairs. Just as Trump rejected nearly every policy objective close to his predecessor's heart, so too did his own successor promise a rejection of his own. "America is back," Joe Biden said soon after replacing Trump. "We will repair our alliances and engage with the world once again," beginning by rejoining international climate accords from which Trump had pulled the United States early in his tenure, and by reassuring nervous allies in Asia and Europe that the promise of American security offered since 1945 remained intact. The past four years, Biden claimed, were nothing more than a blip and an anomaly.

The rest of the world had good reason to question Biden's claim, especially as challenges to the post–World War II international order appeared to mount. The number of democratic states in the world retreated during the 2010s for the first time since the Cold War's end; uneven economic development and population growth destabilized large swaths of Asia, Africa, and Latin America; and global climate change offered an omnipresent fear for those who believed it was occurring. Trump was hardly the first American politician to question whether the supposed benefits of American international leadership were worth the cost, but internationalists had largely held sway since 1945. Perhaps, as the twenty-first century's second decade ended, the world was left to wonder if the persistent forces of nationalism, isolationism, and authoritarianism that had always colored political debate in Washington had finally managed to flip the script for good.

Document 16.1

LEADING FROM BEHIND

As president, Barack Obama faced a range of challenges, some new and emerging but others a revival of older problems. After dealing with the global financial crisis of 2008–2009, which had both domestic and international dimensions, Obama's overall task was to come up with a coherent grand strategy that would distinguish his foreign policy from George W. Bush's "war on terror" while also putting his own philosophical stamp on American engagement with the world. The difficulty was that Obama's foreign policy instincts were more pragmatic than ideological, and more in tune with recognizing the limits of American power than declaring bold ambitions. This New Yorker *article, about the Obama administration's internal debates over how to respond to the 2011 revolution in Libya, illustrates just how tortuous the strategic process really was.*

The debate then narrowed to whether the United States and others should intervene militarily. The principal option was to set up a no-fly zone to prevent Libyan planes from attacking the protest movement, which had quickly turned into a full-scale rebellion based in the eastern half of the country. The decision about intervention in Libya was an unusually clear choice between interests and values. "Of all the countries in the region there, our real interests in Libya are minimal," Brent Scowcroft told me. For a President whose long-term goal was to extricate the U.S. from Middle East conflicts, it was an especially vexing debate.

Within the Administration, Robert Gates, the Defense Secretary, was the most strenuous opponent of establishing a no-fly zone, or any other form of military intervention. Like Scowcroft, Gates objected to intervention because he did not think it was in the United States' vital interest. He also pointed out a fact that many people didn't seem to understand: the first step in creating a no-fly zone would be to bomb the Libyan air defenses. [Secretary of State Hillary] Clinton disagreed with him and argued the case for intervention with Obama. It was the first major issue on which she and Gates had different views.

The days leading up to Obama's decision were perplexing to outsiders. American Presidents usually lead the response to world crises, but Obama seemed to stay hidden that week. From the outside, it looked as though the French were dragging him into the conflict. On March 14th, Clinton arrived in Paris, but she had no firm decision to convey. According to a French official, when Clinton met with President Nicolas Sarkozy she declined to endorse the no-fly zone, which Sarkozy interpreted as American reluctance to do anything. "We started to wonder where, exactly, the Administration was going," the official said. . . .

The one consistent thread running through most of Obama's decisions has been that America must act humbly in the world. Unlike his immediate predecessors, Obama came of age politically during the post–Cold War era, a time when America's unmatched power created widespread resentment. Obama believes that highly visible American leadership can taint a foreign-policy goal just as easily as it can bolster it. In 2007, Obama said, "America must show—through deeds as well as words—that we stand with those who seek a better life. That child looking up at the helicopter must see America and feel hope."

In 2009 and early 2010, Obama was sometimes criticized for not acting at all. He was cautious during Iran's Green Revolution and deferential to his generals during the review of Afghanistan strategy. But his response to the Arab Spring has been bolder. He broke with Mubarak at a point when some of the older establishment advised against it. In Libya, he overruled Gates and his military advisers and pushed our allies to adopt a broad and risky intervention. It is too early to know the consequences of these decisions. Libya appears to be entering a protracted civil war; American policy toward Mubarak frightened—and irritated—Saudi Arabia, where instability could send oil prices soaring. The U.S. keeps getting stuck in the Middle East.

Nonetheless, Obama may be moving toward something resembling a doctrine. One of his advisers described the President's actions in Libya as "leading from behind." That's not a slogan designed for signs at the 2012 Democratic Convention, but it does accurately describe the balance that Obama now seems to be finding. It's a different definition of leadership than America is known for, and it comes from two unspoken beliefs: that the relative power of the U.S. is declining, as rivals like China rise, and that the U.S. is reviled in many parts of the world. Pursuing our interests and spreading our ideals thus requires stealth and modesty as well as military strength. "It's so at odds with the John Wayne expectation for what America is in the world," the adviser said. "But it's necessary for shepherding us through this phase."

Document 16.2

THE PIVOT TO ASIA

U.S. troops left Iraq in December 2011, and a year later Obama announced that most American forces would be gone from Afghanistan by the end of 2014. The Middle East and Central Asia remained important, but in the long withdrawal from these two war zones the Obama administration declared it would pivot back to East Asia, the region in which the United States had fought three much larger wars and which in many ways now seemed to represent the center of gravity of international security and world economics. With the dramatic rise of Chinese economic and military power, Americans could no longer take for granted their preeminence along the Pacific Rim. And, as Obama laid out in a speech to the Australian parliament, for the foreseeable future the world's destiny would be shaped by the relationship between China and the United States.

I'd like to address the larger purpose of my visit to this region: our efforts to advance security, prosperity, and human dignity across the Asia-Pacific.

For the United States, this reflects a broader shift. After a decade in which we fought two wars that cost us dearly in blood and treasure, the United States is turning our attention to the vast potential of the Asia-Pacific region. In just a few weeks, after nearly 9 years, the last American troops will leave Iraq, and our war there will be over. In Afghanistan, we've begun a transition, a responsible transition so Afghans can take responsibility for their future and so coalition forces can begin to draw down. And with partners like Australia, we've struck major blows against Al Qaida and put that terrorist organization on the path to defeat, including delivering justice to Osama bin Laden.

So make no mistake, the tide of war is receding, and America is looking ahead to the future that we must build. . . .

Our new focus on this region reflects a fundamental truth: The United States has been, and always will be, a Pacific nation. Asian immigrants helped build America, and millions of American families, including my own, cherish our ties to this region. From the bombing of Darwin to the liberation of Pacific islands, from the rice paddies of Southeast Asia to a cold Korean Peninsula, generations of Americans have served here and died here so democracies could take root, so economic miracles could lift hundreds of millions to prosperity. Americans have bled with you for this progress, and we will not allow it—we will never allow it to be reversed.

Here, we see the future. As the world's fastest growing region, and home to more than half the global economy, the Asia-Pacific is critical to achieving my highest priority, and that's creating jobs and opportunity for the American people. With the world—with most of the world's nuclear power and some half of humanity, Asia will largely define whether the century ahead will be marked by conflict or cooperation, needless suffering or human progress.

As President, I have therefore made a deliberate and strategic decision: As a Pacific nation, the United States will play a larger and long-term role in shaping this region and its future by upholding core principles and in close partnership with our allies and friends.

Document 16.3

DON'T DO STUPID SHIT

As much as Obama wanted to pivot away from the Middle East, events on the ground determined otherwise, and the chaos of the Libyan revolution dragged him into launching yet another U.S. war in the Middle East. Like many other states of North Africa and the Middle East, Libya's turmoil was a product of the Arab Spring, a regional revolt against corrupt, authoritarian regimes that had begun in Tunisia in December 2010. Within a month, protests had spread to Syria, which in turn triggered a violent struggle for power that caused the outbreak of civil war that was still ongoing more than a decade later. The situation in Syria resurrected the debate within the Obama administration over how to respond. Chastened by the failure to achieve much of anything in Libya, this time Obama opted not to intervene. In this excerpt from a wide-ranging interview with The Atlantic *magazine, Obama was clearly at pains to articulate a grand strategy that would do enough, but not too much, in the world.*

The current U.S. ambassador to the United Nations, Samantha Power, who is the most dispositionally interventionist among Obama's senior advisers, had argued early for arming Syria's rebels. Power, who during this period served on the National Security Council staff, is the author of a celebrated book excoriating a succession of U.S. presidents for their failures to prevent genocide. The book, *A Problem from Hell*, published in 2002, drew Obama to Power while he was in the U.S. Senate, though the two were not an obvious ideological match. Power is a partisan of the doctrine known as "responsibility to protect," which holds that sovereignty should not be considered inviolate when a country is slaughtering its own citizens. She lobbied him to endorse this doctrine in the speech he delivered when he accepted the Nobel Peace Prize in 2009, but he declined. Obama generally does not believe a president should place American soldiers at great risk in order to prevent humanitarian disasters, unless those disasters pose a direct security threat to the United States.

Power sometimes argued with Obama in front of other National Security Council officials, to the point where he could no longer conceal his frustration. "Samantha, enough, I've already read your book," he once snapped.

Obama, unlike liberal interventionists, is an admirer of the foreign-policy realism of President George H. W. Bush and, in particular, of Bush's national-security adviser, Brent Scowcroft ("I love that guy," Obama once told me). Bush and Scowcroft removed Saddam Hussein's army from Kuwait in 1991, and they deftly managed the disintegration of the Soviet Union; Scowcroft also, on Bush's behalf, toasted the leaders of China shortly after the slaughter in Tiananmen Square. As Obama was writing his campaign manifesto, *The Audacity of Hope*, in 2006, Susan Rice, then an informal adviser, felt it necessary to remind him to include at least one line of praise for the foreign policy of President Bill Clinton, to partially balance the praise he showered on Bush and Scowcroft.

At the outset of the Syrian uprising, in early 2011, Power argued that the rebels, drawn from the ranks of ordinary citizens, deserved America's enthusiastic support. Others noted that the rebels were farmers and doctors and carpenters, comparing these revolutionaries to the men who won America's war for independence.

Obama flipped this plea on its head. "When you have a professional army," he once told me, "that is well armed and sponsored by two large states"—Iran and Russia—"who have huge stakes in this, and they are fighting against a farmer, a carpenter, an engineer who started out as protesters and suddenly now see themselves in the midst of a civil conflict . . ." He paused. "The notion that we could have—in a clean way that didn't commit U.S. military forces—changed the equation on the ground there was never true." The message Obama telegraphed in speeches and interviews was clear: He would not end up like the second President Bush—a president who became tragically overextended in the Middle East, whose decisions filled the wards of Walter Reed with grievously wounded soldiers, who was helpless to stop the obliteration of his reputation, even when he recalibrated his policies in his second term. Obama would say privately that the first task of an American president in the post-Bush international arena was "Don't do stupid shit."

Obama's reticence frustrated Power and others on his national-security team who had a preference for action. Hillary Clinton, when she was Obama's secretary of state, argued for an early and assertive response to Assad's violence. In 2014, after she left office, Clinton told me that "the failure to help build up a credible fighting force of the people who were the originators of the protests against Assad . . . left a big vacuum, which the jihadists have now filled." When *The Atlantic* published this statement, and also published Clinton's assessment that "great nations need organizing principles, and 'Don't do stupid stuff' is not an organizing principle," Obama became "rip-shit angry," according to one of his senior advisers. The president did not understand how "Don't do stupid shit" could be considered a controversial slogan. Ben Rhodes recalls that "the questions we were asking in the White House were 'Who exactly is in the stupid-shit caucus? Who is pro–stupid shit?'" The Iraq invasion, Obama believed, should have taught Democratic interventionists like Clinton, who had voted for its authorization, the dangers of doing stupid shit.

Document 16.4

SECURE OUR BORDER

No real political consensus on immigration policy existed in the decades after the Cold War, with Republicans and Democrats alike championing reform. The only agreement was that the system required an overhaul. For some that meant providing an easier path to citizenship for children of undocumented immigrants. For others that meant a clamp-down on what they dubbed "illegal" immigration, and deportation of those who had come to the country without proper paperwork or who had overstayed their visas. One vocal proponent of a crackdown was Joseph

Arpaio, sheriff of Arizona's Maricopa County (the border state's most populated) from 1993 to 2017. Self-described as "America's toughest sheriff," Arpaio's opposition to "illegal immigration" was well-known—and frequently litigated—making his support for Donald Trump in the 2016 campaign, including at that year's Republican National Convention, vital to the candidate's own promises to better patrol and control the country's southern border.

We need a strong leader who will stand up for America, and put the interests of her citizens first. Unfortunately, we are losing the battle. We are the only country in the world whose immigration system puts the needs of other nations ahead of ours. We are more concerned with the rights of illegal aliens and criminals than we are with protecting our own country. That must change. We need a leader who will protect our border and enforce our laws, because a nation without borders, and a nation without laws, is no nation at all. And now, more than ever, we must respect, and have respect, for the police.... I can tell you first hand about the dangers of illegal immigration and drugs. We have terrorists coming over our border, infiltrating our communities, and causing massive destruction and mayhem. We have criminals penetrating our weak border security system and committing serious crime. I am supporting Donald Trump because he is a leader. He produces results. He's the only candidate for president ready to get tough in order to protect Americans. I have fought on the front lines to prevent illegal immigration, and I know Donald Trump will stand with me and other proud Americans to secure our border. Donald Trump will build the wall. [Chants of "Build the Wall."] And restore law and order and keep drugs and illegal immigrants from entering into OUR country.... Let's elect a leader who will stand up for America. And protect our border. And support law enforcement. And the military. And in doing so, unite our country. Let's elect Donald Trump.

Documents 16.5 and 16.6

PIVOTING AWAY FROM OBAMA'S PIVOT TO ASIA

President Obama promised a "pivot to Asia" and a reorientation of American interests and policy away from Europe. Trade formed a key component of his administration's plans, which spent years constructing a broad "Trans-Pacific Partnership" between the United States and eleven other Pacific nations that collectively represented more than 40 percent of global trade. Its stated goal was a reduction of trade barriers and improved regulation of both industry and working conditions, but its real purpose was to solidify American leadership in opposition to China's rising economic and geopolitical might. Signed in February 2016, this signature achievement of Obama's diplomacy was never ratified by the U.S. Senate and thus became a political football in the 2016 campaign between Trump and Obama's first secretary of state, Hillary Clinton, who voiced her own concerns with the deal when running for office. Trump promised to pull the United States from the deal if elected, and made good on that campaign promise in early 2017, leaving Asian leaders such as Japan's long-time prime minister Shinzo Abe to wonder not only what would become of the economic pact, but also about America's role in their region. Soon into Trump's time in office, they seemed to have their answer.

As for aiming to bring the [Trans-Pacific Partnership trade deal] into effect without the United States, at the 12-nation meeting there was no such discussion. TPP is meaningless without the United States. Just as a renegotiation is impossible, this would disturb the fundamental balance of benefits. On the policies of the incoming administration of the United States, I would like to refrain from commenting at this stage based on free judgment.

. . . . . .

We have finally come to an agreement on the rules of free and fair trade. We hoped to utilize that agreed framework. Unfortunately, the US has declared withdrawal from the TPP. Since we have come thus far, Japan must take on a leadership role, and bring the talks forward. We would like to capitalize upon the results of our long years of effort. I think the important point is to ensure a fair and free trading regime between Japan and the United States. We have agreed that it is very important to create a trading framework which will enable the development of this region as a whole, for free and fair trading activities. So momentum should not be lost. In the upcoming TPP Ministerial Meeting in Vietnam, I wish to seek the solidarity and the unity of the 11 countries, so we can come up with a clear direction of where we want to go from this point forward. . . . Eleven countries have made their judgement on the assumption that the U.S. will be in TPP. We need to consider what is best, and the eleven countries must be united. Since the U.S. understands the importance of having free and fair rules in the trading world, our wish is that the U.S. will return to the TPP.

Document 16.7

THE RETURN OF AMERICA FIRST

In 1940, during the national debate over how the United States should respond to the outbreak of World War II, a diverse group of anti-interventionists gathered in an umbrella organization known as the America First Committee (see document 5.11). Afterward, the term "America First" became synonymous with isolationism, nationalism, and even xenophobia. U.S. entry into the war, and then the Cold War that followed, discredited isolationism even as it legitimated internationalism. But the difficulties of the post–9/11 "forever wars" saw a revival of the isolationist spirit, alongside a new right-wing populism that distrusted political elites (conservative as well as liberal) for dragging Americans into global crusades and neoliberal economic policies that seemed to harm middle-class Americans. Donald Trump campaigned on this populist platform in his successful run for president in 2016. Here, in his January 2017 inaugural address, he explains just what that meant.

The oath of office I take today is an oath of allegiance to all Americans.

For many decades, we've enriched foreign industry at the expense of American industry, subsidized the armies of other countries while allowing for the very sad depletion of our military. We've defended other nations' borders while refusing to defend our own and spent trillions and trillions of dollars overseas while America's infrastructure has fallen into disrepair and decay. We've made other countries rich while the wealth, strength, and confidence of our country has dissipated over the horizon.

One by one, the factories shuttered and left our shores, with not even a thought about the millions and millions of American workers that were left behind. The wealth of our middle class has been ripped from their homes and then redistributed all across the world.

But that is the past. And now we are looking only to the future.

We, assembled here today, are issuing a new decree to be heard in every city, in every foreign capital, and in every hall of power. From this day forward, a new vision will govern our land. From this day forward, it's going to be only America first. America first.

Every decision on trade, on taxes, on immigration, on foreign affairs, will be made to benefit American workers and American families.

We must protect our borders from the ravages of other countries making our products, stealing our companies, and destroying our jobs. Protection will lead to great prosperity and strength. I will fight for you with every breath in my body, and I will never, ever let you down.

America will start winning again, winning like never before. We will bring back our jobs. We will bring back our borders. We will bring back our wealth. And we will bring back our dreams.

We will build new roads and highways and bridges and airports and tunnels and railways all across our wonderful Nation.

We will get our people off of welfare and back to work, rebuilding our country with American hands and American labor. We will follow two simple rules: Buy American and hire American.

We will seek friendship and good will with the nations of the world, but we do so with the understanding that it is the right of all nations to put their own interests first. We do not seek to impose our way of life on anyone, but rather to let it shine as an example—we will shine—for everyone to follow.

We will reinforce old alliances and form new ones and unite the civilized world against radical Islamic terrorism, which we will eradicate completely from the face of the Earth.

At the bedrock of our politics will be a total allegiance to the United States of America, and through our loyalty to our country, we will rediscover our loyalty to each other. When you open your heart to patriotism, there is no room for prejudice. The Bible tells us, "How good and pleasant it is when God's people live together in unity." We must speak our minds openly, debate our disagreements honestly, but always pursue solidarity. When America is united, America is totally unstoppable. There should be no fear: We are protected, and we will always be protected. We will be protected by the great men and women of our military and law enforcement, and most importantly, we will be protected by God.

Documents 16.8, 16.9, and 16.10

ALLIANCE TENSIONS

America First did not sit well with America's traditional allies, but it was never intended to do so. In fact, Trump was often more critical of U.S. allies, especially in Europe, than he was of long-standing U.S. adversaries, such as Russia and North Korea. Yet as president, Trump discovered what Obama had discovered before him: The demands of being president are more complicated than the president's own plans. Here, in a series of tweets—his preferred means of public communication—and a major speech at NATO headquarters in Belgium, Trump seeks to work with Europeans while simultaneously berating them for what he criticizes as inadequate military spending and unfair trade practices. Even at the dedication ceremony for two memorials at NATO headquarters—to victims of communist rule in Cold War Europe and 9/11 in America—Trump cannot help but criticize his allies' spending priorities.

Donald Trump (@realDonaldTrump)

March 18, 2017,13:15:41

Despite what you have heard from the FAKE NEWS I had a GREAT meeting with German Chancellor Angela Merkel. Nevertheless Germany owes. . . .

March 18, 2017,13:23:37

. . . vast sums of money to NATO & the United States must be paid more for the powerful and very expensive defense it provides to Germany!

• • • • • •

Thank you very much, Secretary General Stoltenberg. Chancellor Merkel, thank you very much. Other heads of state and government, I am honored to be here with members of an alliance that has promoted safety and peace across the world. . . .

The NATO of the future must include a great focus on terrorism and immigration, as well as threats from Russia and on NATO's eastern and southern borders. These grave security concerns are the same reason that I have been very, very direct with Secretary Stoltenberg and members of the Alliance in saying that NATO members must finally contribute their fair share and meet their financial obligations, but 23 of the 28 member nations are still not paying what they should be paying and what they're supposed to be paying for their defense. This is not fair to the people and taxpayers of the United States. And many of these nations owe massive amounts of money from past years and not paying in those past years. Over the last 8 years, the United States spent more on defense than all other NATO countries combined. If all NATO members had spent just 2 percent of their GDP on defense last year, we would have had another $119 billion for our collective defense and for the financing of additional NATO reserves.

We should recognize that with these chronic underpayments and growing threats, even 2 percent of GDP is insufficient to close the gaps in modernizing, readiness, and the size of forces. We have to make up for the many years lost. Two percent is the bare minimum for confronting today's very real and very vicious threats. If NATO countries made their full and complete contributions, then NATO would be even stronger than it is today, especially from the threat of terrorism.

I want to extend my appreciation to the 9/11 Memorial and Museum in New York for contributing this remnant of the North Tower, as well as to Chancellor Merkel and the German people for donating this portion of the Berlin Wall. It is truly fitting that these two artifacts now reside here so close together at the new NATO Headquarters. And I never asked once what the new NATO Headquarters cost. I refuse to do that. But it is beautiful.

. . . . . .

Donald Trump (@realDonaldTrump)

May 30, 2017, 10:40:36

We have a MASSIVE trade deficit with Germany plus they pay FAR LESS than they should on NATO & military. Very bad for U.S. This will change.

Document 16.11

AMERICA ALONE?

Merkel did not respond as Trump expected. Instead of adapting to the new politics of America First, she and other NATO allies immediately began to reflect about the endurance of the transatlantic alliance itself. Merkel herself publicly wondered whether Europeans should take more control over their own defense, even if that meant a partial withdrawal of the U.S. presence in Europe. Later, French president Emmanuel Macron criticized NATO as "brain dead." In Canada—perhaps America's closest ally—foreign affairs minister Chrystia Freeland used a speech to parliament to warn that America First could in fact mean America alone.

International relationships that had seemed immutable for 70 years are being called into question. From Europe, to Asia, to our own North American home, long-standing pacts that have formed the bedrock of our security and prosperity for generations are being tested.

And new shared human imperatives—the fight against climate change first among them—call for renewed, uncommon resolve.

Turning aside from our responsibilities is not an option. Instead we must think carefully and deeply about what is happening, and find a way forward. . . .

Since before the end of the Second World War, beginning with the international conference at Bretton Woods in 1944, Canada has been deeply engaged in, and greatly enjoyed the benefits of, a global order based on rules.

These were principles and standards that were applied, perhaps not perfectly at all times by all states, but certainly by the vast majority of democratic states, most of the time.

The system had at its heart the core notions of territorial integrity, human rights, democracy, respect for the rule of law, and an aspiration to free and friendly trade.

The common volition toward this order arose from a fervent determination not to repeat the immediate past.

Humankind had learned through the direct experience of horror and hardship, Mr. Speaker, that the narrow pursuit of national self-interest, the law of the jungle, led to nothing but carnage and poverty.

Two global conflicts and the Great Depression, all in the span of less than half a century, taught our parents and grandparents that national borders must be inviolate; that international trading relationships created not only prosperity but also peace; and that a true world community, one based on shared aspirations and standards, was not only desirable but essential to our very survival.

That deep yearning toward lasting peace led to the creation of international institutions that endure to this day—with the nations of Western Europe, together with their transatlantic allies, the United States and Canada, at their foundation. . . .

As I have said, we Canadians can rightly be proud of the role we played in building the postwar order, and the unprecedented peace and prosperity that followed.

Yet even as we celebrate our own part in that project, it's only fair for us to acknowledge the larger contribution of the United States. For in blood, in treasure, in strategic vision, in leadership, America has paid the lion's share.

The United States has truly been the indispensable nation, Mr. Speaker. For their unique, seven-decades-long contribution to our shared peace and prosperity, and on behalf of all Canadians, I would like to profoundly thank our American friends.

As I have argued, Canada believes strongly that this stable, predictable international order has been deeply in our national interest. And we believe it has helped foster peace and prosperity for our southern neighbours, too.

Yet it would be naive or hypocritical to claim before this House that all Americans today agree. Indeed, many of the voters in last year's presidential election cast their ballots, animated in part by a desire to shrug off the burden of world leadership. To say this is not controversial: it is simply a fact.

Canada is grateful, and will always be grateful, to our neighbour for the outsized role it has played in the world. And we seek and will continue to seek to persuade our friends that their continued international leadership is very much in their national interest—as well as that of the rest of the free world.

Yet we also recognize that this is ultimately not our decision to make. It is a choice Americans must make for themselves.

The fact that our friend and ally has come to question the very worth of its mantle of global leadership, puts into sharper focus the need for the rest of us to set our own clear and sovereign course. For Canada that course must be the renewal, indeed the strengthening, of the postwar multilateral order. . . .

First, we will robustly support the rules-based international order, and all its institutions, and seek ways to strengthen and improve them. We will strongly support the multilateral forums where such discussions are held—including the G7, the G20, the OAS, APEC, the WTO, the WHO, the Commonwealth and La Francophonie, the Arctic Council, and of course NATO and the UN.

Document 16.12

TRUMP'S GRAND STRATEGY

Even more than Obama's foreign policy, Trump's approach to the world lacked ideological consistency—was it isolationist? unilateralist? populist? nationalist? militarist?—in large part because Trump's politics were driven by his own personality more than they had been, arguably, for any previous president. For example, unlike most other modern presidents, Trump lacked a foreign policy "doctrine." On July 13, 2017, two of his key officials—national economic council director Gary Cohn and national security advisor H. R. McMaster—took up the task of trying to define the Trump administration's grand strategy.

President Trump just concluded a second overseas trip to further advance America's interests and values, and to strengthen our alliances around the world. Both this and his first trip demonstrated the resurgence of American leadership to bolster common interests, affirm shared values, confront mutual threats and achieve renewed prosperity.

Discussions with world leaders highlighted extraordinary potential: vast supplies of affordable energy, untapped markets that can be opened to new commerce, a growing number of young people seeking the chance to build better futures in their homelands and new partnerships among nations that can form the basis for lasting peace. At every opportunity abroad, President Trump articulated his vision for securing the American homeland, enhancing American prosperity and advancing American influence. . . .

Central to President Trump's approach is that the United States will seek areas of agreement and cooperation while still protecting American interests. At the G-20, the United States supported open trade but insisted that it be fair. The G-20 communiqué recognized "the importance of reciprocal and mutually advantageous trade," and all leaders agreed to do more to eliminate excess capacity in industrial sectors such as steel. Because of American leadership, all G-20 nations joined together in making an urgent call "for the removal of market distorting subsidies and other types of support by governments" to "foster a truly level playing field."

The G-20 leaders agreed that a strong economy and a healthy planet are mutually reinforcing. America will continue to lead by example in demonstrating that market forces and technology-driven solutions are the most effective means of protecting the environment while fueling economic growth. . . .

Perhaps most important, President Trump affirmed on this trip that America First is grounded in American values—values that not only strengthen America but also drive progress throughout the world. America champions the dignity of every person, affirms the equality of women, celebrates innovation, protects freedom of speech and of religion, and supports free and fair markets. . . .

America First is rooted in confidence that our values are worth defending and promoting. This is a time of great challenge for our friends and allies around the globe—but it is also a moment of extraordinary opportunity. The American delegation returned from the trip with tremendous optimism about the future and what the United States, our allies and our partners can achieve together.

Document 16.13

AN ALTERNATIVE AMERICA FIRST

Republicans were not the only ones to criticize the broader trajectory of American foreign policy since 1945. The left wing of the Democratic Party featured critics of its own, including Vermont senator Bernie Sanders. Technically an independent who merely caucused with Democrats, Sanders nonetheless sought the party's presidential nomination in 2016 and again in 2020. He too thought globalization and recent trade deals in particular had unfairly punished American workers, but he also believed the nation's obsession with economics as a foreign policy rationale was itself misguided. The total sum of American (and global) economic strength mattered less than its fair distribution, he argued in a populist vein that would have sounded familiar to supporters of William Jennings Bryan or Robert LaFollette. Unable to secure his party's nomination, his campaign and frequent critiques nonetheless forced Hillary Clinton in 2016 and Joe Biden four years later to recognize that their own base of voters felt the need for change as well.

What Eisenhower said over 50 years ago is even more true today.

Foreign policy is about whether we continue to champion the values of freedom, democracy and justice, values which have been a beacon of hope for people throughout the world, or whether we support undemocratic, repressive regimes, which torture, jail and deny basic rights to their citizens.

What foreign policy also means is that if we are going to expound the virtues of democracy and justice abroad, and be taken seriously, we need to practice those values here at home. That means continuing the struggle to end racism, sexism, xenophobia and homophobia here in the United States and making it clear that when people in America march on our streets as neo-nazis or white supremacists, we have no ambiguity in condemning everything they stand for. There are no two sides on that issue.

Foreign policy is not just tied into military affairs, it is directly connected to economics. Foreign policy must take into account the outrageous income and wealth inequality that exists globally and in our own country. This planet will not be secure or peaceful when so few have so much, and so many have so little—and when we advance day after day into an oligarchic form of society where a small number of extraordinarily powerful special interests exert enormous influence over the economic and political life of the world.

There is no moral or economic justification for the six wealthiest people in the world having as much wealth as the bottom half of the world's population—3.7 billion people. There is no justification for the incredible power and dominance that Wall Street, giant multi-national corporations and international financial institutions have over the affairs of sovereign countries throughout the world.

At a time when climate change is causing devastating problems here in America and around the world, foreign policy is about whether we work with the international community—with China, Russia, India and countries around the world—to transform our energy systems away from fossil fuel to energy efficiency and sustainable energy. Sensible foreign policy understands that climate change is a real threat to every country on earth, that it is not a hoax, and that no country alone can effectively combat it. It is an issue for the entire international community, and an issue that the United States should be leading in, not ignoring or denying.

My point is that we need to look at foreign policy as more than just the crisis of the day. That is important, but we need a more expansive view.

Document 16.14

TRUMP'S "MUSLIM BAN"

Donald Trump knew how to garner attention, and he did so in late 2015 while campaigning for the Republican nomination by promising a "total and complete shutdown of Muslims entering the United States until our country's representatives can figure out what is going on." Critics deemed the pledge unconstitutional, or at least antithetical to the country's promise as a beacon for freedom. His supporters countered that the War on Terror had since 9/11 focused on enemies motivated by their version of Islam. Some even argued Muslims could never become loyal Americans in the first place, a charge that echoed earlier contentions that immigrants from Ireland, Germany, Japan, and elsewhere would prove incapable of properly assimilating into the country's dominant culture. Elements of the ban went into effect soon after Trump took office, leading the state of Hawaii (among others) to question its constitutionality in federal court. A federal judge in the Ninth District soon ruled the ban illegal. The Trump administration appealed this decision to the Supreme Court. The case was argued before the Court in late 2017, with the justices siding with the administration in the summer of 2018, less on the grounds of the ban's merits (ethical or otherwise) than based on their view that the Constitution indeed gave the president the power to regulate the country's borders and ports-of-entry in this manner. The vote was 5–4. Every justice nominated to the Court by a Republican president supported Trump's plan. Every Democratic nominee opposed.

(b) Plaintiffs allege that the primary purpose of the Proclamation was religious animus and that the President's stated concerns about vetting protocols and national security were but pretexts for discriminating against

Muslims. At the heart of their case is a series of statements by the President and his advisers both during the campaign and since the President assumed office. The issue, however, is not whether to denounce the President's statements, but the significance of those statements in reviewing a Presidential directive, neutral on its face, addressing a matter within the core of executive responsibility. In doing so, the Court must consider not only the statements of a particular President, but also the authority of the Presidency itself. . . .

(c) . . . The Court need not define the precise contours of that narrow inquiry in this case. For today's purposes, the Court assumes that it may look behind the face of the Proclamation to the extent of applying rational basis review, i.e., whether the entry policy is plausibly related to the Government's stated objective to protect the country and improve vetting processes. Plaintiffs' extrinsic evidence may be considered, but the policy will be upheld so long as it can reasonably be understood to result from a justification independent of unconstitutional grounds.

(d) On the few occasions where the Court has struck down a policy as illegitimate under rational basis scrutiny, a common thread has been that the laws at issue were "divorced from any factual context from which [the Court] could discern a relationship to legitimate state interests." . . . The Proclamation does not fit that pattern. It is expressly premised on legitimate purposes and says nothing about religion. The entry restrictions on Muslim-majority nations are limited to countries that were previously designated by Congress or prior administrations as posing national security risks. Moreover, the Proclamation reflects the results of a worldwide review process undertaken by multiple Cabinet officials and their agencies. Plaintiffs challenge the entry suspension based on their perception of its effectiveness and wisdom, but the Court cannot substitute its own assessment for the Executive's predictive judgments on such matters. Three additional features of the entry policy support the Government's claim of a legitimate national security interest. First, since the President introduced entry restrictions in January 2017, three Muslim-majority countries—Iraq, Sudan, and Chad—have been removed from the list. Second, for those countries still subject to entry restrictions, the Proclamation includes numerous exceptions for various categories of foreign nationals. Finally, the Proclamation creates a waiver program open to all covered foreign nationals seeking entry as immigrants or nonimmigrants.

Under these circumstances, the Government has set forth a sufficient national security justification to survive rational basis review. Reversed and remanded.

ROBERTS, C. J., delivered the opinion of the Court, in which KENNEDY, THOMAS, ALITO, and GORSUCH, joined. KENNEDY, and THOMAS, filed concurring opinions. BREYER filed a dissenting opinion, in which KAGAN, joined. SOTOMAYOR, filed a dissenting opinion, in which GINSBURG, joined.

Document 16.15

AMERICA (FIRST) IN THE WORLD

Perhaps the clearest expression of Trump's worldview came in this 2018 speech to the United Nations. This was ironic, given the mutual disdain Trump and the UN had for each other—but it also helps explain the unusual reaction the speech evoked among the foreign dignitaries in the audience.

We are standing up for America and for the American people. And we are also standing up for the world. This is great news for our citizens and for peace-loving people everywhere. We believe that when nations respect the rights of their neighbors and defend the interests of their people, they can better work together to secure the blessings of safety, prosperity, and peace.

Each of us here today is the emissary of a distinct culture, a rich history, and a people bound together by ties of memory, tradition, and the values that make our homelands like nowhere else on Earth.

That is why America will always choose independence and cooperation over global governance, control, and domination. I honor the right of every nation in this room to pursue its own customs, beliefs, and traditions. The United States will not tell you how to live or work or worship. We only ask that you honor our sovereignty in return. . . .

America's policy of principled realism means we will not be held hostage to old dogmas, discredited ideologies, and so-called experts who have been proven wrong over the years, time and time again. This is true not only in matters of peace, but in matters of prosperity. We believe that trade must be fair and reciprocal. The United States will not be taken advantage of any longer.

For decades, the United States opened its economy—the largest, by far, on Earth—with few conditions. We allowed foreign goods from all over the world to flow freely across our borders. Yet other countries did not grant us fair and reciprocal access to their markets in return. Even worse, some countries abused their openness to dump their products, subsidize their goods, target our industries, and manipulate their currencies to gain unfair advantage over our country. As a result, our trade deficit ballooned to nearly $800 billion a year. . . .

I spoke before this body last year and warned that the U.N. Human Rights Council had become a grave embarrassment to this institution, shielding egregious human rights abusers while bashing America and its many friends.

Our Ambassador to the United Nations, Nikki Haley, laid out a clear agenda for reform, but despite reported and repeated warnings, no action at all was taken. So the United States took the only responsible course: We withdrew from the Human Rights Council, and we will not return until real reform is enacted.

For similar reasons, the United States will provide no support in recognition to the International Criminal Court. As far as America is concerned, the ICC has no jurisdiction, no legitimacy, and no authority. The ICC claims near-universal jurisdiction over the citizens of every country, violating all principles of justice, fairness, and due process. We will never surrender America's sovereignty to an unelected, unaccountable, global bureaucracy.

America is governed by Americans. We reject the ideology of globalism, and we embrace the doctrine of patriotism. Around the world, responsible nations must defend against threats to sovereignty not just from global governance, but also from other, new forms of coercion and domination.

In America, we believe strongly in energy security for ourselves and for our allies. We have become the largest energy producer anywhere on the face of the Earth. The United States stands ready to export our abundant, affordable supply of oil, clean coal, and natural gas.

OPEC and OPEC nations are, as usual, ripping off the rest of the world, and I don't like it. Nobody should like it. [Laughter] We defend many of these nations for nothing, and then they take advantage of us by giving us high oil prices. Not good.

We want them to stop raising prices, we want them to start lowering prices, and they must contribute substantially to military protection from now on. We are not going to put up with it—these horrible prices—much longer.

We recognize the right of every nation in this room to set its own immigration policy in accordance with its national interests, just as we ask other countries to respect our own right to do the same, which we are doing. That is one reason the United States will not participate in the new Global Compact on Migration. Migration should not be governed by an international body unaccountable to our own citizens. Ultimately, the only long-term solution to the migration crisis is to help people build more hopeful futures in their home countries. Make their countries great again. [Laughter]

Document 16.16

"AMERICA IS BACK"

More than any president since World War II, Donald Trump denigrated multilateralism and questioned the value of alliances. He embraced instead a transactional approach to international affairs rooted in a clear-eyed sense of America's material and strategic interests. Critics charged that the Trump administration's approach undercut the leading role that the United States had played on the global stage for seventy-five years. After replacing Trump in the White House, president Joe Biden sought to reassure the world that the United States would revert to older patterns of principled leadership. Some of his most forceful words came in the following speech, which Biden delivered at the State Department two weeks after taking office.

[This] is the message I want the world to hear today: America is back. America is back. Diplomacy is back at the center of our foreign policy.

As I said in my inaugural address, we will repair our alliances and engage with the world once again, not to meet yesterday's challenges, but today's and tomorrow's. American leadership must meet this new moment of advancing authoritarianism, including the growing ambitions of China to rival the United States and the determination of Russia to damage and disrupt our democracy.

We must meet the new moment [of] accelerating global challenges—from the pandemic to the climate crisis to nuclear proliferation—[that] will only . . . be solved by nations working together and in common. We can't do it alone. . . .

[W]e must start with diplomacy rooted in America's most cherished democratic values: defending freedom, championing opportunity, upholding universal rights, respecting the rule of law, and treating every person with dignity.

That's the grounding wire of our global policy—our global power. That's our inexhaustible source of strength. That's America's abiding advantage.

Though many of these values have come under intense pressure in recent years, even pushed to the brink in the last few weeks, the American people are going to emerge from this moment stronger, more determined, and better equipped to unite the world in fighting to defend democracy, because we have fought for it ourselves. . . .

Over the past two weeks, I've spoken with the leaders of many of our closest friends—Canada, Mexico, the UK, Germany, France, NATO, Japan, South Korea, Australia—to being [begin] reforming the habits of cooperation and rebuilding the muscle of democratic alliances that have atrophied over the past few years of neglect and, I would argue, abuse.

America's alliances are our greatest asset, and leading with diplomacy means standing shoulder-to-shoulder with our allies and key partners once again.

By leading with diplomacy, we must also mean engaging our adversaries and our competitors diplomatically, where it's in our interest, and advance the security of the American people.

Document 16.17

THE END OF THE FOREVER WARS?

In the summer of 2021, almost twenty years after the 9/11 attacks and the U.S. invasion of Afghanistan, and nearly ten years after the killing of Osama bin Laden, Biden withdrew all U.S. personnel from Kabul, the Afghan capital, and acquiesced in the country coming under Taliban rule. In a nationally televised speech defending his decision, Biden gives an overview of the troubled history of what was now America's longest war and the dilemmas he faced in deciding whether to escalate further or withdraw completely.

In April, I made a decision to end this war. As part of that decision, we set the date of Aug. 31 for American troops to withdraw. The assumption was that more than 300,000 Afghan national security forces that we had trained over the past two decades and equipped would be a strong adversary in their civil wars with the Taliban.

That assumption, that the Afghan government would be able to hold on for a period of time beyond military drawdown, turned out not to be accurate. But I still instructed our national security team to prepare for every eventuality, even that one. And that's what we did. So we were ready when the Afghan security forces, after two decades of fighting for their country and losing thousands of their own, did not hold on as long as anyone expected.

We were ready when they and the people of Afghanistan watched their own government collapse and the president flee amid the corruption and malfeasance, handing over the country to their enemy the Taliban and significantly increasing the risk to U.S. personnel and our allies. . . .

Let me be clear: Leaving Aug. 31 is not due to an arbitrary deadline. It was designed to save American lives. My predecessor, the former president, signed an agreement with the Taliban to remove U.S. troops by May 1, just months after I was inaugurated. It included no requirement that Taliban work out a cooperative governing arrangement with the Afghan government. But it did authorize the release of 5,000 prisoners last year, including some of the Taliban's top war commanders, among those who just took control of Afghanistan.

By the time I came to office, the Taliban was in its strongest military position since 2001, controlling or contesting nearly half of the country. The previous administration's agreement said that if we stuck to the May 1 deadline that they had signed on to leave by, the Taliban wouldn't attack any American forces. But if we stayed, all bets were off.

So we were left with a simple decision: Either follow through on the commitment made by the last administration and leave Afghanistan, or say we weren't leaving and commit another tens of thousands more troops. Going back to war. That was the choice, the real choice. Between leaving or escalating. I was not going to extend this forever war. And I was not extending a forever exit. . . .

The bottom line is, there is no evacuation from the end of a war that you can run without the kinds of complexities, challenges, threats we faced. None. To those who would say we should have stayed indefinitely, for years on end, they ask: "Why don't we just keep doing what we were doing? Why do we have to change anything?"

The fact is everything had changed. My predecessor had made a deal with the Taliban. When I came into office, we faced a deadline, May 1. The Taliban onslaught was coming. We faced one of two choices: follow the agreement of the previous administration and extend it to have more time for people to get out, or send in thousands more troops and escalate the war.

To those asking for a third decade of war in Afghanistan, I ask: What is the vital national interest? In my view, we only have one: to make sure Afghanistan can never be used again to launch an attack on our homeland.

Remember why we went to Afghanistan in the first place? Because we were attacked by Osama bin Laden and Al Qaeda on Sept. 11, 2001, and they were based in Afghanistan.

We delivered justice to bin Laden on May 2, 2011. Over a decade ago. Al Qaeda was decimated.

I respectfully suggest you ask yourself this question: If we had been attacked on Sept. 11, 2001, from Yemen instead of Afghanistan, would we have ever gone to war in Afghanistan? Even though the Taliban controlled Afghanistan in the year 2001? I believe the honest answer is no. That's because we had no vital interest in Afghanistan other than to prevent an attack on America's homeland and our friends. And that's true today.

We succeeded in what we set out to do in Afghanistan over a decade ago. Then we stayed for another decade. It was time to end this war.

This is a new world. The terror threat has metastasized across the world, well beyond Afghanistan. We face threats from Al Shabab in Somalia, Al Qaeda affiliates in Syria and the Arabian Peninsula, and Isis attempting to create a caliphate in Syria and Iraq and establishing affiliates across Africa and Asia.

The fundamental obligation of a president, in my opinion, is to defend and protect America. Not against threats of 2001, but against the threats of 2021 and tomorrow. That is the guiding principle behind my decisions about Afghanistan.

I simply do not believe that the safety and security of America is enhanced by continuing to deploy thousands of American troops and spending billions of dollars a year in Afghanistan. But I also know that the threat from terrorism continues in its pernicious and evil nature. But it's changed. Expanded to other countries. Our strategy has to change, too.

We will maintain the fight against terrorism in Afghanistan and other countries. We just don't need to fight a ground war to do it. We have what's called over-the-horizon capabilities, which means we can strike terrorists and targets without American boots on the ground, very few if needed. . . .

As commander in chief, I firmly believe the best path to guard our safety and our security lies in a tough, unforgiving, targeted, precise strategy that goes after terror where it is today. Not where it was two decades ago. That's what is in our national interest.

And here is the critical thing to understand: The world is changing. We're engaged in a serious competition with China. We're dealing with the challenges on multiple fronts with Russia. We're confronted with cyberattacks and nuclear proliferation. We have to shore up American competitiveness to meet these new challenges and the competition for the twenty-first century. And we can do both: fight terrorism, and take on new threats that are here now and will continue to be here in the future. And there's nothing China or Russia would rather have, would want more in this competition, than the United States to be bogged down another decade in Afghanistan.

As we turn the page on the foreign policy that's guided our nation the last two decades, we've got to learn from our mistakes. To me there are two that are paramount: First, we must set missions with clear, achievable goals, not ones we'll never reach. And second, we must stay clearly focused on the fundamental national security interest of the United States of America.

This decision about Afghanistan is not just about Afghanistan. It's about ending an era of major military operations to remake other countries. We saw a mission of counterterrorism in Afghanistan, getting the terrorists to stop the attacks, morph into a counterinsurgency, nation building, trying to create a democratic, cohesive and united Afghanistan. Something that has never been done over many centuries of Afghan's history. Moving on from that mind-set and those kind of large-scale troop deployments will make us stronger and more effective and safer at home.

Documents 16.18, 16.19, and 16.20

GHOSTS FROM THE PAST

The chaotic manner by which the United States evacuated Afghanistan caught Americans, and people elsewhere, by surprise. In document 16.18, Osama Hajjaj, a Jordanian editorial cartoonist, portrays the U.S. withdrawal in an ironic light: Biden is depicted pulling down a statue of a U.S. soldier in Afghanistan, literally cutting him off at the knees, in a direct emulation of U.S. soldiers pulling down a statue of Saddam Hussein in Baghdad in 2003 (document 16.19). Even though Hajjaj drew this cartoon after Biden announced his intention to withdraw but before U.S. forces actually pulled out, he presciently anticipated the chaos that would ensue—just as chaos had ensued in Baghdad following the overthrow of Saddam Hussein. The U.S. evacuation from Afghanistan unleashed widespread panic that quickly descended into anarchy, leading editorial cartoonist Scott Stantis (document 16.20) to compare the distressing scenes in Kabul to an iconic image from the U.S. withdrawal from Saigon in April 1975.

NEXT TIME! WE'LL LEARN OUR LESSON NEXT TIME!!!
Vietnam
AFGHANISTAN

17

Great Powers and Global Challenges

When the Cold War ended, politicians, pundits, and scholars speculated intensely about what would come next. What kinds of threats to American interests were likely to arise in the new international environment? How should U.S. foreign policy be altered to meet them and assure a new global order that would serve American purposes? Some commentators speculated that unconventional new challenges—environmental crises, resource scarcity, human migrations, and pandemic disease—would dominate global affairs in the post–Cold War era, necessitating a fresh concept of national security. Others suggested that the resolution of the East-West rivalry, far from ending the era of geopolitical rivalry and military conflict, would give way to a new, potentially more dangerous period of confrontation among powerful nations.

The fixation on international terrorism in the first decade of the twenty-first century muted this sort of speculation. Terrorism stood out as easily the most urgent threat to the nation and seemed to offer a new central theme for American foreign policy. Under the banner of the "War on Terror," U.S. leaders expended vast resources in impoverished nations of the Middle East and South Asia.

When terrorism receded as Washington's central preoccupation, however, the old uncertainties returned: what were the fundamental threats confronting the nation and how should U.S. policy adapt? Increasingly, it became clear that both lines of thinking dating back to the 1990s had proved prescient. Warming temperatures, rising seas, and devastating storms focused more attention than ever on climate change as a profound challenge to humanity that necessitated bold diplomacy on a global scale. Meanwhile, waves of refugees fleeing environmental collapse as well as war and economic misery fueled political movements skeptical of open borders and liberal principles more generally. And then in 2020, the COVID-19 pandemic demonstrated the potential of infectious disease to stir international tensions, empower authoritarian regimes, and wreak havoc on the global economy.

Predictions of a new era of rivalry among the world's great powers also came true. Optimism about the possibility of folding Russia and China into a Western-led global order committed to democracy, multilateralism, human rights, and unfettered trade crumbled as those two nations grew increasingly powerful and hostile to the United States. By the 2020s, new cold wars with ideologically hostile, militarily adventurous great powers appeared to be at hand. Western notions of freedom, openness, and rights came under broad attack as at no point since the Cold War.

Led by autocrat Vladimir Putin, Russia signaled its expansionist ambitions in 2008, when Russian forces invaded parts of neighboring Georgia and established pro-Russian governments in those areas. The United States and other Western governments condemned these moves, but Russian belligerence continued. Russia invaded the Crimean Peninsula, then a province of Ukraine, in 2014 and quickly annexed it. A major invasion of Ukraine followed in early 2022, sparking a grueling war against Ukrainian forces armed by the West.

Meanwhile, an increasingly confident, powerful, and nationalistic China challenged Western interests all over the world. In the Western Pacific Ocean, the Chinese navy confronted long-standing Western dominance by operating far from shore and building new bases. In South and Southeast Asia, sub-Saharan Africa, and even Latin America, China sought influence by distributing development assistance and undertaking massive projects to build roads, dams, and other infrastructure.

The combination of dire global threats and renewed great-power tensions confronted the United States with increasingly urgent and complex questions by the third decade of the century. How could Washington pump more resources into foreign policy at a time of economic weakness and declining public interest in international affairs? How should the nation balance the need to confront China and Russia with the obvious need for multilateral innovation to confront problems that threatened human existence? Was a coherent national strategy possible in a moment of profound political polarization?

Document 17.1

KENNAN REDUX

George F. Kennan has loomed large over the events covered in this book. After mobilizing Washington into action against Soviet communism with his 1946 "Long Telegram" (document 7.3), his "X" article in the July 1947 issue of the journal Foreign Affairs *laid out the strategy of containment that would guide U.S. foreign policy during the Cold War (document 7.9). After serving in the State Department for decades, Kennan became a historian at the Institute for Advanced Study, Princeton, where he wrote prize-winning books and commented frequently on current problems in international relations. In 1985, at the age of eighty-one, he returned to the pages of* Foreign Affairs *to lay out his vision of the problems of a new era. In this valedictory article, excerpted below, Kennan identified two of the phenomena that he predicted—accurately, as it turned out—would define international security into the next century: environmental crisis and the resumption of great-power competition.*

Except perhaps in some sectors of American government and opinion, there are few thoughtful people who would not agree that our world is at present faced with two unprecedented and supreme dangers. One is the danger not just of nuclear war but of any major war at all among great industrial powers—an exercise which modern technology has now made suicidal all around. The other is the devastating effect of modern industrialization and overpopulation on the world's natural environment. The one threatens the destruction of civilization through the recklessness and selfishness of its military rivalries, the other through the massive abuse of its natural habitat. Both are relatively new problems, for the solution of which past experience affords little guidance. Both are urgent. The problems of political misgovernment, to which so much of our thinking about moral values has recently related, is as old as the human species itself. It is a problem that will not be solved in our time, and need not be. But the environmental and nuclear crises will brook no delay.

The need for giving priority to the averting of these two overriding dangers has a purely rational basis—a basis in national interest—quite aside from morality. For short of a nuclear war, the worst that our Soviet rivals could do to us, even in our wildest worst-case imaginings, would be a far smaller tragedy than that which would assuredly confront us (and if not us, then our children) if we failed to face up to these two apocalyptic dangers in good time. But is there not also a moral component to this necessity?

Of all the multitudinous celestial bodies of which we have knowledge, our own earth seems to be the only one even remotely so richly endowed with the resources that make possible human life—not only make it possible but surround it with so much natural beauty and healthfulness and magnificence. And to the degree that man has distanced himself from the other animals in such things as self-knowledge, historical awareness and the capacity for creating great beauty (along, alas, with great ugliness), we have to recognize a further mystery, similar to that of the unique endowment of the planet—a mystery that seems to surpass the possibilities of the purely accidental. Is there not, whatever the nature of one's particular God, an element of sacrilege involved in the placing of all this at stake just for the sake of the comforts, the fears and the national rivalries of a single generation? Is there not a moral obligation to recognize in this very uniqueness of the habitat and nature of man the greatest of our moral responsibilities, and to make of ourselves, in our national personification, its guardians and protectors rather than its destroyers?

This, it may be objected, is a religious question, not a moral-political one. True enough, if one will. But the objection invites the further question as to whether there is any such thing as morality that does not rest, consciously or otherwise, on some foundation of religious faith, for the renunciation of self-interest, which is what all morality implies, can never be rationalized by purely secular and materialistic considerations.

Document 17.2

CHINA'S RENEWED CHALLENGE

Words can have multiple meanings, and the varied understandings of the word "democracy" found around the world offers a case in point. George W. Bush famously made democracy promotion the centerpiece of his foreign policy, yet Chinese officials brought a quite different sense of the word to their political discussions as the twenty-first century progressed, exemplified by the article below. Yu Keping's "Democracy Is a Good Thing" appeared in an influential government-sponsored journal in 2006. Written by a well-placed official, it signaled the Beijing regime's determination to legitimize its policies, and its spreading influence throughout Asia and beyond, as a new brand of democracy promotion with, as he put it, "Chinese characteristics."

Democracy is a good thing, but this is not to say that democracy comes unconditionally. Implementing democracy requires the presence of economic, cultural, and political preconditions; the unconditional promotion of democracy will bring disastrous consequences to the nation and its people. Political democracy is the trend of history, and it is the inevitable trend for all nations of the world to move toward democracy. But the timing and speed of the development of democracy and the choice of the form and system of democracy are conditional. An ideal democratic system must be related to the economic level of development of society, the regional politics, and the international environment, and it must also be intimately related to the national tradition of political culture, the quality of the politicians and the people, and the daily customs of the people. It requires the wisdom of the politicians and the people to determine how to pay the minimum political and social price in order to obtain the maximum democratic effects. In that sense, democratic politics is a political art. To promote democratic politics, one should have an elaborate system design and excellent political techniques.

Democracy is a good thing, but that does not mean that democracy can force the people to do things. The most concrete meaning of democracy is that it is government by the people who get to make choices. Even though democracy is a good thing, no person or political organization has the right to regard itself as the embodiment of democracy and therefore able to force the people to do this and not to do that in the name of democracy. Democracy requires enlightenment; it requires the rule of law, authority, and sometimes even coercion to maintain social order. The basic approach to developing democracy is not the forceful imposition of a democratic order by the government, but rather the emergence of such an order from among the people. Since democracy is rule by the people, it should respect the people's own choice. If a national government employs forceful means to make the people accept a system that they did not choose, then this is national autocracy and national tyranny masquerading as democracy. When one country uses mostly violent methods to force the people in other countries to accept their so-called democratic system, then this is international autocracy and international tyranny. National tyranny and international tyranny are both contrary to the nature of democracy.

We Chinese are presently building a strong, modern socialist nation with unique Chinese characteristics. For us, democracy is not only a good thing but an essential one. The classical authors of Marxism said, "There is no socialism without democracy." Recently Chairman Hu Jintao pointed out further, "There is no modernization without democracy." Of course, we are building a socialist democracy with unique Chinese characteristics. On the one hand, we want to absorb the best aspects of human political culture from around the world, including the best of democratic politics; on the other hand, we will not import wholesale an overseas political model. Our construction of political democracy must be closely integrated with the history, culture, traditions, and existing social conditions in our nation. Only in this way can the people of China truly enjoy the sweet fruits of political democracy.

Document 17.3

RUSSIA'S RENEWED CHALLENGE

Russia underwent a difficult period of transition in the decade following the end of the Cold War and the breakup of the Soviet Union. Upon becoming the country's president in 2000, Vladimir Putin went about restoring Russian power, at first through continuing his predecessors' policy of maintaining cordial relations, and even at times cooperation, with the West. However, once he returned Russia to the front rank of the world's great powers, Putin adopted a more adversarial stance, especially toward the United States. Using the Syrian civil war as his backdrop, Putin used an article in the New York Times *to signal a more assertive Russian presence by voicing direct criticism about U.S. intervention in the Middle East and the legitimacy of American exceptionalism.*

Recent events surrounding Syria have prompted me to speak directly to the American people and their political leaders. It is important to do so at a time of insufficient communication between our societies.

Relations between us have passed through different stages. We stood against each other during the cold war. But we were also allies once, and defeated the Nazis together. The universal international organization—the United Nations—was then established to prevent such devastation from ever happening again. . . .

Syria is not witnessing a battle for democracy, but an armed conflict between government and opposition in a multireligious country. There are few champions of democracy in Syria. But there are more than enough Qaeda fighters and extremists of all stripes battling the government. . . .

It is alarming that military intervention in internal conflicts in foreign countries has become commonplace for the United States. Is it in America's long-term interest? I doubt it. Millions around the world increasingly see America not as a model of democracy but as relying solely on brute force, cobbling coalitions together under the slogan "you're either with us or against us."

But force has proved ineffective and pointless. Afghanistan is reeling, and no one can say what will happen after international forces withdraw. Libya is divided into tribes and clans. In Iraq the civil war continues, with dozens killed each day. In the United States, many draw an analogy between Iraq and Syria, and ask why their government would want to repeat recent mistakes. . . .

My working and personal relationship with President Obama is marked by growing trust. I appreciate this. I carefully studied his address to the nation on Tuesday. And I would rather disagree with a case he made on American exceptionalism, stating that the United States' policy is "what makes America different. It's what makes us exceptional." It is extremely dangerous to encourage people to see themselves as exceptional, whatever the motivation. There are big countries and small countries, rich and poor, those with long democratic traditions and those still finding their way to democracy. Their policies differ, too. We are all different, but when we ask for the Lord's blessings, we must not forget that God created us equal.

Document 17.4

A NEW COLD WAR?

In 2014, a year after the publication of Putin's New York Times *article, Russia annexed the Crimean Peninsula, home to a large Russian population but at the time an integral part of another sovereign nation-state, Ukraine. Undeterred by international law, and fearful that Ukraine was becoming closer to the European Union and NATO, Russia sponsored a referendum in Crimea on whether its people wanted to remain part of Ukraine or secede and join Russia. In his response to*

Russia's annexation of Crimea, Obama announced a series of countermeasures designed to punish Russia without provoking the outbreak of war. Take note of two things in particular: First, Obama's repeated invocation of a concept, the "international community," that emerged during the Cold War and exploded in usage during the globalization of the 1990s but steeply declined following the U.S. invasion of Iraq in 2003; and second, Obama's reliance on an old tool of internationalist statecraft, economic sanctions, that was becoming an even more frequent weapon of choice as American officials grappled with the revival of fierce competition between nuclear powers in the twenty-first century.

Good morning, everybody. I wanted to provide an update on the situation in Ukraine and the steps that the United States is taking in response.

Over the last several days, we've continued to be deeply concerned by events in Ukraine. We've seen an illegal referendum in Crimea; an illegitimate move by the Russians to annex Crimea; and dangerous risks of escalation, including threats to Ukrainian personnel in Crimea and threats to southern and eastern Ukraine as well. These are all choices that the Russian government has made—choices that have been rejected by the international community, as well as the government of Ukraine. And because of these choices, the United States is today moving, as we said we would, to impose additional costs on Russia.

Based on the executive order that I signed in response to Russia's initial intervention in Ukraine, we're imposing sanctions on more senior officials of the Russian government. In addition, we are today sanctioning a number of other individuals with substantial resources and influence who provide material support to the Russian leadership, as well as a bank that provides material support to these individuals.

Now, we're taking these steps as part of our response to what Russia has already done in Crimea. At the same time, the world is watching with grave concern as Russia has positioned its military in a way that could lead to further incursions into southern and eastern Ukraine. For this reason, we've been working closely with our European partners to develop more severe actions that could be taken if Russia continues to escalate the situation.

As part of that process, I signed a new executive order today that gives us the authority to impose sanctions not just on individuals but on key sectors of the Russian economy. This is not our preferred outcome. These sanctions would not only have a significant impact on the Russian economy, but could also be disruptive to the global economy. However, Russia must know that further escalation will only isolate it further from the international community. The basic principles that govern relations between nations in Europe and around the world must be upheld in the 21st century. That includes respect for sovereignty and territorial integrity—the notion that nations do not simply redraw borders, or make decisions at the expense of their neighbors simply because they are larger or more powerful. . . .

In Europe, I'll also be reinforcing a message that Vice President Biden carried to Poland and the Baltic states this week: America's support for our NATO allies is unwavering. We're bound together by our profound Article 5 commitment to defend one another, and by a set of shared values that so many generations sacrificed for. We've already increased our support for our Eastern European allies, and we will continue to strengthen NATO's collective defense, and we will step up our cooperation with Europe on economic and energy issues as well.

Let me close by making a final point. Diplomacy between the United States and Russia continues. We've emphasized that Russia still has a different path available—one that de-escalates the situation, and one that involves Russia pursuing a diplomatic solution with the government in Kyiv, with the support of the international community. The Russian people need to know, and Mr. Putin needs to understand that the Ukrainians shouldn't have to choose between the West and Russia. We want the Ukrainian people to determine their own destiny, and to have good relations with the United States, with Russia, with Europe, with anyone that they choose. And that can only happen if Russia also recognized the rights of all the Ukrainian people to determine their future as free individuals, and as a sovereign nation—rights that people and nations around the world understand and support.

Document 17.5

IS CHINA A PARTNER?

If a newly assertive Russia was one challenge for American foreign policy makers, China was another matter entirely. Following Richard Nixon's opening in 1971–72 (see documents 12.2 and 12.8) and Jimmy Carter's normalization of official relations in 1979, the People's Republic of China became a key strategic and economic partner of the United States. Even the Tiananmen Square massacre in 1989 (see document 13.14) did little to damage relations between Washington and Beijing. But in the new century this relationship oscillated between cooperation and confrontation, and by 2016 it was at a crossroads. As we see in this exchange from 2017, Trump and his Chinese counterpart, Xi Jinping, initially sought to overcome growing tensions and reset the U.S.-China partnership.

President Xi Jinping:

The development of China and the United States is mutually reinforcing. Without contradicting each other, our respective success serves the common interests of both countries. We believe that facing the complex and changing international landscape, in maintaining world peace and stability, in promoting global development and prosperity, China and the United States, being two large countries, share more common interests, shoulder greater responsibility, and enjoy broader room for cooperation.

A healthy, stable, and growing China-U.S. relationship is not only in the fundamental interest of the Chinese and American people, it also meets the expectations of the international community. For China and the United States, win-win cooperation is the only right choice and the pathway toward a better future. . . .

As two distinctive countries, our two sides may have different views or differences on some issues. This is only natural. The key is to properly handle and manage them. There is far more common interests between our two countries than differences. It is important to respect each other's sovereignty and territorial integrity, respect each other's choice of development path and our difference. As long as the two sides commit to a constructive approach, we can put aside undiffused differences, while at the same time build common ground and advance cooperation. . . .

President Donald Trump:

President Xi, I want to thank you for an incredible welcoming ceremony earlier this morning. It was . . . truly memorable and impressive and something I will never forget. Melania and I are honored to visit your country, with its ancient history, dynamic people, and thriving culture. I also want to thank you and Madam Peng for a tour that was given to us yesterday of the very majestic Forbidden City. Your people are proud of who they are and what they have built together, and your people are also very proud of you.

I want to congratulate you on the recent and very successful 19th Party Congress. Perhaps now more than ever, we have an opportunity to strengthen the relationship between our two countries and improve the lives of our citizens, as long as we stand together—with others, if necessary—against those who threaten our civilization. That threat will never happen. It doesn't even have a chance. . . .

In addition to improving the safety and security of our citizens, President Xi and I discussed improving our economic relationship. We want a vibrant trade relationship with China. We also want a fair and reciprocal one. Today I discussed with President Xi the chronic imbalance in our relationship as it pertains to trade and the concrete steps that we'll jointly take to solve the problem of the massive trade distortion.

This includes addressing China's market access restrictions and technology transfer requirements, which prevent American companies from being able to fairly compete within China. The United States is committed to protecting the intellectual property of our companies and providing a level playing field for our workers. At the same time, our relationship with you and China is a very important one to me and to all of the people of our country. And just by looking at the tremendous, incredible, job-producing agreements just signed by those major companies, we're off to a very, very good start.

As part of our commitment to regional stability and peace, the United States also continues to advocate for reforms that advance economic freedom, individual rights, and the rule of law.

The United States, working with China and other regional partners, has an incredible opportunity to advance the cause of peace, security, and prosperity all across the world. It's a very special time, and we do indeed have that very, very special opportunity. A great responsibility has been placed on our shoulders, President—it's truly a great responsibility—and I hope we can rise to the occasion and help our countries and our citizens reach their highest destinies and their fullest potentials.

Document 17.6

"HOW DARE YOU!"

The return of great-power rivalry was only one of the new global challenges facing the United States. The twenty-first century brought others too, chief among them the problem of climate change. Experts had already been warning about the likely effects environmental crisis would have on international security (see documents 14.1 and 14.9), but by the 2010s the issue was still not considered a top priority by many countries, including the United States. Environmental protest intensified in response, epitomized by the Swedish teenage activist Greta Thunberg, speaking here to the United Nations.

My message is that we'll be watching you.

This is all wrong. I shouldn't be up here. I should be back in school on the other side of the ocean. Yet you all come to us young people for hope. How dare you!

You have stolen my dreams and my childhood with your empty words. And yet I'm one of the lucky ones. People are suffering. People are dying. Entire ecosystems are collapsing. We are in the beginning of a mass extinction, and all you can talk about is money and fairy tales of eternal economic growth. How dare you!

For more than thirty years, the science has been crystal clear. How dare you continue to look away and come here saying that you're doing enough, when the politics and solutions needed are still nowhere in sight.

You say you hear us and that you understand the urgency. But no matter how sad and angry I am, I do not want to believe that. Because if you really understood the situation and still kept on failing to act, then you would be evil. And that I refuse to believe. . . .

How dare you pretend that this can be solved with just "business as usual" and some technical solutions? With today's emissions levels, that remaining CO2 budget will be entirely gone within less than 8 1/2 years.

There will not be any solutions or plans presented in line with these figures here today, because these numbers are too uncomfortable. And you are still not mature enough to tell it like it is.

You are failing us. But the young people are starting to understand your betrayal. The eyes of all future generations are upon you. And if you choose to fail us, I say: We will never forgive you.

We will not let you get away with this. Right here, right now is where we draw the line. The world is waking up. And change is coming, whether you like it or not.

Document 17.7

THE FALL AND RISE OF THE WEST?

By 2020, the combined effects of the rise of China, the resurgence of Russia, the strength of authoritarianism worldwide, and the various crises that beset the United States—disastrous wars in the Middle East, financial crisis and recession, domestic turbulence during the Trump presidency—had produced a powerful sense of decline among NATO allies. The uncertainties of climate change only added to the general sense of foreboding. In this report from that year's Munich Security Conference, analysts use a play on words—"westlessness," which hinted at both a world order without the West but also the restlessness of the western allies themselves—to reflect on this crisis of confidence.

A century ago, Oswald Spengler published his book *The Decline of the West* ("Der Untergang des Abendlandes"), in which he predicted the impending decay and ultimate fall of Western civilization. Today, "the West" is the subject of a new declinist literature, as a cottage industry of politicians, pundits, and public intellectuals has produced speeches, books, reports, and articles discussing the decay of the Western project.

In the past, the Munich Security Conference (MSC) was often referred to as a kind of "family reunion" of the West. While it has evolved to bring in a much broader spectrum of the international community, it continues to provide a prime opportunity to take the temperature of not just the state of international peace and security in general but of the West in particular. Judging from the reporting on last year's conference, the West is indeed in serious trouble. The *New York Times* even labeled the gathering a "requiem for the West." And while the MSC has traditionally been a venue for the coordination of Western policies, in recent years "the focus has shifted to the schisms within the West." Those rifts were on full display when Chancellor Angela Merkel and Vice President Mike Pence took to the stage and offered different responses to key challenges—from the future of the Iran deal or the pipeline project Nord Stream 2 to NATO defense spending and transatlantic trade imbalances. To a certain degree, such policy disagreements have always existed, and the Munich Security Conference has been known as a key venue for an open and frank exchange of different views. Today, however, it is evident that something more fundamental is at play. Listening to Merkel and Pence, it appeared that the small and crowded ballroom of the Bayerischer Hof was home to two different worlds. The audience came away with the distinct impression that there was no common understanding of what the West represents.

Far-reaching power shifts in the world and rapid technological change contribute to a sense of anxiety and restlessness. The world is becoming less Western. But more importantly, the West itself may become less Western, too. This is what we call "Westlessness." . . .

[T]he defenders of an open, liberal West, caught on the wrong foot, so far seem unable to find an adequate answer to the illiberal-nationalist challenge, which researchers describe as having both cultural and economic causes. Part of the reason for the seeming liberal inability to successfully confront nationalist populism may be found in the long, almost unshakable conviction that all obstacles to liberalization were only minor setbacks, as liberalism's eventual triumph was seen as inevitable. In the long run, liberal-democratic values would take hold everywhere: Europe would soon be "whole, free, and at peace," Russia and China would over time adopt liberal values and become "responsible stakeholders" in the Western-led liberal world order. Critics of "liberalization" were sometimes seen as "backward." In that sense, the liberal triumphalism of the post–Cold War period lacked necessary self-reflection. . . .

Critics often blame the United States for the lack of Western assertiveness, as Washington is said to abandon its traditional role as a guardian of the international order. For some, recent events underline "a rapid decline in the ability and willingness of the United States to shape events in the Middle East—leaving a gap that is being filled by other powers, such as Russia, Iran, and Turkey." In an unusually blunt statement, Angela Merkel asked: "Is it good for the Americans to want to pull out of Syria immediately and quickly, or is that not also a way to strengthen the opportunities for Iran and Russia to gain influence there?" Others complain that "these days, neither friend nor foe knows quite where America stands." President Trump's decision to withdraw US troops from Northern Syria, although repeatedly hinted at, came as a shock to many and triggered a new debate about the reliability of the Trump administration. The lack of consultation and deconfliction among allies, when it finally happened almost overnight, was a key reason for Emmanuel Macron's assertion that we are experiencing "the brain death of NATO."

While Europeans have been quick to criticize the United States, their own approach is, as critics point out, "even more impotent and inward-looking than that of the United States." The few proposals that were launched recently, such as the new German defense minister's call for a safe zone in northern Syria and for a European naval mission in the Strait of Hormuz, were more consequential for the debate in Berlin and other European capitals than for the situation in the region itself. While appreciated by some as honest attempts to address the deteriorating security situation in the region, the proposals did not gain traction due to a lack of domestic consensus and international support. In effect, they underlined the European inability to jointly shape Europe's neighbourhood. . . .

In a period shaped by the relative decline of the West and the relative rise of the non-Western world, it would seem even more important to have a common Western strategy. Alas, recent years have seen estrangement and diverging positions on crucial policy challenges—ranging from arms control and global trade to climate change or the role of international institutions. Unsurprisingly, others are keen on exploiting these rifts for their own purposes. At last year's Munich Security Conference, representatives from China, Iran, and Russia were quick to point out transatlantic differences and offer themselves as the seemingly better partners to Europe. . . .

These days, it is hard to escape the impression that the West is in retreat, in decline, and under constant attack—both from within and from without. Yet, there are still many reasons for liberal optimism. Despite a frightening illiberal *zeitgeist*, autocratic governments are not necessarily on a never-ending winning streak. After all, a closer look reveals that those countries that Western strategists have identified as the main challengers are facing their own domestic crises that may easily dwarf the challenges that Western countries have to deal with. Russia remains "a 'one-crop economy' with corrupt institutions and serious demographic and health problems." And China's increasingly authoritarian policies and Xi's "imperious style" have also triggered a new wave of criticism at home—both among intellectuals and the party cadres. For them, it may become ever more difficult to deal with large-scale discontent at home. In contrast, Western countries, at least in theory, possess the necessary ideational, material, and institutional resources for a revitalization that will provide them with long-term advantages in a competitive environment.

Most importantly, liberal ideals are still powerful, autocrats' proclamations of the death of liberalism notwithstanding. While the liberal triumphalism of the early Cold War period exaggerated the ease with which liberal values would take over the whole globe, a requiem for the West as a set of ideas is premature. Quite strikingly, people outside the traditional world remind us of the unabated power of Western ideals. In Hong Kong, millions of people take to the streets to demand their democratic rights. And in Lebanon, citizens protest by singing Beethoven's *Ode to Joy*. People may be dissatisfied with how liberal ideas have been translated into political practice. But liberal ideas themselves will always be attractive.

Moreover, despite the relative decline of Western economic strength, the combined powers of the world's liberal democracies will remain second to none for a long time to come. The members of the D10, an informal group of nine key democratic countries and the EU, alone accounted for 57 percent of global GDP in 2018. If they are able to muster their combined political, economic, and military power they can maintain a version of the liberal order—and even improve it.

As recent years have made all too clear, Western liberal democracies are far from perfect. Checks and balances have been weakened, democratic values and traditions undermined. A revitalization of the West in the world must start at home. But, in contrast to autocratic regimes, liberal democracies have built-in mechanisms that allow for course corrections and democratic renewal. There may be bugs in the system, but it is not the system itself that is the bug.

Defenders of the West would do well to pursue what Thomas Kleine-Brockhoff calls "robust liberalism"—a modern liberalism that, being aware of its limits, stays clear of overreach but is more determined to defend the core of the liberal project. The West should be able to defend the liberal international order while accepting that global power shifts will bring competing models with which the liberal order will have to coexist. The transatlantic partners will have to reach out even more proactively to like-minded states across the world and think about new ways to ramp up cooperation among liberal democracies, revitalizing the West for the 21st century. The West may then continue to "decline" successfully, allowing the next generation of Spenglerians to reexamine the future of the West in the 22nd century.

Document 17.8

PANDEMIC

The global pandemic that began in 2019 was just that: global. Peoples around the world were more connected than ever before, not only digitally but also physically. Large-scale commercial air travel simply did not exist the last time a deadly virus so dramatically struck the world, and leaders on every continent struggled to meet a crisis none had ever witnessed in their lifetimes. COVID-19 originated in China before spreading abroad, leaving American policy makers the hope that they could contain the contagion before it reached their shores. In truth, it was already there. U.S. mitigation efforts began in March 2020. Having already limited travel from Asia, president Donald Trump addressed a nationwide audience on March 11 to announce new travel restrictions on Europe.

My fellow Americans, tonight I want to speak with you about our nation's unprecedented response to the coronavirus outbreak that started in China and is now spreading throughout the world.

Today, the World Health Organization officially announced that this is a global pandemic.

We have been in frequent contact with our allies, and we are marshaling the full power of the federal government and the private sector to protect the American people.

This is the most aggressive and comprehensive effort to confront a foreign virus in modern history. I am confident that by counting and continuing to take these tough measures, we will significantly reduce the threat to our citizens and we will ultimately and expeditiously defeat this virus.

From the beginning of time, nations and people have faced unforeseen challenges, including large-scale and very dangerous health threats. This is the way it always was and always will be. It only matters how you respond, and we are responding with great speed and professionalism.

Our team is the best anywhere in the world. At the very start of the outbreak, we instituted sweeping travel restrictions on China and put in place the first federally mandated quarantine in over fifty years. We declared a public health emergency and issued the highest level of travel warning on other countries as the virus spread its horrible infection.

And taking early intense action, we have seen dramatically fewer cases of the virus in the United States than are now present in Europe.

The European Union failed to take the same precautions and restrict travel from China and other hot spots. As a result, a large number of new clusters in the United States were seeded by travelers from Europe.

After consulting with our top government health professionals, I have decided to take several strong but necessary actions to protect the health and well being of all Americans.

To keep new cases from entering our shores, we will be suspending all travel from Europe to the United States for the next thirty days. The new rules will go into effect Friday at midnight. These restrictions will be adjusted subject to conditions on the ground.

There will be exemptions for Americans who have undergone appropriate screenings, and these prohibitions will not only apply to the tremendous amount of trade and cargo, but various other things as we get approval. Anything coming from Europe to the United States is what we are discussing. These restrictions will also not apply to the United Kingdom.

At the same time, we are monitoring the situation in China and in South Korea. And, as their situation improves, we will reevaluate the restrictions and warnings that are currently in place for a possible early opening.

Document 17.9

IMMIGRATION AND HUMAN RIGHTS

Immigration has been one of the most contentious issues in American politics for more than a century, but in the twenty-first century it became increasingly central to questions of national security. This stemmed in large part from the fact that since the 1980s immigrants arrived via U.S. land borders rather than on transoceanic journeys to U.S. ports, which made the flow of people much more difficult to control. The increase of transnational drug trafficking and terrorism led some Americans to fear that these migrant flows were actually security concerns (see document 16.4). But others pushed back, interpreting the strict control of U.S. borders as a problem of human rights, which was also a central component of U.S. foreign policy in the twenty-first century. In this press release, four congresswomen call for the defunding of the agency tasked with policing the nation's borders.

WASHINGTON, D.C.—Today, Representatives Alexandria Ocasio-Cortez, Ilhan Omar, Ayanna Pressley, and Rashida Tlaib released a statement urging House Leadership to significantly reduce the budget for Customs and Border Patrol (CBP) in the upcoming Appropriations bills. This call follows a recent report from the Government Accountability Office (GAO), which found that the additional funds appropriated by Congress to CBP in 2019, which the four Congresswomen voted against, were misused.

"As we continue through appropriations season, it is important to remember the lessons of last year. In 2019, as thousands of migrant families were held in cages and detained in horrific conditions along the southern border, the President requested and Congress handed over an additional $112 million in funding to CBP, which was intended to be used for food and medical care. In June, a report unveiled by the GAO, an independent government watchdog, found that these taxpayer funds were instead used on dirt bikes, ATVs, and other unnecessary items.

"Last year, the four of us voted against this CBP funding, clear eyed that CBP and ICE [Immigration and Customs Enforcement] are rogue agencies that act to inflict harm on our communities and have a pattern of behavior of abuse and mismanagement of funds. This year, the House must hold CBP accountable for their egregious violation of the law by withholding any further funding and imposing additional accountability measures with real consequences."

Document 17.10

THE PANDEMIC AND GLOBAL AFFAIRS

The COVID-19 pandemic presented the United States and other countries with urgent policy decisions about how to control their borders, develop vaccines, and distribute protective equipment. But it also raised questions about the long term. How would the pandemic interact with other trends to alter economics, politics, and diplomacy on a global scale in the decades to come? In March 2021, one year after COVID had emerged as a worldwide emergency, the Office of the Director of National Intelligence, the bureaucracy charged with coordinating information gathered by various intelligence agencies, addressed these questions in a report entitled "Global Trends 2040," one of its periodic assessments of world trends.

The COVID-19 pandemic emerged globally in 2020, wreaking havoc across the world, killing more than 2.5 million people as of early 2021, devastating families and communities, and disrupting economies and political dynamics within and between countries. Previous *Global Trends* editions forecasted the potential for new diseases and even imagined scenarios with a pandemic, but we lacked a full picture of the breadth and depth of its disruptive potential. COVID-19 has shaken long-held assumptions about resilience and adaptation and created new uncertainties about the economy, governance, geopolitics, and technology.

To understand and assess the impact of this crisis, we examined and debated a broad range of our assumptions and assessments related to key global trends. We asked a series of questions: Which existing trends will endure, which trends are accelerating or decelerating because of the pandemic, and where are we likely to experience fundamental, systemic shifts? Are the disruptions temporary or could the pandemic unleash new forces to shape the future? Much like the terrorist attacks of 11 September 2001, the COVID-19 pandemic is likely to produce some changes that will be felt for years to come and change the way we live, work, and govern domestically and internationally. How great these will be, however, is very much in question.

ACCELERATING, SHARPENING SOME TRENDS

The pandemic and corresponding national responses appear to be honing and accelerating several trends that were already underway before the outbreak. COVID-19 brought global health and healthcare issues into sharp relief, exposed and in some cases widened social fissures, underscored vast disparities in healthcare access and infrastructure, and interrupted efforts to combat other diseases. The pandemic also highlighted weaknesses in the international coordination on health crises and the mismatch between existing institutions, funding levels, and future health challenges.

Catalyzing Economic Trends. Lockdowns, quarantines, and the closing of international borders have catalyzed some preexisting economic trends, including diversification in global supply chains, increased national debt, and greater government intervention in economies. Moving forward, the character of globalization may retain some of the changes from this crisis period, and debt, particularly for developing economies, will strain national capacities for many years.

Reinforcing Nationalism and Polarization. Nationalism and polarization have been on the rise in many countries, especially exclusionary nationalism. Efforts to contain and manage the virus have reinforced nationalist trends globally as some states turned inward to protect their citizens and sometimes cast blame on marginalized groups. The response to the pandemic has fueled partisanship and polarization in many countries as groups argue over the best way to respond and seek scapegoats to blame for spreading the virus and for slow responses.

Deepening Inequality. The disproportionate economic impact of COVID-19 on low-income earners has caused them to fall further behind. When COVID-19 is finally controlled, many families are likely to have experienced further setbacks, especially those working in the service or informal sectors or who left the workforce to provide dependent care—predominantly women. The pandemic has exposed the digital divide within and between countries while spurring efforts to improve Internet access.

Straining Governance. The pandemic is straining government capacity for services and contributing to already low levels of trust in institutions in countries that have not effectively handled the response. The pandemic is exacerbating the confusing and polarized information environment that is undermining public confidence in health authorities, particularly in open societies. Illiberal regimes in some countries are using the pandemic as a pretext to more severely crack down on dissent and restrict civic freedoms, conditions that may outlive the disease.

Highlighting Failed International Cooperation. The COVID-19 pandemic exposed the weaknesses and political cleavages in international institutions, such as the World Health Organization (WHO) and United Nations, and called into question countries' ability and willingness to cooperate multilaterally to address common challenges beyond infectious disease, particularly climate change. The WHO, which has faced significant funding difficulties and resistance to mandatory surveillance regimes, is facing its gravest shock in nearly two decades. The crisis, however, may ultimately lead actors to make deeper reforms, standardize data collection and sharing, and forge new public-private partnerships.

Elevating the Role of Nonstate Actors. Nonstate actors, ranging from the Gates Foundation to private companies, have been crucial to vaccine research or retrofitting equipment to mass produce medical supplies and personal protective equipment. Nonstate networks will complement national and intergovernmental action in future health crises, including early warning, treatment, facilitation of data-sharing, and vaccine development.

WHILE OTHERS DECELERATE OR REVERSE

COVID-19 is slowing and possibly reversing some long-standing trends in human development, especially the reduction of poverty and disease and closing gender inequality gaps. The longest lasting reversals may be in poverty reduction across Africa, Latin America, and South Asia, followed by losses in gender equality. The resources devoted to fighting COVID-19 and social restrictions could reverse years of progress against malaria, measles, polio, and other infectious diseases by consuming key financial, material, and personnel resources.

The COVID-19 emergency may bring regions together in ways that previous crises have not. Although European countries early in the crisis imposed restrictions on border traffic and exports of critical medical supplies, the European Union has rallied around an economic rescue package and other emergency measures that could bolster the European integration project going forward. COVID-19 could also lead to redirection of national budgets toward pandemic response and economic recovery, diverting funds from defense expenditures, foreign aid, and infrastructure programs in some countries, at least in the near term.

MORE QUESTIONS THAN ANSWERS

The unanticipated second- and third-order effects of the COVID-19 pandemic have reminded us how uncertain the future is—both in the long and short term. As researchers and analysts, we must be ever vigilant, asking better questions, frequently challenging our assumptions, checking our biases, and looking for weak signals of change. We need to expect the unexpected and apply the lessons of this pandemic to our craft in the future.

DOCUMENT 17.11

CLIMATE CHANGE AS A MILITARY PROBLEM

The growing environmental crisis was not just a concern of young activists like Greta Thunberg. From a very different perspective, the Pentagon reached the same conclusion: Climate change was going to have a profound impact on daily life and basic security, including for the military. Here, in this 2021 report to the National Security Council, military officials outline some of their concerns.

Climate change is reshaping the geostrategic, operational, and tactical environments with significant implications for U.S. national security and defense. Increasing temperatures; changing precipitation patterns; and more frequent, intense, and unpredictable extreme weather conditions caused by climate change are exacerbating existing risks and creating new challenges for U.S. interests. Without adaptation and resilience measures, climate hazards, particularly when combined with other stressors, are likely to contribute to political, economic, and social instability around the world. In many cases, the physical and social impacts of climate change transcend political boundaries, increasing the risk that crises cascade beyond any one country or region. . . .

The risks of climate change to DoD strategies, plans, capabilities, missions, and equipment, as well as those of our allies and partners, are growing. Therefore, analyses based on historical frameworks will not be sufficient to prepare for future risks complicated by a changing climate. To train, fight, and win in this increasingly complex strategic, operational, and tactical environment, DoD will consider the effects of climate change at every level of the DoD enterprise. The Department will consider how crises exacerbated by climate change are likely to increase demand for defense missions and impact critical supply chains, infrastructure, and readiness. Mission success will depend on planning and operational adaptability that account for climate-related complexities and contingencies, and on forces, equipment, and capabilities engineered to adapt to and withstand more extreme environments. . . .

Even with aggressive international and whole-of-government action to mitigate future climate change, many effects to the physical environment are now unavoidable and will continue to shape our security environment. DoD will adapt to and mitigate the impacts of these changes to the climate as outlined in the DoD Climate Adaptation Plan (CAP) as well as the Sustainability Report and Implementation Plan (SRIP). The CAP details pathways to achieve an end-state where "DoD can operate under changing climate conditions, preserving operational capability and enhancing the natural and manmade systems essential to the Department's success."

DoD plays an important role in the whole-of-government effort to address climate change security risks, which includes working closely with allies, partners, and multilateral institutions to mitigate future climate change and adapt to those changes that are unavoidable. The challenges posed by climate change demand on-going analysis of evolving risks as well as investments in resilience, international development, and governance. As many areas of U.S. Government (USG) response are primarily the responsibility of civilian agencies, DoD will work closely with state and local governments and other parts of the Federal Government, including the Department of State, U.S. Agency for International Development (USAID), the Department of Homeland Security (DHS), intelligence agencies, and science agencies. DoD will often be in a supporting role to other agencies in working with local stakeholders and governments to counter climate-related risks to U.S. national security.

U.S. allies, partners, and competitors are assessing the implications of climate change on their respective strategic objectives. Malign actors may try to exploit regional instability exacerbated by the impacts of climate change to gain influence or for political or military advantage. Global efforts to address climate change—including actions to address the causes as well as the effects—will influence DoD strategic interests, relationships, and priorities. Cooperation with international partners to address the security implications of climate change can strengthen alliances and partnerships. Building awareness of how other nations are preparing for climate change is critical to understanding the risks and opportunities across strategic, operational, and tactical environments.

Document 17.12

CHINA AS A STRATEGIC THREAT

The ambivalence with which U.S. officials viewed China had disappeared by the time Joe Biden became president, and few in Washington perceived Beijing as a potential partner any longer. As a result, Barack Obama's "pivot" to Asia (document 16.2) moved from being a sound bite to, as secretary of defense Lloyd Austin put it here to an audience in Singapore in 2022, "our center of strategic gravity."

Today, the Indo-Pacific is our priority theater of operations.

Today, the Indo-Pacific is at the heart of American grand strategy.

Today, senior American officials—including the President, the Vice President, the Secretary of State, the National Security Adviser, and so many others—travel constantly in this region.

And today, American statecraft is rooted in this reality: No region will do more to set the trajectory of the 21st century than this one.

And so the Indo-Pacific is our center of strategic gravity. . . .

We'll also stand by our friends as they uphold their rights.

That's especially important as the PRC adopts a more coercive and aggressive approach to its territorial claims.

In the East China Sea, the PRC's expanding fishing fleet is sparking tensions with its neighbors. In the South China Sea, the PRC is using outposts on man-made islands bristling with advanced weaponry to advance its illegal maritime claims. We're seeing PRC vessels plunder the region's provisions, operating illegally within the territorial waters of other Indo-Pacific countries. And further to the west, we see Beijing continue to harden its position along the border that it shares with India.

You know, Indo-Pacific countries shouldn't face political intimidation, economic coercion, or harassment by maritime militias.

So the Department of Defense will maintain our active presence across the Indo-Pacific. We will continue to support the 2016 Arbitral Tribunal ruling. And we will fly, sail, and operate wherever international law allows. And we'll do this right alongside our partners....

We remain focused on maintaining peace, stability, and the status quo across the Taiwan Strait. But the PRC's moves threaten to undermine security, and stability, and prosperity in the Indo-Pacific. And that's crucial for this region, and it's crucial for the wider world.

Maintaining peace and stability across the Taiwan Strait isn't just a U.S. interest. It's a matter of international concern.

So let me be clear. We do not seek confrontation or conflict. And we do not seek a new Cold War, an Asian NATO, or a region split into hostile blocs.

We will defend our interests without flinching. But we'll also work toward our vision for this region—one of expanding security, one of increased cooperation, and not one of growing division.

I continue to believe that big powers carry big responsibilities. And so we'll do our part to manage these tensions responsibly, and to prevent conflict, and to pursue peace and prosperity.

Documents 17.13

HUMAN RIGHTS AND THE NATIONAL INTEREST

In the history of American foreign relations, human rights have had a long but uneasy relationship with the national interest. Liberal values have been at the heart of U.S. foreign policy since at least the days of Woodrow Wilson, but those values have often been honored in the breach, when presidents found it more advantageous to support, or receive support from, highly illiberal countries that were serial human rights abusers but that helped achieve U.S. national security objectives. Which should take priority: the promotion of human rights or the pursuit of stability? Sometimes those two goals aligned, and in this book we have seen many instances in which the promotion of values was designed to create a more secure and stable world order in line with U.S. interests. But sometimes those two goals have been sharply at odds, nowhere more so than with regard to U.S. relations with Saudi Arabia. The Biden administration was already wrestling with the contradiction between its desire to move to greener, carbon-free energy and the world economy's continuing reliance on oil (Saudi Arabia being the world's largest producer). But in this open letter to Biden, sent on the eve of a visit to Saudi Arabia, Hatice Cengiz added a very personal touch to the ongoing dilemma for U.S. foreign policy.

Dear President Biden:

My life turned upside down on Oct. 2, 2018, when my fiancé, *Washington Post* contributing columnist Jamal Khashoggi, entered the Saudi Consulate in Istanbul to obtain a document that would legalize our marriage.

I waited outside the consulate for Jamal, anxious and delighted that our new life was just around the corner, but he never reappeared. Instead, he was cruelly tortured and killed. According to the Central Intelligence Agency, Saudi Crown Prince Mohammed bin Salman himself gave the order for the crime. Since then, the thought of what happened to Jamal and the details of the suffering he endured have haunted me every day.

In the days, weeks and years that followed, I watched in horror as my fiancé's killers roamed free. As I fought to go on with my life, President Donald Trump disregarded the calls to hold Jamal's murderers accountable, and he rewarded them with billions of dollars worth of weapons. Calculating, cold politicians can never be trusted to bring about justice.

As I was on the verge of losing all hope, it was your remarks as you stood on a debate stage in November 2019 that rekindled my drive. You vowed to bring Jamal's killers to justice. "Khashoggi was, in fact, murdered and dismembered, and I believe on the order of the crown prince," you said, adding you would make Saudi Arabia "the pariah that they are." . . .

You can imagine how shocked and disappointed I was to learn that you would break your promise and travel to Saudi Arabia to likely meet with the crown prince—the person who U.S. intelligence determined was responsible for ordering Jamal's murder.

You condemn Russia for persecuting dissidents and committing war crimes in Ukraine. But the Saudis are executing the same horrific human rights abuses. Why are they being given a pass? Is that the price of oil? . . .

President Biden, Jamal would ask you this question if he were still alive: Who will defend freedom, democracy and human rights if the United States doesn't stand up to tyranny? If you don't confront those who make a mockery of these fundamental values at a time when the world needs principled leadership now, then when? . . .

President Biden, rather than helping to heal our anguish and sorrow with justice and accountability, this visit will significantly compound our grief and hopelessness. I implore you to cancel your trip and uphold your promise to pursue justice for Jamal.

Documents 17.14 and 17.15

WAR OF WORDS OVER UKRAINE

U.S.-Russian tensions reached a new peak on September 30, 2022, when the Moscow government granted diplomatic recognition to four parts of Ukraine that Russian forces had occupied in earlier months. Although strong evidence suggested that the Russian war effort was faltering badly, president Vladimir Putin used the occasion to deliver a speech aggressively asserting his country's revisionist goals and denouncing Western—especially U.S.—opposition to his designs. Later the same day, President Biden issued a brief statement rejecting Russia's recognition of the four territories and reasserting American determination to defend Ukrainian sovereignty.

Our compatriots, our brothers and sisters in Ukraine who are part of our united people have seen with their own eyes what the ruling class of the so-called West have prepared for humanity as a whole. They have dropped their masks and shown what they are really made of.

When the Soviet Union collapsed, the West decided that the world and all of us would permanently accede to its dictates. In 1991, the West thought that Russia would never rise after such shocks and would fall to pieces on its own. This almost happened. We remember the horrible 1990s, hungry, cold and hopeless. But Russia remained standing, came alive, grew stronger and occupied its rightful place in the world.

Meanwhile, the West continued and continues looking for another chance to strike a blow at us, to weaken and break up Russia, which they have always dreamed about, to divide our state and set our peoples against each other, and to condemn them to poverty and extinction. They cannot rest easy knowing that there is such a great country with this huge territory in the world, with its natural wealth, resources and people who cannot and will not do someone else's bidding.

The West is ready to cross every line to preserve the neo-colonial system which allows it to live off the world, to plunder it thanks to the domination of the dollar and technology, to collect an actual tribute from humanity, to extract its primary source of unearned prosperity, the rent paid to the hegemon. The preservation of this annuity is their main, real and absolutely self-serving motivation. This is why total de-sovereignisation is in their interest. This explains their aggression towards independent states, traditional values and authentic cultures, their attempts to undermine international and integration processes, new global currencies and technological development centres they cannot control. It is critically important for them to force all countries to surrender their sovereignty to the United States.

In certain countries, the ruling elites voluntarily agree to do this, voluntarily agree to become vassals; others are bribed or intimidated. And if this does not work, they destroy entire states, leaving behind humanitarian disasters, devastation, ruins, millions of wrecked and mangled human lives, terrorist enclaves, social disaster zones, protectorates, colonies and semi-colonies. They don't care. All they care about is their own benefit.

I want to underscore again that their insatiability and determination to preserve their unfettered dominance are the real causes of the hybrid war that the collective West is waging against Russia. They do not want us to be free; they want us to be a colony. They do not want equal cooperation; they want to loot. They do not want to see us a free society, but a mass of soulless slaves.

They see our thought and our philosophy as a direct threat. That is why they target our philosophers for assassination. Our culture and art present a danger to them, so they are trying to ban them. Our development and prosperity are also a threat to them because competition is growing. They do not want or need Russia, but we do. . . .

And all we hear is, the West is insisting on a rules-based order. Where did that come from anyway? Who has ever seen these rules? Who agreed or approved them? Listen, this is just a lot of nonsense, utter deceit, double standards, or even triple standards! They must think we're stupid.

Russia is a great thousand-year-old power, a whole civilisation, and it is not going to live by such makeshift, false rules. . . .

The dictates of the U.S. are backed up by crude force, on the law of the fist. Sometimes it is beautifully wrapped, sometimes there is no wrapping at all, but the gist is the same—the law of the fist. Hence, the deployment and maintenance of hundreds of military bases in all corners of the world, NATO expansion, and attempts to cobble together new military alliances, such as AUKUS and the like. Much is being done to create a Washington-Seoul-Tokyo military-political chain. All states that possess or aspire to genuine strategic sovereignty and are capable of challenging Western hegemony, are automatically declared enemies. . . .

They do not give a damn about the natural right of billions of people, the majority of humanity, to freedom and justice, the right to determine their own future. They have already moved on to the radical denial of moral, religious, and family values.

Let's answer some very simple questions for ourselves. Now I would like to return to what I said and want to address also all citizens of the country—not just the colleagues that are in the hall—but all citizens of Russia: do we want to have here, in our country, in Russia, "parent number one, parent number two and parent number three" (they have completely lost it!) instead of mother and father? Do we want our schools to impose on our children, from their earliest days in school, perversions that lead to degradation and extinction? Do we want to drum into their heads the ideas that certain other genders exist along with women and men and to offer them gender reassignment surgery? Is that what we want for our country and our children? This is all unacceptable to us. We have a different future of our own.

Let me repeat that the dictatorship of the Western elites targets all societies, including the citizens of Western countries themselves. This is a challenge to all. This complete renunciation of what it means to be human, the overthrow of faith and traditional values, and the suppression of freedom are coming to resemble a "religion in reverse"—pure Satanism. . . .

The world has entered a period of a fundamental, revolutionary transformation. New centres of power are emerging. They represent the majority—the majority!—of the international community. They are ready not only to declare their interests but also to protect them. They see in multipolarity an opportunity to strengthen their sovereignty, which means gaining genuine freedom, historical prospects, and the right to their own independent, creative and distinctive forms of development, to a harmonious process.

• • • • • •

The United States condemns Russia's fraudulent attempt today to annex sovereign Ukrainian territory. Russia is violating international law, trampling on the United Nations Charter, and showing its contempt for peaceful nations everywhere.

Make no mistake: these actions have no legitimacy. The United States will always honor Ukraine's internationally recognized borders. We will continue to support Ukraine's efforts to regain control of its territory by strengthening its hand militarily and diplomatically, including through the $1.1 billion in additional security assistance the United States announced this week.

In response to Russia's phony claims of annexation, the United States, together with our Allies and partners, are announcing new sanctions today. These sanctions will impose costs on individuals and entities—inside and outside of Russia—that provide political or economic support to illegal attempts to change the status of Ukrainian territory. We will rally the international community to both denounce these moves and to hold Russia accountable. We will continue to provide Ukraine with the equipment it needs to defend itself, undeterred by Russia's brazen effort to redraw the borders of its neighbor. And I look forward to signing legislation from Congress that will provide an additional $12 billion to support Ukraine.

I urge all members of the international community to reject Russia's illegal attempts at annexation and to stand with the people of Ukraine for as long as it takes.

Sources

1. Motives of Expansion

Document 1.1: Ulysses S. Grant, "Second Annual Message," December 5, 1870, American Presidency Project, http://www.presidency.ucsb.edu/ws/?pid=29511.

Document 1.2: Arnold Guyot, *Physical Geography* (New York: Scribner, Armstrong, 1873), 114–18.

Document 1.3: Josiah Strong, *Our Country: Its Possible Future and Its Present Crisis* (New York: American Home Missionary Society, 1885), 161, 173–76, 180.

Document 1.4: "A Vindication of Cuba," letter to the editor, *New York Evening Post*, March 25, 1889.

Document 1.5: Alfred Thayer Mahan, "The United States Looking Outward," *Atlantic Monthly* 66, no 398 (December 1890), 816–21.

Document 1.6: Frederick Jackson Turner, "The Significance of the Frontier in American History," in *The Frontier in American History* (New York: Henry Holt, 1920), 1–2, 32, 37–38.

Document 1.7: Carl Schurz, "Manifest Destiny," *Harper's New Monthly Magazine* 87 (October 1893), 737–46.

Document 1.8: *Beiblatt zum Kladderadatsch* (Berlin) 47, no. 28 (July 15, 1894), 1.

Document 1.9: Richard Olney to Thomas Francis Bayard, July 20, 1895, in U.S. Department of State, *Papers Relating to the Foreign Relations of the United States, with the Annual Message of the President, Transmitted to Congress December 2, 1895,* part 1 (Washington, D.C.: Government Printing Office, 1895), 554–55, 557–58.

Document 1.10: Charles R. Flint, "Our Export Trade," *The Forum* 23 (May 1897), 290–93.

Document 1.11: Liliuokalani, *Hawaii's Story by Hawaii's Queen* (Boston: Lothrop, Lee & Shepard, 1898), 354–56.

Document 1.12: Charles Jay Taylor, "Another Shotgun Wedding, with Neither Party Willing," *Puck* vol. 42, no. 1082 (December 1, 1897), cover. Library of Congress Prints and Photographs Division, Washington, D.C., Reproduction number LC-DIG-ppmsca-28757, http://www.loc.gov/pictures/item/2012647635/.

Document 1.13: Henry Childs Merwin, "On Being Civilized Too Much," *Atlantic Monthly* 79, no. 476 (June 1897), 838–40.

2. Imperial America

Document 2.1: Statement of Senator Redfield Proctor, March 17, 1898, printed in Clara Barton, *The Red Cross* (Washington: American National Red Cross, 1899), 534–39.

Document 2.2: *New York Journal*, February 17, 1898, 1.

Document 2.3: Theodore Roosevelt to George Dewey, February 26, 1898, Record Group 45, Naval Records Collection of the Office of Naval Records and Library, File Unit: 1989, 02/1898–02/1898, National Archives and Records Administration, College Park, Md.

Document 2.4: Stewart Woodford to William McKinley, March 17, 1897, telegram, in U.S. Department of State, *Papers Relating to the Foreign Relations of the United States* (Washington, D.C.: Government Printing Office, 1901), 687–88.
Document 2.5: Cartoon, in *Cartoons of the Spanish-American War*, ed. Charles Lewis Bartholomew (Minneapolis: Journal Printing, 1899), 7.
Document 2.6: Cartoon, in Bartholomew, ed., *Cartoons of the Spanish-American War*, 39.
Document 2.7: Cartoon, in Bartholomew, ed., *Cartoons of the Spanish-American War*, 69.
Document 2.8: Walter Hines Page, "The War with Spain, and After," *Atlantic Monthly* 81, no. 488 (June 1898), 721–29.
Document 2.9: "Shall Cuba Be Taken for Christ?" *American Missionary* 52, no. 3 (September 1898), 106–7.
Document 2.10: James Rusling, "Interview with President William McKinley," *Christian Advocate*, January 22, 1903, 17.
Document 2.11: William Jennings Bryan, *Republic or Empire: The Philippine Question* (Chicago: Independence, 1899), 41–46.
Document 2.12: Rudyard Kipling, "The White Man's Burden," *McClure's*, February 1899, 290.
Document 2.13: *The Statutes at Large of the United States of America from March 1897 to March 1899 and Recent Treaties, Conventions, Executive Proclamations, and The Concurrent Resolutions of the Two Houses of Congress*, vol. 30 (Washington, D.C.: Government Printing Office, 1899).
Document 2.14: *Annual Report of the War Department for Fiscal Year Ended June 30, 1899*, Report of the Major General Commanding the Army, part 2 (Washington, D.C.: Government Printing Office, 1899), 95–96.
Document 2.15: Murat Halstead, *Pictorial History of America's New Possessions* (New Haven, Conn.: Butler and Alger, 1899), 603.
Document 2.16: "Aguinaldo Shot by American Troops?" *New York Times*, June 4, 1900, 1.
Document 2.17: *The Statutes at Large of the United States of America from March 1897 to March 1899 and Recent Treaties, Conventions, Executive Proclamations, and The Concurrent Resolutions of the Two Houses of Congress*, vol. 30 (Washington, D.C.: Government Printing Office, 1899).
Document 2.18: Mark Twain, "Salutation to the Century," *Minneapolis Journal*, December 29, 1900, 2.
Document 2.19: Mark Twain, "The Battle Hymn of the Republic, Updated," *The Complete Works of Mark Twain*, vol. 20 (New York: Harper Brothers, 1917), 465.

3. Varieties of Empire

Document 3.1: William Graham Sumner, "The Conquest of the United States by Spain," January 16, 1899, in *War and Other Essays by William Graham Sumner*, ed. Albert Galloway Keller (New Haven, Conn.: Yale University Press, 1919), 297–334.
Document 3.2: John Hay to Joseph Choate, September 6, 1899, in U.S. Department of State, *Papers Relating to the Foreign Relations of the United States, 1899* (Washington, D.C.: Government Printing Office, 1901), 131–33.

Document 3.3: Brooks Adams, *America's Economic Supremacy* (New York: Macmillan, 1900), 50–53.
Document 3.4: Circular from John Hay to U.S. embassies in Berlin, Paris, London, Rome, and St. Petersburg, July 3, 1900, in U.S. Department of State, *Foreign Relations of the United States, 1901, Affairs in China Appendix* (Washington, D.C.: Government Printing Office, 1901), 12.
Document 3.5: Samuel D. Ehrhart, after a sketch by Louis Dalrymple, "Columbia's Easter Bonnet," *Puck* 49, no. 1257 (April 6, 1901), cover, Library of Congress Prints and Photographs Divisions, Washington, D.C., Reproduction number LC-DIG-ppmsca-25515, http://www.loc.gov/pictures/item/2010651396/.
Document 3.6: "The Water Cure Described: Discharged Soldier Tells Senate Committee How and Why the Torture Was Inflicted," *New York Times*, May 4, 1902, 13.
Document 3.7: "Relations with Cuba," in U.S. Department of State, *Treaties and Other International Agreements of the United States of America, 1776–1949*, vol. 6, ed. Charles I. Bevans (Washington, D.C.: Government Printing Office, 1971), 1116–17.
Document 3.8: Wilhelm von Polenz, *The Land of the Future*, trans. Lily Wolffsohn (Chicago: Brentano's, 1904), 280–82. Originally published as *Das Land Der Zukunft* (Berlin: Fontane, 1903).
Document 3.9: Liang Qichao, "Notes from a Journey to the New Continent," in *Land without Ghosts: Chinese Impressions of America from the Mid-Nineteenth Century to the Present*, trans. and ed. R. David Arkush and Leo O. Lee (Berkeley and Los Angeles: University of California Press, 1989), 89–90.
Document 3.10: Moorfield Storey, "The Recognition of Panama," address delivered at Massachusetts Reform Club, December 5, 1903 (Boston: G. H. Ellis, 1904), 14–19.
Document 3.11: Theodore Roosevelt, "Fourth Annual Message," December 6, 1904, American Presidency Project, http://www.presidency.ucsb.edu/ws/?pid=29545.
Documents 3.12 and 3.13: Albert Shaw, ed., *A Cartoon History of Roosevelt's Career* (New York: Review of Reviews, 1910), 134–35.
Document 3.14: Jane Addams speech, October 5, 1904, in *Official Report of the Thirteenth Universal Peace Congress* (Boston: Peace Congress Committee, 1904), 121–22.
Document 3.15: William Howard Taft to U.S. Senate, "Message from the President of the United States Transmitting a Loan Convention between the United States and Honduras," January 26, 1911, in U.S. Department of State, *Papers Relating to the Foreign Relations of the United States with the Annual Message of the President Transmitted to Congress December 3, 1912* (Washington, D.C.: Government Printing Office, 1919), 555–60.
Document 3.16: Robert Lansing to Woodrow Wilson, June 21, 1916, in U.S. Department of State, *Papers Relating to the Foreign Relations of the United States: Lansing Papers, 1914–1920* (Washington, D.C.: Government Printing Office, 1940), 558–59.

4. The Rise and Fall of Wilsonianism

Document 4.1: Woodrow Wilson, Fourth of July Address, in July 4, 1914, *The Papers of Woodrow Wilson*, vol. 30 (Princeton, N.J.: Princeton University Press, 1979), 248–55. © Princeton University Press.
Document 4.2: Woodrow Wilson, Remarks to the Associated Press, April 20, 1915, in *The Papers of Woodrow Wilson*, vol. 33 (1980), 37–41. © Princeton University Press.

Document 4.3: "I Didn't Raise My Boy to Be a Soldier," words: Alfred Bryan; music: Al Piantadosi, Archeophone Records.

Document 4.4: Woodrow Wilson, Address to the Senate, January 22, 1917, in *The Papers of Woodrow Wilson*, vol. 40 (1982), 533–39. © Princeton University Press.

Document 4.5: Woodrow Wilson, Address to a Joint Session of Congress, April 2, 1917, in *The Papers of Woodrow Wilson*, vol. 41 (1983), 519–27. © Princeton University Press.

Document 4.6: Woodrow Wilson, Address to a Joint Session of Congress, January 8, 1918, in *The Papers of Woodrow Wilson*, vol. 45 (1984), 534–39. © Princeton University Press.

Document 4.7: Anatole France, "Salut au Président W. Wilson," *L'Humanité*, December 14, 1918, 1.

Document 4.8: Cartoon, *Literary Digest* 60, no. 1 (January 11, 1919), 13.

Document 4.9: Raymond Poincaré, "Remarks to Assembled Delegates," in Charles F. Horne, ed., *Source Records of the Great War*, vol. 7 (New York: National Alumni, 1923), 37–43.

Document 4.10: Nguyen ai Quac [Ho Chi Minh] to Robert Lansing, June 18, 1919, Record Group 256: Records of the American Commission to Negotiate Peace, File Unit 851G.00, MLR I9 27, National Archives and Records Administration, College Park, Maryland.

Document 4.11: Henry Cabot Lodge, "League of Nations," August 12, 1919, *Congressional Record: Proceedings and Debates of the First Session of the Sixty-Sixth Congress of the United States of America*, vol. 58, part 4 (Washington, D.C.: Government Printing Office, 1919), 3778–84.

Document 4.12: Cartoon, *Punch* 157 (September 3, 1919), 203.

Document 4.13: Woodrow Wilson, Address in the City Auditorium in Pueblo, Colorado, September 25, 1919, in *The Papers of Woodrow Wilson*, vol. 63 (1990), 500–513. © Princeton University Press.

Document 4.14: Henry Cabot Lodge, "Reservations with Regard to Treaty," *Congressional Record*, vol. 58, part 9 (Washington, D.C., 1919), 877–78.

Document 4.15: Clark McAdams, "Panatela," *St. Louis Post-Dispatch*, November 19, 1919, 26.

Document 4.16: Cartoon, *Chicago Tribune*, November 20, 1919, 1.

Document 4.17: Advertisement, *New India* (Madras), January 11, 1919.

Document 4.18: Muhammad Husayn Haykal, *Fi Awqat al-Faragh*, originally published in Cairo as *al-Siyasah*, February 5, 1924, 149–56.

5. Isolation and Intervention

Document 5.1: Marcus Garvey, Address at Philadelphia, November 13, 1921, in *The Marcus Garvey and Universal Negro Improvement Association Papers*, vol. 4 (Berkeley and Los Angeles: University of California Press, 1985), 173–74, 176–77.

Document 5.2: Treaty on the Renunciation of War as an Instrument of National Policy, signed August 27, 1928, in *Treaties and Other International Agreements of the United States of America, 1776–1949*, vol. 2 (Washington, D.C.: Government Printing Office, 1969), 732–35.

Document 5.3: "The President Begins to Carry Out the Good-Neighbor Policy," April 12, 1933, in *The Public Papers and Addresses of Franklin D. Roosevelt*, ed.

Samuel I. Rosenman, vol. 2, *The Year of Crisis, 1933* (New York: Random House, 1938), 129–33.

Document 5.4: Cordell Hull, "William and Mary College Commencement—Address by the Secretary of State," *Congressional Record 1934*, June 13, 1934, 11349–50.

Document 5.5: *Report of the Special Committee on Investigation of the Munitions Industry* (Washington, D.C.: Government Printing Office, 1936).

Document 5.6: C. Van H. Engert (Addis Ababa) to State Department, May 12, 1936, in U.S. Department of State, *Foreign Relations of the United States, 1936*, vol. 3, *The Near East and Africa* (Washington, D.C.: Government Printing Office, 1953), 76.

Document 5.7: Franklin D. Roosevelt, Address at Chicago, October 5, 1937, in *The Public Papers and Address of Franklin D. Roosevelt, 1937: The Constitution Prevails*, ed. Samuel I. Rosenman (New York: Macmillan, 1941), 406–11.

Document 5.8: "Statement by the Japanese Prime Minister (Prince Konoye)," July 7, 1938, in U.S. Department of State, *Foreign Relations of the United States, Japan, 1931–1941*, vol. 1 (Washington, D.C.: Government Printing Office, 1943), 467–70.

Document 5.9: "Hoover's Address on 'New Departure' in Our Foreign Policy," *New York Times*, February 2, 1939. Used by permission of the Herbert Hoover Presidential Library Association, http://www.hooverassociation.org.

Document 5.10: George Buttrick and Samuel McCrea Cavert to Franklin D. Roosevelt, October 9, 1939, Presidential Papers, Official File 213, Franklin D. Roosevelt Library, Hyde Park, N.Y.

Document 5.11: Ruth Sarles, *A Story of America First: The Men and Women Who Opposed U.S. Intervention in World War II* (Westport, Conn.: Praeger, 2003; originally published 1942), 65–68.

Document 5.12: Franklin D. Roosevelt to Joseph C. Grew, January 21, 1941, in U.S. Department of State, *Foreign Relations of the United States, 1941*, vol. 4, *The Far East* (Washington, D.C.: Government Printing Office, 1956), 6–8.

Document 5.13: Joint Statement by President Roosevelt and Prime Minister Churchill, August 14, 1941, in U.S. Department of State, *Foreign Relations of the United States, 1941*, vol. 1, *General: The Soviet Union* (Washington, D.C.: Government Printing Office, 1941), 367–69.

Document 5.14: Franklin D. Roosevelt, Navy and Total Defense Day Address, October 27, 1941, in *The Public Papers and Address of Franklin D. Roosevelt, 1941: The Call to Battle Stations*, ed. Samuel I. Rosenman (New York: Harper and Brothers, 1950), 438–45.

6. World War II

Document 6.1: "Discussion of the Tripartite Pact, September 19, 1940," in Nobutaka Ike, ed., *Japan's Decision for War: Records of the 1941 Policy Conferences* (Stanford, Calif.: Stanford University Press, 1967), 4–10. © Stanford University Press.

Document 6.2: "Acting Secretary of State, Sumner Welles' Statement on the German Reich's Attack on the Soviet Union," in U.S. Department of State, *Foreign Relations of the United States*, 1941, vol. 1, *General: The Soviet Union* (Washington, D.C.: Government Printing Office, 1941), 767–68.

Document 6.3: "The Director of the War Plans Division of the Navy Department (Turner) to the Chief of Naval Operations (Stark), July 19, 1941 [The Possible

Effects of an Embargo]," in U.S. Department of State, *Foreign Relations of the United States*, 1941, vol. 4, *The Far East* (Washington, D.C.: Government Printing Office, 1956), 839–40.

Document 6.4: Memorandum of Conversation by the Under Secretary of State (Welles), August 11, 1941, in U.S. Department of State, *Foreign Relations of the United States*, 1941, vol. 1, 364–367.

Document 6.5: "Joint Declaration by the United States of America, China, Great Britain, the Union of Soviet Socialist Republics and Other Signatory Governments," in U.S. Department of State, *Foreign Relations of the United States*, 1942, vol. 1 (Washington, D.C.: Government Printing Office, 1960), 4.

Document 6.6: "Don't Sit Under the Apple Tree (with Anyone Else But Me)," words and music by Charlie Tobias, Lew Brown, and Sam H. Stept © 1942 (Renewed) CHED MUSIC CORPORATION and EMI ROBBINS CATALOG INC. All Rights for CHED MUSIC CORPORATION. Administered by WC Music CORP. Exclusive Print Rights for EMI Robbins Catalog Inc. Administered by ALFRED MUSIC. All Rights Reserved. Used by Permission of ALFRED MUSIC.

Document 6.7: "Mr. Mohandas K. Gandhi to President Roosevelt," July 1, 1942, in U.S. Department of State, *Foreign Relations of the United States*, 1942, vol. 1, 677–79.

Document 6.8: "President Roosevelt to Mr. Mohandas K. Gandhi," in U.S. Department of State, *Foreign Relations of the United States*, 1942, vol. 1, 703.

Document 6.9: "Airways to Peace Exhibition with Text by Wendell L. Willkie," Museum of Modern Art Archives, Press Releases, June 30, 1943. © Museum of Modern Art, New York.

Document 6.10: "Roosevelt-Stalin Meeting, November 29, 1943, Bohlen Minutes," in U.S. Department of State, *Foreign Relations of the United States*, 1943, vol. 3, *The Near East and Africa* (Washington, D.C.: Government Printing Office, 1953), 529–33.

Document 6.11: "Memorandum by President Roosevelt to the Secretary of State, January 24, 1944," in U.S. Department of State, *Foreign Relations of the United States*, 1944, vol. 3 (Washington, D.C.: Government Printing Office, 1965), 773.

Document 6.12: Franklin D. Roosevelt, press conference, February 23, 1945, American Presidency Project, http://www.presidency.ucsb.edu/ws/index.php?pid=16589.

Document 6.13: A. Leon Kubowitski to John J. McCloy, August 9, 1944, General Correspondence of John J. McCloy, 1941–45, War Refugee Board (file 400.38), Records of the Office of the Assistant Secretary of War (RG 107), National Archives and Records Administration, College Park, Md.

Document 6.14: John J. McCloy to A. Leon Kubowitski, August 14, 1944, General Correspondence of John J. McCloy.

Document 6.15: "Anglo-Russian Political Conversations at Moscow," Prem 3 434/4 9565, The National Archives, London.

Document 6.16: Pamphlet No. 4, in *Pillars of Peace, Documents Pertaining to American Interest in Establishing a Lasting World Peace: January 1941–February 1946* (Carlisle Barracks, Penn.: Army Information School, 1946).

Document 6.17: *Post-War Economic Policy and Planning: Hearings before the Special Committee on Post-War Economic Policy and Planning*, House of Representatives, 78th Congress, Second Session (Washington D.C.: Government Printing Office, 1944), 1081–83, 1098.

Document 6.18: Henry L. Stimson, "The Decision to Use the Atomic Bomb," *Harper's*, February 1947, 97–107.

Document 6.19: "The 36 Hour War: The Arnold Report Hints at the Catastrophe of the Next Great Conflict," *Life* 19, no. 21 (November 19, 1945), 27–36.

7. The Beginnings of the Cold War

Document 7.1: Wendell L. Willkie, *One World* (New York: Simon and Schuster, 1943), 53–54, 80, 84, 87. By permission of the Indiana University Foundation.

Document 7.2: W. Averell Harriman to Harry L. Hopkins, September 10, 1944, in U.S. Department of State, *Foreign Relations of the United States, 1944*, vol. 4 (Washington, D.C.: Government Printing Office, 1944), 988–90.

Document 7.3: George F. Kennan to James F. Byrnes, in U.S. Department of State, *Foreign Relations of the United States, 1946*, vol. 6 (Washington, D.C.: Government Printing Office, 1946), 699–700, 706–7.

Document 7.4: "The Way to Peace," September 12, 1946, Papers of Henry A. Wallace, Collection MsC 177, University of Iowa Libraries, Iowa City, Iowa.

Document 7.5: "Telegram from Nikolai Novikov, Soviet Ambassador to the US, to the Soviet Leadership," September 27, 1946, History and Public Policy Program Digital Archive, AVP SSSR, f. 06. op. 8, pp. 45, 759, published in *Mezhdunarodnaya Zhizn'* 11 (1990), 148–54, trans. for the Cold War International History Project by Gary Goldberg, http://digitalarchive.wilsoncenter.org/document/110808.

Document 7.6: "Special Message to the Congress on Greece and Turkey: The Truman Doctrine," March 12, 1947, in *Public Papers of the Presidents of the United States: Harry S. Truman, 1947* (Washington, D.C.: Government Printing Office, 1963), 176–80.

Document 7.7: David Low, cartoon, British Cartoon Archive, University of Kent, reference number LSE4889. By permission of DMG Media Licensing.

Document 7.8: "European Initiative Essential to Economic Recovery," June 5, 1947, *Department of State Bulletin* 16, no. 415 (June 15, 1947), 1159–60.

Document 7.9: X [George Kennan], "The Sources of Soviet Conduct," *Foreign Affairs* 25, no. 4 (July 1947), 575–76, 582. Reprinted by permission of *Foreign Affairs*. Copyright 1947 by the Council on Foreign Relations, Inc., http://www.foreign affairs.com.

Document 7.10: "Hearings before the Committee on Un-American Activities," House of Representatives, 80th Congress, 2d session, on Public Law 601 (Washington, D.C.: Government Printing Office, 1948), 504–11.

Document 7.11: Draft Report by the National Security Council on United States Policy toward China, February 28, 1949, in U.S. Department of State, *Foreign Relations of the United States, 1949*, vol. 9 (Washington, D.C.: Government Printing Office, 1949), 492–94.

Document 7.12: Alexander Paniushkin to Dean Acheson, March 31, 1949, in U.S. Department of State, *Foreign Relations of the United States, 1949*, vol. 4 (Washington, D.C.: Government Printing Office, 1975), 261–63.

Document 7.13: "Are We Afraid of Freedom?" *Hartford Courant*, June 19, 1949, A2. © *Hartford Courant*. All rights reserved. Distributed by Tribune Content Agency, LLC.

Document 7.14: *Congressional Record*, 81st Congress, 2d Session, vol. 96, part 2 (Washington, D.C.: Government Printing Office, 1950), 1954.

8. The Korean War and the Cold War of the 1950s

Document 8.1: "Statement by the President on the Situation in Korea," June 27, 1950, in *Public Papers of the Presidents* (Washington, D.C.: Government Printing Office, 1963), 173.

Document 8.2: "Substance of Statements Made at Wake Island Conference on 15 October, 1950," in U.S. Department of State, *Foreign Relations of the United States, 1950*, vol. 7 (Washington, D.C.: Government Printing Office, 1963), 948–60.

Document 8.3: "The Commander in Chief, Far East (MacArthur) to the Joint Chiefs of Staff, November 9, 1950, in U.S. Department of State, *Foreign Relations of the United States, 1950*, vol. 7, 1107–8.

Document 8.4: "United States Delegation Minutes of the First Meeting of President Truman and Prime Minister Attlee," December 4, 1950, in U.S. Department of State, *Foreign Relations of the United States, 1950*, vol. 7, 1361–74.

Document 8.5: William Faulkner, "Banquet Speech, December 10, 1950," http: //www.nobelprize.org/nobel_prizes/laureates/1949/faulkner.speech.html. Copyright © The Nobel Foundation (1950).

Document 8.6: "Memorandum by the Chairman of the National Security Resources Board (Symington) to the Executive Secretary of the National Security Council (Lay), September 5, 1950, in U.S. Department of State, *Foreign Relations of the United States, 1950*, vol. 1 (Washington, D.C.: Government Printing Office, 1977), 395–97.

Document 8.7: Dwight D. Eisenhower, "Text of the Address Given by Dwight D. Eisenhower, Republican Nominee for President, Delivered at Detroit, Michigan, October 24, 1952," http://www.eisenhower.archives.gov/research/online_documents/korean_war/I_Shall_Go_To_Korea_1952_10_24.pdf, reprinted with thanks to the Dwight D. Eisenhower Presidential Library.

Document 8.8: "Address, 'The Chance for Peace,' Delivered before the American Society of Newspaper Editors," April 16, 1953, in *Public Papers of the President, 1953* (Washington, D.C.: Government Printing Office, 1960), 179–82.

Document 8.9: James C. Hagerty, diary entry, Dwight Eisenhower Presidential Library, James C. Hagerty Papers, Diary Entries Series, Box 1, April 26, 1954.

Document 8.10: Raymond Aron, "Europe and Airpower," *Annals of the American Academy of Political and Social Science* 299 (1): 95–101. Copyright © 1955 by American Academy of Political & Social Science. Reprinted by permission of SAGE Publications.

Document 8.11: Edwin Marcus, "Awake at Last," Reproduction Number LC-Z62–108455, Library of Congress Prints and Photographs Division. By permission of the Marcus Family.

Document 8.12: "The Last Message of Imre Nagy," November 4, 1956, in *The 1956 Hungarian Revolution: A History in Documents* (Budapest: Central European University Press, 2003), 383. © National Security Archive and Central European University Press.

Document 8.13: "Memorandum of Discussion at the 303d Meeting of the National Security Council, Washington, D.C., November 8, 1956," in U.S. Department of State, *Foreign Relations of the United States, 1955–1957*, vol. 25 (Washington, D.C.: Government Printing Office, 1990), 1070.

Document 8.14: Senator John F. Kennedy and Vice President Richard M. Nixon First Joint Radio-Television Broadcast, October 7, 1960, John F. Kennedy Speeches, John F. Kennedy Presidential Library, Boston.

Document 8.15: "Memorandum of Conference on January 19, 1961, between President Eisenhower and President-Elect Kennedy on the Subject of Laos," in U.S. Department of State, *Foreign Relations of the United States, 1961–1963*, vol. 24 (Washington, D.C.: Government Printing Office, 1994), 20–22.

9. The Nationalist Challenge

Document 9.1: "The World's Colonies and Ex-Colonies: A Challenge to America," October 30, 1953, G. Mennen Williams papers, box 16, Bentley Library, University of Michigan, Ann Arbor, 1–5.

Document 9.2: "Speech before the Political Committee of the Asian-African Conference," April 22, 1955, in *The Asian-African Conference*, ed. George McT. Kahin (Ithaca, N.Y.: Cornell University Press, 1956), 64–67. Kahin indicates that this version of the speech, which is slightly different from other versions published over the years, was taken from a mimeograph distributed by the Indian delegation at Bandung.

Document 9.3: William J. Lederer and Eugene Burdick, *The Ugly American* (New York: W. W. Norton, 1999), 11–14. Copyright © 1958 by William J. Lederer and Eugene Burdick, renewed 1986 by William J. Lederer. Used by permission of W. W. Norton & Company, Inc., and Harold Ober.

Document 9.4: Michael Cummings, cartoon, British Cartoon Archive, University of Kent, reference number MCO524A. By permission of Express Newspapers.

Document 9.5: "Analysis of the Khrushchev Speech of January 6, 1961," Hearing before the Subcommittee to Investigate the Administration of the Internal Security Act and Other Internal Security Laws of the Committee on the Judiciary, U.S. Senate, 87th Congress, 1st session (Washington, D.C.: Government Printing Office, 1961), 52–78.

Document 9.6: "Inaugural Address," January 20, 1961, in *Public Papers of the Presidents, John F. Kennedy, 1961* (Washington, D.C.: Government Printing Office, 1962), 1–3.

Document 9.7: "Guerrilla Warfare in the Underdeveloped Areas," *Department of State Bulletin* 45, no. 1154 (August 7, 1961), 234–36.

Document 9.8: "The Port Huron Statement of the Students for a Democratic Society" (New York: Students for a Democratic Society, 1962), 27–30.

Document 9.9: U.S. Senate Committee on Commerce, Hearings on S. 1732, "A Bill to Eliminate Discrimination in Public Accommodations Affecting Interstate Commerce," 88th Congress, 1st Session, 281–83.

Document 9.10: Kwame Nkrumah to Lyndon Johnson, February 26, 1964, in U.S. Department of State, *Foreign Relations of the United States, 1964–1968*, vol. 24 (Washington, D.C.: Government Printing Office, 1999), 426–27.

Document 9.11: Speech by Herman Talmadge, Herman Talmadge Papers, Series II, Press Office Series, 1965 Subseries, box 280, Richard B. Russell Library, Athens, Ga.

Document 9.12: Herblock, cartoon, *Washington Post*, May 2, 1965, A24. A 1965 Herblock Cartoon, © The Herb Block Foundation.

Document 9.13: "Huey Newton Talks to the Movement about the Black Panther Party, Cultural Nationalism, SNCC, Liberals, and White Revolutionaries," *The Movement* (San Francisco) 4, no. 7 (August 1968), 8–9.

Document 9.14: "Alleged Assassination Plots Involving Foreign Leaders: An Interim Report of the Select Committee to Study Governmental Operations with Respect to Intelligence Activities," U.S. Senate, 94th Congress, 1st Session, November 20, 1975, xiii–5.

10. Years of Crisis

Document 10.1: Pat Frank, *Alas, Babylon* (New York: Harper Perennial, 1999), 90–91. First published 1959. Copyright © 1959 by Pat Frank. Reprinted by permission of HarperCollins Publishers.

Document 10.2: National Intelligence Estimate, "Estimate of the World Situation," January 17, 1961, in U.S. Department of State, *Foreign Relations of the United States, 1961–1963,* vol. 8 (Washington, D.C.: Government Printing Office, 1996), 3–9.

Document 10.3: Memorandum of Conversation, "Vienna Meeting Between the President and Chairman Khrushchev," June 3, 1961, in U.S. Department of State, *Foreign Relations of the United States, 1961–1963*, vol. 5 (Washington, D.C.: Government Printing Office, 1998), 183–85.

Document 10.4: "Radio and Television Report to the American People on the Berlin Crisis," July 25, 1961, in *Public Papers of the Presidents of the United States: John F. Kennedy, 1961* (Washington, D.C.: Government Printing Office, 1962), 533–36.

Document 10.5: Excerpts from Khrushchev's speech, August 4, 1961, History and Public Policy Program Digital Archive, Storage Center for Contemporary Documentation, miscellaneous documents of the CC CPSU International Department, trans. for the Cold War International History Project by Vladislav Zubok, http://digitalarchive.wilsoncenter.org/document/114837.

Document 10.6: John F. Kennedy to Willy Brandt, August 18, 1961, National Security File, Folder: Germany, Berlin, General, 8/19/61–8/20/61, John F. Kennedy Library, Boston.

Document 10.7: Memorandum for General Maxwell Taylor, Military Representative to the President, by Carl Kaysen, "Strategic Air Planning and Berlin," September 5, 1961, National Security Archive Electronic Briefing Book no. 56, ed. William Burr, September 25, 2001, document 1, http://www.gwu.edu/ sarchiv/NSAEBB/NSAEBB56/BerlinC1.pdf.

Document 10.8: "Off the Record Meeting on Cuba," October 16, 1962, in U.S. Department of State, *Foreign Relations of the United States, 1961–1962*, vol. 11 (Washington, D.C.: Government Printing Office), 60–61, 72.

Document 10.9: Report by advisory group led by Douglas Dillon, "Scenario for Airstrike against Offensive Missile Bases and Bombers in Cuba," October 25, 1962, Digital National Security Archive, item number CC01334, Document Set: the Cuban Missile Crisis, 1962, ed. Laurence Chang (Alexandria, Va.: National Security Archive and Chadwyck-Healey, Inc. [now ProQuest], 1990).

Document 10.10: Record 195, READD-RADD collection, Cuban Missile Crisis file, National Security Archive, George Washington University, Washington, D.C. (original archive: Archive of Foreign Policy of the Russian Federation), trans. Michelle Reeves.

Document 10.11: "Minutes of Conversation between the Delegations of the CPCz and the CPSU, the Kremlin (excerpt)," October 30, 1962, History and Public Policy Program Digital Archive, National Archive, Archive of the CC CPCz, (Prague); file: "Antonín Novotný, Kuba," Box 193. http://digitalarchive.wilson center.org /document/115219.

Document 10.12: David Low, cartoon, British Cartoon Archive, University of Kent, reference number LSE9141. By permission of DMG Media Licensing.

Document 10.13: John F. Kennedy, "Commencement Address at American University in Washington," June 10, 1963, *Public Papers of the Presidents of the United States: John F. Kennedy, 1963* (Washington, D.C.: Government Printing Office, 1964), 460–62.

11. The Vietnam War

Document 11.1: Dwight D. Eisenhower, The President's News Conference, April 7, 1954, in *Public Papers of the Presidents: Dwight D. Eisenhower, 1954* (Washington, D.C.: Government Printing Office, 1960), 381–90.

Document 11.2: Letter from the President's Military Representative (General Taylor) to the President, November 3, 1961, in U.S. Department of State, *Foreign Relations of the United States, 1961–1963*, Vol. 1, *Vietnam, 1961* (Washington, D.C.: Government Printing Office, 1988), 477–79.

Document 11.3: John F. Kennedy, Transcript of Broadcast with Walter Cronkite, September 2, 1963, in *Public Papers of the Presidents: John F. Kennedy, 1963* (Washington, D.C.: Government Printing Office, 1964), 650–653.

Document 11.4: Telephone conversation between President Johnson and National Security Adviser McGeorge Bundy, May 27, 1964, in *The Presidential Recordings: Lyndon B. Johnson*, vol. 6, *Toward the Great Society, February 1, 1964–May 31, 1964* (New York: W. W. Norton, 2007), 886–92.

Document 11.5: McGeorge Bundy to Lyndon Johnson, February 7, 1965, in U.S. Department of State, *Foreign Relations of the United States, 1964–1968*, vol. 2, *Vietnam, January–June 1965* (Washington, D.C.: Government Printing Office, 1996), 174–85.

Document 11.6: Hubert Humphrey to Lyndon Johnson, Washington, February 17, 1965, in U.S. Department of State, *Foreign Relations of the United States, 1964–1968*, vol. 2, *Vietnam, January–June 1965* (Washington, D.C.: Government Printing Office, 1996), 309–13.

Document 11.7: Lester B. Pearson, *Mike: The Memoirs of the Rt. Hon. Lester B. Pearson*, vol. 3, *1957–1968* (Toronto: University of Toronto Press, 1975), 138–39. © University of Toronto Press 2015. Reprinted with permission of the publisher.

Document 11.8: Lyndon Johnson, Address at Johns Hopkins University, "Peace without Conquest," April 7, 1965, *Public Papers of the Presidents: Lyndon B. Johnson, 1965* (Washington, D.C.: Government Printing Office, 1966), 394–99.

Document 11.9: Pham Van Dong, "The Four-Point Position of the Democratic Republic of Vietnam Regarding a Political Solution of the Vietnam Question," in *American Foreign Policy: Current Documents, 1965* (Washington, D.C.: Government Printing Office, 1968), 852–53.

Document 11.10: Bob Dylan, "Masters of War," on *The Freewheelin' Bob Dylan*, Columbia Records, 1963. © Bob Dylan/Special Rider Music. Reprinted with permission.

Document 11.11: Martin Luther King Jr., "A Time to Break Silence," speech at Riverside Church, New York, April 4, 1967. © 1967 Martin Luther King, Jr., copyright renewed 1995, Coretta Scott King. Reprinted by arrangement with The Heirs to the Estate of Martin Luther King, Jr., c/o Writers House as agent for the proprietor, New York, NY.

Document 11.12: Rolando E. Bonachea and Nelson P. Valdes, eds., *Che: Selected Works of Ernesto Guevara* (Cambridge, Mass.: MIT Press, 1969), 170–82. © Che Guevara Studies Center and Ocean Press. Reprinted with permission.

Document 11.13: Harold Ockenga, "Report from Viet Nam," *Christianity Today*, March 15, 1968, 35. © Gordon-Conwell Theological Seminary. Reprinted with permission.

Document 11.14: Richard M. Nixon, Address to the Nation on Southeast Asia, April 30, 1970, in *Public Papers of the Presidents: Richard M. Nixon, 1970* (Washington, D.C.: Government Printing Office, 1971), 405–10.

Document 11.15: Gerald R. Ford, Address at Tulane University, April 23, 1975, in *Public Papers of the Presidents: Gerald R. Ford, 1975* (Washington, D.C.: Government Printing Office, 1977), 568–73.

12. The Era of Détente

Document 12.1: "Text of Interview with the President Published in *America Illustrated* for Distribution in the Soviet Union," September 27, 1966, *Public Papers of the Presidents: Lyndon B. Johnson, 1966*, book 2 (Washington, D.C.: Government Printing Office, 1967), 1066–71.

Document 12.2: Richard M. Nixon, "Asia after Viet Nam," *Foreign Affairs* 46 (October 1967), 111–25. Reprinted by permission of *Foreign Affairs*. Copyright 1967 by the Council on Foreign Relations, Inc., http://www.foreignaffairs.com.

Document 12.3: Richard M. Nixon, Informal Remarks in Guam with Newsmen, July 25, 1969, in *Public Papers of the Presidents: Richard Nixon, 1969* (Washington, D.C.: Government Printing Office, 1971), 544–56.

Document 12.4: Richard M. Nixon, First Annual Report to the Congress on United States Foreign Policy for the 1970s, February 18, 1970, in *Public Papers of the Presidents: Richard Nixon, 1970* (Washington, D.C.: Government Printing Office, 1971), 116–90.

Document 12.5: President Nixon to Secretary of Defense Melvin Laird, February 4, 1969, in U.S. Department of State, *Foreign Relations of the United States, 1969–1976*, vol. 1, *Foundations of Foreign Policy, 1969–1972* (Washington, D.C.: Government Printing Office, 2003), 56–58.

Document 12.6: Richard M. Nixon, Address to the Nation Outlining a New Economic Policy, "The Challenge of Peace," August 15, 1971, *Public Papers of the Presidents: Richard Nixon, 1971* (Washington, D.C.: Government Printing Office, 1972), 886–91.

Document 12.7: Anatoly Dobrynin, *In Confidence: Moscow's Ambassador to America's Six Cold War Presidents, 1962–1986* (New York: Times Books, 1995), 197–98, 270–71. Copyright © 1995 by Anatoly Dobrynin. Used by permission of Crown Books, an imprint of Random House, a division of Penguin Random House LLC. All rights reserved.

Document 12.8: Henry Kissinger to Richard Nixon, July 14, 1971, in U.S. Department of State, *Foreign Relations of the United States, 1969–1972*, vol. 17, *China, 1969–1972* (Washington, D.C.: Government Printing Office, 2006), 453–55.

Document 12.9: "Vote and Debate on S.J. Res. 241," *Congressional Record, 1972*, September 14, 1972, 30623–27.

Document 12.10: House of Representatives Committee on Foreign Affairs, Subcommittee on International Organizations and Movements, *Human Rights in the World Community: A Call for U.S. Leadership—Report, March 27, 1974* (Washington, D.C.: Government Printing Office, 1974).

Document 12.11: Speech by Henry Kissinger, "The Moral Foundations of Foreign Policy," to the Upper Midwest Council, Minneapolis, July 15, 1975, *Department of State Bulletin*, August 4, 1975, 161–68.

Document 12.12: Jimmy Carter, "Address at Commencement Exercises at the University of Notre Dame," May 22, 1977, *Public Papers of the Presidents: Jimmy Carter, 1977*, vol.1 (Washington, DC: Government Printing Office, 1977), 954–62.

13. Escalating and Ending the Cold War

Document 13.1: Charter 77 Collection (MS 124), Archives and Special Collections, University of Nebraska–Lincoln Libraries.

Document 13.2: The Hostage Crisis in Iran, Iran Hostage's Diary, Robert C. Ode, Documents and Photographs On-Line Collection, Jimmy Carter Library, Atlanta.

Document 13.3: "Stasi Note on Meeting between Minister Mielke and KGB Chairman Andropov," July 11, 1981, History and Public Policy Program Digital Archive, Office of the Federal Commissioner for the Stasi Records (BStU), MfS, ZAIG 5382, 1–19, trans. for the Cold War International History Project by Bernd Schaefer, http://digitalarchive.wilsoncenter.org/document/115717.

Document 13.4: National Security Council Minutes (Poland), December 22, 1981, NSC Country File Box 91283, Ronald Reagan Presidential Library, Simi Valley, Calif.

Document 13.5: Ronald Reagan, "Address to Members of the British Parliament," June 8, 1982, *Public Papers of the Presidency* (Washington D.C.: Government Printing Office, 1983), 742–48.

Document 13.6: "The Challenge of Peace: God's Promise and Our Response: A Pastoral Letter on War and Peace by the National Conference of Catholic Bishops," http://old.usccb.org/sdwp/international/TheChallengeofPeace. © 1983 by United States Conference of Catholic Bishops, Washington D.C. Used with permission. All rights reserved.

Document 13.7: Memorandum of Conversation, December 28, 1984, NSC Records, European and Soviet Affairs Directorate, Box 90902, File: Thatcher Visit, December 1984 [1], Ronald Reagan Presidential Library, Simi Valley, Calif.

Document 13.8: "Gorbachev's Economic Agenda: Promises, Potentials, and Pitfalls," National Security Archive, http://www.gwu.edu/ sarchive/NSAEFF/NSA EFF1722/ doc13.pdf.

Document 13.9: Mikhail Gorbachev, memorandum, reprinted in *Masterpieces of History: The Peaceful end of the Cold War in Europe, 1989*, ed. Svetlana Savranskaya, Thomas Blanton, and Vladislav Zubok (Budapest: Central European University Press, 2010), 231–32. © National Security Archive and Central European University Press.

Document 13.10: Mikhail Gorbachev, notes, reprinted in Savranskaya, Blanton, and Zubok, eds., *Masterpieces of History*, 234–36. © National Security Archive and Central European University Press.

Document 13.11: Reykjavik (Reagan-Gorbachev) Summit, 4th Session, October 12, 1986, Matlock MSS, Box 92140, Ronald Reagan Presidential Library, Simi Valley, Calif.

Document 13.12: "Address by Mikhail Gorbachev at the UN General Assembly Session (Excerpts)," December 7, 1988, History and Public Policy Program Digital Archive, CWIHP Archive. http://digitalarchive.wilsoncenter.org/document/116224.

Document 13.13: Brent Scowcroft to George H. W. Bush, March 20, 1989, National Security Council Files, Arnold Kanter Files, Subject Files: NATO Summit-May 1989, George Bush Presidential Library, College Station, Tex.

Document 13.14: U.S. Embassy in Beijing to State Department, June 3, 1989, China-US Relations FOIA 00–00116, George Bush Presidential Library, College Station, Tex.

Document 13.15: Michael Edwards, "Right Here, Right Now," on Jesus Jones, *Doubt*, EMI Records, 1990. © 1991 by EMI Music Publishing Ltd. All rights administered by Sony Music Publishing (US) LLC. International copyright secured. All rights reserved. Reprinted by permission of Hal Leonard LLC.

14. Globalization after the Cold War

Document 14.1: Jessica Tuchman Mathews, "Redefining Security," *Foreign Affairs* 68, no. 2 (Spring 1989), 162–77. © 1989. Used with permission of the Council on Foreign Relations.

Document 14.2: George H. W. Bush, Address before a Joint Session of the Congress on the Persian Gulf Crisis and the Federal Budget Deficit, September 11, 1990, in *Public Papers of the Presidents: George Bush, 1990*, vol. 2 (Washington, D.C.: Government Printing Office, 1991), 1218–22.

Document 14.3: Anthony Swofford, *Jarhead: A Marine's Chronicle of the Gulf War and Other Battles* (New York: Scribner, 2003), 123, 244–45, 250–51. Copyright © 2003 by Anthony Swofford. Reprinted with the permission of Scribner Publishing Group. All rights reserved.

Document 14.4: Bill Clinton, Remarks at the Signing Ceremony for the Israeli- Palestinian Declaration of Principles, September 13, 1993, in *Public Papers of the Presidents: Bill Clinton, 1993* (Washington, D.C.: Government Printing Office, 1994), 1475–77.

Document 14.5: Tony Lake, "From Containment to Enlargement," Johns Hopkins University School of Advanced International Studies, Washington, D.C., September 21, 1993, http://www.fas.org/news/usa/1993/usa-930921.htm.

Document 14.6: Samuel P. Huntington, "The Clash of Civilizations?" *Foreign Affairs* 72, no. 3 (Summer 1993), 22–49. © 1993. Used with permission of the Council on Foreign Relations.

Document 14.7: "Meeting with the UN on Proposed Resolution for Rwanda, ca. 16 May 94," doc. 44, in William Ferroggiaro, *The U.S. and the Genocide in Rwanda 1994: Information, Intelligence and the U.S. Response* (Washington, D.C.: National Security Archive, March 24, 2004), http://www.gwu.edu/~nsarchiv/NSAEBB/NSAEBB117/RW44.pdf.

Document 14.8: Mark Alan Stamaty, cartoon, *Washington Post*, May 3, 1993, A19. © Mark Alan Stamaty. Reprinted with permission.

Document 14.9: Robert Kaplan, "The Coming Anarchy," *The Atlantic*, February 1994, 44–76. © 1994 by the Atlantic Monthly Group, Inc. All rights reserved. Distributed by Tribune Content Agency.

Document 14.10: Mahathir bin Mohamad, "Asian Values," speech at the Just International Conference on Rethinking Human Rights, Kuala Lumpur, Malaysia, December 6, 1994, Koleksi Arkib Ucapan (official website, Office of the Prime Minister of Malaysia), http://www.pmo.gov.my/ucapan/?m=p&p=mahathir&id=1206.

Document 14.11: Letter opposing NATO expansion, June 26, 1997, Arms Control Association, https://www.armscontrol.org/act/1997-06/arms-control-today/opposition-nato-expansion.

Document 14.12: Naomi Klein, *No Logo* (New York: Picador, 1999), xvii, xx–xxi, 442. © 2000, 2002, 2009 by Naomi Klein. Reprinted by permission of Picador, Vintage Canada/Alfred A. Knopf Canada, a division of Penguin Random House Canada Limited. And International Creative Management.

Document 14.13: Madeleine Albright, interview with Matt Lauer, NBC *Today Show*, February 19, 1998, http://www.fas.org/news/iraq/1998/02/19/98021907_tpo.html.

Document 14.14: Tony Blair, "Doctrine of the International Community," speech in Chicago, April 23, 1999, http://www.econclubchi.org/Documents/Meeting/1afd70f3–4eb6–498d-b69b-a1741a5a75b1.pdf.

Document 14.15: World Islamic Front, "Jihad against Jews and Crusaders," February 23, 1998, http://www.fas.org/irp/world/para/docs/980223-fatwa.htm.

15. The Age of Terror

Document 15.1: William Kristol and Robert Kagan, "Toward a Neo-Reaganite Foreign Policy," *Foreign Affairs* 75, no. 4 (July–August 1996), 18–32. Reprinted by permission of *Foreign Affairs*. Copyright 1996 by the Council on Foreign Relations, Inc., http://www.foreignaffairs.com.

Document 15.2: George W. Bush, Address to a Joint Session of Congress and the American People, September 20, 2001, in *Public Papers of the Presidents: George W. Bush, 2001*, vol. 2 (Washington, D.C.: Government Printing Office, 2003), 1140–44.

Document 15.3: *The 9/11 Commission Report: Final Report of the National Commission on Terrorist Attacks upon the United States* (New York: W. W. Norton, 2004), 330–31, 334–35.

Document 15.4: George W. Bush, State of the Union Address, January 29, 2002, in *Public Papers of the Presidents: George W. Bush, 2002*, vol. 1 (Washington, D.C.: Government Printing Office, 2004), 129–36.

Document 15.5: National Security Strategy, September 2002, http://georgewbush-whitehouse.archives.gov/nsc/nss/2002/.

Document 15.6: George W. Bush, "President Discusses the Future of Iraq," American Enterprise Institute, Washington, D.C., February 26, 2003, in *Public Papers of the Presidents: George W. Bush, 2003*, vol. 1 (Washington, D.C.: Government Printing Office, 2006), 216–20.

Document 15.7: Tom Toles, cartoon, *Washington Post*, March 26, 2003. TOLES © 2003 *Washington Post*. Reprinted with permission of Andrews McMeel Syndication. All rights reserved.

Document 15.8: *Return to an Address of the Honourable the House of Commons, dated 14th July 2004, for the Review of Intelligence on Weapons of Mass Destruction: Report of a Committee of Privy Counsellors* (London: Stationery Office, 2004), 105–6. The original version of this document had alternating normal and boldface type, which made it difficult to read. As far as we could determine, the boldface did not signify any additional importance or unusual meaning to the document. Thus, for the purposes of clarity and readability, we have reprinted this document without the boldfacing.

Document 15.9: Nick Anderson, "Statue of Liberty," May 5, 2004, http://www.cartoonistgroup.com/store/add.php?iid=7219. Nick Anderson editorial cartoon used with the permission of Nick Anderson, the Washington Post Writers Group and the Cartoonist Group. All rights reserved.

Document 15.10: Anthony Shadid, *Night Draws Near: Iraq's People in the Shadow of America's War* (New York: Henry Holt, 2005), 94, 150–53. Copyright © 2005, 2006 by Anthony Shadid. Reprinted by permission of Henry Holt and Company, LLC. All rights reserved.

Document 15.11: Larry Diamond, *Squandered Victory: The American Occupation and the Bungled Effort to Bring Democracy to Iraq* (New York: Times Books, 2005), 290–94. Copyright © 2005 by Larry Diamond. Reprinted by permission of Henry Holt and Company, LLC. All rights reserved.

Document 15.12: George W. Bush, Second Inaugural Address, January 20, 2005, in *Public Papers of the Presidents: George W. Bush, 2005*, vol. 1 (Washington, D.C.: Government Printing Office, 2007), 66–69.

Document 15.13: Andrew J. Bacevich, "I Lost My Son to a War I Oppose. We Were Both Doing Our Duty," *Washington Post*, May 27, 2007, B01. © Andrew J. Bacevich. Reprinted with permission.

Document 15.14: Barack Obama, Remarks by the President at the Acceptance of the Nobel Peace Prize, December 10, 2009, in *Public Papers of the Presidents: Barack Obama, 2009*, http://www.presidency.ucsb.edu/ws/index.php?pid=86978&st=oslo&st1=.

16. The Liberal Order in Crisis

Document 16.1: Ryan Lizza, "The Consequentialist," *The New Yorker*, May 2, 2011, https://www.newyorker.com/magazine/2011/05/02/the-consequentialist.

Document 16.2: Barack Obama, "Remarks to the Parliament in Canberra," Online by Gerhard Peters and John T. Woolley, *The American Presidency Project*, https://www.presidency.ucsb.edu/node/297536.

Document 16.3: Jeffrey Goldberg, "The Obama Doctrine," *The Atlantic*, April 2016, https://www.theatlantic.com/magazine/archive/2016/04/the-obama-doctrine/471525. Copyright © 2016 The Atlantic Monthly Group, Inc., All rights reserved. Distributed by Tribune Content Agency.

Document 16.4: Sheriff Joe Arpaio RNC Full Speech 7/21/16 Republican National Convention, https://www.youtube.com/watch?v=ayr3a_2su9U. Courtesy of the Republican National Convention.

Document 16.5: "Prime Minister Shinzo Abe (Japan) Expresses Disappointment in Trump Administration Plans to Leave TPP," November 22, 2016, https://www.wsj.com/video/japan-abe-tpp-is-meaningless-without-the-us/973FA32A-8C2B-47C2-B60B-721D6A7080A0.html.

Document 16.6: Nyshka Chandran, "Japanese PM Abe Says It Is His 'Strong Wish' that the US Returns to the TPP," CNBC, May 17, 2017, https://www.cnbc.com/2017/05/15/japanese-pm-abe-says-it-is-his-strong-wish-that-the-us-returns-to-the-tpp.html. © 2022 by CNBC (UK) Limited. All rights reserved, used with permission.

Document 16.7: Trump inaugural, January 20, 2017, Online by Gerhard Peters and John T. Woolley, *The American Presidency Project*, https://www.presidency.ucsb.edu/node/320188.

Document 16.8: Donald J. Trump, Tweets of March 18, 2017 Online by Gerhard Peters and John T. Woolley, *The American Presidency Project*, https://www.presidency.ucsb.edu/node/340256.

Document 16.9: Donald Trump, "Remarks at the Dedication Ceremony for the Berlin Wall Memorial and the 9/11 and Article 5 Memorial in Brussels, Belgium," May 25, 2017, Online by Gerhard Peters and John T. Woolley, *The American Presidency Project*, https://www.presidency.ucsb.edu/node/328698.

Document 16.10: Donald J. Trump, Tweets of May 30, 2017, Online by Gerhard Peters and John T. Woolley, *The American Presidency Project*, https://www.presidency.ucsb.edu/node/340329.

Document 16.11: Foreign Affairs Minister Chrystia Freeland, Address to the House of Commons, "Canada's Foreign Policy Priorities," June 6, 2017, https://www.canada.ca/en/global-affairs/news/2017/06/address_by_ministerfreelandoncanadasforeignpolicypriorities.html.

Document 16.12: Gary D. Cohn and H. R. McMaster, "The Trump Vision for America Abroad," *New York Times*, July 13, 2017, A23.

Document 16.13: Senator Bernie Sanders, "Westminster College Address," September 20, 2017, in "Bernie Sanders's Big Foreign Policy Speech," Vox, September 21, 2021, https://www.vox.com/world/2017/9/21/16345600/bernie-sanders-full-text-transcript-foreign-policy-speech-westminster.

Document 16.14: Supreme Court of the United States, October Term 2017, "Trump v. Hawaii," June 26, 2018, www.supremecourt.gov/opinions/17pdf/17-965_h315.pdf.

Document 16.15: Donald J. Trump, Remarks to the United Nations General Assembly in New York City, September 25, 2018, Online by Gerhard Peters and John T. Woolley, *The American Presidency Project*, https://www.presidency.ucsb.edu/node/332698.

Document 16.16: President Biden speech at the State Department, February 4, 2021, https://www.whitehouse.gov/briefing-room/speeches-remarks/2021/02/04/remarks-by-president-biden-on-americas-place-in-the-world/.

Document 16.17: "Remarks by President Biden on the End of the War in Afghanistan," August 31, 2021, https://www.whitehouse.gov/briefing-room/speeches-remarks/2021/08/31/remarks-by-president-biden-on-the-end-of-the-war-in-afghanistan/.

Document 16.18: https://cartoonmovement.com/cartoon/withdraw-all-us-forces-afghanistan.

Document 16.19: Wathiq Khuzaie / Stringer https://www.gettyimages.co.uk/detail/news-photo/marines-and-iraqis-are-seen-on-april-9-2003-as-the-statue-news-photo/57272427?adppopup=true.

Document 16.20: Scott Stantis, Tribune Content Agency, https://www.syracuse.com/opinion/2021/07/editorial-cartoons-for-july-11-2021-afghanistan-pullout-olympics-runup-delta-variant.html.

17. Great Powers and Global Challenges

Document 17.1: George F. Kennan, "Morality and Foreign Policy," *Foreign Affairs* 64 (Winter 1985/86), 205–18. George F. Kennan Papers, MC076, Public Policy Papers, Department of Special Collections., Princeton University Library.

Document 17.2: Reproduced from Yu Keping, *Democracy Is a Good Thing: Essays on Politics, Society, and Culture in Contemporary China*, Foreword by John L. Thornton and Introduction by Cheng Li. Copyright © 2009 The Brookings Institution. Reproduced by arrangement with The Rowman & Littlefield Publishing Group.

Document 17.3: Vladimir V. Putin, "A Plea for Caution from Russia," *New York Times*, September 12, 2013, A31.

Document 17.4: Statement by the President on Ukraine, March 20, 2014, https://obamawhitehouse.archives.gov/the-press-office/2014/03/20/statement-president-ukraine.

Document 17.5: Donald J. Trump, "Remarks to Members of the Press with President Xi Jinping of China in Beijing," November 9, 2017, Online by Gerhard Peters and John T. Woolley, *The American Presidency Project*, https://www.presidency.ucsb.edu/node/331569.

Document 17.6: Transcript: Greta Thunberg's Speech at the U.N. Climate Action Summit, September 23, 2019, https://www.npr.org/2019/09/23/763452863/transcript-greta-thunbergs-speech-at-the-u-n-climate-action-summit?t=1659521625636.

Document 17.7: Munich Security Report 2020, "Westlessness," https://securityconference.org/assets/user_upload/MunichSecurityReport2020.pdf

Document 17.8: Donald J. Trump, "Address to the Nation on the Coronavirus," Online by Gerhard Peters and John T. Woolley, *The American Presidency Project*, https://www.presidency.ucsb.edu/node/341491.

Document 17.9: Press release, "'The Squad' Calls for Reductions to U.S. Customs and Border Patrol Budget," July 16, 2020, https://ocasio-cortez.house.gov/media/press-releases/squad-calls-reductions-us-customs-and-border-patrol-budget-0.

Document 17.10: Office of the Director of National Intelligence, "Global Trends 2040: A More Contested World," March 2021, https://www.dni.gov/index.php/gt2040-home.

Document 17.11: Department of Defense, Report to the National Security Council, "Climate Risk Analysis," October 2021, https://media.defense.gov/2021/Oct/21/2002877353/-1/-1/0/DOD-CLIMATE-RISK-ANALYSIS-FINAL.PDF.

Document 17.12: Remarks at the Shangri-La Dialogue, Singapore, by Secretary of Defense Lloyd J. Austin III, June 11, 2022, https://www.defense.gov/News/Speeches/Speech/Article/3059852/remarks-at-the-shangri-la-dialogue-by-secretary-of-defense-lloyd-j-austin-iii-a/.

Document 17.13: Hatice Cengiz, "Dear President Biden: Please Don't Break Your Promise to Shun Saudi Arabia," *Washington Post*, July 6, 2022, https://www.washingtonpost.com/opinions/2022/07/06/hatice-cengiz-biden-should-not-go-saudi-arabia-jamal-khashoggi/.

Document 17.14: Putin speech, September 30, 2022, http://en.kremlin.ru/events/president/news/69465.

Document 17.15: Biden press statement, September 30, 2022, https://www.whitehouse.gov/briefing-room/statements-releases/2022/09/30/statement-from-president-biden-on-russias-attempts-to-annex-ukrainian-territory/.

Index

Page numbers in *italics* indicate an illustration.

Printed in the USA
CPSIA information can be obtained
at www.ICGtesting.com
JSHW081921090224
57032JS00007B/62

9 780691 2487